THE NEW
CAMBRIDGE MODERN HISTORY

ADVISORY COMMITTEE

G.N.CLARK J.R.M.BUTLER J.P.T.BURY

THE LATE E.A.BENIANS

VOLUME III

THE COUNTER-REFORMATION AND
PRICE REVOLUTION

1559–1610

THE NEW CAMBRIDGE MODERN HISTORY

VOLUME III

THE COUNTER-REFORMATION AND
PRICE REVOLUTION
1559-1610

EDITED BY
R. B. WERNHAM

CAMBRIDGE
AT THE UNIVERSITY PRESS
1968

Published by the Syndics of the Cambridge University Press
Bentley House, 200 Euston Road, London, N.W. 1
American Branch: 32 East 57th Street, New York, N.Y. 10022

Library of Congress Catalogue Card Number: 57–14935

Standard Book Number: 521 04543 6

Printed in Great Britain
at the University Printing House, Cambridge
(Brooke Crutchley, University Printer)

CONTENTS

v

CONTENTS

CHAPTER IV

PROTESTANTISM AND CONFESSIONAL STRIFE

By T. M. PARKER

I. LUTHERANISM AFTER LUTHER

2. THE DEVELOPMENT AND SPREAD OF CALVINISM

CONTENTS

CHAPTER V

SOCIAL STRUCTURE, OFFICE-HOLDING
AND POLITICS, CHIEFLY IN WESTERN EUROPE

By J. HURSTFIELD, *Astor Professor of English History, University College, London*

CHAPTER VI

INTERNATIONAL DIPLOMACY AND
INTERNATIONAL LAW

By the late G. MATTINGLY, *formerly Professor of History, University of Columbia*

CONTENTS

CHAPTER VII

ARMIES, NAVIES AND THE ART OF WAR

By J. R. HALE, *Professor of History, University of Warwick*

CONTENTS

ix

CONTENTS

CONTENTS

CHAPTER X

THE AUSTRIAN HABSBURGS AND THE EMPIRE

By G. D. RAMSAY, *Fellow and Tutor in Modern History, St Edmund Hall,*
Oxford

CONTENTS

CHAPTER XI

THE OTTOMAN EMPIRE 1566–1617

By V. J. PARRY, *Lecturer in the History of the Near and Middle East,*
School of Oriental and African Studies, University of London

CHAPTER XII

POLAND AND LITHUANIA

By P. SKWARCZYNSKI, *Reader in Central European History, School*
of Slavonic and East European Studies, University of London

CONTENTS

CHAPTER XIII

SWEDEN AND THE BALTIC

By I. ANDERSSON, *lately Director, the Riksarkivet, Stockholm,
Member of Swedish Academy*

CONTENTS

xiv

CONTENTS

CONTENTS

2. ASIA AND AFRICA

By J. B. HARRISON, *Reader in History of South Asia,*
School of Orientaland African Studies, University of London

CHAPTER I

INTRODUCTION

THE half century between 1559 and 1610 must assuredly rank as one of the most brutal and bigoted in the history of modern Europe. The massacre in Paris on St Bartholomew's day in 1572; the calculated savagery of the duke of Alba's Council of Blood and the wild atrocities of the Calvinistic Beggars in the Netherlands; the persecution of the Moriscos in Spain—these were merely the more spectacular barbarities of an age unsurpassed for cruelty until our own day.

Yet what, in the history of the later sixteenth century, is just as striking as man's inhumanity to man is man's impotence before events, his inability to control his circumstances or to dominate his destiny. Thus in the political field the greatest monarch of his time, Philip II of Spain, was unable to conquer a weak England or a disunited France; could hold only half his rebellious Netherlands; and ended his reign, as he had begun it, in bankruptcy.[1] His noblest opponent, William the Silent, died knowing that a union of his beloved fatherland upon a basis of mutual toleration between rival religions was a dream as remote as the hopes that Sir Edward Kelley and Marco Bragadino cherished of transmuting base metals into gold. With others the gap between aspiration and achievement was narrower only because they pitched their ambitions lower, and indeed for the most part the rulers of this time did pitch their ambitions much lower than those of the preceding generation. Was not one of the most successful of them, Elizabeth I of England, renowned above all for her chronic indecision and her dexterity in avoiding action?

If, however, European rulers and statesmen of the later sixteenth century seemed lesser men than their fathers, this was precisely because their fathers had aimed too high and attempted too much. At the beginning of the century a series of fortunate—or perhaps unfortunate?—marriages had made the young ruler of the Netherlands king of Spain in 1516 and then in 1519 head of the Austrian Habsburg house and, by election, Holy Roman Emperor. So, for the next forty years this man, the Emperor Charles V, became involved, almost continually and generally as a principal, in almost every conflict in every corner of Europe—in that in Hungary, the Mediterranean, and North Africa between Christians and Moslems; in that, centred mainly in Germany, between Protestants and Catholics; in that, centred mostly in Italy, between the French monarchy and the Spaniards; even, through his sister's marriage to the Danish king, in the struggle for Baltic supremacy. Every local quarrel, therefore, easily

---

[1] See also the description of Philip II, below, pp. 239 ff.

took on a European significance and princes' ambitions readily swelled to continental dimensions. While Charles V took his imperial role very seriously, the French king, too, saw visions of empire and even Henry VIII of England dreamed of marrying his daughter to the emperor with 'the whole monarchy of Christendom' as their inheritance.

Yet while the ends that princes pursued grew ever higher and wider, the means of pursuing them grew vastly more expensive every year. The expense of the new spreading network of diplomatic and intelligence agents could perhaps by itself have been borne easily enough by all except the poorest. But the cost of the new armies and navies, made necessary by the increasing use of firearms, was so great that by mid-century it had brought even the emperor and the king of France up to and over the edge of bankruptcy. The Turks, too, had almost shot their bolt by the time that Sulaimān the Magnificent died in 1566, while lesser powers had long since abandoned all attempts at keeping up with the Habsburgs and the Valois. England, for example, exhausted by the efforts of Henry VIII and Protector Somerset to dominate Scotland, had become first little better than a French satellite under Northumberland and had then seemed doomed to absorption in the Habsburg aggregate under the half-Spanish Mary Tudor.

So the great conflicts that had torn Europe during the first half of the sixteenth century died away as the combatants one by one sank down exhausted. In the east the long struggle between Christians and Moslem Turks slowly cooled into a bickering and still explosive co-existence. In the centre, in the Holy Roman Empire, the Augsburg settlement of 1555 consecrated a triple balance, precarious but generally treasured, between Lutheran princes, Catholic princes, and a Habsburg emperor whose power (such as it was) rested more and more upon the far eastern frontiers of the empire, on the Austrian duchies and Bohemia. In the west the settlement of Cateau-Cambrésis in April 1559 recognised a rough and unstable balance between the French monarchy and the Spanish branch of the house of Habsburg, the two leviathans that still towered over all the other powers and whose long quarrel was now rather suspended than ended.

Each of these conflicts, as it died away, thus left behind it its own particular political system and after 1559 each of these systems went more and more its own way in growing isolation from the rest. Their insulation from one another was further encouraged by the fact that Charles V, when he abdicated (1555–6), divided his unwieldy inheritance between his son Philip II—who received Spain, Spanish Italy, Franche-Comté, the Netherlands, and the New World—and his brother Ferdinand I—who, with Bohemia, the Austrian lands, and the title of Emperor, was left to salvage what he could of imperial authority in Germany and on the eastern marches of Christendom. The partition removed the link between the various systems and conflicts which had given unity to the political history of Charles V's time, and for fifty years and more after 1559 there is no longer one focal point or personality through which we can view the affairs of Europe as an interrelated whole. And the change also lessened the temptation for statesmen of the time to look too far afield and encouraged them to confine their ambitions to their own particular part of the continent.

Other circumstances further encouraged, almost imposed, such a limitation. The financial difficulties, the near-bankruptcy, which governments had brought upon themselves by their wars and their over-ambitious foreign policies, were continued and often worsened after the mid-century by monetary inflation. We no longer regard the 'price revolution' as solely the product of the sudden influx of silver from America after the opening of the Potosí mine in 1543, any more than we think of the Renaissance as caused by the sudden influx of Greek scholars after the fall of Constantinople in 1453. Nevertheless, the flood tide of American silver, pouring in on top of other deeper and longer-term movements of population, of trade, and of finance, did quicken and steepen the price rise and make this a more than ever difficult time for governments and for all whose incomes were comparatively inflexible.

It was the more difficult because the dying down of the wars left many of the nobility and gentry without employment in the only profession for which most of them were trained, the profession of arms. They now looked to their government for lucrative occupations, or at least for subsidies and rewards that would enable them to go on living in the style to which they had grown accustomed. When government failed or fell short in its expected role of aristocratic provider, nobles and gentry were ready enough to turn against it. So did many of Mary Tudor's subjects turn against her and look hopefully to the heir presumptive Elizabeth who was thought—before her accession—to be 'a liberal dame and nothing so unthankful as her sister is'. Much of the discontent of the French noblesse against their Valois kings, and of the Netherlands nobility against their Spanish overlord, sprang from similar sources. Aristocratic discontent, indeed, became a major cause of tension in almost every country, at least of western Europe.

What made it the more dangerous was that government, while drawing in its horns abroad, was becoming more and more active and interfering at home. It was intruding more and more into those local affairs which the landed aristocrats had long regarded as their own peculiar concern, as franchises where the royal writ ran in practice only by their consent. As its intrusions often threatened other local interests and classes as well, and invariably brought to both townsman and peasant an increased burden of taxes and exactions, the landed nobility and gentry often found themselves standing forth as popular leaders of local particularism and ancient liberties against an encroaching central power.

Nor was that all. The growing activity of government required a growing number of government servants. Their loyalty and efficiency had to be assured by adequate rewards. Yet few governments had sufficient revenues to be able to pay their servants proper salaries, and few could now dare to staff their civil service so largely with ecclesiastics as they had done in the past. More than ever, therefore, they appointed men to offices upon the tacit understanding that they might supplement a nominal stipend by such fees, gifts, or plain bribes as their consciences would allow and their clients would pay. From this it was but a short step to selling offices, monopolies, privileges, and functions, the purchasers recouping themselves at the expense of the public without too many questions asked. It was an even shorter step thereafter to the creation of offices, even inheritable offices, for the admitted purpose —even the sole purpose—of making money by their sale. This venality of offices, this sale of privileges and prerogatives of government, was common, though in varying degrees, to the whole continent. Abuse of it was all too easy, for the thing itself was an expedient born of poverty-stricken necessity. How great an outburst of anger it could provoke, even where its abuse was by no means most flagrant, was shown by the uproar over patents of monopoly in the 1601 English parliament. Moreover, around the system there grew a tangled connection of patronage and 'clientage' that could all too easily degenerate into internecine faction, as again was shown during the last years of Elizabethan England by the Essex–Cecil rivalry.

Equally, however, common burdens and shared grievances could spread local and aristocratic discontents nation-wide and weld them into something like a national opposition. This happened most easily where the ruling dynasty was alien and absentee, as in the Netherlands against Philip of Spain, and in Sweden against Sigismund of Poland; or where the marriage of a female sovereign threatened to absorb her realm in some wider political combination, as with England under Mary Tudor and with Scotland under Mary Stuart. It was in such places that the ancient and largely negative hatred of foreigners was most readily and rapidly transmuted into something not far removed from a new and positive spirit of nationalism.[1] Yet everywhere this new spirit was beginning to show itself more or less strongly and wherever it appeared it gave men a new awareness of the distinction between love of country or nation and personal loyalty to prince or dynasty. William Shakespeare's 'blessed plot, this England', and William the Silent's 'entire fatherland' were beginning to inspire in men affections and loyalties not much less ardent than those inspired by a Virgin Queen or a Most Catholic King. The sharper the distinction became, the more readily and the more dangerously opposition to the central government could spring up.

Moreover, while disgruntled aristocrats could thus provide the leaders

---

[1] For a somewhat different view, however, see chapter VI below.

4

for wide movements of political discontent, there were always hungry poor to provide those movements with a dangerously undisciplined rank and file. The great majority of mankind have always lived very close to the borders of starvation and the later sixteenth century was no exception to this rule. Indeed, the growth of population was then, it seems, outstripping the growth of industrial and agricultural production. And the growth of trade, if it enabled the surplus of one region rather more often than before to relieve the dearth of another, also left a larger number of people at the mercy of market fluctuations, tended to depress or hold down real wages, and increased the gap between rich and poor. Much of England's trouble in the late 1540s and the 1550s resulted from the economic and social repercussions of a glut in the Antwerp cloth market; some at least of the violence of Netherlands disorders in the middle 1560s sprang from the dearth of corn caused by Baltic wars and from the unemployment in the cloth industry caused by a quarrel with England. Indeed, it was never very difficult anywhere to start a riot and the fears of social revolution aroused by the German Peasants' Revolt and by the excesses at Münster were kept keenly alive by such episodes as the Netherlands' image-breaking riots of 1566 or the later violence of the Paris mob and the banditry of the peasants in other parts of France. In the long run, no doubt, these fears of mob rule helped to drive the propertied classes back into support of the central governments—we can see that happening both in the Netherlands and in France. Nevertheless, it was the opposition of those propertied classes, or portions of them, to the central power that had opened the fissures through which these under-surface social discontents could erupt. And their eruption added still further to the tensions that were straining the fabric of government.

Last and not least among the problems that caused uneasiness in crowned heads, there was religious opposition, and in particular Calvinist opposition. For now, in western Europe especially, the conservative, compromising, and generally prince-loving Protestantism of the Lutherans and the anarchic and fragmenting radicalism of the Anabaptist sects were both being shouldered aside by a radical and uncompromising Calvinism. The leadership of active Protestantism was passing to men who put their trust not in princes but in the strength and resilience of their own church organisation and who, despite Calvin's own hesitations, became increasingly quick to assert themselves by force of arms. Flowing outwards from the fountain-head at Calvin's Geneva, this militant faith spread fastest along the lines of least political resistance, through those regions where governments were weakest or most heavily challenged. Its chief successes thus came in the politically fragmented Rhineland; among the nation-wide oppositions to Spanish rule in the Low Countries and to French rule in Scotland; and in France itself, where feeble rulers and royal minorities gave it the chance to link up with and exacerbate the mounting feuds of noble and local factions. To the Huguenot faction in France, to the 'Lords of the Congregation' in Scotland, to the Beggar party in the Netherlands, Calvinism gave a cohesion and a driving force that no mere political or economic or social grievances could have provided. For, by a bond of faith that was stronger than any bonds of blood or interest or connection, it bound noble and burgher and peasant, men of one province and men of another, in a common cause that overrode class distinctions and local particularism. It gave an unprecedentedly effective organisation, and the self-confidence of an uncompromising faith, to factions that were already beginning to adopt violent methods to achieve political ends.[1]

But violence begets violence and the vigour of Calvinism soon provoked vigorous reactions. The German Lutheran princes hated its theology, feared its missionary work among their subjects, and trembled lest its militancy should upset the precarious peace prevailing in the empire since Augsburg. Soon, in Germany, the controversies between Lutheran and Calvinist became sharper than the disputes between Protestant and Catholic. In England, too, Elizabeth I, despite her reluctance to make windows into men's souls, had to set the Anglican bishops and the Court of High Commission upon those Puritan agitators who 'would deprive the Queen of her [ecclesiastical] authority and give it to the people'. In Scotland James VI found considerable support, and not only among the northern conservatives, for his resistance to the kirk's attempt to treat him as 'God's silly vassal'. Even in tolerant Poland the Roman church was by the end of the century mounting its counter-attack and calling the government to its aid.

It was, however, in France and the Netherlands that the influence of religion was seen at its most vicious and that the reaction to Calvinist violence was sharpest. The Calvinists' resort to arms and their desecration of churches in the image-breaking riots of 1566 provoked a Catholic reaction that ruined the first Netherlands opposition and opened the way for Alba to come in unopposed with the Spanish army and the Council of Blood. Catholic alarm at Calvinist aggression a decade later undermined the Pacification of Ghent and in 1579 split the momentarily united Netherlands into the rival Unions of Arras and Utrecht. In France in 1572 the mobs of Paris and other cities needed little incitement to vent their fury upon a Huguenot minority that looked like becoming more influential than the Catholic majority could tolerate. Later the prospect of a Huguenot succeeding Henry III upon the throne provoked the last, longest and bitterest of all the French wars of religion, that between Henry of Navarre and the Catholic League, a war that saw Spanish troops invited into Paris by French rebels and that threatened to sacrifice France's independence upon the altar of religious fanaticism.

From the 1550s onwards an acute awareness of all these various

[1] See also below, chapter IX.

tensions and passions combined with a plain lack of money to restrain most rulers to modest ambitions in their foreign policies. In the far north kings of Sweden and of Denmark might still dream of, and fight for, *dominium maris Baltici*; and kings of Poland, having achieved a union with Lithuania, might still regard wider unions, first with Sweden, then with Muscovy, as practical aims. But the Baltic countries had been less crippled by wars than the lands farther south and in the Swedish kings and Sigismund of Poland the tendency of the Vasa family to megalomania was always liable to break surface. Most of Europe's rulers were more restricted by circumstances and less adventurous by temperament. Well aware of how limited were their means for dealing with the growing strains and discontents within their own dominions, the last things that most of them wanted to do were to add a large-scale foreign war to their burdens or to offer their foreign rivals any opportunity to send assistance to their own rebels. The English intervention in Scotland in 1560, the Anglo-French meddlings in the Low Countries in 1572 and 1578, the Spanish assistance to the Catholic League in France during the earlier 1590s, showed only too clearly how dangerous could be the combination of foreign hostility with domestic opposition.

There was therefore a widespread, indeed for many years an almost universal, desire to avoid any renewal of the general large-scale warfare that had been so common during the first half of the century. Yet dynastic and national jealousies did not, of course, now cease; commercial rivalries still exploded from time to time; strategic interests remained as sensitive as ever and princes as prickly about personal and dynastic prestige. Moreover, the existence of discontent and organised opposition within a country was a standing temptation to its neighbours. And as there was, in greater or less degree, discontent and opposition in almost every country of Europe, the governments of the later sixteenth century could almost always expect to find friends, even perhaps armed allies, within their enemy's camp, such as the previous generation had found only upon rare occasions. The fostering of 'fifth columns', the underhand helping of rebels, thus became regular and recognised instruments of later sixteenth-century statecraft. They were instruments resorted to all the more readily because it was so easy for one government to give help to another's rebels unofficially and without committing any overt act of war. Yet they were dangerous instruments precisely because the line between underhand help to rebels and open war between governments was so blurred and uncertain that even the most cautious and skilful statesmen could easily overstep it unintentionally.

So a mood of nervous and irritable timidity ruled the foreign policies of most governments and dominated much of the diplomatic correspondence of their agents—Alba's letters from the Netherlands in 1567–73, at least so far as they concern the danger of an open break with England, are a remarkable example. In domestic matters, on the other hand, there was an increasing tendency to rush into panic measures and violent solutions—Philip II's despatch of Alba and his army to the Netherlands in 1567; Catherine de Medici's drastic attempt to remove Admiral Coligny, which led into the massacre of St Bartholomew's day; the severity of the English parliament's legislation against the Catholic missionaries; the growing resort to arms by Rhenish and south German Catholics to uphold their endangered cause at Cologne, Aachen, and Donauwörth. Yet these desperate remedies did not by any means always solve the problems and did almost always make the internal conflicts far more bitter and irreconcilable. They thus served all too often only to make the rebels more ready to call foreign powers to their aid and to strengthen the temptation for foreign powers to answer their calls.

Worse still was the ready way in which political factions tended to identify themselves with rival international religious sects—the Guise faction in France with the church of Rome, the Beggars in the Low Countries with Calvinism. The tendency did not, of course, prevail everywhere, for religious faith was still a stronger force than political or party allegiance—hence the reluctance of the Catholic Portuguese to accept the help of Protestant England against Catholic Spain after 1580 and rebel Aragon's lack of interest in a Huguenot king of France in 1591. Nevertheless, it did mean that all Protestant rebels—French, Netherlands, Scottish—looked more and more to protestant England for help; all the Catholic rebels—French, English, Scottish, Irish—looked to Catholic Spain. By the 1580s the role of Protestant champion was being thrust upon the very reluctant Elizabeth I; that of Catholic champion upon Philip II, who until recently had been hardly less reluctant. Unofficial and underhand intervention now turned gradually into open war and the various local and national feuds began to coalesce into a new general conflict.

As yet, during the period with which we are concerned in this volume, this conflict involved only western Europe directly, only that part of the continent whose statute had been laid down at Cateau-Cambrésis in 1559. The central, 'Augsburg', area for the most part slumbered on in uneasy peace. The Baltic states, too, still went their own way, not greatly affected by the turmoil of western Europe, though the Protestantism of the north German Hanse towns was sorely tried during the 1590s by English interference with their lucrative trade to Spain in naval stores and corn. Yet already that turmoil was beginning to spread into the western fringes of Germany, to the Rhineland, where the establishment of Calvinism in the Palatinate and the spread of militant Tridentine Catholicism from Bavaria were striking sparks that could easily touch off a conflagration. The danger was all the greater because of that region's importance to the communications of the Spanish army in the Netherlands. Trouble in the Rhineland might well not only spread rapidly eastwards through the rest of Germany but also draw in Spain and Spain's enemies to the west.

These things did not, in fact, happen until the years from 1618 onwards, until the Thirty Years War. For the western conflicts at the end of the sixteenth century provided some of the more spectacular illustrations of the inability of European statesmen and commanders to impose their pattern upon events. In 1588 the Spaniards failed to land a single soldier upon English soil and the English sailors failed to destroy in battle more than half a dozen ships of the great Armada. Next year the English counter-stroke did put an army ashore, first at Coruña, then in Portugal; but in the end it withdrew without being able to take a single town of any consequence. English efforts to cut off Spain's supplies of silver from America were as unavailing as Spanish efforts to exploit rebellion in Ireland. Henry of Navarre's stirring victories over the League at Arques and Ivry proved as barren of decisive effect as Parma's interventions to save Paris in 1590 and Rouen in 1592. In the Netherlands likewise the war came to stalemate along the line of the great rivers. It is true that in naval warfare the new fleets of sailing warships, relying upon gunfire instead of boarding to destroy their enemies, were novel weapons whose use and tactics needed time to be properly elucidated and made effective. It is also true that it was not for purely military reasons that Henry of Navarre and Parma failed to gather the fruits of victory. Nevertheless, the striking thing about this long-drawn-out war—even for England it lasted nineteen years—was its indecisiveness. In the end all the combatants had to pause out of mere exhaustion. Yet, just because the pausing was due to mutual exhaustion, the treaties between France and Spain in 1598 and England and Spain in 1604 and the truce between the Dutch and Spain in 1609 left most of the great questions unsettled. One by one the powers had drawn out of the battle, but for most of them (England under James I was perhaps an exception) this was only to repair their damage and replenish their strength for fresh onslaughts.

All through this period, then, the tensions within states and between states, although for many years they deterred governments from risking war, were mounting towards a fresh European conflict. They encouraged attitudes of mind, nervous and fearful, yet violent, that often mistook movement for action and were often unduly obsessed by present troubles and short-run problems. Men's capacity for solving the underlying long-term problems was thus seriously lessened. Caught up in surface tensions, they had insufficient time and energy to devote to deeper problems of population growth and price inflation; of commercial change and industrial development resulting from them; of government finance and methods of recruiting and rewarding its servants; of constructing a coherent system of international relations, working out agreed principles of international law, and creating an effective diplomatic service. Above all, there was the problem of persuading people of differing religious faiths to live together in peace (if not in amity).

Here and there some progress in these deeper matters was indeed made. No one had much success in restraining prices, though the English did succeed in reforming their currency, creating a system of poor relief, and redeploying their overseas trade when Antwerp failed them as a distributing and collecting centre. Yet even Elizabeth I's thrifty administration could not find a real answer to the problem of government insolvency, and its efforts to make ends meet during the Spanish war provoked the first round of the constitutional conflict that was to end in civil war in 1642. Dutch commerce prospered and expanded more notably than English, yet the States made very little headway towards the development of a truly effective system of government. The Spaniards found ways to increase greatly the American mines' output of silver and to bring that silver safely across the Atlantic. Yet they could not prevent the downward turn of the Spanish economy that marked the beginning of its long decline. In Germany, although the Augsburg principle of *cuius regio eius religio* made it possible for Lutheran and Catholic princes and cities to live side by side fairly peaceably in one empire, it was much more rare for Catholic and Lutheran subjects to be allowed to live side by side under one prince. In 1598 the Edict of Nantes compelled the Catholics to share France with Huguenots, yet it had to leave the Huguenots as an armed and organised minority within the state.

It is not surprising that the men of the later sixteenth century had so limited a success. The problems that faced them were, in all conscience, difficult enough in themselves. They were made doubly difficult by their novelty. The preceding century, and more particularly the preceding half-century, had opened new continents for Europeans to conquer and had provided them with new, if costly and more complicated, weapons of conquest. While it had thus expanded geographical horizons and revolutionised the art of war, it had also brought a faster, an unwontedly fast, rate of economic and social development and of political evolution. It had brought changes and challenges to almost every human activity and institution. Above all, it had brought a veritable nuclear explosion of new or refurbished ideas in religion. Such an age of innovation and expansion could only be followed by an age of assimilation and consolidation.

We have already seen how in political affairs the years after 1559 witnessed a contraction of ambitions in the foreign policies of most European powers and a growing concentration upon asserting authority and overhauling techniques in the more restricted field of domestic government. Outside Europe the story was the same: the great age of discovery and conquest gave place to an age of settlement and exploitation—at least this was so for the Spanish and Portuguese colonies which English and French and Dutch adventurers were as yet more concerned to plunder than to copy. We have seen, too, that the soldiers and sailors had problems enough in learning to master their new weapons and in feeling their way towards tactics that would make them effective. In economic activity also, although the long upswing of expansion that had started in the mid-fifteenth century was still carrying business forward, the pace was slowing markedly by the 1590s. The questions that puzzled the business world—and governments, too—were, here again, for the most part questions that the preceding half-century had posed but had hardly begun to answer. The men of the later sixteenth century lacked the technical invention and the scientific advancement to answer the challenges of growing population, rising demand, and rising prices, so that in this field, too, signs were beginning to appear of a coming contraction.

Just why they should not have been able to respond to these technical and scientific challenges as their eighteenth-century descendants were to respond, it is not altogether easy to say. Technology and science, like the arts, do of course obey the separate and distinct rhythms of their own being. Those rhythms may differ widely from the contemporary economic and social and political rhythms, and certainly at this period neither science nor technology had reached a stage in its own development where it was ready or equipped to offer solutions to the problems of the day. It is also true that at the universities, and in education generally, the main concern was to work out and apply the flood of new ideas which the preceding generations had poured forth. For in this field, too, this was an age of assimilation. Nevertheless, it does seem as if the natural advance of science, of technology, indeed of thought and experiment in most secular subjects (except perhaps those connected with warfare), was re-tarded by the almost universal preoccupation with the great debate about religion. For, in the minds of most men of those times, religion was the dominant concern, and we shall never make sense of their thoughts and their doings if we try to analyse them only in political and economic terms.

In religion, of course, the great outpouring of fresh ideas also ebbed away with the passing, first of Zwingli, then of Luther, and finally of Calvin. Here as elsewhere the concern was now to digest and to define—a concern manifest equally in Calvin's Geneva and in the Catholic Council of Trent. Even the Lutherans were driven into writing down their own sectarian Formula of Concord. The rival churches had chosen their battle-grounds and were digging themselves in along more and more carefully prepared positions, ready for a long period of theological trench warfare, in which there would be little of the scope for manœuvre that had existed down to the middle of the century. What most people wanted now was certainty, to find among all the doubts and challenges to faith an authority that could be accepted and obeyed. And certainty was most readily provided in the closing ranks of churches that became more and more sharply set apart one from another by more and more precisely defined creeds and ceremonies. But separation bred hostility, the more so as all—except for a few small and despised sects—had inherited from medieval Christianity a conviction that there could be only one true church and that this church had the right, indeed the duty, to use force to uphold and impose its faith.

This intolerant exclusiveness and this readiness to resort to force led almost every church sooner or later into close alliance with the secular power and eventually into dependence upon it. This happened not only to the Anglican church in England and to the Lutheran churches in the German principalities, but also to the Catholic church in Spain and to a great extent to the Calvinist kirk in Scotland. In France *une foi, une loi, un roi* was widely accepted as the ideal, though for most of the time the king was too weak to impose either faith or law. A necessary result of thus identifying church and state was that heresy and treason were also identi-fied—it was as traitors that the Catholic missionaries to Elizabethan England suffered the barbarous penalty of being hanged, drawn, and quartered. We have seen already how this identification embittered quarrels between nations by injecting into them religious hatreds; how it made faction feuds within nations almost irreconcilable; and how the international character of both Calvinism and Tridentine Catholicism tended to link up local squabbles into general continental conflicts.

There was another result. The united pressure of church and state drove or attracted overmuch intellectual effort into narrow theological and sectarian channels. Education and learning came to be regarded too much as primarily instruments for producing sound Protestant Englishmen or sound Catholic Spaniards. Those branches which contributed most directly and most obviously to those ends were the most favoured and the best endowed. Thus theology replaced law and medicine as the dominant faculty in the universities, and learning the catechisms became one of the more insistent of school exercises. Theological studies, moreover, were more and more straitjacketed by sectarian orthodoxy and too often became merely an expense of spirit in a waste of controversy. The controversies did sometimes stimulate enquiry in wider fields, as with the Magdeburg Chroniclers and Baronius; yet the scholarship that they encouraged could not be entirely disinterested nor the enquiry entirely free. All this does not, of course, mean that independent thought was altogether stifled or in-tellectual progress brought to a halt. To speak in that way of the times of Bodin and Hooker, of Tycho Brahe and Gentili, would be absurd. Never-theless, the rewards for the advancement of secular learning were not usually very great and the dangers were often considerable in an age which found it hard to differentiate between science and magic and mere witch-craft. Not until the ideas and the knowledge of the learned had been assimilated by men of affairs, by businessmen and merchants, navigators and engineers, could there anyway be that blend of theory and practice which was later to produce first the 'scientific revolution' and then the 'industrial revolution'. The scholars and teachers of the later sixteenth century were mostly absorbed in the humbler task of trying to sort out those ideas and of diffusing that knowledge. Their main efforts were expended in popularising and describing; in defining and pointing out the problems rather than in breaking through to new solutions.

It is tempting to see here a reason for the successes of this age, and particularly of its later years, in the one field where its achievements rose far above mediocrity. For in imaginative literature and the drama, in those arts that hold a mirror up to human nature, the late sixteenth century and the first years of the seventeenth century soared to heights that in other fields seemed quite beyond the reach of the men of those times. In vernacular literature and drama, and in music, Cervantes and Shakespeare, Palestrina and Byrd, and their fellows, brought to brilliant maturity the strivings of the preceding generation. In painting and architecture, too, the inspiration of the High Renaissance was passed down, as by way of Titian and El Greco, to the seventeenth century. It has been possible in this volume to do little more than mention these achievements, but it was in these realms of the imagination that such creative spirit as the age possessed chiefly found its expression. In the other aspects of its intellectual life, as in its political and economic activity, it was a time when the questions loomed larger than the answers and the problems looked greater than the men.

CHAPTER II

THE ECONOMY OF EUROPE 1559–1609

ON 2 and 3 April 1559 at Cateau-Cambrésis the powers of western
Europe once more agreed to make peace. The settlement then
achieved after prolonged manœuvres and hesitations was destined
to find its place among the decisive treaties in European history. Historians
have accepted it as such, confirming its importance with that fanfare of
trumpets so often reserved for the great acts of peace-making which check
the persistent quarrelling in Europe. And they have done so with good
reason.

In the first place, this great political event marked a turning-point.
Although Charles V had died the year before, on 21 September 1558, the
treaty of Cateau-Cambrésis was the effective closure to his dramatic reign.
With the accession of Philip II to power and majesty, a new epoch opened,
certainly not less dramatic but of a different and harsher texture. It seemed
as if an outdated style of empire, largely medieval in character and justifiable as such, maintained by imponderable and time-honoured traditions,
was being directed by a more realistic and oppressive hand, henceforth
devoid of political *raison d'être* and hesitant to show its true purpose.
Such was the political importance of the treaty of Cateau-Cambrésis. Can
we assume that its economic importance was just as great?

Certainly the coincidence was more than slight. The peace allowed the
international economy to recover its strength, and this brought considerable benefit. As the major conflict between France and the Habsburgs did
not officially return to open warfare until 17 January 1595, almost half a
century later, the economic activity of western Europe enjoyed a period of
prolonged ease and recuperation. On this occasion, as often happens with
the disbanding of armies, there were the pleasures of peace: the wines of
the south once more found their way northwards in regular abundance.
It would be tedious to linger over such details, if the international economy,
about 1559 or perhaps a little later, had not surmounted the immediate
post-war problems and entered a phase of constructive activity, carried
forward by a long upsurge of prosperity. Such an oversimplification of the
reality carries with it many dangers, but it is evident that during these
years there was a distinct change from the conditions characteristic of the
age of Charles V. Prices continued to rise, but the inflation of the cost of
living was also accompanied by rising wage-rates. This has been established
for the Low Countries, Florence, Spain, Germany, Austria, England, and,
as we shall see, has important implications.

Yet after the treaty of Cateau-Cambrésis—the first boundary of this study—we can turn to the other political pause, the truce of April 1609 between Spain and the insurgent United Provinces. This constituted an event of outstanding importance not only, inevitably, in the political but also in the economic sphere. It meant a substantial return to more normal peacetime conditions. It crowned a prologue of three other treaties: between Spain and France (at Vervins on 2 May 1598); between France and Savoy (1601); and between Spain and England (1604). This round of peace-making had perhaps even more profound consequences. Far beyond the storm-centre of affairs in western Europe, and rising above the alarms, hesitations and rebuffs, peace spread across the seven seas as the mercantile nations set claim to the resources of the world, in more or less peaceful competition.

Nevertheless, it must not be assumed that the activities of the international economy remained completely subordinate to the traditional rhythm of political events. Their importance cannot be denied, but politics were one thing, and economics another.

The development of the economy of Europe was distinguished, as in the political sphere, by a series of striking dates: the bankruptcy of the Spanish monarchy in 1557, for example, although this was mainly a Spanish affair. The two bankruptcies which followed in 1575 and 1597 were both profound disturbances which shook the European economy to its very foundations. There soon followed another bankruptcy, that of 1607, for which the conspicuous spending at the court of Philip III must largely bear the responsibility. But just as in the case of the treaties, wars, and accidents which were the main constituents of political history, these events were only a preliminary indication of economic change. A closer examination reveals fairly long-term movements, now in one direction, now in another, forming an alternating theme of recession and expansion. The evidence of this sequence of cycles is still far from conclusive, but it is clear that aggregate production tended to rise and fall. This ebb and flow in the material output is fundamental to the study of economic affairs at that time. In all probability it did not have the same incidence from one end of Europe to another. The economy of France, for example, turned away from the continent and the Mediterranean to invest in the Atlantic, and thus experienced a change in direction in the years roughly from 1536 to 1564. The Low Countries did not recover until about 1590. If we look at the earlier period, it is clear that the profound crisis of the mid-sixteenth century, from about 1540 to 1560, was particularly severe in the case of England, but scarcely made its presence felt in Spain during the last years of Charles V and the early reign of Philip II. If these differences in chronology turn out to be correct from current studies, they will have deep significance in the analysis of basic trends. At least, the main features are generally apparent and already show signs of being different from the chronology of political history. An economic historian, following these indicators, would prefer to open his study not in 1559 but rather about 1565–6; and close it not with the Twelve Years Truce of 1609 but about the commercial crisis of 1619–20 or even at the end of the Thirty Years War, when long-term recession proved inevitable, this time for the whole European economy. And, for good measure, we can add that these phases in economic expansion were not in themselves exclusive boundaries. Over and beyond the surface movements, the general economic activity was consolidated by a secular trend, a long upswing sustained by its own momentum. Indeed, few will deny that this period forms part of the pervasive resurgence of Europe which gathered strength about the mid-fifteenth century and lasted until the catastrophes of the mid-seventeenth century. The years 1559–1609 float in a much larger span of time, prolonged in the wider perspectives of the 'long' sixteenth century, as Fernand Braudel has termed it, from the mid-fifteenth century to the *débâcle* of the Thirty Years War.

Yet, complementary to this economic chronology, there are considerations of historical geography. It is a difficult task even to indicate the complexity of Europe in the second half of the sixteenth century, with its diverse regions relegated to partial autonomy and constituting economies very different in evolution, substance and motivation. In the south and east, Italy was on the point of emerging from the long tribulations of the Italian Wars with their windfall gains and their destructions. For the Italian peninsula the trumpets of Cateau-Cambrésis heralded a long peace. And it need hardly be added that the reconstruction there required concentrated investments. In south-western Europe, Spain and Portugal were still relatively young economies: in the late fifteenth century they threw themselves into the adventure of lucrative colonial exploration. The rich possibilities of the Atlantic put them ahead in the race for wealth. The port of Lisbon, for a brief spell, and then Seville became dominant centres and *foci* of growth for the whole of Europe. In the north, Antwerp, another seaport, effectively prolonged the Spanish fortune. Among the countries of the north, the southern Netherlands, the Italy of the north, were particularly well endowed with merchants, craftsmen and rich cities. By the mid-sixteenth century their golden age was already overcast. And England, inevitably moulded to the pattern of the Low Countries, gave the impression of having relatively small resources. After 1543–4, the Low Countries became a battlefield in the war against France, open to the conflicts of others, which soon, as if in compensation, were involved in their own civil troubles. It seemed that war, suppressed in one theatre of Europe, was ready to burst out in another. After the middle of the century, after the religious Peace of Augsburg in 1555, Italy and Germany became territories of relative peace. On the other hand, France and the Low Countries were soon submerged in civil war. They became cockpits for

Europe, almost as Italy had been during the first half of the sixteenth century. The disputes never remained entirely local, and invited neighbours to intervene. The resulting invasions inevitably gave the history of France and the Low Countries a special character. To the north and east of Germany and the Low Countries, there were the marches of Europe— Scandinavia and Poland: these were also economic zones apart, less well provided with men, focal cities, and free or almost free lands. The civilisation of Europe was spread thinly over these vast frontier territories. Here, the wars were waged with greater brutality than in the west, and brought a way of life subordinated to pillage and constant alerts. More than Germany, already mentioned, Poland endured a wasting role as bastion of Europe.

This sketch in historical geography is far too rapid to be complete. Europe was not alone. The continent was not sufficient in itself. It lived and grew increasingly as part of a world economy to the extent that sea trade could mobilise its resources. There were colonial empires seized with vital energy by the Portuguese and Spaniards. Europe thrived on the extension of these empires: the Portuguese established themselves officially in Macao in 1557 after years of tolerated occupation. In 1565, Miguel Lopez de Legazpi linked Acapulco to Manila and thus opened a route of outstanding importance for trading the silver of the New World against the silks and porcelains of China. These were important events in empire-building, but there were many others, for the Spaniards and Portuguese were not alone in widening the economic range of Europe. In 1553 English ships under the command of their 'pilot general' Richard Chancellor sailed into the Arctic, making port at Archangel, to pay homage to the Czar. Through his protection and favour, the Muscovy Company, chartered in 1555, had access to the roads and river routes of Russia, and so to the riches of Persia and the East.

Established within these periods and geographical limits, our study can now turn to the economic life of Europe between 1559 and 1609. The customary tests of prices, money, production and population can be applied to outline the salient features of a development, difficult to appraise in all its complexity.

I

First, the problem of prices and wages. At the outset it should be noted that this double-sided, classic history is not enough in itself to explain the diverse economic development of Europe, even after numerous studies during the last thirty or so years. Wage levels in general are not known with sufficient exactitude; sometimes wages were paid in kind, sometimes in money, so that it is difficult to estimate their true value. Price series, moreover, represent a series of equilibrium points between supply and demand, and, since all the information is not available, the interplay of forces must be inferred. It is not unfair to say that the combined history of prices and wages presents far more problems than it can hope to settle with the present information. It is, at best, a preliminary appraisal of economic reality in constant evolution, and already fairly well known. In the period from 1559 to 1609 prices and wages rose progressively. Although this price rise was well established perhaps a century before the mid-sixteenth century, it became far more rapid, far more pronounced, after the 1550s. And it did not fail to impress contemporaries confronted with persistent economic difficulties.

The sudden awareness of these realities was indeed a remarkable feature of the period, and historians have rightly used the reactions of the 'economists' of the sixteenth century to explain the creeping inflation. The precious metals of the New World (at first gold and then after 1519 silver as well) made their début in Europe through Spain, and Spain was first to experience the problem. The effects of the prolonged inflation were particularly felt with the new wave of silver after the middle of the century. Martín Azpilcueta de Navarro published his *De usuris* in 1556. This scholar from the school of Salamanca in all probability first set the responsibility squarely on the consignments of precious metals to Europe. The crux of the matter lay in their abundance. In 1566–8, ten years after the tract of Azpilcueta, the famous controversy between the Sieur de Malestroit and Jean Bodin exploded in France. The former maintained the proposition that there was a rise of prices in terms of money of account, but that in reality prices when calculated in gold and silver remained the same. In his *Response*, Bodin adroitly demolished the logic of his adversary. 'I find', he said (in the edition of 1568), 'that the high prices which we see appear for three reasons. The chief and almost only cause (to which until now no one has referred) is the abundance of gold and silver which is greater in this kingdom today than it was four hundred years ago...The second cause of high prices comes partly from monopolies. The third is the dearth, which is caused as much by trading as by spoilage. The last is the extravagance of kings and great nobles, which raises the price of things they like.' In England, the *Discourse of the Common Weal of this Realm of England*, apparently written in the autumn of 1549 but published in 1581, presented a series of conversations dealing with the same problems.

I perceive [said the Merchant] we be neither the wealthier but rather the poorer; whereof it is longe I can not well tell, for theare is suche a generall dearthe of all thinges as I never knewe the like, not only of thinges growinge within this Realme, but also of all other merchandise that we bye beyonde the seas, as silkes, wynes, oyles, woode, madder, iron, steyll, wax, flax, lynnen clothe, fustians, worstedes, coverlettes, carpettes, and all arrasies and tapestrie, spices of all sorts and all haberdashe wares as paper, bothe whyte and browne, glasses as well drinkinge and lookynge as for glasinge of windowes, pinnes, nedles, knives, daggers, hattes, cappes, broches, buttons, and lases; I wote well all theise doe cost me more now by the third parte well, then they did but seaven yeares agoe. Then all kynde of victuall are as dear or dearer agayne, and no cause of godes parte thereof, as farre as I can perceyve; for I never sawe more plentie of corne, grasse and cattel of all sorte, then we have at present, and have had theise iij years past continually, thanked be oure Lord.

They all faced the same problems and, inevitably, sooner or later arrived at the same conclusions.

To this rapid résumé of contemporary opinions of the 'economists' of the sixteenth century, we must add those of the historians. The calculations and observations of Luigi Einaudi on the same controversy between Bodin and Malestroit are particularly revealing. It is true that his study surveys prices in France, the actual scene of the controversy, for much of the 'long' sixteenth century, from the middle of the fifteenth to the end of the sixteenth century. His estimates are open to discussion, but in general are valid. They attempt to apportion the responsibility of each sector for the inflation.

Table 1. *Analysis of the 'real' and 'nominal' price rise in France, 1471–1598* (reference: L. Einaudi)

Period	1471–2	1473–86	1487–1514	1515–54	1555–75	1590–8
Price index (1471–2 = 100)	100	111·5	106·6	161·6	265·2	627·5
Index of the intrinsic value of the *livre tournois* in gold and silver (1471–2 = 100)	100	91·0	78·8	65·5	51·4	47·7
Price index (1471–2 = 100) taking into account only the devaluation of the *livre tournois*	100	109·8	126·9	152·7	194·6	209·6
Price index (1471–2 = 100) with the *livre tournois* retaining its equivalent in precious metals and allowing other causes to take effect	100	101·5	84·0	105·8	136·3	299·4
Percentage of price rise due to the devaluation of the *livre tournois* (nominalist theory: Malestroit)	—	86·73 %	—	90·09 %	72·27 %	35·47 %
Percentage of price rise due to other causes including the devaluation of precious metals after the imports from America (realist theory: Bodin)	—	13·27 %	—	9·91 %	27·73 %	64·53 %

Yet, in spite of the apparent success of this exercise, the essential problem of inflation in the second half of the sixteenth century remains unsettled. Its ramifications are more extensive, and finally such an explanation would not really be appropriate. This, no doubt, is what Carlo Cipolla was attempting to establish when he discussed the 'so-called price revolution' and argued to minimise the impact of inflation. It would indeed be an exaggeration, as we have already implied, to consider the period from 1559 to 1609 as separate and self-contained. It belongs implicitly to a wider and more general movement extending well beyond these limits. The particular characteristic of this period lies in the acceleration of the different inflations across Europe. During these years everything was upset by the movement of prices. In the sixteenth century the world was faced, perhaps for the first time, with a persistent inflation of exceptional magnitude, and this fact must be kept in mind. The rise in prices, to be sure, was not uniform across the different regions of Europe, as is shown briefly and clearly in the two graphs in Fig. 1, reprinted from the *Cambridge Economic History of Europe*. In addition, all prices did not follow the same trend: those of metals, textiles and industrial products in general, of fuel and lighting, of drink and cereals—each had an individual movement. There was a fairly clear divergence between the prices in the industrial sector and in agriculture. This was a major feature—perhaps the touchstone of the whole economy of the century. All that was destined to feed men, above all grainstuffs, came under the heaviest inflationary pressures. The solution of this difficult problem for Europe entailed changes in both structures and habits, and these will be examined later. For the moment, it is enough to underline the disparity between the different sectors, as shown on the one hand by the cost of food, which was highly sensitive to inflation, and on the other hand by the prices of 'industrial' products, which remained relatively unresponsive.

Eventually, all this resolved itself into the problem of the standard of living. By comparison with the more or less satisfactory state of our knowledge of price movements, the information on wages is far from reassuring. Any attempt to estimate the level of employment and personal incomes only from the evidence of daily wage-rates in money is bound to be difficult, particularly when employment was paid sometimes in money and sometimes in kind. On this complex question, the conclusions of E. H. Phelps Brown and Sheila Hopkins are very interesting. They have shown more skill than their predecessors in measuring the interplay of prices and wages, to reveal the consequent deterioration of real wages and standards of living. The violent rise in prices from the mid-sixteenth century led to widespread readjustments in wage levels, but these rarely, if at all, succeeded in keeping up with the rise in prices. As a result there are grounds for inferring a generalised fall in living standards. This fact has been established, for example, in the evidence from England, France,

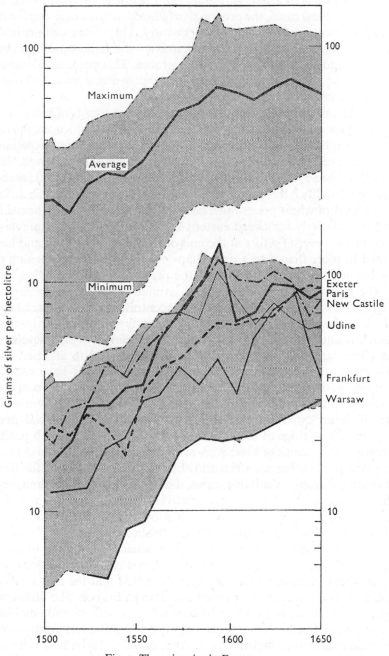

Fig. 1. The price rise in Europe.

Alsace, Valencia, Vienna, Augsburg, and Münster in Westphalia. In the majority of these cases, the progressive fall in standards of living continued until the opening of the seventeenth century. This state of affairs has been closely associated with another movement—the build-up of commercial fortunes and the inflation of trading profits. This paradox coloured the whole of the sixteenth century, when prosperity was achieved all too often to the detriment of large numbers of people.

Apart from the considerations of wages and standards of living, a major question for economic history remains: the extent to which the movement generally affected the continent of Europe. It meant, first, a pressure to closer economic unity in Europe, and, although not fully achieved, this was certainly more evident in the different sectors along the Atlantic seaboard. In all probability it did not prevail over the whole of Europe. The difference in the level of wheat prices in terms of silver between the advanced Spain and the relatively backward eastern Europe—Poland, for example—had been of the order of 7 to 1 at the end of the fifteenth century and had not closed to more than 6 to 1 or perhaps even 5 to 1 by the opening of the seventeenth century. Nevertheless, the pressure to unity, carried forward by the great upsurge in price levels, stimulated a general expansion of mercantile activity. This meant the concentration of commercial capital, which in the past had not enjoyed the same opportunities for investment. Such unification flowed directly from the differences in price levels, which permitted large trading operations from one market to another. Indeed, this mechanism is clear enough. Economic historians have established that international trading balances were often adjusted in terms of bullion. Spain, with the deliveries of gold and silver from the New World, found herself in an extremely favourable position. The commercial network responded to a ridge of high monetary pressure in the Spanish peninsula, where prices in terms of silver were at a higher level. The prices of the same commodities in other countries and above all the countries on the frontiers of western Europe—the Baltic states, the Balkans, the Levant (and, beyond, the countries of the East)—were relatively lower. There was a vast price system after the zones of a Von Thünen model, in which the prices of goods when valued in silver progressively diminished as they were further from Spain. This state of affairs frequently attracted the attention of travellers and writers. When Jacques Esprinchard, a Protestant gentleman from Saintonge, arrived in Cracow in 1597, he noted that the cost of living in Poland was as much as four times less than in France. The differences in price levels stimulated trading in commodities and, indeed, mobility of labour. Jean Bodin observed the migration of labourers from Auvergne to Spain in search of higher wages. And, more recently, historians report the extent of this movement of small craftsmen, pedlars and itinerant peasants towards Spain. The peasants in particular succeeded in repopulating the abandoned lands of Aragon. In Castile, French workmen were reported at cross purposes with the authorities of the Inquisition, whose records frequently indicate that these poor folk became victims as much of their faith as of their reaction to the rigorous inflation of living costs.

It would be, however, an oversimplification to say that prices rose continuously in the sixteenth century. The secular trend suffered repeated interruptions for various reasons. In the middle of the century, there was the depression of the 1540s and 1550s already mentioned. Even after 1560, the rising trend in prices was not a smooth and continuous upswing in material conditions. There were, for example, harvest failures and epidemics which broke the long-term trend with short disasters. In the Netherlands, according to W. S. Unger, the dearth of 1556–7 was the worst winter experienced in the sixteenth century: it was also felt in Denmark, England, north-west Germany, but less acutely in Sweden. In Siena in 1557, suffering from the closing phases of the Italian Wars, there were also catastrophic famine prices. The huge dearths in France came in 1573, in the wake of the vendettas and massacres of St Bartholomew the year before; in 1586–7 and again in 1590–1 in the time of the League. From 1595 to 1597, years of famine prices brought complaints from wide areas over Europe. These shortages, although not as disastrous as those in the following century, were nevertheless severe tests for large sections of the international economy.

In the wake of hunger came disease, epidemics and, above all, plague. Here the same remarks can be made as in the case of famines: in spite of its prosperity, the general health and well-being of Europe hung in a delicate balance. The more heavily populated regions with their brilliant cities were all too often the victims. In Italy the plagues of 1576–7 appeared in Sicily and soon spread to the Peninsula. The estimated ravages were huge: 17,329 deaths in Milan; 28,250 in Genoa; 47,721 in Venice; 16,000 in Pavia—although some exaggeration in these figures must be taken into account. In 1580, so it was reported, plague carried off 120,000 in Paris and 30,000 in Marseilles. In 1565 Hamburg lost a quarter of its inhabitants; and another 6,213 in 1597. In the latter year, 7,737 died in Lübeck. In London in 1563, according to John Stow, plague accounted for 17,404 out of a total 20,372 deaths; and later, in 1593, 10,662 out of a total 17,844 deaths, figures which are roughly valid. These were indeed heavy blows.

Beyond such passing crises and their repercussions on the trend of growth, the mercantile system of Europe at the end of the century began to show signs of stress, of being unable to maintain the same rate of progress. After 1590, after the defeat of the Invincible Armada, weaknesses in the structure began to become apparent. Here was the essential crisis of Spain, the dominant economy, confronted with the prospect of waning power, due in no small measure to the diminishing imports of bullion after the peak years of the 1590s. Such a crisis implied modified rates of growth, and, inevitably, serious consequences for the mercantile system and those networks of merchants who thronged the markets of Europe. All these matters require closer examination.

II

The question of changes in price levels naturally raises the problem of money and credit. Although this has claimed historians' attention, it is nevertheless clear that it is not confined to the simple problem of bullion and money but implies more crucial questions of credit. To put these developments clearly in perspective, we must go back beyond the limit of our chapter, at least to the fifteenth century. Already at that time, the European economy experienced a slow, almost imperceptible inflation of gold. Gold, the noblest and rarest of the precious metals, was produced by the primitive but effective technique of panning. It was found in many parts of Europe, along the rivers Rhine and Seine for example, and even in the eighteenth century these continued to attract small groups of gold-panners. By far the most important source, however, was Africa. The placer gold was found there more abundantly; it was brought to the shores of the Mediterranean by caravans across the Sahara, or by an alternative route down the valley of the Nile. This African trade was partly but not completely diverted to the Atlantic by the Portuguese, when they arrived on the Guinea coast in 1474 and guarded their interests with the massive fort of São Jorge da Minha (1481). All this reinforced the economic power of Portugal in the years before 1497–8 and the discovery of the route by Cape of Good Hope.

The monetary circulation of Europe, however, was not entirely tied to gold: it was also supplied with silver. Although this was less valuable, it was more difficult to produce. Its value increased with the relative abundance of gold, which in turn stimulated silver production. Out of all this emerged the profits of central Europe at the turn of the fifteenth century and the astonishing fortunes of merchant financiers such as the Fuggers and Welsers of Augsburg. Although silver-mining brought handsome returns, it also required heavy inputs of capital for the sinking of new mine-shafts and the application of new methods of extraction. In 1451, when the duke of Saxony authorised the use of lead to extract silver from the mixed copper and silver ores, no mine in Germany produced annually more than 10,000 marks weight. In 1530, there were eight mines claiming an annual production of 10 to 15,000 marks. The scope of this achievement can be seen in the engravings, so often reproduced, from Georgius Agricola's *De re metallica*, written about 1533 but published in Basle in 1556. The coinage and circulation of heavy silver coins were further evidence of this industrial development: the *taler* appeared in the Tyrol in 1484, in Saxony in 1500, in Austria in 1524, and not least at Joachimstal in 1518, origin of the famous *Joachimstaler*.

24

Thus, the situation was basically simple: abundant gold and relatively scarce silver. This was not reversed until the depression of the mid-sixteenth century, which marked a turning-point. It revealed changes in the terms of trade between the different regions of the international economy, changed relationships filled with surprises and individual disasters. These were particularly severe in the markets long accustomed to trading silver from Germany against gold from Spain and Portugal or, more precisely, relayed by Spanish and Portuguese merchants from Africa and later from America (which at the outset supplied mainly gold). This

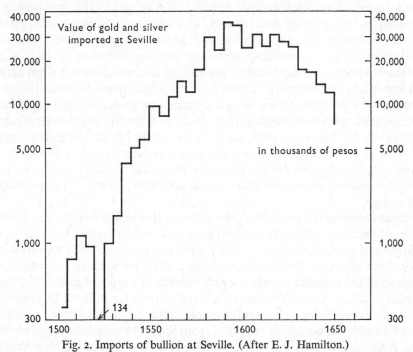

Fig. 2. Imports of bullion at Seville. (After E. J. Hamilton.)

came in sufficient abundance to capture the market from the more expensive gold from Guinea. With the second half of the sixteenth century, however, silver mines were opened up in the New World, first in the arid lands of north Mexico: at Zacatecas (1546), Compostela de la Guadalajara (1553), Sombrete and Durango (1555), Trestrillo (1562), Parral (at the end of the sixteenth century). Then, in Peru, the astonishingly rich lodes of the mountain at Potosí were 'discovered' in 1543. The introduction of methods of treating the ore with mercury (by amalgamation, or the *patio* process as the Mexicans called it) in Mexico after 1556 (really effective after 1562), and in Peru after 1572 (effective in the 1580s), brought progressively larger quantities of silver to the wharves and warehouses of Seville. They certainly increased, as is shown in Fig. 2, from the classic study of

Earl J. Hamilton, who sets the maximum for these imports in the decade 1591–1600. The studies of Huguette and Pierre Chaunu, however, place this peak at a later date, in the following decade, 1600–9, which is possible but not proved beyond all doubt.

In brief, during the period covered by this chapter, the international economy was in a phase of silver inflation. Its first consequence was to undercut the prosperity of the German mines: they never really recovered from the difficulties already apparent in the 1530s. Secondly, it stimulated the economy of Europe as a whole. And finally, but by no means least in importance, it entailed a rapid appreciation of gold. The two precious metals had in effect changed places, and now gold tended to disappear from circulation. The appreciation of gold was a long-term affair, and the full effects in the international economy were not felt until the beginning of the next century. Nevertheless the change in conditions was soon acute in the market of Antwerp, which covered adjustments between the two metals. The peculiar nature of this situation at its turning-point did not escape the attention of the Royal Merchant in Antwerp, Thomas Gresham: 'Here ys no kinde of gold stering', he wrote on 20 December 1553, 'which ys the strangest matter that ever was seyn upon the Bowesse of Andwerpe having no nother payment but silver Spanish ryalls; as for angelles and sovereynes, here is nonen to be gotten...for that the exchange ys so hye.'

Spain became the unchallenged master in this new phase in the circulation of precious metals. It received large deliveries of silver together with cargoes of gold. Although the latter were not comparable in weight with the silver delivered from New Spain and the Tierra Firme, nevertheless they enabled Spain to remain the great source of supply of gold in Europe. Spain in effect became the strongroom of Europe for bullion. By contrast the other economies—near and far—faced the problem of how to join in the scramble for bullion re-exported from Spain. In principle, Spain closed her frontiers, with the purpose of keeping the treasures of the New World for herself: but this was merely in principle. The gold and silver soon found their way abroad, not least through an unfavourable balance of trade, which contemporaries only vaguely appreciated. Spain did not produce sufficient meat for herself, sufficient wheat, cloth and other manufactured goods to supply her own needs. Her exports of salt, wool and oil did not compensate for the imports she bought for herself and for her hungry colonies.

This paradoxical situation was most serious in countries with apparently the greatest advantages. In the seventeenth and eighteenth centuries, the matter engrossed the attention of economists and advisers not only in Spain but in other countries as well. They discussed the subject endlessly: bullion did not create wealth. Yet, in reality, the situation in Spain should not be painted darker than necessary. Her textile industries in Segovia,

Córdoba, Toledo, and even in such rural centres as Cuenca, did not lose vitality until the end of the sixteenth century, about 1590, when Spain was finally obliged to open her coffers and allow the bullion to escape. From that moment, if we follow the conclusions of Felipe Ruiz Martin, the great international merchants and financiers, who had until then invested part of their profits in the products of Spanish industries, now preferred to export them in form of specie or even in bullion. The exports of silver— the *sacas de plata*—had become so convenient.

The reason for these increasing exports may be found in the imperial policy of Spain. By the occupation of Portugal in 1580, Spain was drawn more deeply into the vast and costly politics of the Atlantic. After the defeat of the Invincible Armada, the control of the seas slipped more and more from her grasp. She was obliged to fall back and consolidate her strength in the great cockpit of Europe, the Low Countries. In this situation, her future became entangled in the power politics of Europe, in Germany, in the Baltic States, in England, in Ireland, and not least in turbulent France. To sustain this gigantic struggle, she was obliged to arrange great payments to the Low Countries, where Antwerp still remained one of the great banking centres of Europe, even though over-shadowed with the futility and uncertainties of war. Such credits were only effective when followed up by huge deliveries of silver to pay the armies and settle the bills of exchange falling due in the fairs. Indeed, the cargoes of treasure which arrived at irregular intervals in the Casa de la Contratación in Seville were soon spread to the markets of Europe, including Antwerp, according to a set time-table. These irregular shipments were changed into a continuous stream by means of loans and transfers—in particular the *asientos*, or loans arranged between the merchants of Madrid and the *Corte*. Such operations were only made possible by means of a 'float' of bills of exchange, and sales of silver crossed the Mediterranean in convoy from Barcelona to Genoa, for the route through the Channel became in practice half closed to Spain after 1569. The Genoese bankers excelled in these financial operations. They controlled the huge trans-actions in coin and paper and organised the concomitant trading arrange-ments. After about 1570 the heyday of the Genoese began,[1] opening a century when they took over the running from the Fuggers, whose financial pre-eminence declined with the fading prosperity of the German mines after 1530.

In addition to these ways of draining silver from Spain, there was smuggling. Without exaggerating its importance, it undoubtedly played a persistent role: bullion in contraband slipped from Spain to France by way of the Pyrenees, a veritable paradise for smugglers. The lines of mules carrying bullion crossed the mountains to reach Toulouse, St-Jean-de-Luz, and that remarkable entrepôt city, Bayonne, a great centre for smuggling,

[1] See also below, p. 257.

thus brought into the forefront of affairs. In such ways, gold and even the more bulky silver were constantly on the move.

As a result, the monetary systems of Europe were reinforced. All or at least almost all these systems had suffered disastrously, particularly after 1540 and the beginning of the decade of the 1550s, from the difficulties of debased coinage, from the flood of small coins (of mixed copper and silver). These clogged the markets, and drove the more valuable coins from circulation. The seriousness of the situation was all too clear, for example, in the region of Hamburg; and in France, where the famous silver *testons* were converted into *douzains* of much lower alloy. England also suffered extensive debasements under Henry VIII and even more disastrously under Edward VI. With the growing deliveries of silver in Spain, these strains were generally relieved. In France the minting of *testons* was resumed after 1553; the coinage of heavier silver typical of the late sixteenth century came with the silver *franc* in 1575 and the *quart d'écu* in 1577. The United Provinces, although hostile to Spain, were still prepared to accept her silver: their *rijksdaalder* weighing 29·28 grammes appeared in 1583. But, as was to be expected, the greatest success was reserved for the coins of Spain. Along with the gold *escudo* or *pistollet*, first issued in 1537, came waves of silver *reals*: the heaviest, the famous piece of eight, invaded the whole of Europe. In Poitou, the studies of Paul Raveau show the abundance of *reals* circulating after 1575, although this was a time when the monetary system of France particularly favoured silver currency. However, the same coins were also flooding the Low Countries (both loyal and insurgent) in the wake of the Spanish armies on campaign to win obedience for Philip II. From the great ports of Italy—from Genoa, Leghorn, Venice—and not only from Italy but also from the great port of Marseilles, they filtered into the markets of the Levant, and thence to the Far East: in China the merchants accepted them with eager enthusiasm.

However, these coins, whether allowed to circulate or kept in coffers, did not represent the whole monetary stock in the sixteenth century. In addition to real coins, a large place was taken by the type of money called money of account, whose role—contrary to the opinions of many historians—was by no means insignificant. Indeed, it was a factor of exceptional importance.

These imaginary and fiduciary moneys of account had particular names in the different countries—the *pound sterling* in England, the *livre tournois* in France, the various *lire* of Italy, the *maravedí* of New Castile, the *florin* of Flanders. In these units it was customary to keep accounts. Naturally, such moneys of account were convertible into actual gold and silver coins, but the conversion rate was not fixed. In brief, their intrinsic value was variable. Any alterations inevitably indicated profound economic movements and changes in structure.

At the time, theorists were aware of the problem, and the controversy in 1566–8 between the Sieur de Malestroit and Jean Bodin affords ample proof of this. It has often been customary to give Bodin credit for clear thinking in elaborating a quantity theory of money, in asserting that the flood of precious metals from the New World was directly responsible for the rise in prices. On the other hand, Malestroit was not entirely wrong. It ought to be said at the outset that the inflation of the moneys of account did not follow exactly the rise in prices in terms of precious metals. There was a gap. Nominal prices certainly proved to be far more sensitive than other prices. In reality, the moneys of account must be considered as representing the level of transactions of a region, of an economy with a certain way of living and activity, of the effectiveness with which its income covered consumption. If, in a particular economy, this balance between revenue and consumption fell out of line on the international level, an element of weakness entered the monetary system and devaluation followed. The changes in the relative positions of the different moneys of account, when measured against an international currency such as silver, were thus unmistakable evidence of disorders and internal deteriorations. They showed that the different sectors of the European economy were not only intimately tied together, but also underwent a process of progressive adjustment. Such relative changes in the long run established a hierarchy: the dominant economy remained stable, while the others devalued. Table 2 gives a glimpse at this immense problem, setting out the changes in position of some of the major currencies:

Table 2. *Index of the devaluation of selected silver currency systems in Europe 1530–1614*

Country	Name of money of account	Index of silver values in 1610–14 (1530–9 = 100)
New Castile	Maravedí	98·03
Würzburg	Rechnungsgulden	91·87
Naples	Carlino	87·34
Frankfurt	Rechnungsgulden	84·06
Augsburg	Rechnungsgulden	83·02
Austria	Rechengulden	76·33
Poland	Grosz	75·71
England	Pound sterling	72·59
Venice	Lira	69·72
Genoa	Lira	67·71
France	Livre tournois	66·57
Strassburg	Pfund	62·97
Holland	Guilder	60·13
Spanish Netherlands	Florin	46·55
Turkey	Asper	44·19

Spain remained relatively stable until the turn of the century. But among the more seriously affected currency systems were those of France and the Low Countries (both south and north), which paid a heavy price for the disturbances of civil war. The Ottoman empire, long accustomed to putting a high price on silver, inevitably lost a great deal of ground with the changes in the second half of the sixteenth century provoked by the rising deliveries of silver from the New World.

The expansion in the level of economic activity, however, demanded ever greater quantities of gold and silver. But the arrivals of both gold and silver in the Casa de la Contratación in Seville, as we have seen, reached a culminating point in the decade 1591–1600. However, the retardation of this huge movement was even more important than the actual quantities involved. For this, it is necessary to attach the greatest significance to the decade 1581–90, during which the decennial rate of increase of the arrivals of bullion reached its peak. In other terms, after the difficult years about 1590, the whole movement had already begun to mature.

This is important, for, as a result of the slowing pace of economic change at the close of the sixteenth century, Europe began to experience monetary conditions which in general were to be typical of the seventeenth century. At a time when the economy continued to expand, even at a slower rate, and required increasing quantities of money, the supplies began to slacken and then decline. There was an overriding need to supplement the existing facilities, to adopt a new attitude to instruments of credit, and to return to a system of inferior coins—of copper and silver, and then of pure copper—which gained increasing circulation. Even in Amsterdam, the famous Wisselbank was established partly to overcome the difficulties arising from the confusion of varying and defective coins which hampered large-scale trade.

These new conditions were first evident in Spain. After the crisis and bankruptcy of 1596–7, the government turned to minting copper money. Between 1599 and 1606, 22 million ducats worth of these coins were issued from the mints in Spain (each ducat equalled 375 maravedís). This tampering with the economic system had immediate and serious consequences, and even a century later Spaniards considered this monetary policy a disaster of the first magnitude. Other countries in Europe did not escape the same difficulties, but the effects in Spain made them more cautious. France was a case in point: she had minted pure copper coins since 1577, but in 1608–9, in the face of the new conditions, the royal officials approached the problem with prudence. The same experience warned the authorities in Sweden, in north Germany, in the Low Countries; and other countries—England, Venice, Portugal (included in the Iberian group until 1640)—were infinitely more prudent when faced with an inflation of copper.

A more significant inflationary force, though not always successful, was that of credit. The volume of credit in Europe was naturally a function of the level of transactions themselves. The movement of commodities, the progressive settling of trading balances, all demanded confidence and eventually credit, even though, as we have seen with the devaluations of the moneys of account, the credit system was never able to escape very far from the requirement of large bullion reserves. The mass of bills of exchange which circulated in Europe at the end of the sixteenth century bore witness to the fact. These requirements were aided by the wider use of more sophisticated techniques—the endorsement of bills of exchange, the use of the *patto di ricorsa* (which offered a brief period of credit during the time the bill circulated before settlement), and of the public banks. These developments, although apparent at the close of our period, belong rightly to the early seventeenth century.

In another respect, the extent of credit was intimately linked with the network of trade, with the associations of merchants, in ports, markets and fairs all over Europe. The activity of the merchant financiers of Genoa was an outstanding example. Established in Italy, the traditional focus of Europe, and involved in the great Atlantic venture of Spain, with agents all over the continent, they were the channels through which the shift in emphasis was effected in the international economy from the south to the north of Europe and the Atlantic. They thus prepared the way for the extraordinary success of Holland.

Holland indeed became a notable place of refuge in Europe. The thirteenth article of the Union of Utrecht (1579) proclaimed religious toleration, a feature of outstanding importance, for refugees to Holland automatically brought with them established sets of contacts throughout Europe. The Sephardic Jews, harried from the Iberian Peninsula, were an excellent case in point. The first direct arrival of Portuguese Jews in Amsterdam came in 1598 or late 1597; and by 1609 they numbered 200. By 1630 there were altogether about 1,000 Jews in Amsterdam. Bringing their riches and business acumen to supplement the prosperity of the mercantile states of the north, such an emigration became by definition a European phenomenon. A case study of this great movement can be found in the itinerary of the wealthy Mendes family of Lisbon, who in 1536 went by way of London, Antwerp, Lyons, Venice and Ragusa to establish themselves finally in the commercial and financial world of Constantinople. One member, later the duke of Naxos, carved out an astonishing career. This diaspora and others served to establish a brilliant network of family and business relationships across the continent.

III

Although the problems of prices, wages and precious metals have their own particular importance, the main discussion of this chapter turns on the subject of aggregate supply and demand. Total effective demand was in the first instance a mass of needs and necessities expressed within the framework of traditional and relatively unchanging societies, which allowed little alteration. They were marked by insufficiencies, inelasticities, and barriers to development rarely overcome. These structures, by definition, tended to make population movements the principal factor in the formation of demand. Over the course of time, it dominated the scene.

The population of Europe, according to the evidence available, certainly increased from the middle of the fifteenth to the beginning, even the middle, of the seventeenth century. About this time a general decline set in. It is not possible to offer an exact estimate of this growth in the short period covered by this chapter, more especially since quantitative comparisons are very approximate. About 1450, according to the estimates of historians, Europe counted some 50 to 60 millions; about 1600, perhaps 80 to 85 millions, though Joseph Kulischer put the population of the Europe west of the Urals as high as 95 millions. These estimates thus give a growth of 30 millions in a century and a half (or roughly an increase of half) or an almost imperceptible annual increase of perhaps 0·3 per cent. It was, however, cumulative. It gave strength to all the progress accomplished in the material and even non-material life of men. Indeed, it has been said that in perhaps two or three generations the Renaissance added some 10 million more people to Europe. This Europe can be defined as the narrow continent, even if unified only in theory, reaching from the Atlantic to the conventional limit of the Urals, from Scandinavia to the Mediterranean. To this area we must also add European Turkey with perhaps, at a conservative estimate, 8 million persons in 1600. In all, some 95 or at most 100 million human beings. This suggests an average density of about 25 per square mile. For the time, it was a very high concentration. It meant that Europe was more than able to counterbalance the weight of decadent China (which under the Mings, according to some estimates, claimed 56–60 million persons). Europe, at a guess—and it is certainly stretching the evidence—represented about a fifth of the world's population, and this constituted a dense, dynamic human mass.

Although the density and size of population cannot be said to have ordered everything in human history, a great deal nevertheless depended on this factor. In the first place, after a century of expansion, Europe revealed a general vitality in the world in the late sixteenth century. Men were abundant in Europe. The cities, the wars, the colonial empires, and the expansion even in the second half of the sixteenth century, were fed from this reservoir. More men meant more hands to work, more transport on the roads distributing both merchandise and people, ever on the move from place to place. Also during this development, money loans increased considerably; during the whole of the sixteenth century, the level of prices could have increased five times. And, after all, the price rise and the increasing deliveries of precious metals were due to some extent to the effects of this impressive growth in numbers.

At this particular stage in economic development, human labour could be a measure of value. And the countries of Europe can be classed in these terms. Julius Beloch has already measured the size and densities of the different countries in Europe at the end of the sixteenth century. First of all, size. About 1600, the most populous country was Germany (some 20 millions); then France (slightly smaller in area than at the present day), which claimed 16 millions; Italy, 13 millions; Spain and Portugal (united after 1580), 10 millions at the most. England and Wales cut a small figure—4·5 millions; Scotland and Ireland, 2 millions. The Scandinavian countries, 1·4 millions, to which Denmark contributed 0·6. The four provinces of Poland, according to Beloch, probably contained 3 million inhabitants, but more recent estimates for the larger area of Poland/Lithuania propose a figure of 8 millions.

The densities of the different countries, however, give another classification. Italy heads the list with 114 per square mile; then the Low Countries with 104; France with 88; England and Wales with 78; Germany with 73; and Spain and Portugal trailed behind with 44. The last figure is most remarkable, in view of the world power of the Spaniards and Portuguese. The Peninsula, however, was mountainous, its climate arid; and inevitably emigration played its part. In 1572 the Venetian Ambassador in Lisbon wrote to the Senate, 'In the Province of Portugal there can hardly be more people than there are, so long as this region is deprived of people to send to the Indies.' The observation could have been made equally well for Spain.

These figures of density and population appear low, at least to modern eyes. But the same can be said of the price revolution in the sixteenth century, when seen in the light of the twentieth century. Everything was relative, and the sixteenth century must be judged in the first instance by the limits of its own dimensions and vitality. In this way France with its sixteen millions and a density of eighty-eight was apparently an over-populated country, endowed with an explosive force. Similarly in the case of Italy, which had a still higher density. This meant pressures only partly relieved by emigration, although the extent of the problem is difficult to estimate. The low figures must not be considered as without importance (a thousand emigrants went annually from Spain to America in the sixteenth century). They indicate the tensions inherent in the general expansion, not least in the cities.

In the Europe of 1500 five cities probably had a population of about 100,000 inhabitants or more: Paris, Naples, Venice, Milan and Constantinople. By 1600 Paris and Naples had passed into the class of more than 200,000 inhabitants. In the group of cities of above 100,000 inhabitants, Venice and Milan were joined by seven others: London, Lisbon, Rome,

Amsterdam, Palermo, Seville and Antwerp. These towns played a decisive role in the course of the century; almost all of them were ports and five of them in particular on the shores of the Atlantic Ocean. As for the special example of Constantinople, at the end of the century it claimed for certain 400,000 and perhaps as many as 700,000 inhabitants.

Further information on the great cities of Europe is given in Maps 1 and 2. Their growth stimulated the long and prosperous economic activity associated with the sixteenth century. But on the other hand it should be noted that these cities did not reach the level of great urban agglomerations. The great fortune of London began to emerge only with the seventeenth century.

Many other remarks can be made on the complex subject of the cities. Not all were of the same rank. In the sixteenth century, Paris and London changed from being cities of wooden buildings to triumph with brick and stone—'from sticks to bricks', as James I is supposed to have said. Closer studies of the remarkable achievements of these cities show, for example, how London succeeded in imposing the Reformation; how Paris, in spite of the triumphal entry of Henry IV in 1594, carried the day, for the king had already 'received instruction' and accepted the *sine qua non*, the Catholic church. These robust cities bear excellent witness to the huge economic systems which they served and guided. Lisbon soon reached 100,000 inhabitants and then, as Pierre Chaunu has shown, levelled out with the middle of the century. In contrast, Seville, which claimed 73,522 inhabitants in 1530 and 114,738 in 1594, continued to expand in the seventeenth century, until it could no longer resist the collapse of the great days of America and the loss of that easy flow of bullion to Spain.

Yet changes in population were not always as favourable to economic development as may at first be imagined. More men brought more vagabonds and bandits to live on the fringe of society and the law; they also raised the demand for employment, which created another difficult problem. In short, the growth of population implied a whole series of advantages, mixed with burdens and inconveniences. It is possible, as Alfred Sauvy has shown, that at a given moment human production follows the laws of diminishing returns, a process of deterioration. In the seventeenth century the concentration of population in Europe sooner or later suffered severe setbacks according to the region, and first of all in Spain. Europe at the end of the sixteenth century had become relatively overpopulated, more especially in the western countries, the most dense and the most wealthy. A technological revolution such as the Industrial Revolution might have saved the situation but this came two centuries later. In other words, it is possible that the level of production could not reach the required capacity, and was insufficient for the population. In effect, supply did not respond to the increasing demand.

Map 1. Urban centres in Europe *c.* 1500.

◯ , cities with over 100,000 inhabitants

⬤ , cities with over 200,000 inhabitants

Map 2. Urban centres in Europe *c.* 1600.

IV

In the final assessment, the crux of the international economy in the six-teenth century was how production could respond to the powerful up-surge in demand. This entails a review of the production and productivity of Europe.

For the first sector, agriculture, the quantitative estimates are imperfect. There are some samples here and there, but they are of local interest and importance. One of the more recent is the study of Hans-Helmut Wächter for some East Prussian estates in the sixteenth and seventeenth centuries. This shows the relative importance of the different cereals: wheat remained a luxury, rye was a basic commodity, barley and oats were spring crops of secondary value. The average returns per hectare (slightly less than two and a half acres) were: wheat, 870 kilogrammes; rye, 760; barley, 700; and oats only 370. Higher returns no doubt existed, but these tended to be exceptional. The returns in general were mediocre, for grain tended to be smaller and, sown more thickly, gave a thinner return than today. In reality, as the conclusions for East Prussia show, the harvest yields, when compared with the seed sown, were often very low—four to one, five to one, or six to one—and, moreover, the seed required for the next sowing considerably diminished the grain available for immediate consumption. These poor yields, indeed, were a barrier for agriculture. The area under cultivation could be extended but, each time the total volume of the harvest was thus increased, the average returns were systematically reduced. The study of Hans-Helmut Wächter demonstrates this very clearly, as the graph reprinted from his study shows. This emphasises the contrast between the area cultivated and the percentage yield, and by implication the barriers to increasing the production of grain.

Yet what has been shown for cereals—and, after all, bread was the basic need of Europe—can equally well be shown in the case of livestock. This sector too could not satisfy the growing demand for meat without having artificial pastures, largely unknown in the sixteenth century. It is not surprising therefore that, except in the plains of the east and in the Balkans, cattle were scarce in Europe. In one respect, however, the sixteenth century was favoured: there was a huge rise in pig-raising, and so in the consump-tion of preserved pork in various forms.

In general, whether we consider agriculture or livestock husbandry, the sixteenth century was clearly hampered by limits and barriers. As a general rule, if an annual minimum ration of three hectolitres of grain—wheat, or rye, or a mixture of wheat and rye—is assigned to each person, then every year Europe consumed some 300 million hectolitres of cereals. Or, if the lower figure of 85 millions is used for the population of Europe, the amount would be 255 million hectolitres. It is clear also that the needs of Europe were by no means regularly satisfied, for the records of the period are filled with complaints of famines and high prices. Apparently grain production did not perfectly meet the demand.

In the past, historians have devoted a great deal of attention to the huge traffic in wheat which the trends of the sixteenth century encouraged and enlarged. Large cargoes of wheat and rye were exported from the Baltic during the course of the sixteenth century and shipped to the Low Countries, to Portugal and Spain. After the crisis of 1590, grain from the

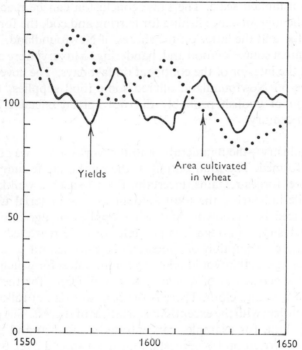

Fig. 3. Grain production in East Prussia. (After H.-H. Wächter.)
(Index base: 1549–1697 = 100)

north invaded the Mediterranean, from Gibraltar to Genoa, to Leghorn, to Venice. This was paid for by great remittances of silver settled through the Exchange of Antwerp, the focal point in these financial operations, while Amsterdam had charge of storage and shipment of this bulky merchandise. Wheat was also exported from Provence and Languedoc. Evidence of these long- and short-haul distributions of grain is recorded in numerous documents. They were extremely important, but their total volume represented a small part of the needs of Europe. The shipments by sea probably amounted to one or two per cent of the total consumption of grain. The problem of grain remained largely a local affair. The hunger of the cities and the countryside was generally satisfied at short range. The impressive wheat shipments were to all intents and purposes a phenomenon of minor importance when related to the overall appetite of Europe. However, years of crop failures and famines could bring about huge modifications to such a system. These pressures were infinitely greater in the seventeenth century.

A similar situation existed in the remarkable successes of Schleswig-Holstein and the United Provinces, which specialised in the production of beef cattle and edible fats. Bacon, butter and cheese were the foundation of some huge local fortunes. This production remained geographically and socially on a limited scale. The same conclusion can be reached on the subject of the long-distance fishing for herring and cod, the former on the Dogger Bank, and the latter off the shores of Newfoundland. These were certainly a great source of food and, pandering to luxury, were appreciated not least in the interior of the continent on fast days. The development of the fisheries off Newfoundland offered some food supplies, though the consumption of codfish probably did not spread effectively until the seventeenth century.

As for industry—the handicrafts and the workshops—we are also only partially informed. The total output of the mines, the foundries and the iron and steel forges remains uncertain. Even in such a well-known field as the textile industries, the total amount of raw material used and of cloth produced is unknown. And what applies in agriculture is also valid for industry. Although it is possible to make reasoned guesses for the aggregate consumption of foodstuffs in Europe and to arrive at an approximate figure, this would relate to commodities for which there were relatively low elasticities of demand. It was different for the mass consumption of iron and cloth. There is the constant risk of following those studies which deal with the exceptional instances of success. The production of woollen cloth, for example, concentrated craftsmen and workshops, but was also carried on by domestic industries spread over the countryside—as in the case of many regions in England. And very often these concerned high-class products. The 20,000 cloths which Venice manufactured yearly at the end of the sixteenth century were luxury cloths. The cloths of Segovia (13,000 about 1580) or of Córdoba (17,000 about 1566), like the sturdy English cloth, were also quality productions. In Riga at the end of the sixteenth century, Gunnar Mickwitz has shown that the English and Dutch cloths, and even more the silk fabrics, were destined for the use of a rich clientele, while the peasants had to remain content with the coarser local weaves. In the same way, in Spain during the whole of the sixteenth century, there were the fashionable Aragonese cloths, woven in the countryside—the *cordeletes*—and the increasing use of local cloths, such as those spun and woven in the little town of Cuenca, in the centre of Manca. It is scarcely possible to take account of the heterogeneous clientele in the lower ranks of society, all too often accustomed to linen and hempen cloth produced locally or even by the family. In France the peasantry began to use coarse woollen cloths only in the eighteenth century. Thus there is little chance to estimate the volume of woollen, or mixed woollen and cotton, cloth used by the inhabitants of Europe, although the limited market for luxury fabrics is relatively well known. The industries in effect did not yet produce for mass consumption. They did not possess the low final costs to reach the poor on the verge of subsistence, to which the grey mass of people were confined at that time. Although naturally this statement is only valid for the sectors considered, in general it carries considerable weight.

In the second place, these industries were not concentrated. Each economic zone could more or less cover its requirements. Spain herself, to take an example, had mines and ironworks, silver and mercury mines, salt-pans, shipbuilding yards, manufactures of saltpetre, gunpowder and arms, and indeed a whole line of textile industries, both rural and urban, to which even large towns such as Segovia, Toledo and Córdoba were devoted. Some needs, however, were not met locally. Salt from the sea was a monopoly of the countries of the south, and there was a considerable trade in salt to England (where the high price undoubtedly encouraged salt-boiling), to the Netherlands, Germany and the countries of the Baltic, either by sea from Setúbal or San Lúcar, or from Brouage in France— the 'Bay'. In the same way there was a monopoly of tin, lead and copper (Hungary excepted) to the profit of the countries of the north and Germany (whose wealth in silver reached its heyday about 1530). Philip II had even considered bringing the insurgent Low Countries to heel by putting a blockade on salt but this only resulted in pushing the rebels to develop the American salt from Araya on the coast of Venezuela.[1]

All these products were competitive in the great markets unless their special qualities had assigned them in advance to particular zones of custom. Venice produced fine cloths and quality silks, but the Tierra Firme wove cloths of second quality. The kersies of England passed by way of Venice to the Levant, but, in general, did not compete with the fine cloths of Venice, which were of a different style. It was the same with the serges and light cloths of Hondschoote in Flanders, which were marketed with the fustians (linen and cotton) of southern Germany, but were not substitutes. It is possible that the expansion of the sixteenth century brought a spread in the location of industries, maintaining and reinvigorating the old. The exceptions, however, confirm the rule: the siting of industry in Europe was widespread. Later, in the seventeenth century, industries— to confine our remarks to this sector—tended to become concentrated in more restricted areas.

Everywhere industrial expansion was the rule. How did it grow? We

[1] See also below, p. 523.

can follow the situation in some cases from year to year. The exports of shortcloths from London, for example, which had known a spectacular boom during the debasements of Henry VIII and Edward VI, recovered the same level at the end of the century: an average of 103,032 pieces were exported annually during the years 1598–1600. In Venice, the production of woollen cloth rose from an average of 8,563 pieces in 1540–9 to 22,428 in 1600–9 (see Fig. 4). In Leiden in the United Provinces, another spectacular increase: 23,047 serges in 1587 and 45,557 in 1610; 1,200 fustians in 1589 and 14,522 in 1610; 2,389 'ras' in 1600 and 2,726 in 1610; 250 cloths (*laken*) in 1574 and 1,422 in 1610; 3,033 baizes in 1584 and 8,202 in 1610. In effect the total production of Leiden doubled in a quarter of a century.

Table 3. *Average annual production of cloth in Venice*

Period	Number of pieces
1540–9	8,563
1550–9	13,240
1600–9	22,428

Table 4. *Average annual exports of shortcloths from London*

Period	Number of pieces
1500–2	49,214
1542–4	99,362
1545–7	118,642
1550–2	110,148
1598–1600	103,032

Inevitably, these are isolated figures. There was also the stable tin production in Devon and Cornwall during the second half of the sixteenth century, the silver production of Potosí in Peru, the slump in the cloth industry of Hondschoote in the 1580s, which however began to show signs of recovery by the end of the century. But it is the general movement of production which must be kept in mind. There are two particularly long series, those of the Sound tolls edited by Nina Bang and Knud Korst; and those of the port of Seville, published by Huguette and Pierre Chaunu. These, admittedly, are figures for trade and not production. However, it is probable that trade moved largely in association with the general level of economic activity in Europe. For the movement through the straits of Denmark, the Sound, the estimates are not conclusive, for the extent of smuggling remains an unknown factor. If, however, we accept that the type of ships used did not diminish in displacement (which is more than probable since they began to increase noticeably in size at the turn of the

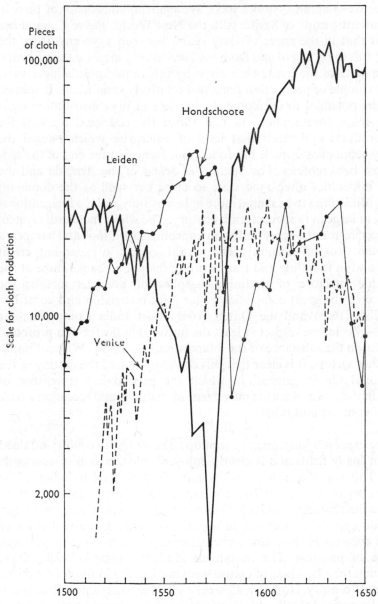

Fig. 4. Cloth production in Venice, Leiden and Hondschoote.

century), then the *number* of ships recorded as passing through the Sound trebled between about 1550 and 1600. We again find this factor of three in the transatlantic trade of Seville with the New World. Pierre Chaunu has estimated that in the space of sixty years, between 1550 and 1610, the shipping *tonnage* going to and from the New World increased three times.

Yet, in spite of the impression given by this remarkable achievement, the total volume of production remained relatively insufficient. It seemed to lack the potential to overcome the barriers of high distribution costs and low mass consumption, to rise above the restricted markets for luxury products and reach that level of enterprise which offered the necessary economies of scale in production. Hence, at the end of the century, came bankruptcies. For Spain, the defeat of the Armada and the years of difficulties after 1590 were to close her spell as the dominant economy, difficulties to be shared more or less by Italy and the international economy at large in the seventeenth century. The whole mercantile system experienced restraints, depressed by an unpromising outlook and hampered by a certain lack of ingenuity. The partial success in expanding credit facilities and in founding and transforming the public banks came at the unfortunate juncture of declining supplies of precious metals; the emergence of the great companies under joint ownership and control— the English (1600) and the Dutch (1602) East India Companies, for example—was in one respect at least the outward indicator of a profound adjustment in the substance of the international economy. Without implicating other sectors, it is clear that this economy shared the destiny of the international life in general, in which the paradoxical emergence of Holland in the midst of a wide movement of maturity and recession struck a note of contrast and relief.

Can we express a judgement to sum up? The sixteenth century attained success in many fields and it clearly enjoyed an expansion of economic activity. This expansion, however, was destined to tend to a limit. The great tide began to ebb, as if its rise lacked the requisite momentum to overcome the obstacles and impediments which it itself had raised. Large-scale trade apparently was not in a position to reach the vast mass of potential consumers. Few new technical changes were made to reinforce the surge of progress. The movement gradually turned to disunities, tensions and rebuffs. These of course were not lacking in the course of the late sixteenth century. However, after the 1590s the bankruptcies increased, state bankruptcies as well as those of companies and merchants. In Spain and in Italy especially, the signs of economic maturity and the shadows of recession multiplied, forecasting the stagnation of the seventeenth century. The whole economy of Western Europe suffered powerful checks as if it had passed the peak of its effort and begun to experience falling marginal returns.

In the sector of credit, however, the patterns of the future were beginning to show, although the expedients adopted were not always successful in remedying the inherent difficulties in the international economy. It had grown accustomed to a flood of bullion and, in attempting to enlarge the system of credit, in effect proposed a huge reform. The seventeenth century did not invent but rather increased the mass of bills of exchange in circulation. This filled or tried to fill the gap left by the insufficiencies of coin and bullion. There were other techniques in the establishment of the public banks. Venice introduced her Banco della Piazza di Rialto in 1587; Spain attempted unsuccessfully to do the same in 1604, and France in 1607. Then in 1609, in the last year of our study, in Amsterdam, the famous Wisselbank was founded, token of the rising trade and finances of expanding Holland. Another sign of mixed progress and prudence, this time in England, was the greater use of regulated and joint stock companies; there was the Levant Company of 1581, which in turn was destined to nourish the foundation of the East India Company (1600), a powerful instrument of colonial trade. There were the Dutch, English, Danish and French companies and others which at the beginning of the seventeenth century crossed the Atlantic to tap the trade of the West Indies and plant colonies on the mainland of North America. These institutions ran counter to the traditions of the great merchant dynasties.

Thus, the close of this period revealed a certain adroitness in the trading sectors of Europe, but forecast with equal certainty the difficult times ahead. Thirty years of war were about to strike the foundations of Europe. And then there were difficulties for all, not least for the golden fortunes of the small United Provinces, that hub to the international economy, all drawn into the slow, unrelenting troubles which characterised the seventeenth century.

CHAPTER III

THE PAPACY, CATHOLIC REFORM, AND CHRISTIAN MISSIONS

'THEY are wretched Tridentines everywhere.' Thus Hurrell Froude, in one of his epigrammatic and often contradictory judgements, described the Roman Catholic church of the early nineteenth century. How true is the implication that the Council of Trent created modern Roman Catholicism? In one sense the conclusion is inescapable. The fact that after Trent closed in 1563 the Roman church summoned no further general councils until 1869 tells its own story. In the three hundred years between there was much development. Doctrinal disputes evoked papal condemnations of certain types of theology. Although the canon law, destined to be codified in 1918, was not fundamentally changed, yet the development of the supervisory powers of the papal curia by means of the Roman congregations was a post-Tridentine innovation. Missionary work in and far beyond Europe vastly increased the area of Roman Catholic influence. Yet no comprehensive review or reform of Catholic teaching and practice comparable to that effected by Trent was attempted until the Second Vatican Council of our own day—for the First Vatican Council of 1869–70 was limited in its aims and in any case was cut short. Trent, then, was certainly formative. Was it innovatory? It is far too easy to overlook the extent to which it merely codified and defined medieval teaching and practice. On the doctrinal side this is very apparent, and even the disciplinary reforms, which seemed to many at the time revolutionary and for that reason aroused the suspicion of Catholic states jealous of their lucrative control over ecclesiastical institutions, were often in essence attempts to restore old principles, such as the episcopal control of the lower clergy and religious, so much undermined by medieval exemptions and privileges. Only in its invalidation of clandestine marriages, contracted in the absence of a priest, did Trent appear to be abandoning a traditional principle and there, although perhaps unconsciously, it was inclining towards the attitude of the Eastern Orthodox church, which regarded an ecclesiastical ceremony as an indispensable requirement for Christian marriage.

Indeed the Tridentine fathers did not regard their task primarily as an *aggiornamento* in the style of Pope John XXIII in our day. On the contrary they saw Protestantism as a revolt from historic Christianity. Catholic doctrine and practice had to be rescued from its iconoclastic hands, not adjusted to its criticisms. In this they directly contradicted the Protestant

44

reformers, who held that the true gospel had been perverted and hidden for centuries, chiefly, as they claimed, because of the 'Babylonish Captivity' suffered by the church through the usurpation of the papal monarchy. To the Protestants medieval Catholicism and all its most characteristic doctrines and customs were 'popery', to be combated and destroyed by those who had rediscovered true scriptural teaching. How could such an idea be endorsed or even compromised with by a council summoned by the pope and presided over by his legates? Nor was Trent, composed predominantly of south European prelates, likely to be attracted to the new doctrines which had proved so attractive to some northern minds; in their own countries Protestantism had either not been able or not been allowed to take root. It is worth recalling that at the opening ceremony only two bishops from France and one from Germany were present, whilst it has been calculated that at the end of the long council three-quarters of the members came from the Mediterranean area and most of these from Italy. Only a year before its closure was it strengthened by a respectable contingent of French bishops, headed by the cardinal of Lorraine; before that France had virtually boycotted it. As Alphonse Dupront puts it, a council called to deal with dangers coming from northern and western Europe turned out to be an assembly of southern Europe.

Thus most of its members saw Trent's task as the condemnation of heresy and the defining of disputed doctrines in opposition to it. Not that they were blind to practical abuses which, in addition to their deleterious effects upon the church, provided ammunition for Protestant critics. Indeed the bishop of San Marco in Calabria said as much in his sermon after the opening Mass of the second session, on 7 January 1546, which was followed by Cardinal Pole's famous exhortation, written at the request of his fellow legates to be read by the conciliar secretary. In this the blame for the rise of heresy and the collapse of Christian morality was laid squarely upon the shoulders of the episcopate. 'We are like salt that has lost its savour.' Nor was this avowal of guilt repudiated by the bishops addressed.

This, however, does not mean that the very plausible view favoured by many laymen, and by the Emperor Charles V in particular, that a purging of abuses would of itself reconcile the Protestants, was accepted by the fathers. For one thing it overlooked the theological radicalism of the Protestants, who thought these abuses merely symptoms of the disease resulting from the medieval distortion of the gospel. Here in fact opinion was divided, as the initial debate about the order of procedure revealed. The majority did indeed want reform given priority over doctrinal definition, as did the emperor. But Paul III had ordered his legates to adopt the contrary procedure and this plan was not without its supporters. In the end a compromise, first suggested by Tommaso Campeggio, bishop of Feltre, in accordance with which dogma and reform would be dealt with *pari passu*, was almost unanimously adopted, although it was a hard task to gain the pope's consent to this. Thereafter, throughout the long proceedings, each doctrinal decree was accompanied by decrees on practical reform.

No general council has lasted as long as Trent. Opened at the end of 1545, it held its last session eighteen years later, in December 1563, and then against the view of the king of Spain, who wanted it to continue still longer. The primary reason for its length was not the length of the debates, but the fact that the disturbed condition of Europe compelled the suspension of sessions for two long periods. In March 1547 the Council was transferred to Bologna, much to the wrath of Charles V, whose supporters ridiculed the official, but probably genuine, excuse of an outbreak of typhus in Trent. They thought the real reason was a desire to move the sessions from imperial territory at a time when Charles, having defeated his Protestant rebels at Mühlberg, thought that this turn in their fortunes would induce them to send representatives to the Council and accept an agreed church reform. A minority of Spanish bishops defied the pope and stayed on at Trent, and Paul III was reduced to preventing the fathers at Bologna from passing any decrees, and in 1549, shortly before his death, he formally suspended the Council. His successor, Julius III, came to terms with the emperor and summoned the Council back to Trent in 1551, where a little later Protestant representatives were allowed to visit it and present their case.

It was at this stage that the logical difficulty in the theory held by some, that a dialogue between the protestants and the Council would restore unity, became apparent. For it was quickly clear that the adherents of the reformers were in no mood to compromise. They demanded in effect that all the work of the Council should begin over again, its earlier decisions being annulled; and the Württembergers wished the issues to be tried by neutral judges rather than by the fathers of the Council. One can understand this attitude when what has already been said about the Mediterranean predominance in the Council is recalled, as well as the fact that in its earlier sessions it had already rejected the central dogma of the Protestants, justification by faith only, at least as they read the decrees. Moreover, as early as 1520 Luther had rejected the authority of general councils summoned by the pope; the appeal to Scripture only was an axiom of Protestantism. And, as the demands for adequate safe-conducts now made showed, in the background lay the memory of how Hus had been treated by the Council of Constance. But the impasse illustrated vividly the shallowness of the idea that mere practical reform would satisfy Protestant complaints about the Catholic system. It was dogma that was really at issue, a fact which politically minded laymen from Constantine onwards have always been slow to see in ecclesiastical disputes. It is possible for the eirenically minded theologian today to maintain that many of the sixteenth-century theological disputes were rooted in misunderstanding, sometimes in mere logomachy. It was not so easy then for those, on the one hand, who thought they had rediscovered the gospel and those, on the other, who clung to unbroken tradition to think in such terms. Moreover, to suggest that a canonically summoned council could go back upon its solemnly affirmed decisions was to undermine the whole hierarchical theory upon which Catholicism was based; the conflict was ultimately one between private judgement and acceptance of ecclesiastical authority and could not be treated as a matter of bargaining, as the ambassadors of Ferdinand of Austria, brought up in the traditions of Renaissance diplomacy, thought when they urged the acceptance of the Protestant demand for a new beginning to the Council. The time for dialogue was at the opening of the Council and then, for various reasons, the chance had been lost. So attempts at religious peace on these lines in 1551–2 were predestined to failure.

Indeed, within a very short time, the Council's very existence was threatened by a renewed outbreak of the argument by force. In March 1552 the second Schmalkaldic War broke out. Maurice of Saxony, earlier the emperor's ally against his fellow Protestants, now joined them in revolt and, in alliance with Henry II of France, made war, defeated and almost captured Charles V and by May had forced him to conclude the treaty of Passau. Fear of the possible advance of the Protestant armies on Trent induced the pope to invite the Council to break off its sittings, which, in spite of the opposition of some Spanish and other bishops, it resolved to do on 28 April 1552. Not for ten years was it to meet again. In this second brief period of action it had indeed done a good deal of work. It had defined the Real Presence in the Eucharist, maintaining as against the Protestants the doctrine of transubstantiation (although avoiding committing itself to any one philosophical interpretation of the doctrine), and it had dealt also with the sacraments of penance and extreme unction. On the side of reform, it had strengthened the disciplinary powers of bishops and tried to restrict lay patronage of ecclesiastical benefices. But much more remained to be done if all matters needing definition and purging were to be dealt with. For a long time it looked as if hope of further progress must be deferred, if not abandoned. Julius III died in 1555, to be succeeded, after the brief pontificate of Marcellus II, by Paul IV, the fiery and unbalanced Caraffa, already known as the stern, unbending leader of the reforming party, opposed to all compromise or negotiations with Protestantism of the kind formerly patronised by Contarini. Cursed with ambitious and unscrupulous relations, who used him for their own purposes (especially his nephew Charles, whom the pope allowed to conduct papal secular policy), Paul involved himself in a war with Philip II of Spain and eventually had the humiliation of discovering and having to acknowledge the malpractices of his nephews. His genuine if harsh zeal for reform was overshadowed by the scandals for which he was only indirectly responsible and it was perhaps fortunate for the reputation of the Council that no serious attempt was made to revive it during his pontificate. On his death in 1559 the new Medici pope, Pius IV, who was to have as his secretary a very different cardinal nephew, St Charles Borromeo, later to be the famous pastoral and reforming archbishop of Milan, almost immediately set about the recalling of the Council.

By now the political background was different. In 1555 Charles V had been compelled to give up all hope of re-Catholicising Germany and by the Peace of Augsburg to acquiesce in the control of religion in each princely state by its ruler, thus canonising the religious divisions of the empire which were to continue until the present day. Next year he abdicated, to be succeeded as king of Spain by his son Philip and as emperor by his brother Ferdinand, already since 1522 the ruler of the Habsburg family territories. The link between Spain and the Empire was thus broken and the already noticeable tendency of Spain towards Erastian, nationalist Catholicism increased. Ferdinand, who although he made use of the Jesuits to reform and revive Catholicism in his lands, was far from favourable to the reopening of the Council, thinking that it would exacerbate Protestant feeling, at one point demanded a new council at some place other than Trent and only reluctantly agreed to the pope's plan. France, always suspicious of Trent and faced by the Huguenot problem, took a similar line and was with difficulty restrained from holding a national Gallican council of its own.

By persistent diplomacy the obstacles were overcome and the Council reassembled at Trent early in 1562. Its final group of sessions were to last not quite two years. In that time it cleared up the controversial questions left undecided earlier, including those of the restriction of communion in both species to the celebrant of the Eucharist and the doctrine of the sacrifice of the Mass. It was strange that these two matters, storm-centres from the beginning of the Reformation disputes, had been left so long outstanding. Now, in the face of strong demands for the restoration of the chalice to communicants, communion in both kinds was forbidden as a normal practice, whilst the doctrine that the Mass was a true sacrifice was affirmed. By both these decrees the breach with Protestantism was widened, but indeed by this time it was recognised that restoration of religious unity in Europe by means of the Council was a vain hope. The closing sessions of Trent were devoted rather to rounding off the scheme of reform by which it was hoped that a renovated Catholicism would win back the dissidents individually. This was not chimerical in view of the success already being achieved by the Jesuits and others in central Europe and it is noteworthy that, although he was resolutely opposed to doctrinal concessions to the Protestants, St Peter Canisius, the chief Catholic apostle of the German lands, was convinced that the chief obstacle to conversions was the lax morals, ignorance and lack of a sense of duty of the native priests. Small wonder that Trent's XXIInd Session passed a comprehensive decree about the standard of life required of the clergy, whilst the next laid down the principle which, long as it took to be fully implemented, was eventually to have most influence upon post-Tridentine Catholicism, namely, that clerics should be carefully trained in theology, spirituality and regularity of life in diocesan seminaries. It was in fact the haphazard character of medieval clerical training which was perhaps most of all responsible for the scandals of the priesthood and the often low standards of pastoral care and efficiency. There was no room in a reformed priesthood even for the well-meaning amateur, still less for the half-converted drifter with no clear sense of vocation, or for the avaricious careerist. Nothing could wholly guard against the danger of such men infiltrating into the clergy, as much subsequent history was to show; but careful training could eliminate many of them before ordination and, still more important, equip adequately the zealous aspirant who would otherwise have little idea of what he was to teach and how he was to carry out his priestly duties.

In the process of regulating clerical life bishops, no less than priests and perhaps more, needed marching orders. In the process of giving these, the underlying question never fully faced at Trent, namely, the relationship between papal and episcopal authority, came up once again at the end of the Council as it had done earlier on in an indirect way. One clamant need was to prevent the constant and sometimes habitual absence of bishops from their dioceses, which had been such a feature of the later middle ages, bound up as it was with the political and secular avocations to which many of them were attracted. This originated largely from the earlier monopoly of learning by the clergy, which had once made them the only source of literate servants of the state; but, as in so many cases, the tradition lingered on when the need for it no longer existed. The duty of bishops to reside with their flocks was inevitably admitted as a principle, but controversy arose as to whether this was based upon a divine law. This in turn raised the theological issue of whether the jurisdiction of bishops came direct from God, as many (and especially the Spanish) bishops held, or whether the episcopate was really a delegation of papal authority. After much hot dispute at various phases of the Council, this issue, which touched the whole theory of Catholicism, had to be left in the air, to be once again raised at the First Vatican Council in 1870, after a great deal of dispute in the interval, and only finally resolved by a full statement of the 'collegiate' nature of the episcopate and papacy at the Second Vatican Council. From this curious fact, more than anything else, came the anomaly that the Council of Trent made no comprehensive statement of the papal claims, although these were such a burning issue in the Protestant–Catholic confrontation of the time, the matter being left as it had been generally defined at the Council of Florence in 1439 when reunion with the Eastern church was under debate. On the practical side the reforms of Trent did much to canonise and establish still further that centralisation of the Roman church which had been more and more built up during the middle ages, even if Philip II's *mot* that his bishops had gone to Trent as bishops and returned as parish priests was exaggerated. Moreover, various matters with which the Council did not find opportunity to deal were formally remitted to the papacy for final decision. This was the case with liturgical reform, designed largely to reduce the wide varieties of diocesan usage which characterised the middle ages, and in 1568 and 1570 Pius V issued conservatively revised editions of the Roman breviary and missal, the use of which was imposed in all dioceses and religious orders which could not claim an antiquity of more than two centuries for their peculiar rites. This measure, in the nature of the case, fell far short of producing complete uniformity. Even more important was the *Catechismus Romanus*, published by the same pope in 1556, which put into simple form the teaching of Trent and provided parish priests with a standard of doctrine to be taught to their flocks. For the purpose of interpreting authoritatively the conciliar reforms, a papal congregation of cardinals was set up in 1564, received wider powers in 1566 and 1587, and became a permanent feature of the Roman church, holding in particular the powerful responsibility of issuing dispensations in special cases from the disciplinary rules of Trent. Already in 1542 Paul III had set up the Congregation of the Holy Office, the Inquisition in its post-medieval form, which, besides hunting down and punishing heresy, had wide powers of passing doctrinal judgements. It was complemented in 1587 by the Congregation of the Index, which took over from it the duties of supervising the Index of books judged immoral or heretical which Catholics were forbidden to read, published by Pius IV in 1564 in accordance with decisions of the Council. By means of these bureaucratic institutions a closer control of the whole working of the church by the Roman curia than had been possible earlier was gradually established.

The centralisation brought about by the post-Tridentine Roman system has been subjected to much criticism in our own day. Whatever may have been its long-term results, an historical assessment of it is bound to take into account the obstacles to reform which it was, at least in part, intended to circumvent. It was not mere lust for power which induced the papacy to assume more and more a constant supervisory and directive influence from Rome. It was apparent to any observant man, and had been so for at least a century, that one of the chief difficulties in restoring order and efficiency to the church was the control exercised over local churches by the secular power. From the days of the *Eigenkirchen* of the dark ages, the notion that church property and institutions should remain ultimately at the disposal of the lay magnates who had established and endowed them had never really died out. In England this was made very obvious in the Provisors legislation of the fourteenth century and the same idea is enunciated in the Henrician Statute of Appeals of 1533. It lay equally behind the French Pragmatic Sanction of Bourges of 1439, which virtually eliminated papal control of benefices in France. It is one of the ironies of history that the surrender by Francis I in 1516 of the national rights acquired in this way at a time of papal weakness was made in exchange for a concordat which in fact gave the French crown a virtually absolute control over all higher ecclesiastical appointments in the realm. Well may Willaert compare the Concordat of 1516 with the *plat de lentilles* for which Esau sold his birthright. The papacy gained a right of formal confirmation of episcopal nominations, but at the cost of having to accept the choice of the monarch. The same author not unfairly sums up the results, to be balanced against the occasional royal nomination of worthy prelates, as 'clerks and religious, unworthy or without vocation, nominated by intrigue or favour; episcopal sees turned into hereditary fiefs of ambitious families; the spiritual abandonment of dioceses and religious houses; misuse of enormous revenues intended for charitable uses and in fact devoted to lives of scandalous luxury; and, in sum, a church life in which the élite struggled with limited success against torpidity and indifference'. One result was the frequent granting of abbeys *in commendam* to abbots who were not monks and who were clerics only in name, who used their revenues for a wholly secular way of life—a practice which has left its mark upon nomenclature in the colloquial title of *abbé* used to this day of French secular priests who are not *curés*, in much the same way as all German waiters are politely assumed to be *Oberkellner*.

A lay society which looked upon ecclesiastical benefices primarily as prizes to be bestowed upon its servants or favourites was not likely to look too kindly upon a reform which aimed, as did the Tridentine, at restricting ecclesiastical posts to priests and bishops carefully trained and tested for their spiritual duties. A good example of how the Tridentine plan appeared to ecclesiastics familiar with the workings of the existing system can be gained from the comments of the theologians advising the Emperor Ferdinand on the scheme worked out at Trent for reforming episcopal elections and the constitution of cathedral chapters by which, and normally from which, new bishops were chosen. In a document of May 1563 they pointed out the difficulties the proposals would meet with in Germany. They recalled that some German cathedral chapters were closed to all but princes, counts and barons, from whom alone bishops could be chosen. In others membership was restricted to nobles and members of military orders, excluding 'plebeian doctors'; whilst in those to which doctors not of noble birth were admitted, their numbers were in practice less than those of the noble canons, and their voting rights limited. Moreover, noble canons would object to undergoing examination before they were admitted to major orders. The theologians agreed that cathedral customs of this kind were open to criticism and that the proposed reforms were very right and proper (*justissimos*), but asked the pertinent question how they were to be put into operation. The type of person who could carry them into effect was now lacking. The nobles regarded cathedrals as *hospitalia* for their sons and would not agree to their exclusion from canons' stalls, even if they were mere children. As those to be elected from the chapters to the episcopate became electors or princes of the empire, the nobility would consider it improper that plebeian doctors should attain these ranks. Finally, the effect of all this would be that the cathedral churches would lose the protection they had hitherto received from the German nobility. Indeed they pointed out earlier in their comments that in some metropolitan churches many nobles were infected with heresy, interested more in secular and military affairs than in ecclesiastical matters. If the attempt were made to enforce the examination of canons for major orders, the innovation would be resented, the archbishops and senior bishops would not willingly carry out the examination and some chapters, or a large part of them, would go over to Protestantism rather than submit to examination.

This of course reflected the peculiar circumstances of German ecclesiastical society where, partly because of the prevalence of prince-bishops ruling territories resembling miniature papal states, the higher reaches of the hierarchy were intensely aristocratic. But it throws light upon the extent to which all over western Europe the lay and clerical societies, however much theoretically separate, were intimately linked by ties of kinship, political and social responsibility, and economic interdependence. The German situation was extreme, but not unique.

The course of events after Trent indeed showed clearly that the obstacles to the implementation of its reforms were to be found quite as much in the vested interests of Catholic governments as in those of the clergy who had come to accept long-standing anomalies and scandals as normal. France provides the outstanding example of this—not unnaturally, in view of what has been said of the control exercised over the French church by the monarchy. France, too, had to deal with the danger to national unity presented by Huguenotism and the wars of religion. As these developed it became more and more apparent that the Calvinists, who believed strongly in the right of the church (as they understood it) to self-government by means of its presbyteries of ministers and lay elders, would, if successful, set up an ecclesiastical power able to challenge the state as effectively as did the medieval church with its ultimate loyalty to the supranational authority of the papacy. On the other hand, the ultra-Catholics, who gathered round the house of Guise and were willing to seek the alliance of Spain in order to further the aims of the Counter-Reformation, equally represented a threat to the national monarchy. It was against these forces that the attitude of mind known as *politique* grew up, in the conviction that toleration was essential for the preservation of national unity, and it is not difficult to see that this attitude almost inevitably went with a desire to keep state control over the church in order to curb fanaticism—an attitude which could equally easily rationalise the desire of laymen to take a share of ecclesiastical revenues. Many factors went to make up the phenomenon called Gallicanism, which was to be such a strong force in France down to the nineteenth century. Going back to the determination of the medieval French kings not to admit any control of their power in temporal matters by the papacy, it had been strengthened by the anti-papal and nationalistic trends of the fifteenth-century Conciliar Movement, centred very largely in France. In the sixteenth century it took its stand largely upon the supposed 'privileges' of the Gallican church, claimed to derive from the early ages of the church and to give the church of France a large measure of freedom from papal control. Such a view of church history had the double advantage of stimulating nationalism and at the same time offering some kind of sop to the Huguenot hatred of the papacy. Two instruments in particular lay ready to hand in propagating it—the *parlement* of Paris, the closed circle of royal lawyers who had built up the judicial monopoly of the French crown and by now claimed the position of watchdogs preventing the king himself from abdicating any of his rights; and the Sorbonne, with its long-standing theological prestige, which by now thought of itself as the doctrinal authority of the French church. The *parlement* had opposed the Concordat of 1516 because, whatever rights over the church it gave to the king in collaboration with the pope, it seemed to bargain away the national Gallican rights secured by the Pragmatic Sanction of 1439. After Trent it opposed the promulgation of the Council's decrees in France on the ground that they exalted the power of the Holy See and made ecclesiastical jurisdiction independent of state control, an attitude in which it was often supported by powerful elements in the Estates General and by some of the theologians of the Sorbonne. It was indeed not until 1615, and then in the teeth of lay opposition, that the assembly of the French clergy formally accepted the administrative reforms of Trent and ordered the provincial synods to receive them. The whole question was symbolised by the parallel opposition of Sorbonne and *parlement* to the Jesuit Order, thought of, not without reason, as the praetorian guard of the Holy See and as the chief opponents of lay control of the church. It was only against great opposition, both from those who feared the Jesuit invasion of their monopoly of theological instruction and of those who thought of them as enemies of nationalism and monarchy, that the Jesuits were able to establish and maintain themselves in France.

The result of all this was that down to the Revolution the church of France remained a centre of opposition to the centralisation of the Roman church which Trent did so much to further, and at the same time suffered from many of the administrative and pastoral abuses from which the Council had sought to free it. In this it was not unique. Indeed in every Catholic state of Europe much the same pattern was repeated with variations. Spain, commonly thought of as the spearhead of the Counter-Reformation, in fact kept the papacy at arm's length. True, the decrees of Trent were formally received less than a year from the closure of the Council, but only with a reservation of the rights of the king and country, and by 1582 the provincial synods, the revival of which was an essential part of the Tridentine reform, after being watched by royal commissioners, were silenced altogether. Papal bulls could be implemented in Spain only after they had received the royal consent; and students of the efforts of St Teresa and St John of the Cross to reform the Carmelite Order will remember that nothing could be accomplished without the favour of Philip II. It would be unfair to suggest that Spanish Erastian Catholicism hindered reform to the same extent as did French, but it did not make it easier, and the national policy was the more difficult to resist because the Spanish church had largely been reformed long before Trent by the co-operation of Ferdinand and Isabella with Cardinal Ximenes. In the Spanish European dominions, Milan and Naples, state interference with church affairs was as stark as in Spain and not always exercised with as much wisdom.

In short, whatever Trent had intended, the Roman Catholic church outside the papal states was everywhere dependent upon the goodwill of the state in applying the plan of reform and all the more so in a religiously divided Europe in which Catholicism seemed destined to survive only if supported by the arms of Catholic states in which religion appeared primarily as a facet of national policy. Unlike the thirteenth-century Lateran reforms of Innocent III, the Tridentine reform could not be carried through by an episcopate taking its orders from Rome. Fortunately there was a limiting factor. In so far as Catholicism was a national palladium, it needed to be free from too much tarnish in a world in which every spot upon it was noted by heretics and made a controversial weapon. Individual reformers at least could approach professedly Catholic monarchs with pleas for support in making respectable the religion which the autocrat claimed to protect and extend, and much could be done by those who, like St Peter Canisius in Bavaria and the Habsburg dominions, could win the ruler's ear.

Most of all perhaps was this true in the New World which discovery had opened to Catholic missions and in which the staunchly Catholic Spanish and Portuguese nations were the pioneers and where, from the beginning, the spread of the faith had been an avowed purpose of the explorers and *conquistadores*. In many ways the beginnings had not been auspicious. The exploitation of the Indians of the Caribbean had roused the wrath of Las Casas, and St Francis Xavier found one of the greatest obstacles to his work in India in the unedifying lives of the Portuguese colonists of Goa. Nevertheless it is significant that protests could be made by missionaries, and to some extent heard, and in any case the development of the external framework of the church, the formation of dioceses, the building of churches and the planting of mission stations, received the blessing and support of the state. Here the revival of theology in the Spanish Peninsula, which is such a striking feature of the later sixteenth century, played its part, for the great theologians had much to say about rights of conquest and great teachers like Vitoria and Suárez energetically defended the rights of non-Christian natives on the basis of natural law, and *a fortiori* of those who became Christians. Colonisation they allowed on the theory of the unity and sociability of the human race, which ruled out exclusiveness; but that same principle implied that the colonists had a duty to share their good things, and notably the faith, with the original inhabitants and thus in a sense missions were a condition of lawful imperialism.

This did not of course mean that social and religious conditions were ideal in the Spanish and Portuguese colonies. Exploitation of the natives continued in spite of denunciation, nor could the insistence of popes, bishops and church councils upon the natural and spiritual rights of Indians, and condemnations of slavery in principle, prevent cruelty and abuses. Yet it is probable that without them matters would have been even worse and at least the authorities and colonists could not plead the authority of the church in defence of their misdoings. Moreover, one may suspect that uneasy consciences tried to find appeasement by material support of the church and to that extent aided the dissemination of the Catholic faith.

The centralisation of missionary effort under papal supervision saw only its beginnings in this period. It was not until 1622 that Gregory XV set up the Congregation of Propaganda and it was his successor, Urban VIII, who in 1627 founded the Propaganda College for the training of missionaries, with its polyglot printing press. Nevertheless the papacy was fully aware of the vital importance of foreign missions and encouraged them in every way possible. *Propaganda* had its precursors. In July 1568 Pius V, at the suggestion of St Francis Borgia, set up a congregation of cardinals to promote the faith in pagan areas, parallel to another established at the same time to work for the conversion of heretics in Europe. Nevertheless, in practice the power of the state was the controlling force in the most extensive Roman Catholic mission fields, the overseas dominions of Spain and Portugal, and it must be remembered that from 1580 onwards Portugal was ruled by the kings of Spain, who brought to their new dominions the Spanish Erastian tradition to support that which already existed in Portugal. Latourette has summed up the Spanish monarchy's absolute control of missions.

To the crown belonged the selection of all the missionaries. No missionary could go to the New World or, when once there, leave it, without royal permission—usually granted, of course, through the Council of the Indies or one of its associated bureaus...The pope granted to the crown the right of appointment to all ecclesiastical benefices in the colonies. In theory Rome reserved the power to confirm the choice, but in fact it often happened that a bishop entered upon the administration of his diocese without awaiting the papal bulls. All bishops, heads of religious houses, and parish priests were named by the king. The king created new dioceses and determined their boundaries. Sometimes a diocese was created and filled before the pope was even apprised of its existence. No church, convent, or school could be erected without royal permission...In spite of emphatic protests from Rome, the king would allow no communication to pass from the Holy See to ecclesiastics in the colonies without his *imprimatur*. Nor could a bishop in Spanish America write to Rome without presenting the letter for royal censorship. Actions of ecclesiastical synods in the Americas were all to be submitted to the viceroy or governor. These royal officials had power to overrule them or to send them to the Council of the Indies for such action as that body chose to take.

The success or otherwise of the missions, especially in the New World, must therefore be attributed as much to state as to ecclesiastical authority. Certainly, on the face of things, overseas Catholic missions show an almost continuous story of success in the sixteenth century. Mass baptisms, recalling in their size those of dark-age Europe, were common, although the more sensational took place before the turn of the half-century. Even if figures were exaggerated, the numbers were certainly large. In 1541 the bishop of Tlaxcala claimed that he baptised and confirmed three hundred persons a week and it is not surprising to learn that by the beginning of the seventeenth century the greater part of the population of Mexico south of the Rio Grande was reckoned to be Christian. These facts naturally gave rise to the questions of whether, as centuries before in Europe, converts submitted to baptism in fear of *force majeure* or in hope of government favour, and of how genuine their new-found Christianity was. Of their nature these questions cannot be answered with assurance but certain facts make one pause before giving the entirely cynical answer. Thus, mass baptisms were a feature of the mission work of St Francis Xavier, often in regions to which the authority of the Portuguese government did not effectively reach. In some cases his work was dependent upon the goodwill of non-Christian potentates. Writing of a village in south India, he says that, when he urged the headmen to accept baptism,

they replied that they dare not become Christians without the permission of the raja, their overlord. There was an official of that ruler in the village who had come to collect taxes for his master, and him I sought out. When he heard what I had to say, he agreed that to be a Christian was a good thing and gave the villagers leave to accept the faith, but he would not follow his counsel to others and embrace it himself. I thereupon baptized the chief men of the place and their families, and afterwards the rest of the people, young and old.

It does not therefore follow that where Christian governments possessed direct power all, or even most, conversions were the result of fear or worldly hope. Moreover, there is plenty of evidence that the need of instruction was realised and met. Catechisms and summaries of the faith were produced on a large scale in the native tongues and must have had effect. The survival to this day of Indian pagan customs with a veneer of Christianity in Latin America warns one against a naïve view of the thoroughness of conversions; but, on the other hand, the continuing devotion of the Indians to Christianity as they understand it makes one equally hesitant to suggest that the work of the Catholic missionaries in the New World (or in the East) was wholly superficial. The parallel with Europe holds good here also. Even if the mass baptisms effected by Charlemagne's missionaries were a direct result of conquest, and even if pagan survivals, more or less baptised into Christianity, abounded in medieval Europe, contributing considerably to the superstition of which sixteenth-century reformers were to make so much, nevertheless it would be a bold historian who denied that Europe of the middle ages was in any real sense a Christian continent. Indeed the strategy of Gregory the Great, in advising Augustine of Canterbury to invest old pagan customs with Christian meaning, was probably followed out to some extent by sixteenth-century Catholic missionaries in some areas. Nor need it be supposed, even by those who do not themselves accept the Christian position, that Christianity could have had no attraction to those whose former religions were primitive and sometimes crude. It has been pointed out that Scandinavian paganism in the Viking age was already thinking of itself as obsolescent and that the Vikings were willing to examine the claims of Christ, as were the Shamanist Mongols in the thirteenth century. The same factors were probably at work in the sixteenth-century New World and, in spite of the strength of Hinduism and Buddhism and the competition of Islam, in the East at the same time.

However this may be, the visible and apparent success of Catholic missions and the devoted heroism of missionaries, chiefly from the new and reformed religious orders, who went in large numbers to the field overseas, did much to restore and increase the prestige of Catholicism and redress the balance upset by the Reformation. Catholicism had secured a long start over Protestantism in the mission field and was never to be fully overtaken there in succeeding centuries. Territorially in the struggles between Catholicism and Protestantism the New World redressed the balance of the Old, for the Catholic areas overseas became increasingly wider than the areas lost in northern Europe.

What of those areas themselves? Here, too, the later sixteenth century saw much Catholic progress. A swift comparison between the situation as it was when the Council of Trent was drawing to a close and at the end of the century tells its own story. Although by 1563 the Jesuits and other Catholic missionaries had been for some little time at work in the districts where the struggle between Catholicism and Protestantism swayed in the balance, yet the tide of the Reformation could barely be seen to have turned. The Peace of Augsburg had, as it seemed, put an end to the efforts of Charles V to restore religious unity in Germany and the Lutheranism of many important states of the empire was guaranteed. Even in the Habsburg lands it did not seem clear that official policy would remain Catholic, whilst the church itself was opposed by quite large elements of the population. Ferdinand I, their ruler since 1522 and emperor since 1556, died in 1564. His policy, although cautious, had been basically Catholic; his son and successor, Maximilian II, was not without reason suspected of a desire to compromise with Protestantism and the Jesuits of Vienna expected to be expelled the moment his father died. Moreover, the Catholic church in Germany, even where it retained power, was far from being morally reformed and was still a byword to many. In March 1564 a parish priest, Martin Eisengrein, wrote to Laynez, the General of the Jesuits, expressing gratitude for the work done by the Society in Germany, by which he had himself been converted back to Catholicism. But he draws a dismal picture of the Catholic clergy.

The rest of the clergy in Germany would seem to be fast asleep and as free of care as if nothing of the havoc which confronts us, nothing of the lamentable downfall of many souls, could be laid to their charge. Your Reverend Paternity could not look without tears upon the wretched condition of some German dioceses, or upon so many of the clergy, rendered utterly hateful to Catholics and a mockery to heretics by the enormity of their wickedness. Up to this hour, they cling to their vices and neither the merited detestation of Catholics, the derision of heretics, nor the destruction of religion avails to make them amend their lives. Rather do they pile evil upon evil and daily more and more provoke the wrath of God...Take for example, also, the famous cathedral of Regensburg...You might say that the diocese of Regensburg is a sink of all iniquity. You can see there not only priests living in concubinage but adulterous and incestuous ones, and priests who have committed rape and homicide. And who is there to call attention to their crimes, by which very many are frightened away from the Catholic faith and all heretics are confirmed in their heresy?

As late as 1585 it could be said of Germany: 'The chapters are for the most part composed of heretics or simoniacs or *concubinarii* or drunkards or men infected with some other vice.' Such testimonies could be multiplied.

In France, in which a schism from the papacy had narrowly been averted at the time of Trent, Calvinism was growing, gaining influential supporters and organising itself; the Wars of Religion were beginning, the massacre of Vassy having taken place in 1562. Despite all Charles V's attempts to suppress Protestantism in the Netherlands by persecution, when Philip II succeeded his father there in 1555 it was on the increase as much in the south as in the north and was to become increasingly Calvinist, with all the strength of organisation and purpose which that would imply. In Poland the senate which formed part of the parliament of 1569 had 58 of its 133 seats occupied by Protestant notables; in 1570 the Lutherans, Calvinists and Bohemian Brethren formed a political union to such effect that by 1573 they had secured formal religious toleration and equality before the law with Catholics. King Sigismund II had only with reluctance been persuaded to accept the Tridentine decrees and it was only in 1564 that the Jesuits began their work in the country. Hungary, divided since 1547 into a narrow western crescent ruled by the Habsburgs, a Turkish Hungary and a Transylvanian principality subject to the Turks, was divided religiously, and Protestantism had been enabled to spread by the confusion caused by Turkish occupation. Although Archbishop Nicholas Oláhus of Gran introduced the Jesuits, the compromising policy of Maximilian II, who governed the country from 1564 to 1576, and his failure to fill the see of Gran after Nicholas's death in 1568, resulted in the conversion to Protestantism of a majority of the great nobles.

Thus, when Trent came to an end, the position of Catholicism in northern, eastern and central Europe was by no means promising, whilst in England the Marian reaction had given place to the Protestant revival under Elizabeth, and France might well have seemed destined to become Huguenot. Italy and Spain might seem secure, but in both religious dissidence had shown its head and persecution was needed to keep it from surviving and spreading.

By the end of the century the picture was very different. In France Henry of Navarre had realised that Paris was worth a Mass or, in less flippant language, that only a Catholic dynasty could hold the throne and both obtain toleration for the Huguenots and curb the anti-national fanaticism of the Catholic League. In the Netherlands Philip II's foolish policy, if it had lost the north, had ended by consolidating Catholicism in Belgium, nor had Catholicism wholly died in the United Provinces. In Germany the Catholic church had regained at least a measure of respectability and the spread of Protestantism had been held. Protestant solidarity, too, had been gravely weakened by the internal theological disputes of the Lutherans and their dislike of Calvinism which, both in its pure form and as crypto-Calvinism, had caused a spread of the Swiss Protestant radicalism against which Luther had fought all his life. The policy of the Habsburgs and of the Bavarian Wittelsbachs in their territories had hardened in favour of repressive Catholicism and in the case of the former family this had also involved the beginning of a turning of the tide in Hungary. In Poland the successive reigns of Stephen Bathory and Sigismund III had caused a revival of Catholicism, even if Protestantism had to be allowed toleration; whilst in 1596 the position of Catholicism was much strengthened by the Union of Brest-Litovsk, by which a large part of the Eastern Orthodox church of the Ukraine was united to the Roman church though retaining its old rites and customs. Even in Sweden King John III (1568–92), who had a Catholic wife, had envisaged the possibility of reunion with Rome, although this in the end came to nothing. In England and Scotland, whilst Catholic missionaries had done no more than hold to the faith a dwindling minority of faithful, they had at least prevented the total extinction of Roman Catholicism which seemed a real possibility in the 1560s. It was sufficient of a force for James I to play with the idea of toleration or even of reunion. In Italy and Spain Protestantism had been virtually eliminated. Small wonder that the opening of the seventeenth century saw the Protestants almost everywhere in a state of almost hysterical alarm about the possibility of a final reversal of the Reformation; the situation which led to the Thirty Years War, a fight for survival, was already building up.

What had caused this change of fortune? The most obvious answer, dealt with from another angle at the beginning of this chapter, is the political attitude of the Catholic states, which identified the faith with national policy. They, after all, were collectively more powerful, or so it then seemed, than the Protestant states. It is certainly true that in the empire and the lands adjoining it on the east Catholicism would never have attained its triumph without political help, just as earlier on Lutheranism would have succumbed but for the support of the German princes who adopted it. For the *cuius regio, eius religio* principle, which affected Catholicism just as much as it did Protestantism, necessarily equated religious dissidence with sedition if not with treason, and ensured that the state would persecute or harass opponents of the national religion to the limit imposed by the fear of rebellion. Even though the idea persisted that it was a Christian prince's duty to uphold what he regarded as truth and to suppress error, it is a commonplace that the predominant motive behind state persecution of religion in the sixteenth century was political, fear that religious dissidence would undermine the unity and power of the state and also lead to treasonable alliances of the minorities with foreign powers. Experience seemed to bear this out. In the empire the Schmalkaldic League had sought the alliance of other states against Charles V. In France both the Catholic League and the Huguenots had sought aid abroad from their respective co-religionists. In Elizabethan England one section of the Catholic recusants had thrown in their lot with Spain. On the Catholic side this both explains the tight hold kept by governments over ecclesiastical affairs, described earlier on, and also their conviction that it was their duty to support the evangelistic and educational work of the church. It also explains why, not only for fanatical reasons, Protestant governments regarded the toleration of Catholicism as out of the question, at least without very strong guarantees. It was the fate of later sixteenth-century Catholicism to be tied up with nationalism, positively in Catholic states and negatively in Protestant ones. The observer today can see the evil effects of this upon its life and development; at the time it must have seemed to most Catholics natural and inevitable.

This does not mean that without state support Catholicism would have been tolerant and eirenical. The feeling for rigid orthodoxy was too strong among even saintly characters for this to be possible. The fact that the Inquisition was an integral part of the church's structure, as reformed by the Council of Trent, shows this. Trent had not legislated about the Inquisition. It was unnecessary for it to do so, since this medieval institution had been reorganised by Pope Paul III in 1542 under the *Sacred Congregation of the Roman and Universal Inquisition or Holy Office*, a committee of cardinals who acted as final judges in all matters of faith and supervised the work of discovering and punishing heresy throughout the Roman church, so far as the civil power would allow. For here also the limitations imposed by Erastianism operated; secular rulers often preferred to do their own persecuting without interference from Rome. Of this tendency the notorious Spanish Inquisition is the supreme example— a case in which an institution nominally dependent on the pope was captured by a national government. Here the secular invasion of the ecclesiastical sphere goes back to the fifteenth century. It arose quite naturally out of the mood engendered in Spain by its medieval history of continual struggle against the Moslems, together with the fact that the Iberian Peninsula was one of the chief centres of medieval Judaism. 'At the heart of racial and religious persecution in mediaeval Spain', a recent author has said, 'lay the problem of coexistence between the three great faiths of the peninsula: Muslim, Christian and Jewish.' It was after a bad outbreak of anti-Jewish fanaticism in 1391, resulting in large-scale massacre, that there arose the problem of the *conversos*, the Jews who, under duress or for prudential reasons, accepted baptism. As always, conversion, especially in the circumstances which had caused it, did not remove Christian suspicions, which were exacerbated by Jewish prosperity and by the vital roles Jews played in the national economy and administration. Another factor was the degree to which intermarriage with Jews had affected the proud Spanish nobility, in reaction to which grew up a pseudo-scientific racialism of a type familiar in our own century, the Spanish concept of *limpieza de sangre*, purity of blood, which added fuel to the religious fanaticism engendered by Spain's history. Into such an atmosphere, prone to hysteria, the Inquisition, dormant since the fourteenth century in Aragon and no longer existent in Castile, was reintroduced in 1478 at the request of Ferdinand and Isabella by a bull of Sixtus IV, with the purpose primarily of searching out Jewish *conversos* believed to be practising Jewish rites in secret. It started operations in 1480 and soon claimed to have unearthed evidence of the prevalence of underground Judaism and of its dangerous character, with the result that a network of courts was set up all over the country. From the beginning the ruthlessness of its behaviour alarmed Rome, and as early as 1482 Sixtus IV himself issued another bull moderating the methods of procedure allowed and permitting appeals to Rome. Ferdinand protested, made Sixtus suspend it and in 1483 secured the appointment of the Dominican Tomás de Torquemada (whose name was to become a byword), who was already Inquisitor General of Castile, to the same position in Aragon. Significantly the friar became, as has been pointed out, 'the only individual in the peninsula whose writ extended all over Spain', since at that time Castile and Aragon were only loosely united by the marriage of their monarchs.

The beginnings of the Spanish Inquisition being thus so bound up with real, if exaggerated, national problems in a country seeking unity, it is not surprising that it continued to be a national as much as an ecclesiastical institution. Drawing its ultimate authority theoretically from the pope, it was in fact controlled by a council, the *Suprema*, the members of which were nominated by the king and were headed by the Inquisitor General who, though appointed by papal bull, was in fact also the royal nominee. Although the papacy never gave up the struggle to keep some authority over the institution it had been forced to create, and although it sometimes had some success, for the most part it had to let the Spanish crown run what was supposed to be the chief instrument for safeguarding the faith in Spain. The most sensational example of its power of defying Rome was seen in the case of Archbishop Carranza of Toledo, the primate of Spain, who, ironically enough, had occupied himself in 1554-7, during Philip II's occupation of the English throne as husband of Mary Tudor, with crushing heresy in England. Hardly had he been appointed to the Toledan see in 1557 than he was attacked as a heretic by the Inquisitor General Valdés, a fellow Dominican and a great enemy of Erasmianism and Protestantism. Valdés launched his attack on the strength of a denunciation by yet another Dominican, Melchior Cano, who disliked Carranza, of a book of commentaries on the catechism published by the archbishop in 1558. Carranza's looseness of expression—he was no great theological scholar—afforded some grounds for this, as did the fact that he had earlier been suspect of Erasmianism and had shown himself at Trent as a reformer. What is striking, however, is that, after his arrest by the Inquisition in 1559, despite the formal approval of his *Commentaries* by the Council of Trent and the representations and threats of Pope Pius IV, it was not until 1566 that Pius V succeeded in getting Carranza released from the grip of the Spanish Inquisition and sent to Rome for papal judgement. Even there the long arm of Spain reached. It was not until 1576 that Gregory XIII gave a sentence which, though it did not proclaim the archbishop a formal heretic, put his *Commentaries* on the Index as a dangerous book and banished Carranza, who had obediently abjured those of his statements judged erroneous, for five years to the Dominican house at Orvieto. He died, however, in Rome eighteen days after sentence had been pronounced. When the Spanish monarchy, by use of the Inquisition, could thus stand so long between the pope and the highest ecclesiastic in Spain, it is not surprising to find royal customs officers being disciplined by it for allowing horses to cross the frontier, allegedly for the use of the French Huguenots. The Spanish Inquisition may have promoted the Catholic faith according to its lights, but it did so with a pronounced Spanish accent and, like all other ecclesiastical institutions in Spain, was closely bound to the throne.

It is perhaps worth remark, too, that the massacres, notably that of St Bartholomew, which stain the record of Catholicism in this period, were also bound up with political nationalism. Sir John Neale's comment upon Catherine de Medici's attitude after the failure of the attempt to assassinate Coligny is very much to the point.

In such situations people are thrown back on their deeper promptings, and in her desperation Catherine seized on an idea that was then in the air. Her daughter's marriage, by bringing the leading Huguenot noblemen from all over the country to court, had presented a unique opportunity of getting rid of them all at a blow; an opportunity which a generation that knew its classical history and recalled the story of Tarquin and the poppies could not fail and had not failed to perceive. It was this idea that Catherine seized upon. In other words, a frantic woman determined to save herself and rescue France from its deadly plague of religious strife by the wholesale murder of the Huguenot leaders in Paris.

Religious violence, legal or extra-legal, went hand in hand with *raison d'état* in sixteenth-century Europe and it is difficult indeed to disentangle motives of religious fanaticism and nationalist panic in the religious wars, massacres, and persecution of the time. Indeed, as the experience of our own century shows, ideologies and political calculation form a psychological amalgam which it is difficult, if not vain, for the historian to try to analyse.

Is one therefore to ascribe the notable success of Catholicism in the later sixteenth century solely to political or military factors? No one acquainted with the facts could so simplify the issue. Faith can never rest upon, or be developed solely or even chiefly by, statecraft; whatever Thomas Hobbes may have thought, men will not simply accept as true what the state commands them to believe. The Counter-Reformation, if it owed much to Catholic rulers, could never have succeeded by their efforts alone, as they themselves realised by their support of Catholic education and Catholic preachers and missionaries. It was men like St Peter Canisius (1521–97), the apostle of Germany and second St Boniface as he has been described, or St Francis de Sales (1567–1622), missioner in the Protestant Chablais, subsequently bishop of Geneva, residing in inevitable exile from his see at Annecy in Savoy, but also exercising a profound influence upon the court of the newly converted Henry IV and all France, who were primarily responsible for the restoration of Catholicism. They are but outstanding examples of a host of apostolic labourers, largely, but not entirely, from the religious orders, of whom only a proportion have acquired historic fame, who worked tirelessly and often with great courage to attract Protestants back to the Catholic fold and, no less necessary a task, to instruct and build up traditional but lukewarm or discouraged Catholics in the faith. Such men, if they shared the general belief of the age in the lawfulness of force in religious matters, did not pin their faith primarily to its efficacy. St Francis de Sales himself wrote: 'I have always said that whoever preaches with love is preaching effectively against the heretics, even though he does not say a single controversial word against them.' Not all Catholic missionaries were as averse to direct controversy as the bishop of Geneva, but all realised the importance of positive instruction. The great defect of medieval Catholicism had been the religious ignorance of the laity, which both nurtured superstition and left them at the mercy of heterodox preachers, and this in turn stemmed largely from the inadequate learning, as well as the often unedifying character, of the bulk of the clergy. Trent's effort to overcome this last defect by its seminary legislation has already been mentioned. It bore fruit slowly. Pope Pius IV set the example by opening a seminary for the Roman diocese itself early in 1565. St Charles Borromeo, cardinal archbishop of Milan from 1560 to 1584, founded no less than three seminaries for his vast diocese. He was in many ways the model bishop of the Tridentine reform, having played a prominent part in its last stage, and his great aim was to reorganise his diocese upon the pattern set by Trent. In himself an example of how much reform was needed, Charles, the nephew of Pius IV, was made a cardinal at the age of 21, having been titular abbot of a monastery since the age of 12, and at the same time was made administrator of the archdiocese of Milan. It was not until 1563 that he was ordained priest and consecrated bishop, and it was 1566 before, after the death of his uncle, he was allowed to abandon the heavy duties he had carried out in the papal curia since 1560 and actually reside in his see, which hitherto he had had to supervise by means of deputies. Once there, he not only lived a life of great austerity, almsgiving and pastoral work, personally ministering to the sick in the great plague of 1576–8, but carried on energetically the huge task of reform. He aroused the opposition both of the Spanish governors[1] and of the relaxed clergy; the religious order of the Humiliati upon whom he imposed much needed reforms tried to assassinate him. For a concrete example of the obstacles facing the Tridentine 'new deal', the career of St Charles could hardly be bettered. (It may be noted that when he reached Milan in 1566 he was the first resident archbishop for eighty years.) Equally his policy and activities show the directions in which reform was primarily needed. Beyond the removal of unworthy priests and the raising of the whole standard of clerical education and spirituality,

[1] See below, pp. 258–9.

he realised the need for better instruction of the laity and not only pressed upon his clergy the duty of catechising, but founded the Confraternity of Christian Doctrine, the prototype, as has often been pointed out, of the Sunday schools begun in England 200 years later by Robert Raikes. His schools are said to have numbered 740, with 3,000 teachers and 40,000 pupils.

Outside Italy similar work was done against the same and other obstacles. Even in disturbed Germany a seminary was founded at Eichstadt in 1564. In France the successful establishment of diocesan seminaries had to wait until the next century, although in Spain progress was much more rapid. It was in these circumstances that the religious orders, and especially the Jesuits, effected much that was beyond the power of individual dioceses. Indeed the Jesuit work for education, of both clergy and laity, was in every way as important as their pastoral activities and missionary efforts. Their colleges were 'pontifical', since the Society depended directly upon the Holy See; and, provided the good will of the secular authorities could be obtained, their work was not hindered by the inertia or traditionalism of local ecclesiastical authorities. The content, no less than the organisation, of Jesuit teaching was of vital importance. For future priests they provided a full grounding in theology of the traditional scholastic type, reinforced by studies of immediate pastoral importance, such as moral theology and the technique of preaching and instruction. For the same men at an earlier stage of their training and for those destined for the life of laymen, they made full use of the humanist ideals of the Renaissance and of the educational techniques developed by the humanists. The *Ratio Studiorum*, published by the Society in 1599, superseded an earlier edition of 1591, which in turn derived from the work of a committee of six experienced schoolmen set up by the great Jesuit General, Acquaviva, in 1584, which reported in 1586. It contained a full scheme of regulations for both lower and higher education, based equally upon theory and experience, and its solidity can be judged by the fact that it was felt to need no further revision down to the suppression of the Society of Jesus in 1773. It covered every aspect of education, from classroom technique and discipline, together with provision for games and exercise, to the content of studies. The principle underlying all the earlier stages of education envisaged by the *Ratio* has been described as that of *efformatio ingenii*, a general training of the mind, an end to which the various subjects prescribed are a means. 'The training given by the *Ratio* was not to be specialized or professional, but general, and was to lay the foundation for professional studies.' Liberal education was the initial aim, both for members of the Society itself and for future priests, and also for the future lay élite of the church. The success of this may be judged, not merely from the galaxy of scholars—in mathematics, astronomy, history, linguistics and other disciplines as well as in the theological field—produced within the Society, but also from its distinguished lay alumni, including such names as Calderón, Tasso, Galileo and Descartes. Whatever the achievements of Protestantism in the field of education, the work of the Jesuits and other Catholic educationalists ensured that they were rivalled, if not surpassed.

Here one must turn to the part played by the universities in the Catholic revival. The Reformation of necessity brought a schism in what had been the international comity of the medieval universities.[1] Willaert has pointed out the remarkable way in which the frontier between the opposing lines of Catholic and Protestant universities in Europe at this time corresponds to the old *limes* of the Roman Empire along the Rhine and Danube— on the Catholic side Louvain, Cologne, Mainz, Dilligen, Ingolstadt and others, facing the Protestant Leyden, Erfurt, Marburg, Tübingen and their allies, a geographical symbol of an intellectual schism. The Catholic universities of the north certainly played their part in maintaining and developing Catholic theology, yet it was in Spain that Catholic thought flourished most, as such names as Salamanca, Alcalá, Valladolid, with Coimbra in Portugal, remind one. Here the scholastic tradition had not been so battered by Protestant opposition as in the regions where religious conflict had hindered detached academic thought. As Copleston has said:

One might perhaps have expected that the life and vigour of Aristotelian scholasticism would have been finally sapped by two factors, first the rise and spread of the nominalist movement in the fourteenth century and secondly the emergence of new lines of thought at the time of the Renaissance. Yet in the fifteenth and sixteenth centuries there occurred a remarkable revival of scholasticism, and some of the greatest names in scholasticism belong to the period of the Renaissance and the beginning of the modern era.

He goes on to point out the predominance of Spaniards in the revival, listing the great names of Vitoria, Dominic Soto, Melchior Cano, Dominic Bañez, Gabriel Vasquez and Francis Suárez. It is a reflection of the intellectual schism produced by the Reformation that to this day the work of these giants, who are comparable to the great scholastic names of the middle ages, is scarcely known outside the Roman church. Yet Suárez, for example, a prodigious writer whose works fill twenty-eight volumes in the Paris nineteenth-century edition, not only knew all the metaphysicians of the past, from Greek to Renaissance thinkers, but was ready both to amalgamate and to criticise their systems in a synthesis to which his own genius added much originality. Moreover, his studies and writings extended far outside pure philosophy into the realms of theology, moral philosophy and political thought. Vitoria, who is perhaps the most widely known today of this great group of Spaniards because of his pioneering work in the realm of international law, is really a figure of the earlier sixteenth century, since he died in 1546. He presents, indeed, the humanist

[1] See also below, chapter xiv.

attitude of Erasmus, whom he greatly admired, before the advance of the Reformation made Erasmus suspect and caused the Inquisition to persecute Erasmians in Spain; but he was to a great extent the author of the Spanish revival of theology, the teacher of, among others, Melchior Cano and Soto. Both of these latter died in 1560, and the outstanding lights of the later generation were Bañez (1528–1604), Vasquez (c. 1551–1604), Suárez (1548–1617), and Molina (1535–1600). Nor must we forget the eminent men who lectured and wrote outside Spain, but were closely connected with the general revival of technical theology, notably St Robert Bellarmine (1542–1621), who lectured at Louvain from 1570 to 1576, spending nearly all the rest of his life in Rome, first as professor of controversial theology at the Jesuit Roman College, then as a theological adviser to the papacy. He became a cardinal in 1599 and, after a brief period as archbishop of Capua, ended his life in the service of the curia, becoming involved both in the argument between James I of England and the papacy and in the case of Galileo. His whole career lay more in the field of applied than of pure theology and is the outstanding example of the tendency of Catholic theology to become unduly obsessed with the Protestant–Catholic dialectic of the day and thus less purely creative than it might have been.

Indeed it was one of the aspects of this which was destined before the century ended to sow the seeds of controversy within the Catholic camp itself, seeds which were to develop into the passionate disputes over Jansenism in the next century. The Reformation quarrels all sprang fundamentally from differing views about divine grace and its role in the salvation of man, views which in origin can be traced back to medieval disputes and further still, since they took their rise from the teaching of St Augustine of Hippo, which ever since the fifth century had had such a profound influence upon western Christian thought. It was St Augustine's interpretation of St Paul which had such a profound effect upon Luther's theology, even if he added to it convictions arrived at by personal experience. Thus it was that justification by faith became the central concept common to all Protestantism, to which directly or indirectly practically all other Protestant convictions can be traced. As this represented in part a reaction against the tendency in some forms of later medieval theology to minimise the action of God in man's attainment of salvation, it was not unnatural that some types of Catholic thought, even in combating Protestantism, should tend to return to more rigid Augustinianism. Augustine was too great a figure, too much entrenched in the tradition of the west, to be ignored or even apparently surrendered to the Protestants. As Willaert puts it, in the sixteenth century Protestants and Catholics competed for Augustine. In our period this showed itself in the dispute over the teaching of Baius, who was a leading light of the university of Louvain from 1541 to his death there in 1584. Without going into the complex details of his views, it may be said that they sprang from a feeling that medieval theology had glossed patristic teaching, notably that of St Augustine, and that the teachings of the Protestants could best be corrected and refuted by bypassing scholasticism and appealing to the early fathers 'who still enjoy some credit with the heretics'. On this basis Baius found himself arriving at a position which emphasised the helplessness of fallen man, minimised his free will and made of God's grace merely a force controlling concupiscence rather than a source of positive transformation of his nature, an attitude which seemed to his opponents virtually indistinguishable from the Protestant view of salvation. His views were condemned without mention of his name by Pius V in 1567. Baius at first accepted the papal bull in common with his colleagues at Louvain, but later claimed that it did not really condemn his views. After various complicated manœuvres during which Baius appeared to submit without doing so at heart, he was compelled by Pope Gregory XIII in 1580 to recant unequivocally. But Baianism was not dead. He had given rise to a school at Louvain and after his death his followers actually founded a chair there to combat the teaching of the Jesuits, regarded as the chief opponents of his opinions. The first holder of this chair, James Janson, was destined to be the teacher of the better known Cornelius Jansen, the posthumous founder of Jansenism. Nor was this the end of disputes within the Roman church during the century upon the vexed questions of grace, predestination and free will, which from the time of St Augustine had exercised such a fascination upon western theology, with its passion for logic and concentration upon the practical issues of personal religion, both of which seemed to be involved in these deep problems. The always latent rivalry between the older Dominican Order and the new Society of Jesus came into the open with the Molinist controversy. Molina (1535–1600), a Jesuit theologian of the Portuguese university of Evora, evolved a highly subtle theory designed to harmonise human free will with divine omnipotence. This was first published in full at Lisbon in 1588 in his famous book, *Concordia*, which came out in a second edition at Antwerp in 1595. In the interval there had been a lively controversy stirred up by the Dominicans, who held firmly to the Thomist teaching which, in its main aspects, was firmly Augustinian; and both the Inquisition and the king of Spain had concerned themselves with the matter. Rome took cognisance, but declined to condemn either side. Not unexpectedly, Molina's views were censured at Louvain in 1587, nor did they gain the full approval even of his most distinguished fellow Jesuits, Bellarmine and Suárez. The issues involved, however, were too much bound up with the practical pastoral teaching of the Jesuits for Molinism not to gain popularity in the Society. For the Jesuits, following the *Exercises* of their founder St Ignatius Loyola, laid great stress upon the need for man to take firm decisions if he wished to be saved—precisely what Protestants, Baianists and, to some extent, traditional Thomists denied that he could do without the overpowering grace of God. Violent debates in the Spanish universities eventually forced the papacy to take action and in 1598 the famous Congregation *De Auxiliis*, set up by Clement VIII, began investigating the dispute. Its work dragged on into the pontificate of Paul V, who in 1607 ended the matter with a decree which allowed both parties to retain their opinions and forbade them to censure or condemn each other until the Holy See issued a final judgement—which it never did. Arid as the whole dispute must seem to all except those who think that the precise relationship between the power of God and the will of his creature, man, is capable of definition in human terms and involves no ultimate mystery, it illustrates vividly the intense mental activity with which theology was being pursued in the Roman fold in this period. Thought was certainly not stagnant and, even if one feels that it might have been devoted to more constructive ends than violent controversy, yet the matters in dispute were not, as has been said, irrelevant to practical religion. It is curious that the Protestant world was at the very same time involved in closely similar quarrels and the student of English puritanism, for example, will realise that the concept of predestination had a deep influence upon both the religious and political action of Calvinists.

These episodes bring out also the extent to which the universities still, as in the middle ages, played a vital role in Catholic life and were the ultimate force behind pastoral training. The foundation of seminaries, which indeed were often closely associated with them, did nothing to undermine their influence and often enhanced it, for the days had gone by when the ordinary parish priest was often barely literate and thereby isolated from academic life. As in medieval times, too, the religious orders, which played such a big part in evangelisation and specialised pastoral work, were closely associated with university life and to some extent dominated it. The great theologians were almost all members of one or other of the orders. Thus from the universities there spread down to the layman through the clergy, regular or secular, religious instruction of a far more systematic and intensive type than had been available before the Reformation. The system established itself only slowly and ignorance was not dissipated everywhere or at once, as, for example, St Vincent de Paul was to find when he established his parochial missions in seventeenth-century France. But something like a revolution had been accomplished in great areas of the Roman obedience by the end of the sixteenth century in making religion intelligible and vital.

Behind this lay something much deeper. No account of the period would be complete without a consideration of the forces which brought not merely knowledge but also piety to the ordinary man. It was not only popularised theology which the religious orders and the parochial clergy endeavoured to bring to the layman. Those of them who had really absorbed the principles of reform wished to make him pray, value the sacraments, practise the Christian virtues and by all these means attain sanctity as well as orthodoxy. The ultimate power of the Counter-Reformation lay in the revival of spirituality, which had begun before the middle of the century, but which went on with increased vigour afterwards. Perhaps the best example of what was aimed at lies in the long lifework of St Philip Neri (1515–95), the Florentine who from 1533 until his death lived in Rome, entering the priesthood in 1551 and founding the Congregation of the Oratory, a body of priests living as religious, although not under vows. The whole object of his apostolate, exercised partly through the confessional, partly by assembling layfolk in informal meetings for prayer, discussion and recreation, was to lead ordinary persons to live not merely respectable but sanctified lives. His influence extended into the papal court, and, although he refused any official position, he could and did guide papal action on various occasions. He was known to and revered by almost all those concerned with Catholic revival at the centre, for there could be no better strategic base than Rome for the kind of influence wielded by St Philip, little as his remarkable humility aimed at controlling the revivification of the church.

What St Philip Neri aimed to do in Rome was done elsewhere by a whole series of saintly figures. The remarkable number of ecclesiastics and others of this time who were destined to become after their deaths canonised saints must strike anyone familiar with the period, especially since the standards required for canonisation by the post-Tridentine Roman church were by no means low, as the official rules show. The 'heroic sanctity' which is the basic requirement has to be strictly heroic and go far beyond ordinary piety and good works. It is no exaggeration to describe the later sixteenth century, compared with other times, as an age of saints, and in that lies the real secret of what Catholicism achieved during it.

Partly, no doubt, this increase of sanctity can be attributed to the often heroic response brought out in any community by a challenge to its existence and way of life. *L'église en danger* can be as stimulating a rallying call as *la patrie en danger*. But the church historian, aware of the relationship between spiritual practice and theory in earlier ages, will tend to look for a deeper reason and to identify it with another striking feature of this period of Catholic life, the revival and development of the ascetic and mystical traditions. The later sixteenth century was an age of spiritual reading, which had much to do with the conversion to a more real and deeper spiritual life of some of the outstanding figures of the age and doubtless also of many others less well known to us. The story is well known how St Ignatius was first turned to his vocation by the enforced reading, through sheer boredom, of a life of Christ and a series of lives of the saints when he was recovering from his wounds sustained at Pamplona and none of his favourite romances of chivalry were available in the house. In her autobiography St Teresa of Avila makes it clear how much she owed, in progressing beyond the lax piety of an earlier sixteenth-century cloister, to such books as the *Tercer Abecedario* of the Franciscan Francisco de Osuna, which opened fresh horizons of the possibility of contemplative prayer to her. Equally the age was one of spiritual writing. Had it produced no more than the works of St Teresa herself and of her associate in the reform of the Carmelite Order, St John of the Cross, by common consent the deepest analyses of the mystical life ever written, it would stand out as a time of exceptional productivity in spiritual theory. But in fact these are only the peaks of a whole range of spiritual literature which rivalled and at times surpassed the classics written in the age of the Desert Fathers and the middle ages. The fact that St John of the Cross, in particular, had been educated in the heart of the great Spanish theological tradition at Salamanca and shows in his writings an accurate knowledge of scholastic theology demonstrates that the Spanish universities were capable of producing something better than arid logic-chopping in the theological field, contrary to what might be supposed from what has been said of the wearisome controversies about grace and free will. Like all apparent novelties in Spain, the mystical movement came under the suspicion of the Inquisition—a fact partly to be excused by the prevalence of groups of heretical *Alumbrados*, who claimed special illumination and held that immorality did not stain the soul—but the fact that it survived and established its orthodoxy again shows that Spanish religion was not the mere militant fanaticism combined with unthinking conformity it is often thought to have been.

Late sixteenth-century Catholicism is today as much under fire from Catholicism of the *aggiornamento* as it has been in the past from Protestantism and agnostic humanism. It is fashionable to describe it disparagingly as 'baroque Catholicism', and indeed it had something of the flamboyance of its favourite architectural style. But not all aesthetic taste rules out Baroque or fails to distinguish it from Rococo. There is a strength and solidity beneath the exuberant decoration of the Baroque which is not to be despised. In the same way there is a difference between the stern self-sacrifice of the men of the Counter-Reformation, decked as it may have been with an almost swaggering parade of the uncompromising affirmations of the Council of Trent and the kind of sentimental pietism at which Pascal was to mock in the next century. Stained as it was by fanaticism and cruelty and too often chained to Machiavellian nationalism, lacking as it now seems to have been in what is now known as the oecumenical spirit, there was a depth, a realism and above all a zeal inspired by deep spirituality about later sixteenth-century Catholicism which makes it impossible for the historian to dismiss it as an aberration of Christianity.

CHAPTER IV

PROTESTANTISM AND CONFESSIONAL STRIFE

1. *Lutheranism after Luther*

A<small>T</small> the beginning of the second volume of his massive *Histoire générale du Protestantisme* Émile Léonard describes the disappearance of Luther as a *coup d'arrêt* for Lutheranism, contrasting it in this way with the effects of Calvin's death upon Calvinism. There is a real aptness in this comparison. For Lutheranism was, and to a great extent remains, the religion of a personality, of an often stormy and erratic genius, but one capable of influencing and inspiring his followers to an almost unique degree. That Luther's influence has survived his death is apparent from the endless stream of books upon his thought produced by Lutherans in Europe and America and could never be doubted by anyone who has heard a committed Lutheran decide a problem with the reverential words, *Luther sagt*... Nevertheless, Léonard is not mistaken in seeing Luther's death as a calamity for the confession he had founded, in contrast to the comparatively calm way in which Calvinism reacted to the death of the Genevan reformer in 1564, less than a year after the ending of the Council of Trent. For Calvin created a system; he lived in his works and in the clearly defined church polity he had established in Geneva, which formed a pattern for all Calvinist churches. Luther was not a man of system; one might almost say that he abhorred systems and organisation as much as did St Francis of Assisi. Indeed it was a principle with him that, provided the gospel as he understood it, centring in the justification of man by faith alone, was purely preached and the sacraments administered in accordance with it, church organisation and the details of worship were matters indifferent and could be variously decided in different places according to local and temporal preference and utility—a principle which explains the variations to be observed in Lutheran churches today.

The comparison with St Francis, however, has a further applicability, for just as his death was followed quickly by disputes and divisions within his Order, which indeed had been present in germ even earlier, so the death of Luther in 1546 released and exacerbated divisive tendencies already operative within the Lutheran fold. The temperamental and intellectual contrasts between Luther himself and his most important disciple, Melanchthon, had led to differences of opinion between them in Luther's lifetime, which only their personal affection for each other prevented from becoming schismatic. Luther always considered Melanchthon too charitable towards opponents of all kinds. 'I am Isaiah, Philippus is Jeremiah; he always worried that he scolded too much, just like Philippus!' Yet he had for Melanchthon's mildness the wistful respect that the stormy petrel often feels for the man of peace. 'Philippus proceeds in charity, and I in faith. Philippus suffers himself to be eaten up, I eat up everything and spare nobody.' But this only partly explains the differences between not merely the men, but their policies, which became so apparent, for example, both when the Augsburg Confession was discussed at the Diet of 1530 and later at the time of the Colloquy of Ratisbon in 1541, when agreement between Catholics and Protestants seemed so near to achievement. In both cases Luther felt that Melanchthon had sold the pass. The Confession of Augsburg, largely Melanchthon's own composition, Luther at first appeared to accept cordially, writing to the Elector of Saxony: 'It pleases me well, and I know not how to better it . . . for I cannot tread so softly and gently.' Peacemaking he had always recognised as Melanchthon's forte, seeing in it the complement to his own intransigence. As he wrote in his preface to his colleague's commentary on Colossians: 'I am rough, boisterous, stormy, and altogether warlike. I am born to fight against innumerable monsters and devils. I must remove stumps and stones, cut away thistles and thorns, and clear the wild forests: but Master Philip comes along softly and gently, sowing and watering with joy, according to the gifts which God has abundantly bestowed upon him.' Yet Luther's second thoughts about Melanchthon's policies were usually less accommodating. Melanchthon had admittedly made further concessions at Augsburg, in an attempt to win the legate Campeggio to agreement; he even expressed willingness to accept the authority of the pope and bishops, at least until a council could meet, if in return communion in two kinds and clerical marriage were allowed. Luther, writing from Coburg, condemned concession, on the ground that the Catholics were reluctant to grant more than minimal concessions themselves, adding characteristically: 'We do not come to learn whether they approve our ideas or not, leaving them free to remain as they are.' There is no doubt at all that if he had had the penning of the Confession it would not have been the conciliatory document it was, and certainly he would not have gone a step beyond it. The difference between the two men appeared more clearly still when in 1541 an even more conciliatory statement was debated with the Catholics at Ratisbon, with Melanchthon as one of the Protestant representatives. Although, surprisingly enough, agreement was reached upon the central point at issue, justification by faith, Luther himself rejected this agreement as 'a patched-up thing', demanding that the Catholics should explicitly change their doctrine on the subject. Melanchthon had thought the agreed formula 'shorter than the importance of the subject demands' but yet *mediocris*, not too bad.

This excursion into events before our period is necessary if one is to

understand the mind of Melanchthon and its difference from that of
Luther. For Melanchthon, the disciple, was to survive his master by fourteen years, dying as he did in 1560, and thereby was to experience bitterly
the hitherto more or less hidden cleavages in the Lutheran fold, which
only the prestige of its acknowledged leader had prevented from becoming
chasms during his lifetime. Quite apart from his controversies with the
left-wing 'Anabaptist' sects and with the Zwinglians, Luther had had to
deal with divergencies in his own following. On the one hand there was
the antinomianism which pushed Luther's own paradoxical conception
of justified man as *semper justus, semper peccator* to the extent of holding
that sin does not separate from God, so that the Christian is not really
subject to the moral law. On the other, there was the attitude which came
to be known as synergism, which questioned Luther's absolute denial of
free will and tried to find some place for human co-operation in the work of
salvation. The former position, set forth by Agricola and Schenck, Luther
attacked in 1537–8. The latter, represented chiefly by Osiander, the
Nuremberg reformer, who believed that justification was bound up with
the indwelling of Christ in the souls of those who accepted him as Saviour,
Luther left alone, perhaps, as Léonard suggests, because his beloved
Philip Melanchthon was accused of holding similar views. Melanchthon
certainly watered down the view he had originally held, with Luther, of
the absolute incapacity of man to forward his own salvation, and he
became less of a predestinarian. 'God saves whom he wishes', said
Luther once at table; to be contradicted by Melanchthon in the words:
'No, him who wishes to be saved.'

Nor was this the only deviation of Melanchthon. When the Augsburg
Confession was revised in 1540 he altered the definition of the Eucharist
in a sense favourable to the Swiss denial of the Real Presence, a doctrine
to which Luther always held fast. Indeed the friendship of the two men
became strained in Luther's last years. Luther was warned that Melanchthon was secretly at variance with his views, which in fact he was criti-
cising behind Luther's back, even in correspondence with Catholics, but
refused to take notice. For his part, Melanchthon, fearful of the bad temper
which grew upon Luther more and more as he aged, also kept silence.

The fact was that Luther and Melanchthon, however closely associated
they had been, were men of fundamentally different temperaments and
outlooks. Melanchthon was always the academic, the close scholar, the
don, concerned about exactitude of teaching, a humanist, with a respect
for public order which went far beyond Luther's view of the prince as set
up by God to keep the wicked in fear. He was willing to make concessions
at the Diet of Augsburg primarily, as he said, for the sake of 'maintaining,
strengthening and establishing peace, concord and the authority of the
ecclesiastical order' and, for the same reason, in Luther's last days he was
anxious to make peace if he could with Catholics on the one hand and the

Swiss Reformation on the other. Franz Hildebrandt has enumerated the concessions which led him to diverge from Luther as those made to tradition, to reason, to law, to power and to opposition. Luther, on the other hand, emotional and fiery by nature, was the academic turned prophet—always a dangerous change of trade, although one which, as in his case, can enhance personal influence upon others. We have already seen Luther's consciousness of the contrast in temperament and attitude between himself and the friend he both loved and mistrusted. This, and the realisation that Melanchthon was in no way fitted to succeed him in the task of holding Lutheranism together, may have lain behind the words he wrote to him in 1538:

How many different masters will the next century follow? The confusion will reach new heights. None of them will be willing to be governed by the opinion or authority of the others. Each will want to set up as his own *rabbi*: look at how Osiander and Agricola are already behaving...And what terrible scandals there will be! What excesses! The best course would be for the princes to avert such evils by means of a council. But the Papists would avoid this: they are so afraid of the light!

It was a true prophecy so far as Lutheranism was concerned. The years following Luther's death were a time of bitter conflict within the Lutheran party, a conflict in which the unhappy Melanchthon was destined to be an unwilling central figure. They began precisely because of Melanchthon's zeal for peace, as an outcome of the *Interim* which Charles V, after his defeat of the Lutheran Schmalkaldic League at Mühlberg in 1547, two years after Luther's death, tried to impose upon the empire. It was a compromise intended, as its name suggested, to maintain a temporary balance between Catholics and Protestants until their differences could be permanently resolved in a council. Concessions were made to the Protestants in certain respects, but they were required to maintain, or rather to reintroduce, a large number of Catholic practices and ceremonies. It caused violent indignation and led to the voluntary exile of many prominent reformers who could not in conscience accept it—a fact which explains Cranmer's success in attracting some of them to England to assist the Edwardian Reformation—and it was resisted by most of the Protestant princes. But Melanchthon and his associates lent themselves to a project launched by Maurice, duke of Saxony, who, although a Protestant, had allied himself with the emperor before the Schmalkaldic War and received from him the Electorate of Saxony, confiscated from his relation, John Frederick, which included Wittenberg. John Frederick reconquered the Electorate in 1547, but lost it again after the battle of Mühlberg, at which he was made prisoner. Maurice, whose religion was flexible, attended Mass after the battle and willingly accepted a papal dispensation allowing him to retain secularised ecclesiastical property. But he knew the difficulties he would encounter in persuading his Saxon subjects to accept the emperor's *Interim* of 1548 and began to strive for a compromise within a compromise in the form of an *Interim* of his own which the Saxon Diet might be willing to agree to. This was the origin of the Leipzig *Interim* of December 1548, so called to distinguish it from the imperial Augsburg *Interim*, already mentioned, which had been published with papal approval the previous May. In view both of the collapse of the Schmalkaldic League and, on the other hand, of the resistance put up by the more intransigent Protestants, it seemed to offer a possible way out. Some of the more recalcitrant reformers, notably Amsdorf and Flacius Illyricus, took refuge in Magdeburg, a Lutheran stronghold since 1521, which was destined to be captured by Maurice on behalf of the emperor in 1551, after a siege which, like that of Londonderry in 1689, became a Protestant epic. It is noteworthy also because it caused the first break in the Lutheran theory of passive obedience to rulers, since the besieged pastors issued a solemn declaration justifying resistance.

It was to the Leipzig *Interim* that Melanchthon and his Wittenberg supporters lent their co-operation, Melanchthon himself becoming the Elector's religious adviser in the matter. It is possible that he found this easier for his conscience in that Maurice's chief lay adviser was Christopher Carlowitz, an Erasmian who always maintained a middle course in religious matters. This was an attitude Melanchthon understood, and one must also remember the Lutheran principle of obedience to the godly prince. Moreover, as he revealed in a letter of April 1548, Melanchthon was under the influence of a reaction against the violence and intransigence of Luther, under whom he had suffered what he now described as a slavery. He spoke of his old master as often forgetting his dignity—one can well imagine that the cultured Melanchthon had often shuddered at Luther's coarser polemics—and, significantly, as not paying attention to the general weal. (Melanchthon, as has been said, had the scholar's love of civic peace.) Nor, probably, was he speaking untruly when he regretted the foundation of the Evangelical church and denied his own responsibility for schism, or avowed his lifelong affection for Catholic ceremonies. Many of his other words and actions suggest this psychological trait, even though he was not always consistent and in a private letter had criticised the Augsburg *Interim* and spoken of the ceremonies commanded by it as stupid. (When the letter was printed without his knowledge he tore up a copy publicly in order to dissociate himself from it!) Nor was he the only one to feel that Luther's Reformation was not necessarily to be adhered to in all its details when circumstances called for compromise; he was supported by other Lutherans of note, such as Bugenhagen and George Major, the latter a Wittenberg professor since 1536, who was later to proclaim the necessity of good works for ultimate salvation.

The Leipzig *Interim* itself was a document in fifteen articles which attempted to bring into harmony Catholic and Protestant doctrine upon faith and works, authority in the church, the sacraments, the use of images, the canonical Hours, prayers for the dead and fasting. Its practical effect in Saxony seems to have been minimal. Melanchthon himself wrote that things went on in the church there as they had done for the previous twenty years; no one thought of alteration. Nor would it appear that he really believed in it; to a critic who described it as collusion with the devil, Melanchthon is alleged to have said that this was true, but what else could one do? In any case even the idea of compromise was not to last. Although in 1550 Charles V, at the second session of the Diet of Augsburg, persuaded the Protestants to send delegates to plead their cause at the Council of Trent, their appearance there in 1552 did nothing to influence the Fathers to accept their demands, which amounted to asking for a new start to the Council on the basis of Scripture as the sole standard of truth, lay participation in voting, and the rejection of papal presidency and right of veto. By 1551 Maurice of Saxony had broken with the emperor and allied himself with the other Protestant princes, the coalition receiving the help of Henry II of France. The advance of Maurice upon Innsbruck caused the Council of Trent to break up in confusion, not to meet again for ten years, and at Passau that August Charles V had to come to terms with the Protestants. Next year Maurice of Saxony was killed in action against Albert Alcibiades of Brandenburg and in 1555 the Peace of Augsburg, which gave each territorial prince the right to decide religious matters in his own territories, made all *Interims* otiose.

Nevertheless the split between Lutherans prepared to compromise and the fundamentalists, revealed by the temporary victory of Charles V, was to add rancour to the differences of outlook current even in Luther's lifetime and to cause serious quarrels in the Lutheran fold for the thirty-two years between 1548 and 1580. Yet these quarrels, though by their divisive character they weakened Lutheranism at a critical time, ended in the establishment of a defined corpus of Lutheran doctrine and so led to a unity which might well have seemed an impossibility at the time of Luther's death. It should, however, be added that many would claim, with some support from the subsequent history of Lutheranism, that this was a doubtful benefit, in that it tended to freeze a type of religion which was essentially more concerned with devotional attitudes than with dogma as such, into a scholastic pattern which deprived it of the *élan* and attractive power of its salad days.

As already said, Melanchthon found himself the unhappy centre of the controversies which now raged. In one sense this was inevitable. For Melanchthon, in virtue of his influential *Loci communes*, had become the systematic theologian of the Lutheran Reformation; moreover, he was the chief author of what had become the title-deed of Lutheran belief, the Augsburg Confession. The paradox has been remarked that in the long run his desire for systematisation, in contrast as it was with the emotional and sometimes illogical character of Luther himself, by force of circumstances imposed itself in the end upon his opponents, the Gnesiolutherans, as they are known, who violently opposed what they regarded as his revisionist tendencies. Melanchthon, the prince of Luther's apostles and the chief intellectual of the original movement, was a figure who could not be ignored, but at the same time was suspected of the wavering and halfheartedness nearly always attributed to intellectuals by active revolutionaries. Nor, as we have seen, were these suspicions without foundation from the point of view of those to whom Lutheranism was and must remain a permanent break with the *ancien régime* of the Catholic church.

The series of quarrels which now arose, with the patriarchal figure of Luther no longer there to act as arbitrator or to impose peace by an appeal to personal loyalty to himself (if indeed the disillusioned, crossgrained and increasingly irritable figure which Luther presented in his last years could have done this), began with the Adiaphoristic controversy, set off in 1549 with the publication of Flacius Illyricus's *De veris et falsis adiaphoris*. Flacius, it will be remembered, was the most prominent of those intransigent Protestants who had withdrawn northwards to Magdeburg to defy the Augsburg *Interim*. To them the Leipzig *Interim* was scarcely less anathema than its predecessor and they reacted sharply when Melanchthon and his supporters defended it on the ground that the Catholic ceremonies to which it had agreed were *adiaphora*, things indifferent, in that they rested merely upon human tradition, so that compromise over them was not treason against the word of God. To them there was no halfway house between good and evil, truth and falsehood. It must be recalled that they were attacking a claim, not that these things were good or valuable in themselves, but that they were practices of no deep moment which, although unnecessary and perhaps even undesirable, could be allowed for the sake of peace, much as Calvin in another context was to describe some of the details of the Anglican prayer-book as *tolerabiles ineptiae*. Those who defended this attitude could claim some standing in Lutheran tradition, for Luther in the early days at Wittenberg had opposed the radicalism introduced by Karlstadt and others during his absence in the Wartburg and restored on his return the traditional practices swept away by them, most of which he later abandoned. Moreover, it was a Lutheran principle that only the centre of the gospel, justification by faith and the view of the sacraments which resulted from it, was absolutely obligatory; almost all else in religious practice and organisation was of secondary importance and could be accommodated to circumstances. The violent opposition to the Interim proposed by Wittenberg theologians of the mid-century not only witnessed to the development of a party resolved not to retrace one step of the path already trodden, but also to the growth of a Jacobin type of Lutheranism more akin to the attitude of the Swiss reformers than to the conservatism which to some extent marked Luther all his life. Indeed this radicalism perhaps indicates a slow spread of the spirit, if not the actual doctrines, of the Swiss into Lutheran Germany from the south-west, where from a very early date Swiss ideas had taken possession of the Reformation. It is noteworthy that in the Adiaphoristic dispute not only Brenz, the Lutheran reformer of Württemberg and strong opponent of Zwinglians and Calvinists on the Eucharistic issue, but Calvin too, took sides against the Wittenbergers. Indeed the resemblance between this dispute and that between Hooker and the radical puritans in England, over the question of whether only things specifically approved in Scripture were lawful, will be at once apparent to students of the period.

It was ironic that on the Eucharistic issue Melanchthon was sympathetic to the Swiss 'sacramentarian' view, which denied any change in the elements after consecration, and was to oppose Brenz when he set forward the Lutheran doctrine of the Real Presence in a very precise form, based upon Luther's view that the humanity of Christ had communicated to it the property of omnipresence belonging to his godhead and so could be made present in the sacrament. The Reformation had indeed reached a stage in which the cross-fertilisation of ideas and the pressure of the Catholic reaction were making strange bedfellows.

Melanchthon by 1552 had, as was often the case with him, abandoned his defence of *adiaphora* in the face of opposition and indeed, as already pointed out, the question became irrelevant as the effects of Charles V's temporary victory of 1547–8 faded with the Protestant resurgence. But the issue had already tended to split Lutheran opinion into the two parties of 'Philippists' and 'Gnesiolutherans', who tended to find their strongholds in Wittenberg and the new university of Jena (founded in 1548) respectively. The fact became apparent in the related disputes which followed the Adiaphoristic, which turned upon points central to the Lutheran conception of salvation, the necessity or otherwise of good works for salvation (really the old antinomian issue in a slightly different form) and on the problem of free will, in which those who held fanatically to Luther's conception, maintained by him against Erasmus, of the servile will of man enslaved either to God or the devil, were opposed by 'synergists' who wished to allow man some title to co-operation with God in the process of salvation. It is hardly necessary to say that in each case the Philippists were to be found upon what the Gnesiolutherans regarded, not without reason, as the revisionist or deviationist side. There is indeed a certain resemblance here to the conflicts among Marxists in our own day, between those who will tolerate no departure from the letter of Marx and those who are alleged to depart from it. The parallel extends further, since, as today there are those who appear to be more Marxist than Marx, so then there were those prepared to be more Lutheran than Luther, such as Amsdorf, who was prepared to assert that good works were a positive hindrance to salvation.

The effect of all this upon the unity of Lutheranism, even upon the political side, does not need to be stressed. The 'godly prince' was, in Lutheran thought, expected to interest himself in and maintain the purity of religion. The long quarrel between the Ernestine and Albertine branches of the Saxon family thus translated itself into theology at the middle of the century. John Frederick of the Ernestine line, from whom the Electoral dignity had been taken by the Albertine Maurice, backed the extreme Lutherans against the Philippists who were favoured by Maurice's brother and successor, the Elector Augustus. John Frederick authorised the putting forth in 1559 of the Confutation of Weimar anathematising not only all opponents of Lutheranism but also those who favoured the positions of Melanchthon and his friends as against a formula of union agreed by the other Protestant princes at Frankfurt in 1558. Fortunately the intricacies of the theological conflict prevented the development of what could have been a real political schism. Even in the university of Jena opposition to the extreme opponents of free will developed. The fiery Flacius Illyricus, who had become a professor there in 1557, was attacked for his view that man was as passive in the hands of God as wood or stone by Strigel, a disciple of Melanchthon and another of the professors. The university superintendent banned the Confutation of Weimar and imprisoned the rival divines for six months, releasing them only at the request of the rank and file of the university, backed by the Protestant princes and the Emperor Ferdinand I himself. The quarrel continued and Strigel was dismissed from his chair. Long arguments between him and Flacius at Weimar in 1560 effected nothing more than to make Duke John Frederick adopt a neutral position. Flacius and his partisans continued to rage against their opponents and the duke adopted an Erastian solution, by setting up a consistory to take over the powers of excommunication and censure of books from the pastors. Flacius, with about forty supporters, was deposed from office. In 1561 Strigel was recalled to Jena and reinstated but, perhaps wisely, accepted a chair at Leipzig the following year.

Clearly these embittered disputes were endangering the very survival of Lutheranism, faced as it also was with a spread of Calvinism in Germany. The princes were aware of it and saw a chance of restoring unity when the Emperor Ferdinand put forward his son, Maximilian, for election as king of the Romans and his own successor. Ferdinand himself favoured concessions to the Protestants; but his son, who had been educated by Lutheran tutors, was actually negotiating with the Protestant princes, promising to support the Augsburg Confession provided that the Protestants established unity among themselves. This they failed to do in a conference of princes at Naumburg in 1561, chiefly because Philip of Hesse succeeded in getting the majority to accept Melanchthon's view of the Eucharist, which was too much akin to the Swiss attitude for the strict Lutherans. They were not even unanimous in backing Maximilian's election, the Count Palatine, as a favourer of Calvinism, being opposed to him, so that he had to win election by pretending to the Catholics to be fully at one with them in faith. Even the removal of Duke John Frederick of Saxony did not bring peace among the Lutherans. He was imprisoned for life for his support of the plotter Wilhelm von Grumbach who, having brought about the assassination of the Catholic bishop of Würzburg, involved the duke in a wild plan for a revolution which would make him emperor with the aid of Sweden and of prominent figures in the Netherlands and France, a project supported by the pretended revelations of a wild prophet, Tausendschön.

His brother and successor, John William, supported the men of Jena down to his death in 1573, when the Ernestine lands fell under the administration of the Albertine Elector, Augustus, a supporter of the Philippists. Augustus pursued Flacius with unrelenting hate, causing him to be banished from one city after another, whilst Flacius continued to uphold everywhere extreme views about the utter corruption of man, maintaining that sin had become the actual substance of human nature. Controversy indeed had reached a degree of almost unimaginable bitterness, its spirit represented by one of Flacius's associates, Wigand, who held that 'he who is not a zealot does not love Christ'. At a disputation between theologians at Altenburg in 1568 before Duke John William, in which this last worthy took part, the vituperation between the Gnesiolutherans and the Philippists became so scandalous that it was popularly believed that heaven itself was shocked and showed it by the appearance of prodigies. (Apocalyptic and astrological interests were never far from the sixteenth-century Lutheran mind; Melanchthon himself had an interest in astrology, from which even Luther could not wean him.)

Increasingly, too, the struggles within Lutheranism became connected with the Lutheran fear and dislike of Calvinism, which went back to Luther's own opposition to Zwingli, a dislike which must have increased considerably after Bullinger, Zwingli's successor, came to an agreement with the Calvinists in the *Consensus Tigurinus* of 1549. The *Consensus* denied the Real Presence in the elements, a basic belief which the thoroughgoing Lutherans shared with Catholics, even though they rejected transubstantiation. It described as *praeposteros interpretes* those who took literally the words of Christ, 'This is my Body. This is my Blood'—as Luther had done at the Marburg Conference of 1529, when he chalked the words *Hoc est corpus meum* on the table and refused to budge an inch from their literal sense. 'Better to be Catholics than Calvinists' became a Lutheran slogan and the fundamentalists described those Lutherans who seemed to them unsound on the doctrine of the Sacrament as 'crypto-Calvinists'. The opposition to such men was fierce. When in 1574 Joachim Curaeus, of the Philippist school, published a treatise on the Lord's Supper setting forth the Swiss doctrine and the Wittenberg theologians approved it and used it in teaching, the horrified Elector Augustus, who does not seem to have realised how far the school opposed to the Gnesiolutherans was prepared to go, had the book condemned in the *Articles of Torgau*. He also put the leaders of the crypto-Calvinists on trial, tortured one to death and kept another in prison for a long time. Indeed persecution of Protestants by Protestants was becoming general. When the Count Palatine Frederick III, who had patronised Calvinism at Heidelberg, died in 1576, his son Ludwig demanded from his subjects a return to Lutheranism and expelled from his territory about 500 or 600 Calvinist leaders who refused to conform. The Palatinate became Lutheran until 1583, when John Casimir, Ludwig's brother, acting as Administrator for his young nephew Frederick IV, restored the Calvinist faith.

It must be remembered in this connection that the Emperor Maximilian (1564–76), himself nominally a Catholic, favoured Lutheranism, even encouraging it in his own territory of Austria, but had no use for Calvinism. He summoned a Diet at Augsburg in 1566 with the intention of proscribing all sects outside the Catholic and Lutheran folds, but failed to get the support of a majority of the Lutheran princes in his effort to make the Count Palatine, Frederick, abandon Calvinism. Led by the Elector Augustus of Saxony, they persisted in regarding Frederick as loyal to the Augsburg Confession apart from his views on the Sacrament of the Altar. Maximilian's hostility to Frederick stemmed, no doubt, from the latter's opposition to his election as king of the Romans in 1562, but he had also imbibed from his Lutheran tutors a belief in the positive merits of Lutheranism, and probably thought that two religions in the empire were enough, especially as a reconciliation of right-wing Protestantism with Catholicism at which he aimed would be wrecked if the left wing gained ground.

It may well be that the succession to the throne after Maximilian's death in 1576 of his son, Rudolf, a thoroughgoing Catholic, was one of the factors impelling the Lutherans to set their house in order and achieve unity. The overthrow of Calvinism in the Palatinate on Frederick III's death must also have made the time seem propitious. The first steps had already been taken. Christopher, duke of Württemberg, was a devout Lutheran and his dominions were less troubled by the current disputes than was Saxony. He became the patron of James Andreae, chancellor of his university of Tübingen, who was a devoted worker for unity. Andreae produced in 1567 five articles to form a basis of unity and gained support for them from both Philippists and Gnesiolutherans, but the death of Duke Christopher in 1568 and the estrangement from Andreae of William of Hesse-Cassel, who had shared Christopher's zeal for unity, stopped further progress. In 1573 Andreae returned to the task by publishing six eirenical sermons, which gained him the support of some important north German Lutheran divines, notably Martin Chemnitz, who interested his secular ruler, Julius of Brunswick, with the result that

Andreae formed out of his sermons the *Swabian Concord* of eleven articles, to which Lower Saxony subsequently adhered. An independent initiative was taken by Augustus of Saxony, whose theologians produced in 1576 the *Formula of Maulbronn*. Later in the year a conference summoned by Augustus at Torgau amalgamated the *Swabian–Saxon Concord* and the *Formula of Maulbronn* into the *Formula of Torgau*, the work very largely of friends and disciples of Melanchthon. Too long in itself to serve the purpose needed, the Torgau Formula was abbreviated by Andreae into what became the *Epitome* of the final *Formula of Concord*, published in German at Dresden in 1580, thus appropriately marking the jubilee of the Augsburg Confession of 1530. Criticisms made of the *Formula of Torgau* were utilised to form a *Book of Bergen*, which became in turn the immense *Solida Declaratio* which forms the second part of the *Formula of Concord*.

Thus was produced the definitive statement of Lutheran theology. The first Latin translation of it by Osiander was found defective and was revised, a final authentic Latin edition being published at Leipzig in 1584. It is a formidable document of some 17,000 words, preceded by a long preface which was signed by the Lutheran princes, nobles and city authorities. It is verbose and studded with Scriptural quotations and, whilst declaring that, after Scripture itself and the three traditional creeds, the original unaltered Augsburg Confession of 1530 forms the norm of Lutheran doctrine, goes in great detail into the controversies which had arisen since then, controversies which a recent writer on the *Formula of Concord* has enumerated as no less than ten, although they could be differently divided. As we have seen, they were numerous, interrelated and bitter; nor is it necessary, for the purpose of tracing the fortunes of Lutheranism in this period, to describe all of them. This, to a great extent, the *Formula* does itself, for, to quote Léonard, 'it has for the historian the great merit of being conceived in terms of history, as the reply to problems raised by the evolution of the Reformation, each of these being preceded by an impartial explanation of the circumstances, in which the opposing theses are defined soberly but precisely'. By its very nature it is impartial, condemning the various parties in some matters and not canonising any of them, although, as was to be expected, it is most severe when attacking Calvinism, and it is interesting that the most severe passage comes, not on the Eucharistic issue, but in its criticism of Calvinist doctrines of predestination, which it declares to be 'all false, horrifying and blasphemous'. 'By them all consolation, which they ought to gain from the gospel and the use of the sacraments, is snatched away from pious minds, and therefore they are in no way to be tolerated in the Church of God.' To authentic Lutheranism, predestination, however strongly believed in, was a doctrine of comfort, not of potential despair.

It must seem little less than a miracle that out of the turmoil of violent controversy which had embroiled Luther's followers ever since his death, and indeed had begun before, such detailed agreement could come, so completely and in a sense unexpectedly, twenty years before the end of the century. Controversy did not cease of course immediately. Voices were raised in criticism of the *Formula* from theologians in different parts of Germany, which necessitated an *Apology* for it by Selnecker, Chemnitz and Kirchner, published at Dresden in 1584.[1] But eventually it was accepted by the majority of Lutheran churches in Germany and Scandinavia. Attacked vigorously by the Calvinists, it was, partly for that very reason, regarded more and more as a second basis, after the Augsburg Confession, for that essentially Teutonic form of Protestantism which, although it never made serious progress elsewhere, captured and retained the affection of so many Germans and virtually all Scandinavians and retains it today, even when Teutons are transplanted into other backgrounds, as the vigour of modern American Lutheranism shows.

If one asks, as one must, what enabled Lutheranism to survive this time of troubles and to emerge as still the predominant form of Protestantism in Germany, part of the answer probably lies precisely in this psychological kinship between it and the Teutonic mind. Luther, both in his strong points and in his weak ones, has always been seen to be profoundly German, as indeed the rapidity with which he gained national popularity between 1517 and 1521 shows. It was not only that he appealed directly and intentionally to German national feeling: it is even more significant that he knew exactly how to do so. If he lost popularity later, especially at the time of the Peasants' War, if he failed in the end to retain more than a part of the German people on his side, yet he remained influential in Germany to the end, and, significantly, virtually nowhere else. Lutheran ideas influenced other parts of Europe, but not Luther the man, and it is a plain fact of history that outside Germany and Scandinavia Calvinism reaped the whole of the harvest that Lutheranism had sown. The internal tensions of Lutheranism we have been describing no doubt help to explain this; German Lutheranism became introverted, absorbed in its controversial efforts to understand itself; it could not easily also be a missionary religion. But anyone who has experienced, even briefly, the peculiar, indeed unique, atmosphere of Lutheran worship and piety will suspect a deeper reason. Lutherans themselves are accustomed to see in these the essence of their faith, much as do the Eastern Orthodox. Their objections to Calvinism spring quite as much from the cold, intellectual character of Calvinist worship as from their dislike of Calvinist doctrines, and that in turn, as is evident from the passage from the *Formula of Concord* about predestination quoted above, comes largely from the feeling that the characteristic Calvinist theology is cold, legalistic, rationalising, and ministers nothing to the warm confidence in God manifested in Christ which is perhaps the deepest thing in the authentic Lutheran attitude to religion.

[1] See below, p. 333.

Lutheranism has never been ascetic, in either the Catholic or the Calvinist way; its notions of sanctity are largely its own and are not very easily understood by those of other backgrounds.

It is noteworthy, too, that Lutheranism retained much of the devotional background of medieval German Catholicism, however freshly it interpreted it. Unlike Zwinglianism and Calvinism, it was not iconoclastic, as Lutheran churches in some parts of Germany, and still more in Scandinavia, witness today; it had not the fear of the sensuous in worship which dominated other forms of Protestantism. Some of the survivals of medieval practice in Lutheranism are striking. It is not only the retention of medieval vestments in many places which surprises those familiar with the Calvinist zeal against 'rags of popery': Lutheranism did not always keep strictly to the principle of the vernacular in worship and the Latin office continued to be recited in some Lutheran cathedrals down to the eighteenth century and was then abandoned, not on any Protestant principle, but under the influence of the *Aufklärung*. Such things are straws which show the direction of the wind. Lutheranism remained rooted in the traditions of the German past more perhaps than it fully realised. One cannot but suspect that the underlying psychological reason for the Lutheran retention of the doctrine of the Real Presence, badly as it seemed to other Protestants to square with Luther's total rejection of the Sacrifice of the Mass and effectively as it prevented an alliance with the Swiss Reformation, lies, at least partly, in the prominence of the cultus of the Host in medieval Germany, where exposition was more or less perpetual, and elaborate 'sacrament houses' were features of the churches. From another point of view, the resemblances between German Catholicism and Lutheranism in such features as delight in popular hymn-singing and a combination of ceremonial with homeliness suggest that Lutheranism retained much that was German rather than specifically Catholic or Protestant. If this be so, one can understand why to this day Lutheranism remains, both in the Old World and in the New, a Teutonic religion, with a theology and a practice which have never had a wide appeal to other peoples. One can understand also that perhaps the strongest survival factor during the later sixteenth century, which has been described as the gravest crisis in its history, lay in the appeal of its worship and devotional attitude, anchored as these were in the national consciousness. With this, of course, goes the fact, which emerges clearly from the history of this period, that the close link between church and state, characteristic of Lutheranism from the time when Luther had found his chief patron and shield in his Elector, seems rarely to have been found oppressive by theologians and that it was through the Lutheran princes that Lutheranism recovered its compromised unity in the *Formula of Concord*.

The same conclusions are borne out if one turns briefly to the Scandinavian countries in this period. It is true that they were to a great extent isolated from the storms which blew in Germany, echoes of which reached them faintly. It is significant that it was not until 1686 that the *Formula of Concord* was officially embodied in Swedish church law; the need for it had not been felt urgently there. In Denmark even the Augsburg Confession was not formally accepted until 1574, and later still in Sweden. Medieval survivals were even more obvious in the Scandinavian countries than in German Lutheranism and yet in worship and devotional outlook the Scandinavians followed the Lutheran pattern and felt a strong kinship with their brethren in Germany. Calvinism never obtained a footing among them, even though King Eric XIV of Sweden (1560–8) had been educated under Calvinist influence. The famous archbishop of Uppsala, Laurentius Petri, wrote strongly in favour of Lutheran principles and against Calvinist ideas in his book of 1566 *On Church Ordinances and Ceremonies*. In the following reign, that of John III (1568–92), Eric's brother, a movement towards reunion with Rome proved equally unsuccessful. John, who before his deposition of his brother in 1568 had been duke of Finland and in 1562 had married the Catholic Catherine of Poland, had also imbibed in Poland the theology of George Cassander, which combined elements of both Catholicism and Protestantism. A Polish Jesuit, Stanislas Warszewicki, visited Stockholm in 1574 and had audiences with the king, upon whom he made a great impression. An outcome of this seems to have been the attempt of John in 1576 to introduce a new liturgy known as the *Red Book* which, following upon the *Nova Ordinantia Ecclesiastica* of the previous year, showed the king's Catholicising tendencies. In 1576 also a Jesuit mission arrived in Stockholm and Laurentius Norvegus, its leader, a man of Scandinavian origin, was placed by the king in charge of a theological college, the *Collegium Regium Stockholmense*, he was founding. With his help the king forced through his new liturgical policy. In 1577 an even more notable Jesuit, Antonio Possevino, reached Stockholm, where he stayed until 1578 as papal legate, before he left formally receiving the king into the Roman church.

The conversion was not lasting, however. John had plans to restore Roman Catholicism as the religion of Sweden, but the obstacles were immense and the Roman curia would not grant the concessions the king thought necessary. Possevino was made vicar apostolic for Scandinavia and many other territories of northern and eastern Europe, returning to Stockholm in 1579. But the king had changed his mind when he learned that Rome was not going to prove as accommodating as he had hoped in relaxing some matters of Catholic discipline for the sake of the conversion of Sweden. So at the very time of Possevino's return he had publicly returned to the communion of the Lutheran church. A Catholic mission was maintained in Sweden until 1583 and enjoyed considerable success, but, after the death of his wife in that year, King John expelled it. He continued his general policy of semi-Catholicising the Swedish church, against much opposition, until his death in 1592, but soon afterwards it was apparent that he had failed. For early in the following year a large council of the clergy, summoned by the regent, the Duke Charles of Södermanland, at Uppsala, formally accepted the Augsburg Confession, restored the Church Order of 1571 (the work of Archbishop Laurentius Petri which had preceded King John's *Nova Ordinantia*), and elected as archbishop of Uppsala Abraham Andreae Angermannus, formerly principal of the Stockholm grammar school, who had been the chief ecclesiastical opponent of the *Red Book* and had been in exile for more than ten years. The whole episode had very much the nature of a political *coup d'état*, for the successor to the throne was John's son, Sigismund, who had been elected king of Poland in 1587. He had been educated in the Roman Catholic religion of his mother, to which he remained faithful despite efforts by his father to make him conform to Lutheranism, and in Poland he was a promoter of the Counter-Reformation and a close friend of the Jesuits. Duke Charles, on the other hand, King John's brother and a younger son of Gustavus Vasa in whose reign the Reformation had been established in Sweden, was a zealous Protestant and had strongly resisted his brother's religious policy. As in other cases in Europe at this time, the issue was the double one of religion and the possibility of foreign rule. In opening the assembly of 1593, the royal High Steward, Nils Gyllenstjerna, after pointing out the dangers of religious division, as illustrated in France and the Netherlands, ended his speech with the words:

If the king in Poland comes hither he must not be lord over our faith and conscience, but we must abide in that agreement as to doctrine which is here determined. Whatever is here agreed on in accordance with God's pure Word and will must be set forth in a Christian manner, and be subscribed by all. Finally, I pray that the living God may be the highest ruler in this Church Council, that he may govern all things in it, so that they may turn to God's praise and honour, and be a strong support and an eternal benefit to ourselves and our descendants.

And, after the detailed examination of the Augsburg Confession clause by clause and its acceptance by all the nobles, bishops and clerics present, the ecclesiastical president of the assembly, Nicolaus Olai Botniensis, exclaimed: 'Now has Sweden become one man, and we all have one Lord and God.'

The plan for a national subscription to the decisions of this *Uppsala-Mote* was carried into effect by sending copies of it to the provinces and 1,934 signatures of prominent persons are extant on the copies preserved. When Sigismund reached Sweden to assume the crown he was required to take an oath confirming the Uppsala decisions as a condition of coronation by the Swedish bishops, although they included provisions against the toleration of Catholic worship. His attempts to rule by means of Polish ministers were resisted and in 1595, against Sigismund's will, Charles was recognised as regent by the Riksdag. He fell out witht he aristocratic council of the realm, which claimed a right to share his powers, and raised the lower classes against them, with the result that most of the council fled to Poland. Sigismund in 1598 invaded Sweden to restore his authority, but was defeated by Charles at Stångebro. In 1599 the Riksdag deposed Sigismund and in 1600 Charles was elected king of Sweden as Charles IX.[1] He proved himself to have Calvinistic leanings and attempted to change the service-book and to introduce a catechism based upon the Heidelberg Catechism of 1563, which had been jointly composed by Philippist Lutherans and Calvinists. Charles, whilst regent, had already fallen foul of Archbishop Abraham Angermannus, to whose violent methods of enforcing church discipline by such methods as birching followed by the deluging of the culprit with icy water, or by fines for more serious offences he apparently objected. In 1599 Abraham, who had supported King Sigismund against Duke Charles, was suspended from office by the clergy and imprisoned. The clergy were unwilling to depose him from his see, but Nicolaus Botniensis was elected archbishop by secular authority; he died, however, before he could be consecrated. In 1601 the Riksdag chose Olaus Martini in his place, the chapter of Uppsala accepted the election, and he was duly consecrated and remained in office until his death in 1609. He proved a strong opponent of Charles's Calvinising policy, controverting the royal theological writings and standing up to the Scottish Calvinist, John Forbes (exiled by James I in 1605 for his resistance to royal ecclesiastical policy), who in 1608 was invited by the king, under the influence of Micronius, his Calvinist chaplain, to take part in a disputation at Uppsala. Forbes had to withstand the general hostility of the archbishop, professors, nobles and students who made up the assembly, even though he disclaimed any intention of trying to convert Sweden to Calvinism and said that he merely wished to explain and defend the Scottish Calvinist faith. His proclamation of absolute predestination was received with horror and Olaus Martini declared that the assembly's ears were tired out 'with hearing the abuse of God which has been uttered by this stranger', adding: 'Let us pray God that he may convert this misguided man', to which Forbes courteously, but with true Scots pertinacity, replied, 'May God convert us all!' The king apparently felt that his champion had gone too far and let him leave Sweden. He returned in 1610 with a project of reunion between Lutherans and Calvinists, but this came to nothing. By the time of his death in 1611 Charles IX had signally failed to make Sweden Calvinist.

These episodes of Swedish religious history, which present some striking analogies with the politico-religious struggles in seventeenth-century

[1] He did not actually assume the throne until 1604, as his nephew, John, son of King John III by his second and Protestant wife, had not attained his majority and it was considered decent when he came of age to offer him the kingship, which he wisely declined, accepting a duchy instead. Charles's coronation took place in 1607, the throne being entailed upon his descendants, provided they were Protestants.

England and Scotland, serve to illustrate the fact that Lutheranism, outside Germany as well as within, was indeed a religion with an ethos of its own, distinct alike from Catholicism and Calvinism, and not, as Calvinists liked to think, a halfway house between popery and logical Protestantism. Despite the Erastianism which one too easily tends to think its outstanding characteristic, it had stood up successfully in Sweden to the Catholicising tendencies of one king and the Calvinist tendencies of another, proving in the process a centre of national unity. And the central part played in these controversies by liturgical questions confirms the opinion already put forward that the real hidden strength of Lutheranism lay in its ways of worship and its warm piety. It was a religion of practice rather than of theory.

Thus, the theological crisis of later sixteenth-century Lutheranism, dangerous and nearly destructive as it proved to be, was in the last resort irrelevant to a religion whose future really lay in the hearts rather than the heads of its adherents. It is not without reason that historians of Lutheranism tend to agree that the era of 'scholastic Lutheranism', introduced by the controversies which have been described, was a distortion of the true ethos of Luther's reformation and presented a desiccated version of his principles. The coming of the Pietist movement in the next century did much to restore the balance. But that is another story and it remains only to suggest that the survival of Lutheranism between the upper and nether millstones of the Counter-Reformation and Calvinism, torn as it was by its own internal struggles, is perhaps one of the most striking instances of success against what appear to be overwhelming odds to be found in history.

2. *The development and spread of Calvinism*

A recent historian, Alain Dufour, has written of 'The Myth of Geneva', by which he means the idea held by Calvinists of Geneva as the Holy City: the mirror and model of true religion and true piety, as the Englishman, William Whittingham, described it; 'the most perfect school of Christ that ever was in the earth since the days of the apostles', in the famous phrase of John Knox, the Scot. Certainly it was in this sense a myth which inspired Calvinists everywhere. To them Geneva was the Protestant Rome, and indeed it meant more to them in one sense than Rome did to Catholics, since, however firmly he might believe in the aura of the see of Peter, the candid Catholic had to admit the scandals of Rome as a city even after the Catholic Reformation had taken effect, whereas Geneva claimed, with some justification, that it presented a model of morality and piety as well as of pure doctrine. Nevertheless, as Dufour points out, there was also a counter-myth of Geneva as the throne of error and narrow heartless discipline which influenced Catholics and also those Protestants who were disgusted by the burning of Servetus in 1553, resented the restriction of evangelical freedom by the Genevan discipline, or thought of the lakeside city as the home of sedition where doctrines dangerous to civil obedience were taught.

There was a core of solid fact behind the myth. For Geneva was a religious centre to a degree which Luther's Wittenberg and Zwingli's and Bullinger's Zürich never became, influential as they were. Not only was Geneva the home of a systematic Protestant theology embodied in Calvin's *Institutes*, and of a church organisation and discipline increasingly thought of as what Calvin claimed them to be, the pattern set out in the New Testament and the primitive church. It was international to a remarkable degree, controlled largely in Calvin's day by a nucleus of exiles from France, who were long looked upon by the native Genevese with jealousy as foreign interlopers changing the city's old ethos; but filled also both with refugee Protestants from almost all other parts of Europe and increasingly with those who came to study what they regarded as the purest form of evangelical truth at its fountain-head. The Genevan Academy, built by the city at Calvin's request between 1559 and 1563 on the hill of Sainte-Antoine overlooking the lake, had assembled a complete staff by 1559, with Theodore Beza, destined to be Calvin's successor, as its first rector, and was formally inaugurated in a great ceremony in St Peter's church on 5 June that year. It began with no less than 162 students, three-quarters of them from France, only four native Genevese, the rest from most of the other countries of western Europe. By 1564 there were 1,200 collegians and 300 advanced students, for the university was divided into two sections, the College or *Schola Privata* for beginners, the Academy proper or *Schola Publica* for advanced students. In the College the classics were taught in a series of seven graduated classes. In the Academy students could select their own lectures from the series offered on theology, Hebrew, the Greek poets and moralists, dialectic and rhetoric, physics and mathematics. As in the Jesuit schools, the education was a combination of Renaissance humanism and theology, a combination which ensured the respect of the age and, as in the case of Jesuit education, intellectual instruction was accompanied by devotional exercises. The primary object of the university was to supply trained ministers, for whom incessant demands reached Calvin, especially from France; but those with a lay vocation were welcome and, as the institution grew, faculties of medicine and law were added. It was from the Academy that there went forth, not only to France, but to many other parts of Europe, the trained élite of Calvinism, to whom its impressive spread during the whole of the later sixteenth century was ultimately due. By their means faithful adherence to the principles and organisation of the most tightly knit form of Protestantism was assured, so that with the minimum of compromise or adaptation to local conditions Calvinism was monolithic in its attitude and structure all over Europe. Small wonder that, except in Germany, it swept into its own net the much vaguer reforming tendencies spread earlier in the century by Lutheran propaganda and could stand in effective opposition to the left-wing sects which, although largely driven underground by persecution, still attracted the simpler and less sophisticated of those dissatisfied with conventional religion.

Naturally it was in Calvin's native France, close as it was to Geneva and linked to it by language, that the most immediate progress was made. Calvin had known the earlier stages of the French Reformation at first hand and had been in constant touch with Protestants there ever since he had taken refuge abroad. His religion reflected French intellectualism and love of definition; indeed it is doubtful whether, even had he never existed, French Protestantism would ever have rested content with the largely unsystematised Lutheranism which so slowly evolved into any kind of theological system in the heat of the controversies described in the first half of this chapter. France, too, was a country in whose development law and lawyers had played and were always to play a great role, and Calvin's theology reflected the effects of his own early legal studies and therefore appealed to the French instinct for order and discipline. The idea of law in religious matters which Luther, influenced as he was by the Pauline contrast between the law of the Old Testament and the spiritual freedom and power of the New, deeply suspected, and which some of his followers, who embraced antinomianism, rejected wholly, was to Calvin axiomatic. In the *Institutes* he sees the function of the moral law of God as threefold: first, to exhibit the righteousness which God demands of us, to show us, as in a mirror, our impotence by ourselves to fulfil this requirement and our consequent sinful condition, together with the curse upon us which this implies; secondly, to curb our wickedness by dread of punishment; and, thirdly, to map out for justified believers the way to the sanctity which God expects from them. Luther would not necessarily have disagreed with all this; indeed, part of it echoes what he says in his *Liberty of a Christian Man*: 'Now when a man has learned from the commandments, and perceived his own incapacity, then he will be anxious to know how to keep the commandment, for unless he fulfils the commandment he will be damned.' Moreover, Calvin lays even more stress upon the power of divine grace than Luther, regarding it in a way rather closer to the Catholic idea as a transforming agency. But the emphasis is different. To Luther the law was primarily written in the heart of the believer; he saw less need than did Calvin for its enforcement by church discipline. Hence probably one of the reasons for Calvin's greater appeal to the French temperament which hated anarchy and had come to look upon strong government as the prerequisite of a strong nation; a church which left too much to the initiative of the individual would have appeared suspect to Frenchmen.

It might be thought that the grim character of the Calvinist discipline, as evidenced at Geneva, with its tendency to repress not merely obvious sin but also amusements which could be occasions of sin and almost, if not quite, to equate them, would have offended the Gallic temperament, which always revolts against what seem to be irrational taboos. But to think thus is to overlook another side of the Gallic mind, its intense realism. In time of war the Frenchman will consent to the limitation of his liberty, and Calvinism tended to look upon the spiritual life, especially in a licentious age, as a kind of holy war. Indeed French Calvinism, almost from its birth, was destined to be engaged in material warfare, for it had from the beginning to meet the challenge of persecution in France, which led on to the Wars of Religion. The last years of Francis I and the reign of Henry II were marked by an increase in persecution of Protestants. In 1547 was created the *chambre ardente*, the name of which reveals its purpose, and in 1551 those accused of heresy were banned from municipal or judicial office. But for fear of opposition from the organs of state, always jealous of ecclesiastical power, Henry II and his advisers would probably have introduced the Inquisition. Protestantism, however, was growing and had made important converts among the nobility and even in the royal family itself. It was during his captivity in the Netherlands after the battle of St Quentin in 1557 that the future Huguenot leader, Gaspard de Coligny, the Admiral, finally adopted the Protestant faith; his brother, François d'Andelot, was converted to it about 1556; and a third brother, Odet de Coligny, cardinal prince-bishop of Beauvais, caused a sensation in 1561 by becoming 'the Protestant cardinal', for he did not at once resign his papal title. In 1557 a Protestant assembly of some 400 persons, largely of the *noblesse*, was surprised and broken up, and 130 arrests made, in a house in the rue du Faubourg Saint-Jacques in Paris itself. In May of the following year for three evenings running 4,000 Protestants held open-air meetings and sang psalms on the further bank of the Seine, overlooked by the Louvre and Tuileries. They were headed by Antoine de Bourbon, king of Navarre, and son-in-law of Margaret, Francis I's sister. A year later still was held in Paris a Protestant 'synod', which drew up a confession of faith that some leading Huguenots wished to present to the king in a body in order to bring pressure to bear upon him, although in fact, for prudential reasons, the confession was kept secret, ready to be shown to the authorities at the right moment. Legend has made of this gathering the formal organisation of a national Calvinist church, but in reality its scope does not seem to have been quite so wide.

Nevertheless, in the years just before, a whole series of local churches had been built up in different parts of France on the Genevan model and often with the aid of ministers sent by Calvin from Geneva.[1] By 1557 there was an organised church in Paris; in other places, such as Tours, Bourges and Angers, churches had come into existence even earlier. Calvin took a personal interest in these developments, although his cautious spirit

[1] See also below, pp. 282-4.

made him deprecate public manifestations of the kind which had taken place in Paris. After the affair of the rue Saint-Jacques he advised the Parisian Calvinists to keep under cover. He was by no means pleased when he learned of the plans for the assembly of 1559, which he thought unwise, too late to modify them, although he consented to send three delegates, who arrived when the gathering was almost over. Even if it had not quite the importance later attached to it, this assembly was certainly significant, for, not only was its confession authentically Calvinist, but it adopted at the same time a plan of church order on the model of Geneva and, significantly, since France was not a mere city state, provided for provincial and general synods to co-ordinate and control the work and decisions of the local consistories of ministers and lay elders. If it did not create a national Calvinist church it showed the way to one; and in this it was building upon the work of a synod held at Poitiers in 1557 or 1558— the exact date is disputed—which assembled to decide a local dispute there about the evergreen subject of predestination but took the opportunity of also drawing up a scheme of discipline to avoid similar happenings. This was basically Calvinist, although it gave the deacons, at Geneva subordinate officials, powers there reserved to the pastors and allowed for popular election of them, the lay elders, and the ministers themselves. In Geneva the ministers were chosen by those already ordained and the choice was subsequently approved by the civil power and finally by the people, after they had heard them preach. Lay elders Calvin had wished to be chosen by the laity, but he had been unable to get his way and had had to agree that they should be chosen from the three civil councils which governed the city. The scheme adopted at Poitiers therefore reflects the greater democracy possible in a minority body in a Catholic nation and this plan was only slightly modified in 1559. The *Discipline* adopted then retained the popular election of deacons, but made the consistory the body which chose pastors, with, as in Geneva, a right of final approval vested in the laity. Significantly, the Paris assembly refused to allow the purely clerical synods, meeting frequently, which were a vital feature of the Genevan church. To each synod the ordained minister of a congregation must take with him one or more elders or deacons of his flock, who would have the right to speak at it.

French Calvinism abhorred anything which savoured of the Catholic hierarchical system, with episcopal sees grouped in provinces under archiepiscopal authority, all subject to the Holy See. The *Discipline* of 1559 laid down in its very first article that 'no church can claim principality or dominion over another' and went on in the next to lay down that the authority of the president of every provincial or national synod should end with the synod itself. At the same time it insisted, as Poitiers had done before it, that no local church should 'do anything of great importance in which the benefit or damage of other churches might be involved without the judgement of the provincial synod'. Thus the Calvinist system, now to be applied on a national scale, was prevented from being either hierarchical or purely congregationalist. All, as will be seen, was based upon a plan of mutual deliberation of clergy and laity alike; Calvinism rejected utterly any system of episcopacy which implied that the episcopate was a separate order of the ministry and, in respect of the government of the church, refused to allow ordained ministers any absolute monopoly of power. This was the system which Calvin had claimed in the *Institutes* was laid down in the New Testament and which, with local modifications such as those proposed for France, was to be set up wherever Calvinism succeeded in gaining freedom of action. The strength and sense of unity which it gave to the faithful is obvious, even if it could also lead, as can any system based upon debate and deliberation, to factiousness and embittered dispute. To some extent it did so in France, for the national synod held at Orléans in 1562 had to deal with a demand for greater democracy. By this time political events momentous for the future of the Huguenots had occurred.[1] In July 1559 Henry II died after a wound accidentally received at a tournament and was succeeded by his son, Francis II, aged 15. The powerful family of Guise, to the end of the Wars of Religion the leaders of the fanatical Catholic party, saw the chance to seize power and did so by the expedient of proclaiming the boy king technically of age and, with the agreement of the Queen Mother, Catherine de Medici, persuading him by means of his wife, their niece Mary, Queen of Scots, to entrust the government to them. Both family rivalry and the obvious danger to Protestantism made Louis de Bourbon, prince of Condé, claim that there ought to be a regency and that his elder brother, Antoine de Bourbon, the king of Navarre and heir to the French throne should the direct Valois line die out, had a right to be regent. He could not persuade the weak Antoine to take any effective steps himself. Some of the Guises' opponents therefore fell back upon the plot known as the Conspiracy of Amboise, which aimed at capturing the king and the Guise brothers, Duke Francis and Charles, the cardinal of Lorraine, after which an army secretly gathered round Amboise would enable Condé to seize power. But the plan leaked out and the government was able to mop up the contingents of the plotters' army one by one.

Although neither in personnel nor in motives solely Huguenot, the Conspiracy had religious repercussions of some importance, quite apart from the role it played in the events leading up to the Wars of Religion. It alarmed the Guises and induced them to moderate their ecclesiastical policy to the extent of easing persecution and even listening to Huguenot demands for a nationalist settlement of religion by means of a council of French bishops and the Estates General. This project was carried further when, after the death of Francis II (December 1560) and the accession of

[1] For a fuller account of these events, see below, pp. 283-5.

Catherine de Medici to power as regent, the Estates General were actually summoned in 1561 and the *tiers état* called for a national council in which the laity should have votes. This meeting was accompanied by the Colloquy of Poissy between Catholic and Protestant divines, with Beza leading for the Calvinists, by means of which Catherine hoped, but failed, to secure religious unity. After its failure a degree of toleration was granted by edict to the Huguenots in 1562. The massacre of Huguenots at Vassy soon after by the duke of Guise wrecked even this plan of compromise and, after the duke had seized the young king, Charles IX, and made Catherine de Medici accept his policy, the first War of Religion broke out, to end in an uneasy truce, the Pacification of Amboise,[1] in 1563.

All of these events brought out clearly the intimate bond between political and religious tensions in France and raised for the more conscientious Calvinists the issue of how far political action, extending to violence, revolution and war, was consonant with their principles. They consulted their mentors at Geneva about this during the planning of the Amboise Conspiracy, and it is an interesting testimony to the effects of the *Consensus Tigurinus* of 1549 in bringing together the Calvinists and the Zwinglians of Zürich that one finds Beza writing to Bullinger about the matter. Calvin himself gave a cautious approval to the scheme, provided that it avoided bloodshed, even though afterwards he endeavoured to disclaim having favoured it; and La Renaudie, the leader of the rising, was able to recruit in Geneva some sixty or seventy French 'crusaders' for the enterprise. It was Jean Morelli de Villiers, who had, much to Calvin's annoyance, spread the report that the reformer had approved of the whole plan, who was responsible for the debate about the rights of the laity in the Calvinist national synod at Orléans in 1562, probably because he resented the interference of Calvin and Beza in French politics at the time of the Conspiracy. The year before, he had published a book designed to show that the early Christian church had been democratically governed and demanding a return to this principle. When he submitted his manuscript to Calvin before publication, he received the reply that the Genevan system was in accordance with the Word of God. When the book appeared it was publicly burned at Geneva and its author excommunicated, and the synod of Orléans pronounced against it.

Morelli, however, was only expressing the feelings of a considerable part of the Calvinist laity of France who were coming to think, as Milton was later to do, that 'new presbyter was but old priest writ large' and who resented clericalism as much in the Reformed church as they had in the Catholic. Coligny sympathised with them although he, like the other Huguenot aristocrats, tended to ride roughshod over the rights of the lesser laity. This was only the beginning of controversy on this subject. The partisans of lay rights were joined by two important academic figures,

---

[1] For its terms, see below, p. 286.

Charles du Moulin and Pierre Ramus, the inventor of a new and, as most modern logicians would hold, unfortunate system of logic. The latter, in a book which appeared in 1576, four years after his death in the massacre of St Bartholomew, appealed to the Zwinglian discipline, which he had known at first hand through his friendship with Bullinger, against the Genevan. He demanded that the civil magistrates, whom Calvin had tried to exclude as such from ecclesiastical affairs, should be allowed a say in church matters. Before this, however, Ramus had, by tongue and pen, vigorously expressed his anti-clericalism, and the dispute had caused a personal visit of Beza to the synod of La Rochelle in 1571, at which the *Discipline* was revised in such a way as to give even less power to the laity in the choice of ministers. The dispute dragged on right up to the massacre of St Bartholomew, which brought home to the Huguenots the dangers of disunity. The intensification of religious war thereafter made the primary problem seem one of survival. The synod of Sainte-Foy in 1578, the first following the massacre and, significantly, the last of the century to be fully representative of the various local churches, which thereafter showed little interest in synodical government, was almost entirely concerned with military matters. The six which followed it, the last in 1598 at Montpellier, never contained representatives of all the provinces of the church at any one time and never numbered as many as thirty delegates in all, of whom in each case more than half were clerical although the *Discipline* provided for equal representation of clergy and laity.

As Romier has pointed out, the fact is that from 1560 onwards the Huguenots, now necessarily a military party, were increasingly governed in each region by lay nobles as 'protectors' on a quasi-feudal basis, a system which, after the catastrophe of 1572, hardened into a Huguenot state composed of local civil communities, united in an army and in civil assemblies of parliamentary type which put in the shade the ecclesiastical synods. Huguenotism became a lay-controlled movement, but of a different type from that envisaged by those who had first pleaded for an equal share for the laity in church affairs. It resembled rather the religious army into which the persecuted Waldenses organised themselves in the seventeenth century, or the military religious brotherhood of the Sikhs in India. The Calvinist polity was not abandoned at local level, but the original idea of a national church working through synods was virtually shelved under the stress of the siege political structure demanded by the need of survival in the Wars of Religion. This system was in a sense incorporated into the machinery of the French state by the Edict of Nantes in 1598. Henry IV, having abandoned Protestantism personally in 1593, had found impossible the revived project of a Catholic–Protestant reunion in a Gallican church, independent of Rome and dominated by the king, which was discussed in the conference at Nantes that year. So in 1598 by the Edict of Nantes he granted to the Calvinists, besides liberty of conscience and the right to hold public office, some 150 cities of refuge, of which a large proportion were garrisoned by Protestant troops paid by the state, with a Protestant governor. Thus was preserved that Huguenot state within a state which Richelieu was to find such a danger and was to destroy. The Huguenot movement, as has often been pointed out, was from the beginning as much political as religious. It was headed by a section of the nobility and a number of towns, both elements which resented the increased centralisation of French government during the later fifteenth and early sixteenth centuries, with the monarchy absorbing more and more of the power earlier exercised by nobles and communes. The monarchy's attempt to suppress the new religion only added fuel to a resentment which might in any case have led to rebellion. That being so, it is not surprising to find Huguenotism becoming more and more a lay movement, with considerable elements in it determining not to be under the tutelage of their clergy and resenting the tendency of Geneva to act as a Holy See to which French Calvinists must turn for detailed spiritual guidance.

Yet it would be wrong to imagine that as a national rebellion Huguenotism was deserting Calvinist principles. Calvin may have seemed evasive in his attitude to the Conspiracy of Amboise. In reality he was faced by a dilemma posed by his own teaching. To the doctrine he inherited from Luther, based upon the teaching of St Paul in the Epistle to the Romans and of the First Epistle of St Peter about the Christian's duty to obey rulers even if they were non-Christians or tyrants, Calvin had added in the *Institutes* two escape clauses. Not only did he hold that God sometimes specially inspired individual men, like Moses and Othniel to lead his people against tyrants: he also allowed that in states having in their constitution officials akin to the Spartan ephors, with a right and duty to regulate the behaviour of kings, these magnates might rightfully lead the people in rebellion against tyrants. Such a position could easily be claimed by the nobility and town authorities who stood at the head of the Huguenots. After his death, his successor as religious leader of Geneva, Theodore Beza, considerably enlarged this right of rebellion. In the anonymous tract of 1576, which can be ascribed with some certainty to his pen, *Du droit des magistrats sur leurs sujets*, he both allows a right of rebellion against tyrannical and idolatrous rulers, provided it is led by subordinate magistrates who have a duty to maintain the health of the state, and goes further, in speaking of a contract between the ruler and these subordinate magistrates who, as representatives of the people, choose the ruler. Should the ruler break this by misgovernment, the power which set him up has a right to depose him. The date of the book is of course significant. It was published four years after the massacre of St Bartholomew, and with the realisation that now the only choice before the Huguenots lay between continued military resistance and extinction. It was a similar situation to that which had faced the Lutheran pastors besieged in Magdeburg for their defiance of the *Interim* of 1548,[1] and Beza's treatise was almost certainly based partly upon a reading of their *Bekenntnis Unterricht und Vermanung*. This, published in 1550, had claimed that if the supreme power in a state (the *Hohe Obrigkeit*) attempted to destroy true religion, the subordinate powers (the *Unter Obrigkeit*), which also held authority direct from God, were bound not only to withhold help from it, but to help the faithful in resisting it. (This, of course, had a peculiar appositeness in Germany, where the emperor was trying to enforce a measure of Catholicism and the Lutheran princes were the patrons and protectors of Protestantism.) Simon Goulart, who printed Beza's treatise in his *Mémoires de l'estat de France sous Charles IX* in 1576, actually describes it as *publié par ceux de Magdebourg l'an MDL et maintenant reveu et augmenté de plusieurs raisons et exemples*, although it is by no means the same book.

There can be little doubt that the ideas of the Magdeburg pastors had a great effect upon subsequent Protestant thought, all the more so since, in other countries besides Germany, the dilemma of passive obedience and death or resistance and possible survival was presenting itself. Thus the exiles from Marian England, John Ponet, John Knox and Christopher Goodman, all wrote between 1556 and 1558 against the doctrine of absolute obedience to princes canonised by Luther, urged by the early English Lutheran, John Tyndale, in his *Obedience of Christian Man*, and so strongly preached in England under Henry VIII and Edward VI. In France the circulation of Beza's work is but one incident in a whole series of Calvinist publications designed to justify Huguenot resistance, in which among other things the theory of social contract is often applied to the right of resistance for conscience' sake. Famous among them are Hotman's *Franco-Gallia*, published during his exile in Geneva in 1573; the anonymous *Réveille Matin des Français*, published in two parts in 1573 and 1574; and the anonymous *Vindiciae contra Tyrannos* (usually attributed to Duplessis-Mornay) of 1579.[2] It has been pointed out that a strange *renversement des alliances* occurred after 1584 when, by the death of the duke of Anjou, Henry of Navarre, the Huguenot leader, became heir to the throne. Henceforward, as Figgis says, the Huguenots were turned into thoroughgoing supporters of legitimism. 'Hereditary right and the Salic Law became their watchwords henceforth, and we must seek elsewhere for the succession to their older theories of liberty.' In French affairs it was the Jesuit writers who, on similar theories of popular sovereignty and social contract, maintained that an heretical king had no right to the throne, whilst 'Rossaeus' (who was perhaps the English Catholic exile, William Reynolds) in his *De Justa Reipublicae Christianae Potestate* of 1592 upheld similar theories and classed Henry III of France as a tyrant comparable with Nero and Queen Elizabeth. Thus came about that curious

[1] See above, p. 76.   [2] See below, p. 500.

98

coincidence of ideas between one aspect of Calvinist thought and ultramontane Catholicism which enabled Filmer in the next century, when attacking the doctrine of popular sovereignty, to say epigrammatically: 'Cardinal Bellarmine and Mr Calvin both look asquint this way.'

In the Revolt of the Netherlands, although this was not in origin nor for a long time exclusively a Calvinist movement, the same problem of the right of rebellion had to be faced. The Declaration of the States deposing Philip II in 1581 is a document not dissimilar from the American Declaration of Independence of 1776. As that was to accuse George III of violating the rights of the colonists and to appeal to 'the Laws of Nature and of Nature's God', so the Netherlanders appealed to the Law of Nature and accused Philip II of destroying their privileges, significantly adding that it was only on condition of accepting their customs that he had obtained their allegiance. They did not appeal to theological ideas and indeed hardly could do so in view of the mixed religious allegiance of the insurgents. The only considerable political treatise produced by the Revolt, Althusius's *Politica Methodice Digesta* (1603), not only came after the turn of the century, when Dutch freedom had been secured, but is secular in tone, not even making provision for the church as a society distinct from the state. Its author, although he had studied theology, was primarily a lawyer. Moreover, he was German, not Dutch, although he became a citizen of Emden, which ecclesiastically was a German province of the Dutch Calvinist church, subject to the Netherlands general synod. Though his book reproduces the familiar arguments against tyranny, including in his definition of it régimes which establish idolatry, and defends the right of the people to depose tyrants, he is far more interested in expounding his corporative theories of the state. Although Pierre Mesnard may be right in describing him as 'one of the most eminent representatives of Calvinist political thought', the same author admits that his ideas derive more from the views of Hotman, whose *Franco-Gallia* is based almost entirely upon arguments drawn from the constitutional history of France, than from the more theologically minded Huguenot pamphleteers. 'In the *Politica* there are many thousands of citations of the Bible, and yet one scarcely scents there the religious breeze of Calvin or even of Duplessis-Mornay.' As Mesnard points out, errors in the scriptural quotations and the unexpected way in which they are sometimes used, have raised the question of whether many of them may not have been derived at second hand. In any case, the Bible is for him chiefly a mine of historical examples rather than an authoritative source of politico-theological principles. He is one of the first of the new generation of secular political theorists leading on to Hobbes who, incidentally, was also a great quoter of Scripture. It is difficult to believe that the Netherlands Revolt, still less its religious side, was the real inspiration of Althusius's thought, however much it may have influenced it. The Netherlands Calvinists in fact, partly because they had not to confront a traditional national monarchy for which divine right was claimed, as did the earlier Huguenots in France, but a ruler thought of as alien in a country with a long tradition of municipal and provincial self-government, did not need to find theological justification for their rebellion to the same extent as did their French brethren.

The Netherlands were, of course, the second great area of Calvinist penetration in our period. Calvinism began to enter there in the 1540s, at a time when Charles V had mitigated his policy of fierce persecution, although this had raged more against the Anabaptists than against less unorthodox Protestants. (It has been calculated that, between 1523 and 1555, out of 1,500 to 1,700 martyrs in the southern Netherlands, some 1,000 were Anabaptists; in the north, 178 out of 240.) Calvinism thus arrived at a time when it could establish itself in relative peace before the storm broke out again. It did not come into a virgin field. Lutheranism had rapidly spread to these lands so closely connected with Germany by political history, language and economic relations; the first Lutheran martyrs were executed as early as 1523. But the Lutheranism of the Netherlands quickly began to take on a form of its own. It may have been the importance of the Rhine as a commercial waterway, offering comparatively easy communications between its headwaters in Switzerland and the Netherlands, which explains the spread of Swiss reforming ideas there. In any case we know that by the 1540s Bullinger's works met with a ready sale in the Netherlands and Geyl is justified in claiming that, even before the advent of Calvinism in its pure form, Netherlandish Protestantism had a character of its own, being largely sacramentarian in eucharistic doctrine. Indeed, after the *Consensus Tigurinus* of 1549, it was a comparatively short step from the developed Zwinglianism of Bullinger to full-blown Calvinism. The difference between them lay chiefly in the Calvinist 'discipline'. As that had been derived largely from Bucer's system at Strassburg, where Calvin had spent his exile from Geneva from 1538 to 1541, it is conceivable that Bucerian influences could have reached the Netherlands direct, by way of the Rhine, quite early. One must also remember Calvin's special interest in the Low Countries. Born himself not far from their frontier, at Noyon, his mother came from Cambrai; his wife, Idelette de Bure, whom he married in Strassburg, was the widow of a refugee from Liège who had once been an Anabaptist; and he had many Netherlandish friends. He could even say, in a letter to Bullinger, 'I am a Belgian myself.' In 1544 we find him in correspondence with Poullain, a refugee from Lille to Strassburg, about 'Nicodemism', the practice of concealing one's Protestantism, which was not unusual in the Low Countries. Calvin's condemnation of it had been thought too severe there. At Poullain's request Calvin also wrote against the Anabaptists, who formed such a large element in Netherlandish dissidence. An outcome of this contact was the despatch to Belgium of Pierre Brully, a man of Luxemburg, who had succeeded Calvin as pastor of the French congregation at Strassburg. His ministry at Tournai and Valenciennes, where he prepared the ground for churches on the model he had learned in contact with Calvin at Strassburg, was short, for he was quickly arrested and burned at the stake in February 1545. But he had had time to combat the left-wing sects and his appearance was connected with a considerable migration of southern Netherlanders to Geneva to absorb Calvinist principles.

The establishment of Calvinism as a system, however, owes most to Guy de Brès, born at Mons, who, after a sojourn in England in the days of Edward VI, fled from the Marian reaction to Switzerland and became acquainted with Calvin and Beza. He returned to Belgium, basing himself first at Antwerp but in 1560 settling at Tournai, where he built upon Brully's work and founded a fully fledged Calvinist congregation, from which others, notably at Lille and Valenciennes, were established, with de Brès as superintendent of the whole area. In 1561 he composed the *Confessio Belgica*, or *Confession de Foi des Eglises Reformées Wallonnes et Flamandes*, which was naïvely sent to Philip II next year for authorisation or rejection, with the claim that it represented the belief of 100,000 of his subjects 'who were never found in arms or plotting against their sovereign', an attempt presumably on the part of the Calvinists to dissociate themselves from the wilder sectaries of the Low Countries, and perhaps also from the Catholic opposition to Philip's methods of rule which had manifested itself in 1559 at the States General held at Ghent. It naturally made no impression at all on the severely orthodox Philip, but it speedily became the standard of doctrine and discipline of the Low Countries' Calvinists, replacing the formularies borrowed from the Walloon congregation in London in 1550. Revised in 1566, it was adopted by a synod at Antwerp that year and finally made compulsory by the synod of Emden in 1571. It closely followed the French confession of 1559, although it added to it and was a faithful statement of Calvin's doctrine. But it reflected the democratic ideal by laying down that the consistories of ministers, elders and deacons which were to rule each church should be elected by the congregation. It was to remain throughout the official standard of Netherlandish Calvinism.

It will be seen from all this that the original home of pure Calvinism in this corner of Europe was the south Netherlands, the modern Belgium, not the north with which it was later to be exclusively associated as the result of accidents of history in the course of the long struggle for freedom from Spain. In the north there was a separate focus of general Calvinist influence from outside the boundaries of the Netherlands, the church of Emden, already mentioned in connection with Althusius. This had grown up in the 1540s. It was organised by the Pole, John Laski (or à Lasco), who fled to London when Charles V introduced the *Interim* but returned to Emden after Mary Tudor's accession, although he afterwards moved on to other parts of north Germany. Although Laski had no very direct contact with Geneva, he was sympathetic to the Calvinist discipline and the church at Emden was modelled on it. It thus became a 'northern Geneva' and was a mission centre of Calvinism to the northern Netherlands. But before 1566 the full Calvinistic system of consistories and synods did not extend to the north.

It was the events of 1566 which altered everything.[1] The league of nobles, formed in 1565 by the signing of the Compromise, was then pressing upon Philip's regent, Margaret of Parma, a protest against Philip's earlier refusal to summon the States General and give more power to the native nobility, who were opposed to the promulgation in the Low Countries of the decrees of Trent and to persecution of heretics. Philip, to whom the petition was forwarded, made a temporising answer about the heresy laws, but flatly refused to summon the States General. This no doubt raised popular feeling, but it was the violent preaching of fanatical ministers that encouraged an outburst of mob violence, spreading from the south and bringing destruction of altars and images in churches all over the Low Countries in August and early September 1566. How far this was premeditated and how far spontaneous is still disputed, but its results were both to deter many Catholics from the national movement, with which they had hitherto co-operated, and also to antagonise them against the Calvinists, upon whom they laid the blame. It led also ultimately to Philip's despatch of Alva to the Netherlands in 1567 and to the savageries of the 'Council of Blood', which he set up on arrival. Before Alva arrived, the more militant confederate nobles, for the most part Calvinists, had risen in arms, but had been defeated; they knew that they would be held responsible for the iconoclastic riots, even though they had not been directly concerned in them. They were not supported by the national leaders, William of Orange and the Counts Egmont and Hoorn, who had already shown their disapproval of the riots. The regent soon regained control of the country and William of Orange, knowing in advance of the coming of Alva, retired to Nassau.

Nevertheless, this apparent disaster to the Protestant cause set forward the progress of the Calvinist discipline, as ministers, no doubt realising the necessity of organisation in the face of further troubles to come, set up consistories for their congregations. Largely abandoned by the *gueux d'état*, by those nobles who had joined the confederation for patriotic rather than religious reasons, and unable to unite with the Lutherans, a party to which William of Orange, after his marriage to Maurice of Saxony's daughter, inclined, the Calvinists appeared isolated and so not unnaturally tried to perfect their church organisation.

This situation was to be altered again by the blood bath into which Alva plunged the Netherlands after the execution of Egmont and Hoorn in

---

[1] For a more detailed account of the Revolt, see below, pp. 264–81, 297 ff.

1568. William of Orange's first attempt to invade the country and raise it against the Spaniards failed. But in 1572 the insurrection proper began with the seizure of Brill by the Calvinistic Sea Beggars. Help began to come from the French Huguenots and from English Protestants in consequence and the 'Eighty Years War' against Spain (1568–1648), as Dutch tradition has rather inaccurately named it, was well under way. It was never the wish of William of Orange that it should be a religious struggle. It was only in 1573 that he himself formally accepted the Calvinist faith and he always wanted Catholics to be tolerated in the national interest. But the failure of the 1572 insurrection outside Holland and Zeeland, and the continued resistance in those two provinces of the Calvinistic Sea Beggars, who persisted in plundering churches and monasteries, murdering priests and expelling magistrates thought to be favourable to Catholicism, increased the tendency for the national cause to be identified with violent Calvinism. We are not concerned here with the details of the struggle, but rather to notice its effects upon religious matters in the Netherlands. In 1576 there seemed a good chance of establishing a religious truce when the sack of Antwerp by the mutinous Spanish army shocked the rest of the provinces into an agreement with Holland and Zeeland. By the Pacification of Ghent all foreign troops were to be removed and the laws against heresy suspended. Holland and Zeeland, where the Calvinists' dominance was tacitly recognised, undertook not to attack the Catholic faith established in the other provinces. The new Spanish governor, Don John of Austria, in his Perpetual Edict of February 1577, also agreed, if reluctantly, to send away the Spanish troops, restore the Netherlands' privileges, and rule with the consent of the States General. In return, the provinces were to recognise him as governor, disband their own troops, and maintain the Catholic religion. The Calvinist rulers of Holland and Zeeland clearly could not accept these conditions, which said nothing about the toleration of their own faith, and soon Don John's impatience brought a renewal of the war and the recall of the Spanish army. Even now William still hoped for religious peace and nearly secured it in the proposed *Religionsfrid* of 1578, which would have assured freedom of conscience everywhere. The plan was wrecked, however, upon the suspicions of the Catholic Walloon nobles and the aggressive intransigence of the Flemish Calvinists, those at Ghent in particular, who were ruthlessly destroying the visible signs of Catholicism there and elsewhere in Flanders so far as they could.

Out of this there came in 1579 the two rival unions—that of the Catholic Walloon provinces (Artois and Hainault) in the Union of Arras and that of the northern provinces with Flanders and Brabant in the Calvinist-dominated Union of Utrecht. The fact that this original 1579 division coincided roughly with the linguistic boundary between Dutch–Flemish and Walloon–French speech shows, as Geyl has remarked, that a feeling of rivalry between two cultural groups was involved, exacerbated no doubt by religious differences in the sense that Protestantism had now become dominant in the north, Catholicism in the south. This does not, however, support the further conclusion, fashionable in the days not far back when half-baked racialism dominated the minds of some historians, that there is some natural affinity between Catholicism and the Romance languages and between Protestantism and Teutonic tongues. Even if language were a reliable indication of race—and race is an unscientific concept in itself—the theory is disproved in Germany, where Protestantism has never eradicated Catholicism and where, broadly speaking, Catholicism has been at its strongest in those parts least affected by Slavonic admixture in the past. It is more difficult still as an explanation in the Low Countries. For even as late as 1587 the Calvinists were reckoned to form not more than a tenth of the population of Holland itself. Moreover, the final boundary between north and south was decided by the rival military fortune and prowess of Alexander Farnese and his successors on the Spanish side and of Maurice of Nassau for the north. In places it departed widely from the linguistic frontier, and today the Flemish Belgians are notably more attached to Catholicism than their Walloon neighbours, while in Holland Catholicism has remained predominant in the south and west, so that something like a third of the present population is Catholic. Historical circumstances have far more to do with religious allegiance than language or genes.

As in France, so in the Netherlands, war diminished the power of the Calvinist ministry. William of Orange had always been unwilling to let the clergy have much say in affairs of state, all the more so because his sympathies remained Lutheran rather than Calvinist most of his life. Even the devotedly Calvinist Philip Marnix de Saint-Aldegonde resented clerical domination, saying once of the ministers: 'They may well advise, but they cannot command. They cannot dominate; they should leave consciences free.' So the establishment of the United Provinces and their ultimate success in casting off the Spanish yoke did not entail a victory for Calvinist ecclesiasticism. Thus in 1581 the synod of Middelburg censured Gaspard Coolhaes, a Leyden professor and a pastor, for refusing to accept the Belgic Confession and for having criticised the Calvinist discipline in arguments with a strictly Calvinist fellow professor and pastor, the Frenchman, Lambert Daneau. The council of Leyden intervened, one member declaring that he would resist the Genevan Inquisition just as much as the Spanish. As a consequence, Daneau, who had tried to regulate the Walloon church in Leyden, of which he had charge, on strict Calvinist lines and to extend the same principles to the whole territory, left the city. In 1591 the States General appointed a commission to draw up a new *Discipline* by which local magistrates should have equal rights with the consistories in the choice of ministers, who were to be approved in each case by the burgomasters. On one occasion five ministers of Alkmaar who refused to subscribe to the official confession and catechism were protected both by their civic authorities and by the Estates of Holland.

Indeed it was in the United Provinces that the first big challenge to Calvinist orthodoxy was to emerge, in the shape of Arminianism, which denied the doctrine of absolute predestination. It took its name from Jakob Hermandszoon, trained at Geneva under Beza, who was ordained a minister at Amsterdam in 1588. Called by the Amsterdam church to confute the views of Coornaert, who had challenged the accepted doctrine of predestination, Arminius (as he is generally known from the Latinised form of his name) came to the conclusion that he sympathised with the views he was expected to condemn. Attacked by Peter Plancius, Arminius denied that he had contravened either the Belgic Confession or the Heidelberg Catechism, but at the same time made it clear that he did not feel bound to accept any Calvinist interpretation of Scripture without question. The burgomaster of Amsterdam attempted to settle the dispute by calling a council of ministers, but all he could effect was a request to both parties not to air their controversies in public. As the disputes continued, Arminius demanded that definite charges should be preferred against him by Plancius and these he was able to answer, so that a reconciliation was effected. But Arminius's doubts about the high doctrine of predestination increased and he was willing to quote even Catholic theologians such as Bellarmine and Contarini in support of his views. His appointment as a professor at Leyden in 1603 caused fresh controversies, his leading opponent being Francis Gomar (Gomarus). The disputes involved the highest authorities in both church and state and in 1608 Arminius defended his teaching before a special meeting of the States General at the Hague. He died the next year, but the controversy went on, becoming involved in Dutch politics, which were disturbed at the time by the rivalry between Maurice of Nassau, William of Orange's son, the Stadtholder, who opposed the Twelve Years Truce made with Spain in 1609, and John of Oldenbarnevelt, the Advocate of Holland, who favoured it. Oldenbarnevelt was for the Remonstrants, as the Arminian party was called; Maurice for the Counter-Remonstrants. The affair ended in a kind of oecumenical council of Calvinism held at Dordrecht, the synod of Dort, in 1618. Before it opened, Oldenbarnevelt was imprisoned on a charge of conspiring with Spain, and the famous Grotius, an Arminian, was also imprisoned together with others of that opinion. The synod condemned Arminianism and three days after its close Oldenbarnevelt was executed. Doctrinally the whole dispute shows that Calvinist orthodoxy was now being questioned, and largely by those who held views opposed to clerical domination of the state. From the point of view of history it demonstrates the extraordinary complexity of church–state relations in the United Provinces and the degree to which the laity, as in France, were concerning themselves with ecclesiastical affairs. Calvin's fight to secure ecclesiastical independence of the state at Geneva was narrowly won; as the movement he had begun spread to large nations faced by big problems of statecraft, it was almost inevitable that the state would more and more control the church. The situation in which contemporary Catholicism found itself, of having to depend for protection upon national governments and in return having to submit to their control, was to a great extent being experienced by Calvinism also.

The fact can be further illustrated from the fortunes of Calvinism in England and Scotland, where, once again, it was involved in the complications produced by nationalism. English Calvinism in the proper sense of the word began with the return of the Marian exiles after Elizabeth's accession in 1558. Calvin had not been altogether without influence upon the Edwardian Reformation, especially as Bucer, his preceptor at Strassburg, had then ended his days as an exile for his faith in England, whilst Peter Martyr and John Laski, amongst those invited to England by Cranmer, together with some English reformers, had in one way or another come under Calvinist influence. Yet the Calvinist polity in Geneva was not established before Calvin's return there in 1541 and there was scarcely time between that date and the reign of Edward for its influence to be more than general. It was the contacts with Geneva made by English exiles during Mary's reign which were really influential, when Englishmen could see at first hand how it worked. This was especially so when the troubles at Frankfurt between those English refugees who kept to the second Edwardine prayer-book and those who preferred a more reformed liturgy caused the latter group to migrate to Geneva, where they found themselves more at home. It is, however, sometimes overlooked that the Frankfurt heartburnings did not turn only upon liturgical issues. From the beginning the English church there, free on the continent from the limitations imposed upon church organisation by the episcopacy maintained in England even under Edward VI, adopted the kind of polity which they had seen in the foreign exiles' churches in England, which was essentially very similar to the Calvinist scheme. In 1554 they elected a minister and deacons 'to serve for a time' and drew up a code of discipline which all had to pledge themselves to accept. This included a presbytery of lay elders and ministers and also provided for public satisfaction by notorious sinners and excommunication of the recalcitrant—all features of the Strassburg–Genevan discipline and all alien from anything which had been practised in the established church of England in Cranmer's day. Nor, as the city was Lutheran, could the civil power play any part in all this, although during the disputes its intervention was in fact sought by both parties. It is worth while observing that the presbyterian system was maintained after the departure of John Knox and his followers, the anti-prayer-book party, in 1555. There seems to have been no question of anything else being substituted for it and in fact the only change made in the new *Discipline*, instituted in 1556, was the giving of ultimate authority to the whole congregation, the earlier being criticised as permitting 'all to the Pastor'. It was expressly declared that the new arrangement was not unchangeable, since it was not desired to set up a system under which 'men's pleasures' should be 'holden for and unmoveable: as the Papists would'. Here already was a move towards that greater democracy which, as we have already seen, was to characterise Calvinism the more it developed outside Geneva and was to be the root of later Congregationalism. It must also be remembered that even the party which stuck to the Edwardine liturgy did not conform to every detail of it, partly because it was felt that certain features of the prayer-book would offend the French congregation, whose church the Frankfurt magistrates permitted the English to share.

These points deserve emphasis, since the impression is sometimes given that only the Genevan exiles, when the return to England came after 1558, were in favour of what came to be called puritanism. On the contrary, none of the exiles, wherever settled, seem to have regretted greatly the loss of episcopacy and virtually all were to a greater or lesser degree prepared for a more radical Reformation than that which had been reached in England by 1553. In the outcome, when the settlement of religion was being discussed in the parliament of 1559, the returned exiles had difficulty in obtaining even the immediate restoration of the 1552 prayer-book against the Queen's wish to proceed with caution, and then with slight but significant changes designed to make it more palatable to those who still believed in the Real Presence in the sacrament. Of the abolition of episcopacy there could be no question and in 1559 the government speedily set about filling up vacant sees, and those made vacant by the deprivation of the remaining Marian bishops. The paradox was that, although Matthew Parker was available for the see of Canterbury, yet for the most part it was exiles upon whom Elizabeth had to rely to create a new episcopate and these, as they later said, accepted very much *à contre cœur* the settlement they were expected to administer, feeling that, had they refused preferment, popery might have returned. This weakened their position when they were expected to enforce the prayer-book rubrics against radicals unhampered by the restraints of high office who refused to conform—a fact very evident in the Vestiarian controversy in the 1560s, when authority had to come to grips with those who objected to wearing the 'rags of popery' prescribed by the 1559 prayer-book, or to other ceremonial matters ordered in it. Complete conformity was never secured throughout Elizabeth's reign, despite deprivation of some of the more obstinate among the clergy, partly because bishops, faced in any case with a shortage of suitable men for the ministry, were often willing to turn a blind eye towards an incumbent who was zealous and not outrageously defiant of the law, even if his conformity was not complete. As time went on, however, even the more Calvinistically inclined of the first bishops, stung by resistance to their authority, lost sympathy with what came to be called puritanism, whilst succeeding generations, with no personal memories of it retained from exile, thought of Calvinism on its organisational side—for Calvinist theology long reigned supreme—as an alien system not fitted for England.

This was the more true as constant efforts were made to introduce both new liturgies and a Calvinistic discipline by parliamentary means. Here one sees once again, although in a different way, the emergence of that lay predominance already noted in the development of Calvinism else-where. The ecclesiastical Convocations, dominated by the bishops who formed their upper houses, and by no means wholly puritan in the lower houses, were not suitable vehicles for introducing Calvinist worship and discipline, although in the lower house of Canterbury in 1563 six articles proposing changes in the prayer-book in a puritan direction were defeated only by the narrow majority of one vote. It was this setback which seems to have done much to turn the minds of the puritans to parliament, which had enacted the original settlement and had the power to undo it, pro-vided the queen agreed—a proviso which experience showed to be in fact the ultimate obstacle. For the queen probably always resented the way in which the Commons in 1559 had forced upon her a liturgical settlement more Protestant than she then wanted by holding up the bill for restoring the royal supremacy until it was accompanied by one enforcing substan-tially the second Edwardine liturgy. At all events she never showed any sign of consenting to further change.[1] Nevertheless the puritans could always rely upon a substantial body of puritan gentlemen in the Commons ready to bring forward bills to reform the prayer-book, introduce Calvinist discipline or increase the persecution of Roman Catholic recusants. Only in the last case was there any success and then because the government, alarmed by the dangers of Catholic co-operation with Spain, was itself willing to stiffen penalties. To all other proposals about religion the queen turned a deaf ear, despite the puritan sympathies of some of her advisers.

It was the early experience of this deadlock which induced some of the puritans to turn to more direct action. The first generation, however much they might admire the Genevan discipline, did not regard it as strictly obligatory. By 1570, however, a new spirit arose, caused by indoctrination at a later date of younger men by a Geneva which, under Beza, tended to think the Calvinist system even more essential than Calvin himself had thought it to be. They regarded it, not merely as set forth in Scripture, but as commanded there, so that it was treason to the word of God to reject it. In England the leader of this absolutist position was Thomas Cartwright, who became Lady Margaret Professor of Divinity at Cambridge in 1570 and immediately began to attack episcopacy as it existed in the church of

---

[1] See also below, p. 212.

England as wrong in principle, since the church should be governed by consistories. He based his case upon the Acts of the Apostles, upon which he was lecturing. Strangely enough he had never been in exile or seen Geneva—a fact which illustrates the effectiveness of Calvinist propaganda in print or by word of mouth. Only when he was deprived of his chair and forbidden to preach by John Whitgift, the future archbishop of Canterbury, then master of Trinity, Cartwright's college, and vice-chancellor that year, did he depart to Geneva for a time in order to drink in Calvinistic truth at its source. Attempts by puritans to implement his policy in the parliament of 1571 failed, as they did again in 1572, with the result that the party turned to a campaign in print. The opening salvo was fired by their *Admonition to the Parliament*, published while the 1572 parliament was still sitting, which gave rise to a long series of literary exchanges, begun by Whitgift's *Answer* to the *Admonition*.

It was at this stage that the puritans looked like having some chance of obtaining their desires by the use of ecclesiastical authority. The government were concerned at the strengthening of recusancy by the arrival of seminary-trained English priests from the continent and not unnaturally were more disposed to be lenient to puritans who, if disobedient and argumentative subjects, were violently opposed to popery. Moreover, in 1575 Archbishop Parker, who had done his best to maintain the Elizabethan settlement since he had become archbishop in 1559, died. He was succeeded next year by Grindal, archbishop of York, who, unlike Parker, had been an exile and who, though not an outright puritan, was in favour of practical reform in the church. Apart from its constitution and liturgy, the Elizabethan church was unpopular with the puritans, not without reason, because of its many administrative abuses, most of them survivals of medieval bad habits which had never been changed. Had Grindal been able to carry through his programme, much of the ground might have been removed from beneath the extreme puritans' feet and the moderates more or less satisfied. But it was not to be. Grindal fell foul of the queen on the issue of 'prophesyings', regular gatherings of clergy and laity much favoured by the puritans, at which the clergy expounded passages of Scripture and criticised each other's expositions while the laity listened. The view taken of these exercises naturally varied. To the puritans a thorough knowledge of Scripture was all important, and this was a way for ministers to acquire it and learn how doctrine could be derived from the Bible, whilst the laity benefited from their expositions. On the other hand, the dangers of controversy were obvious and an illiterate or uneducated laity—and learning was not widespread in Tudor times—could well be bewildered, misled or scandalised. From the royal point of view prophesyings were occasions which could well be used for religious, if not political, sedition. Within a year of his translation to Canterbury Grindal was ordered by the queen to suppress them and at the same time to reduce the number of licensed preachers in each county. He refused to obey, setting out the value of sermons and prophesyings as he saw it and at the same time taking up the attitude, classical in Calvinist as in Catholic tradition, that it was not for a lay sovereign to dictate religious matters but to be guided and limited by her clergy. This was a dangerous doctrine in England, where the royal supremacy was looked upon as the keystone of the established church, and certainly not one welcome to the imperious Elizabeth. Her reply was to order the bishops by royal letter to suppress the prophesyings, and to place Grindal under house arrest and suspend him from office in June 1577. He remained adamant, finally offered his resignation, but died in 1583 before it could be accepted.

His successor was none other than Whitgift, now bishop of Worcester, the chief anti-puritan controversialist. Going up to Cambridge in Edwardian days, he had successfully stayed there under Mary, partly, it would seem, because of the protection of Perne, the Master of Peterhouse, where he became a Fellow in 1555, who advised him to keep silence about his opinions when the Marian visitors came to the university. He was evidently prudent, although not perhaps timeserving, with a strong sense of the duty of respect for authority—a valuable asset in Tudor times. It was this attitude which marked his policy as archbishop. What he demanded of the puritans was obedience to the ecclesiastical laws. Calvinist theology he shared with them, although not in its extreme form; but he had already shown that he had no sympathy with those who held that the Calvinist discipline was the only legitimate form of church order. Armed with the extraordinary powers of a new Commission for Ecclesiastical Causes to administer the executive powers of the royal supremacy, which reinforced his own rights of metropolitical visitation, Whitgift withstood the royal council, some important members of which had puritan sympathies, when they tried to hinder his proceedings. He harried those clerics who would not conform, although he also attempted a policy of practical church reform. Parliamentary attempts to legalise puritan policies he resisted with the aid of the queen, whose favour he won and who used to refer to him as her 'little black husband'. Baulked here, the more firmly presbyterian puritans attempted direct action. The suppressed prophesyings were replaced by semi-secret meetings called *classes* that were intended to become eventually the consistories or presbyteries which strict Calvinists regarded as the right form of church government. For the time being, until they could act as such, they tried to carry out the functions of presbyteries on a voluntary basis in the districts in which they were established. Attention was publicly called to what was going on by Richard Bancroft, a canon of Westminster Abbey, later to be Whitgift's right-hand man and to succeed him as archbishop, in a sermon at Paul's Cross in 1589. The episcopate was already annoyed by the appearance of the Martin Marprelate tracts, which began in 1588, attacking various bishops by name in a witty, but scurrilous, fashion. Next year the secret press which produced them was discovered near Manchester, its fourth hiding-place, and eventually those responsible were tracked down and prosecuted, though the authors were never found. Among others Cartwright was arrested and imprisoned on the ground that, besides preaching illegally and speaking against the prayer-book, he knew the authors of the tracts but would not give their names. Eventually, although he declined to sign a form of submission condemning presbyteries, Cartwright and other leading puritans who had been in custody were released in 1592 on declaring their belief in the royal supremacy. They had been the leaders of the *classis* movement, the secrets of which Bancroft had ferreted out, and, those secrets once revealed, the movement died a natural death. An execution in 1593, that of John Penry, who had taken refuge in Scotland and then unwisely returned to England, marred what by the standards of the age was a merciful treatment of the extreme puritan leaders.

By the end of Elizabeth's reign puritanism was no longer in a position to challenge her government. It was by no means a spent force, as the events of the seventeenth century were to show; but its lack of success earlier and Whitgift's firm handling of it had driven it to desperate courses which proved self-defeating. Some of the rigid Calvinists formed separatist movements which tried to opt out of the national church altogether and, in some cases, these met persecution by emigrating abroad like their Marian predecessors. Their attitude was, however, regarded by the main body as wrong, for most puritans held fast to Calvin's principle that no amount of corruption in a national church, short of the actual errors of popery, justified one in schism from it, any more than the corruptions of the church of the Old Covenant would have justified the prophets who denounced them in deserting the Temple. In saying this it must also be remembered that the term puritan covered a wide variety of opinion. By no means all who demanded reform of the church of England were utterly committed to presbyterian principles in the manner of Cartwright. All were firmly Protestant, fiercely anti-papist; nearly all disliked some features of the prayer-book, although the chief motive of some was probably a not unjustifiable dislike of the undoubted administrative and financial abuses which disfigured the Elizabethan church. Had these been reformed, it is quite possible that their consciences would have swallowed the ceremonial and prayers they disliked, or would at least have tolerated them. Although the theology of all was Calvinist, it was only a minority who held the Calvinist view of church order in its full rigour.

Calvinism had indeed failed in the sixteenth century to conquer England. By the end of the century it was losing ground both as a theology and as a theory of the church. Hooker's famous *Ecclesiastical Polity* undermined in the view of many the Calvinist ecclesiology and gained positive support for the Anglican system. At the same time, especially at Cambridge, criticism of Calvinist predestinarianism was growing in the latter part of the century and independently of the Arminian movement in the Netherlands. As Dr H. C. Porter has written: 'The Cambridge school was an indigenous growth. It would be improper to use the word "Arminian" of any English theologian before 1610.'[1] Calvinism had a great influence upon England in the later sixteenth century and was to have a violent and revolutionary effect in the seventeenth. But it failed permanently to capture the national church, largely because, as in France, it came into collision, although not as yet by way of war, with a national monarchy which refused to adopt it.

In Scotland it was a different story, although by the end of the century the outcome looked like being not wholly dissimilar. The decisive factor there was that the Scottish monarchy was weak as compared with the English and had not secured the absolutist tradition of the French kings, weakened though that was at the time of the Wars of Religion. It is hardly an exaggeration to say that Scottish kings ruled by sufferance of the nobility and this was why the Scottish Reformation was from the first a movement from below, not, as in England, a state-controlled affair. Later, in the reign of James VI, the monarchy was to gain power, a gain overestimated perhaps by James himself, with his theoretical passion for autocracy. It is against this political background that the vicissitudes of Scottish Calvinism must be seen. The effects also of the 'auld alliance' of Scotland and France were of decisive importance. Scotland's nearest Protestant neighbour and potential ally in the Reformation was the traditional enemy, England, and therefore Scottish Protestants had to make their own decisions between nationalist patriotism and religious affiliation. There was, too, the additional complication that Mary, heiress to James V, was the daughter of a French mother, Mary of Lorraine, who belonged to the Guise family, the leaders of French Catholicism, and that she was herself dauphiness, and for a brief time queen, of France as well as being a convinced Catholic. The dilemma of choice between France and England was no new phenomenon when John Knox started off the decisive phase of the Reformation of Scotland. Henry VIII had tried to lead his cousin James V in the direction of a breach with Rome and a dissolution of the monasteries; had built up by means of bribes to nobles a not very dependable party favourable to him in Scotland; and had tried to secure the marriage of the future Edward VI to the young Mary. This policy had been continued after Henry's death by Protector Somerset, who had plans for an actual union of the kingdoms into a realm of Great Britain. Indeed the Protector's Pinkie campaign of 1547, as well as earlier campaigns before Henry VIII's death, had their effect upon the Scottish Reformation, with the destruction of monasteries they involved and even the distribution of Bibles to the Scots.

[1] H. C. Porter, *Reformation and Reaction in Tudor Cambridge* (Cambridge, 1958), p. 408.

The campaign of 1547 brings into the picture John Knox. He had already been converted to the Reformation and was making a name for himself as a preacher. As in England, Lutheran ideas had first entered Scotland from the continent by way of the east coast ports and the first martyr, Patrick Hamilton, was burned as early as 1528. There is earlier evidence of a certain degree of penetration by English Lollardy in the south-west. The Reformation was likely to have success, for the Catholic church in Scotland was morally and financially corrupt to a degree greater than in many other parts of Europe, with many of its clerics incontinent and with a good proportion of its higher offices used for the maintenance of royal and noble bastards. Indeed lay encroachments upon ecclesiastical revenues remained a tradition which was to hinder the proper endowment of the Reformed church later. By the 1540s Protestant opinions had won the favour of a number of nobles and lairds, classes who were always to form the real bastion and controlling power of the Scottish Reformation. Support from town burgesses was almost as important; whilst the poorer classes, who suffered from the financial exactions of the church, so visibly ill spent, were not deeply attached to the old religion. In view, however, of what has already been said about the degree to which the upper classes had already invaded church property, one must not imagine that those who came to be the 'Lords of the Congregation' were motivated simply by the thought of financial gain. They already had largely appropriated church property.

Knox's own conversion came chiefly through George Wishart, whom he accompanied on a preaching tour in Lothian in 1545. Shortly afterwards Wishart was arrested and burned at the stake at St Andrews in 1546. From him Knox imbibed Swiss ideas, for Wishart had fled Scotland in 1538 after being charged with heresy and had quite probably visited Germany and Switzerland before, after a sojourn at Cambridge, he returned to his native land about 1543. He had translated the Helvetic Confession of 1536, in which Bullinger had had a hand. His mentor's martyrdom had an effect upon Knox which is reflected in his *History of the Reformation within the Realm of Scotland*. Knox, who always believed in the answering of religious violence by violence, joined the assassins of Cardinal Beaton, murdered in the same year partly in revenge for Wishart's death. They were then besieged in the castle of St Andrews at Easter 1547. The hoped-for intervention by England in their support came too late and Knox with many others was captured by the French, who reduced the castle in July. He spent the next two years as a French galley slave. Released in 1549, he made his way to England and played an active part in the Edwardian Reformation on the left wing of the movement. His activities among the English Marian refugees at Frankfurt have already been mentioned. They caused his withdrawal to Geneva and his lifelong committal to Calvinism, even though his support of the principle of revolution and war on behalf

113

of religion did not please Calvin. During his absence from Scotland the Reformation had made further progress. The noble group supporting it, the Lords of the Congregation, were pressing the Queen Regent, Mary of Guise, for changes in religion, were gaining ground, and were almost in control of the country. Some of them had already invited Knox back to Scotland in 1557—he had spent a brief time there in 1556–7, preaching and establishing congregations in which the Lord's Supper could be celebrated according to the principles he thought right—but to his annoyance when he reached Dieppe he found other letters advising him not to come, which he interpreted as signs of half-heartedness on the part of the supporters of the Reformation. After Elizabeth's accession he found with equal annoyance that he was *persona non grata* to the queen on account of his pamphlets against the 'monstrous' nature of female rule, written at a time when Mary Tudor, Mary Queen of Scots, and Mary of Guise seemed the protagonists of Catholicism. There was no question, therefore, of a return to England, nor was he even allowed to travel through the country. This was an additional reason for accepting the further invitation back to his own land which he had received at the end of 1558. He took passage and landed at Leith in May 1559.

The political situation he met was ripe for revolution whether Knox realised it or not. On 12 May ('flitting Friday'), ten days after his arrival, the friars were due to quit their houses according to the terms of an unofficial notice, the so-called 'Beggars' Summons' posted on their doors at the beginning of the year, warning them to give place by then to the poor and infirm. Moreover, news was reaching Scotland of the passing of the English Acts of Supremacy and Uniformity. Mary of Guise had summoned the Protestant preachers to appear at Stirling, apparently with the intention of taking legal action against them. The townsmen of Dundee and neighbouring lairds had determined to go with their preachers and protect them. They moved on to Perth, which had recently adopted Protestantism, which its provost, Lord Ruthven, declined to suppress when so ordered by the regent. Thus it was that on Thursday, 11 May, the day after the preachers should have presented themselves at Stirling on pain of 'horning' (outlawry), Knox preached in St John's church at Perth to a congregation already in a revolutionary frame of mind. He was, as he says, 'vehement against idolatry', a statement which, given the usual violence of Knox's speech, means much. Immediately afterwards, and, as Knox thought, in contempt of him, a priest started to say Mass and a boy called out a protest. The priest struck the boy and he retaliated by throwing a stone towards the high altar which broke an image above it, whereupon the congregation immediately wrecked all the images in the church. Following this, what Knox calls 'the rascal multitude' attacked the Franciscan friary, first breaking images and then looting the house, enraged, according to Knox, to find it luxuriously furnished and stocked in spite of the Franciscan claim to a vocation of poverty. The same treatment was meted out to the Dominican house and the Carthusian priory, so that within two days nothing but the walls of these impressive buildings was left standing. A general uprising followed, with more destruction, as the insurgents marched upon Edinburgh. There a truce was made, allowing the city to choose its own religion and forbidding the restoration of 'idolatry' wherever it had been abolished, on condition that no further attacks were made upon churches. Mary of Guise brought in French troops to protect her policy and the Protestants entered into secret negotiation with Cecil in England for support, Elizabeth (who had her doubts about supporting rebellion) professing no knowledge of them. In October military operations began with a march by the insurgents on Edinburgh, which they occupied. Then the Lords, presided over by James Hamilton, duke of Châtelherault, formally suspended Mary of Guise from her regency in the name of the king and queen of Scotland, Francis II of France and his wife Mary Queen of Scots. However, as they were short of money, and money sent from England was intercepted, their forces melted away, and they had to retreat ignominiously to Stirling. Soon afterwards, however, English intervention, at first naval but later military as well, forced the French to agree to the treaty of Edinburgh and withdraw from Scotland. The Reformation was saved. Mary of Guise had died just before the treaty and the way was now open for the introduction of Protestantism as the national religion.[1]

In August 1560 the Scottish parliament accepted a confession of faith, forbade the saying of Mass and renounced the pope. Next year a *Book of Discipline* was adopted by an ecclesiastical synod, and subscribed afterwards by a number of nobles and lairds who, however, showed their fears for their own hold upon ecclesiastical benefices by stipulating that all clerics should hold their existing benefices for life, providing that they contributed to the support of the Protestant ministers who would now do the actual pastoral work. (The *Book* had laid down that ecclesiastical revenues should be used for the adequate support of the new ministry, the upkeep of church buildings, the relief of the poor and the education of children.) Thus began the curious situation, which lasted so long, by which the old ecclesiastical benefice structure remained, but was not for the most part in the hands of what had now become the national church. In 1562, after the return of Queen Mary to her kingdom following her husband's death—she had been in France since 1550—negotiations took place between the beneficed clergy and the royal privy council and early next year it was decided that a third part of all benefice income should be paid over for the support both of the crown and of the Protestant kirk, the remainder being formally secured to the benefice-holders. As this third was collected by the crown, it is not surprising to find that as time

[1] See below, pp. 215–6.

went on the royal share increased and the kirk's share diminished. So the reformed establishment was dogged almost from the beginning by shortage of means, much as was the Elizabethan church in England for somewhat similar reasons. Its position in this respect was improved in 1573–4 by the regent, Morton, who caused a survey of parishes to be made, brought to light concealed revenues, and had a proper distribution of the proceeds of the thirds made to the parish ministers. Earlier on, in 1566, it was laid down that benefices, as they became vacant, should be given to reformed ministers, although an attempt to take the logical step of dispossessing benefice-holders who were not qualified for the reformed ministry failed.

All this illustrates the degree to which, in Scotland, as elsewhere, the pure theory of Calvinism had to bow to the wishes of the laity. On the face of things Scotland had become a fully Calvinistic nation in 1560–1, the first to do so; but in practice things were different. The confrontation between Knox and Mary Queen of Scots after her return, her inability to preserve Catholicism as more than her private religion and the attacks made upon even that—these are an often told story, as is also the series of follies and accidents by which she lost her crown and had to take refuge in England in 1568. Nevertheless, she was not without her supporters in Scotland and a religious reaction was always a possibility if they should win, especially if her English Catholic supporters should ever make good her claim to the English throne. It was not until Mary's party, which had already been breaking up, was finally crushed by the reduction of Edinburgh Castle in 1573 by a combined English and Scottish force, that this danger seemed remote. Even after that, James VI from time to time seemed to be coquetting with Rome and with Scottish Roman Catholics. The Scottish Reformation could never feel wholly secure, however much it seemed to rest upon popular support, especially in a country where so much depended upon the varying inclinations of the nobles, whom the shrewd Knox always regarded with suspicion.

The settlement of 1560–1 was broadly Calvinistic. The confession of faith not only used violent language in rejecting the church of Rome, described as 'the horrible harlot, the kirk malignant', but stated Calvinist doctrine on the sacraments and the nature of the church, without, however, laying great stress upon predestination. Nevertheless, the *Book of Discipline*, whilst insisting upon reformed ideas of preaching and the administration of the sacraments, did not dogmatise unduly about church order and repeatedly spoke of the arrangements it made for government as 'expedient'. It prescribed the familiar Calvinistic system of ministers, lay elders and deacons, although it is a remarkable contrast from the later presbyterian system that these two latter categories of church officials were to be elected annually. As elsewhere in Calvinist lands, an element of anti-clericalism is apparent, especially as the elders and deacons were given the right to admonish and correct their minister and, if necessary, depose him with the consent of the superintendent. The very setting up of these superintendents, whose areas of rule corresponded to a great extent to the old dioceses, was in itself a break with the general practice of Calvinism, for in many respects they carried on the functions of the former bishops. They were not regarded as a separate order of the ministry or as the indispensable bestowers of ordination, although they played an important part in the examination of ministerial candidates chosen by the congregations and could themselves, with the aid of the councils who assisted them, choose a minister if a parish failed to do so within forty days of a vacancy. It was they too who admitted a minister, after election and examination, to serve in a parish. The ultimate authority in the new kirk was the general assembly, but this included nobles, barons and representatives of burghs, as well as superintendents and ministers. Ministers had no prescriptive right to attend and were not encouraged to leave their parishes for the purpose without good cause. Those who came normally did so either because the business to be done concerned them personally or because their superintendent ordered them to attend. As a result the ministerial element was often far outnumbered by the laymen. This is not surprising, considering the vital part that had been played by the leading laity in the formation of the kirk, although it should be added that the local synods were on the accepted pattern, ministers of the area attending, as in France, each accompanied by an elder or deacon from his parish.

This was not presbyterianism as later understood and the change came with the arrival in Scotland in 1574 of Andrew Melville. He had spent the last five years at Geneva in direct contact with Beza, whose view of church polity had grown much more rigid than that of Calvin, the latter having allowed for differences in discipline in different places. Melville had the same views as Cartwright, whom he may well have met at Geneva, and was, like him, the leader of a younger and more radical generation. Those who thought with him had a special grievance in the appointment by the state of bishops (actually so called), who would replace the superintendents. This was a scheme approved by the assembly in 1572, on condition that this and the retention of the titles of archbishop, archdeacon, dean and so forth did not seem to be approving popery, although they preferred that for strictly ecclesiastical purposes archbishops should be known as bishops only. (It must be remembered that, because of the agreement in 1561 respecting the vested interests of existing beneficeholders, these titles had not died out and some of the holders of them had accepted the reformed faith and taken part in the work of the kirk.) This was anathema to men like Melville who believed in the principle of the 'parity of ministers'. He carried the day by the adoption in 1578 by the assembly of the *Second Book of Discipline*, but the Scottish parliament refused its assent and only to a degree was the establishment of presbyteries of the classic type, courts of ministers and lay elders for the administration of discipline, realised. In 1584 there was a government reaction against Melville's ideas. The 'Black Acts' passed by parliament then reinforced the authority of the bishops and, to make matters worse from the presbyterian point of view, they were declared subject to the king rather than to the general assembly, whilst the authority of parliament over the church, 'of late years called in some doubt', was affirmed. A compromise, providing that bishops should act administratively only with the advice of committees of ministers and should be subject to the general assembly, and allowing the erection of presbyteries, was worked out in 1586 and accepted reluctantly by the general assembly. Between then and 1592, when a parliamentary statute formally authorised the presbyterian system, the tendency was for episcopal power to diminish in favour of the presbyteries, but even after 1592 presbyterianism was not universal in practice, nor were bishops abolished. After his accession to the English throne as James I in 1603, James VI was to establish an episcopate nearer to the English model, having at the Hampton Court conference of 1604 expressed violently his detestation of presbyteries as incompatible with monarchy.

Indeed the basis of Andrew Melville's programme was a belief in church and state as separate communities, even if composed of the same persons, and a denial of the right of the latter to control the former. He struggled for the paramount rights of the general assembly over the kirk, just as much as for the establishment of presbyteries, and his outlook was summed up in his famous interview with an irate James VI at Falkland in 1596, as one of a committee protesting against the return to Scotland of the banished Catholic earls of Huntly and Erroll. Melville answered James's denial of the right of ministers to meet without his consent, by seizing the king by the sleeve, calling him 'God's sillie [simple or weak] vassal' and informing him in the course of a lengthy harangue that 'thair is twa Kings and twa kingdomes in Scotland. Thair is Chryst Jesus the King, and his kingdome the Kirk, whase subject King James the Saxt is, and of whase kingdome nocht a king, nor a lord, nor a heid, bot a member.' It was Calvin's principle at Geneva being applied to a monarchy. Never perhaps has been put more succinctly one side of the thesis and antithesis which lie behind so many of the problems of this period, the claim of the state on the one hand to dictate or at least to regulate the religion of its subjects, the claim of the church on the other to pronounce upon the word of God and to expect conformity to it even from rulers. James, with his exalted ideas of divine right and his attachment, which he was to make so clear later in England, to the principle of the royal supremacy over the church, must have regarded Melville's outburst as heretical and blasphemous, as well as insulting.

In a sense James had the last word, for about the same time David Black, minister of St Andrews, not only preached that 'all kings are devil's children', but also called Queen Elizabeth of England an atheist, thus producing an international incident. Elizabeth complained to James, who summoned Black before the privy council. Black denied the council's competence to judge his case, but was banished to the Highlands. The king was at odds with the kirk on other issues. Churchmen had rebuked him for his habit of swearing and his wife for vanity. In November a demand was made that the king's ministers of state should be censured for negligence in hearing sermons and next month commissioners of the kirk insisted that they should be constantly in attendance upon the king because they feared that he might alter religion or bring in 'liberty of conscience at the least'—probably a dig at James's alleged willingness to tolerate Catholicism. All this roused the government, which declared the powers of the commissioners of the assembly illegal and ordered them to leave the capital; laid down that ministers accused of sedition must submit to the council; and revived an act forbidding speech against king and council. A riot in Edinburgh gave them a chance of further action. On 17 December a mob raised the cry that the papists were in revolt and would massacre the king and government and make disturbances. James removed to Linlithgow and ordered the removal of the law courts from Edinburgh, which would cease to be the capital city. The city authorities surrendered to the king's wrath, imprisoned the ministers in the castle and undertook not to receive them back or admit other ministers in future without the king's consent, in addition paying a heavy fine. On 1 January 1597 James re-entered Edinburgh in triumph and later parliament allowed him the right to forbid church courts to meet or ministers to preach whenever he should deem it necessary. It was not the end of strife, for in 1600 there came the mysterious story of the Gowrie Conspiracy, in which the king alleged that he had been enticed by the earl of Gowrie, a man of strongly Protestant views and much in the confidence of the presbyterian party, and his brother to their house at Perth with a view to kidnapping him. Five Edinburgh ministers, who evidently disbelieved the story—the Gowrie brothers had been killed by those who rescued the king—refused to give thanks for James's escape in the terms he wanted. Four finally submitted and the remaining one, Robert Bruce, who held out, was banished to the north of Scotland. Thus, on the eve of his departure to England, James seemed on balance to have got the better of a church recalcitrant to state control. Later he was to do so still more, even if his son was to reap the effects of the unpopularity of his father's policies.

The reformed church of Scotland, it has been said, 'started its career in rebellion against the crown and had been associated with a revolution which deposed the sovereign'. It might be thought that here at least Calvinism had escaped from state control; but as we have seen, not only did the century end with the kirk curbed, but in fact its earlier victories against monarchy were won under lay leadership and would have been impossible without it. In view of the power of the Scottish nobility, the situation was not so unlike that in Germany, where the Reformation was accomplished only because it was backed by some of the princes against the emperor. Not even in Scotland could Calvinism escape what Léonard has described as 'the secularisation of the Reformation'.

Something has been said of German Calvinism in the earlier section of this chapter and this perhaps permits one to add only a little here. As was said there, the victories of Calvinism in Germany were due as much to internal penetration of Lutheranism by 'crypto-Calvinism' as to an actual spread of Calvinist churches. Calvinism was faced by an earlier and popular reforming movement with which it had, at least tacitly, to come to an accommodation. Even in the Palatinate, as we have seen, its outstanding work, the *Heidelberg Catechism*, although it became a standard Calvinist formulary, was composed in collaboration with Melanchthonists. It did, however, prevail in certain states, although no German city became Calvinist in Calvin's lifetime and even Strassburg, Calvinism's real birthplace, became strongly Lutheran and anti-Calvinist after Bucer had retired to England in 1549 rather than accept the *Interim*. As related before, it triumphed in the Palatinate, though not fully, during the reign of Frederick III, his successor expelling it. It was there, too, that in 1568 Erastus, destined to give his name to an attitude of mind which he would not really have endorsed, protested against the Calvinist claim to the right of excommunication by the church without the concurrence of the civil power. Indeed Calvinism would always be regarded with suspicion in a country in which the Lutheran doctrine of the 'godly prince' was so current. Nevertheless, John Casimir, who was regent for his nephew Frederick IV after Ludwig VI died in 1583, restored Calvinism as the state religion of the Palatinate, and it was maintained when Frederick came of age. Other German states and cities also adopted Calvinism. Nassau (under the influence of the preachers driven from the Palatinate by Ludwig VI together with that of Melanchthonists driven from Wittenberg by the Elector of Saxony), Bremen and Wesel had all been won for Calvinism before the end of the century and Anhalt and Hesse were tending the same way. Its greatest triumph, however, was not to come until the next century, when the Elector of Brandenburg embraced it. Its conquests were small in comparison with those of the Lutheran Reformation. Indeed it may be said that in Germany Calvinism was chiefly a refuge for Lutherans dissatisfied with the *Formula of Concord*, which had retained Lutheran teaching on the Real Presence. In consequence, churches which became Calvinist often retained the Augsburg Confession in Melanchthon's revision of 1540, which modified the teaching of the original confession of 1530 on the sacrament. Although it possessed to some degree at least the characteristic Calvinist church order, German Calvinism was to some extent *sui generis*.

Further east in Europe, Calvinism made much more progress. It appeared in Poland,[1] where King Sigismund II Augustus (1548–72) entered into correspondence with Calvin and read the *Institutes*, although he never adopted Calvin's plan, sent to him in 1554, for a reformed church under an archbishop and bishops—one of the many indications that Calvin himself was not opposed to episcopacy if understood in his sense. Polish Calvinism, once again, tended to be syncretistic. In 1555 the Calvinists of Lesser Poland, where Calvinist churches had multiplied in the 1550s, held a joint synod with the Hussite Bohemian Brethren of Greater Poland, who had fled there from Bohemia, accepting the confession of faith of the Brethren as a common statement of belief and entering into intercommunion with them. Calvinism was strengthened by the return to Poland of John Laski in 1556. He worked for the union of Calvinists with both the Brethren and the Lutherans and, although he did not succeed in his lifetime, his work bore fruit in 1570 when, by the Consensus of Sandomierz, Calvinists, Lutherans and Brethren united on a basis of mutual recognition of each other's confessions of faith, adopting on the vexed question of the eucharist the confession of the Saxon churches presented to the Council of Trent in 1551, which had observed a prudent vagueness. The union was motivated very largely by the pressure of the Counter-Reformation, then increasing considerably in Poland after the entry of the Jesuits in 1564, and also by the competition on the other side of Socinianism and other left-wing sects.

In Bohemia also, Calvinism, brought in by students from noble families who had gone to Geneva and other Calvinist universities, found it desirable to unite with Lutherans, Neo-Utraquist Hussites and Hussite Brethren in the Bohemian Confession of 1575, which was Melanchthonian rather than purely Calvinist. In Hungary, where Calvinism appeared about the middle of the century, it had the advantage of being free from Germanism, which Magyars disliked for political reasons; but, perhaps for the same reason, found it impossible to co-operate with the Lutherans there. In 1564 the government gave permission for a separation and the setting up of a Calvinist church, which adopted Calvin's Catechism and the Second Helvetic Confession. A synod of 1576 adopted a code of discipline which had affinities with the Scottish, in that the churches were grouped under superintendents or bishops, with a synod of the whole church as the ultimate authority. The local churches had the ordinary consistorial constitution characteristic of Calvinism, but lay influence was strong. In the seniorates, the territorial organisations intermediate between the local churches and the superintendencies, a clerical and a lay official stood at the head side by side, and each bishop had likewise a lay *curator* as colleague. In Transylvania Socinianism was a serious rival, obtaining as it did in 1564, together with Catholicism, Lutheranism and Calvinism, the protection of the law. (A large part of Hungary, it must be remembered,

---

[1] See also below, chapter XII.

was under Turkish overlordship.) In the part of Hungary under Habsburg control the Counter-Reformation prevailed and toleration was not to be expected after the accession of the Emperor Rudolf in 1576, whilst even Maximilian II, his predecessor, was no friend to Calvinism, although he favoured Lutherans.

Except, then, for Hungary, classical Calvinism hardly existed in central and eastern Europe. Its influence was strong, but it could not maintain itself free from admixture from other Protestant traditions. In one sense this may have been a cause of strength. Calvin had been much more tolerant of local variations and much more willing to seek co-operation and unity with other Protestants than the Genevan tradition showed itself to be when it was inherited by Beza. However much Calvinism gained in internal unity from this attitude—and the Arminian controversy was to show that that unity could be precarious—it largely lost in the west the chance of creating a united Protestantism which could confront Tridentine Catholicism everywhere. Too rigid an orthodoxy, whether in doctrine or in church order, can make for defeat in the face of adverse circumstances, as the failure of radical puritanism in Elizabethan England shows. It was an utter refusal to compromise which was primarily responsible for the downfall of the movement headed by Cartwright, and much the same might be said of Melville's programme in Scotland. Calvinism, in fact, showed itself the least tolerant of Protestant creeds; from the days of Calvin himself insistence upon the duty of the state to punish heresy was an outstanding feature of it. Its increasing tendency also to adopt warlike violence, originally forced upon it by persecution, was in the long run to damage it severely, for violence begets violence. If the Catholic League in France set its face against toleration, so also did the Huguenots, and also the Dutch Calvinists whenever they gained power. It is this strain in Calvinism which too easily causes the observer to overlook the genuine atmosphere of worship and devotion which Calvinism at its best could produce and, together with its insistence upon the rigid disciplining of the faithful, has created the impression of Calvinism as a harsh, rigid, unloving and cold religion, which undoubtedly at times it was, an impression strengthened by the ruthless logic with which the doctrine of predestination and reprobation was often taught. All this, however, is but the reverse side of a creed which could and did create a heroism and self-sacrifice which explain much of its success. Yet, even so, the last reflection left with the historian is perhaps the fact that even this uncompromising religion, as appears wherever one looks at its development, could not ultimately withstand the control of nationalistic statecraft, any more than could Catholicism or Lutheranism. This is one more testimony to the power of *étatisme* in sixteenth-century Europe. The Leviathan, of which Hobbes was to write, had come into existence in practice, whether in monarchical or republican form, long before he described it.

Two possible, if ultimately impracticable, ways for religious bodies to try to escape this confrontation with the state are, either to set up a Utopia according to their own hearts' desire, a self-sufficient church-state in which religion and politics will be one; or, alternatively, to try to contract out of the territorial state by playing no part in it and as far as possible refusing the obligations it imposes. Both of these expedients were tried at different times by bodies of left-wing dissidents in religion during the sixteenth century, some of which were so far from central Protestantism that it is perhaps misleading to describe them as Protestant at all. They formed what has been called the 'Radical Reformation' and many of them were movements of social reform or protest as well as religious schisms. Without some account of them no description of religious attitudes in the years following 1559 would be complete.

Chief among them stood the series of sects and groups called at the time Anabaptists, from the fact that most of them denied the validity of infant baptism, holding that a personal response was necessary for true baptism, and therefore rebaptized any of their converts who had been baptized before the age of reason. The name is not a happy one, both because it suggests more unity and homogeneity among these groups than they ever attained and also because anabaptism was not really the centre of their faith, which usually lay in a belief in personal inspiration by the Spirit, with a corresponding devaluation of the written word of Scripture and of outward rites, the attitude often described as 'enthusiasm' in the strictly technical sense of the term. Indeed at this time the word 'Anabaptist' was largely a term of abuse used by their Catholic and Protestant enemies, much as the word 'Bolshevik' was popularly used after 1917, and partly for the same reason. It was the Anabaptist revolution at Münster in 1531–6 which discredited the Anabaptists finally, both in Catholic and Protestant opinion, all the more so as enthusiasm of the same type had been associated with the Peasants' War earlier on. The practice of community of goods, and later polygamy, as well as the violence and fanaticism shown, shocked all Europe and the memory lasted long after the revolution had been suppressed and Münster secured again for its prince-bishop by combined Catholic and Lutheran forces. More than ever after this, Anabaptism had to become an underground movement, and the persecution of its adherents was fiercer than any others of the time and was approved by almost all shades of religious opinion to its right.

We have seen already something of this in the Low Countries, which became comparatively early a great centre of Anabaptism. Indeed some of the more radical leaders of the Münster revolution had come from the Netherlands. It was there also that the most noteworthy and attractive Anabaptist leader of this period, Menno Simons, exercised part of his ministry. He was born in west Frisia. Ordained a Catholic priest in 1524, he followed his vocation until 1536, although he had come to disbelieve in transubstantiation and subsequently in infant baptism; in the former case his doubts began the year after his ordination. Paradoxically, what finally persuaded him to throw in his lot with the Anabaptists was precisely their violence at Münster, which shocked him and against which he wrote. He felt that they lacked proper guidance and that he, who might give it, was still living a lie by continuing as a priest of the Roman church. At first he tried to preach the truth as he saw it from his pulpit, but in 1536 quitted his parish and took up the career of a pastor to the Anabaptists, itinerating ceaselessly and gathering up into organised groups the scattered Anabaptists of the Netherlands and north Germany, disheartened and in many cases shocked by the excesses at Münster. In 1540 he published his *Foundation of Christian Doctrine* as a manual of instruction in Dutch, which came out in new editions in 1554 and 1558. It displays unorthodoxy in regard to the received doctrine of the Incarnation, holding that Christ was a heavenly man sent from the Father, who passed through Mary but did not take his flesh from her. On this basis Simons urged the importance of excluding all unworthy communicants from the Lord's Supper, in which the faithful fed upon the heavenly flesh of Christ. Anabaptists must be a society withdrawn from the world, excluding all sinners, even though Menno urged the readmission of the repentant. He died in 1559, but his work lived on, for it was chiefly owing to it that Anabaptism survived as in any sense an organised movement. Nevertheless, even he could not maintain unity in what was by its very character a fissiparous movement. In competition with his followers were the Familists, founded by Henry Niclaes (1502–c. 1580), who taught first at Amsterdam and later at Emden, although he too travelled a great deal. He founded the Family of Love, which laid great stress upon personal religious experience and put services and ceremonies upon a lower level, although they formed well-organised communities controlled by elders chosen for their supposed high degree of spiritual enlightenment. Moreover, after Menno Simons's death, some of his followers, called Waterlanders from the fact that they lived chiefly in the region between Leyden and Haarlem, besides adopting an extremely liberal attitude to belief—they decided in 1579 not to excommunicate anyone, whatever his interpretation of any articles of faith not expressly laid down in Scripture—also gave up the characteristic Anabaptist separation from ordinary society. In 1572 they contributed liberally to William of Orange's funds for the war against the Spaniards and they were willing to undertake obligations imposed by the state. They adopted the distinctive name of Baptists (*Doopsgezinden*) and it was from them that the English seventeenth-century Baptists originated, for their contacts with the English Brownist Separatists who took refuge in the Netherlands later encouraged some Waterlanders to migrate to England.

It was, as we have seen, in eastern Europe that the sects which broke most fully from traditional Christianity, by adopting heterodox views of the Trinity and Incarnation, found both most support and most refuge. Such ideas tended to come from southern Europe, where the logical Italian or Spanish mind, once it had broken with Catholicism, saw no reason not to question the most long-standing traditions of the church. From Spain came both John de Valdés and Servetus, Calvin's victim— the former accepting orthodoxy but regarding the articles of faith as subjective, only to be understood by experience; the latter denying that either the doctrine of the Trinity or that of the two Natures of Christ could be found in Scripture.

It was, however, the Italian Lelio Sozzini, his name latinised to Socinus, who founded the anti-Trinitarian movement called Socinianism, which had most influence of all and gave its name to all tendencies of this kind. Attacking first the Calvinist doctrine of the eucharist and then that of predestination, from his refuge at Zürich, he published in 1563 his *Trente dialoghi*, which denied the received doctrine of the Trinity, even though his alternative explanations were by no means fixed or clear. The scandal caused by the book compelled him to leave Zürich and eventually to seek refuge in Poland with Prince Nicolas Radziwill, to whom his *Dialogues* had been dedicated. Forced to leave Poland by an edict against heretics, he sought refuge in Moravia, where he died in 1565 at Austerlitz. To describe the complicated history of Socinianism and its relationship with Anabaptist movements is impossible in a chapter of this compass. As we have seen, it became a denomination of considerable size and importance in various parts of central and eastern Europe, whilst it had a continuing influence upon individuals and groups in the west. It was one of the evidences of the way in which, once the revolt against medieval orthodoxy had begun, there was virtually no aspect of it which was not considered open to question by some minds, even if the majority of dissidents kept their heterodoxy within strict limits. Just as Anabaptism shows the extent to which many, especially among the socially depressed classes, added to their dislike of medieval religion a dislike of the society in which it had flourished, so other sectaries saw no reason why the doctrinal decisions of the early church had more claim to respect than those of its medieval successor. All Protestantism was in the broad sense revolutionary; but, as in all revolutions, there were degrees of radicalism, the gamut in this case running from Lutheranism on the right through Calvinism to the sects on the left. The whole situation boded ill for the peace and unity of Europe in the coming century, and experience was to show that such fears were to be realised.

CHAPTER V

SOCIAL STRUCTURE, OFFICE-HOLDING AND POLITICS, CHIEFLY IN WESTERN EUROPE

POST-REFORMATION Europe displayed on the surface a large measure of political diversity. The fragmentation of the universal church, it would appear, completed a process of political fragmentation which had been going on for centuries. With medieval natural law in decline, and the emergence of the modern sovereign state still in the future, the nations of western Europe became locked in conflict within—and with their neighbours—in search of a system of government which would lead them away from confusion and anarchy. Yet the historian who looks at western Europe at the end of the sixteenth century is, in general, impressed not by the diversity of the political systems in the process of formation but by their striking similarity. In the constitutional issues which confronted them, and in the manner of their solution, all the governments of the day had much in common, because the pressures upon them were more or less the same. The general pressure of economic and social forces burst through and flowed beyond the frontiers of the new nation states.

The whole of Europe was at this time, to a greater or less degree, subject to a double upward pressure: of prices and of population. The rise in population far outdistanced the rise in productivity and inevitably commodity prices were driven sharply upwards. In Spain, for example, the 1540s saw a savage rise in prices and the succeeding decades would see a tragic worsening of the whole situation as the Spanish economic system sagged under heavy overseas commitments, a debilitating war in the Netherlands, and a war of attrition at sea. In France inflation added its own severe stresses at a time when she was entering upon four decades of civil war. In England inflation in the middle years of the century gave momentum to the process of social dislocation and at a most delicate time of religious and constitutional experiment. Thereafter this pace of inflation slackened: but it was renewed in the last dozen years of the century at the very period when her political insecurity in relation to Spain deteriorated into a war for survival itself. Inflation spread on into the third decade of the seventeenth century.

If then a relatively underdeveloped European economy proved unequal to the demands of a rising population, there were other social consequences no less powerful. London, for example, during the second half of the sixteenth century doubled its population, in spite of the heavy incidence of endemic disease. It was a pressure on both town and country. 'We have not, God be thanked', wrote William Lambarde in 1594, 'been touched with any extreme mortality, either by sword or sickness, that might abate the overgrown number of us.' But even when sword and sickness did intervene with tragic force, the rise was still largely unabated. Over a considerable part of Europe the combined effects of war, famine and disease proved inadequate to bank up the social system against the accumulating tide of population, a tide which did not begin to ebb until the fourth decade of the seventeenth century.

The pressures of population upon the scarce and underdeveloped resources of Europe were irregular in their effect; some areas might have to endure the powerful thrust of an enclosing landlord, others might remain wholly remote from the uneven stresses of agrarian change. In England the west and north saw little alteration in the traditional agricultural techniques and aims, while the central plains and the home counties were more responsive to contemporary economic demands, especially for wool in the midlands and dairy and market gardening products in the satellite regions of the capital. If the changes were not as rapid or extensive as contemporaries were willing to believe, they were more unsettling and socially radical than historians were, until recently, willing to acknowledge. In France the economic pressure was less; there is no story of a movement from corn to sheep or of eviction to meet the requirements of agrarian reconstruction. But politics took a more vigorous hand in the proceedings. With the long devastation of the Hundred Years War still not wholly repaired, the French landscape endured once more during the civil wars the remorseless tramp of the soldiery, more especially in the north-east and south. Hence—in the intervals of peace—the lords themselves sought to repopulate the abandoned lands. The old tenures became increasingly impracticable, as they had been in England for some time. The new men were more free—at least in the tenurial sense. This process could not be significant until the early seventeenth century, when the civil war was over. In the second half of the sixteenth, the pressure was working the other way. War drove men from the land.

But whatever the economic causes and consequences, the social effects were clearly manifest. Population was on the move. The 'push' and 'pull' elements were present in most of western Europe: the push from the land either because of conversion from corn to wool, with a diminished demand for labour, or simply because numbers grew beyond the capacity of the soil to bear them. The pull came from the demand for labour as industry developed, sometimes in old towns, sometimes in new. That pull, of ever increasing power, stretched beyond endurance the social services of the recipient towns. For, if many were drawn to the towns in the hope of work, a good proportion did not find any—or did not hold it for long. And some of course did not want work at all. So the great cities of Europe, as well as the smaller ones, were confronted with a settlement problem of ever growing dimensions. There was shortage of work, shortage of houses, shortage of food, shortage of social relief. The problem respected neither national boundary nor ecclesiastical doctrine. It emerged in powerful proportions whether the monasteries were dissolved or intact. Paris no less than London, Ypres no less than York, found that their social apparatus was unequal to the calls made upon it; while philosophers and theologians alike sought for the principles which should govern social amelioration. These principles concern us less than the basic facts which evoked them, namely, that population was significantly mobile and that it was impossible to contain the vagrant poor within their local restraints. All this underlined the fears of the governing classes that physical dislocation and social instability would breach the slender walls of their internal political security. The revolt of the *Germanía* in Valencia, the Anabaptist rising in Münster—these things had happened in the lifetime of the middle-aged men who held power now in the central years of the sixteenth century. The French civil wars of the second half of the century confirmed their gravest social anxieties.

These anxieties were reflected and reaffirmed in the legislation of the time. In England, the Statutes of Weavers of 1555, and of Apprentices of 1563, looked back to a somewhat imaginary past of settled, socially immobile and unexpanding populations, a past conjured up to justify an impracticable, economic conservatism. The English statute-book displays a gathering volume of economic and social legislation against a thrusting textile capitalism; against uncontrolled movement from one trade to another or from one district to another and in some cases from one class to another; against the wearing of excess apparel—silk was the status symbol of social aspirants below the rank of knighthood who sought to ape their betters. In Germany and France alike the knightly class was expected to live in a manner appropriate to its rank; while in Spain the social divisions had so hardened as to raise unsurmountable barriers between the leisured classes, secular and clerical, on the one hand, and all those engaged in commercial and industrial enterprise, on the other.

Here was a paradox. At the very time when an expanding economy—albeit slowly expanding—called for a reservoir of mobile labour, whose freedom to move might therefore have reduced the call for unemployment relief, government opinion was in general hostile to such uncontrolled expansion. And where such hostility was not fully effective, bad roads and generally deficient communications imposed insuperable handicaps. So much stood in the way of the full exploitation of human and physical resources. Meanwhile, unemployment and instability dogged each other's heels round the vicious circle of the contemporary social outlook.

There is, of course, no fundamental distinction between social and political instability; but they exacerbate each other. This was clearly marked during the sixteenth century; and of all classes the princes of Europe were most vulnerable to the disruptive forces of the age. For the very inflationary movement which stimulated industry and trade—as well as disturbed order and stability in time of slump—struck the monarchies where it could damage them most: in their treasuries. Faced with the growing cost of armies, of domestic administration and of diplomacy, they found that the revenues from their land, and the taxation from their political assemblies, were woefully inadequate for the needs they were alleged to meet. Hence the bewildering assortment of devices, obscure and contorted, illegal sometimes, to which the governments resorted at a high cost in unpopularity and maladministration; hence the heavy confiscations of the possessions of attainted noblemen and, most of all where possible, of the wealth of the church; hence the pious calls for retrenchment, faintly heard and rarely answered. Throughout Europe it is the same lamentable story of the increasing impoverishment of the monarchy. In Scotland the young James VI had experienced the greatest difficulty in raising sufficient money to go to Denmark to bring back his bride; and, in due course, the baptism of his son had to be delayed because he could not find the money to pay for a ceremony appropriate to his rank. In England the cautious queen was better supplied but she was also more heavily committed and, when she took measure of the cost of war, and the cost of her household, she bitterly directed against her ministers—at one time the earl of Leicester, at another the comptroller of her household—the full volume of her horrified surprise. In France Sully seriously tried to carry through a policy of fiscal reform; in England under James I, Robert Cecil. But what could one minister do in England against the extravagance of a glamorous court and an irresponsible king? The Swedish pattern was exceptional. There monetary inflation came lightly and late. The confiscated revenues of the church proved invaluable. Whereas the Swedish monarchy was poorer than that of Scotland before the Reformation, it was relatively richer than that of England after the Reformation. For when ecclesiastical wealth came to the Swedish king it came to stay—at least until well into the seventeenth century. In Scotland and in England it did not. The Spanish monarchy received substantial taxation from the church, as well as a vast accession of riches from the confiscated treasures of the Incas and from the exploitation of the American silver mines. But the wealth never stayed; and by the end of the century the Spanish monarchy was, at one and the same time, the most powerful and the most poverty-stricken of all the monarchies of Europe.

A complex of crises emerged in Germany. Here the redistribution of ecclesiastical wealth was of no benefit to the Habsburgs; and it carried one stage further the dissolution of central authority. For it came at a time when the whole constitution was crying out for reform, and the whole notion of imperial rule was under fire. To the north German princes in particular the Reformation had brought a relative increase in power in two separate senses: against the church and against the emperor. Such visions as the princes had had early in the century of a federated German nation under a German-orientated emperor had vanished. Instead, the centrifugal process of princely consolidation continued apace. Increasingly, as the Reformation spread in Germany, its hostility to a universal Rome reinforced the hostility to an emperor whose claims to universal rule, however tenuous, confused the aims and issues of German nationalism. But the aggressively Catholic-Spanish possessions of the emperor—a far greater source of wealth and a far greater reservoir of power than the whole of Germany put together—made it likely that he would choose Rome rather than the Reformation. The Protestant Reformation which might have unified Germany against the pope in fact divided Germany against the emperor. The Augsburg doctrine of *cuius regio eius religio* confirmed and extended political particularism into the sphere of religion. On the eve of the Thirty Years War Germany was divided into a mosaic of principalities which needed only the treaties of Westphalia to give them the powers of endurance. But, before this, the governments of Germany endured a century of consuming instability.

The instability of the monarchies reflected the deeper instability of the classes with whose fortunes their own were so closely intermingled. For if the new monarchies had to fight hard to retain and extend their hold on power, the old aristocracies found their resources under even greater strain. These two sectors of the governing classes were linked in a curious relationship. The monarchies, it is true, found it hard to rule without the nobility; but they found it equally hard to rule with them. Developments in Scotland made this abundantly clear, where, for example, the office of justiciar was hereditary in the nobility—and justice was therefore hard to come by. But all over western Europe the function of the aristocracy in society was inherently self-contradictory. As barons they had traditional ambitions and rivalries which frequently ran counter to the interests of the king's peace. But as hereditary office-holders—as many of them were—they were expected to enforce a legal and political system whose continuing strength depended upon the curbing of their own selfish powers. In Poland the crown's authority lay under constant threat of the aristocracy, and here was a barrier to good government as effective as any exercised by the Polish *sejm*. In Sweden the nobility was bent on aggrandising its privileges at the expense of the crown. In France during the last years of the sixteenth century there was re-enacted, in conditions of incomparable ferocity, the same factious conflict which had been fought out a century earlier in England during the Wars of the Roses. In England the Rising of the Northern Earls in 1569 was, in one sense, the rising of an *old* aristocratic group whose political power had been sterilised by the centralisation of the Tudor crown; while the rebellion of the earl of Essex in 1601 was, in many respects, the rising of the leaders of the *newer* aristocracy who had failed to inherit the powers enjoyed by the first generation, the founders of their line. But the belief that the new monarchs were hostile to the older aristocracy is an oversimplification—and distortion—of their attitudes. Even the first of the new Tudor dynasty, it has recently been shown, far from decimating it, employed the older aristocracy in the service of the state. The last of the Tudors clearly regarded a stable aristocracy as an essential part of her régime. Her refusal to inflate and dilute it with the easy creation of peerages, her policy of reserving some of the major offices of state—so far as possible—for noblemen, were all part of her inherent traditionalism. The divine queen needed the trappings of a high nobility about her throne. But it had to be an aristocracy whose teeth had been drawn. Her declaration to the earl of Leicester that England would have but one mistress and no master might have been addressed to the whole aristocracy. Yet the fact remains that a pivotal office like the lord lieutenancy tended to become hereditary in the leading aristocratic family in the shire. The Herberts were lords lieutenant of Wiltshire from the 1550s until the Civil War, with only one interruption. A large part of the nobility remained loyal to the Stuarts throughout; but it is perhaps symbolic of the dualism and contradictory role of the aristocracy that it was a Herbert, lord lieutenant of Wiltshire, who in the 1640s turned his forces against the king.

In France during this period the tension between monarchy and nobility flared up into a long and bloody struggle. It is, of course, well known that the French civil wars derived from powerful secular no less than religious causes, though the issue has been obscured by the intense religious emotions which intervened in the contest. The Calvinist movement in France had first, in the mid-sixteenth century, taken hold upon the merchant and the artisan; and its early martyrs—as in Marian England—came from the humblest stock. But by the time the civil wars began in 1562 the nobility, both high and provincial, had joined in and indeed taken over control.[1] Contemporaries in France recognised the importance of distinguishing between the two wings of the movement, describing the one group as 'Huguenots of religion', and the other group as 'Huguenots of state'. These latter stood for much more than religious dissent. They represented the long-standing hostility of the ruling families of provincial France to the power of Paris; to the crown and its ally, the Catholic church; and, above all, to the Guises, the family most closely identified with that church and most bitterly opposed to the aims and interests of these provincial and often decaying noble houses. (The traditional use of the expression 'provincial nobility' in part confuses the issue: most of its members would be regarded in England as belonging not to the nobility but to knightly and gentry families.) It was no wonder that many of them—

---

[1] See below, p. 282.

dissident politically—became the patrons of religious dissidence in the shape of the local Protestant sects; no wonder also, that the crown, whose control over the church was considerable, should resist the emergence of an alternative ecclesiastical system which was a federation of self-governing synods. In France, as in England, it could be assumed that 'no bishop' meant 'no king'. The French crown in the second half of the sixteenth century, like the English crown, had nothing to gain from a puritan revolution, and a good deal to lose.

To many members of the provincial nobility who joined the Huguenots, ideology probably meant less than the simple fact that they were impoverished, and therefore threw in their lot with one or other of the great aristocratic patrons. The same thing happened in Scotland (as in England a century earlier). In Scotland, however, the threat to the provincial baronage came not from over-mighty Catholic magnates like the Guises but from a pseudo-democratic organisation like the Calvinist kirk. Hence in Scotland there was built against the kirk a natural alliance between the old baronage and the old church. In France the tendency was in the opposite direction: but even at a time when Frenchmen's religious emotions were most deeply engaged, the constitutional disorder lay close to the heart of the matter. In France, during these last decades of the Valois rule, bastard feudalism flared up into civil war. In England a century earlier it had been a struggle between two warring houses, in France it was now a struggle between three: Guise, Montmorency and Bourbon, with the feeble government of Catherine de Medici vainly trying to hold the ring. The struggle for power became, in essence, a struggle for the throne. At the end it became also a struggle for the independence of France, more especially as the Guises prepared to lead France into the Spanish orbit. Faced from the 1560s onward with the threat that the French system of government might completely dissolve, men like Jean Bodin sought to shift all authority to the father king, *la grande puissance souveraine*. Bodin's powerful appeal aimed also at minimising the differences between the various faiths, an attitude which, to the faithful, looked like minimising the faiths themselves. The chancellor l'Hôpital however reminded his listeners of what he described as the old French proverb, 'one faith, one law, one king'. It is at this time, writes Henri Hauser, that 'the nations, like the princes, remain attached to the barbarous doctrine of unity of faith'. It was a heavy price to pay in the search for unity in the state.

The impoverishment of the French nobility, like that of the Scottish, tempted—or drove—them into military adventures. In all aspects of these French wars, the economic problems of inflation and poverty intervened, although it is impossible to isolate the economic from the other causes of social change, or estimate the part they played in the vast reduction of local self-determination which the Valois sought and the Bourbon achieved. In England, the economic decay of a section of the aristocracy is equally clear. But in the present state of knowledge about the structure of English society, it is impossible to establish how far this decay took place, and what were its major causes. Undoubtedly, as Professor Lawrence Stone has recently brought out with an abundance of evidence, the cost of living, of eating and drinking, of marrying, of building—and even of dying—drained away whole fortunes. The notorious earl of Oxford, it was said, squandered his inheritance in a bitter and distorted revenge against his wife and his father-in-law, the eminent Lord Burghley. Others lost theirs through incompetence of agrarian administration; and still others may have spent their energies—and perhaps their wealth—in the public service, at the sacrifice of their private estates. But who precisely composed this latter group it is difficult to establish. For, if the royal service drained their income, it was also the source of their wealth, patronage and power. The earl of Leicester's complaint that he was sent without resources to fight in the Netherlands for the queen reads strangely when his handling of the war chest is closely examined. The earl of Essex was given by the queen large grants of land and the profits of office—for example, the farm of the sweet wines—but never enough. The earl of Oxford was also rewarded by the queen, but in this case at the expense of the bishop of Ely. It has recently been suggested that such aristocratic decline as took place may have derived from social rather than economic causes, for example, the heavy burden of finding dowries which might face a nobleman unluckily possessed of a group of daughters of marriageable age. Recusancy in religion and the fines that went with it might complete the decline of a nobleman's estate. Yet, whatever the causes of aristocratic decay, there were also powerful causes of aristocratic advance: the fortunate discovery of minerals on the estate; the application to the lands of newer techniques, and up-to-date methods of administration, by no means the monopoly of the progressive merchants and lawyers who came out from the towns. But in some cases, undoubtedly, it was the holding of public office which yielded the richest rewards to those who could gain access to it. Office, having been gained by patronage, was itself the instrument of patronage. Patronage meant the ability to build up and hold a following; it meant the access to funds from private suitors and, unofficially, through the public treasury. Through patronage, if successfully operated, lay the path to wealth and the extension of power. But it was a delicate and complex instrument of government. If it could add to the strength of a Burghley, its absence could exacerbate the weakness of an Essex. Its full effects upon the aristocracy of western Europe have yet to be assessed. But, whereas in France Henry IV consciously aimed at bringing the provincial aristo-cracy under a tight centralised rein, a policy ultimately fulfilled by his descendant Louis XIV, in England James I turned aristocratic patronage away from a system of government, as under Elizabeth, into a system of courtly favouritism. Patronage and favouritism, on the surface, seem largely the same. But in fact, the one, patronage, was a system of rule appropriate and practical for its day. The other, favouritism, was merely the reward from the public resources for irrelevant personal qualities. Favouritism is patronage in a condition of utter decadence. But the causes for the rise or decline of the nobility as a class are still surrounded by obscurity. Perhaps Thomas Wilson's vague summary, which he recorded at the end of the sixteenth century, is about as far as, at present, we can go: 'Some daily decay, some increase according to the course of the world.'

If the causes are obscure, the slow decline of the role of the aristocracy in the constitution is clear enough. The end of the sixteenth century and beginning of the seventeenth saw in England the continuation of a process which can be traced back to at least the Reformation Parliament of 1529–36. The disappearance of the abbots from the House of Lords, the reduction in status of the bishops, the dilution of the lay aristocracy by large creations of a new peerage—all these played their part. Thomas Wilson declared that the monarchy deliberately helped the middle class in their upward climb at the expense of the aristocracy, and thereby clipped the wings of their insolencies. Wilson's hindsight oversimplifies the issue. It reflects more a situation which had arisen than the policy which caused it. But another commentator on this decline went so far as to say, at the beginning of Elizabeth's reign, that the crown and Commons alone constituted a parliament. If this was an extreme, indeed a ludicrous opinion, as was the assertion that a member of the Commons carried greater weight than a peer, it was followed, in the next century, by the more realistic observation that the House of Commons could command three times the wealth of the House of Lords. More significant still, Francis Bacon was arguing in 1593 that the grant of taxation was exclusively the concern of the elected house, a doctrine which, only in the present century, and not without difficulty, was at last written into the British constitution.

Here was the crux of the issue; and it divided the constitutional history of England from that of France. For the English parliamentarians tightened their grasp upon the revenue system at the very time when the members of the French Estates General were forced to relax theirs. The English system of taxation was—at least in theory—based firmly on consent. In France, there remained a good deal of obscurity. Claude de Seyssel, writing at the beginning of the sixteenth century, argued that royal necessity did not have to wait for popular consent: the monarch and people were so bound together by mutual obligation that the royal necessity, and therefore the royal right to taxation, overrode the property rights of the subject. The crown should, of course, be prudent. But prudence in politics is elusive of definition. In England extraordinary taxation—that is, taxation beyond what the crown took by custom—was *ipso facto* within the jurisdiction of parliament. Extraordinary demands required the special consent of the nation. In France, theorists like

Chasseneuz argued the precise opposite. They claimed that extraordinary taxation was determined by the extraordinary conditions of the time and these justified the emergency rights of the crown to tax without consent. This, it was held, was not arbitrary taxation. Chasseneuz is quite clear that necessity alone justified the royal exercise of this right to taxation; otherwise it was indefensible. But since this opportunity existed—with the prince the sole authority on when an emergency could be said to have arisen—the whole constitutional defence against arbitrary taxation could be washed away. The English parliamentarians saw this danger clearly enough. So did John Bates in the celebrated case of 1606 when, in effect, he resisted the right of the crown to determine the need for special taxation without parliament. Bates lost the battle but—when their time came—the parliamentarians won the war. In France constitutional resistance to the fiscal prerogative crumbled. In England constitutional resistance brought deadlock in government for half a century—and then victory to the constitutional opposition. It is true that 1614, the year of the last meeting of the Estates General until the French Revolution, is also the year of the Addled Parliament. (It was called 'addled' presumably because it was even more addled than the others under the early Stuarts.) But in England parliament possessed impressive powers of recovery and, a quarter of a century later, carried through the greatest constitutional revolution in English history. In France, the Estates General, serving no financial purpose and exercising no financial control, was not summoned again after 1614. Its demise made possible the rise of the Bourbon absolutism of the *Ancien Régime*: its reassembly in 1789 symbolised the end of the *Ancien Régime*.

It was on this very issue of taxation that the survival and strength of the assemblies of western Europe depended. For, unless the power to grant taxation was vested in the assembly, the prince had no incentive to summon it. But if it possessed that power, it could use it to extort a share in the crown's authority to govern. The crown must either lose money or lose power. The notion of a close marriage between the sixteenth-century monarchies and the parliamentary bourgeoisie scarcely exists outside the text-books. It was at most a chequered honeymoon. In Spain that partnership never came into being, nor did it in Germany. In France the provincial assemblies were often responsive to the royal demands; but the Estates General arrived without a mandate to grant funds and departed without the gratitude of the monarch or any wish on his part to see it again. Even in England, the so-called love-play between Elizabeth I and her faithful Commons finished up sometimes with the lady in tears. The association between crown and estates was at best an uneasy relationship and at worst an unseemly brawl.

To meet its administrative bills and pay its official salaries, a government could do one of two things. It could seek to increase its taxes upon the nation; or it could in one way or another leave the officials to collect their own fees from the public. Or the government could try a combination of both methods. To increase direct taxation—with or without the approval of the estates—raised formidable problems at every stage. For its impact, uneven and clumsy, often fell heaviest on those least able to bear it. In those countries, such as France and Spain, where the crown was not dependent on the assembly of the estates for grants of supply, a large proportion of the taxes came from those sections of the community whose resistance was weakest—for example the peasantry—but whose resources were equally slender. From the whole community it came through taxes upon trade and industry, for example the Spanish *alcabala*: crude expedients, shortsighted, unimaginative, harmful to the national economy. In England the system of direct taxation, with all its faults, fell more broadly upon the nation—here it was the aristocracy which was not exempt and the poorest section of the peasantry which was—but it was held more tightly within the parliamentary grasp. So the English government, too, had to fall back on indirect taxation.

The Elizabethan and early Jacobean system of indirect taxation had a longer continuous history in this country than had direct taxation. But it had become an unstable amalgam of medieval expedients modernised in a half-hearted way to do service in a later age. The customs dues are a striking example of this. The *ancient customs*, dating back to 1275, provided an export duty on wool, hides, tin and leather. To these had been added the subsidies of the middle of the fourteenth century, better known as *tunnage and poundage*, on wine and other commodities imported and exported. From the early fifteenth century, the practice was to grant them for the life of the monarch. This was in itself a compromise, for the merchants, as well as the baronial opposition, had resisted the crown's sporadic imposition of these taxes upon trade without the consent of parliament. By this compromise, the crown acknowledged that such consent was necessary while parliament acknowledged the royal necessity to enjoy these taxes for life. But there were still loose ends in the system. The Hanseatics had the special privilege of paying lower rates than the native English. At the same time goods were universally underestimated for customs purposes. Valuations were made somewhat more realistic by the new book of rates issued shortly before the end of Mary's reign in 1558. But they were not significantly raised again until 1608. Meanwhile the whole customs system, quite apart from smuggling, was riddled with mismanagement and corruption. Hence the development of customs farming by which the crown leased out some of these indirect taxes for a lump sum for each year and left the lessee to seek greater rewards from customs than the crown had hitherto been able to obtain. Farming was employed during the middle years of Elizabeth's reign, then more or less discarded, revived at the end of the reign, and used extensively under

James I. And then in 1625, at the beginning of Charles I's reign, parliament broke an old precedent by granting him tunnage and poundage for only one year. He ignored it, but the basic political weakness of the whole revenue structure was laid bare for all to see.

This marshalling of the forces by both sides in the matter of taxes upon trade was merely one of many signs that the Commons recognised that the central weakness of the early Stuart monarchy lay in its revenue system; and that the monarchy recognised it too. The other taxes upon trade were of less importance. Purveyance and pre-emption (rights of the royal household to obtain transport and to purchase provisions at favourable prices) caused a good deal of irritation for a very limited reward to the crown. Some revenue came also from the issue to private individuals of monopolies in industry and trade. But these bred for Elizabeth I a major constitutional crisis in the last parliament of her reign and fed the discontents of the opposition throughout the whole of the next reign. Meanwhile, on the one side resistance and on the other incompetence and corruption cut back sharply whatever modest expectations from indirect taxation the government still clung to. On top of this the severe depressions in trade, for example at the end of the sixteenth century and in the second decade of the seventeenth, drained at the source the inadequate revenue from commerce. In Spain the burden was heavier, in the shape of the notorious *alcabala*, a 10 per cent tax on nearly all commercial transactions. It had, at various times, been converted into an annual lump sum, the *encabezamiento*, which under Philip II came to be worth the equivalent of well over half a million pounds sterling. It bled white the state of Castile, the most industrious of the Spanish kingdoms; and when in 1572 a comparable system was imposed in the Netherlands, it tore to shreds their threadbare patience. Already a rebellious Calvinism had taken root in a number of industrial and commercial centres, including Antwerp; but in the *alcabala* the whole merchant class saw their very economic existence laid under menace. Freedom, autonomy and prosperity thus shared a common peril and bred a doughty and unconquerable resistance. As a result, war and the heavy cost of maintaining distant armies shifted the Netherlands from the credit to the debit side of the Spanish fiscal balance sheet. Netherlands unity in resistance proved ephemeral but the drain upon Spain's resources lasted on into the next century.

In France, as in metropolitan Spain, the crown's revenues were limited less by constitutional restraints than by its physical incapacity to gather in its revenues. The Estates General could neither grant nor withhold taxes but could only recommend their grant by local estates. From the Estates General of 1560 the crown came away without even the promise of this aid. Instead it was given gratuitous advice from the second and third orders that the first order, the clergy, could be called upon to play a larger part in meeting the national debt. The clergy took the warning

and made a substantial contribution. The king too drew his own conclusion and without ado—since consent was not forthcoming—imposed
a wine tax as an executive decision and, at the same time, continued to
collect the *taille*. The Estates General of 1576 recited anew the lessons of
its predecessor and indeed went a good deal further. But it was itself
trapped in a contradiction. Representing as it did aggressive Catholic
opinion, and committed to a policy of extinguishing the Huguenot forces,
it displayed no comparable zeal in recommending funds for the purpose.
(In this its members resembled the English parliamentarians of the early
seventeenth century who wanted an aggressive foreign policy without
yielding the supply to sustain it.) In an assembly confronted with this
dilemma, Jean Bodin emerged as the spokesman in the third estate of that
minority opinion hostile to a religious uniformity imposed by force, and
as a spokesman also of that majority opinion hostile to the fiscal immunities enjoyed by the nobility and the clergy. If in the first of these objectives
Bodin failed to carry the third estate with him, in the resistance to taxation
he succeeded. The polite refusal to grant the royal demands for funds was
couched in language which made the constitutional position plain beyond
dispute: 'The deputies were *without the power* to act otherwise.' It was a
categoric declaration of *non possumus*.

That, too, had its price. The Estates General never came to a true
maturity in any way comparable to the English parliament. Instead provincial autonomy, deeply embedded in the French constitution, history
and psychology—and shown in the unwillingness of the local electors to
allow their deputies to be anything more than delegates—starved the
Estates General of the life-blood of power. Hence, lacking the authority
to grant money, the Estates General never gained the capacity to make
political bargains with the crown or enter into any share in political
control. Having no authority to pay the piper, it never acquired the right
to call the tune. The great incursions into the sphere of the prerogative,
so characteristic of late Elizabethan and early Jacobean England, were
impossible in contemporary France. The struggle around and against the
French throne took place instead on the battlefield in the last third of the
sixteenth century; and as victory went to the Bourbons, the prospects of
effective national self-government were extinguished for centuries. In
England, too, in the middle of the seventeenth century, the issue was fought
out on the battlefield; but the cause had already been won in the first
months of the Long Parliament. Victory had gone the other way.

In Spain, the constitutional conflict took another form. In both Castile
and Aragon the Spanish kings had been faced with assemblies which made
far more extensive claims than did the Estates General of France. The
Cortes of Castile traditionally claimed that no new tax should be imposed
without its being consulted; but in general it was not obstructive, although
a group of proctors might declare that the grant would not be upheld

in their own province. Yet, although the Cortes of Castile were much less representative than the French Estates General—only some of the towns were represented and the nobility and clergy were in practice not summoned—its deputies none the less *could* commit the towns which had sent them. However, in any case the amounts received from these sources were proportionately small compared with the total commitments of the Spanish crown. In Aragon there was a sharp contrast. There were four estates in the Cortes (with the nobility divided into a greater and lesser section) and its powers were considerable. Led by the vigorous, politically conscious nobility, the Cortes had stubbornly and successfully held fast to its privileges and its purse-strings. But, by the end of the century, after the Perez fiasco of 1591–2,[1] its powers declined. With the collapse of the rebellion, the king seized the opportune moment to reduce Aragonese self-determination, exploited in any case for noble interests. The aristocracy's rights of voting, though not of representation, in the Cortes were diminished. More important, the Cortes' control over the use of the national revenue—essential to any control of policy—was largely reduced.[2]

The governments of sixteenth-century Europe found themselves faced with relatively slender resources against ever-mounting commitments. Philip II had begun his reign with a virtual declaration of bankruptcy; Henry II of France was likewise hastened towards the treaty of Cateau-Cambrésis by the yawning deficit in his revenues. Elizabeth I of England inherited a large debt from her sister and a corrupt currency to make things worse. It was possible, during the middle years of her reign, to combine stringent economies at home with minimal commitments abroad; but, even so, the balance between income and expenditure was a fragile one and did not survive until the end of the reign. Yet even this modest achievement never came into sight for other monarchies. The French civil wars sapped the limited resources of the crown and bled the monarchy white; the Spanish king's imperial burdens far outweighed even the heavy yield of bullion coming in from the New World. Flung hither and thither in search of ready cash, driven to piecemeal expedients of the most primitive kind, the governments were obliged to seek relief by putting up for auction the machinery of government itself. The distortion of public office for fiscal gain—a phenomenon familiar throughout western Europe—was a desperate and bankrupt device, in part to run government on the cheap, in part to make a profit—if not a virtue—out of necessity. Such a clumsy manœuvre was inescapable. For the governments of Europe were faced with a situation in which the middle classes could not, or would not, carry the major share of the costs of national government.

But if the middle classes proved uncooperative, the monarchies themselves, in relation to the middle classes, were ambiguous to a degree. In

[1] See below, pp. 250–1.
[2] See also below, pp. 253–8, for Spain's Italian possessions.

France the crown sometimes opposed the oligarchical powers of the gilds and aimed at bringing them more directly under national control. But the policy was only unevenly carried through. And at other times the crown quite simply sold *lettres de maîtrise* which in fact gave men the necessary authority to set up as masters of gilds. In Spain the history of the Mesta—the powerful corporation of sheep-breeders—in the later sixteenth century provides an interesting example of the government on the one hand, and the powerful sheep-trading gilds on the other, endeavouring to profit at each other's expense. For example, the Mesta had purchased outright from the exchequer the sheep-tolls collected for the crown. In time of inflation this arrangement showed a handsome return to the Mesta. So did various other privileges purchased from the impoverished exchequer. But having sold privileges to the Mesta, the government now proceeded also to sell privileges *against* the Mesta, that is, to independent sheep masters. At the same time, having sold exemptions to the Mesta from old dues, it proceeded to impose new taxes upon sheep, thus requiring the whole process of exemption purchase to begin all over again. This process was useful at first but it was coming within sight of killing the goose which was laying the golden eggs. The early seventeenth century saw the emergence of a thoroughly decadent Mesta, with no compensatory improvement in agriculture outside the corporation to set in its place.

These manœuvres are merely examples of a widespread series of attempts made throughout Europe to tax the economy by subterfuge; to use existing commercial and industrial processes as a fiscal sponge. They necessarily involved the distortion of the economy; and this was proceeding on a massive scale. The best manifestation is the widespread sale of office. The term itself is a very broad one. It covers a variety of different procedures instituted for a variety of different purposes. In its simplest form it meant the sale of existing public offices by the government or indeed the erection of special offices simply in order to sell them. It could take the more indirect form of the sale of economic controls—for example, customs farming or monopolies—so that the purchaser guaranteed a capital sum or an income in return for a free hand to use his executive and administrative skills to extract such profits as he was able. Finally, it could take the form of the canalisation of the grant of office through ministers or their dependants, who charged fees for their services—fees variously and loosely described as gifts, rewards, perquisites and bribes. In practice the existing system, if so diffuse and diverse a method can be thus described, often partook of more than one of these processes. But it owed its importance fundamentally to its dual purpose: it brought in a revenue to the crown at the same time as it transferred the burden of administration to private persons. For example, the customs system was notoriously inefficient and the government was forced to resort to customs farming.

Thus, the farm allotted to Mr Customer Smythe in 1570 extended over all the import duties of London and its satellite ports. It lasted nearly twenty years and proved rewarding to both the crown and Smythe. But critics of the farm considered that the government was being underpaid and the farm was brought to an end in 1588. There followed a thoroughly disappointing period of direct government control with the result that the end of the century saw a reversion to customs farming. Here was a clear admission that an indirect civil service could prove more useful to the exchequer than one operated by the government itself. This, of course, does not apply to the creation of a sinecure or to the grants of patents of nobility. They brought in revenue but they rendered no service.

The need for a bureaucracy was, of course, nothing new. But in the post-Reformation period the problem assumed urgent and growing proportions. For the medieval monarchies always, as it were, had at their disposal a bureaucratic reservoir. But the bureaucrats had been supplied and paid elsewhere, namely, by the church. This was less true of the payments to the military class, which had to be met largely out of feudal lands or the king's revenues—or out of those of a conquered people. But the administrative class had consisted of churchmen and was paid for by the church; and without this rudimentary framework of a civil service, the king's government could never have gone on. But the sixteenth century saw a severe weakening of the church, in Catholic as well as Protestant nations—with exceptions such as Spain on the one hand and Geneva on the other. The natural reservoir of administrators began to go down: in any case, the mood of the time made intolerable the whole notion of an ecclesiastical monopoly of government office. In other words, the crown could no longer hope to run the state with a civil service paid for by the church. At this very time, also, the volume of administrative duties vastly increased, as the governments assumed enlarged responsibilities at home and abroad, in church and state, locally and centrally. The sixteenth century saw, therefore, the rise of the secretary of state all over Europe. Through him flowed a mass of directives to all corners of the realm; back to him came a mass of information from all parts of the continent. In England in the second half of the century the office of the secretary of state became a highly sophisticated, elaborate machine; in France it remained primitive, with the secretaries leading a wretched, overworked, hand-to-mouth existence. Meanwhile the output of official papers reached staggering proportions. If Philip II of Spain is rightly called *le roi paperassier*, the surviving manuscripts in the English Public Record Office, and in the *Archives Nationales* in Paris, give some measure of what was going on elsewhere. Administration multiplied itself, grew diversified, technical—and costly. Each government in its turn was faced with the appalling task of meeting a spendthrift demand for manpower and money with the ancient and restricted revenues of government. This indeed was the crisis of government in the late sixteenth century. It formed an intimate part of the political crisis of the age.

It was perhaps natural enough that the holder of a public office, if the grant was for life or if he held it for a long period, should come in time to regard his office as almost a piece of property, a kind of freehold which he could pass on to his heirs. This was all the more likely when, in spite of the protocol and extreme formality of the documents produced, the important part of the work was in fact done on an informal, intimate basis between monarch and minister, or between minister and trusted assistant. This was the case with the secretary of state in both France and England. It was a common practice in the France of Catherine de Medici for the secretaries of state to bring in their relations to carry some of the burdens of administration and to be trained as their successors. In England in the later part of Elizabeth's reign, Lord Burghley brought in his younger son, Sir Robert Cecil, to help in the general work of political management, as well as in the more specialised duties of the Court of Wards. An able and apt pupil, Robert Cecil became secretary of state in 1596 and, after his father's death, Master of the Court of Wards in 1599. Within that same institution the family of Hare held the office of clerk for several generations. The succession from father to son could, in some cases, be defended since the funding of experience in one family could make for the more efficient conduct of affairs. But the sixteenth century had seen the increasing use of 'reversions', with officials disposing of their appointments to other men— at a price. This widespread practice alarmed the monarchies who saw the control of appointments, in effect, passing from their hands without any certainty as to the ability or probity of the successor. Elizabeth I was hostile to the practice but could do nothing to stop it. In France, in spite of restraining legislation, the practice continued.[1] Indeed here, having failed to stop it, the government decided to take a share in the proceedings, as for example did Charles IX in 1568 by imposing a tax on the transfer of office. But more important than any share that the government might have in the profits of the business conducted privately was the profit to be gained by itself selling—and creating for sale—numerous offices of state. The *Paulette* of 1604 was not an innovation but completed this process under which the holders of many offices were virtually guaranteed their right of inheritance in return for an annual fee to the crown. Since the profits of office came from the public at large, this was one more example of the crown taxing the nation at one stage removed. But this process had a considerable influence on the economy and structure of contemporary society. The creation of an elaborate vested interest in officialdom which was self-regarding was often of no help to the crown. It necessarily set bounds to the advancing autocracy of the early seventeenth-century kings; and the crown was forced in France to discover new officials and new

[1] See also below, p. 316.

taxes outside the existing bureaucracy. The office of *intendant* was the answer; but the imposition of the new taxation in the middle of the seventeenth century was one of the causes which turned the established bureaucracy against the crown in the internal struggles of the period.

In Spain, where the crown had been selling offices over a wide field, central and local (but not senior administrative ones or any judicial offices), numerous inessential posts were created simply in order that they might be sold. In France, likewise, this process became so extensive that Loyseau could allege that half the citizens of towns were functionaries. In England the sale by the crown of local offices was unknown; but in Switzerland the bailiffs of the Grisons, who had bought their appointments for substantial sums, proceeded to mismanage their offices in pursuit of gain. This commerce in administration reached up into the heart of government itself: Henry III of France sold four seats in the council at 15,000 francs apiece. Moreover, the general rise of the *noblesse de robe* to a veritable fourth estate in the realm carried also tax exemptions, as it did in Spain; while the sale of patents of nobility was one more of the disastrous ways of selling the future for immediate gains. (On the other hand, the sale in Spain of patents of legitimacy to the children of clerics was at least fiscally innocuous.) In England the sale of titles did not begin until the coming of James I, which led also to the creation of the hereditary title of baronet, specifically for revenue purposes. But these sales were not at the expense of the future, for nobility in England carried no exemption from tax. Indeed, the sale of baronetcies, significantly enough, began only in 1611, after a major attempt at fiscal reconstruction, the 'Great Contract', had collapsed. But if the English government never put its great offices of state up for auction, throughout its lesser officialdom and its quasi-civil service private enterprise was rampant.

A striking example of the interplay of government and private enterprise in fiscal matters was displayed in the right enjoyed by the English crown in wardship and the related feudal dues. The end of the middle ages had of course not seen the end of feudalism in Europe: in varying degrees the holders of feudal rights—as well as those who had bought their way into them—extracted where they could the increasingly irrelevant profits from these ancient tenures. But only in England were the rights of the crown as feudal overlord raised to a significant position in the revenue system and given a special court to develop and safeguard them. The mere possession of land held in chief by knight service imposed upon the heir, if under age, the full burden of feudal wardship, including the obligation to marry at the will of the crown or of the person who had purchased the wardship: a refusal could mean a crushing forfeit. Thus the right of feudal marriage survived beyond its feudal context and was imposed, in irrelevant circumstances, upon a considerable number of land-holders. This was largely a royal right—with scattered relics surviving among other lords; and it was a right which was on many occasions sold to strangers for a capital sum, and for a further rent charge for the wards' lands. It led in some cases to grave social abuses and it raised a considerable outcry. But it brought in money to the crown and it brought in even more in fees and profits to the crown servants. In very many cases the crown was simply transferring to the landed classes the task of paying the salaries of the civil service. But far more was involved than this. For, in exploiting these sources of indirect and unparliamentary taxation, the crown was parrying the increasing efforts of the opposition, especially in the early seventeenth century, to bring policy—and ministers—under parliamentary control. Such fiscal contortions on the part of the crown were particularly necessary in a country like England where parliamentary consent was essential for direct taxation as well as for new taxes upon trade. Hence the increasing importance of disguised indirect taxation of which monopolies furnish one example and wardship another.

A further consequence followed from this extension of private control in public administration: the distrust of public administration itself. For it looked like the subversion of public interests to private ends: in short, corruption. But the word corruption is rarely defined and has been as much bandied about by historians as it was indiscriminately used by contemporaries. There were of course numerous examples of justice being subverted by fraud or force. 'The law is ended', said a contemporary rhyme, 'as a man is friended.' There were examples of the despoiling of the crown by those who had been called to its service. These practices are, of course, corrupt; and an immature—or ill-paid—administration anywhere in the world, at any time, displays precisely these qualities. But the expression 'corruption', as used of the sixteenth and seventeenth centuries, has been extended and applied to the whole range of official perquisites, gifts and favours; and the structure of society and government has thereby been obscured. For, in many cases, these gifts were virtually fees, and no more than another facet of that indirect and inefficient taxation upon which the governments perforce depended. In all cases they were a double sign, of the rudimentary and incomplete control of the crown over its civil service and of the gross inadequacy of the public revenues to provide sufficient taxes to sustain its civil service by direct salaries. It is true that many of these gifts were to obtain favours at public expense. But far more were routine payments, made by all and taken by all. This was not corruption but something inherent in the faulty revenue system of the day. In any state in the modern period, the extent to which this defective system survives varies inversely with the success of the government in taxing the nation.

But what happened when the recipients of gifts were not civil servants but royal favourites—the *mignons* of Henry III of France, the Carrs and Villiers of James I of England? It was only then that the system was indeed distorted into corruption. It was only then that these indirect revenues seeped away into the thirsty soil of luxury and greed. Then the system became barren and twisted; and national interests were sacrificed to a decadent court. As a result the very word courtier acquired the attributes of corruption itself. But that, too, is to confuse the whole with the part. For the 'court' in the age of personal government meant two things. It meant, in its narrow sense, that section of the aristocracy and the household servants called to the immediate service of the palace, with all its luxury, ceremonial and gilded artifice. In this milieu the personal favourite flourished. But the court meant also the whole substantial body of ministers and civil servants called to the public service of the crown. Sometimes a man was a personal favourite as well as a minister, as was the case with the earl of Leicester in Elizabethan England. Many contemporaries correctly understood this, as did, for example, the journalists of the eighteenth century who spoke of 'court' and 'country'. By 'court' they meant simply that party which was in public office at the time. By the 'country' party they meant those out of office. 'Court' meant the palace at Westminster; but it also meant the civil service of Whitehall.

The pattern of politics at the centre was reproduced on a smaller scale in the provinces. A local magnate had enormous resources of power and profit both in offices under him on his estates and in his recommendation for public office in the capital. Such a man was the duke of Norfolk in the first decade of Elizabeth I's reign; but with his execution in 1572, no aristocrat emerged in East Anglia to take his place. Instead, the whole patronage system became the battlefield for bitter local feuds among the upper gentry, with prestige no less than profit in the balance. For example, to be placed on the commission of the peace—or to be evicted from it— raised or reduced a man's social standing to an impressive degree. In the west country the earls of Pembroke were continually pressed by suitors for office. On the other hand the office of deputy lieutenant was in some counties difficult to fill while in others it was much sought after. The degree of patronage in English local society is difficult to assess; but it was clearly widespread and served to nourish a flexible yet firm relationship on a local territorial basis. That is to be seen in religion as well as politics, where the country-house might serve as a local centre for religious dissent, whether Catholic in England or Huguenot in France. This quality is reflected no less in the economic than in the social structure of the provinces. In western Europe at this period, there was a far greater measure of free cultivation than in eastern Europe and beyond. In those regions a new and tougher form of agrarian feudalism was emerging at the very time when in western Europe many of its harsh qualities were passing away. None the less, the power of the local gentry in the west survived and sometimes grew stronger, but it was power sustained by their role as *rentiers* and by a new kind of social cohesion. It is true that the pressure of rent could in its way be as burdensome and inexorable as the earlier pressure of personal serfdom; but the quality of society was changing. The lord of the manor was becoming the squire of the village.

In France those with vested interests in office—at least in its upper ranges—emerged as a fairly distinct class, the *noblesse de robe*: but this applied to only one sector of the administration. It could not link them as a class to the holders of the innumerable petty offices diffused throughout France. In England, even at the centre, the government servants lacked that constancy of interest and attitude needed to ensure a stable following to the privy council, in parliament and in the country. Parliamentary patronage, and patronage of office, could guarantee no certain support to a magnate in a Commons' debate over some great religious or other issue which divided the nation. Lord Burghley gathered into his clientage men like James Morrice, who later on embarrassed the government by taking a minority view. In successive decades in the first half of the seventeenth century, as the conflicts between their loyalty to crown and to principle intensified, many officials followed principle—or interest— against the will of the king. In France likewise, at the time of the Fronde, many office-holders identified themselves with the local population against the government, for the mixed reasons of interest and tradition. The lesson of these years and what went before demonstrates the social complexity of office-holding. The office-holders of the governments of Europe formed neither a coherent body of vested interests nor a uniform class or caste. In England the local government was in the hands of amateurs from the lord lieutenant down through the justices of the peace and on to the parish constable. In France it was much more professionalised from the *intendant* downwards. But in neither case could a national directive override the interests of the provinces without splitting the loyalty of the officials. Moreover, those without access to the profits of office had cause to deepen their discontent; and this was especially strong against court favourites with little to commend them except their charm. But in the absence of party politics, patronage provided—however inadequately— the broad channels of political command.

It is the practice to speak of this large and growing body of bureaucrats, drawn to the service of the government, as belonging to the middle class. The term is quite imprecise; but it has some utility in that it differentiates its members from the older aristocracy who, by a rapidly fading tradition, claimed an hereditary right to govern and advise. It also differentiates the bureaucracy from the artisan and peasant classes. But it was essentially an open class, not a caste. It led on quite often to fairly rapid promotion into the aristocracy at one end (cemented often by marriage) and at the other end it gave access to the talented man of humble birth. The medieval church had always supplied a channel such as this, of which the career of Cardinal Wolsey is the best and last exemplar in England; but by the end of the sixteenth century the secularisation of political power had proceeded far. It was still possible in the middle of the seventeenth century for ecclesiastics like Laud and Juxon to rise high in the Protestant state, and for cardinals to rule in Catholic France. But in most high offices the cleric was giving way to the lawyer and the businessman. After Wolsey came Thomas More, Thomas Cromwell, Gresham, the Seymours, the Dudleys and the Cecils. In France the secretaries of state such as de Laube-spine, Pinart and Villeroy were laymen. John Maitland of Thirlstane, appointed chancellor of Scotland in 1587, was the first to hold that office without being either a bishop or a great lord. Against this process there was an outcry, not from the weakened church but from the older aristocracy and their dependants. In England, the rising of the northern earls in 1569 had as one of its declared objects the elimination of the corrupting influence of upstarts like Cecil, thereby echoing the slogan of a generation before when the Pilgrimage of Grace aimed at eliminating the upstart Cromwell. In Sweden, Charles IX was criticised by the aristocracy for relying on secretaries of menial birth. It was, indeed, in Sweden, a nation far less supplied with lawyers, merchants and industrialists than were England and the Netherlands, that the growth of a professional bureaucracy was too long delayed. In this Sweden resembled Catholic Spain rather than Protestant England or Holland. But in western Europe the situation was changing decisively in favour of the professional middle class. In contrast, a state like Poland, with no bureaucratic middle class at the disposal of the government, was obliged to function mainly through an irresponsible aristocracy, with results which are well known.

All over western Europe the monarchies suffered a severe decline of wealth, either absolutely, or relatively to the wealth of the leading sections of the commercial, industrial and landed classes. This disparity was intensified as the governments found themselves obliged to take on the heavier, and more expensive, tasks of domestic administration, diplomacy and war. In the second half of the sixteenth century, England, France, Spain and the Netherlands assumed burdensome military commitments and, in its last two decades, they were continuously at war. By one means or another taxation had to be increased; and, in all cases, indirect taxation (either on trade or by the exploitation of technical anachronisms, like wardships) offered the most elastic source. But it could be stretched beyond endurance as the response of the Low Countries to the *alcabala* showed, in which case it could hasten the advance towards costly and disastrous war. In Spain resistance to indirect taxation was weak, but the whole economy of the nation was already enfeebled, with its society distorted into preferences for non-productive pursuits, of which the most important were the church and the armed services. Yet if this period saw the beginning of the decay of the Spanish economy, it saw also the culmination of the decay of the Spanish Cortes, as the crown emancipated itself from their consent for taxation. The same thing was happening in France. In England the constitution allowed to the monarchy only limited powers of manœuvre in the field of taxation. Hence the advent of war in 1585, with its call for money, gave parliament an increasingly strong claim to influence government policy, a claim it would never again renounce. Elizabeth tried to counter this by economies in expenditure, the early Stuarts by stretching to breaking-point the dubious devices of the prerogative. Indeed so fragile was the fiscal prerogative of the early Stuarts that it needed only a minor war on the Scottish border in 1638–9 to shatter it beyond hopes of recovery.

In England the aristocracy never became a caste and the landed gentry never became a lesser nobility. Hence the middle and upper classes stood in much closer relation to each other than they did to the monarchy; and, in time of crisis, had much more in common with each other than they had with the crown. That was the case in the shires, and it was the same men who felt at ease with each other in the House of Commons. The institution of justices of the peace, said Francis Bacon, 'knits noblemen and gentlemen together, and in no place else but here in England are noblemen and gentlemen incorporated: for abroad in other countries noblemen meddle not with any parcel of justice, but in martial affairs; matter of justice that belongs to the gownmen; and this is it that makes those noblemen the more ignorant and the more oppressors; but here amongst us they are incorporated with those that execute justice, and so being warriors are likewise made instruments for peace; and that makes them truly noble'.

This, of course, was an idealistic picture; but, as ever, Bacon put his finger on the crucial point. There can be little doubt that English society was more closely knit at this time than was true of most countries in Europe. This was a major social fact. Alongside it was the major constitutional fact that direct taxation required parliamentary consent and indirect taxation was relatively inelastic. These two things preserved the English parliament at a time when comparable institutions elsewhere were passing into desuetude.

CHAPTER VI

INTERNATIONAL DIPLOMACY AND INTERNATIONAL LAW

THE treaties of Cateau-Cambrésis signed at the bishop's château on the outskirts of Cambrai on 2 and 3 April 1559 marked the abrupt end of one era of European diplomacy and the beginning of another. The signatories were the delegates of the three major Atlantic powers, Spain, France and England. The main issue that was settled was the one that had dominated European power politics since 1494: who was to be paramount in Italy? And it was symptomatic of the new times that the fate of Italy was finally decided around a conference table at which sat not one Italian negotiator, not even a representative of the pope, while the ambassadors and agents of vitally interested parties, Florence and Mantua and the Republic of St Mark's, scrounged for crumbs of information on the fringes of the court at Brussels seventy miles away. Along with the pope and the Italian powers the potentate until recently most concerned about the fate of Italy had been the Holy Roman Emperor, but there was no representative of the empire at the conference either, not even though the next most important question on the agenda was the disposition of the three cities of Metz, Toul and Verdun. With the transfer of the imperial title to the cadet branch of the house of Habsburg, the emperor assumed the role of warden of the eastern marches, vigilant on the Danube, but for the next seventy years intervening only occasionally and feebly in western affairs. Philip II of Spain's willingness to settle the question of Metz, Toul and Verdun if necessary without his uncle Ferdinand's agreement, bartering them away to France in return for French evacuation of Piedmont and Savoy—also imperial, not Spanish, fiefs—was an early indication of his fixed belief that whoever might toy with the imperial sceptre and wear the title of Holy Roman Emperor Elect, the temporal sword of Christendom, the sword of Charlemagne and Frederick Barbarossa, had been handed on to him by his father. This Spanish belief that the substance of imperial power had been transferred to Spain, and with it the emperor's primary responsibility for the defence of the Catholic faith, was another sign of the new times.

Seen from the watershed of Cateau-Cambrésis, and with a view of the country ahead as well as of that behind, the diplomatic history of western Europe in the sixty-five years 1494–1559 shows an essential unity which reduces the differences between its subdivisions to small consequence. Although it was posed in various ways and the immediate stake was now

COUNTER-REFORMATION AND PRICE REVOLUTION

one area and now another, the real question until 1559 was: who is to be master in Italy? A series of dynastic accidents turned the confused battle royal of the earlier wars, in which combatants were always appearing and disappearing and those in the ring were constantly changing sides, into the long grim Habsburg–Valois duel. The manifold responsibilities of the Emperor Charles V complicated the duel with all sorts of extraneous diversions—the theological squabbles of German monks, the domestic embarrassments of an English king, the ancient quarrels of France and Burgundy and the constantly more dangerous intrusions of the Ottoman Turks. Nevertheless, the chief duellists were still, as they had been since Gonzalvo de Córdoba crossed the Straits of Messina, Spain and France, and the prize for which they fought was always Italy. It seems sensible, therefore, as well as convenient to label the whole sixty-five years following Charles VIII's expedition to Naples, the age of the Italian wars.

It did not matter that neither Spain nor France had any rational interest in Italian conquests, and that, whichever won, foreign domination would be a curse to Italy without benefiting the victor. Then, as later, there was nothing rational about the origins of war. War was a way of life, an ingrained habit of late feudal society. The landed aristocracy, who were almost everywhere the ruling class, had no other serious occupation and indeed no other valid excuse for existence. Kings existed to lead them from one war to another, and thus keep them from one another's throats. And for what should the two most powerful kings of Europe fight, except for Europe's most glittering prize? When they had fought until they were both exhausted, the Peace of Cateau-Cambrésis awarded the prize permanently to Spain.

The age of the Italian Wars saw more than forty years of open war between the principal contenders and their chief allies, as against scarcely more than twenty years of uneasy and ill-kept peace. Naturally, in that time, the art of war underwent a considerable development. The army that Charles VIII led over the Alps, with its serried masses of Swiss pikemen, its quick-stepping Gascon light infantry, its train of heavy guns, all to supplement the companies of *gens d'armes d'ordonnance* which were its backbone, was farther ahead of the army of Formigny in its development towards modern efficiency than the professionals of Formigny were ahead of the feudal levies of Agincourt. But the armies that fought at Metz and St Quentin and Gravelines and in the valleys around Siena in the 1550s were so much more modern still as to make the forces that clashed at Fornovo only sixty years before look like medieval hosts. In the interval fire-arms had come into their own, and field entrenchments, the art of siege warfare had been revolutionised, artillery was becoming manœuvrable, and horsemen were beginning to rely on the pistol instead of the lance.[1] Perhaps the change may be summed up by saying that not cavalry but

[1] See vol. II, ch. XVI.

infantry was now the decisive arm and that, in consequence, the leading military power was no longer France, but Spain.

During the whole period of the Italian Wars negotiations played a role not less important than the fleets and armies. At frequent intervals the wars were interrupted by treaties of peace or truce, none of them very durable, and further punctuated by announcements of broken alliances and the conclusion of new ones, by proclamations of fresh Holy Leagues, and the assembly of congresses meant to settle some question or other forever. Meanwhile, all during the fighting, diplomatic conversations went on, always among allies, usually with wavering neutrals, and often between enemies. Under the stimulus of this intense activity the art of diplomacy experienced a development at least as striking as the parallel development of the art of war.

By the later middle ages, western Europeans had developed four means of diplomatic action. First, they used unofficial and semi-official agents for a wide range of more or less tentative contacts. These agents might be mere spies, ostensibly private persons, who could be completely disavowed at need, like some of the servants of Giangaleazzo Visconti and later of Louis XI and, in Italy, of Ferdinand of Aragon. Or they might be privately accredited as Nicodemo da Pontremoli was in the first phase of his residence in Florence. Or they might have some sort of public and quasi-diplomatic status, be legal procurators, perhaps, or even heralds. They could be used to transmit all sorts of confidential communications and conduct all kinds of preliminary negotiations, to cement old alliances or feel out the grounds for new ones, to reassure a friend or keep an eye on a potential enemy. Their chief advantages were secrecy (in the case of procurators and heralds an ostensible mission might mask a real one; less official agents might, with luck, be kept entirely under cover), informality and speed. Their gravest disadvantages were the vulnerability of the agent to attack either *en route* or, if he aroused distrust, at the place of his mission, and his lack of authority to press an agreement home.

These disadvantages were met by the second and commonest means of diplomatic action, the public embassy, in which one or more ambassadors were armed with documents which gave them a special status with atten-dant privileges and immunities, and empowered them to negotiate a particular piece of business or to deliver a particular message. Such embassies were generally held necessary for the settlement of disputes and the conclusion of treaties, and desirable for the paying of official compliments and the delivery of very formal messages or requests.

These two means of diplomatic action, through informal agents and through accredited ambassadors, were frequently supplemented in the fifteenth century by two others at a higher level. To settle a dispute, conclude a peace, or concert a common course of action, congresses were assembled, like the congress of Arras which made peace between France and Burgundy, or the congress of Mantua which Pius II called to arrange a crusade against the Turks. Sometimes the effort was to assemble delegates of all the interested powers, all the powers of Italy, for instance, or all the powers of Christendom, or all those involved as allies in the quarrel to be ended; sometimes only the principal disputants were represented. Usually, though not always, there was a presumably neutral mediator presiding. But regularly each power sent a team of from four to eight delegates with their secretaries, interpreters, couriers and industrious seconds; the headings of the agenda were agreed upon in preliminary discussions; and the congress proceeded thereafter by alternations of public speech-making and private dickering.

Finally there was the face-to-face interview between chiefs of state. For such meetings there were no fixed rules. They might be as stiff with protocol and precaution as Louis XI's conversation with Edward IV on the bridge at Picquigny, or as impromptu and informal as Lorenzo the Magnificent's visit to Naples. They might be surrounded with the pomp and magnificence with which Charles the Bold went to meet the emperor at Trier, or clad in the shabby simplicity with which Frederick III attended the same occasion. The conversations they initiated might be so wary and distant that the same business could have been done more quickly by ambassadors, or so intimate and private that even today historians can only guess at what was actually decided. Only one thing about them was certain: they were desperately risky. It was not just that the prince's person was endangered, though that could be true, as Louis XI discovered at Peronne. More generally undesirable was the excessive publicity which inevitably accompanied them, making their failure far more damaging than any other kind of failure, and so tempting both parties to impracticable commitments, ambiguous agreements and a willingness to accept vague, partial solutions which often led to grave subsequent misunderstandings. Besides, there was the likelihood that two mature politicians with incompatible aims, having discovered that neither would bend to the other's will, would end by disliking each other more bitterly than ever, so that Commines advised princes who wanted to keep friends with one another never to meet.

The fifteenth century knew about these risks. But such is the perennial optimism of politicians and the indestructible confidence of rulers in their own sagacity that sixteenth-century princes continued to seek personal interviews just as they continued to exploit all the other traditional means of diplomatic action. Among sixteenth-century royal interviews one thinks first of the glittering débâcle of the Field of Cloth of Gold and the brilliant successes of Charles V's two visits to England, successes which nevertheless carried within them seeds of trouble more poisonous for the future than the flat failure in France. But though the consequences of those interviews took less than a decade to unfold themselves, Henry VIII was still willing to cross the Channel to talk to Francis I; both Francis and Charles were able to persuade themselves for a season that in personal conversations at Aigues-Mortes they had found solutions which had eluded the patience of their negotiators and the dexterity of the pope; and almost to the day of his abdication Charles V continued to believe that if only he could talk to the king of France face to face, he might win back what diplomacy and arms had failed to recapture.

International congresses had hardly had more success than royal interviews, but the half century which opened with one at Cambrai announced as aiming at a general peace, though all it achieved was a league against Venice, closed with another in the same place again intending a general peace. Equally the age of the Italian wars saw a constant coming and going of special embassies, sometimes as ostentatious as Wolsey's mission to France in the summer of 1527, sometimes quiet and routine. And as had been the earlier practice, the sixteenth century employed unofficial and semi-official agents to supplement exchanges of public embassies during delicate negotiations, or as a substitute for them where publicity would have been dangerous or inappropriate. Sir Thomas Spinelly, during his first years in the Netherlands, may have been an agent of this sort, but better examples are Gian Giacomo Passano, coming to England to talk to Wolsey on behalf of Louise of Savoy, or Christopher Mundt, sounding out the Lutheran princes of Germany for Thomas Cromwell. In the first half century or so of the modern European power struggle, the rival dynasts found all the diplomatic devices inherited from their medieval past useful, but still inadequate for the tasks their ambitions imposed.

The continuous tension in European affairs after Charles VIII's invasion of Italy obliged the greater powers to find machinery for continuous diplomacy. Fortunately the machinery was at hand. A hundred years earlier the Italian states had been held together by the continuous tensions of the last phase of the Visconti effort to dominate the peninsula, and had responded to the pressures and dangers of their situation by beginning to establish permanent resident embassies with one another, at first only for the sake of diplomatic liaison between allies, then, after the Peace of Lodi (1454), regularly among all the major powers and their principal satellites, except for the interruption of war. Before Charles VIII crossed the Alps, the major Italian powers had been exchanging resident ambassadors for nearly forty years, and the first Italian residents had already begun to appear at transalpine courts. The chanceries of the greater dynasties had only to adapt the Italian system to their own not very different practices and needs, adding another to the cluster of importations from Italy which marked the sixteenth-century Renaissance. During the first thirty-five years of the Italian wars they did so. Spain, which had inherited through Aragon the closest experience of Italian diplomacy, led the way; France, until the humiliation of Pavia too confident of its unaided strength, brought up the rear. At first, as had happened in Italy a hundred years before, resident ambassadors were exchanged only between allies; but, as Italian experience had shown, patterns of alliance tend to shift and before 1559 it had begun to seem normal for monarchs with a major stake in the European power struggle to maintain permanent embassies at each other's courts whenever they were at peace, just as this had begun to be the rule in Italy by the time of the Peace of Lodi.

After the Peace of Cateau-Cambrésis one might have expected the transalpine state system to conform to the next phase of the Italian development and establish networks of resident embassies throughout western Europe. Cateau-Cambrésis was, after all, a more definitive peace than Lodi. Its territorial provisions lasted for almost a century. It inaugurated a period in which there was no formally declared war between major European powers for thirty-six years. And although it left Spain in a position clearly paramount, with all the provinces of the Burgundian Netherlands, Franche-Comté, Milan, the Tuscan *Presidios* and Naples added to its older Mediterranean and peninsular dominions and its empire in the New World, yet France, the solid bulk of its territory undiminished and strengthened by the bastions of Metz, Toul and Verdun and the reconquest of Calais, was by no means in a position of hopeless inferiority. Moreover, the reconstitution of an independent Savoy-Piedmont and the detachment from Spain of the Holy Roman Empire and the Austrian hereditary lands broke up the division of western Europe into two irreconcilable blocks, and seemed to promise a period of freer diplomatic manœuvre and a policy, as in Italy after Lodi, of something like a balance of power.

The promise proved false. Instead of widening, the area of diplomatic action constantly narrowed. Perhaps it was not altogether a loss that the era of personal interviews between sovereigns closed abruptly. Queen Elizabeth never left England. Once he got back from the Netherlands, Philip II never left Spain. And Charles V was the last of the Habsburg emperors for a long time to cross the Alps or the Rhine. Catherine de Medici's attempt in 1564–5 to revive personal diplomacy achieved no greater result than her conversations with the duke of Alba at Bayonne; it was fruitless and had no sequel. Similarly the age of great European peace congresses seemed over. If there were no fully declared wars between the great powers in the thirty-six years after Cateau-Cambrésis, there were mounting diplomatic tensions; but almost the only attempt to resolve them by full-scale, formal discussion in the style of the diplomacy of the Italian wars was the curious Anglo-Spanish conference which opened at Bourbourg in the early spring of 1588 and lasted until the guns of the Armada were heard in the Channel. The history of that abortive negotiation shows clearly the change in the atmosphere. No neutral mediator was selected or even seriously considered. Both sides knew that there were no neutrals. The English from the first were pessimistic about any agreement. The Spanish—or rather the delegates sent by the duke of Parma—knew that the whole conference was a ruse, acted in bad faith throughout, and they never even had proper powers or accreditation. The Dutch, whose interests were the hinge of the conference, contemptuously refused to attend at all. But it had been so long since the delegates of two powers of opposing faiths had talked to each other at all that all Europe watched the conversations with the keenest interest, and the zealots of both parties denounced the negotiations as fatal confessions of weakness and evident treason to the principles (the opposing principles) which the two monarchs were supposed to champion.

Throughout the second half of the sixteenth century diplomacy declined because an ideological issue, the difference between Catholics and Protestants, divided Europe into two camps more bitterly irreconcilable and more firmly aligned than any that had ever rallied behind Habsburg and Valois. After the breakdown of the colloquy at Ratisbon and the return of Calvin to Geneva, the lines had begun to harden on both sides, and every subsequent event, the Schmalkaldic War, the triumph of the curialists at Trent, the revenge of the German princes under Maurice of Saxony, the sharp leftward turn of the English Reformation under Edward VI, even an act about the piety and morality of which Catholics and Calvinists were as completely agreed as they were about the burning of Michael Servetus—all served to widen the cleavage and stiffen the ranks.

In the Genevans and their converts and allies in Britain and on the continent, Protestantism had found its militants. Their sense of their election set them free for the work of bringing nearer God's kingdom on earth, and gave them the unflinching courage of early Christian martyrs or Jesuit missionaries. Every refugee from England, Scotland, France and the Netherlands trained for the pastorate at Lausanne and Geneva was not just a man chosen for sound learning, pulpit eloquence and seemly behaviour as a fit bearer of the gospel to his native land, but a man sustained in his dedication to his appointed task by his confidence that God had chosen him to rescue at least some of his fellow-countrymen from error and idolatry. By proudly refusing to subject the church to the dictation of the civil magistrate, by reasserting the essential thesis of Gregory VII that the end of human society is the salvation of souls and that God's appointed means to that end is his church, which must be free and independent to perform its function, Calvin had made sure that wherever there was a minority of his followers strong enough to do so, they would resume the ancient struggle of the spiritual against the temporal power.

With this foundation to build on, it mattered less that Calvin paid the customary lip service to the verse in Romans bidding every soul be subject unto the higher powers than that he provided the Reformed church with an organisation simple, compact and flexible enough to infiltrate across frontiers without the support of such powers, and even in defiance of them. Each Calvinist community of the elect, with its own pastors, teachers, elders and deacons, was an autonomous self-sufficient cell, capable of multiplying by fission or of sustaining itself indefinitely in isolation, but capable, too, of linking itself to all like cells in any given area, within territorial boundaries or across them, by a system of synods and a network of correspondence, as closely and as widely as the dictates of prudence permitted. By the early 1560s these cells had overthrown a government and a church in Scotland, attempted to do the same in France, were preparing something similar in the Netherlands, were influencing public policy in England, and penetrating as far eastward as Bohemia, Poland and Hungary, while all of them, everywhere, vibrated to any impulse which stirred their connecting web. At the centre of the web, Geneva, training school of potential revolutionaries and asylum for unsuccessful ones, could always disavow responsibility for movements beyond its own narrow boundaries, while at the same time supplying its activists with the ideas and exhortations which were their spiritual sustenance, and the books and pamphlets, and sometimes the arms and gunpowder with which, according to opportunity, they sought to advance the common cause.

To this mature, dynamic organisation for religious revolution by political means, with its oecumenical claims and its exclusive dogmas, Rome, before the end of the last session at Trent, was able to oppose a counter-revolutionary force no less rigid in its doctrinal system and no less flexible in its practical politics. Like Geneva, Rome was prepared to use secular rulers whenever it could, and defy and overthrow them whenever it had to. The re-animated church of Rome had not needed Geneva to remind it that Christ's church is universal and coterminous with Christian society, and that every Christian soul owes to it primary allegiance. Long before the treaties of peace were signed at Cateau-Cambrésis, both Calvin's Geneva and the Rome of the Counter-Reformation had gone far beyond the Teutonic pietism and quietism, the Renaissance scepticism and syncretism and the general deference to temporal authority which had seemed to open vistas of possible compromise and ultimate reconciliation in almost every year between Luther's appearance at Worms and the colloquy of Regensburg. By the 1550s neither Rome nor Geneva could envisage any end of their struggle short of the other's complete extermination. Compromise and toleration, when they were not anathema, were accepted simply to gain a breathing spell and the chance to look for a fresh hold. As religious issues came to dominate political ones, any negotiations with the enemies of one's faith looked more and more like heresy and treason. The questions which divided Catholics from Protestants had ceased to be negotiable. Consequently, instead of increasing, as they had done in Italy after the Peace of Lodi, diplomatic contacts diminished. Special embassies continued to go back and forth from time to time between powers in opposing ideological camps, but they were less frequent and, instead of expanding, the network of resident embassies actually contracted.

A chief contributory cause of interruptions in the network of continuous diplomatic contacts was the embassy chapel question. In the first half of the century, even a staunch anti-papalist and anti-clerical like Sir Thomas Wyatt could kneel before the high altar at Valladolid with no more sense of incongruity than his opposite number, Eustache Chapuys, seems to have felt at taking communion at the hands of one of Henry VIII's tame bishops. The question of special services in the embassies first became acute in 1551 when Edward VI's ambassadors to the emperor insisted on using the new English Book of Common Prayer, and Charles V's sense of outrage at the celebration of a heterodox service at his court almost led to a breach of diplomatic relations. Eight years later, the embassy chapel question was important, perhaps decisive, in ending the exchange of resident ambassadors between England and Venice, the only Italian state with which England had maintained continuous diplomatic relations after 1533. In the latter part of her reign Mary I had used as her ambassador her husband's representative, the Spanish resident in Venice. When, shortly after her accession, Elizabeth I prepared to accredit an ambassador of her own to the Republic of St Mark's, the pope solemnly warned the Signory that it must forbid the inclusion of an Anglican clergyman in the ambassador's train, and refuse permission for the performance of any but Catholic rites, even in the privacy of the ambassador's dwelling. The queen's government naturally could not grant the Venetian resident a privilege which the Signory denied hers, and consequently neither party maintained a resident ambassador with the other throughout the queen's reign. The Counter-Reformation papacy seems not to have been as sure as a good many subsequent historians have been that the Italian soul was naturally Catholic and so immune to Protestant propaganda; at any rate, the popes were determined to prevent the establishment of any Protestant chapels at all on Italian soil. Spain agreed heartily, and as a result, throughout the second half of the sixteenth century, there was no resident ambassador of any Protestant power anywhere in Italy.

In 1568 the English embassy in Spain was discontinued in consequence of a dispute over the same question. Dr John Man was a tactless and irritable person at a post where tact and calm were essential, and Anglo-Spanish relations were so bedevilled that it seems likely that whatever the occasion, Dr Man would have managed to embroil himself with Philip II's government or the Inquisition or both before long. But the actual explosion was over whether embassy servants might be permitted to attend services allowed for the ambassador and his immediate personal and official family, and about this the Holy Office and Spanish officialdom were as arbitrary and provocative as Dr Man. Man's reaction was violent enough to justify his punitive detention and subsequent expulsion, and Philip II was careful to make it clear that he did not wish to deny to English ambassadors in Spain a privilege granted to Spanish ambassadors in England, but only to limit the privilege so as to avoid scandal to the orthodox and the possible infection of his Catholic realms with heresy. Nevertheless, Dr Man was not replaced, perhaps because the queen's council believed Man's own view that his troubles were part of a deliberate policy of harassing the English embassy, and that to continue the embassy would be to invite further trouble.

If the harassment of the English embassy was a deliberate policy, it was not Philip II's, any more than the harassment of the Spanish embassy in London was a deliberate policy of Elizabeth I's. Perhaps the most striking development in international relations in the second half of the sixteenth century is the gradual, apparently irreversible deterioration of relations between England and Spain, in spite of the fact that both countries were ruled by strong monarchs who assumed and were conceded the right to direct their own foreign policies, and that both monarchs were sincerely anxious for peace with one another. As dynasts, neither Elizabeth I nor Philip II had any sound reason to want to make war on the other, and many sound reasons not to. Both dreaded the expense of war, Elizabeth because of the slenderness of her purse and her reluctance to tax her subjects, Philip because of the staggering burdens which his inheritance had thrust upon him. Both had urgent immediate reasons to want to continue the old alliance of their ancestors against France, Philip because rebellion in the Netherlands was a constant invitation to French intervention, Elizabeth because her heir presumptive, and in Catholic eyes the rightful tenant of her throne, was Mary Queen of Scots, half French by blood and wholly French by culture and sympathy, on whose behalf there was always the danger that her Valois brother-in-law or her uncles and cousins, the Guises, would take arms. Strategically, England and Spain were necessary to each other. Without Spanish troops to defend them the southern Netherlands would sooner or later be overrun by the French, and England would find her hereditary foe in possession of the whole coastline from Ushant to the mouth of the Scheldt, an intolerable threat. Without England's alliance or, at the very least, neutrality, Spain could not keep touch with the Netherlands by sea and would be forced to depend on a long, roundabout, expensive and basically indefensible line of communications through the Alpine passes and Alsace or Franche-Comté. Meanwhile, England and Spain were each other's best customers. English cloth and tin and corn found a ready market in Spain and through King Philip's Antwerp the Merchant Adventurers reached all the other markets of western Europe. At the same time Castile soap and merino wool were indispensable to some branches of the English textile industry, and if Bilbao cutlery was less in demand than formerly, English consumers took eagerly Spanish oil and fruits and Jerez wines. England was perhaps the one country of Europe where Spanish merchants did not normally have to balance their accounts with hard cash.

Religion finally made irreconcilable enemies out of natural allies. How this came about can be seen most clearly in the development of what, ever since Elizabeth's reign, historians have been pointing to as quite a different *casus belli*, the conflict over the Spanish claim to exclusive control of the commerce of the Americas. Further studies of the customs rolls and of notarial archives at Seville and elsewhere will be necessary before any-one can say with certainty how far the usual annual profits of the English merchants of Sanlúcar de Barrameda from 1558 to 1585 exceeded the average return from privateering and unlicensed trading in the Caribbean and along the Spanish Main in the following eighteen years. There can scarcely be any doubt that they were greater, since the English merchants trading to Seville consistently got rich, while most of the backers of privateering expeditions lost money or, if they kept at it, eventually went bankrupt.[1] But no further study at all is necessary to note that the English puritans and their Huguenot allies were responsible for the notion that the Spanish commercial monopoly of the western Indies and the Portu-guese monopoly of the eastern ones was sustained by the terrors of papal bulls, to defy which required a peculiarly Protestant form of courage.

In fact, as the leading Catholic canonists, civilians and theologians unanimously agreed, all that the popes had power to confer on Spain and Portugal was supervisory authority over religious establishments and missionary activity in the new-found lands. Even the so-called 'lines of demarcation' themselves, the meridian three hundred and seventy leagues west of the Azores and the parallel of Ferro in the Canaries (apparently the northern quadrants of the globe were always excluded), were agreed upon explicitly or tacitly by the two secular powers concerned in the treaty of Tordesillas, without the intervention of any ecclesiastical authority at all. The subsequent confirmation of the lines by papal authority gave the treaty of Tordesillas just as much force as any other such agreement voluntarily registered with the papal curia, neither more nor less. The greatest Spanish jurist theologian of the first half of the sixteenth century was quite clear that the pope was powerless to grant to Spain any sovereignty over the people of the Indies or any control of the commerce and navigation of its seas. The only valid claim to sovereignty (*dominium*) over lands in the New World, Francisco de Vitoria insisted, must rest on effective occupation of territory previously vacant. As for penalizing or prohibiting commerce, no one had any right to do that anywhere, since by natural law and *ius gentium* trade was everywhere free. This was, in fact, the customary late medieval position. Sixteenth-century canonists and civilians concurred, and Francis I, when he rejected Spanish and

---

[1] [For a somewhat different view, see K. R. Andrews, *Elizabethan Privateering* (1964)— *Editor's note.*]

Portuguese protests against French interloping in the Americas and down the coast of Africa was, for once, on a sound legal footing. Throughout the Habsburg–Valois wars, the French insisted that the 'lines of demarcation' were merely a private agreement between the crowns of Castile and Portugal, and in no sense a part of the public law of Christendom, and French captains defied the Iberian monopolies whether their sovereigns were at war or at peace. At Cateau-Cambrésis, the stubborn refusal of the French delegates to sign anything which in any way admitted the validity of Spanish and Portuguese claims in the southern seas practically established the rule 'no peace beyond the lines' as part of the law of nations. It was just a political accident that the challengers of Spain in the New World after 1559 were mostly Protestants, Huguenots leading for the first decade and Englishmen thereafter.

By the 1580s, however, European public opinion was beginning to forget that the conflict in the Caribbean had not always been a part of the religious conflict. *Piratos luteranos* had become almost a single word in Spanish, and English captains, recruiting men and money for their raids, regularly held out the double bait of fantastic profits (seldom realized) and the opportunity to assert a sturdy Protestantism by defying the pope of Rome's arrogant prohibitions. In one sense, English incursions into the West Indies did serve a Protestant purpose. They did not seriously impoverish Philip II and Drake's great raid of 1585–6 seems to have amused Pope Sixtus V much more than it annoyed him. But each such episode pushed England and Spain nearer to open war.

To precipitate open war between England and Spain was the chief aim of the puritan activists, and of all the zealots of the Common Cause, in England and on the continent. It was also the chief aim, after 1569, of the English Catholic exiles, one of the chief aims of Pope Pius V and his successors, and an increasingly important aim of the Jesuits and all the other Catholic activists of the Counter-Reformation. In their pursuit of this aim the zealots of both religious parties could deploy, as the century wore on, increasingly formidable resources. Both could now command the services of agents with a talent for intrigue and a thirst for martyrdom. Both were now served by scholars and gentlemen, fit for the company of magnates and the cabinets of princes. And in the 1550s and 1560s the Catholics had learned to use the printing press and the popular pulpit with as much skill and as few scruples as the reformers. Consequently, both were able to create currents of public opinion strong enough, eventually, to sweep along with them reluctant governments and rulers.

In the sixteenth century religion was still the one force powerful enough to move masses and to override the selfish interests of dynasts and oligarchs, as it had been in western Christendom in every century since the tenth. Intermittently, in the feudal monarchies, among the aristocracy and even among the commons, there was a recognition of a bond of fealty to the person of a sovereign. But there was as yet no sense of the nation, no sense even of the state (outside of Italy, anyway) as an abstract entity to be loved and served. Humanists might talk of the *patria* and arouse in themselves for the moment something of the same feeling of idolatrous worship for an abstraction called 'France' or 'England' that ancient Romans said they felt for Rome, but for most men throughout most of the sixteenth century one's *patrie* was simply one's *pays*, and one's country was not France or England, but Anjou or Devonshire. Except for England, bound in by the triumphant sea, none of the larger territorial states even had clearly defined frontiers, and certainly no part of their populations had any notion of 'natural boundaries' or of 'national interests' different from the dynastic interests of rulers and the associated interests of immediate subordinates.

Strong religious emotions might act on these societies in one of two ways. They might rally them around their sovereigns, unify them, or the significant part of them, and give them a sort of proto-nationalism. So most Englishmen (legend says 'all') were rallied around Elizabeth I by the menace of a Catholic crusade, and most Spaniards, or at least most Castilians, were rallied around Philip II by pride in Castile's mission to reconquer Christendom from the heretics as once their forefathers had reconquered Spain from the Moors. This effect could operate only when the national sovereign went along with the prevailing current of religious emotion. When he did not—the classic example is France under Henry III— the nation, instead of being unified, was bitterly divided, and confessional solidarity replaced loyalty to the crown. Throughout western Europe the total effect of the religious conflict was to create two hostile camps, one Catholic, one Protestant, bent on the triumph of one or the other of their incompatible ideologies.

In diplomacy the effect of the ideological conflict was most obvious in respect to the new institution of resident ambassadors. Like standing armies, resident ambassadors were the institutional expressions of the power drives of the new egotistical sovereign states, and, in a society accustomed to thinking of diplomats as the servants of an oecumenical society, residents had always been the objects of a certain amount of suspicion. The schism in Christendom hardened that suspicion to a certainty. The popular view was that if the celebration of religious rites in a manner contrary to that sanctioned by the law and custom of the country was so displeasing to God as to make it an offence punishable by death, it could not be less displeasing simply because it went on behind the closed doors of an embassy. Besides, since there could be no peace, no real truce even, with the powers of darkness, what purpose could the residents of an infidel power have in the realm except espionage and subversion? So reasoned earnest puritans in London and earnest Catholics in Madrid and Paris and Rome, and where their pressures did not lead to a complete rupture of diplomatic relations, as sometimes they did, they made the surviving resident ambassadors extremely uncomfortable.

Unhappily, the popular view was not without justification. If Dr John Man was not conspiring with Spanish Protestants before he was expelled from Spain it was only because in Spain he could find no Protestants to conspire with. Every English ambassador in Paris from Throckmorton to Stafford was thicker with leading Huguenots, even when the Huguenots were in open rebellion, than any government would be likely to tolerate these days; and every Spanish ambassador in London in the reign of Queen Elizabeth was deep enough in treasonable conspiracy to justify, by modern standards, handing him his passport, as, by late medieval law, every one of them, except the adroit de Silva, was in deep enough to justify his execution. Don Bernardino de Mendoza, who, after he was expelled from England for his part in a plot to murder Queen Elizabeth, was given credentials for France and there helped organise the Holy League, planned the Day of the Barricades, and ended his career as ambassador as the open chieftain of the Paris rebels, was only too apt an instance of what was happening to diplomacy in the period of the religious wars. Even the French envoys, who were expected to be *politiques*, and so above the religious mêlée, were trapped by the opening abyss. Châteauneuf in London, suspected of complicity in the Babington plot largely because he was a Catholic, was practically under house arrest and quite deprived of influence or contacts for months before his recall, while at almost the same time Longlée, in Madrid, was so deeply distrusted because of his master's willingness to negotiate with heretics that, even before the murder of the duke of Guise completed his isolation, he had almost no one to talk to, and nothing important to do. By the time the pressures of their subjects had pushed Elizabeth I and Philip II into war with one another, diplomatic contacts between the Catholic and the Protestant worlds were almost completely broken.

The disruption of diplomatic communications and the increasing disuse of the diplomatic machinery developed in the preceding three centuries was accompanied by a reversion to the less formal methods of an earlier period. In her relations with continental powers Queen Elizabeth increasingly made use of agents with only quasi-diplomatic status, or with no status at all, either because the states concerned were reluctant, like Florence and Venice, for instance, to receive formally accredited envoys from a heretic prince, or because the queen could not bring herself to recognise as sovereign equals the powers, like the Dutch States General, the duke of Bouillon and the Elector Palatine, with whom she had to deal. Her agents varied in dignity downwards from her residents at the Hague and her envoys to the German princes, who were ambassadors in all but name, to her merely tacitly recognised 'pensioners' in Venice and Florence. At the same time she received agents from the French Huguenots and the

Dutch rebels although she was at peace with France and Spain, just as these groups kept in touch with one another although the agents who shuttled back and forth between Holland and the south of France would have been accorded no diplomatic status whatever by the Catholic sovereigns through whose lands they had to pass.

On the Catholic side the technique was somewhat different. Philip II himself sent only open ambassadors or secret spies, although, as the tensions of 'war underhand' increased, he acquiesced more and more readily in the relations which his accredited ambassadors established with treasonable and subversive groups. But his governors and deputies, especially in Milan and the Netherlands, were permitted and sometimes ordered to employ semi-official or private agents to communicate with foreign powers, friendly or hostile. Philip and Elizabeth before the ends of their reigns had reverted to diplomatic techniques more like those of Edward III and Pedro the Cruel than like those of Henry VIII and Charles V.

The disruption of diplomatic contacts within the disintegrating society of Latin Christendom was not offset by any significant extension of contacts outside it. English merchants, seeking Cathay by way of the Arctic waters beyond North Cape, found their way instead to Moscow and a Christian ruler eager for western goods and western allies. In the reign of Elizabeth, the Muscovy Company initiated a series of quasi-diplomatic missions to the tsar, aimed at securing commercial concessions and monopolies, the company normally selecting and paying the envoy, who was accredited and instructed by the queen. English diplomacy evoked a livelier response in Moscow than English trade goods, and its apparent success led to attempts by competing Dutch and French merchants similarly to involve their governments in negotiations with Russia, but the genuine anxiety of Ivan the Terrible and his immediate successors to find western support against Poles and Swedes led to no treaty of alliance, not even to any exchange of resident ambassadors. The eastern Baltic and the Polish plain were too remote from the Rhine and the Channel, and the habits and values of Muscovy too remote from those of the west. Russia was not to be drawn for a long time to come into the circle of western diplomacy.

Nor was the Turk, not though he could exert, through his fleets of Mediterranean galleys and his armies in Hungary, military pressures of the first importance against the preponderant Habsburgs, not though his ancestors had been negotiating as well as fighting with the Franks since the fourteenth century, not though Francis I, after his chastening at Pavia, had struck with Sulaimān the Lawgiver a firm alliance and sealed it by establishing a resident ambassador at Istanbul. In fact, the activities of the French ambassador at the Sublime Porte had less and less to do after the 1540s with spurring or checking the movements of Turkish fleets and armies, and the war that raged through the Greek islands and along the shores of North Africa in the 1560s and 1570s was scarcely at all a reflex of western politics and very much a resumption of the perennial struggle between the Crescent and the Cross. After the death of King Sebastian at Alcazar-el-Kebir in 1578, Spanish diplomacy became as active at Istanbul as French had once been, and for some years Philip II was almost continuously represented there. His ambassadors negotiated an armistice which kept the peace between the Turk and Christendom for more than a decade, and were credited in the west with a diplomatic triumph, but it seems likely that they deserved the credit as little as French and English diplomats deserved blame for the renewal of the Turkish attack on the Habsburgs in 1593. In 1578 Turkey was drawn towards Persia and the steppes as Spain was drawn towards Portugal and the ocean, and turned, like Spain, from war with infidels to war with heretics. As Fernand Braudel has pointed out, that Turkish swing eastward and the counter-swing westward fifteen years later were responses to a rhythm of history whose impulses did not correspond to those of the west, and whose pattern we shall not begin to understand without a great deal more work in the Turkish archives. It may be that the capricious negligence with which western ambassadors were treated at the Sublime Porte and the consistent refusal of the sultans to return the compliment of resident embassies can be explained by more solid reasons than barbaric arrogance or Byzantine pride.

If western diplomacy made no permanent impression on Russians or Turks, elsewhere, outside of Europe, it made no impression at all. Before 1559 Spaniards and Portuguese had furrowed all the temperate and tropical oceans of the globe and visited every civilised land, and in the next half century Frenchmen and Englishmen and Dutchmen followed them. But although efforts were made to open diplomatic channels of communication with the greater oriental potentates, they came to nothing. It was not so much that Europeans were negligible in oriental power politics, although to the greatest sovereigns, the Mogul emperors of India and the Ming emperors of China, they must have seemed of very little account. It was rather that there was not enough mutual understanding to provide a basis for conversations, much less for any sort of co-operation. The cultural distance was even greater than the physical. So the Spanish and Austrian efforts to strike an alliance with the shah of Persia, though based on the rule of making friends with the power on the other side of your enemy, a rule as well understood in Islamic as in European diplomacy, bore no fruit, and the second half of the sixteenth century saw Henry the Navigator's dream of an alliance between the westernmost and the easternmost of Christian kings finally disappointed after a moment when it seemed likely to be realised. In the end, Portugal and Ethiopia took separate paths less because the Turkish capture of Massawa denied the

Portuguese access to the Abyssinian highland than because the more the Roman and the Abyssinian clergy saw of one another, and the more learnedly and earnestly they sought to assimilate their rituals and creeds, the wider the gulf between the Latin and the Coptic churches proved to be. If religious differences among the heirs of a common tradition threatened to split the long-established diplomatic community of western Europe, the gaps between the heirs of different traditions proved, for the time being, unbridgeable by diplomacy.

In western Europe, towards the beginning of the seventeenth century, the strained and loosened diplomatic network began to be re-spliced. After Henry IV had bought Paris with a Mass, the veteran Villeroy began to restore the French diplomatic service to something like its old efficiency. The failure of the Enterprise of England, the English subjugation of Ireland, the hopeless division of the Netherlands, had awakened in Madrid and Rome some sober second thoughts about the profitableness of religious war, and when the pacific James I came to the throne he was able to re-establish the previous English resident embassies in Spain and Italy while, at the same time, Spanish resident ambassadors reappeared in London and made their first bows at the Danish and Swedish courts. But the mutual suspicions of the religious wars would not down, and it was not until after the treaties of Westphalia that the modern style of diplomacy became as firmly established throughout Europe as it had been throughout Italy after the Peace of Lodi almost two hundred years before. The diplomatic community of Europe re-knit itself only slowly.

The rules under which the new community was to live, the rules we call 'international law', formed themselves more slowly still. It is really too early to speak of 'international law' before 1610; still too early even after Hugo Grotius, who used to be called its founder, had published his *Laws of War and Peace* (Paris, 1625); perhaps too early at any time before the third quarter of the seventeenth century. A system of international law had to wait until Europeans had got accustomed to living in one or another of a congeries of independent, completely autonomous, completely self-regarding sovereign states, and had established habits of speech and behaviour in relation to such a way of life. For although a Cartesian-minded society might prefer to believe that it could be governed by a code produced by establishing axioms and deducing the consequences, what it actually wanted was an acceptable rationalisation of its usual patterns of acting and feeling. Since there was no agency to enforce rules of international behaviour anyway, any system of international law had to depend for whatever measure of acceptance it received on its compatibility with prevailing sentiments. Obviously, no system of international law for western Europe could have much relation to reality until the people concerned had made up their minds what, as far as international relations were concerned, they were doing and how they felt about it.

This is not to say that western society had previously lacked a reasonably adequate body of rules corresponding to what we should call public and private international law. Only it thought of those rules, not as a separate body of law applicable to the relations of a special class of sub-societies to one another, or of the individuals belonging to one sub-society when temporarily under the jurisdiction of another, but simply as a part of the common law of Latin Christendom. For instance, canonists and civilians between 1250 and 1500 had a good deal to say about justifiable causes for war, the propriety of declarations of war, limits to be observed in its conduct, the rights of neutrals and so forth, but they rarely said these things in separate treatises on the laws of war. They said them for the most part under rubrics concerning just quarrels, duels, and trials by battle, the right of self-defence, and the impropriety of involving women, minor children, clerks and peaceable merchants in the violent settlement of disputes. Treaties are discussed in the glosses and commentaries on contracts. A *concilium* on the liability of the city of Perugia to a suit for damages refers once to a case involving a crowned head and again to one involving a tanners' guild as if both were equally useful by way of illustration. So indeed they were. The common law of Christendom was respectful of special privileges, of a hierarchically ordered society and of local and regional customs, but it held, or rather it assumed, that every individual and every corporate society was subject in certain matters to the canon law and in others to the civil law. Consequently it is only on certain special topics, such as letters of marque and reprisal or the privileges and immunities of ambassadors, that one is likely to find tractates immediately recognisable as being about what we should call international law.

The elaboration of the common law of Christendom, the combined system of the canon and the civil law, was largely the work of Italian jurists, notably of the Bartolists, but it is in a country like England where the provincial customs were generalised and defended by powerful royal courts that its role as international law appears most clearly. In the theory of the canonists, and sometimes in actual practice, the church took a leading interest in the observance of treaties, the maintenance of peace among Christians and the regulation of intercourse with infidels; but the chief business of church courts was with ecclesiastical property and privileges and with the sacraments, and it was only occasionally that people noticed that the sacramental system bound England into a larger society, and more rarely still, as for instance in a famous trial at Blackfriars, that a church court emerged clearly as an international tribunal.

As the monarchy grew stronger in the fifteenth and sixteenth centuries, it was natural for royal servants trained in the civil and the canon law to use Roman procedures to reinforce royal authority and cut through the inequities and obstructive delays which distorted and clogged the operation of the common law. But quite aside from the domestic uses and abuses of courts like Star Chamber, there were times when the courts representing the king's personal justice were obliged to employ the rules of the civilians because they were functioning as tribunals of what served the middle ages as international law. So the Court of Admiralty, one of the offshoots of the king's council, administered maritime law as it was administered everywhere else in Europe, according to the procedures of the civil law and the interpretations of the post-glossators, and another offshoot, the Court of Chivalry, mixed cases about precedence and heraldry with cases about contracts for mercenaries and supplies, about capitulations, hostages, and ransoms, all decided according to principles as familiar to the Frenchmen, Italians and Germans involved as they were to the Englishmen. Certain civil law cases were reserved for the un-delegated authority of the king in council, including all those touching ambassadors and their suites, and miscellaneous actions not otherwise provided for, involving conflicts of laws and therefore referable for settlement under the Roman civil law.

Throughout the later middle ages there were no significant differences in the ways these matters were handled as between one European country and another. The west had, as far as it needed to have, a common legal system, and the law schools of northern Italy had equipped it, so its students thought, against every emergency. By 1559 it had survived for half a century the strain of the continuous power struggle with its con-comitant of a system of resident ambassadors for which its elaborators had failed to prepare it. It had survived, too, the shock of the Lutheran revolt. Then, in the half century after 1559, it melted away and had become in another hundred years so completely forgotten that men could talk as if the inter-state relations of the middle ages had been an anarchy, subject only to jungle law, and as if the rule of reason in the conduct of European affairs was a discovery of the age of reason.

Let it be emphasised that what disappeared were not modes of action or sentiment, but modes of thought. States and individuals still acted, most of the time, as if the great society of the west lived under the rule of law, and most of the courts charged with administering and interpreting segments of this law continued to operate. Patterns of international behaviour did change in response to changing pressures and opportunities, in particular in response to the growing power and self-sufficiency of the state, but the change was a gradual one, with no sudden leaps or breaks, and on the whole less than one might expect unless one has noticed that human behaviour is usually less liable to change than are the standards by which it is judged. In the long run sentiments changed more than actual behaviour, since sentiments at any given moment of time are necessarily more uniform, but for that very reason they always tend to lag behind the events which change them. What changed drastically and abruptly was the mode of thinking, or rather of verbalising, about international relations. The difficulty was less in knowing what one ought to do in a given situation than in explaining why one ought to do it.

In the fourteenth century the Bartolists had confronted a similar difficulty. Respect for law in the sphere of international relations depended then as later upon rational persuasion, since neither the popes nor the emperors had the power to enforce obedience. In the interest of persuasion the Bartolists drew from the arsenal of the Roman jurists the same linked weapons which later the seventeenth century used: the belief in the Stoic's Natural Law which imbued all human minds with the same fundamental moral principles, and the consequent willingness to draw on *ius gentium*, the customs of the gentiles, to supplement deficiencies in the corpus. But the Bartolists possessed two auxiliary weapons which their successors lacked. They could base their arguments on the unquestioned assumption that, no matter how fragmented the sources of temporal and spiritual authority, Latin Christendom was one, with a common end and a common scale of values, and that the interest of the whole overrode the interest of any part. The religious revolution struck this weapon from the legists' hands. In addition, the Bartolists could reinforce their arguments and enrich the exiguous materials available in the *Corpus Juris Civilis* for regulating international relations by appealing to that part of *ius gentium* available in the tradition of the immediate past of Latin Christendom. By the late fifteenth century, the compilers of legal manuals could draw on a rich store of glosses, commentaries, opinions, cases decided and precedents established to help settle almost any point, no matter how minor and obscure, of inter-state relations. This powerful weapon the legists of the age of transition, of the century between the treaties of Cateau-Cambrésis and the Peace of the Pyrenees, voluntarily let fall from their hands.

They were moved by the same logic that impelled architects and philosophers, grammarians and theologians, physicians and painters to turn their backs upon their medieval past. They did not abandon the patterns of behaviour or the techniques which they had inherited from that past. Had they done so they would have been lost and helpless, the legists and diplomats as much as the architects and painters. But they did their best to forget whence they had their habits and their skills, and to base themselves directly upon antique culture, leaping over the intervening centuries with eyes deliberately closed. The Protestant insistence on the Scriptures and only the Scriptures as the sole theological authority was merely an exaggerated aspect of the Renaissance's veneration for antiquity and yearning to return to the original sources. So the legists of the period of transition, Ayrault and Gentili and Braun, Kirchner and Warszewicki and Ayala, Selden and Grotius and Zouche, suffered a special handicap in their attempt to deal with problems which were unprecedented and difficult enough even for men unhampered. The questions raised in Europe by the emergence of self-conscious, omnicompetent, absolutely sovereign states were complicated by the bitterness of the religious war. There were diplomatic questions. The agents of the sovereign states, the resident ambassadors, their consciences freed by religious zeal from whatever scruples they might otherwise have entertained, too frequently abused the privileges and immunities conferred on their predecessors in quite another context. How far could they be justified? How sharply must they be condemned? How could they be punished? Gentili and Hotman and Paschalius all struggled with this problem. There were questions of the laws of war. When were rebels entitled to the status of belligerents? To diplomatic representation? To the protection of the ordinary laws of war in capitulations and truces? And how much faith should be kept with heretics, anyway? Ayala and Kirchner and Warszewicki all found different answers in the same decade. And there were commercial questions. Can a known heretic claim payment on a contract? Interest on a loan? And how far ought the seas of the world to be free to the commerce of all nations and how far may a trade monopoly be maintained by force? The theologians of Louvain, Salamanca and Geneva did not find these questions easy. Neither did Selden nor Grotius.

What the legists were trying to do, of course, was to rationalise the usual conduct of European governments, or justify the position of a client or patron in a dispute. But their rejection of the recent European past prevented them from citing the precedents and authorities which were really pertinent, even though most of them probably knew them well enough. They could not have recourse to Bertachinus or Gonzalvo de Villadiego or Jason Mainardus; they had to quote Cicero and Plutarch and Livy, no matter how inappropriate. They could not illustrate their points by the conduct of Alphonso the Wise or Louis XI or even the Emperor Charles V; they needed the support of Cincinnatus and Lycurgus and David, king of Israel. No wonder that even the best of them seems to babble and stammer and wander from the point, and compares unfavourably with the crisp, dry, down-to-earth post-glossators.

The whole argument about how to justify the conduct of the European powers and their agents scarcely breaks out into the light and air before Richard Zouche's *Jus Feciale* (1650). It was Zouche, too, who first used the expression *jus inter gentes* in token of his appreciation of the change that had taken place since the fourteenth-century jurists had given a new flavour to *jus gentium*. But for all that, perhaps Hugo Grotius does deserve his reputation as the founder of international law. He was only trying, like most of his contemporaries, to justify what men were doing or thought they ought to be doing, and his standards and value judgements and the rules of international conduct for which he argued were drawn, like most other peoples', largely from a medieval past which he never mentioned. But he was the first person to see, or to make it clear that he saw, that, to be persuasive, the argument must be couched in the terms not of the interests of a single unitary commonwealth of which the princes and republics of Christendom were subordinate members, but in terms of the interest in their own self-preservation of the independent, ego-centred, absolutely sovereign states whose aggregate composed the heterogeneous, pluralistic international society of western Europe. That was what the future was going to be like. And to come to terms with the future, one had to forget the medieval dream.

CHAPTER VII

ARMIES, NAVIES AND THE ART OF WAR

IN every year of the two generations that followed the treaty of Cateau-Cambrésis in 1559 European soldiers were somewhere engaged in battle, skirmish or siege. Few of these actions were on a large scale and none of them was decisive. Christian fought Turk and Catholic power fought Protestant by land and sea; France was distracted by civil wars for thirty years, the Netherlands for forty. Yet when the fighting petered out, the frontiers ran as geography, economic vitality, religion and patriotism dictated, not in patterns cut out by the sword. The costs of war continued to grow, and the sums raised were never enough to release into effectiveness the tactical lessons or the technical advances of the previous period, let alone the flood of advice offered by a new race of military experts. The need for regular pay, increased professionalism and something like a permanent establishment was recognised, but little was done about it. Ambitious plans laid at home were passed to the front in sieves of peculation and inefficiency. It was not a period of achievement, it was not in any real sense a period of transition, yet in no previous age had war loomed so large in men's lives and, through the pulpit, the stage, the fine arts and the press, in their imaginations.

The recurrence of wars was taken for granted. 'To speak of peace perpetual in this world of contention', wrote Thomas Digges, 'is but as *Aristotles foelix, Xenophons Cyrus, Quintilians Orator,* or *Sir Thomas Moores Utopia,* a matter of mere contemplation, the warre being in this iron age *si bien enracinée qu'il est impossible de l'en oster, si non avec la ruine de l'universe.*'[1] But if there was less pacifism than in the first half of the century, there was a greater self-consciousness about the legitimacy of war as such, and a more widespread urge to explain the difference between a just and an unjust war. Another military primer pointed out that notwithstanding texts that exhort the Christian not to kill, and to turn the other cheek, Christ did not come to cancel the justice of natural and civil law but to fulfil it, and a distinction must be drawn between private vengeance and public revenge, executed at the magistrate's order to secure justice and bring peace. The assumption that God used war to work his judgements was gladly accepted by the popes of an age of counter-attack; Trent, while condemning private duels, was silent on the score of national ones. New military religious orders were founded and military literature suggested, if it did not openly promise, that the soldier who fell in defence of his religion had an especially favourable chance of salvation. God was,

---

[1] *Foure paradoxes, or politique discourses* (London, 1604), p. 109.

after all, the Lord of Hosts, and one Italian treatise went so far as to extol the military art above all others on four counts: its constantly changing conditions challenged the intellect, it was the supreme test of personal worth and honour, it brought undying fame on earth, and, after a brief martyrdom, it took the soul to Paradise—'for which sole purpose we are created'.[1] The humanist tradition added its quasi-philosophical assent to this taking of war for granted with its doctrine of cycles of war and peace, its acceptance with Cicero that *rei militaris virtus praestat ceteris omnibus*, and with Sir Walter Raleigh that 'the ordinary theme and argument of history is war'. The mere observer took war for granted because of the ambitious nature of princes, and could accept this the more readily if he heeded three popular arguments which stressed the utility of war: it kept down surplus population, it tautened a flabby civic morale, and as (in Daniel's phrase) 'the foul refiner of a state' it purged the body politic of its viler elements. When to these were added arguments like Botero's praise of foreign war as a safety-valve for the political passions of the great, the popularity of Lucan's *et multis utile bellum* can be understood.

Increasing publicity was given to the theme of war by literature and playhouse. All but the austerest theorists of the epic allowed that not only was war its foremost subject matter but that it might be treated with a wealth of realistic detail. At the other extreme the ballad-writer could be sure of the extent of his audience when he addressed himself to

> You that be desirous
> and therein take delight:
> to hare of bloudie battailes
> and worthy warlike fight.[2]

Accounts of sieges and battles were published in verse and in the prose of the military newsbooks that became increasingly popular as the century wore on. The drama sometimes reported current events, but a more constant preoccupation was with the glamour and terror of war, with the virtue of the upright soldier and the shame of the cowardly one, and with the nobility of militant patriotism. Nor was peace an excuse for putting war out of mind. Peace, indeed, was commonly taken to be no more than an uneasy absence of war.

If war as such was taken to be inevitable, glorious and remedial, there was still a feeling that it should be waged for a just cause. When Shakespeare made Henry V ask the archbishop, before attacking France, whether it could be done 'with right and conscience' he was echoing enquiries made of divines on behalf of the crown when English intervention in the Netherlands was contemplated in 1585. The Aquinan 'just war' had come by the end of the sixteenth century to cover the following

[1] Anon., *Istruzione per i cavallegieri* (Florence, BNF. XIX, 142(1), f. 1ʳ).
[2] 'Newes from Flaunders', quoted by G. G. Langsam, *Martial Books and Tudor Verse* (New York, 1951), p. 141.

situations: a lawfully instituted government might go to war in defence of land, faith, goods or liberty; by way of reprisal for acts of piracy; to avenge insults to ambassadors; to defend its friends and allies; when treaties were broken by another party; to stop other nations supplying an enemy with men, munitions or food. Underlying these conditions was the guiding principle that war was legitimate only as a means of defence. This picture was complicated by the division of Europe into hostile religious groups and by the recognition of something like a balance of power, and the concept of the just war was broadened to allow military aid to be sent to co-religionists in other countries, and to anticipate changes in the balance by a preventive campaign. When Lazarus von Schwendi wrote that a prince might justly go to war whenever he judged that his country's essential supplies were endangered and could only be protected by arms, the just war concept had been stretched nearly to breaking point. The Spanish theologians Molina and Gregorius de Valentia relaxed the rules to permit a prince to go to war if his cause was probably, and not demonstrably, just; and international lawyers, recognising that few causes are, in fact, demonstrably just, that opposing causes may be equally just, and that the issue of wars does not prove the relative justice of the causes, granted the right of war to any belligerent who declared war formally and waged it moderately. It was the lack of moderation with which wars were waged in the following century which moved Grotius to take up once more the distinction between just and unjust causes. But though it was widely recognised that 'every man will seeme to make his cause good, and to do nothing without just cause',[1] governments were still careful to justify their decisions to go to war, and the writers of military handbooks kept the old values in sight by explaining to the ordinary soldier that he was dispensed from observing them as an individual if the prince ordered him to fight for a cause he suspected to be unjust. 'We know enough,' as Shakespeare makes the English soldier Bates say on the eve of Agincourt, 'if we know we are the King's subjects. If his cause be wrong, our obedience to the King wipes the crime of it out of us.' We hear protests against war's cruelties, denunciations of men who live only to fight without considering the cause and scorn any life but of the camp, cries of longing for the days when swords can be beaten into ploughshares, but no protest against war as such, no denial, save from the Anabaptists, that causes exist which license Christians to use sword and gun.

Nor, among the protests that continued to be levelled against the use of gunpowder was there any strong enough to amount to a positive restraint. Guns were still denounced as devilish and cruel, their threat to chivalry debated—as though knights had not been laid low by anonymous missiles since the far-off days of Crecy—by authors of military textbooks as well

[1] Matthew Sutcliffe, *The Practice, Proceedings and Lawes of Armes* (London, 1593), p. 2.

as by the author of *Don Quixote*. There is no proven case of a new or improved weapon being suppressed as a result of moral scruple. The reaction to the blowing up of some eight hundred persons by Giambelli's famous infernal machine during the siege of Antwerp was one of appalled admiration. In an age of much casual cruelty, and of much calculated atrocity, in an age, too, which placed a high value on technological ingenuity, the only effective brake on the more widespread use of guns could come from the military conservatives, the snobs of the *armes blanches*, and they sacrificed what might have been a valuable attack on the overdoing of missile at the expense of shock tactics for the sake of a gallant but anachronistic defence of the bow. In fort and battlefield, in the pageantry of peace and in the imagery of literature, the gun was welcomed; guns appealed strongly to the emotions as well as to military calculation, and in spite of their inefficiency and costliness they played an increasing part in the warfare of the sixteenth century.

In the *pinacoteca* of Turin hangs one of the age's most misleading allegories. Painted by Lukas de Heere, it depicts the fate of 'The Seven Liberal Arts in Time of War'. They are shown sleeping, in shapely disarray, on a hillside. In the valley below a battle is in progress. From a council of the Gods in heaven Mercury descends with a message of peace to tell the Arts that they can wake again. In cold fact he would have found the hillside bare, his lovely colleagues in the thick of the fighting; Rhetoric urging on the troops with harangue and broadsheet, Mathematics embattling them by the square root, Music encouraging them with fife and drum (encouraged by a concept which saw war as a musical harmony), Architecture putting the final touches to a flanking fortress, Astronomy lending her telescope to the general she favoured, Grammar taking notes for the victory's celebration, Philosophy for its justification. War and the arts, war and learning, were no longer, even as a topic of after-dinner debate, seen to be in conflict.

Yet for all the sanction given to military activity by ecclesiastical and lay thinkers, for all the welcome extended to it by science and the arts, the mass of society was apathetic in the face of its appeal. Governments found it difficult to obtain troops save from malcontents from all classes, a cosmopolitan group of amateur adventurers, the professionally organised mercenary bands, and the noble classes of France and Spain, though their tradition that arms was the only respectable occupation outside the church was fast losing its force. Spain increasingly had to promote foreigners and Sully considered setting up aristocratic military schools to re-inculcate the military virtues. Attempt after attempt failed to augment these nuclei with native troops recruited from town and country. England, mourned Geoffrey Gates, was full of 'secure rustickes and dayntie citizens' who used every subterfuge to avoid military service, and in the same way the French chancellor, Michel de l'Hôpital, complained that his nation were turning their backs on arms and cultivating instead their gardens and their businesses. In theory, war was still a fine thing for fine men, but every campaign added force to Erasmus's bitter glosses on the tag *dulce bellum inexpertis*. Pay was irregular, food and lodging even more uncertain as old methods of supply struggled to keep pace with armies which had far out-stripped them in size and complexity. Material incentives over and above normal pay were few. The military entrepreneurs, the suppliers of mer-cenary bands, might make fortunes,[1] and the lesser men who invested their own small units with them at least a profit, but except for these men, the expense of going to war was likely to exceed the gain. Soldiers no longer retired on fortunes made from booty, and ransom was by no means simple to obtain, especially as many men fought as substitutes for richer 'dayntie citizens'. Looting was theoretically legal as soon as war had been formally joined, but the clutter this produced on the march, and the temptation to break formation before an action was finished, led to stringent attempts to regulate it. (The Protestants lost the battle of Dreux (1562) in this way, as did the Christians to the Turks at Kerestec (1596).) Cities, besides, usually fell after protracted sieges which gave the citizens time to conceal their valuables, and shortage of transport made it necessary to dispose of loot at give-away prices to the civilian traders who followed armies for this purpose.

While the rewards were low, casualty rates were high. Precise figures are difficult to obtain and are, in any case, misleading; many died after-wards from inadequate medical care, and the actual battle casualties are but one item in a long train of deaths and sickness due to privation. Of the English expeditions to Lisbon and Brittany, it has been calculated that well under half returned from the first and about one-half from the second. More important, besides, than battle casualties in affecting a man's inclina-tion to go to war, was the lack of provision for his welfare. As Botero put it, 'men usually avoid the dangers of war not so much for fear of death, which usually brings little pain and suffering, but for fear of disablement and the misfortunes which are brought about by wounds and accidents'. And he went on to say, 'If the ruler is able to assure his soldiers that not only will they be well treated if misfortune befalls them, but that their wives, sons, sisters or other relations will be remembered if they are killed, then he will have done all that he can to induce them to face fire, arrows and death itself.'[2] The only nation to approach this ideal was that of the Turks, who had a pension system, and granted leave with pay to garrisons abroad, and whose model barracks in Algiers were the admiration of European travellers. In France, the widows and children of soldiers might be exempted from imposts, and in 1601 the *Maison de charité chrétienne*

---

[1] Details in Fritz Redlich, *The German Military Enterpriser and his Work Force* (Wies-baden, 1964), vol. I.

[2] *The Reason of State* (trans. P. J. and D. P. Waley; London, 1956), bk. x, c. 11, p. 192.

was built in Paris for old and invalid soldiers; but throughout the religious wars men were mobilised and, when a campaign was over, demobilised with no attempt to help them back into civilian life. Elizabeth's government was forced to tackle this problem when ex-soldiers came to be a dangerous element in the ranks of those sturdy beggars to whom the country owed so much of its social legislation. Employers were directed to take back their men, a system of passes was devised to distinguish the real from the fake veteran, to gain him admission to a hospital, if he could find one, and to a pension raised by a parish rate; but inefficiency and peculation, together with the abuse of every privilege by those not entitled to them, prevented this exiguous welfare system from bringing real relief. When Marina in *Pericles* upbraided Boult for being a bawd, his answer was, 'What would you have me do? Go to the wars, would you, where a man may serve seven years for the loss of a leg, and not have money enough in the end to buy him a wooden one?' The failure of states to select men with care, train them properly, pay them regularly and assure them some degree of security when the wars were over led to a state of affairs where even statesmen who knew how much a nation depended on the profession of arms could speak out against it. 'Never, by my consent,' wrote Elizabeth's great minister Burghley in a letter of advice to his son Robert on the bringing up of his family, 'shalt thou train them up in wars. For he that sets up his to live by that profession can hardly be an honest man or a good Christian. Besides it is a science no longer in request than use. For soldiers in peace are like chimneys in summer.'[1]

Alarmed by civilians' reluctance to take arms and by the failure of governments to force them to, pulpit and press rang with warning. Preachers cited the nemesis that visited lazing Nineveh; the authors of military books cited the fatal surrender of Roman armies to the wanton unarmed combats of Capua. For England the sack of Antwerp by the Spaniards provoked a monitory propaganda which reached its peak in the crudely effective play *A Larum for London*, whose story was hardly more than an excuse for introducing blood-curdling episodes like the one in which, while the sack is at its height, two little children, Martin and Lenchy, run on and discuss where to hide. Two Spaniards enter running, with drawn swords, shouting, 'Kill, Kill, Kill.'

> MARTIN: I pray you M. Spaniard hurt us not,
>   We are poore children, we have done no harme.
> LENCHY: Good gaffer doe not kill my little brother.
> 1ST SPANIARD: Fuora villiaco, sa, sa, sa, sa.
> MARTIN: Ah Master Spaniard doe not kill my sister,
>   My father is a poore blinde man, and he will dye, if you kill her.
> 2ND SPANIARD: Cut the Bastards throates.

[1] Quoted by Joel Hurstfield, *The Queen's Wards* (London, 1958), p. 257, from Peck's *Desiderata Curiosa*.

The Armada set off a similar wave of hate propaganda. With disturbing relish Thomas Delony described the cargo of special whips the Spaniards had brought with them in order to ravish the women of England before their husbands' eyes and then fall on them with these instruments, which were

> Strengthned eke with brasen tagges,
>   and fild so rough and thin,
> That they would force at every lash
>   the bloud abroad to spinne.[1]

The English naval victory, the military preparation that accompanied it, the publicity given to the queen's triumphal review of the troops at Tilbury: none of these things could give the sense of security that a permanent army could have given. Yet beside a wish for protection there was a lively fear of such an army, potentially a tyrannous instrument, and of any man who voluntarily chose a soldier's life, for the chances were that he would come back from the wars a licentious and anti-social hooligan. An attempt to solve this impasse in a creative manner was made by a class of books dedicated, as the title of Geoffrey Gates's work of 1579 had it, to *The Defence of Militarie Profession*, which extolled the virtues not so much of the real-life, but the ideal, soldier. This prodigy—devout, enduring, moderate, brave, faithful, intelligent, healthy, well-read, eloquent, handsome and fortunate—stood in ludicrous contrast to the misfits lugged off to the wars as 'fit for powder' by captains like Sir John Falstaff, but the existence of such a model, fitfully illuminated from time to time by the exploits of a de La Noue or a Sidney, did something to keep alive the glamour and seriousness of purpose of the military life, and achieved some contact with reality by references to contemporary wars.

The second half of the sixteenth century, indeed, saw more books published on military topics than were to be published for a century and more. Military practices were still unstandardised and, in the absence of permanent armies, instruction in arms had in part to be derived from books. There was, besides, an avid army of stay-at-homes who liked to read of the wars in comfort, and master without danger the fascinating complexities of drill, battle-order and encampment. Some sensitiveness was felt on the score of the relevance of books to a trade so practical as that of arms, and authors and translators were careful to stress the utility of books to soldiers, to give their own war record, and to mock captains who could not drill their men without breaking off to shout to their servants, 'Hola sirrah, where is my book?'[2]

It is difficult to guess what influence this literature had on the practice of war. Some nations, it is safe to say, were entirely untouched, especially those countries whose mode of warfare differed radically from Roman

---

[1] Quoted by Langsam, *Martial Books and Tudor Verse* (New York, 1951), p. 132.
[2] Robert Barret, *The Theoricke and Practike of Moderne Warres* (London, 1598), p. 6.

practice, which remained the common denominator of most military literature. Such a country was Poland, where war books were widely read, but where practice was governed by the use on her great plains of predominantly cavalry forces against marauding Tartars. It is to be doubted if men with the authority to alter the methods of their countries' armies read widely in these books, but there is no doubt that Machiavelli's *Art of War* remained a perceptible influence and that classical authors either in their own dress or through interpretative works like Justus Lipsius's *De Militia Romana* (1598) were responsible in part for the innovations of Eric in Sweden and Maurice of Nassau in the Netherlands. It is likely that, on a larger, less influential audience, the effect of this literature was to substitute a view of warfare as something orderly, complex and professional for the older vision of the battlefield as a theatre for displays of personal valour. It would be tempting to go further, to explain the increasingly hesitant and cautious attitude to battle, the increasing preference for campaigns of manœuvre rather than shock in terms not only of an increased dependence on missiles at the expense of pike and lance but on the growing assumption, reflected in the titles of military books, that war was an Art. In origin the Art of War was a classical phrase; it was used sparingly during the first half of the sixteenth century but more frequently in the second. This period, too, saw the use of model soldiers and of model fortifications, and whereas the older analogy for war had been the hunt, it was now frequently compared to chess.

Though blunt Iago could scornfully dismiss Cassio as 'a great Arithmetician', there is one concept which military books undoubtedly fostered: that war calls for a knowledge of mathematics. Mathematical knowledge was considered necessary for the calculation of ranges for guns, the plotting of mines, the surveying and mapping of enemy positions, the design of fortifications and the embattling of troops, determining, that is, how shot, pike and halberd were to be distributed among a required number of tactical units. Thus the first book of Girolamo Cataneo's treatise on fortification took the reader through the basic principles of Euclidean geometry, Alexandre Vandenbyssche's *L'arithmatique militaire* (1571) dealt with the practical mathematical problems likely to face the soldier, and the title of another of Leonard Digges's works can be left to speak for itself: *An arithmeticall Militare Treatise, named Stratioticos: compendiously teaching the science of nūbers, as well in fractions as integers, and so much of the rules and aequations algebraicall and arte of numbers cossicall, as are requisite for the profession of a Soldiour* (1579). After so daunting a title it is reassuring to find, in the section addressed to the Master of the Victuals, a type of problem familiar to schoolchildren. 'If 1200 quarters of corne suffise 400 souldyoures for 9 weekes, how muche ought to be provided to serve 2500 souldyours for 40 weekes?' The existence of commanders' batons in the form of calculating machines which showed how many men could occupy any given space, and vice versa, suggests that this dependence on arithmetic in the disposing of an army was not simply a recreation of the textbooks, and after the invasion scare of 1588 one of the measures taken by the City of London was the setting up of a public lectureship in mathematics for the benefit of volunteer officers. It is to be remembered, too, that the greatest of Dutch mathematicians, Simon Stevin, was also the author of an influential work on fortification, and that Galileo taught the theory of fortification at Padua. Apart, perhaps, from the stimulus it gave to the study of ballistic problems, war certainly gained more from the mathematicians than it gave them, but it is equally certain that the military textbooks popularised mathematics, and that, through their emphasis on mensuration and statistics and the use of instruments like the quadrant and telescope, they helped to extend the sympathetic reception of scientific ideas.

The ideal soldier, parade-ground formations, textbook tactics, resolute morale: all these aids to victory existed in the literature—and seemed condemned to remain there. The gap between theory and practice began at the very first stage of raising an army—recruitment. Governments were not prepared to pay for an effective body of men and, moreover, were determined to use recruitment for the additional purpose of social cleansing; local authorities charged with raising conscripts took the opportunity of ridding themselves of vagabonds and suspicious characters— they were, indeed, reluctant to take men out of steady employment because of the difficulty of finding them jobs on their return. When volunteers came to the drum on local recruiting drives no attempt was made to distinguish between the likely man and the misfit. Thanks to the greater effectiveness of the legislation which provided for the supply of military equipment by all substantial citizens, than the provision for drill and arms instruction, far more recruits had arms than had acquired any training in their use.

The unattractive nature of military service led to widespread draft-dodging. The local authorities and licensed private individuals on whom governments relied to collect recruits were open to bribery and confidently expected it. Some degree of control was attempted by checking the original muster-rolls against the men turning up at a transport centre or in camp, but so many substitutions could take place that socially and physically the unit appeared to have suffered a sea-change en route. As the government supplied pay, rations and equipment on the basis of the muster-rolls, it was in the interest of the pay clerks and captains of companies who handled the money to create as many vacancies as possible in the ranks while keeping the paper strength intact. The devices used to this end, varying from bribing men to desert to the hiring of substitutes to stand in the vacant places when the muster-master made his rounds, were legion, as were the ways in which money and supplies destined for men in the ranks could be diverted from them by their officers. Squeezed between a

179   12-2

government that allowed but little pay in the first place and officials and captains who kept part of it from reaching its destination, the troops willingly deserted or bought forged leave passes or surrendered to the enemy in return for a safe passage home. In this way, while the cost to the state of a company remained the same, there was a steady drain on its numbers and quality. Long-term planning, moreover, was inhibited by a commander's ignorance of how many men he could bring on to the field, or how many he would be left with in the course of a siege or on emerging from winter quarters.

The state was forced to employ three hierarchies at this time to perform functions it would later do itself: local authorities to see to the raising of local levies and the functioning of the laws obliging individuals to provide arms and equipment; the officials who escorted the companies thus raised to the front; and the contractors who transported, clothed and fed them and organised the carriage and distribution of their pay. Each of these hierarchies took its cut, from justice's clerk and captain to treasurer-at-war. There was little public respect for the national forces and every civilian hand was against them; prices rose, transport mysteriously disappeared, money was produced more and more grudgingly.

Military efficiency was further hampered by a shortage of trained officers and the tendency to make birth a more important qualification for the highest rank than military experience. The raising and dismissing of troops on an *ad hoc* basis, from crisis to crisis, meant that there was little time for steady progress up the ranks, from company officer (sergeant, ensign, lieutenant, captain) to regimental officer (sergeant-major, colonel or camp-master), let alone beyond that to sergeant-major general, master of the ordnance, camp-master general, captain general of the cavalry, or general of the army. At each transition from the level of company to regiment or regiment to general staff, a different concept of the sort of man required was introduced, with greater emphasis on the administrative and political side of his office. So, while no stigma attached to the rank of captain (colonels retained companies of their own within the regiment they commanded, and captain remained the highest substantive rank), there was no easy movement from one stratum to another and, as a result, there was a grave shortage of trained men at the regimental and staff level. Nor was it easy to appoint to general rank men who combined high birth, political maturity and military experience. Only in the Spanish army which was in the field for generations rather than months at a time, and which was run on professional, mercenary lines, did these problems come near to being solved, and it was their experience that was passed on through the military textbooks to the less professional nations. Their greatest generals, on the other hand, were appointed on political grounds, and it is doubtful whether any purely military nominee could have coped with the administrative problems of keeping a restless cosmopolitan army in the field, or the political decisions which had to be taken without the advice of a trained civilian staff.

Europe was divided into nations that were at war but were unable to raise enough troops to wage it and nations that were at peace but had large numbers of men that were eager to fight. From the nations in the second category, especially Italy, Germany, and Switzerland, there was a steady flow into those in the first, especially France and the Netherlands. In 1573 Alva besieged Haarlem with an army of Spaniards, Italians, Germans, Burgundians and southern Netherlanders, while it was defended by Scots, French, Germans, English and Walloons. The muster-list of Maurice of Nassau's camp at Juliers in 1610 shows that his army consisted of nineteen French companies, six German, sixteen Walloon, eight Frisian, thirty-five English, and twenty-nine Scottish companies. Among the twenty-five thousand troops on the Catholic side at Moncontour (1569) six thousand were Swiss, some four thousand Italian, three thousand German and there were a few companies of Walloons lent by Alva. The army with which Sebastian of Portugal invaded North Africa in 1578 consisted of Portuguese, Spaniards (recruited secretly in Castile), Germans, Walloons, and papal troops under the command of an Englishman, Thomas Stukely. There was a constant exodus of volunteers in spite of spasmodic attempts on the part of governments to stop them. Frenchmen defied the Franco-Turkish alliance and went to fight the infidel in North Africa or Hungary. Germans defied the imperial ban and fought in France. Scots fought in the guard of the rulers of Poland, Englishmen fought on both sides in the Netherlands and sometimes changed from one to the other. As a result of the mercenary and volunteer systems it was not only in the civil wars of France that fellow nationals fought one another. Germans fought for both sides there; and the Swiss who fought by treaty for the French king fought by private contract for his enemies. From the Swiss Protestants who opposed the Huguenots to renegade Christians who fought for the bey of Algiers, the mercenary soldier continued to maintain the role in which Machiavelli had condemned him, putting profit and personal convenience before country or faith.

Respect for Machiavelli's military ideas continued to increase as his political reputation became more alarming. In England, France, Germany and Sweden his trenchant denunciation of mercenary arms and defence of national troops helped to guide debate on three keenly argued topics: Were native troops to be preferred to hired soldiers? Was a permanent army preferable to an *ad hoc* one? And were volunteers preferable to conscripts? The arguments against mercenaries can be reviewed in a summary written by an Italian author[1] for a French audience in 1558. A native soldier fought best because he fought for a cause; he kept faith and showed greater patience in adversity; he shunned mutiny or treachery

[1] Gabriele Simeoni, *César renouvellé* (Paris, 1558), pp. 114–16.

because his goods and family were in the prince's power; he was less likely to rob and plunder; he did not bring 'wife' and children with him to burden the camp as mercenaries did; he was more obedient; he could be dismissed more easily at the end of a campaign; his pay would remain in the country. And other reasons for preferring native troops could be added: mercenary contracts were commonly too short to allow for any long-range planning, their regimental officers treated each contract as a means of getting as much personal profit as possible, and thus added another layer of peculation to those represented in native regiments. And it could happen that mercenaries of the same nation could meet on either side on a battlefield, with incalculable results.

On the other hand, since the proved success of the pike and of firearms, armies had become increasingly specialised, as these weapons were only effective when employed in a strictly disciplined way and indeed with a certain temperamental predisposition which led certain nations to be identified with the best use of a given weapon. The ideal army, it seemed, was one that hired specialists in the various branches—light and medium cavalry, shock and missile infantry, artillery, engineers—to supplement their nation's own best arm. In practice, moreover, native troops showed to poor advantage when matched against mercenaries, and those countries which attempted to raise large numbers of native troops, as did Sweden and some of the German princes, were forced by administrative difficulties, and by the reluctance of the men to serve, to modify or abandon their plans. Faced by the time and money required to turn a peasant into a trained soldier, it was tempting to pay for the packaged product and be done with it.

Among advocates of a national, or largely national, army there was a difference of opinion as to whether the national element should be permanent or not. There was no opposition to permanent garrisons, such as those along the sea and land frontiers of France; though their numbers were considerable, they were too scattered to be a danger, and they were a patriotic necessity. To some the phrase Praetorian guard sprang to mind whenever a standing army was suggested, while others felt that to arm a section of the people was to incite them to revolt. Another view was that if subjects were to be armed, they should be chosen from rural and distant areas—Dalmatia and Albania, in the case of Venice; yet another, that, while there might be a permanent cavalry force, gentlemen with a stake in the country in fact, the socially less dependable infantry should be armed and trained only in time of war. A proposal for something like compulsory national service was made, without consequence, for England in Sir Henry Knyvett's *Defence of the Realme* (1596). French reformers like de La Noue, Vigenère and Duplessis-Mornay made suggestions based on permanent cadres of infantry and cavalry which could be supplemented by conscripts and mercenaries in case of war, but nothing came of these until the Peace of Vervins, when Henry IV retained the organisational nucleus of a small standing army, though as the men themselves were raised and dismissed from alarm to alarm its efficiency was erratic. Lazarus Von Schwendi proposed to transform the *lansknechts* back into the national infantry they had once been and prevent the mercenary cavalry from serving foreigners for pay without specific licence, and to supplement this professional core with compulsory military training, especially in danger areas like the Turkish-threatened eastern frontier. His plan was adopted in part by the Reichstag in 1570, but shortage of money and the lack of a proper administrative machinery prevented it from being put into effect. The impatience of Gustavus Vasa with mercenaries, however, had produced by mid-century an actual example of a national standing army in Sweden.[1] It was composed for a short while of volunteers, then of conscripts, and this represents a tendency general in Europe to prefer the conscript to the small numbers and the unreliability of volunteers. But the end of the century found the mercenary more firmly ensconced than ever. As armies continued to grow in size, and steadiness became the crucial factor in tactics dominated by firearms, the hired specialist was found both more reliable and more capable of adjusting himself to change than the soberest conscript. Gustavus Vasa's successor, Eric, returned to using them, and 'perhaps the weightiest testimony of all against the conscript army was the experience of the Dutch: the great reforms of Maurice [of Nassau] were carried through (and contemporaries believed that they could only have been carried through) by an army of punctually paid mercenaries'.[2]

In the matter of command, some lessons had been learned from the Italian Wars. Military leaders were less frequently shadowed by civilian commissaries; the idea of divided military command was a positive bogy. But the problem of preventing an army, once wound up by the state, from running away on its own was still grave, especially for countries which, like England, tempered periods of inactivity with ambitious long-range amphibious operations. Only in the Netherlands was a solution reached, where the captain general of the Spanish forces was also governor of the country. The captain general had, moreover, what the leaders of other national armies lacked: a general staff capable of keeping a firm control over the whole administrative and military structure of his force. The chief of this staff, the camp-master general, disposed the army in camp, on the march, and in order of battle. He and his own staff were responsible for knowing where every man should be at all times. Under him was a quartermaster, in charge of a camp once established, and a provost who, with his men, was responsible for justice, order, and the prices and sale

[1] Michael Roberts, *Gustavus Adolphus*, vol. II, p. 191, calls it 'the first truly national standing army of modern times'.
[2] *Ibid.* p. 203.

of foodstuffs. The high quality of these men and their representatives in each *tercio* was a vital element in the success of campaigns that involved long periods in quarters, in winter and during sieges. The scope of their organising ability went as far as the prostitutes which accompanied the army. There should be eight for each hundred men, a Spanish writer, himself a *maestro di campo*, wrote, 'for, accepting the fact that well organised states allow such persons in order to avoid worse disorders, in no state is it as necessary to allow them as in this one of free, strong and vigorous men, who might otherwise commit crimes against the local people, molesting their daughters, sisters and wives'.[1] Attached to the captain general's staff, on the more active side, was a *corps d'élite* of officers, some directly appointed for special merit, not merely for noble birth. These men were used for special duties, from holding reviews to leading a particularly hazardous reconnaissance. With this staff, and a flying squadron of cavalry to carry orders, the general could control, guide and repair the force brought into the field by the camp-master and his men.

For massive efficiency the Spanish army had no rival. The Turks, whose discipline and morale had once been held up as a model, had declined as a fighting power. The Janissaries had fallen off in efficiency and gained in obstreperousness, and the quality of the feudal horse had worsened with the granting of fiefs to civilians who sent substitutes instead of fighting themselves, and as cavalry remained the predominant arm, the Turkish army was doomed to mark time in a war of sieges waged in the steep hills and valleys of the empire's eastern border.

The Spaniards, however, were not beyond criticism. In the important matter of brigading, they had been pioneers. The *tercio* of some three thousand men had provided a rational organisation for blocks of men roughly the same size as the older, haphazardly composed combat block, the 'battle'. Administratively a unit, it commonly fought as a whole, its morale strengthened by the nearest thing to regimental tradition outside small picked corps like the Scots guard of the French kings. From an administrative point of view the size of the regiment did not matter, but from the point of view of tactics, the massive groups, which had evolved early in the century when the prestige of the dense infantry column was at its height, had become anachronistic now that caliver and musket and horse pistol dictated the manner in which battles were fought, rather than pikes and the lances of heavy cavalry. Now that the infantry formation seldom had to withstand massive charges, large numbers of men in its centre were reduced to the status of passengers. Other formations were required which would enable every man to develop his striking power. At the other end of the scale the *tercio*, like the regiments of England and France, was composed of companies of about one hundred men, micro-

---

[1] Sancho de Londono, *Discours sur la forme et maniere qu'on devroit user, pour reduire la discipline militaire à meilleur et son ancien estat* (Brussels, 1589), f. 35ʳ.

cosms of the *tercio* in that they combined pike, halberd and shot. These companies could be combined in fighting formations that were designed to bridge the gap between company and regiment. However, thanks to a natural conservatism and to the shortage of officers intermediate in rank between the captain of a company and the colonel of a regiment, the tactical unit tended to coincide with the administrative one, and it is noteworthy that as the *tercio* was copied by the French *légion* and then by the English regiment, each of these units became smaller than the last. The company of a hundred men was convenient from the point of view of recruitment and training, the regiment as an administrative unit; the reformers of the age, notably Eric of Sweden and Maurice of Nassau, preserved the small company and the large regiment but introduced an intermediate tactical unit, the battalion, which in Sweden comprised five hundred and twenty-five and in the United Netherlands five hundred and fifty men, and trained a new class of officers to train and command it. At last armies had enough hands to grasp all the weapons available to them, and were potentially able to submit them to serious experiment.

For all the attempts to improve their organisation, however, armies remained inadequately trained and officered, and lacking in unity. There was nothing like a regimental uniform, let alone a common dress for an army. If certain units looked alike it was because of the whim of a wealthy captain or nobleman, or because of the order of a local recruiting authority, or because of the bulk purchase of a particular cloth by an army contractor. While national characteristics could be identified amid all the variety of armour, costume and weapons, matters were complicated when mercenaries of the same nation fought for both sides and, for combat, scarves or tunics were used as distinguishing marks. They also made impersonation easy, and were the cause of many a successful surprise. As battlefields became noisier and armies ever more multilingual, the use of drums to give orders to the infantry and trumpets to the cavalry became more elaborate. Increasingly a semblance of unity was given to an army by the practice of marching in step, 'just and even with a gallant and sumptuous pace',[1] and more strenuous attempts were made to subject every man to a code of laws binding for the duration of a campaign. Such codes, promulgated by the war council and passed down from the general to the captains and from them to their men, commonly forbade the soldier to gamble, to blaspheme, to smuggle any unauthorised woman into camp, to get drunk, to leave the line of march or the camp in search of food or drink, to loot ecclesiastical buildings or use them as billets, to kill or rape non-combatants, to change his company or leave it without permission, to be absent from musters or use a false name, to join a mutinous assembly

[1] William Garrard, *The Arte of Warre* (1591), quoted by H. G. Farmer, 'Sixteenth and Seventeenth Century Military Marches', in *Journal of the Society for Army Historical Research* (1950), p. 49.

or lack a proper respect for his superiors. Provisions were made to guard against mutiny, desertion or failure to perform military duties, and also to prevent trouble between men of different nationalities, to prevent infection (latrines to be used; dead animals buried), to stop the disorder caused by unregulated looting, and to prevent soldiers from antagonising the civilian population to a degree that would hinder billeting and the purchase of local supplies. These military laws, whose fundamentals were common to all nations, even played a part in overseas expansion, where military discipline not only helped in conquest but sustained civilian morale, as in Virginia where, a contemporary writer reported, if it had not been for the military laws learned in the Netherlands by Sir Thomas Gates and Sir Thomas Dale, 'I see not how the utter subversion of the colony could have been prevented'.[1]

The presence of poorly trained men, and a mixture of nations, led to attempts to supplement the unifying bond of law by strengthening morale. There is an element of parody in the decision made by the Turkish vizier on the eve of Alcazar to have the recently deceased sultan taken round the army in a litter while his attendants pretended to keep up a conversation with him. But similar devices were used in the north, down to the issuing of nooses to men about to go on a raid, with instructions not to take any prisoners. The textbooks emphasised that men fought best when they had been taught to hate their enemy and believe in their own cause, and urged that one of the qualities needed by a military commander was eloquence with which to encourage his men. The harangue, whether delivered by the general and passed down to the men through the captains, or delivered at some crucial moment to a small group of waverers, undoubtedly helped to give troops a sense of purpose and confidence, and of contact with that otherwise remote person, their general. These harangues —to men whose emotions were still most susceptible to the spoken word— varied from complex appeals to hasty promises or threats. So far was the harangue from being merely a literary device that the literary harangue, as in Ronsard's appeal to the Catholics to save Paris from the Huguenots, owed its force to its reflection of battlefield practice.

> Vous, guerriers asseurez, vous, pietons, vous soldars
> De Bellone conceus, jeune race de Mars,
> Dont les fresches vertus par la Gaule fleurissent,
> N'ayez peur que les bois leurs fueilles convertissent
> En Huguenots armez, ou comme les Titans
> Il naissent de la terre en armes combatans.
> Mais ayez fort pique et dure et fort espée,
> Bon jacque bien cloué, bonne armure trempée,
> La bonne targue au bras, au corps bons corselets,
> Bonne poudre, bon plomb, bon feu, bons pistolets,

[1] Ralph Hamor, *A true discourse of the present state of Virginia* (1615), quoted by A. L. Rowse, *The Elizabethans and America* (New York, 1959), p. 76.

Bon morion en teste, et sur tout une face
Qui du premier regard nostre ennemi desface.
    Vous ne combattez pas (soldars) comme autrefois
Pour borner plus avant l'Empire de vos Rois,
C'est pour l'honneur de Dieu et sa querelle sainte,
Qu'aujourd 'huy vous portez l'espée au costé ceinte.[1]

In spite of firearms, most soldiers still wore armour, and, as this poem suggests, it helped to sustain morale by giving protection as well as by presenting a glittering and alarming spectacle to the enemy—a factor which prompted military writers to prefer a polished to a blackened surface. In face of the threat of firearms, however, armour was modified. Vital pieces were made pistol- or caliver-proof, and to compensate for the increased weight, inessential pieces, especially for the leg, were dispensed with. The horseman's armour changed less than that of the infantryman, who found himself so weighed down by pieces of proof that he got rid of them when he could, provoking cries of foreboding from those who remembered that the Romans had in this way made themselves an easy prey for the Goths, while others, though deploring the practice, reflected gloomily that the regular wearing of proof could crook the back and exhaust the manhood of a warrior in his thirties. Leather was used for unimportant pieces, and wide use was made of various forms of armoured doublet. But if firearms tended to simplify armour, another influence, that of the tilt and the parade, worked in the opposite direction. Only the very rich could afford different suits for civil pageantry and for war, and while some pieces—head-pieces, for instance—could not be interchanged, some of the most splendid parade armour was designed for use in battle as well.

This generation, which has seen increasing sympathy for other forms of late *cinquecento* art, may come to be lenient towards the lavishly decorated armour of this period, so much deplored by admirers of the Gothic and Maximilian styles. At no period was armour so utilitarian as to be unmodified by artistic fashion, and while too much embossing and reheating in order to obtain complex decorative effects could weaken the metal, the technical mastery of the late sixteenth-century armourer was as great as ever, and, in designing pieces that were to resist bullets rather than sword blows, he could afford to roughen the glancing surfaces with decoration. The demand on the great centres of production, Augsburg, Landshut, Innsbruck, Milan and Greenwich, was so heavy that simplifications— fewer overlapping plates, for instance, duplicated pieces for the left and right sides, helmets made in halves joined in the centre—were introduced for the mass market. There was an increasing need for sapping helmets and other specially heavy pieces for siege work. On the other hand, the

[1] 'Remonstrance au peuple de France', printed in *Discours des Misères de ce Temps* (ed. Jean Baillou, Paris, 1949).

demand for fine armours for parade and pageant, and for the special equipping of princely or municipal body-guards, led to something like the mass production of highly decorated suits as well, especially in north Italy. Though there was possibly little change in the number of complete suits worn, the total production of pieces of armour steadily increased. There was more than mere nostalgia for an era without guns behind the continued popularity of armour as a diplomatic gift and the prominence given it in the tombs and portraits of the period.

In the same way, the number and variety of *armes blanches* increased in response to the demands of war, sport and pageantry. On the battlefield the main weapons were the pike and sword—the handguard of the latter becoming elaborate to compensate for the declining use of plate on the arm—with dwindling numbers of halberds and cavalry lances. In sport, the sabre, the two-handed sword and the javelin increased in popularity, and a bizarre multiplicity of hafted weapons based on the halberd were used for ceremonial purposes to make a show at once luxurious and martial.

Though crossbows were used against the Turks in Malta and by some Spanish units in the Netherlands, and though Leicester took a company of longbowmen with him to the Low Countries in 1585, and they were used until the end of the century against the Irish, the bow was an obsolescent weapon. Arguments in favour of its tactical superiority to the gun on the score of a faster rate of fire, convenience in wet weather and lightness, which enabled more armour to be worn, were less telling than the fact that they already existed in large numbers, were cheap to replace, and cost nothing for use in practice, while firearm training consumed powder and shot. However, the armies of this period could not afford to support units which were worth little in siege work or defence. There were two standard infantry missile weapons, the caliver—an improved, standard-bore arquebus—and the longer, heavier musket, which could only be fired from a rest. Though the wheel-lock had been invented in the first quarter of the century, and the more reliable snaphaunce towards its end, both weapons relied on the matchlock, whose rough-and-ready simplicity more than compensated for its faults in spite of the wasteful consumption of match, its vulnerability to rain, the difficulty of concealing it by night, the bother of keeping it trimmed to the right length, and the extra movements required to control it while reloading. From its introduction into the Netherlands in the late 1560s and soon afterwards into France, the musket slowly replaced the caliver, except for use on horseback and for infantry duties like skirmishing where the 16–20 pound musket and its rest were too heavy. The rate of fire of both caliver and musket was slow, in spite of the occasional use of made-up cartridges containing charge and shot, and as a result the countermarch was developed, which allowed each rank to withdraw and reload while the one behind moved forward to take its place. The musket could penetrate all but the heaviest proof armour at two hundred yards, and tales of its killing at five hundred yards are common. Its accuracy, however, was poor. Bullets made on the spot from moulds, unstandardised powder, excessive windage between the ball and the barrel: these were some of the factors which made accuracy difficult, and in spite of stories like Ambroise Paré's of the Catholic who stuck his hand over the wall to bait the Huguenot assailants of Bourges and had it promptly shot through, true marksmanship was possible only to the few men who were issued with rifled guns for sniping, and to the wealthy civilian sportsman with his rifled wheel-lock. More inaccurate still were the pistols used by the German *reiters* from the 1540s and growing in popularity thereafter: the bullets sprayed out from their short barrels were so vagrant that point-blank range was hardly more than three paces. In spite of this they were considered effective enough to cause the pistol to be substituted for the lance, and the caracole for the charge home. Besides the great mass of utilitarian guns and pistols, others were produced, especially for sporting purposes, that were marvels of decorative and mechanical skill, with German gunsmiths, especially those of Augsburg and Nürnberg, in the lead. Pistols were made with multiple barrels and double locks, they were concealed in the hafts of maces and war-hammers, ingeniously combined with crossbows, swords and daggers. But these toys of wealthy sportsmen or collectors, though they indicate one aspect of the fascination exerted by gunpowder, are irrelevant to the development of the sturdy, plain military weapons, which remained virtually unchanged in manufacture and accuracy until the invention of the percussion cap and a cheap rifling process in the nineteenth century.

Though the Turks used catapults in their attack on Malta in 1565 and the Italian military engineer Girolamo Maggi recommended that the *balista* should be kept in mind in case normal munitions should run short, guns were the only heavy missile weapons the soldier of the period had to take into account. In spite of attempts to reduce the number of different types of guns in order to ease the problems of supply, the textbooks could still, at the end of the century, list some forty varieties, from a piece hardly weightier than a musket to massive siege and ship cannon. Four main guns, however, emerged as the most useful, and were standardised by edict in France and Spain and by gradual usage elsewhere: large cannon, shooting a heavy ball of fifty pounds or more to a maximum range of about two thousand yards; medium cannon, shooting a thirty-pound ball to a range that was shorter by a couple of hundred yards; the large culverin, longer and lighter than the equivalent cannon, sending a seventeen-pound ball two thousand five hundred yards; and a smaller culverin sending a ball of about half the size to a similar range. Broadly speaking, the cannon were for siege work, to deliver a smashing blow at short range, while the culverins, which combined range with lightness, were used in the field. The smaller type of each class was the most common, and still smaller culverins, especially one corresponding to the English saker, which fired a five-pound ball, remained popular both in battle and in defence works. All of these guns, except for a few small and eccentric pieces, were muzzle-loading (the speed of reloading with removable chambers at the breech had not been found to compensate for the structural weakness involved) and increasing numbers were cast in brass. The quality of gunpowder had improved, and accordingly the thickness of metal had increased. Iron balls were the standard ammunition, stone-throwing guns (periers), formerly popular because a smaller charge was required to expel a stone ball and the gun could be made thinner and lighter, were no longer made, though many remained in use. Red-hot shot was occasionally used, a turf wad being used as an insulator, and chained shot was used at sea and in defence works: to sweep breaches, for instance. Mortars were used even more sparingly in siege work than they had been previously. Explosive mortar shells played a picturesque part in the books devoted to gunnery, but they were hazardous and there were only a few instances in which they were of any real importance. Cartridges of paper or canvas were not unknown, but most loading was done by ladle direct from the keg, the charge being then set off with a burning match held in one of the period's few inventions: the linstock, a combination weapon and tool: a halberd shaped to hold the burning match.

It is easy to list factors which should have made it impossible for the gunner to hit his mark. No two guns were precisely alike as each was made in a different mould. A sizeable gap was allowed for windage between the bore and the ball, so the projectile did not emerge on a true centre line. The quality of the powder was not constant nor the charge (especially when the wind was blowing) uniform. At each discharge the gun's setting was disturbed by the recoil of the entire carriage, sometimes to the extent of several feet. The shape and weight of shot were variable. Guns were tested to make sure that they were not likely to burst, but they were not fitted with sights nor checked for the smoothness or the correct centring of the bore. Yet from accounts of siege and battle there is little doubt that a trained gunner could get to know his weapon (he would only have one in his care) so well that his skill and instinct would compensate to a large extent for its technical inadequacies. The problem was to obtain skilled gunners, and this could only be done if states were willing, as was Spain, to establish schools and pay for the powder used in trial shots. Sea gunnery was especially inaccurate partly because powder was too scarce to be used for practice. The emphasis in gunnery, in any case, was less on marksmanship than on shock, for it was in siege work that the vast majority of shots were fired, and it was assumed that the range would be point-blank, that is, about six hundred feet.

Guns were so necessary that governments attempted to control manufacture and export. On the other hand, they were so profitable to sell that there was constant arguing about export licences and continual smuggling. Countries with few foundries of their own, like Portugal (where import taxes on armaments were waived) and Spain (which relied heavily on imports until the royal foundries at Seville got under way after 1611), bought abroad and welcomed smugglers. Holland was a large importer and so, until the end of the century, was Sweden. France, too, was an importer, for the casting of cannon, in bronze or iron, was a large-scale operation and vulnerable to the dislocations of war. For this reason the flourishing foundries of the southern provinces of the Low Countries also came to lose their trade to England, Germany and Italy from the 1570s.[1] Gunpowder, too, was controlled in the same way, not to keep powerful subjects from revolt but to ensure that the state had enough for its own needs. It was the difficulty of eking out her own saltpetre supplies from Europe that forced Elizabeth's government to trade illicitly with the infidels of Morocco. However, as with men, so with munitions: thanks to the possibility of adding to a nation's own resources by purchase, legal or not, there is no indication that any major politico-military decisions were affected by the state of production at home.

Partly because of crown interest, partly because it was the least aristocratic arm, the artillery had come to surpass the other arms in the efficiency of its organisation. The size of this can be gauged from the number of men and services required to attend one gun of the largest size. At least twenty horses were needed to drag it, thirty if the ground was slippery from rain. Thirty pioneers were required to build its implacements and haul it back into position after firing. It was served by a team of from two to five gunners. It shared the care of the carpenters, blacksmiths and wheelwrights and the protection of the infantry guard who accompanied the artillery train, but its powder and its balls—sixty to a load—required six more carts and up to forty more horses. Each gun was but the striking tip of a ponderous haft of services.

The arm which was most recalcitrant to organisation was the cavalry, still the arm with the highest social prestige—indeed, in the empire it was subject to a separate 'gentlemanly' disciplinary code—though as this prestige was mainly associated with the obsolescent, fully armoured man-at-arms, the gentleman no longer attached so much value to fighting on horseback rather than on foot. But the tradition of independence based on the privileges of birth made the efficient brigading of companies of horse into regiments a comparatively slow business. Cavalry remained an indispensable element on any battlefield; when infantry was left to fend for itself it could seldom stand up to a cavalry attack. A common proportion of horse to foot was rather more than one to three, though in eastern countries like Poland where the chief threat consisted of horsed

---

[1] Much information in C. Cipolla, *Guns and Sails...* (London, 1965).

raids, and in the Ottoman empire cavalry remained the more numerous arm. While men-at-arms were still an element to be reckoned with on occasion, their numbers steadily declined. The three commonest types of cavalry were the lancer, the pistoleer and the carbine. The lancer was armed and mounted to charge home against shaken troops; the pistoleer was armed with two pistols, sword and dagger, and as he did not have to charge home but rode up, fired, and wheeled away, he did not need to be so well mounted; the carbine was more lightly mounted and armoured than the other two, as he would be expected to scout, forage or take messages and also to fight on foot. He carried sword, dagger and a wheel-lock or snaphaunce caliver. He was not expected to come to close quarters with the enemy. As a cross between a light-cavalryman and a foot arquebusier, the carbine was the subject of much debate, being attacked on the one hand for being an arquebusier who had climbed up on a horse to get out of harm's way, praised on the other as the most generally useful of all horsemen; and as early as the 1560s there were élite corps of carbines in the tradition-haunted cavalry ranks of France. Debate raged, too, over the rival merits of lancers on the one hand, pistol- or carbine-armed cavalry on the other. It was a debate that was bound to be protracted, because while in theory an attack by pistoleers should be decisive, in fact, as they usually fired too soon, their caracoles were indecisive, whereas attacks by lancers, hazardous in theory, proved increasingly effective as infantry became less and less used to shock attack.

The predominant role played by infantry since the emergence of the Swiss pikemen after the middle of the previous century had led to a dwindling in the proportion of horse to foot which was a source of satisfaction to nations which found it difficult to breed enough horses, to individuals who could not face the expense of setting up as a cavalryman, and to commanders who found cavalry even less subject to discipline than the infantry. The fact that cavalry had even less part to play in campaigns that increasingly revolved about sieges was accepted with little protest. Only the French still felt that there was something not quite gentlemanly about fighting on two rather than four legs, and their own reformers roundly scolded them for it. The infantry came to wear less armour during this period, and their arms became more standardised: swords (as a sole arm) had entirely, and halberds very largely, given place to the pike or the musket. A normal proportion of pike to musket in a Spanish *tercio* was two to one, but it tended to increase, and in any case the proportion was determined by other factors than a theoretical optimum; the French, for instance, had never taken willingly to the pike: they stuck, for the most part, to the arquebus or musket and paid other nations, when possible, to trail pikes.

In an age like the present, was the example of the ancient world still relevant, the military authors asked? But they asked only to return themselves a ringing affirmative. The use of guns had not exploded the usefulness of the ancients. Fashions in armament might change, but the need for high morale and firm discipline was constant. Constant, too, was the need to reward men's valour and promote them by desert, not birth, to accustom them by drill and gymnastics to the fatigues of war, especially to the strain of wearing armour. It was the Romans who had sounded that so contemporary warning: in peace prepare for war; the Romans who had analysed and decided against the perennial temptation to provide an army with a joint command. It is not surprising that what a supreme fighting race had said about the nature of a fighting man should have remained of value, but it is interesting that an increasing attention was paid to ancient tactics. Wherever men were studying how to use modern weapons most effectively, they appeared to be reading Livy, or Caesar, or the Emperor Leo. Eric of Sweden, Maurice and Lewis William of Nassau studied the military writings of the ancients. 'Our discipline of embattailing our army', wrote Lord Burghley in 1595, 'is according to the Roman dizeniers.' When Henry IV wished to improve the tactics of the French army he asked Sully if he would 'faire une recueil des articles les plus convenables au temps present' from texts both of the modern world and of antiquity.

The need for new tactics was widely recognised. Granvelle, Philip II's most trusted minister in the Netherlands, was reported to have said to an English agent in 1559, 'Your men are hardy and valiant, but what discipline have they had these many years? And the art of war is now such that men be fain to learn anew at every two years' end.'[1] To learn it, however, was not easy. There were to be few pitched battles in the next two generations, and most of those were small, of short duration, and fought not with rationally planned combinations of picked men, but with whoever could be scraped together for the occasion. The armies that were longest in the field, the Spanish, revised their tactics to some small extent—the *tercio* was reduced in size and preceded by a forlorn hope of shot; but, while the old mass formations were wasteful, they were solid, and reforms in the direction of smaller bodies, spread out in thin lines, though rational, appeared hazardous. They required, too, a high standard of drill unit by unit, so that firepower could be maintained steadily and accurately by means of the countermarch, and a high standard of co-operation between units; but not only were the officers who could serve this largely lacking, but a combination of units, let alone an army as a whole, was rarely drilled or manœuvred together. There came to be a wide gap between the literature of the parade-ground, with wedge formations, and shears and stars and saws and windmills and cross-squares, expressed in diagrams based on those in Machiavelli's *Art of War*, and the practice of the battlefield, where tactics were largely determined by the traditions or qualities of the

[1] Quoted by J. U. Nef, *War and Human Progress* (Harvard, 1950), p. 30.

different elements that composed an army. The need for regular, rigorous drill, on which extended order tactics depend, was not properly recognised by men or officers, in spite of the constant vague complaint that the 'Roman discipline' had to be revived or of the example of exceptional men like Maurice of Nassau. The minimum of drill accepted as part of the rather casual, free-lance business of being a soldier was consumed in teaching the musketeer the use of his weapon so that it would be a greater hazard to the enemy than to himself. The nearest approach to the ideal formation of the textbooks was to be seen not in action, but on the march, or in the orderly layout of a camp.

The basic infantry formation of the Spaniards, Swiss, and Germans was a deep solid square of pikes, protected on all sides, and especially in front and at the corners, by shot who were expected to take refuge among the pikes if driven in. It seldom happened that the pike square itself was then broken up, as artillery, which could achieve this, was hardly ever employed in the later stage of a battle, and the square could beat off a numerically superior enemy even when engaged on all sides if its corner and outside men were highly trained. Or it might not be engaged at all. 'It is rarely seene in our dayes', noted an English observer, 'that men come often to hand-blowes, as in old times they did: For now in this age the shot so employeth and busieth the field (being well backed with a resolute stand of pikes) that the most valiantest and skilfullest therein do commonly impart the victorie, or the best, at the least wise, before men come to many hand-blowes.'[1] Both its success in resisting attack and its isolation from hand-to-hand fighting until the moment for its power to be exerted as a reserve helped its practitioners to think kindly of the infantry square in spite of its unwieldiness, and rather than break it up into much smaller bodies they concentrated on surrounding it with more shot, and on providing a hollow in its centre where the shot could take refuge more effectively than amongst massed ranks of pikes. These squares were embattled two or three side by side, in three tiers, advance guard, main body and reserve. Artillery, shot and horse stirred up the patterns an action was to take, while the pike squares stood as defensive rocks, or exerted a steady pressure in attack.

While some countries continued to develop the square as the key tactical unit, others, as we saw when discussing the administration of armies, were forming smaller units in an attempt to increase firepower by confronting an enemy with long thin lines, composed of small shallow blocks. Partly because the French had to use many small, skirmish-seasoned groups, but with a theoretical backing from Roman precedent, the process of subdivision continued until Henry IV was brigading his infantry in battalions of five hundred men, trained to support one another in line or chequer formation, and Maurice's battalion of five hundred and fifty,

---

[1] Robert Barret, *The Theoricke and Practike of Moderne Warres* (London, 1598), p. 75.

each combining separate units of pike and shot, deployed a maximum of firepower while relying in defence on intelligent co-operation, quickness of movement and cavalry support. There was no confrontation on a large scale of the two systems; it was for a later age to decide between the older, static and wasteful but solid, and the new one, flexible, deploying more firepower but more fragile, vulnerable to flank attack, and more difficult to officer and control.

While infantry formation tended to become shallower, that of the cavalry became deeper as the old charge *en haie*, in a thin line, gave way to the attack in columns, with a front of some fifteen horses. Such columns could break through an enemy line either by the weight behind their charge or by the concentration of their pistol fire as each rank came up, fired at close quarters and wheeled aside to let the next rank take its place, or by a combination of the two, making gaps with pistol fire and then forcing them open with a charge. It is easy to exaggerate the striking power of the cavalry of the earlier Italian wars and the decadence implied by the change from lance to pistols; as long as formations remained deep a cavalry charge could do little by lance and impetuosity alone, and the pistol, though less 'chivalrous', and deplored by contemporary tradition-alists, was probably more effective in destroying an enemy's steadiness. In eastern Europe, against fast, mounted enemies, the lance remained the primary cavalry weapon, but it did not return in the west until the search for mobility had produced units capable again of being routed by an unsupported cavalry charge. The placing of cavalry in a battle order depended on the numbers involved, but conventionally cavalry was placed on either wing, to impede the enemy's horse from taking the infantry in flank, and there was commonly a cavalry force kept as a reserve.

Field artillery played a small but important part, especially at the onset of a battle, as neither horse nor foot could stand for long while being fired at. Theoretically, armies were supplied with medium-heavy culverins for a preliminary bombardment, and lighter guns to give support where needed in the course of an action. In practice, it was seldom that an army was in possession of all its equipment when brought to battle, and instances of guns being moved about during an engagement are rare. On the other hand the usual number of guns—three to five—that arrived on French battlefields were on several occasions enough at least to provoke the enemy to attack against his will or even to influence an action once it had begun. In the Netherlands a notable example of both effects was seen at Nieuport. Bombardment from the sea forced the Spanish army to move inland and two guns placed on the dunes by Maurice helped to break up the first line of Spanish cavalry when the battle was under way.

It was only in the realm of fortification that practice and theory joined hands and justified a use of the word Art in connection with War. The volume of building and of theorising was very impressive. Italians continued to write most of the books on fortification and Italian engineers were more widely employed than those of other nations both in Europe and overseas, but gradually the lead was taken by principles associated with the writings of the German Daniel Speckle and the Dutchman Simon Stevin. The achievement of the Italian school had been to suit the medieval curtain wall to an age of firearms by thickening it, altering its plan as much as possible into that of a regular polygon, and covering it with flanking fire from obtuse- or right-angled bastions whose fire was supplemented by cavaliers, raised structures either on the bastions themselves or in the middle of a stretch of curtain wall. The German and Dutch schools, and in their wake the French, turned this system into a predominantly aggressive one, reaching far out towards the enemy with detached or semi-detached external works, deploying a much heavier firepower, and shrinking the size and importance of the curtain while increasing those of the bastion. The regular polygon was retained as the ideal trace. The profile of the defence remained low and, indeed, was masked by glacis which had to be scaled before the assailant could glimpse the base of any part of the defences. Beyond the main *enceinte*, subsidiary works, mostly variants on the ravelin, reached out, keeping the enemy at a distance, preventing his concentrating on the main defences, forcing him to thin his forces in wide lines of circumvallation, and to hack his way forward piecemeal and slowly. Such defence systems, which were provided with as many levels of fire as possible, were conceived as static counterattacks. Speaking in broad, ideal terms, the engineers of the mid-century had built outwards from the place to be defended; the northern school planned inwards from a wide belt of outer defences, taking the nature of the perimeter of the *zone sanitaire* as a starting-point. The curtain and its bastions, and the outworks and their ditches were all designed to be mutually supporting: every surface, every length of ditch was to be swept by the fire of an adjacent work. Stevin emphasised this uniting principle: 'En somme NETTOYER, NETTOYER, dije, est le but & poinct principal de l'ordonnance des forteresses du temps present.'[1]

Speckle and Stevin between them anticipated the main developments in fortification that were to be exploited by Vauban, but their systems involved meticulous surveying, and a lengthy and expensive contouring of the outlying countryside. It was the simpler Italian system that remained in vogue throughout this period. The ideas of military engineers like Maggi and de Marchi achieved an international currency through translations of their books; they were spread by itinerant engineers, like Batista Antonelli, who was sent by Philip II to construct a master plan for the protection of Spain's dominions in the New World. A succession of model, much publicised defences—Malta, Antwerp, Palmanova—maintained the prestige of the Italian school; its basic principle, the polygonal

[1] Trans. of *De Sterctenbouwing* (1594) in *Œuvres Mathematiques* (1608), p. 658.

bastioned trace, was so flexible and could be constructed so quickly and simply that it became a true international style, and from Havana to New Navarino, from Moçambique to Goa and Macao, from Antwerp to Algiers, the fortifications of the late sixteenth century belonged recognisably to the same family.

Fortification in the new manner was more than a military need, it was a fashion. As cities had once competed to build the biggest cathedral, and citizens to have chapels named after them, so now cities attempted to rival one another's fortifications, and individuals were proud to see their names attached to a bastion. Fortification was an inseparable part of the new interest in town planning; both gratified the taste for harmony and rational proportion. There was no barrier between the town planner and the military engineer; the same man commonly fulfilled both functions and was responsible for the whole appearance of the town from ravelins on the perimeter to fountains in the central piazza. Tourists paid increasing attention to the defences of the towns they visited, and from Caprarola near Rome to Kerjean in Brittany, wealthy patrons incorporated something of the modish bastioned trace in the plans of their villas.

The result of need and fashion was a vast programme of building and rebuilding. New fortifications were concentrated in three anti-Turkish zones: one running north–south from Vienna through Karlstadt and down the west coast of the Adriatic and the Ionian seas to Crete; another north–south line consisting of the fortified coasts of the kingdom of Naples, Sicily and Malta, guarding the central Mediterranean; a third running east–west and comprising fortified places along the north African shore and along the southern coast of Spain, the Balearics and Sardinia. And there were other concentrations, either where two frontiers clashed, as on France's north-east border, or where an occupying power was digging itself in, as was Spain in Lombardy and the southern Netherlands. The expense involved in all this building activity was formidable, not only in clearing the ground and building the fortifications but in arranging compensation for the land used, purchasing guns and ammunition and, where necessary, maintaining a garrison. Most expensive of all were those outposts, like the Spanish positions in North Africa, which had to be maintained by sea. The money for fortifications was gained in various ways: by government grant, by local contributions in the form of cash, labour services and special taxes on commodities entering or leaving the town; or the city fathers could raise loans and sell trading or social privileges. All these methods were employed at Antwerp in order to raise the million gold crowns needed to build its *enceinte*. At the other end of the scale, the trifling defences of Plymouth were financed by a grant from the crown, a gift from the lord lieutenant, a local tax on pilchards, and contributions from such interested parties as local inhabitants, gentlemen of the county, and London merchants who had a stake in the trade of the town, but all this did not suffice, and the port had to be put on the budget of the Low Countries. New fortified towns like Rocroi or Freudenstadt were able to repay the loans with which they were built by attracting settlers with the promise of religious freedom, free house sites and building materials, sanctuary for certain crimes and exemption from certain taxes. An assessment of the economic and social consequences of so much fortification, on rents for instance, or on the careers of individuals like Gillebert von Shoonbeke, the contractor mainly responsible for the works at Antwerp, let alone the part played by defence works in war budgets as a whole, has scarcely been attempted.

The extent to which defence had regained the lead it had lost to cannon attack in the previous century cannot be easily summarised. Morale, as always, was an important variable which could increase the resistance of a weak position or reduce that of a strong one. Broadly speaking, no city was strong enough to hold out even to the limits of its food supply if an attack was pressed consistently and in force. It is for this reason that the northern school of fortification aimed to hit back at, as well as to keep off, the enemy and bring savage concentrations of fire to bear on his batteries and troop concentrations; moreover, the wider the circle round which the besieger had to extend his men and counterworks the greater became his problems of communication and supply, and the more vulnerable he became to sorties and to the action of relieving forces from outside. The taking even of small places, however, was likely to take time, and armies could not move forward past towns occupied by the enemy, confident that they could be reduced in a few days. The new fortification was the work of specialists, and siegecraft, too, came to depend increasingly on experts to determine the points to attack and to design the trench systems leading towards them. There was still a reluctance to accept the need for long, painstaking sieges, and commanders until the end of the century were forced to take up a spade themselves to convince their men that the construction of trenches and emplacements was part of the soldier's and not simply of the civilian pioneer's trade. Attempts were frequently made to carry a town by ingenuity or subterfuge rather than by force, and much ingenuity was wasted in the manufacture of special bombs, telescopic firing-platforms, portable bullet-proof screens and the like before commanders and their paymasters accepted the fact that new inventions or old tricks culled from Frontinus could only in very exceptional circumstances take the place of slow, methodically applied pressure.

Most siege-work consisted of getting two or three batteries into emplacements some hundred yards from the most vulnerable part of the curtain, and hammering at the angles of the adjacent batteries until one provided a point of entry and the other was unable to provide flanking fire. But the most sensational siege of the period, Parma's fourteen-month attack on Antwerp, unique for the scale on which it was undertaken as well as the blend of methodical patience and experiment employed,[1] only came in contact with the city's famous bastioned front and pentagonal citadel when their fate had already been decided out in the flooded countryside. Parma's designs on Antwerp were known well before he moved against it. The only direction from which assistance could come to the city was from the north, up the Scheldt, or from the north-west, so long as the dykes were cut in such a way as to provide floodwater deep enough for boats to sail over the tall Kouwenstein dyke which ran east from the Scheldt. This last measure, urgently suggested by William the Silent's representative, Marnix, was defeated by pressure brought to bear on the city fathers by the guild of butchers, reluctant to lose their grazing lands. Before there was time for second thoughts, Parma moved in; and, though the lands to the north were flooded, the Kouwenstein dyke remained above water as a barrier to supplies, which could now only reach the city down the Scheldt. It was to block this route that Parma's engineers built a remarkable bridge. He dug a canal from Ghent, where the preliminary construction was done, and along this came ten thousand locally felled trees and fifteen hundred ships' masts imported from Scandinavia. These were made into a bridge nearly two thousand five hundred feet long, the central portion floating on boats, the end portions, where the water was shallower, built on piles, driven in deeply and braced by cross-timbers secured with great nails and chains. The roadway of the bridge was provided with a musket-proof parapet on both sides, and broadened out at each end into platforms from which artillery could give flanking fire. At each end, on the land, was a powerful fort. On the upstream side, to break the brunt of any attack from the besieged city, a line of boats was moored, clamped together in groups of three, making solid platforms from which projected long masts tipped with iron. Other boats were moored downstream to act as was needed against a relief force.

Against this massive obstacle the Anversois launched even more celebrated projectiles, the infernal machines of the Italian engineer Frederico Giambelli. These were two ships which Giambelli made into floating mines. He lined them with brick, filled them with gunpowder covered by layers of broken tombstones and pieces of iron to act as shrapnel and prevent the force of the explosion from spending itself in the air. Over this he placed a deck covered with inflammable material, so that the machine would look like a common fireship. The fuse of one was a timed match, the other a clockwork device made by a local clock-maker. The plan was to let a group of fireships float down first, to destroy the screen of boats which protected the bridge, then to release the infernal machines (guided by sailors who would swim ashore at the last moment), and finally, if a fortunate result was signalled, to follow up with ships containing enough

[1] Unique in length was the defence of Ostend (1601-4), but in this case the city could be supplied, and counter-measures organised, from the sea.

men to complete the destruction of the bridge and occupy the forts at either end. The attack took place at night. One of the machines drifted harmlessly into the bank, but the other struck the bridge and remained flaming there while Spanish soldiers, thinking it to be a fireship, tried, without too great a sense of urgency, to rake its combustibles into the water. Farnese himself came down to watch, and it was only by a lucky chance that he had walked away when the machine blew up, killing some eight hundred men outright and producing such lurid confusion that had the fleet come down from Antwerp the siege might well have been at an end. The confusion, however, affected the Dutch sailors who had been sent down to observe the bridge, and they failed to make the necessary signals. With the bridge repaired, the only chance for the Anversois was to take the Kouwenstein dyke. When this, too, failed, the city had no option but to surrender, with its walls intact.[1]

There was some feeling among contemporaries that fortification and siegecraft were playing too large a part in the business of war, but in fact the pitched battle was unlikely to be decisive except where the loser was far from his base, as the Portuguese were at Alcazar; armies on European battlefields seldom numbered as much as even twenty thousand men, and, when supply was possible, it was only a question of time before a defeated army could be built up again. As a result, there was no great urgency felt about bringing the enemy's force to an engagement; the aim rather was to compel his withdrawal by the occupation of key points and reduce him to such economic straits that he was unable to continue the struggle. But even so cautious a formulation as this probably suggests more strategic planning than actually existed. The fascination siege warfare held for the majority of military men and the fact that it offered a definite objective doubtless tempted commanders to see campaigns in terms of sieges, but little strategic thinking in the modern sense could exist in an age when the behaviour of armies was inefficient and uncertain[2] and when problems of finance and supply were too great to allow for long-term planning. There was, too, a tendency to think of an army as the concrete expression of a hostile state of mind, a mailed gesture which achieved part of its purpose simply by being made; its use as a precision tool for cutting towards a definitive objective was an extension of this purpose, but not the whole of it. The little armies, heavy with non-combatants, that trailed after one another among the fortified towns of Europe were not expected to settle everything by a glorious victory, or a precise programme of raids on vital spots, but to act as reminders that negotiations had been speeded up to the pace of war. Isolated voices, such as that of Lazarus von Schwendi,

---

[1] See the admirable account in L. van der Essen, *Alexandre Farnèse*, vol. IV, 'Le Siège d'Anvers' (Bruxelles, 1935), *passim*.

[2] For a good impression of the problems facing a commander see the account of de La Noue's service in the Protestant cause in the Netherlands in *Correspondence de François de La Noue* (ed. P. Kervyn de Volkaersbeke, Ghent, 1854).

could emphasise the need to concentrate on the end of a campaign, to bend every nerve towards bringing it about, to reassess constantly the situation as a whole,[1] but for most a campaign was something that could find its own level once it had been set going; only for an amphibious operation, where success depended on timing and a definite quantity of stores and transport, was it necessary to glimpse the end in the beginning. And this tendency to allow military operations to coalesce round the first obstacles they encountered was encouraged, finally, by an almost total lack of any abstract conception of 'strategy' as a way of looking at a military enterprise. On this theme the textbooks which purported to tell a soldier all he needed to know, and which were so expansive on the theme of tactics, were dumb.

The failure to think clearly about military objectives reflects, moreover, the lack of a clear-cut distinction between war itself and peace. There was much unofficial fighting, and, though governments from time to time tried to keep their subjects at home, this was at least as much due to a desire to retain manpower as to abstain from interfering in the wars of other nations. The French fleet which took part in the Portuguese attack on the Azores in 1582 was there without the official sanction of the crown. Many Englishmen fought for the Protestant Dutch, and whole companies were raised in England and crossed to the Netherlands before the country went formally to their aid in 1585. Even when a country was officially at war, there was still room for private enterprise. The project of Sir Francis Drake and Sir John Norris in 1589 to cripple Spain by capturing Lisbon and the Azores was financed as a private company venture, with the queen as chief shareholder. In every possible way, from the supply of victuals to the planning of a campaign, the state eagerly shifted its burdens on to the shoulders of private individuals, and was not concerned that this meant sacrificing any uniform, consistent, overall control.

Volunteer service by land was paralleled by piracy at sea and its next-of-kin, reprisal. With governments impotent to help their subjects if their ships were taken by pirates, the practice had arisen of allowing the injured party to recoup himself, under licence, by seizing goods from the shipping of the pirates' compatriots. Under the veil of reprisal acts of aggression went on from the personal to the national scale, as when English privateering in the Atlantic was encouraged from 1585 as a temporising substitute for open war with Spain. Piracy was rife in every sea: even the Turks had to create a special fleet to keep Christian pirates from wrecking their trade in the eastern Mediterranean. And arms-running was a continuous process, heeding neither alliances nor national policy. The definition of certain war materials as contraband had been agreed upon by the end of the century, and there was general acceptance of the idea that a belligerent was entitled

[1] Kriegsdiskurs (1577), printed in E. von Frauenholz, *Lazarus von Schwendi, der erste deutsche Verkunder der allgemein Wehrpflicht* (Hamburg, 1939), esp. pp. 200, 228 and 236.

to stop them from reaching an enemy state, but uncertainty as to how this might be done, and the precise status of a neutral, led to a high tolerance in international relations of acts which, while aggressive, were not quite acts of war. A country could be at peace with a rival, yet its subjects might be fighting it by land and sea; it could be loaning ships and supplies to the rival's enemies, and allowing those enemies to march troops across its own soil, and still not be, in any formal sense, at war.

Military thought at the middle of the century paid little attention to naval warfare. Ships were looked upon as useful to transport troops and protect them *en route*, to raid up and down an enemy's coast, to blockade his ports, but there was little difference in design, especially in round ships, between the warship and the merchantmen which formed in any case the bulk of a fighting force, and so long as naval tactics consisted mainly in boarding and settling the issue in a soldier's rather than a sailor's way, and so long as actions at sea were planned and executed by soldiers, there was little incentive to think in specifically naval terms. During the next two generations matters changed. Warships came to be designed in a way that distinguished them from merchantmen, broadside tactics made military analogies less useful, more and more heed was given, in planning an action, to the advice of experienced seamen. Yet for all this, at the turn of the century the navy remained a poor relation of the land power. War at sea was little written about; when it was, its place was usually in a final chapter or two, and that this does not reflect merely a copying of the space given to the sea by classical writers was shown by the fact that even in England, an island with rapidly growing oceanic interests and with a unique record for the design and handling of fighting ships, emphasis was placed as in the past on sending troops to the continent or supporting the operations of allies there, and time after time naval operations were starved at the expense of the land forces.

Initiative in design and increase in numbers had shifted from the Mediterranean to the north. The Turkish galley strength increased, it is true, and within two years of Lepanto the Turks attacked Tunis with two hundred and eighty galleys and nearly fifty other craft, but Lepanto had broken the prestige of their fleets, and no attempt was made to revise their manner of fighting. The Italian states had galley fleets ranging in size from those of Venice and Genoa to that of Piedmont, but their duties were restricted to watching for corsairs, and after Lepanto there was no major action in which the Italians could show that they had rejected the cautious, flinching tradition they had inherited from Andrea Doria and from their employment by Spain to contain, but not to favour Venice by seriously weakening the Turks.

The Italian states and the Turks, none of them deeply engaged in the long transoceanic voyages which were occupying the other powers, continued to use the galley as the main, almost the only, type of warship.

It was fast, and could be used when sailing ships were becalmed or hampered by contrary airs, and, as all galleys had much the same handling qualities, the ships of one state combined well with those of another. But in the north the round ship had proved more seaworthy, and the cost of keeping a galley with its large crew at sea, even if, as convicts, they did not have to be paid, was another of the factors which led to the use of galleys being restricted there to river patrol duties. There was, besides, a growing interest in broadside fire, and a galley could only fire its large guns fore and aft. But if the future was with the roundship, it was a round ship modified by the long lines of the galley, and for a while an intermediate type, the galleass, a sailing ship built to galley proportions, decked for broadside fire, with fore and after castles, and propelled at need by some thirty oars on either side, appeared to be the ideal fighting vessel. Its vogue had passed by the end of the century, but though the dominant new type, the galleon, had given up oars, the galley had contributed to its long lines and was a pattern for experiments made to improve its manœuvrability.

The galleon, which became during this period the main fighting ship of all the northern nations, and evolved easily into the later ship of the line, was the product of earnest debate in which practical experience and *a priori* calculation of a type more scientific than had hitherto contributed to ship design both played a part. It was longer in proportion to its beam than a merchantman, and if not flush-decked had only rudimentary castles fore and aft, whereas the merchantman retained its top hamper. Its size could vary from some one hundred to three hundred tons, to eight hundred or one thousand tons, the size respectively of the largest English and Spanish galleons in 1588. (Merchantmen might be half as large again; the Portuguese prize *Madre de Dios* was of sixteen hundred tons.) The length of keel of the warship and its sail plan—also experimented with during this period —made the warship more nimble than the merchantman. But if all these changes had made the galleon specially fitted for war, it shared the sea endurance of the merchant ship and was large enough to carry provisions and armaments and have space left over for prize goods. Nor was it so different that governments need do without merchantmen to combine with it in battle, and subsidies were still granted to the builders of ships large enough to be useful in time of war. There were still spokesmen for the older type of vessel which stood higher out of the water, with lofty superstructures that lent an appearance of might and the reality of vantage point in attack and security in defence against boarding. But from each debate on flush deck or half deck, covered waist or open waist, speed as against weight of guns, the medium-sized, fast, low-profiled, square- or transom-sterned, sail-propelled galleon emerged with greater definition. And if the debate was most brisk in England where its results, thanks to an efficient Navy Board, could most speedily be put into effect, the type was produced from Denmark to Portugal. Debate raged, too, over the type of gun to be used. Up to 1588, while the Spaniards had preferred guns of the cannon type, short-ranged, but firing a large, heavy ball, the English had concentrated on the longer-ranged but lighter-shotted culverin type, with the result that while the Armada was unable to get near enough to the English fleet to smash its ships, the English were able to hit the Spaniards, but with shot that was too light to do much damage. The tendency henceforward was to increase the weight of the broadside, and to deliver it as near point-blank range as possible. The inaccuracy and ineffectiveness of the gunfire during the Armada's run up-Channel was remarkable: 'Throughout the entire action, the sum of the Spanish artillery's achievement was to account for Captain Coxe of the pinnace *Delight*, and a score or two of seamen: and to do it, they fired off upwards of 100,000 rounds of great shot.'[1] Nor did the English gunners do much better, and their performances led to a distrust in some quarters of reliance on the broadside at the expense of boarding. It was a timid and ineffective method of attack, wrote Matthew Sutcliffe in 1593; ships should be equipped for resolute boarding, as well, of course, as being 'made swift of sayle, & sharpe to goe neere the winde'.[2] The sense of progress, however, is clearly conveyed by another contemporary. 'In my own time,' wrote Sir Walter Raleigh, 'the shape of our English ships hath been greatly bettered. It is not long since the striking of the topmasts (a wonderful ease to great ships, both at sea and in harbour) hath been devised, together with the chain-pump, which takes up twice as much water as the ordinary did; we have lately added the bonnet and the drabbler. To the courses we have devised studding-sails, top-gallant-sails, sprit-sails, top-sails; the weighing of anchors by the capstan is also new...and...we carry our ordnance better than we were wont.'[3] Further evidence is the way in which the *Revenge* was able to hold off fifteen Spanish ships, while sinking four of them, and the fact that no Elizabethan warship was lost by wreck.

The broadside, delivered by ships moving in on the enemy's weather quarter in line ahead, holding their fire to point-blank range and aiming near the water line, was to become the main element in sailing-ship tactics. As early as 1574 Philip II was warned that the English had been using broadsides against the hull rather than against rigging for some thirty years, and the lesson of large battles like that of the Azores in 1582 and the Channel in 1588 as well as of small engagements on both sides of the Atlantic had been that fire should be held as long as possible, and that it was best delivered by ships coming up in line and delivering their broadsides one at a time. Precise codification of line-ahead tactics still lay in the future, but the evolving design of the round ship suggested the tactics

[1] Michael Lewis, 'Armada Guns', in *Mariner's Mirror*, XXIX (1943), p. 168.
[2] *The practice, proceedings, and lawes of armes* (London, 1593), p. 280.
[3] Quoted by G. J. Marcus, *A Naval History of England* (London, 1961), vol. I, p. 58.

which could best exploit it. As a defensive formation, on the other hand, the solidity of the Spanish crescent, which became a trap if any enemy ship came to leeward of one of its wings, was redoubtably strong, but, as the product of unique circumstances, it had no lesson for a service which learned by painful iteration. In contrast to the north, basic galley design and, as a result, galley tactics in the Mediterranean remained static. The light galley, the *galeria sottile*, just long enough to straddle three wave crests in brisk weather, became the dominant type, used, with minor variations, by Spain, France, Italy and the Turks alike. The early start given to Venice by the combination of mass production methods and the rivalry of the great shipbuilding clans within the vast Arsenal had become tradition-bound; the shipwrights of Barcelona, Marseilles and Constantinople, less integrated with state policy, had experimented more freely and Venice was now in a position of having to catch up through modifications in sail and oar design, the shape of the prow (which had tended to wallow), and seating arrangements. But these were modest alterations. The affection for the galleon felt in the north, and so clearly discernible in the drawings of a shipwright like Matthew Baker or the narratives of Hakluyt, was paralleled by the southern feeling for the galley; that, too, was an affair of the heart. As the sharpest critic of the mid-century Venetian galley said, 'the perfect galley should in every way resemble a graceful girl whose each gesture reveals alertness, vivacity and agility, while at the same time preserving a seemly gravity'.[1] Lepanto was but the most opulent example of countless minor engagements, all governed by the galley's need to keep its guns and ram pointing at the enemy and by the relevance of land tactics to ships whose oars enabled them to be manœuvred like cavalry. There were round ships with the Christian fleet, but though it was hoped that they would be able to come up to support the wings on either side of the main body of galleys, they were considered extraneous to the main battle formation. The main interest of what might otherwise have been a land engagement was the use of the six galleasses, which had been painfully towed along when they could not make their own way; they were stationed, in pairs, one mile in advance of the Christian ships, and helped by their fire to disturb the Turkish battle-line as it rowed past them, spread out, like that of its adversary, in three main bodies. It was above all trade beyond the oceans that stimulated changes in sea warfare: England's search for seaworthy, long-distance raiders, Spain's search for fast merchantmen and specialised craft for use as messengers, as convoy escorts and as harbour guards, Holland's and Portugal's quest for bulky freighters capable of protecting themselves on voyages to South America or the East Indies. For the galleys, ranging ever less frequently beyond the pillars of Hercules, there was no compelling motive for change.

[1] Quoted by Alberto Tenenti, *Christoforo Da Canal. La Marine Vénitienne avant Lépante* (Paris, 1962), p. 29.

Governments were still eager to leave much of the planning of expeditions to private initiative, but it is in the realm of naval warfare that something like strategic thinking can be best observed, whether in the design of the various English raids on the Portuguese and Spanish coasts, or in the more general ideas that were expressed as to the desirability of keeping small units on permanent guard duty in avenues of special danger, or of using the main body as a striking force to destroy an enemy's ships rather than waiting for them at home, or of concentrating on the destruction of an enemy's fighting ships rather than on the indiscriminate raiding of his commerce. But if plans for sea operations were easier to think of in the round than plans for operations on land, they were almost as difficult to carry out. The same inefficiency, lack of training, and peculation were to be found, and the system of recruitment was haphazard. Conditions on board, with cramped quarters and rotten food, took a drastic toll of the effectives of any enterprise. And there were two additional problems: the lack of a well-defined fleet system—an equivalent to the increasingly efficient brigading of land forces; and how to balance the authorities of the soldier and the sailor elements in a fleet. On this latter score a change took place, most strikingly in England: instead of the sailor being looked on as the chauffeur of a military force which gave the orders, handled the guns and did the fighting, the navy came to be seen as an autonomous, self-sufficient arm, and inter-service rivalries were restricted to combined operations. Even here, no later expedition was remotely as catastrophic as that launched by Spain against Djerba, in 1559–60, where the lack of co-operation between the sea and land forces led to a crippling defeat at the hands of the Turks. If there remained a tendency to entrust the supreme command to a landsman, there was a growing tendency for him to rely on the advice of his seafaring colleagues, a tendency strongest in those countries where there was the sharpest divergence between the techniques of land and naval warfare.

Both on land and sea the atmosphere in which wars took place continued to change. The distinction between war and peace became increasingly blurred as men put ever less trust in written treaties and as national rivalries became complicated by civil and religious issues. The vague common fund of ideas, part legal, part Christian, part social and in part simply humanitarian, that had helped to moderate the soldier's destructive instincts had been sustained by the straightforward causes for which he fought. Now, while in the interest of efficiency a more impersonal obedience was urged on the soldier, his enemy was depersonalised by becoming a heretic or a rebel, a man without rights, and the distinction between soldier and non-combatant was becoming less clear. This changed atmosphere did not affect the battlefield, man's behaviour in actual combat being more or less constant, but it did affect the treatment of civilians, prisoners and the inhabitants of captured towns, and it stained the conduct of negotiations, which proceeded uneasily, haunted by fears of assassination and treachery, demanding each written undertaking to be sealed with hostages. Before the political and legal uncertainties which had resulted from the unprecedented volume of warlike activity of the first third of the century could be resolved, the civil wars in France and the revolt of the Protestant Netherlands from Spain raised even greater problems. Moreover, there was no war now that could not be represented as a crusade. Though toleration was preached and even practised by a handful of sectarians and cranks, the Spanish soldier knew it to be his duty to destroy Protestantism, just as the Protestant was pledged to deracinate the whoredoms and tyranny of Rome. Not only religion and resistance but piety and conquest went hand in hand.

> To arms, to arms, to glorious arms!
> With noble Norris and victorious Drake,
> Under the sanguine cross, brave England's badge,
> To propagate religious piety,
> And hew a passage with your conquering swords
> By land and sea.[1]

War was far from becoming so impersonal that there was no place for chivalrous gestures or generous acts, and campaigns that consisted largely of skirmishes and petty assaults provided plenty of occasions for bravery and enterprise, but the laws and usages of war had been based on a common law of precedents created by men often acting in their individual rather than in their politico-military capacity, and opportunities for commanders to act as individuals rather than as the instruments of a cause were becoming rarer. Challenges to single combat were still issued (though never by Spanish, the most professionally minded, commanders) but there was no longer even the likelihood of their being accepted. The treatment of capitulating towns had been based on a roughly worked-out scale which granted fewer concessions the longer the town defied its assailants, though an extreme of stubbornness might draw gentle terms from an admiring conqueror. Alva's systematic cruelty in the Netherlands, however, and Parma's brutality towards both garrisons and civilians, were the result of a deliberate policy, to allow the Spanish troops to compensate themselves for inadequate pay, and to terrify other towns into subjection. After butchering the garrison of Sichem, Farnese explained in a letter to his mother that this was to teach other towns to surrender as soon as the Spaniards made their first bombardment. Freedom of choice here was given up to a programme of calculated atrocity, like that pursued by the Turks, who killed, tortured or enslaved captives to spread a morale-breaking terror. From time to time a city's fate might be settled by pure whim, as when Sully pardoned the citizens of an obdurate town because

---

[1] George Peele, *A Farewell* (London, 1589), lines 23–8.

they were interceded for by an exceedingly pretty woman, but generally it was agreed that nothing was too bad for heretics or rebels. The wounds of a thousand little scars soon healed over, the recovery of countries with a mainly agricultural economy was quick; if small men suffered, military contracts made the fortunes of their bigger neighbours, and France, Holland and England all emerged richer than ever from their wars. But in that appendix of civilian suffering that is so often missing from the histories of war, there is material enough to explain why this age of expansion was also one of pessimism and dread.

CHAPTER VIII

THE BRITISH QUESTION 1559–69

THE Peace of Cateau-Cambrésis ended a war that had become, if indeed it had not started as, 'a race between spent horses'. It was a peace of exhaustion and it endured because for many years to come none of the states of western Europe felt strong enough to risk another general conflict. Yet although all were afraid to strike, some were still willing to wound. And the internal instability that afflicted all of them,[1] bred of exhaustion and fevered by a crisis of conscience in religion, gave to any dissatisfied power repeated hopes of undermining the foundations upon which the 1559 settlement rested.

In that settlement the British Isles occupied a crucial position. For the treaties left one of the two outstandingly great powers of western Europe, France, hemmed in and all but encircled by the territories of the other, Spain. The dominions of Philip II of Spain ran almost all around France—from Spain itself through the Balearic islands, Sardinia, and Sicily to Naples, the Tuscan ports, Parma, and Milan, with dependent Corsica, Genoa, and Savoy-Piedmont linking on to Franche-Comté and the Netherlands. If the British Isles or at least England could be added to these, as during Mary Tudor's marriage to Philip II (1554–8), then the ring would be complete and virtually unbreakable. If, on the other hand, the French could control England as well as Scotland, then the sea route through the Channel and the Straits of Dover could be closed to the Spaniards. The Netherlands would become an isolated outpost, linked to the main centres of Spanish power only by the long land route through Genoa, Savoy, and Franche-Comté, a route that ran close to the French frontier and was made doubly precarious by France's retention of the three bishoprics of Metz, Toul, and Verdun from which she could dominate Lorraine, and temporarily of certain fortresses in Piedmont as well. The whole Cateau-Cambrésis system might thus be jeopardised if England could be brought over to the French camp.

It was for these reasons that the internal instability of the British Isles made them during the next few years the danger area and focal point in the rivalries of western Europe. The chief political cause of that instability was the uncertainty of the English succession and the claim of Mary Stuart, Queen of Scots, to the first place in it. This Stuart claim had originated in the marriage (1503) of James IV of Scotland to Margaret, elder daughter of Henry VII of England. By that marriage Henry VII, at peace with one of England's ancient enemies, France, had hoped to end the equally

[1] See above, chapter I, and below, chapter IX.

ancient enmity with the other. Henry VIII's first French war (1512–14) undid his father's work in Scotland; but the Scottish disaster at Flodden (1513), the death there of James IV, and the disorders of James V's long minority spared England for twenty and more years from serious trouble on her northern border. Indeed, France's preoccupation with the Italian Wars made many Scots doubt the value of the 'auld alliance' and caused some to dream of a closer amity with England. James V's manhood and Henry VIII's breach with Rome spoiled such dreams. For, while Henry was repudiating the pope, James was relying more and more upon the church to help him to restore order in his realm. The fear that Catholic Scotland might become a base for a papal crusade against schismatical England—a fear made urgent by the temporary alliance of Charles V, Francis I, and the pope in 1538—drove Henry to desperate remedies. As soon as Charles and Francis came to blows again (1542), he attacked Scotland. For a time success looked near. Another Scottish disaster at Solway Moss hastened James V's death (14 December 1542) and brought another long minority, for the new Queen of Scots, Mary Stuart, was but a few days old when her father died. At the same time Henry VIII, by allying with Charles, seizing Boulogne (1544), and forcing Francis out of the war (1546), cut the Scots off from foreign aid.

But Henry VIII died (28 January 1547) before he could complete his work, before he could subdue Scotland or assure the marriage of Mary Stuart to his own son Edward VI. His death plunged England, too, into a royal minority and soon into faction struggles and social disorders. The eventual victor, the duke of Northumberland, too busy at home to be strong abroad, in March 1550 sold Boulogne back to France and withdrew from Scotland. Long before then, Henry VIII's 'rough wooing' had driven the Scots again into the arms of France. Their child queen had been shipped to the French court (August 1548) and affianced to the dauphin, while her mother Mary of Guise, with the help of French troops and French money, secured the Scottish regency (April 1554).

Thus Scotland became almost a province of France and the Stuart claim to the English succession became virtually a Valois claim. That claim was not asserted on Edward VI's death, because Northumberland's last desperate intrigue to exclude the half-Spanish Mary Tudor in favour of his own daughter-in-law, Jane Grey, seemed to be doing the French king's work for him. After that, Mary Tudor's triumph and her marriage to Philip II of Spain placed England as much on the Spanish side as Scotland was on the French. But her death childless (17 November 1558) and the accession of her half-sister Elizabeth I brought the danger again to the fore.

For Elizabeth was the last of the Tudors. No one, of course, yet imagined that she would choose 'to reign a virgin and die a virgin'. Yet in sixteenth-century conditions of hygiene and medicine, life and death were very close neighbours, as Elizabeth's own illness in 1562 was to emphasise. If she, too, died childless, the next heir in blood was Mary Stuart. It was true that Mary would get no welcome from English Protestants and that Henry VIII's will, sanctioned by act of parliament, had excluded the Stuart line from the succession. But with the throne vacant, blood might well prove more potent than parchment or Protestantism. And the hopes that this inspired among Scots and French may be gauged by the agitated petitions of the English council and parliaments for Elizabeth's early marriage.

Nor were the French without more immediate hopes. Elizabeth, the daughter of Anne Boleyn, could hardly recognise the papal authority that had pronounced her mother's marriage adulterous and her own birth illegitimate. Yet to defy Rome might make her, in Catholic eyes, no queen. In that event Mary Stuart could claim to be not merely the next heir but the present sovereign. Indeed, promptly upon Mary Tudor's death, Henry II of France had Mary Stuart and her husband, the dauphin, proclaimed queen and king of England, and they had flaunted the English royal arms upon the plate used at a dinner given to the English peace commissioners. Henry had no intention of jeopardising the peace negotiations, and risking the renewal of his disastrous war with Spain, by pressing this claim in earnest. But it was never formally abandoned and its proclamation showed that France had not altogether given up hope of turning the tables upon her Habsburg adversary by exploiting the instability of British politics.

Here, then, was a situation that must have tempted France as gravely as it alarmed Spain. In the circumstances of 1559, of course, its very gravity was a considerable guarantee against its getting altogether out of hand. For it could not be fully exploited without the risk of another general war, which no power could then contemplate. Even so, before the peace was signed, Philip had been sufficiently alarmed to offer marriage to Elizabeth provided she would live as a Catholic; and after the peace he anxiously encouraged the suit of his Austrian cousin the Archduke Charles. Like her own counsellors, he was chiefly concerned that she should quickly marry and have children. But he also felt that, to be safe, she must in addition reconcile herself to the pope and so deprive the French of the religious pretext against her.

Elizabeth and her counsellors were well enough aware of the danger. They were aware, too, how excessively England still depended upon Spanish Antwerp for the marketing of its one great export, woollen cloth, and for such essential imports as armaments. They knew, too, that England, disordered by eleven years of feeble government and religious revolutions, with an empty treasury, antiquated and ill-equipped military forces, and a navy run down from its former greatness, was in no condition to stand up to France in war. Yet they knew equally well how much Elizabeth's hold over her subjects depended upon her policies being—and being manifestly—'mere English'. She could not afford to repeat Mary Tudor's errors. She durst not save herself from France by becoming a satellite of Spain and queen by the grace of the pope. As a result she soon entered upon courses whose boldness and independence drove the Spaniards near to panic.

Her first major decision, the religious settlement of April 1559, practically coincided with the Peace of Cateau-Cambrésis. Here the original intentions seem to have been only to reassert the royal supremacy over the church and to alter as little as possible else. Her final policy, however, was bolder. Pressure from the puritans and their friends in parliament may have driven her on; or perhaps, when she saw peace with France assured and Spain so anxious for her survival, she chose to go further than she had at first deemed wise. At all events, while the Act of Supremacy again abolished all papal jurisdiction in England, the Act of Uniformity restored the second (1552) prayer-book of Edward VI, with minor modifications, and prohibited all other forms of worship. It is true that uniformity was very laxly enforced and that until 1563 Elizabeth kept secret negotiations going with Rome, so that Philip II was able to persuade the pope to withhold her excommunication. Yet those two Acts placed England fairly clearly in the Protestant camp and made it easier for Mary Stuart to pose as the lawful Catholic claimant against an illegitimate heretical usurper. It was still very unlikely that the French would want to press this claim to the point of war. But their hand might be forced if English aggression seriously threatened their hold upon Scotland.

That possibility was brought very much closer by the revolution that broke out in Scotland in the early summer of 1559.[1] This revolution, like that which for very similar reasons was gathering head against Spain in the Netherlands, was partly religious and partly political, with an undertone of economic discontent. The Scottish church's enormous wealth was coveted, and was already being heavily encroached upon, by an impecunious nobility and an emerging urban patriciate, who saw with envy their counterparts across the border waxing fat on ecclesiastical spoils. Its complacency and lack of charity were a grievance among the poor, whose complaint found bitter utterance in *The Beggar's Summons* (January 1559). Its indiscipline and indifference to parochial work had lost it its hold upon the faithful, as its own leaders recognised too late in the last provincial councils they were permitted to hold. Spiritually and materially, the hungry sheep looked up and were not fed. Many of them accordingly listened with eagerness to the preachers of the new Protestant doctrines that were spreading in over the Border and across the seas. By the end of 1557 some of the leading nobles had joined them—Argyle, Morton, Glencairn, Erskine, and Mary Stuart's half-brother Lord James

---

[1] See also above, pp. 112–15.

Stewart. The adherence of these 'Lords of the Congregation' gave the Protestant Reformation a political force to which it could never have attained without them; but their adhesion was quite as much political as religious.

For it was political discontent that made the 1559 revolution possible, discontent at the alien rule of the queen mother, Mary of Guise, regent since 1554. It was French troops, introduced in 1548, and French money that had enabled her to secure the regency from the duke of Châtelherault, head of the Hamiltons. She had never been more than the leader of the French faction and her efforts to strengthen her control only revived the other faction that had long been hostile to the French connection. French garrisons in the principal fortresses aroused patriotic dislike among the burghers. Frenchmen in the chief offices of state and court, culminating in the virtual replacement of the earl of Huntly, head of the Catholic Gordons, by du Roubay as chancellor, angered the native nobility and some at least of the native episcopate. Now in 1559, by taking a vigorous, if belated, stand against the growth of heresy, the regent fused all the discontents, aristocratic and popular, political and religious. Her attempt to put down a Protestant assembly at Perth accordingly brought her in May 1559 into open conflict with both the lords and the congregations. During that summer a fast-spreading revolt consumed the Lowlands and part of the Highlands. Mary of Lorraine and her Frenchmen were shut up in Leith. John Knox came back to help organise a Protestant reformed church and to inspire it with all the power of Calvin's doctrine. The Lords of the Congregation seemed well on the way to control of the whole country.

Even Henry II, war-weary but worried at the progress of heresy in his own realm, could hardly have ignored such a threat to French influence and the Roman church in Scotland. But at this moment Henry II was accidentally killed in a tournament (July 1559). Mary Stuart's husband, the boy Francis II, succeeded him on the throne, and control of French policy passed into the hands of her uncles, the duke of Guise and the cardinal of Lorraine. Guise, the chief rival of the pacific Montmorency for Henry II's favour, was the man who had seized Calais from the English in 1558 and who was now the budding champion of the French Catholics. He was not the man to let his sister, the regent, perish at the hands of the Lords of the Congregation. From the moment that he came to power, the Scots knew that sooner or later they would have to deal not only with the regent's forces in Leith but also with a powerful army that soon began to gather in Picardy under another of the Guise brothers, Elbœuf. They knew, too, that if once Elbœuf's army reached Scotland, the prospects of their revolution would be dark indeed. For their movement, though violent, lacked staying power. There was a fundamental division in it between those who were against both France and Rome and those who were only against France. Besides that, the nobles were torn by family feuds and neither the lords nor the congregations had the money to keep their men long in the field or the guns and siege equipment to reduce even Leith.

Faced with the prospect of massive French intervention, the Scots turned to the only power that might save them, Protestant England. Elizabeth had already helped them to recover from a setback in July, by sending a secret subsidy which she paid in French coin and lied about brazenly to the French ambassador. But what was needed now was something more substantial and more open—troops and a siege train to take Leith, warships to intercept Elbœuf. England could perhaps provide these essentials. Barring accidents of wind and weather, her fleet should be able to deal with Elbœuf's ships. Thanks to Cecil's economies, to the recruiting of German mercenaries, and to Gresham's exploits in procuring armaments and munitions from Antwerp, her financial and military resources might now suffice for a quick decisive blow at Leith. But there would be little in reserve for a second attempt if the first blow miscarried. War with France must follow, war in which England would be hard put to it to defend herself, the Scots' cause surely doomed, and the French given every excuse to assert in earnest Mary Stuart's claim to Elizabeth's throne. Even if Spain found it possible to come to the rescue of Protestant rebels against the Catholic champion, Spanish intervention could only make the British Isles the cockpit of a new Habsburg–Valois conflict from which neither England nor Scotland could hope to emerge with her independence intact. In short, if Elizabeth answered the Scots' appeal, the whole Cateau-Cambrésis settlement might be brought again into debate and general war ensue in western Europe.

It is therefore small wonder that Elizabeth in December 1559 rejected the somewhat hesitant advice of her privy council that she should intervene immediately both by land and by sea. She would do nothing yet by land, for to send an army into Scotland would mean certain and immediate war with France. But at her Secretary Cecil's prompting she did send Sir William Winter to the Firth of Forth with part of her fleet. He was 'to do some effectual enterprise upon the French navy' at sea or in the Forth, though still 'as of your own courage', finding some pretext that would not commit his sovereign. Whether the French government would accept the pretext and overlook the deed was perhaps doubtful. But at least the destruction of Elbœuf's fleet would gain time, time that might well prove decisive if there were truth in the reports of Throckmorton, the English ambassador in France, about the mounting opposition against the Guises there. Even so, Elizabeth and Cecil were taking a risk that frightened some councillors and terrified the Spaniards.

As usual, fortune favoured her. Storms that Winter's ships rode out undamaged shattered Elbœuf's force as it put to sea. Before another could be made ready, the conspiracy of Amboise (March 1560) gave the Guises their hands full at home. Ill managed and abortive though that conspiracy was, it revealed a situation in France which ruled out any further intervention in Scotland or serious quarrelling with England. Already Elizabeth had taken the Scots under her protection by the treaty of Berwick (27 February). Now at the end of March an English army with a siege train marched over the border.

Philip II, alarmed by this display of Protestant independence and fearful of its consequences, demanded the army's withdrawal and proposed to send Spanish troops to hold the ring while a settlement was reached. Elizabeth, however, had gauged both the Spanish and the French dangers accurately and she was not putting the French out of Scotland to let the Spaniards in. Philip's demand and his proposal were alike declined and the siege of Leith went forward with no more interference from the continent. Mary of Guise died and in July the town surrendered. Ambassadors had been sent from France with full powers to make the best terms they could and it was they who concluded the treaty of Edinburgh. All but 120 of the French troops left at once for home, leaving Scotland in the hands of the Protestant, pro-English faction that their dominance had driven to rebellion. By the treaty Mary and Francis II promised from henceforth to cease using the arms and style of England and to renounce all Mary's claims to that kingdom. In a separate 'concession' they guaranteed the laws and liberties of Scotland, promised never again to send French troops there, and undertook to employ only Scots in high office there.

It is true that Mary and Francis steadfastly refused to ratify the treaty which they had empowered their envoys to conclude. It was nevertheless a considerable step towards assuring Scottish independence and establishing an Anglo-Scottish amity that would close Great Britain to the foreign influences which had threatened it for the past dozen years. A considerable faction among the Scots had been bound to England by common opposition to Rome; another by common fear of France; and for the first time in centuries English troops had entered Scotland as allies and left it as friends.

The foundations, however, upon which Scottish independence and Anglo-Scottish amity rested were not yet broad or secure. Protestantism was not yet the faith of the Scottish nation but only of its dominant faction, a faction that owed its dominance as much to favourable political circumstances as to its own missionary zeal. After the treaty of Edinburgh the political circumstances began to change. The old clergy and the Catholic nobles began to take heart now that they could stand up for the Roman faith without thereby supporting French domination. The Protestant lords, too, especially their leader, Lord James Stewart, and their wiliest politician, Maitland of Lethington, as their fear of France died down, began to take fright at the overweening pretensions of the new kirk.

This rift between the 'lords' and the 'congregation', or at least the ministers, appeared as soon as the estates met to settle the religious question, which the treaty of Edinburgh had shelved. In August 1560 they passed acts that abolished papal jurisdiction in Scotland; accepted the Calvinist confession framed by Knox and his fellows; and condemned any Scot who celebrated or attended Mass to loss of goods for the first offence, banishment for a second, and death for a third. These acts passed with little opposition, though Mary again refused to ratify them. In January 1561, however, the ministers' *Book of Discipline* met with a very different reception. For it was concerned with much more than church services and doctrine. It proposed a system of education under the church and a scheme for the relief of the poor and impotent. It claimed for the church a wide jurisdiction over private morals and conduct and a voice in public affairs. It claimed also all the old church's property, without providing compensation for the old clergy or for the many laymen now occupying church lands. In short, the new kirk was claiming the whole wealth, and more than the whole political and social influence, of the ancient church. So much the estates were not prepared to concede. Some lords agreed, provided that the old clergy were allowed to keep their lands on condition that they subsidised the new ministry. Even this failed to win general acceptance or formal enactment and the long debates served chiefly to reveal the growing rift within the ruling faction.

The continued internal instability of Scotland was, however, offset by the growing internal instability of France. The death of Francis II (December 1560) abruptly ended the Guises' ascendancy. Their rivals, Montmorencies and Bourbons, *politiques* and Huguenots, took fresh hope, and a struggle for power developed that was within two years to plunge the country into a generation and more of civil and religious wars. For the moment the queen mother, Catherine de Medici, ruled as regent for her second son, Charles IX. Desperately seeking to unite the rival factions around the throne and to persuade Huguenots and Catholics to settle their religious differences by amicable discussion, she could not risk needless troubles abroad. Nor could the Guises, fully occupied with their own struggle for power, do much for their niece Mary Stuart, who as queen dowager was a greatly diminished asset to them in France.

Mary, however, might still do something in Scotland for the Guises, for France, and for Rome. She could hardly perhaps take seriously the proposals sent to her by John Leslie from the old bishops and the Catholic earls of Huntly, Atholl, Caithness, and Sutherland—that she should land near Aberdeen, rally the northern Catholics, and lead them against Edinburgh. But she did not therefore have to bow to the dictates of Knox, who would not admit her unless she first turned Calvinist. For, as she learned from Lord James, whom the estates sent to her at St Dizier (April 1561), the Protestant lords were ready to allow her and her immediate attendants to hear Mass in private, provided that she accepted the present religious settlement and themselves as her advisers. Moreover, Lord James made it clear that they would not press her to yield to Elizabeth's reiterated demand for ratification of the treaty of Edinburgh. They were not at all prepared to countenance her claim to present possession of the English throne, but they were fully prepared to uphold her right to the succession if Elizabeth should die childless.

The Guises strongly urged Mary to accept these terms and hasten back to Scotland. Their cause there was almost wrecked but, if she behaved sensibly, she might keep Scottish Catholicism from total extinction and preserve some connection with France. Above all, the mediation of the Protestant lords now seemed the only hope of persuading Elizabeth to recognise her place in the English succession. Whether Mary possessed either the brains or the character for such a task was perhaps doubtful. She was only eighteen. She 'thinketh herself not too wise, but is content to be ruled by good counsel and wise men'. Alone in Scotland, might she not be ruled by Lord James and his allies, as in France she had been ruled by her uncles? That, no doubt, was what Lord James and Maitland hoped. If they could secure her place in the English succession, might she not accept a moderate, Erastian Protestantism after the English model, which many a Scottish lord would anyway prefer to the theocratic pretensions of some of the ministers? A united Great Britain under one, Scottish, queen and one religion should guarantee the Scots against a repetition of either Henry VIII's 'rough wooing' or Mary of Guise's French domination.

What Mary Stuart's own intentions were, when she landed in Scotland on 19 August 1561, we can but guess. Probably she was herself much less clear about them than the multitude of historians who have since debated them so hotly and so long. For the next three years, at all events, she seemed content to be ruled by Lord James and Maitland and to be reasonably faithful to the St Dizier understanding, though she was careful not to commit herself about the future. Her attitude was summed up in the proclamation issued after a Protestant mob had tried to interrupt her private Mass on the first Sunday after her arrival. The proclamation, reissued several times later, promised that as soon as was convenient queen and estates would settle all religious differences; but it did not say when the convenient time would be nor promise that the final settlement would resemble the present one. Meanwhile, it threatened with death not only those who sought to overthrow the form of religion now established, but also any who for any cause interfered with the queen's domestics.

The ministers continued to thunder from the pulpits and their congregations threatened to slay the 'massing priests'. But among the Protestant lords, as Knox had feared, 'the holy water of the court' soon quenched such ardours. They allowed Mary, on progress, to 'pollute' Stirling, Perth, Dundee, and Aberdeen with her private Mass. In November 1561 they rejected the ministers' formal demand for the suppression of this 'idolatry' and denied the suggestion that they were not bound to obey an idolatrous queen. Next month they rejected again the demand for the enactment of the *Book of Discipline*; and, although they did impose a tax of one third on all ecclesiastical property, they allotted half of its proceeds to the state and only half to the maintenance of the new ministers. In fact, the conflict was fast becoming one between the Protestant lords and the Protestant ministers rather than one between the Catholic queen and her Protestant subjects.

This did not mean that the Protestant lords were prepared to share political power either with the Catholic nobles or with those lords who, whatever their religion, were first and foremost royalists. Two expeditions by Lord James, and the exiling of the earl of Bothwell, brought the borderers to heel. The crushing of Huntly and his insubordinate Gordons (October 1562) tamed the northern Catholics. Mary's enthusiastic participation in the campaign against Huntly, crowned by her conferring the earldom of Moray upon Lord James (November), indeed suggested that his St Dizier hopes were justified. In the following spring forty-eight persons, including the archbishop of St Andrews, were arrested, convicted, and half of them imprisoned, on charges of celebrating or hearing Mass. This display of Protestant vigour, reinforced by the attainders of the Gordons and Sutherland, again prevented the ministers from winning enough support, when the estates met, for their clamour for the *Book of Discipline* and a more adequate establishment to achieve any results.

Outwardly, that was another triumph for Moray's policy. He had mastered his political rivals among the nobility. Huntly was dead and his heirs disabled from office; Bothwell was in exile; and Arran, Knox's last noble supporter, had lapsed into total insanity. Now Moray seemed to have mastered also his Protestant supporters, even the kirk itself. But he and Knox were hardly on speaking terms. In refusing to accept the kirk as master, he had gone far to losing it as an ally. Moreover, religion was again becoming a political issue. Everywhere the Catholics were growing bolder in defying the law against the Mass, while Protestants, especially in the west, were uniting in 'bonds' and covenants to enforce it. With tempers rising on both sides, Moray's middle course grew daily more difficult. Worst of all, he was losing his hold over the queen. He may have acquiesced in the release of the archbishop of St Andrews and the other Catholic prisoners as soon as the estates were dissolved. But it is not likely that he willingly allowed the celebration of Mass at Holyrood for the queen's servants while she herself was away on progress in the west in the summer of 1563. And when the privy council acquitted Knox of treason for summoning his Protestant friends to appear in force at the trial of those who had interrupted the Holyrood Mass, Mary's anger betrayed her growing impatience of Moray's tutelage.

What most weakened Moray's hold, however, was his failure to secure recognition of Mary's claim to the English succession. The lords had sent Maitland to England to raise the question almost as soon as Mary returned to Scotland in August 1561. Elizabeth answered with another demand for the ratification of the treaty of Edinburgh. This was only to be expected, for Mary had been formally proclaimed queen of England and, although she had ceased to use the title, she had never formally renounced it. On the other hand, the treaty required her from henceforth (*deinceps*) to renounce the title and arms of England. This form of words could be taken to deny not only her present claim but also her future hopes as well. For Henry VIII's will, authorised by statute, excluded the Stuarts from the English succession and this clause in the Edinburgh treaty might be held to reinforce that exclusion. To ratify it might therefore be to renounce all claim not only to present possession but also to future succession. Now, the Scots' idea, as Maitland had suggested to Cecil as early as December 1560, was that Elizabeth should recognise Mary as her heir if she herself should die childless and that Mary in return should ratify the treaty of Edinburgh, thus amended, and be England's firm friend and ally.

There were, however, serious obstacles to such a bargain. One was Elizabeth herself. She was willing to amend the treaty so that Mary, while renouncing the title, reserved her claims to the succession; but she was most reluctant to recognise the Scottish queen as her heir—indeed, never till her dying day was she to allow her successor to be named. She had experienced in her sister's reign how easily conspiracies gathered round an heir presumptive, even when that heir did not presume too much and was not queen regnant of a neighbouring realm. She feared, as she told Maitland, that to recognise Mary as her heir would be to spread her own winding-sheet before her eyes. Besides, there was another obstacle. Recognition meant setting aside Henry VIII's will. That will, authorised by act of parliament, needed another act of parliament to reverse it. And there was a powerful and vocal part of the English nation, strongly represented in the privy council and dominant in the Commons, to whom the prospect of another Catholic and half-foreign sovereign was utterly abhorrent. In short, Elizabeth had reason to doubt not only the wisdom but also the practicability of formal recognition.

Nevertheless, when Mary herself put forward Maitland's proposal in January 1562, Elizabeth proved not unsympathetic. She seemed, and perhaps was, ready to recognise Mary's claim to the succession provided that sure and effective guarantees could be devised for her own continued possession of the throne. To devise such guarantees was difficult to the point of impossibility, but negotiations went on amicably, if slowly, until in May 1562 a meeting of the two queens was arranged for the early autumn at York or thereabouts.

At this point the affairs of the continent once again intruded. In France

Mary's uncles were again seizing control of king and government, for Catherine de Medici's conciliatory courses had encouraged the Huguenots to such pretensions of supremacy that moderate Catholics like Montmorency laid aside their jealousy of the Guises and allied with them in defence of the old faith. For less creditable reasons Anthony of Navarre, head of the Bourbons, joined them and by the spring of 1562 they were strong enough to challenge the queen mother's authority. Condé and the other Bourbons, Coligny and Châtillon and the other Protestants of the Montmorency clan, could not allow such a challenge to go unresisted; and when Guise's body-guard, not without provocation, massacred a Huguenot congregation at Vassy (March 1562), passions exploded on both sides in the first of the Wars of Religion.

Elizabeth at first tried not to let these happenings affect her Scottish policy. She considered helping Catherine to mediate a settlement between the French factions; even perhaps using concessions to Mary to induce the Guises to compromise. But Catherine's authority had ceased when war began and the Guises were not to be moved. Accordingly the meeting with Mary had to be postponed. For, with news flooding in of Huguenot setbacks and losses in France, an English parliament would have been less likely than ever to accept the Guises' niece as their future sovereign. Indeed, it began to look as if the Guises would soon be masters of France again and able to resume the designs that the Tumult of Amboise and the death of Francis II had interrupted. It seemed possible, too, that Philip II's anxiety to preserve his Netherlands from the contagion of heresy, which now induced him to lend a limited countenance to the French Catholics, might outweigh his secular jealousy of French power. Unless England intervened to save the Huguenots and halt the Guises, Mary might soon have the whole power of France, and even the benevolent neutrality of Spain, to back her. Moreover, Lord Robert Dudley and the war party in Elizabeth's council argued that by intervening now she might build up the Huguenots in France as she had built up the Protestants in Scotland, as a permanent counterpoise to the house of Guise and guarantee against French hostility. She might even get back Calais in exchange for Le Havre and Dieppe, which Condé's envoys in desperation were offering. Elizabeth, perhaps the more ready to listen to Dudley as a statesman now that she had to recognise his unsuitability as a husband, agreed. In August she promised to lend Condé 140,000 crowns and in return received Le Havre until Calais should be restored to her.

Even before English troops occupied Le Havre (October 1562), Condé's betrayal of French soil to the old enemy almost shocked the French factions back to sanity. A few of his followers deserted him, and Guise in September offered the Huguenots a wide toleration if they would not let the English in. Catherine made Condé a similar offer in December if he would help to turn them out. Condé was not yet willing to trust his enemies' promises and sacrifice his only ally. Elizabeth, allowing ambition to override her earlier ideas of mediating a settlement, refused to abandon Le Havre unless Calais were handed back to her. So the war went on, and for a time all in Guise's favour. His victory at Dreux (19 December) drove the Huguenot army from the field and removed most of his rivals. For St André was slain, Condé captured by the Catholics and Montmorency by the Huguenots. Anthony of Navarre had been mortally wounded a month before, so Guise now looked as ascendant in the counsels of the boy Charles IX as he had been in those of Francis II. The alarm that had stirred Elizabeth to intervene was becoming a present danger that must draw her still deeper into French quarrels.

Mary's hope of a meeting was thus receding still further. She had, too, other reasons for impatience. In October 1562 Elizabeth had been near to death from smallpox and it was known that in the privy council's discussions about the succession Mary's name had been barely mentioned. Then in January 1563 the English parliament met. That it would keep silent on this vital question was not to be expected; that it would press Elizabeth to a decision fatal to Mary's claims was by no means impossible. Maitland therefore was again sent to London to press for Mary's recognition and for permission to plead her cause before the parliament. He might, in return, offer Mary's mediation to secure peace with France and the restitution of Calais, an offer made a little more plausible by Guise's similar overtures to the English ambassador in France.

But Maitland was to prepare pressure as well as to apply persuasion. He was to approach the Spanish ambassador in England about the possibility of Mary marrying Philip II's son, Don Carlos, and Catherine de Medici for a match with Charles IX of France. In this, Maitland and Moray were certainly playing a very risky game. It may be that they hoped to move Elizabeth to concede what they wanted by the mere threat of such marriages. But what would their position be, what the fate of Scottish Protestantism and British independence, if the negotiations left Elizabeth unmoved and Mary married to the heir of Spain or the king of France?

As it happened, the risk proved, for a time, justified though unproductive. In February 1563 Guise was assassinated. Of his brothers, Aumale and the grand prior died a few days later, Elbœuf was besieged in Caen, and the cardinal of Lorraine was away at the Council of Trent. The Guises were as leaderless as the Bourbons and the Montmorencies. The heads of all the great families were, in fact, either mere boys, like Henry of Navarre and Henry of Guise, or prisoners, like Condé and Montmorency. The way was clear for Catherine de Medici to take control again, for a union of all factions, Catholic and Huguenot, to expel the English from Le Havre (July 1563) and bring Elizabeth to relinquish her claim to Calais by the treaty of Troyes (April 1564).

Yet, despite its failure, Elizabeth's intervention in France had done much to prevent Anglo-Scottish relations from becoming again dangerously entangled in continental politics. For that intervention had once more reminded governments that were willing to wound how dangerous it still was to strike. Elizabeth had burned her fingers helping Protestant rebels against their Catholic sovereign. Henceforth, although always ready to give underhand encouragement to French, Netherlands, and Scottish Protestants as useful pressure groups, she would abet them in open rebellion only as a last desperate remedy, when she could come to terms with their lawful rulers in no other way. Catherine de Medici and the more moderate French Catholics, too, were ready for an understanding that would prevent another English intervention in their own unstable affairs, even if that understanding meant doing little for Mary Stuart and refusing her Charles IX as a husband. Moreover, whatever legends were to grow around Catherine's meeting with the duke of Alba at Bayonne in 1565, her return to power revived all Philip II's old suspicions of France. And before then, Don Carlos's madness had put an end to the hesitant negotiations for his marriage to Mary. The queen of Scots could no longer hope for the king of France or the prince of Spain and there was no other continental suitor of sufficient greatness to frighten Elizabeth into recognising her claims.

Indeed, even the threat of Don Carlos had moved Elizabeth only a little and only slowly. For, although the 1563 parliament had not driven her to name a successor or to choose a husband, it had made her more keenly aware of the practical obstacles to Mary's recognition. That autumn, while warning Mary that a marriage with 'the children of France, Spain, or Austria' would make recognition impossible, she did suggest rather vaguely that a suitable match abroad or perhaps into the English nobility might make it possible to have Mary's title looked into and, if found good, furthered by such means as Lords and Commons could be content with. In March 1564 she went a little further and named her candidate—Lord Robert Dudley, soon to be made rather more suitable by elevation to the earldom of Leicester. Even then, she would not promise full and unconditional recognition. She must, Cecil wrote (December 1564), be ruled by her country's laws and by the consent of parliament.

There lay the crux. To offer more might be, not only to spread her winding-sheet before her eyes, but also to promise what she could not perform. Given the temper of parliament, as manifested in 1563, the best hope for the Scottish claim was, as it proved later with James VI, to trust to time and to Elizabeth's goodwill, not to force an immediate and clear-cut decision. That, however, called for more trustfulness and more patience than Mary could muster and it is small wonder that logical Scots like Maitland complained of Cecil's 'obscure words and dark sentences' or suspected that 'nothing was intended but drift of time'.

Mary accordingly turned to another suitor, the young Lord Darnley. His father, during Mary's infancy, had been Châtelherault's rival for the regency and for first place after her in the Scottish succession. Baulked of his ambition by Cardinal Beaton, he became leader of the faction that recognised Henry VIII's suzerainty. He fought for the English in the war of 1542-9, was attainted as a traitor, and had lived in exile in England since 1544. There he married Lady Margaret Douglas, daughter of James IV's widow, Henry VIII's elder sister Margaret, by her second husband, the earl of Angus, who had led the English faction in earlier years. Darnley's youth and his mother's inclination to the old religion unsuited him to repeat the role of his father and grandfather in 1559-60, when the Scottish Reformation anyway offered Elizabeth more potent allies. None the less, Darnley could still claim through both his parents next place to Mary in the Scottish succession and, through his mother, next place in the English. By marrying him, Mary could strengthen her right in both kingdoms.

Nor was there any very obvious reason to expect that this match would arouse Elizabeth's hostility. She had sent Lennox to the Tower for practising it in 1562; but he, his wife, and his son were back at court in good favour next year. Elizabeth was well aware, as her clear hint to Mary's envoy Melville showed, that the project was alive again in 1564. Yet it was at her request that Lennox was allowed to return to Scotland (September 1564), where his estates were restored to him; and it was by her leave that Darnley joined him there in February 1565. A month later the English ambassador informed Mary that marriage to Leicester would not bring a declaration of her title as heir to England until Elizabeth had either married or announced her intention never to marry. The English queen could hardly have done more to smooth Darnley's path, short of specifically urging Mary to marry him. His timely bout of measles, which brought Mary on long and frequent visits to his bedside, perhaps hastened matters by reinforcing policy with passion. But Mary's feeling that she had been grossly deceived when Elizabeth forbad the banns may well have been genuine. It certainly made her the more determined to marry Darnley, though she did delay the wedding till the end of July in an effort to placate Elizabeth.

Elizabeth's purposes at this time are indeed more than usually obscure. Throckmorton reported rumours that the Darnley match was not so ill taken by Her Majesty and her council as they pretended; and the French ambassador suspected that Elizabeth 'disguised the pleasure which she really had at heart to see it go on'. It is true that some of her council professed great alarm at the encouragement it gave to supporters of the Scottish claim and the old religion, 'upon which only string the Queen of Scots' title doth hang'. Elizabeth's views, however, can seldom be equated with the opinions of her more puritan councillors. She never shared their distrust of her more Catholic subjects and so would hardly have agreed that 'the peril was greater by this marriage with Lord Darnley...than with the mightiest prince abroad'. On the contrary, she may well have regarded it as another step towards disentangling Anglo-Scottish relations from continental politics. For Mary, married, could only appeal to foreign princes for aid to conquer her English inheritance, while Elizabeth could still offer her own hand with a kingdom as her dowry. Also, if she felt now as she did years later, that only a king was fit to succeed her, she may even have regarded Mary's marriage and its encouragement to her English well-wishers as a step in the right direction. At the same time by making Mary out to be marrying in defiance of her express wishes, she might put an end to the Scottish queen's nagging demands for a recognition that it was not yet practicable to promise.

As it turned out, the marriage falsified all the hopes and fears that it had engendered. For Darnley lacked every quality of statesmanship and his arrogance was so insufferable that even before the marriage Randolph feared 'he can have no long life amongst this people'. Mary's infatuation only encouraged his worst qualities and, as 'no man pleaseth her that contenteth not him', the first to suffer were those councillors who had guided her policy since her return from France. By April 1565 Moray had withdrawn from court and council and with Argyle and Châtelherault was concerting measures for his own safety. By August these and a few more lords were in open rebellion, helped by two or three thousand pounds sent secretly from Elizabeth. They sought to justify their revolt by accusing Darnley of plotting their deaths and by asserting that Mary and he, scorning the counsel of the native nobility in favour of base-born foreigners such as the Italian secretary David Rizzio, were scheming to overthrow the Protestant religion.

It was in vain. The battle-cries that had proved so potent in 1559–60 made little appeal in 1565, for Mary and Darnley had as yet done little to make them ring true. Mary had refused the general assembly's demand that she should abandon her own faith (June), but she had again assured them that she would press no man's conscience and that she would maintain their religion as she had found it until the estates could agree upon a final settlement. Darnley, although he had married Mary by Catholic rites, withdrew before Mass was celebrated and during the next few weeks occasionally appeared at Protestant preachings. The recall and growing influence of Bothwell, the restoration of Gordon to the earldom of Huntly, hardly betokened a popish plot, for Bothwell was now a Protestant and Gordon at least professed to be one. Even Mary's secret appeal to Philip II for aid and protection (September), and the professions of devotion to the old faith which she made to him and to the French court (August), could have been explained away. For, with Elizabeth fomenting rebellion and threatening war, where else could Mary turn for support? Thus, when

Moray rose, many of his Protestant allies—Morton, Ruthven, Maitland—stood aside. The Protestant congregations, even in Edinburgh, proved unwontedly Laodicean. By October the 'Chase-about Raid' was over, the rebel lords exiles in England, and Moray apparently as broken as the Gordons had been three years earlier.

Yet Mary, in thus giving Darnley his head—or, as some would say, in thus allowing her own real but long-concealed intent to break surface—had committed herself to a gamble that cool policy could hardly justify. By breaking what a later century might have called the 'Protestant front', she had discarded the one force organised and powerful enough to make the royal authority respected throughout her realm. Huntly and Atholl might dominate the north again, Bothwell the borders, and Lennox give a new foothold in the south-west. But this was a weak and ill-assorted team to master the sullen Protestant lords who had not risen with Moray, those less committed nobles whose feudal instincts scented confusion at the centre of government, and the Protestant congregations whose militancy revived with each fresh concession to Catholicism. Indeed, Mary's appeal to the pope in January 1566, and even more the language used by her envoy in presenting it, suggest that by then she herself almost despaired of mastering her realm without prompt and substantial outside help.

It is, of course, possible that Catherine and Alba's meeting at Bayonne (June 1565), and the rumours of a Catholic league that it bred, had encouraged Mary to hope that her own Catholicism might now bring her such help. Yet if so, she was soon to be undeceived, for from that point of view her stroke was badly mistimed. The two great Catholic powers remained as ever too jealous of each other to act together, too fearful of each other to act separately, especially now that England had again to be reckoned with. Philip II was nervous lest the French, with Condé installed as governor of Picardy, might foment the mounting opposition in his Netherlands provinces. In October 1565 he told the pope, and Mary's envoy, that he was only prepared to give a little money secretly to help Mary against her rebels. If Elizabeth attacked her, he might do a little more, but still secretly and through the pope. If, on the other hand, Mary claimed the English throne during Elizabeth's lifetime, he would not help at all; and he warned her sternly not to admit a French army into Scotland. The French government had as little intention of jeopardising their own precarious religious peace by crusading for a Catholic queen of Scots. They did warn Elizabeth not to attack her, but their main efforts were directed towards restoring amity between the two queens. In short, unless Elizabeth declared war upon Mary, neither of the great Catholic powers would intervene at all effectively. And Elizabeth had no intention of letting Moray involve her in Scotland as Condé had involved her in France. She allowed him to remain penuriously in England only after a public and carefully staged reprimand for his sinful rebellion.

So the Scottish crisis of 1565–7 worked itself out with no serious interference from abroad and Mary had to make shift with such support as she could rally inside Scotland. Her wisest course might have been that suggested by Throckmorton, though whether he gave it as her sincere wellwisher or as the crafty servant of Elizabeth may perhaps be doubted. If she had forgiven Moray and continued a manifestly moderate course in religious matters, she would have lulled Protestant fears even if she did not rally the whole nation to the throne. But Darnley's enmity and, apparently, Rizzio's counsel ruled out a magnanimity that could have been the truest wisdom. She preferred, or was driven to, measures that could only enflame opposition—the increasing favour to Moray's mortal enemy Bothwell; the restoration of the Gordons; the promotion of the Catholic Atholl and the alien Rizzio to the places in her counsels once held by Moray and Maitland; the summoning of the old Catholic bishops and abbots to the estates that were to meet in March 1566 to attaint the exiled lords; even, it was rumoured, the thrusting of Rizzio into Morton's place as chancellor.

All this was made doubly dangerous by Mary's growing estrangement from her husband. Her first infatuation soon wore off as she discovered how politically inept and personally untrustworthy he was. She dared not satisfy his ambition to succeed to the position, and more, from which he had induced her to expel Moray. More and more she excluded him from knowledge of affairs of state. More and more she leaned for counsel upon Rizzio, closeting him with her often late into the night. The descriptions of Rizzio that have come down to us make it hard to believe that their personal relations were not innocent enough, despite persistent Protestant jibes about James VI's parentage. Mary's easy manners and disregard for local convention had raised Scottish eyebrows before and are no proof of immorality at this time. Still, her conduct, like Elizabeth's with Dudley a few years earlier, was sufficiently indiscreet to inspire malicious rumours and to convince such a man as Darnley. Finding himself baulked of political power and fancying himself deceived as a husband, he allied with the Protestants Morton and Ruthven and through them with Moray. They agreed to help him get rid of Rizzio and secure the crown matrimonial, with the succession if Mary should die childless. He in return undertook to restore Moray and the exiles and finally establish the Protestant religion. On the night of 9 March 1566 the first part of the bargain was completed. Darnley, Morton, Ruthven, and their associates dragged Rizzio screaming from the queen's presence and murdered him outside her door. Next day Moray and the exiles from the Chase-about Raid returned.

The rest of the bargain was not fulfilled. Mary, after welcoming Moray with apparent warmth, wormed out of Darnley the story of the conspiracy and then induced him to escape with her to Dunbar (12 March), where Bothwell, Atholl, and Huntly joined them. Having regained control of the king and gained some measure of personal liberty, she was able to insist upon the banishment of Morton and his fellow assassins. There for the time her vengeance ended. Within three months she would be facing all the perils of sixteenth-century childbearing. Any repetition of the ordeal of 9-12 March could well be fatal both to her and to her child and she had no intention of going out of her way to further her husband's ambition for the crown. So Moray, Argyle, and the exiles of 1565 were pardoned. This was followed by a general reconciliation among the nobles, Bothwell and Huntly with Moray, Atholl with Argyle. By the end of April all were back at court and sitting together in council. This appearance of general harmony continued after the birth of Mary's son, the future King James VI, on 19 June 1566. In September Maitland was allowed back at court and reconciled to Bothwell, while on Christmas Eve even Morton and the murderers of Rizzio were pardoned.

Darnley alone was excluded from the general goodwill. Until the birth of her son, Mary kept up some pretence of harmony, though she excluded her husband from political affairs and warned nobles and ambassadors to have no dealings with him. Afterwards it became daily more obvious that her anger was unquenched, while he absented himself from court for long periods and threatened to flee to the continent. Despair over her marriage, and perhaps fear for the safety of her son, may have helped to bring on her illness at Jedburgh (October) after her long ride to visit the wounded Bothwell. Maitland at least thought so. It was, he wrote to Beaton in Paris, 'a heartbreak for her to think that he should be her husband and how to be free of him she sees no outgate...How soon or in what manner it may change, God knows.'

The words have a sinister ring, all the more when we remember that Mary, who had always leaned heavily upon one or two favoured counsellors, was now singling out ever more markedly the earl of Bothwell. Bothwell might be 'a daring pilot in extremity', but he was given to desperate remedies. It is not necessary to accept all the stories that scandal concocted in order to believe that he aimed to take Darnley's place as well as Moray's and that Mary was coming to view this as a welcome possibility. If so—and the attempts to prove that her regard for him was purely political are not very convincing—it boded ill for Darnley that of all men she should have chosen Bothwell to honour and to love. It boded worse because there were none to curb Bothwell's boldness. Not that he was popular. As early as July he was said to be as much hated by the other nobles as Rizzio had been. But few yet felt ready to challenge their queen's favourite and some may have been only too ready to let him deal with Darnley in his own fashion.

Just what was agreed among the leading nobles at Craigmillar after Mary's return there (November); just how much Mary knew and consented to; and just what happened in the next few weeks—these are among the most bitterly and closely disputed of historical detective problems. Moray and Morton signed nothing; Atholl knew nothing. For the rest, Bothwell, Argyle, Huntly, Maitland, and others agreed in some way or other to 'free' Mary of Darnley. So much at least Mary knew. Late in January 1567, probably on the very day that she wrote in bitter terms about her husband to her ambassador in France, she rode to Glasgow and was apparently reconciled to Darnley, then recuperating from the small-pox or perhaps the pox. She brought him back to Edinburgh and they stayed for some days at Kirk o' Field, just outside the walls. On the evening of 9 February she and the court went off to a wedding, leaving Darnley and his servant alone in the house. About two o'clock in the morning, just before the wedding party got back, a violent explosion wrecked the building, or part of it, and the bodies of Darnley and his man were found some distance away, almost naked and quite unmarked by powder.

Fortunately there is no need to consider here the various explanations of this sensational crime put forward by the legion of historical detectives who have since trampled over the evidence. Its effects upon the course of history depended upon what men thought had happened rather than upon what in truth had happened. And men at the time—Spanish, French, Italian, English, as well as Scots; Catholics as well as Protestants—found it difficult not to be convinced by the overwhelming *prima facie* evidence that Bothwell was the murderer and Mary his accomplice. Moreover, Mary's conduct after the crime could only strengthen the presumption against her. Her less than half-hearted efforts to trace the murderers; her still mounting favour to Bothwell; his attendance at the privy council meeting that arranged his own trial; the farcical nature of that trial (12 April): all this made her well-wishers abroad despair. Even the con-temporary belief in magic and witchcraft could hardly convince men that her 'kidnapping' by Bothwell (24 April), and her marriage to him after his collusive divorce from Huntly's sister (in May), were carried through against her will. For although Darnley's murdering of her servant Rizzio was undoubtedly a greater crime, nevertheless to Mary, brought up in the high traditions of Valois kingship, Bothwell's ravishing of her person should surely have been hardly less infuriating if it were in fact against her will. Certainly Lady Buccleugh's spells must have been potent indeed to make Mary for two years yet to come refuse to save her throne by sacri-ficing her ravisher.

For it was this marriage that cost her her throne. It is true that the populace were already clamouring against Bothwell as the reputed murderer of Darnley. Yet on that ground they would have found few leaders among the nobility. Some had committed themselves too deeply at Craigmillar; others, Morton, for example, had known of Darnley's danger and made no attempt to warn him; and Moray's almost too neatly timed withdrawal, to St Andrews and then to France, strengthens rather than weakens the suspicion that he, too, did 'look through his fingers'. Few except Lennox and Atholl could welcome a full and candid investigation of Darnley's murder. The Bothwell marriage was another matter. It turned popular fury against Mary as well as Bothwell and it provided leadership from the nobility. A few—Argyle, Huntly, and Maitland if Bothwell's threats had not terrified him—still felt too deeply compromised over the murder to oppose the marriage. The Hamiltons, hoping for the succession if the infant James should die, stood with them to exclude Darnley's brother. But when the Protestant Morton and the Catholic Atholl rose in arms, they soon gathered a following that Mary's forces had little spirit to resist. At Carberry Hill on 15 June 1567 she was taken prisoner, while Bothwell fled into exile. Had she even now been willing to renounce him, the confederate lords might have defied popular clamour for her dethronement. Her refusal drove them to compel her abdication in favour of her infant son James VI, with Moray (recalled from his travels) as regent.

Once again, as in 1560, the Protestant lords were in control and their tenure of power looked likely to be of long duration. They had a wide popular support, at least in the Lowlands, the real centre of political and economic power. They had the active concurrence of the Catholic leader, Atholl, as well as that of Lennox. By autumn they had compelled the grudging submission of Argyle, Huntly, and the Hamiltons. They held their deposed queen a prisoner. In 1568, with the Hamiltons' help, she did escape from Lochleven castle; but it was only to suffer a still more disastrous defeat at Langside (May) from which she saw no safety except by flight to England. With Mary a fugitive, and the king still an infant who would be brought up in the Protestant faith, Moray could hope now to complete the work which Mary's impatience and folly had interrupted. In the young James, moreover, he had a candidate for the English succession who might be far more acceptable than his Catholic and half-French mother; one, too, whose young years would restrain his supporters from the temptation to hasten the course of nature by violent means. The revolution of 1567 was another long step towards making Great Britain politically as well as geographically an island.

But for Elizabeth, it might have been the final step. The new rulers of Scotland could look abroad for support to no one but her. The Catholic powers were in no position to contemplate intervention. While Mary was losing her throne at Carberry Hill, the duke of Alba was marching from Genoa towards the Netherlands to exact vengeance for the 1566 rebellion there. With what was virtually the entire field army of Spain thus committed in the Low Countries, Philip II could not think of adventures in Scotland that must involve conflict with England and might tempt the French to meddle in the Netherlands. Alba's march also ruled out any

French help for Mary. The French government, alarmed to see the Spanish army marching along its eastern frontier, raised a force of Swiss to shadow it. The Huguenots, imagining these to be the first moves in the 'conspiracy' plotted at Bayonne, took arms and plunged France into a second civil war (September 1567–March 1568) and, almost without pause, into a third (September 1568–August 1570).

The storm-centres of western Europe were moving away from Great Britain to the Netherlands and France. Henceforward it would be from the internal instability of those continental regions that the challenges to the Cateau-Cambrésis system would arise. And if Great Britain did not at once settle down, the reason lay in the policies of England rather than in the ambitions of the continental powers. It was the personal policy of Elizabeth that kept Mary's cause alive in Scotland; it was the policies for which William Cecil was chiefly responsible that provoked a final crisis in England itself.

When Mary fell, every motive of self-interest, of national and Protestant security, pressed the English government to accept her overthrow, publish her guilt, and ally firmly with Moray, whose rule implied the triumph of Protestantism and English influence throughout Great Britain. But Elizabeth's notions of the divinity that hedged a queen were as exalted as Mary's. She would not betray her order, and set an example for Catholic princes to copy against herself, by allying with rebels and condoning the deposition of a fellow queen. First she tried to mediate a settlement that would restore Mary to nominal sovereignty while leaving all real power in Moray's hands. That broke upon the Scots' uncompromising refusal to take Mary back, except for execution.

Next she urged the Scots to appear before a commission of English councillors and peers to justify their rebellion. Mary or her envoys would answer and Elizabeth would then be able to decide upon her own course. Again the Scots refused, unless assured beforehand of a verdict in their favour. As proof of their cause, they sent copies of the bill of charges against Mary and of the 'Casket Letters' written, as they alleged, from Mary to Bothwell at the time of Darnley's murder. This evidence was damning if it could be proved genuine and again Elizabeth had to concede the Scots' demands. Conferences at York and then Westminster followed. The Scots produced their charges and the original Casket Letters. Those originals disappeared within a generation, so no one can now certainly pronounce upon their authenticity—though all too many have tried. At Westminster in December 1568, however, they were produced at three meetings on three successive days; compared with letters from Mary to Elizabeth of undoubted autheticity; and apparently accepted as genuine by the English commissioners, among them such men of skill and experience (if of Protestant faith) as Cecil, Sir Nicholas Bacon, and the earl of Sussex, the last 'a scholar saturated in the new learning' of the

Renaissance. Conservative, and less learned, peers such as Norfolk and Northumberland also inspected them on the final day and professed to be convinced. Even so, the conference ended without a verdict. Elizabeth had her own justification for not restoring Mary, for keeping her in more or less honourable confinement. Beyond that she would not go. She would not formally pronounce against Mary and it was more than two years before the evidence for the prosecution was printed in Buchanan's semi-official *Detection* (1571). This reticence on Elizabeth's part cloaked Mary's apparent guilt in just that veil of doubt that was needed to make her still a danger, to allow her to be portrayed as an innocent and Catholic queen 'framed' by Protestant rebels who were themselves guilty of the crimes for which they had deposed her. This, and Elizabeth's obvious sympathy, were sufficient to keep the Marian faction alive in Scotland and to make it a magnet for other discontents that accompanied Moray's efforts to restore the authority of the Edinburgh government.

Moreover, Mary's presence in the north of England helped to light the fuse for an explosion there, for which the materials had long been accumulating and for which the peculiar circumstances of 1568-9 provided the appropriate atmosphere. The English north, remote, hilly, sparsely peopled, economically backward, was still not reconciled to government from Westminster and its delegated council in the north. There lords and gentry still maintained a semi-feudal independence: Northumberland, it could be said, knew no prince but a Percy. The whole tendency of Tudor government, towards strengthening central control and limiting local autonomy, was alien to the ethos of the north. The new economic trends, the growth of commerce and industry and state regulation, brought relatively little benefit to this predominantly agricultural region. Above all, the north clung to the old Catholic ways in religion and viewed with alarm the steady taking root of the 1559 settlement and the activities of puritans in parliament to remove it even further from Catholicism. William Cecil, the queen's chief counsellor, who seemed to personify all these trends and policies, was fast becoming as unpopular in the north as Thomas Cromwell had been thirty years earlier.

So far the north had been forced to watch these changes in growing despair. Elizabeth, by avoiding extremes, by avoiding violent coercion, was letting the old ways and the old faith fade away from mere inanition. As the old popish clergy died off, there were none to replace them, for there was nowhere in England where successors could be trained in the Catholic faith. In secular matters, too, the pressure was continual but not intolerable. The northern way of life was being slowly undermined, too gradually and silently to provide urgent excuse or provocation for a present stand to halt the decay. Then Mary arrived, for some perhaps a crowned murderess fleeing from justice, but none the less a Catholic queen fleeing from Calvinist rebels. And their own queen's treatment of her, by blurring the first image, could only encourage them to look favourably upon the second. Even so, some provocative occasion and some real prospect of attaining a more than local support were needed to stir the north to action.

Elizabeth's and Cecil's precipitation of a quarrel with Spain at the close of 1568 provided just such an occasion. To understand this, we must go back to the summer of 1567 and across to the Netherlands. Alba's arrival there, with Spain's main field army, was one of the major turning-points in the history of western Europe. For the next hundred years that army's communications back to Italy and Spain were to be a main consideration in Spanish policy, a main object of French attack, a governing factor in international affairs. For the moment France could do little about it. Her government did not dare to let the Huguenots assist William of Orange's first attempt to break Alba's tyrannous grip in the summer of 1568; and after that, civil war ruled out intervention at least until 1571. But Alba's presence and methods alarmed England too. They were a menace to her trade to Antwerp, even though, as the agreement of July 1567 with Hamburg showed, alternatives to Antwerp were beginning to be found. But the real menace was strategic. The hitherto harmless and largely home-ruling Netherlands, the counterscarp of Protestant England as Cecil was to term them, were being transformed into a military camp for the finest and most Catholic army in Christendom, there just across the Narrow Seas from the nerve centres of English government and economic life. This, too, when bickerings over privateers in the Channel, the Inquisition in Spanish ports, and John Hawkins's voyages to Spanish America were already disturbing Anglo-Spanish relations. Henceforward, therefore, one of the dominant purposes of English policy was to get the Spanish army out of the Low Countries and to restore those provinces to their ancient liberties.

The collapse of France made action by England the more urgent. The opportunity came when ships bearing a loan from the bankers of Genoa to pay Alba's army took refuge in English ports from storms and privateers. Elizabeth seized the money (December 1568) and, as in strict law it still belonged to the bankers of Genoa until it was delivered in Antwerp, she persuaded them to lend it to her instead of to Alba. It was a serious blow to Alba[1] and it brought England and Spain to the brink of war. It brought a stoppage of trade with the Netherlands and Spain and seizures of ships and goods on both sides. And although Alba was begging his master not to add an English war to his other troubles, Englishmen only knew of the fierce protests and threats of Philip's ambassador in London.

In alarm many began to agitate for the dismissal of Cecil and a reversal of his policy. The agitation provided a cover and a focus for many discontents and many projects—for Leicester's jealousy of Cecil, for Norfolk's

---

[1] For Alba's difficulties, see below, pp. 271-3.

ambition to marry Mary Stuart, for the more drastic and treasonable designs of the northern Catholics. Yet, although all were hostile to Cecil, only the northern lords were prepared to use force against Elizabeth. Thus, as soon as it became clear that Cecil's policy was the queen's policy, the opposition collapsed. Norfolk, after much hesitation, obeyed a summons to court and promptly found himself in the Tower. Most of his allies had already fallen away and even the north was discouraged. The earls of Northumberland and Westmorland, egged on by their wives, did rise (November 1569), but Dacre in the north-west would not join them. It was not long before they were fleeing over the border (December) and when Dacre belatedly rebelled, he too was rapidly crushed by Hunsdon (February 1570).

The revolt of the north was over, and with it the British Question as we have been considering it. Elizabeth's government, and Cecil's place in it, were safe from domestic challenge. While Mary Stuart lived, her partisans might trouble the rule of England's friends in Scotland, but their hope of overthrowing it was already small and grew smaller every year. Reaction to the old ways could now hardly come except through foreign invasion, and only a small minority even of the Catholics were willing to see their country restored to the Roman fold by foreign conquest. Moreover, while the Protestant ascendancy in Scotland secured England's only land frontier, the growing maritime power of England gave increasing assurance against sea-borne invasion, and the success of the Merchant Adventurers' trade to Hamburg in 1569 held out good hope for an increasing economic independence of Spanish Antwerp. Great Britain no longer offered by its weakness, divisions, and instability a tempting battleground for the great powers of the continent.

The events of the ten years that followed the Peace of Cateau-Cambrésis assured the independence and Protestantism of Great Britain and prepared the way for its political union. Thereby they made possible the emergence of a third great power in western Europe and the eventual supersession of the twin imperialisms of Habsburg and Valois by a multiple balance of powers.

CHAPTER IX

WESTERN EUROPE AND THE POWER OF SPAIN

THE Peace of Cateau-Cambrésis (2–3 April 1559) was a belated recognition of the end of the imperial plans of the late Emperor Charles V.[1] The last phase of the war between Habsburg and Valois had been precipitated by the octogenarian Pope Paul IV in his hatred of Spanish dominion in Italy. The principal combatants had fought it almost unwillingly, but the struggle had been as bitter as it was inconclusive and even more costly than previous wars. Now a new era was to dawn with the marriage of Philip II to Henry II's daughter, Elizabeth.

> O Paix, fille de Dieu, qui nous viens rejouir
> Comme l'aube du jour...
> Et joindre étroitement l'Espagne avec la France
> D'un nœud qui pour jamais en amour s'entretient...

sang the poet Ronsard.

The change was even greater than men realised at the time. In less than ten years from the abdication of Charles V (1555/6) all political problems moved on to a completely different plane. Until the middle of the sixteenth century, the Reformation had been successful only where it had been allied with the state. When it became revolutionary, as it did in the German Peasants' War and in the Anabaptist movements of the Netherlands and northern Germany, it had been easily put down, because it had been supported only by the lower classes in town and country. Now, for the first time and quite suddenly, revolutionary movements became nationwide and included classes, or elements of classes, ranging from artisans to princes of the blood. Determined minorities tried to impose their views on whole countries.[2] They had to build organised parties to match the power of the state. They either acted through a parliament or assembly of estates, or else, at one time or another, they became openly revolutionary. Only religious belief, held either from fanatical conviction or political expediency, could bring together the divergent interests of nobles, burghers and peasants throughout whole kingdoms. Thus it was with the Huguenots and the Holy League in France, with the Calvinists and Sea Beggars in the Netherlands, and with Knox's 'brethren' and the Lords of the Congregation in Scotland. After the third session of the Council of Trent, with its clear definitions of Catholic dogma and of heresy, only those excessively

---

[1] For the terms of the peace, see vol. II, pp. 249 and 358.
[2] See also above, pp. 155–6, 160–1.

234

optimistic, or as obtuse in matters of religion as Catherine de Medici, could still believe that Catholic and Protestant views might yet be re- conciled. Two alternatives remained: toleration or annihilation of the opposition. For a long time neither side was prepared to accept the first alternative.

At the moment when these formidable forces were beginning to emerge, the governments of western Europe were themselves overtaken by a severe crisis. The long wars between Charles V and his opponents had overstrained the resources of their governments. While the economic life of western Europe was expanding, that part of it which could be touched by taxation had been over-burdened. The fall in the value of money had reduced the value of government revenues and had at the same time pushed expenditure to unprecedented figures. In five years the Netherlands had paid eight million ducats for the war and Castile eleven million in three years. Both the Spanish and the Netherlands governments went bankrupt in 1557, forcibly reducing interest payment on all their debts to 5 per cent. A few months later, the French government was compelled to follow suit. These crises caused the first big international banking crash. Antwerp and Lyons were hardest hit, but Augsburg, Genoa and Florence did not escape disaster. With credit difficult to obtain and ex- pensive, governments had to look for new sources of revenue. In the Netherlands these could be obtained only through grants by the estates. Ruler and subjects alike looked to Spain for relief; but when Philip II returned to Madrid in 1559, he found that the financial situation there was even worse than in Brussels. It soon became apparent that in France, too, the crown could not increase taxes further without the consent of its subjects. As so often in the history of the *ancien régime*, financial crisis led to political crisis. The clash between the ruler's demands for money and the unwillingness of his subjects to pay opened up the whole problem of political power.

Firm and experienced leadership was now essential. But in France and the Netherlands it disappeared at this very moment. In both countries the government passed into the hands of women, as it had already done in England and Scotland a few years earlier. In a political society whose ethos was masculine and military, and whose habits of loyalty were still to the person of the sovereign, the 'monstrous regiment of women' made the political crisis all but unmanageable. Only Elizabeth I overcame it, and she had the immense advantage over Catherine de Medici and Margaret of Parma of being a reigning sovereign in her own right.[1]

The crisis of the governments of western Europe was bound to affect international relations. The old rivalries did not die with Charles V and Henry II. France still had a foothold in Italy through her occupation of

[1] So was Mary Queen of Scots; but much of the damage to the authority of the Scottish crown had been done during the regency of her mother, Mary of Guise.

Saluzzo and five Piedmontese fortresses. At any moment she could threaten Spanish predominance in the peninsula and, as before, she would not lack Italian allies. Her old border quarrels with the Netherlands were dormant, not settled. Both Spain and France had their allies and clients among the German princes. England had not forgotten nor forgiven the loss of Calais. More serious still, neither the English nor the Scottish government appeared to be stable. Both France and Spain might intervene and seriously upset the balance of power in western Europe. These were the bare bones of the Habsburg–Valois struggle, stripped of the idealistic motives of Gattinara and Charles V. Ministers and ambassadors saw them as such and were under no illusions. But few had the strength of mind to follow consistently the austere logic of reason of state. They and their sovereigns were not immune from the religious emotions which dominated their subjects. They were convinced that their religious opponents were moved by purely material and political considerations, and these convictions have misled some modern historians. But they were equally convinced of the honesty of their own religious convictions as a motive force for their politics, and of no one was this more true than of Philip II. In practice, therefore, the springs of political motivation were muddy and policies were not pursued consistently. The national rivalries of the great powers became entangled in the social, political and religious struggles within the different states and in the international patterns of religious loyalties. France, the Netherlands, England and Scotland, all had 'fifth columns' within their boundaries—a deadly weakness which Charles V, Francis I and Henry VIII never had to face, despite occasional rebellions against their rule. Thus, for more than twenty years, the great powers shrank from open war, though they were often on the brink. The internal weakness of France seemed to present Philip II with the opportunity for which his father, the Emperor Charles V, had striven all his life in vain: the alliance of the Catholic powers, under the leadership of the Habsburgs, against the enemies of Catholic Christendom. If, later, William of Orange overdramatised the Habsburg–Valois marriage alliance of 1559 into a conspiracy of the kings of Spain and France against the religious liberties of their subjects, he was at least correct in his appreciation of Philip II's religious policy. But the weakness of France depended precisely on these enemies of Catholic Christendom, the Protestants, who were such a deadly danger to Philip's own authority. Philip II never managed to resolve completely the ambiguity of his aims of keeping France both weak and Catholic, and this ambiguity accounts for much of his tortuous policy during the French Wars of Religion.

Spain still had to face the external enemy of Christendom, the Ottoman Turk. Philip II was the only western ruler who, in the twenty years after Cateau-Cambrésis, was still fighting a major war. He might persuade the French crown to co-operate with him against the Protestants. He could never persuade it to help him against the Turks. The Turks, moreover, had their own potential allies inside Spain, the Moriscos. If the Moslem 'fifth column' could never hope to capture the whole country, as the Huguenots and Sea Beggars might, yet in alliance with the greatest naval and military power of the time they might still be a terrible danger. The political crisis in Spain was therefore only little less severe than in the other countries of western Europe.

I. *Spain and Italy*

Charles V had failed to secure the imperial succession for his son.[1] But the fact of empire was not changed by this failure. Philip II still ruled over Spain and her dependencies in Italy, Franche-Comté, the Netherlands and the Indies. These had been the main sources of Charles V's imperial strength, of his money and his soldiers. Materially, at least, it was to Philip's advantage to disengage Spanish policy from the problems of central Europe while, at the same time, keeping on amicable terms with his uncle and cousins of the Austrian branch of the Habsburg family.[2] His marriage to Mary I of England (1554) was the logical complement to such a policy and even after Mary's death (1558) it was not immediately obvious that England would not remain, or become again, a Habsburg satellite. But the absence of the imperial title raised its own difficulties about the nature of Philip II's empire. Charles V's views of the transcendental nature of his position and of his destiny to create a Christian world monarchy had depended on this title. What was left for Philip II was another part of his father's mission, the defence of the Catholic church. 'You may assure His Holiness', Philip wrote to his ambassador in Rome in 1566, 'that rather than suffer the least damage to religion and the service of God, I would lose all my states and an hundred lives, if I had them; for I do not propose nor desire to be the ruler of heretics.' Even the popes, however, found it sometimes difficult to distinguish between Philip's views as to what was the service of God and what the service of the Spanish monarchy.

This formulation of purpose still left out the empire itself. Neither Philip nor any of his contemporaries ever worked out a comprehensive theory of empire to take the place of the now outlived ideas of Charles V's time. In America the Spaniards had conquered and converted heathen populations. Spanish theologians and jurists debated their rights and those of the conquerors, and the Spanish government codified them as laws. But in Christian Europe Philip himself, and almost every one else, saw in his empire only a *monarchia*, a collection of states under one ruler. From the latter part of Charles V's reign it had become more and more a Spanish empire.[3] Philip's succession gave Spain and Castile an even greater

---

[1] See vol. II, pp. 331 ff.   [2] See vol. II, p. 302.
[3] See vol. II, pp. 332 ff.

predominance; for Philip spoke only Castilian, fixed his residence in Castile, and preferred Castilians to all his other subjects in positions of power.

Inevitably, the Castilians came to regard themselves as the rulers of the empire, though they were well aware of the growing hostility of other nations. The marquis of Ayamonte, governor of Milan, wrote to Philip (2 February 1570): 'I do not know whether there is anyone in the world who is subject to the Spanish nation and empire and who is devoted to them, but does not rather abhor their name.' This, he added, was especially true of the Italians. His view was endorsed by an unsigned comment scribbled on the letter: 'For these Italians, though they are not Indians, have to be treated as such, so that they understand that we are in charge of them and not they in charge of us.' A typical note of a Master Race.

In practice, however, Philip's empire could not be run in quite this way. Philip, like his father, rested his claims to the sovereignty over his different dominions on the laws of these states. When Bernardino de Mendoza, his ambassador in France, tried to reassure the French about a possible Spanish succession to the crown of France after the death of Henry III,[1] he likened Philip's monarchy to one of the great monastic orders which were under one head, but in which no one nation commanded another. Such advances as there were in imperial unification were made to meet the demands of defence and of a more efficient administration, not as the result of any advance in imperial ideas. Thus the Spaniards kept a tight hold on all important military positions in their Italian dominions. The captaincies of the local militia and of the feudal levies were generally reserved to natives, for it was Philip's policy to keep the Italian nobility contented. But only Spaniards commanded the regular *tercios* and the castles and fortresses. The greatest administrative advance in imperial unity was the creation of the Council of Italy, in 1558. Philip did not want to see the old Aragonese empire continue as a separate structure within his possessions. It was compromised, in his eyes, by its Catalan traditions. Its supreme organ, the Council of Aragon, was staffed by Aragonese, Catalans and Valencianos. The new council, with its mixed Castilian and Italian personnel, was to act as supreme court for Sicily, Naples and Milan, and as their administrative link with Madrid. Formally, at least, it was a striking advance over Charles V's system. No other European government was now as well informed about its dependencies, nor able to supervise their administrations with such attention to detail and such concern for the welfare of its subjects. Yet its councillors were nearly always mediocrities, with little understanding of imperial problems. All important political decisions continued to rest with the king and his closest advisers. Philip did not set up a Council of Flanders until 1588, although the Netherlanders petitioned for it as early as 1574. It does not appear to have been very effective. The same was probably true for the Council of Portugal,

---

[1] See below, p. 303.

founded in 1582–3. Even the administrative advance in imperial unity therefore remained a very partial one.

The most effective link between the centre of the empire and its members remained the system of weekly, sometimes daily, correspondence between the king and his secretaries, on the one hand, and the viceroys and governors, on the other. Changes from Charles V's system of personal control were the result less of organisational advance than of changes in personnel. Philip II was less fortunate than his father, who had been able to appoint loyal and capable members of the Habsburg family to rule his dominions in his absence. Like the great merchant houses,[1] the Habsburgs were beginning to suffer from the 'problem of the third generation'. Philip's half-sister, Margaret of Parma, proved herself loyal and not unintelligent, as governor-general of the Netherlands. But she lacked the political insight of her aunt, Mary of Hungary, who had held the same position for Charles V. Philip's half-brother, Don John of Austria, was still too young for office when Philip succeeded to the throne. His brilliant though erratic gifts later gave the king his greatest triumph, the victory of Lepanto. But Don John was a failure as governor-general of the Netherlands and his early death, at 31, may have saved him from disgrace at court. Philip tried to make use of his Austrian relatives by carefully bringing up several of the young archdukes at his court. They proved loyal, but of such depressing mediocrity that their political services consisted in little more than the fading magic of their imperial names.

The king's most terrible disappointments were his own sons. Don Carlos (born 1545), child of Philip's consanguineous first marriage with Mary of Portugal, showed early signs of mental instability, perhaps the legacy of Joanna the Mad which he inherited through both his parents. His tragic death has provided generations of historians, dramatists and librettists with splendidly romantic plots, especially about the prince's supposed love for his young step-mother, Elizabeth of Valois.[2] The truth is more simple. For years Philip tried to induce Carlos to take a responsible interest in affairs of state. Eventually he had to admit that the prince's criminal paranoia, his murderous rages, his physical assaults on the citizens of Madrid and the king's councillors, and his treasonable contacts with the rebels in the Netherlands rendered him unfit for any authority and a danger to the state. On 18 January 1568 he arrested him. He could do no less if he was to fulfil his duties as a Christian prince to his subjects. Thus he wrote to his sister, the empress, and the agony of a father speaks through the stilted prose of a king. Six months later, Carlos was dead. There is no evidence that he was murdered, by Philip's orders or otherwise, though within a few days suspicions were whispered in the court itself.

[1] See vol. II, p. 309.
[2] Thus especially Schiller, and Verdi's librettists J. Méry and C. du Locle.

Philip's only surviving son, the later Philip III, was not mad. But the old king was rightly under no illusions as to his abilities. The one outstanding member of Philip's family and his only successful governor-general of the Netherlands was Margaret of Parma's son, Alexander Farnese. His career, as also that of Don John, was to show the greatest weakness in Philip's own character, his almost pathological suspiciousness and duplicity.[1]

Philip therefore had to fall back on the Spanish and Italian high nobility to fill his viceroyalties and governorships. He could employ lawyers, ecclesiastics and professional administrators in his councils and as secretaries of state and, in general, he preferred to do so, just as his father had done. In the viceroyalties and military commands this was not possible. The native nobility hated the men of the long robe. 'They do not know what it is to be a king,' wrote Juan de Vega, viceroy of Sicily, 'nor wherein lies the greatness and authority of monarchy...nor of chivalry and honour.' The Castilian grandees, naturally, had the lion's share of these appointments. Six of Philip's nine viceroys of Sicily were Spaniards; so were all of his viceroys of Naples with the single exception of Granvelle, and ten out of thirteen of his governors of Milan. In the viceroyalties of Aragon, Catalonia, Valencia and Navarre, and in the captain-generalcy of Granada, the question of appointing non-Spaniards did not arise at all. The days of Adrian of Utrecht were long since past.[2] But for the old Italian nobility, too, there were still splendid prizes if they chose the service of the Catholic king. Gian Andrea Doria was commander-in-chief of the king's Mediterranean fleet. The marquis of Pescara and Marc Antonio Colonna were viceroys of Sicily. So was the duke of Terranova, who also became a grandee of Spain and governor of Milan. Alexander Farnese was governor-general of the Netherlands and, in Philip III's reign, Ambrogio Spinola was commander-in-chief.

Philip II appointed only one northerner to high office south of the Alps: the Burgundian Antoine Perrenot, Cardinal Granvelle, son of Charles V's secretary of state. Granvelle came from the same school of Franche-Comtois lawyers as Gattinara. He had little of the old grand chancellor's imperial vision, yet he had a clearer conception of the nature of the Habsburg monarchy than either Philip himself or any other of his ministers. Philip, like his father, tried to rule his empire through his personal control of official appointments and all forms of patronage. The emperor had tried to overcome the weaknesses of this system by constant travelling throughout his dominions. Thus his subjects could always hope that their grievances would be relieved and their services rewarded.[3] Philip failed to understand this. He criticised his father for having wasted his time, health and money in his constant travels. Margaret of Parma and

---

[1] See below, p. 310. [2] See vol. II, p. 319.
[3] See vol. II, p. 310.

Granvelle pleaded with him to revisit the Netherlands. Philip found ready and logical excuses not to do so. If he came with insufficient money and troops, he said, his authority would suffer rather than gain. But, as his subjects' hopes gradually turned to disappointment, the old bands of loyalty wore out. Men ceased to believe in the time-honoured distinction between the wise and good prince and his wicked ministers who could be blamed for all ills. They turned against the prince himself. Thus it happened in the Netherlands, and thus it happened nearer home, in Granada and Aragon.[1] Granvelle, from his vantage point in Brussels, saw the storm-signals. The general dissatisfaction with the Spanish nation, he wrote to Philip in 1563, arose from the suspicion that the king wanted to reduce the Netherlands to the status of his Italian provinces. Yet he was the common lord of them all, and it would be well to show that he did not regard only the Spaniards as his legitimate sons; for these were the words people used, both in Flanders and in Italy. A few ecclesiastical offices and grants (encomiendas) given to Netherlanders in Spain would confirm the loyalty of the recipients, their families and clients, and would keep another 25,000 in hopes of future rewards. Some of the great lords might be given positions of command in Italy. Orange, for example, would serve well as viceroy of Sicily, far from the bad influences of Protestant Germany, and with greater contentment through advancement in the king's service.

Here was perhaps the clearest appreciation of the nature of the empire in the whole reign of Philip II. In contrast to similar appreciations in the first half of the sixteenth century, it arose, not from a theoretical justification of empire by a humanist scholar or statesman, but from the practical insight into its political problems by a brilliant administrator. In the event, Philip found it, as usual, easy to shelve his minister's suggestions. He could not satisfy even all legitimate Spanish claims for encomiendas, he answered, and it would be too dangerous to experiment, in such important positions as the Italian governorships, with anyone whose religious beliefs were not absolutely above suspicion. Moreover, would Orange not be disappointed after the end of a three-year term as viceroy? For Philip, again unlike his father, was usually unwilling to renew appointments, for fear that his viceroys might become too independent. Thus he lost the opportunity of retaining the loyalty and services of the man who was to become his most able and determined enemy.

In practice, the king did not exercise as much control over patronage as he thought he did. His system of personal government is well known. All work was done on paper, on the basis of consultas, that is, memoranda, reports and advice presented him by his ministers. In Madrid, or in the gloomy magnificence of his monastic palace of El Escorial which he built on the slopes of the Sierra de Guadarrama, the king worked alone in his

[1] See below, pp. 244–7, 249–51.

small office, annotating reports, poring over maps and figures, giving his decisions or, as often, deferring them. We know nothing of his order of work, of his selection of documents or of his system of priorities, if indeed he had any. Philip never attended council meetings, for fear that his presence would inhibit the councillors from speaking their opinions. The effect was the opposite of the one he desired. The councillors knew that their opinions were reported to the king by the president or secretary of the council. They knew that Philip might pretend to accept their advice, yet take a contrary decision. Thus they tried to conform their views to the yet unknown wishes of the king; their advice became conservative, their statements of opinion half-hearted and qualified. Inevitably, a strong president of the Council of Castile or the Council of State, a Cardinal Espinoza or a Cardinal Granvelle, dominated policy-making. Equally inevitably, the already strong position of the secretaries of state was further strengthened in the hands of astute men, like Antonio Pérez, who knew the king better than any councillor. It was such men who effectively dominated royal and imperial patronage; for even such a hard-working and well-informed ruler as Philip II had to rely on their advice. The result of this system was that those whose requests were not granted blamed the king for having specially invented the procedure of the *consulta* to be able to refuse them more easily, while those who obtained what they wanted were more grateful to the ministers and secretaries than to the king himself. Philip's ministers and secretaries, as long as they lasted, tended to become rich men.

The Habsburgs had perfected a courier and postal system which was, perhaps, the best in Europe. Even then, communication between the king and the governors of his dominions remained dangerously slow. But much worse than the geographical handicaps were Philip's own habits. Painstaking and conscientious, his craving for ever more information hid an inability to distinguish between the important and the trivial and a temperamental unwillingness to take decisions. His much admired self-possession covered an occasional tendency to panic, as in 1571, when he suddenly ordered the evacuation of the whole population of the Balearic Islands from fear of a Turkish invasion, or as in 1587, when he ordered the marquis of Santa Cruz to set sail against England in November, regardless of the weather and the number of ships which were sea-worthy. In both cases his ministers refused to carry out his commands. But the reverse was much more common. It was of lack of orders that the viceroy of Sicily, García de Toledo, complained when he wanted to relieve the siege of Malta, in 1565.[1] It was the lack of clear and timely decisions from Madrid which helped to undermine the authority of Philip's government in the Netherlands.[2]

Motion, but little movement, was the characteristic of the internal

[1] See below, p. 252.   [2] See below, p. 276.

history of Castile, as it was that of Philip's system of government. Charles V had effectively solved the internal political problems of the kingdom. The nobility supported the crown enthusiastically.[1] The political power of the towns was broken. Their representatives in the Cortes continued to discuss freely all matters of state, from the baleful influence of foreigners on the country's economy, from over-heavy taxes, to the excessive powers of the Inquisition and even the king's own methods of government. Philip was always willing to receive memoranda and petitions on all these matters; but he would not even grant an audience to the representatives, and he accepted or rejected their petitions entirely as he saw fit. He even abrogated the one really important privilege which the Cortes had managed to hold on to, that of refusing consent to the revocation of laws passed in previous sessions.

The political conflicts of the days of Cardinal Ximénez and of the revolt of the *comuneros* had degenerated into the intrigues of court factions and the jurisdictional quarrels between the different law courts and councils of the kingdom. Two men dominated the now all-Spanish Council of State during the first part of Philip's reign: the duke of Alva and the Hispano-Portuguese Ruy Gómez de Silva, prince of Eboli. Since the Venetian ambassadors first wrote about the rivalry between these two, historians have generally spoken of two parties or factions at the court of Madrid, the Gómez 'peace party' and the Alva 'war party'. Recently, these parties have been identified, perhaps a little too imaginatively, with a 'conservative' *comunero* tradition (Alva) and a 'liberal' monarchical tradition (Gómez) (see G. Marañon, *Antonio Pérez*, Mexico, 1947). They were not so much parties as groups, bound loosely together by family connections, patronage and clientage. In the absence of genuine political conflicts they represented little but their own interests and the clash of personalities. Owing to family intermarriages and personal rivalries there were many cross currents. With the rise of Cardinal Espinoza in the king's favour and, even more, after Gómez's death (1573), the earlier groupings tended to break up. The factions became more complex, but their struggles no less bitter.

The results of these rivalries were only a little less disastrous for Spain than similar rivalries were for France and the Netherlands. They slowed down government business in an already excessively dilatory system, for each party tried to block the proposals made by the other. The connections of the family clans of the Silvas and the Mendozas, the Toledos (Alva) and the Figueroas, the Córdobas, Enríquez and Guzmáns, covered the whole country and involved every quarrel over a sheep-run in the power politics at the court of Madrid. They became entangled in the jurisdictional quarrels between military commanders and civil courts, and of both with the claims of ecclesiastical courts. In Calderón's play, *El Alcalde de*

---

[1] See vol. II, p. 314.

Zalamea, Philip II appears as the *deus ex machina* to settle the dispute between the noble colonel of a regiment and the peasant mayor (*alcalde*) of a small town in the *alcalde*'s favour when the latter declares that the king's justice must be one and indivisible.[1] This certainly accorded with Philip's own views. He was unceasing in his efforts to bring the benefits of efficient centralised government and equal justice to subjects suffering under the privileges and petty tyrannies of the nobility. Yet, precisely because Philip saw himself as the sole fountain-head of justice, he was slow to interfere in the quarrels of his courts. They each had their spokesman at court and in the king's councils. Philip fostered their rivalries. His fear of treachery led him into betraying his own ministers and friends. 'Kings use men like oranges,' said the duke of Alva, 'they squeeze out the juice and then throw them away.' His own career showed the justness of his words, though he never wavered in his loyalty. The king's unreliability poisoned the politics of his court and turned political and personal rivalries into deadly struggles for power and survival. 'No decent man can suffer it,' said the marquis de los Vélez; 'for if you do not have the king's favour, they all will trample on you, and if you have it, they will take your life and your honour.' Philip's system of government was directly responsible for the revolt of the Alpujarras of Granada, for the revolt of Aragon and, at least indirectly, for that of the Netherlands.

Outside Castile, Philip was faced with two major problems: the independence or autonomy of the peripheral states of the Iberian peninsula and the religious and racial diversity within these states. When Philip returned from the Netherlands in 1559, the Inquisition had just saved Spain from a 'most terrible conspiracy', discovered only just in time to prevent the whole country being lost. So said the Inquisitors of the arrest of a handful of poor 'Lutherans' in Seville and Valladolid, probably Erasmian or Illuminist survivals from the freer atmosphere of the emperor's reign. Apart from these, the mighty Inquisition, with its courts and councils, its theologians, judges, prisons and thousands of lay familiars, inquired into the Protestant opinions of about 325 suspects during the half century from 1550 to 1600. Many of even this small number were very doubtfully Protestant. All Spanish traditions, formed in the centuries of struggle against the infidels during the *reconquista*, worked against the success of Protestantism. Heterodoxy had a Moorish or Jewish taint in the eyes of every pure-blooded caballero or townsman. No other nation remained as impervious to Protestant propaganda.[2]

If the Protestants were never a serious problem, the 'New Christians' were. The policy of assimilating the Moriscos into Spanish Christian society had been started soon after the conquest of Granada; but, in more than two generations, it had met with only very limited success, not least

[1] 'Toda la justicia vuestra / Es sólo un cuerpo no más.'
[2] See also above, pp. 61–2.

because of language difficulties and because the Spanish government was unwilling to spend money on an effective system of Christian education. Nor did the policy of assimilation command universal support among the Spaniards themselves. No Morisco could become a priest because he was not accepted in the seminaries, reserved for those with *limpieza*, purity of Christian blood without taint of Mohammedanism, Judaism or heresy in the family. Moriscos could not enter the army nor follow a legal career. They remained second-class subjects and, typically, were hated more by the poor Christians than by the great nobles who employed them on their estates and who, in earlier generations, had almost all mixed their blood with that of Jews and Marranos. Equally typically, large numbers of Moriscos drifted into crime and outlawry.

From the beginning of Philip's reign, the position of the Moriscos in Granada suffered a gradual deterioration.[1] This was not originally due to any policy decision. The silk industry on which many Moriscos depended for their livelihood suffered under export prohibitions, imposed in a vain attempt to halt the rise of prices in Spain. Between 1560 and 1565, the tax on silk was more than doubled and the tax-farmers, to whom the Moriscos were fair game, surpassed even the generous limits of corruption which were generally expected from their activities. A government commission under the efficient Dr Santiago, set up to inquire into all titles of land, confiscated in fact mainly Morisco land. When the Turks launched their great Mediterranean offensives in the 1560s, North African Moors took the opportunity to make raids on the coast of Granada. Every time they were joined by large numbers of Morisco outlaws from the province itself. Spain was swept by rumours of an elaborate spy network, covering the whole country, and of a planned rising by all Moriscos, supported by the Turkish fleet.

The captain-general of Granada, Iñigo López de Mendoza, marquis of Mondéjar, was experienced and respected, even by the Moriscos, who saw in him their only protector against both the rapacious Christians and the murderous *monfís*, the bandits of the Sierra Nevada. But for years he had been quarrelling with the municipal council of Granada and with the royal *audiencia*, the supreme court for the south of Spain, over precedence, rights of jurisdiction and the ownership of the Sierra Nevada pastures. The *audiencia* was at odds with the Inquisition over similar questions and the Inquisition, in its turn, had quarrelled with the captain-general. Archbishop Guerrero of Granada supported Mondéjar in his liberal policy towards the Moriscos, but was engaged in a law suit with his own cathedral chapter. Everyone quarrelled with Dr Santiago and his land commission. As usual, these local quarrels were transferred to

---

[1] This account of the causes of the Morisco revolt is based largely on K. Garrad, *The Causes of the Second Rebellion of the Alpujarras (1568–71)*. I would like to thank Professor Garrad for letting me see his typescript and for permission to use it here.

Madrid, where the captain-general's enemies found a spokesman in the marquis de los Vélez, who had a private feud with Mondéjar over some disputed land.

At this point, the government in Madrid decided to solve, once and for all, both the Morisco problem and the political crisis in Granada. Espinoza, the president of the Council of Castile, persuaded the king to re-enact an edict of 1526, forbidding the Moriscos the use of Arabic, their Moorish names, dresses and ornaments and the possession of arms, besides ordering the destruction of all Moorish baths, so as to make an end to all Moorish ceremonies. The edict was published on 1 January 1567, despite Mondéjar's protests and warnings. Espinoza's protégé, Pedro Deza, had already been appointed president of the *audiencia* of Granada several months before. The *audiencia*, supported by Madrid, now claimed the jurisdiction over the Moriscos which the captain-general had formerly exercised. Its own soldiers took over from those of the captain-general, but they were inexperienced. They failed to hunt the bandits and only oppressed the peaceful Morisco farmers. Public security, precariously maintained by the captain-general's forces up till then, now collapsed. Seeing that their only protector, the captain-general, had lost his struggle with the *audiencia*, the Moriscos threw in their lot with the *monfís*. From 1567 they began to plan their rising. Increased taxation for the purpose of coastal defence, coming on top of a bad harvest in 1567, made rebellion seem the only means of escape from the growing misery of life under Spanish rule. On Christmas Day 1568 they struck, at the very moment when most of the captain-general's troops had been ordered to the coast to guard against Moorish raids.

Spain's Morisco policy, both assimilative and repressive, lay in ruins. The Spanish system of divided authority had caused the paralysis of the Granada administration at the most critical moment. The war of suppression which followed showed up unexpected military weaknesses. Mondéjar won early and brilliant successes. By February 1569 he seemed to have already pacified the province. But the robberies and cruelties of the Spanish soldiers drove the Moriscos to renewed resistance. The behaviour of Philip's soldiers towards civilian populations, especially those who were not regarded as good Catholics, proved to be a recurring and deadly weakness in nearly all Spanish campaigns. Mondéjar's personal enemies persuaded the king to replace him in the supreme command by the young Don John of Austria, under whose nominal leadership the Spanish generals continued to quarrel. The war was waged with appalling cruelty by both sides and it took another two years and much voluntary support from the Spanish towns before it was won.

But Spain had not completely failed. The Moriscos of Aragon and Valencia had remained loyal. When the revolt was over, one more heroic effort was made to make the policy of assimilation a success. The Moriscos of Granada, in their thousands, were sent inland, to be distributed in small groups among the Christian population of Andalusia and Castile. As a feat of organisation it was a remarkable achievement. In its execution it seems to have been rather less harsh than some similar forcible shifts of population in the twentieth century. Many Moriscos seem to have done reasonably well in their new homes and some even intermarried with Old Christians. But as a means of assimilating the two races, the policy was a failure. The lack of Spanish and Christian education was not remedied and, in consequence, mutual misunderstanding between the two races persisted. Both sides remained unforgiving.

From the end of the fifteenth century, it had been the policy of the Spanish crown to unify the whole Iberian peninsula. The preferred method, for the Christian kingdoms, was marriage alliance rather than conquest. Only Portugal still remained independent. There was no hurry about changing the *status quo*. Up to about 1580, Spain's resources were fully extended in her great war with the Moslems and by the revolt of the Netherlands. Portugal was a friendly power. Some Spanish grandees preferred it independent, for where else could their children flee from the king's wrath if the occasion arose? Alva had the temerity to say this to Philip himself and the king never forgot, even though Alva eventually conquered Portugal for him.

King Sebastian of Portugal was, from early youth, determined on a crusade in Morocco. Nothing that cautious and realistic advisers, including his uncle Philip II, could say would dissuade him. Portugal made a tremendous effort. But her naval power and the wealth of the Lisbon merchants were committed to her overseas empire. The country itself was poor and royal finances had been in a precarious state for decades.[1] Sebastian's forces were pitifully inadequate for his ambitious plans. His own leadership was rash and incompetent. On 4 August 1578 the Portuguese army was annihilated by the Moors on the field of Alcazar-el-Kebir. The last Christian attempt, before the nineteenth century, to conquer North Africa had ended in complete disaster. The childless king was among the slain and the Portuguese succession question suddenly became acute.

Sebastian's successor, his 67-year-old great-uncle, Cardinal Henry, was not expected to last long. But it was immediately clear that neither the Portuguese nor the European powers would willingly accept a Spanish succession. Philip had to prepare his ground carefully. He called Granvelle to Madrid, recognising at last the cardinal's political gifts and imperialist spirit. He signed a truce with the sultan (21 March 1580) which he had started to negotiate, without enthusiasm, three years earlier. Both in the Netherlands and towards England, Spanish policy became more accommodating. In Portugal itself, the catastrophe of Alcazar-el-Kebir

[1] See vol. II, pp. 608 ff.

had caused an almost complete collapse of public morale. All the nobility had lost relatives. 'The traders and handie-craftsmen who had not their kinsmen there (and yet many of them had) did venture their wealth in it [i.e. the campaign].'[1] The nobility was divided, mostly for purely personal reasons, between support of Philip and of one or other of the Portuguese pretenders, the duke of Braganza and Antonio, prior of Crato, the illegitimate son of the cardinal king's brother. The representatives of the towns in the Cortes were similarly divided. King Henry tried to play his own game and added to the confusion.

Philip cleverly exploited this situation. His pamphleteers insisted on his hereditary rights. His Portuguese agent, Christóvão de Moura, worked successfully to win over nobles and townsmen, bishops and university professors. When one of Henry's ministers proved impervious to bribes of money or titles, Moura provided him with relics for the nunnery he had founded. Could His Majesty steal some from the monastery of the Escorial? Moura wrote to Philip; otherwise he would get hold of corpses and say they were those of holy virgins. Philip thought the matter could be arranged without going to quite such lengths. But when Cardinal Henry died on 31 January 1580, it became apparent that resistance to the Spanish succession was still too strong. Philip would not succeed without a show of force. Antonio, the prior of Crato, became the recognised leader of the resistance to Spain. His pamphlets proclaimed the disasters that had befallen nations which had accepted Spanish rule. The mass of the common people and the lower clergy supported him enthusiastically. But in Castile nobles and towns now rallied to the support of their own king. The Italian provinces sent ships, money and munitions. Granvelle, who had organised the Castilian war effort, induced Philip to recall Alva from retirement. On 27 June 1580 Philip finally allowed his army to cross the frontier into Portugal.

The Portuguese had no chance. Their troops were no match for Alva's generalship and superior forces. Some of their defences were sabotaged: too many of the upper classes favoured the Spaniards. France and England gave good words but failed to intervene. Lisbon fell on 25 August and Oporto in October. That was the end of organised fighting; but it had been fierce while it lasted, and Alva's troops had committed their usual outrages.

Philip could now claim the rights of a conqueror. He found it prudent not to do so. At the Cortes of Thomar in 1581, and in a subsequent statement of 1582, he promised to uphold Portuguese laws and privileges, to appoint only Portuguese to official positions and not to introduce Castilian taxation. He abolished the customs barriers between Castile and Portugal so that his new kingdom could freely import much-needed grain. It was

---

[1] I. de Franchi Conestaggio, *The Historie of the Uniting of the Kingdom of Portugall to the Crowne of Castile* (translated by E. Blount: London, 1600), p. 55.

Philip's only major move in the economic unification of his empire; but he regarded it less as such than as a special privilege granted to his new subjects. In 1593 the customs points were set up again, mainly for financial reasons. The Portuguese colonial empire continued as a separate empire under the crown. For the moment, the Portuguese were well enough satisfied with this arrangement. Only later, from the last years of the century, the disadvantages of this separatism became apparent. Then Portuguese colonies and shipping were attacked by the enemies of Spain, by Holland, England and France, while the Spaniards made only half-hearted efforts to protect them. They were not altogether displeased to see the Portuguese weakened and attacks diverted from their own colonies.

The Prior Antonio escaped from Portugal and continued to direct a stream of propaganda against Spain, doing his best to spread the 'black legend' of the Spaniards' and Philip's cruelty and perfidy. In fact, he was little more than a pawn in the politics of England and France. His name, however, remained a symbol for anti-Spanish feeling in Portugal. The common people, indeed, had profited by the introduction of Castilian ideas of equal justice, for their nobles had treated them 'like black slaves', as the Venetian ambassador, Matteo Zane, said. But the nobles themselves were disappointed in their extravagant claims on Philip's patronage; the clergy remained hostile, for fear Philip would fleece them like the Castilian clergy; and the educated classes now turned deliberately away from Castile and began to look towards France. Gil Vicente and Camoëns had written some of their work in Castilian. This bilingualism now went out of fashion. The union of the crowns of Portugal and Castile did not produce the hoped-for unification of the peninsula. In 1640 even the formal union broke up again.

Isabella the Catholic once said that she hoped for a revolt in Aragon: it would give her the opportunity of establishing the power of the crown there as firmly as in Castile. Philip II showed no such desire. The eastern kingdoms of Spain were poor and sparsely populated. It would have been much too dangerous to interfere in Valencia where one-third of the population were Morisco. Catalonia was difficult but loyal. Her old imperial traditions fitted well with Philip's Mediterranean policies. The shipyards of Barcelona provided him with galleys and experienced seamen. But Barcelona had little part in the expanding trade of the sixteenth century and the Catalan nobility was allowed little share in the fruits of empire. They ruled their estates like miniature kingdoms, engaged in constant feuds and often made common cause with the ubiquitous bandits. The convoys of American silver, *en route* from Seville to Barcelona and Genoa, were frequently and sometimes successfully attacked. The stolen silver was then used in a profitable smuggling trade across the Pyrenees. The Spanish government suspected, not without cause, that the Catalan robber barons of the northern frontier were in close contact with the French Huguenots.

But Philip did little more than appoint some of his most faithful and competent Castilian grandees as viceroys to battle with these problems as best they could.

In Aragon, the king could not even appoint Castilians as viceroys. Here the unfortunate country population looked to the king to protect them from the arbitrary powers of a tyrannous nobility. Philip was very willing to respond to such an appeal; yet the nobles and the townspeople clung fiercely to their privileges. The old hatred of the Castilians had not abated and Philip had not helped his cause by refusing to visit Aragon. When he finally did so, in 1585, it was at least partly to settle the succession to the large county of Ribagorza whose inhabitants were in revolt against their feudal overlord, the duke of Villahermosa. The Aragonese Cortes, the nobles and the court of the *justicia*[1] were alarmed at this Castilian interference. New quarrels arose over the appointment of a Castilian viceroy and in the years after 1585 tension in the kingdom was rising rapidly.

The explosion of 1591, however, was sparked off by events at the court of Madrid itself. After the death of Ruy Gómez, his widow, Doña Ana de Mendoza, princess of Eboli, tried to maintain the Eboli influence at court with the help of Philip's secretary, Antonio Pérez. It is very unlikely that Pérez and the one-eyed princess were lovers, as historians and novelists have often thought; but the upstart secretary was hated both by many of the grandees and by his rivals in the Spanish civil service. The king's favour was unstable and Pérez knew it. To safeguard himself, he intrigued with all parties: with Don John of Austria and his secretary, Juan de Escovedo, against the king; with the king against Don John; perhaps even with the Netherlands rebels against both. Philip was deeply suspicious of Don John and his romantic ambitions. He vetoed his plans of invading England to liberate and marry Mary Queen of Scots. In 1577 he had determined on a policy of appeasement in the Netherlands and Don John was once more involving him in war.[2] When Don John sent Escovedo to Spain, to press his warlike policy, Pérez began to fear for his influence on the king and was in a panic that Escovedo might expose his intrigues. He reacted in the same way as Catherine de Medici in a similar situation on the eve of the massacre of St Bartholomew.[3] It was easy to represent Escovedo as Don John's evil genius, plotting treason against the king. Philip gave his consent to murder (1 March 1578), just as Charles IX had done. It was not a massacre, as in 1572. But Philip never forgave Pérez for having forced his hand. On 28 July 1579 he had his secretary and the princess of Eboli arrested without warning. Granvelle had just arrived to prepare the Portuguese campaign, and the king no longer needed the Eboli faction.

[1] See vol. II, p. 323.   [2] See below, pp. 276–8.
[3] See below, p. 289.

For the next ten years, Pérez remained a prisoner. But the Escovedo family and his enemies at court wanted his complete destruction. Philip now made his second mistake: he fell in with these plans, having convinced himself both that Pérez had misled him and that he had compromising documents in his hands. All efforts to extract these and a confession failed. In April 1590 Pérez escaped from prison, fled to Aragon and claimed the protection of the *justicia*'s court. Philip's case against him, in this court, he now answered, for the first time, by directly accusing the king of the murder of Escovedo. It was a situation which has become familiar in the twentieth century, that of a man who is driven to treason by a system of arbitrary government in which he himself has played a prominent part. Philip had one more card which could overtrump Aragonese privileges. On a fabricated charge of heresy, the Inquisition now demanded that Pérez be handed over to its prison in Saragossa. Never before had the hated Inquisition appeared so blatantly as the tool of royal absolutism. Twice, in May and September 1591, the populace of Saragossa prevented the transfer of Pérez to the Inquisition prison. The king's special representative was killed in the riots. To the Aragonese it meant the defence of their liberties; to Philip it meant open rebellion which had to be put down by force. In November 1591 a Castilian army marched into Aragon. Aragonese resistance collapsed within a few days and Pérez fled to France, there to continue his polemic against the king.

Philip had the *justicia* and many ringleaders of the rebellion executed, but was remarkably moderate in the constitutional changes he imposed. The *justicia* was, from now on, to be removable at royal pleasure; the viceroy could be a foreigner, that is, a Castilian; and majority voting was substituted for the principle of unanimity in the Aragonese Cortes. These changes, together with some very reasonable reforms of the legal system, gave the crown the ultimate power of decision in Aragon, but they preserved the kingdom's autonomy.

The Peace of Cateau-Cambrésis had left Spain free to concentrate on her most formidable enemy, the Turk. The emperor's campaigns had shown that the Christians could not seriously dispute Turkish supremacy in the eastern Mediterranean, nor the Turks Spanish supremacy in its western basin. A stable balance of power, however, had not yet been reached. Spain was in a much more precarious position than her enemies. The sultan's vassals and allies on the Barbary coast were always a potential threat to the Christian flank. Their raids on shipping and on the luckless fishing villages and small ports of Italy and southern Spain were a constant reminder of this threat. Their contacts with the Moriscos in Granada carried the Moslem danger to the very heart of Spanish power. As long as the Barbary kingdoms remained relatively isolated, the danger they presented could be kept in check. Everything therefore depended on the control of the central Mediterranean and both sides developed their strategy accordingly. For the Spaniards it had to be defensive. They were committed to two naval fronts, the Mediterranean and the Atlantic, on which, for technical reasons, warships were not easily interchangeable. Galley for galley, the Turks could outbuild them. An attempt by the combined squadrons of Spain's Italian dominions and allies to recapture Tripoli for the Knights of St John (1560) ended with the loss of more than half the Christian ships and showed the danger of undertaking even a limited offensive operation without naval superiority. The preservation of his fleet therefore became the main object of Philip's naval strategy. It had the disadvantage that Spain might be forced into a naval action when she least desired it or lose a vital strategic position. This dilemma became painfully apparent during the Turkish siege of Malta in 1565. The Knights of St John were sending more and more desperate appeals for relief as the Turks closed in. Philip's own captain-general, García de Toledo, viceroy of Sicily, was in despair at the silence from Madrid. Without definite orders he could not risk his fleet against the stronger Turkish armada. After weeks of hesitation, Philip decided against it. The island was saved by the heroic defence of the Knights and by the brilliant operation in which Toledo landed reinforcements without engaging his fleet.

It had been a near thing, but it was the turning-point in the Mediterranean war. The Turks had lost the fight for the control of the central Mediterranean. But this was not immediately clear. The Turks were still formidable. On both sides, the shipyards were building warships at full pressure. Uluj Ali, the Calabrian renegade and king of Algiers, did little to help the Moriscos of Granada during their rebellion, but he took the opportunity to overthrow the Spanish vassal king of Tunis (January 1570). Once the Morisco war was won, Philip was bound to react to this setback. With the Netherlands temporarily pacified,[1] he could afford to concentrate on the Mediterranean and join Pius V's Holy League with Venice against the Turks (May 1571). Philip had little of his father's crusading ardour. For him, the League presented the chance of meeting the Turks for once on equal or superior terms and securing the Spanish position in the central Mediterranean and on the Barbary Coast. The gamble paid off brilliantly. At Lepanto on 7 October 1571 the League's fleet, commanded by Don John of Austria, virtually annihilated the Turkish fleet. Yet the effects of Don John's famous victory were moral rather than material. To the Spaniards, from the common soldier Cervantes to the commander-in-chief Don John, Lepanto was their St Crispin's day, with the added glory of having fulfilled Spain's destiny as God's champion against the enemies of His Church. This mood explains much of the continued willingness of the Spaniards to support their king's religious and imperial policies, even in the face of ruinous costs and mounting disasters.

[1] See below, p. 271.

The political and strategic consequences of Lepanto, however, were slight.[1] Bickering between the allies about the direction of the next move wasted most of the sailing season of the next year. Cyprus had fallen and there was no chance of retaking it. In March 1573 Venice concluded a peace with the sultan. The Holy League might help her to win battles, but it could not protect her possessions. The defection of Venice at least left Don John free to concentrate on the central Mediterranean. In October 1573 he took Tunis; less than a year later it was lost again to Uluj Ali, commanding a Turkish fleet of such superior strength that the Spaniards could not risk engaging it in open battle. It seemed as if Lepanto had never been fought. The brief period when Philip had been able to concentrate his forces in the Mediterranean was past. It had badly overstrained his resources. From 1571 to 1573 the small kingdom of Sicily had spent 1,200,000 scudi on Don John's armada, and in 1575 Philip was forced to send 75,000 scudi as a direct aid to the Sicilian government to prevent its financial collapse. The financial position of Naples was even worse, and the Spanish government itself staggered towards its second bankruptcy (1575). Spain was now heavily engaged in the Netherlands. The strategic position in the Mediterranean, back where it was after the siege of Malta, presented a tolerable equilibrium. The naval and financial resources of the Ottoman empire, though still superior to those of Spain, had also been overstrained and the Porte, too, had to turn its attention to problems on its other borders. It was time to conclude a truce. The great struggle between the Spanish and Ottoman empires changed into a 'cold war', with only occasional and indecisive forays. Its final outcome was to be determined, not by the clash of arms, but by the internal development of both empires.

Just as in the emperor's reign, so in that of Philip II, the problem of defence dominated Spain's relations with her Italian dominions. But after 1559 Naples and Sicily, rather than Milan, were in the front line of imperial defence. It is therefore not surprising that a viceroy of Sicily, Marc Antonio Colonna, gave the clearest formulation of the problems of imperial defence. Nor is it surprising that, again, imperial arguments were put forward by an Italian rather than a Spaniard. Members of old and famous Italian families like the Colonna, Doria and Pescara could not accept for themselves any inferior status to the Spanish grandees in the service of the king of Spain. It followed that they had to regard Milan, Naples and Sicily as states ranking equally with the Spanish kingdoms in an international, rather than a Spanish, empire. Characteristically, Colonna's remarks centred on finance. The Sicilians, as he knew from experience, haggled about every ducat to be sent to Spain; yet, in case of a serious Turkish attack, the defence of the island would not depend on some 200,000 ducats more or less. Only the combined resources of all the

[1] See also below, pp. 353-4.

king's dominions could provide safety for each one; for they were all members of one body and must help each other. 'I have never seen Your Majesty's affairs in danger, or lost, for lack of money, men and munitions,' Colonna wrote to Philip in 1582, 'but because there was abundance in one part and want in another', and because the vanity of ministers prevented them from giving full support to their colleagues.

When García de Toledo's galleys set sail from Messina for the relief of Malta, or when Don John's victorious ships returned from Lepanto, it was easy for the Sicilians to see the advantages of the Spanish connection and their parliament contributed willingly to imperial defence. But when the Sicilian galleys were called from the defence of the island's shores against corsair raids to take part in Alva's expedition against Lisbon, the advantages of empire seemed to be all on the side of Spain. Up to about 1580 Sicily's imperial connection served as a stimulus for the reform of her administration and the extension of royal power and justice at the expense of turbulent barons and Mafia-like bandits. After that date, the strain became too great. In 1588, for instance, Sicily supplied more than half a million scudi in cash and provisions for the Armada. The good effects of administrative reform were nullified by the growing practice of selling offices. Philip II managed to keep the sale of the rights of jurisdiction to the nobles within bounds. His son had fewer compunctions. In 1621 the nobles finally obtained, as of right, the ability to buy jurisdictional powers over their fiefs. The instructions to the viceroys to protect the weak from the strong had become an empty formula.

The Sicilian parliament retained its privileges and powers because the crown was never required to attack them. It granted the king as much money as could reasonably be expected from a small country whose only economic assets were its production of grain and raw silk. At the same time, Sicily was preserved by her parliament from the degree of financial exploitation from which Naples and Milan suffered. Spanish rule did not cause the economic ruin of Sicily, as many Italian historians have supposed. It was rather that the crown's tacit support of the privileges of the predatory nobility and propertied classes rendered impossible the solution of the island's social problems. Sicily remained a country with great constitutional liberties but with an anarchical administration. Not surprisingly, the viceroyalty came to be regarded as the graveyard of the reputation of its holders. In Madrid they were judged mainly by the success or failure of their financial policy. They fought a losing battle against the privileges of the nobility and the lawlessness of the countryside. Their opponents could become familiars of the Inquisition and thus escape from the jurisdiction of the secular courts. The jurisdictional quarrels between the viceroys and the Inquisition sometimes came near to paralysing the whole administration. Both sides would appeal to Madrid and both sides would find friends at court. Sooner or later, Philip would listen to the whispers against the viceroy's loyalty and recall him.[1]

In contrast to Sicily, Naples presented far fewer problems to the Spaniards.[2] There was no effective counterbalance to the authority of the viceroys. The nobility remained divided: for, while the feuds between the Aragonese and Angevin factions had lost something of their former virulence, the Spaniards had encouraged the settlement of large numbers of Genoese in the kingdom, some two hundred of whom were nobles. Their position and their property depended on royal favour. The government, moreover, secretly fomented distrust between the noble and the popular *seggi* of the city of Naples. Government officials, from the viceroy downwards, were notorious for their greed and corruption. The count of Miranda was reputed to have amassed a million ducats during his viceroyalty. The figure is, no doubt, exaggerated; but the count of Olivares used to say that one ought not to wish to be viceroy of Naples to avoid the pain of leaving the office.

In the virtual absence of constitutional safeguards against the financial demands of the government, taxes and government revenues rose rapidly, probably more rapidly than prices, to the high figure of 2,000,000 ducats in the 1570s and to almost four million by 1611. Most of these sums were spent on defence and on the Mediterranean fleet. But, as in the case of Sicily, after about 1580 increasingly large sums were spent in support of Spain's commitments in western Europe. The viceroys themselves had to reject royal demands for money, for no more could be wrung from the tax-payers. Naples, like Sicily, remained a poor, semi-colonial country. Its trade was in the hands of Genoese merchants; its nobles tyrannised their vassals, despite all royal instructions to the viceroys to protect the weak against the strong; and its peasants and small traders were held to ransom by the bandits of the Abbruzzi. Yet the Spaniards, unpopular as they were, ruled in Naples because their rule was acceptable. The Venetian, Alvise Lando, marvelled that 'there has never been a kingdom, like this kingdom of Naples, which has fallen so often without having fallen and which, in perpetual bondage...should with the greatness of its foes have always boasted liberty and dominion'.

The attitude of the Milanese was very similar. Lombardy had been the battle-ground of the great powers for sixty years. Against the background of burnt harvests and sacked cities, the Milanese were no longer willing to fight for the doubtful benefits of political independence. The Spaniards were unpopular. They continued to treat Milan as a military outpost of Spain[3] and, now that there was peace, the exactions of the Spanish *tercios* were bitterly resented. But the towns retained both a great deal of their former autonomy and also some representation in the organs of central

---

[1] H. G. Koenigsberger, *The Government of Sicily under Philip II of Spain* (London, 1951).
[2] See vol. II, p. 327.　　　　　　　　　　[3] See vol. II, p. 329.

government. The last vestiges of medieval democracy had disappeared from the town governments, and their leading families who now monopolised all local power looked to the king of Spain to maintain them in their position. Only once was there a serious threat to Spanish power. In 1563 Philip decided to introduce the Spanish Inquisition into Milan. The Milanese reacted as violently as the Neapolitans had done to a similar attempt in 1547.[1] Was not Milan one of the oldest Christian cities and never tainted by even the suspicion of heresy? they asked. There were riots. The archbishop, the Council of Trent, the pope himself supported the citizens. They feared for their own rights of ecclesiastical jurisdiction. And, as his father had done in Naples, Philip had to give way.

We have no detailed study of Milanese finances for this period. It does not seem as if the tax burden increased beyond what it had been in the later years of the emperor's reign. Milan was the fulcrum of Spanish power in Europe. From this position, the king dominated his Italian allies and maintained his contacts with the Austrian Habsburgs. From Milan he could throw his troops south against a Turkish threat or march north and west to intervene in the Netherlands or France. It would never do to antagonise the Milanese beyond endurance. Most of the revenues from the duchy, and large sums sent from Spain, had to be used for the regiments stationed in Lombardy. In spite of his theoretical power to impose taxes at will, the governor had to haggle with the individual towns over every extraordinary grant. The financial position of the government of Milan thus went from bad to worse, but the province itself was recovering from the disasters of the first half of the century. The population of its cities rose rapidly and with it their economic activity. Milan, with its 100,000 inhabitants, was one of the largest manufacturing centres of Europe, famous especially for its metal work and armament manufactures. Some smaller cities, like Pavia or the textile centre of Como, expanded even more rapidly. Alone among Spain's Italian dominions, Lombardy was able to take advantage of the rising prices and expanding markets of Europe. Later, during the plague and war years of the seventeenth century, the Milanese came to look back on the reign of Philip II as almost a golden age.

While for the Milanese, Neapolitans and Sicilians Spanish rule was never more than tolerable, a genuine feeling for Italian independence existed only in the still independent Italian states. Even there, it was usually little more than a literary sentiment. In the Italian comedies, as Boccalini remarked, the Spaniard had replaced the Neapolitan as the stock character representing absolute vanity. The Italian states were too jealous of each other to co-operate against Spain; but even their combined forces were puny compared with the overwhelming military power of the Catholic king. Renewed French intervention, hoped for by some and

[1] See vol. II, pp. 328 ff.

feared by others, was always talked about but was not a practical possibility until the end of the French Wars of Religion.

More than any other state, Genoa had staked her fortunes on those of the Spanish monarchy. Her bankers invested their money in Spanish loans and displaced the Germans as the principal creditors of the Spanish crown and farmers of Spanish revenues. Her merchants and nobles settled in Spain, Naples and Sicily, intermarried with the local nobility and cornered much of the trade between Spain and her dominions. Spinola commanded Philip III's armies in the Netherlands. The Doria family commanded the Spanish Mediterranean fleet while, at home, they maintained with an iron hand the rule of the Spanish faction of the Genoese nobility. As long as Peru sent silver to Seville, the Genoese plutocracy flourished. In the splendid painted palaces which Galeazzo Alessi built for them and in their portraits which Van Dyck painted in the 1620s, one can still catch something of the flavour of this elegant, civilised and ruthless society.

In contrast to Spain's smooth relations with Genoa, those with the papacy were much more stormy. 'There is no pope in Spain', said Figueroa, president of the Royal Council, and in this *bon mot* he epitomised the major cause of friction. Figueroa's claim, however, was true only up to a point. The king of Spain had the right of appointment to all ecclesiastical benefices, estimated by contemporaries at an aggregate value of over six million ducats. In consequence, the Spanish clergy looked to Madrid, rather than to Rome, for advancement. The enormous ecclesiastical patronage of the Spanish crown was one of its most powerful means of assuring itself the loyalty of the high nobility, the hidalgos and the educated middle classes of the towns. Since the days of Ferdinand and Isabella, Spanish kings had pursued a deliberate policy of restricting papal influence on the Spanish church. They claimed the right to prevent the publication in Spain of certain types of papal bulls and briefs. They tried to prevent appeals from Spanish ecclesiastical courts to Rome. The popes of the first half of the sixteenth century had been relatively complaisant in these matters. The popes of the Counter-Reformation, however, attempted to regain lost ground.

The first open clash arose out of the Spanish Inquisition's action against Archbishop Bartolomé de Carranza of Toledo.[1] The case was a kind of ecclesiastical counterpart to that of Pérez. Carranza had made a name for himself by his reconciling and burning of heretics in England during the reign of Philip and Mary, and by his pious zeal in luring suspected heretics from the relative safety of Antwerp into territory where they could be seized by the Inquisition. But, after he had risen to the primateship of Spain, jealous emulators accused him before the Supreme Council of the Holy Inquisition and he himself became a victim of the system of which

[1] See also above, p. 62.

he had been such an ardent and successful protagonist (1559). There were doubts in Spain itself about the justice of the accusations. The Council of Trent eventually declared his opinions to be orthodox. The case, however, hinged hardly at all on Carranza's opinions, but on the papal claim that a bishop could only be judged in Rome and the Spanish Inquisition's claim to complete autonomy in all cases involving heresy. The crown supported the Inquisition, for, as Cardinal Alessandrino wrote to Rome: 'The most ardent defenders of justice here hold that it is better to condemn an innocent man than to let the Inquisition suffer any diminution of its powers.' The case dragged on for seven years. Then Carranza was transferred to Rome. It was a substantial victory for the papacy, even though it was several more years before the pope dared to pronounce his sentence of virtual acquittal.[1]

In Italy the quarrels over ecclesiastical jurisdiction were even more acrimonious. In Naples and Sicily the king's hold over the church was even firmer than in Spain itself. By his right of *exequatur* he could deny the publication of all papal bulls, just as the kings of France could by their *droit de vérification*. In Sicily the king, moreover, exercised the *Monarchia*, the rights and powers of a permanent apostolic legate. The claim was based on an alleged grant by Urban II to Count Roger of Sicily. The papacy, not unnaturally, disputed a claim which gave the king effectively as much power over the Sicilian church as the English kings enjoyed over the English church. The dispute was not resolved and remained alive until Pius IX formally revoked the *Monarchia* in 1867. It was typical of Spanish institutions that the court of the *Monarchia* developed a will of its own and came into conflict, not only with the Inquisition (like itself, claiming to be an ecclesiastical court recognising no superior), but also with the royal power as represented by the viceroys.

It was in Milan that the most dramatic conflicts between church and state arose. Here they were the direct result of the counter-offensive of the reformed Roman church after the Council of Trent. Its leading spirit was the young nephew of Pius IV, Carlo Borromeo, who arrived in Milan in 1566 to take up his duties as archbishop. In the words of Philip's confessor, he wanted 'with excessive severity to impose on the masses that which was the end of the most sublime perfection'. Like the Spanish Inquisition, Borromeo built up an impressive court and organised the city and the duchy into districts under his own officials. His armed guards clapped offenders against his spiritual decrees into the archiepiscopal prison. But when he proceeded to extend his authority from the supervision of the morals of the clergy to those of the laity, he began to fall foul of the civil courts. When he proclaimed the Tridentine decrees and the bull *In coena domini* (which forbade princes to levy further taxes on their subjects) despite the prohibition of the governor, the duke of Alburquerque, he

[1] See above, p. 62.

challenged the royal power itself. Alburquerque arrested the archbishop's agents and sent troops to occupy the Borromeo estates. Borromeo answered with curse and interdict. He won great tactical victories. Alburquerque had to beg the pope for absolution. One of his successors, Don Luis de Requesens, obtained his absolution only because he left Milan to become governor-general of the Netherlands. Borromeo's influence over the populace of Milan was enormous. His charity and fearlessness during the plague won the admiration of friends and opponents alike. But he was too much an aristocrat and authoritarian to wish to become the leader of a popular movement against established authority. Neither Rome nor Madrid could afford to push the quarrel to extremes. Philip depended on the pope for the grant of the *cruzada* and other ecclesiastical taxes in Spain. It was the price the Spanish crown paid for not having to argue about taxes with a clergy organised as an estate of the realm, as other European governments had to do. These clerical taxes could be as much as two million ducats a year. For such sums, Philip could afford to overlook the insults to his representatives in Milan.

Towards the end of Philip's reign, the quarrel broke out again. Federico Borromeo, cousin and successor of Carlo, attempting to imitate his great predecessor in the see of Milan, was ready to excommunicate the governor-general. But Juan de Velasco was no Alburquerque; he refused to be brow-beaten. Nor was Clement VIII a Pius V. The archbishop received no backing from Rome. But the disputes continued and even a compromise, in 1615, did not finally settle them. Fundamentally, however, relations between the papacy and the Spanish monarchy depended less on jurisdictional claims than on the policy of both towards their common enemies, the Turks and the Protestants.

Both the dukes of Florence and of Piedmont-Savoy owed their thrones to Spanish arms and diplomacy. Emmanuel Philibert of Savoy, indeed, argued that he had conquered his states in the battle of St Quentin, where he had led Philip's armies to victory and forced the French to conclude the Treaty of Cateau-Cambrésis. Yet, in spite of this argument and of a French marriage, he never forgot his dependence on Spain. Savoy and Piedmont, freed from French and Spanish occupation, welcomed their duke with enthusiasm. Parliament granted him a huge tax and with the money Emmanuel Philibert could pay his troops. From then on, he no longer had any use for his parliament. The old ruling classes of the towns had been shattered by twenty-five years of foreign military occupation. The nobles were locked in private feuds, their estates were mortgaged, and many were receiving bribes from France or Spain, or from both at the same time. Morally and materially, they were incapable of defending their old political privileges. Emmanuel Philibert, with his own disheartening experience as governor-general of the Netherlands in mind, established one of the most rigid systems of absolutist government in

Europe. The administration of his country was carried on by middle-class functionaries who were completely dependent on the duke. The nobles were compensated for their loss of political power by titles and court positions and by the duke's renunciation of any effective interference in their estates, where serfdom often continued until the eighteenth century.

With the country thus firmly in his control, Emmanuel Philibert was able to increase taxation in a way no governor of Milan would have dared. Government revenues were pushed up from about 90,000 ducats to half a million. All the duke's careful attention to the growth of industrial production in Piedmont could not make up for the stifling rate of taxation and the exactions of his standing army. Throughout his reign the Venetian ambassadors speak of deserted farm lands and almost universal poverty and apathy.

Emmanuel Philibert—he was nicknamed Iron Head—at least kept his country out of war and yet managed to make the French evacuate the towns they still garrisoned. His son, Charles Emmanuel I (1580–1630), added to internal despotism a romantic foreign policy. He dreamt of the crown of Portugal or of Bohemia, of Sicily or of Sardinia, even of the imperial crown. For the absurd hope of the French succession, after the death of Henry III, or of a kingdom in Provence, he gave up the possibility of conquering Geneva, his one aim which had both some historical justification and some chance of success.[1] Charles Emmanuel has become famous as a practical exponent of reason of state who anticipated the role of the House of Savoy during the *risorgimento* in the nineteenth century. His contemporaries failed to see him in such a transcendental light. They only saw that he ruined his country economically and that, if Piedmont-Savoy survived as an independent state, it was due to luck and the interests of the great powers (just as was the survival of Geneva) and not to the policies of its dukes.

In 1530, the Medici, with the help of imperial arms, had overthrown the last Florentine republic. The Florentine aristocracy had suffered badly under the republic. Economically unable to stand on their own feet, and morally unwilling to co-operate with the republicans and *popolani*, they had now no choice but to lean on Medici support. First Alessandro and then Cosimo de Medici brilliantly exploited this situation. They transformed the 'principate' into a dukedom, a police state no less despotic than that of the dukes of Savoy, but more efficiently run. The aristocracy was transformed from an urban patriciate into a service and court nobility. Most of them withdrew their capital from industry and trade, engaging only in banking or, much more frequently, developing their estates outside the city. Their social status remained unimpaired (though Cosimo enforced strict justice for all his subjects and abolished also the special

[1] See below, p. 305.

privileges of the city of Florence) but, as a social group, they lost all political power. The institutions of the republic survived in form only, for the duke bypassed them by relying on his own functionaries. Significantly, the brilliant Florentine historians, from Macchiavelli to Guicciardini and Varchi, found no successors after the deaths of those whose views had been formed under the republic. There was nothing more to write about but tedious court intrigues or the deeds of dukes who played but a very small part in the politics of the great European powers. The creative genius of the Florentines, so closely linked with the life of the city state, wilted in the stifling atmosphere of the rigid court society of the dukes, even though the Medici did not give up their traditional patronage of the arts. But there occurred a shift in creative activity, from literature and the visual arts to natural science and music, activities which in Italy were not traditionally bound up with the artist's life in a city state. In these, Florence became as famous as she had once been in painting and sculpture.[1]

The Medici dukes, true to their origins, were excellent financiers. Almost alone among contemporary princes they were always solvent. The financial resources of Cosimo I enabled him to conquer the republic of Siena (1557) and to maintain a sufficient degree of independence from Spain to be treated as an ally, rather than a satellite. More than this was out of the question. The Spaniards held the *presidios*, five fortresses on the coast of Tuscany, from 1530, and kept a military stranglehold on the duchy. In 1570, Cosimo I obtained from the pope the title of grand duke of Tuscany. The need to have this title recognised by the emperor and Philip II made Francis I (1574–87) even more dependent on Spain. Ferdinand I (1587–1609) was able to act more independently and, like Charles Emmanuel, he tried to fish in the troubled waters of Provence during the wars of the League. In the end he was lucky to withdraw without serious loss.

The price which Tuscany paid for the financial solvency of its rulers was, however, a heavy one. Taxation was crushing and nearly all industries were closely controlled by the state. The grain trade, the oil trade, ship-building and shipping were government monopolies. Under Francis I they were exploited almost exclusively for the benefit of the grand duke's private purse. Under Ferdinand I the duchy recovered, to some extent, from a slump in the 1580s and from the misrule of his predecessor. Leghorn, virtually a free port, became the great entrepôt for the trade of northern and western Europe with the Mediterranean. But most of the great ships calling at Leghorn flew Dutch or English flags. The great days of Italian seafaring were over.

The only truly independent state in Italy was Venice. As Nicolò Contarini and other Venetian statesmen saw it, her continued independence was, in the long run, impossible without an independent Italy. The

[1] Cf. H. G. Koenigsberger, 'Decadence or Shift?', *Transactions of the Royal Historical Society*, 5th ser., x (1960).

republic was therefore bound to be hostile to Spain, a fact which was appreciated as much in Madrid as on the Rialto. But there could be no question of an open breach. In the event of a Turkish attack, Venice needed papal and Spanish help. By the middle of the sixteenth century, Venice had at least partially recovered from the shock of losing the monopoly of the spice trade. Venetian merchants in Alexandria and Aleppo could still buy spices from Arab caravans and supply a large part of an expanding European market.[1] They could also supply at least some of the cloth which the Arab and Levantine merchants wanted for their spices. For the first time in their history, the Venetians built up a major cloth manufacturing industry. Nevertheless, the brightly coloured and cheaper English kerseys and French and Dutch says sold more readily in the eastern markets than the dull and expensive fabrics of traditional Italian manufacture. These products gave the western competitors of Venice an enormous advantage in the Levant trade. Moreover, this trade was precarious. The Cyprus war (1570–3)[2] and the activities of Moslem and Christian pirates interrupted commerce and caused the loss of valuable markets. The Turko-Persian war, following the Lepanto campaign, relieved Ottoman naval pressure in the Mediterranean and thus benefited Spain; but it interrupted the caravan trade with the east on which the supply of spices for Venice depended. In consequence, the Venetian patricians tended more and more to withdraw capital from trade and invest it in their estates on the Venetian mainland. Like the English country gentlemen of the eighteenth century, who rightly felt a close affinity to the Venetian patricians, they improved their estates and built their beautiful palladian villas and, when commercial prospects seemed good, reinvested in trade or industry. Venetian glass, ceramics, metal work, silk and, not least, books were the finest in Europe. When Michaelangelo had painted his last fresco and drawn his last plan for the dome of St Peter's, there remained in the rest of Italy no painter of the stature of Titian, Tintoretto and Veronese, nor any architect to rival Palladio. Unlike Florence, Venice could play her part in the new development of music without suffering a decline in the visual arts. Music had her very own home in Venice, wrote Francesco Sansovino in 1581. It could not truthfully have been said fifty years earlier. There is no clearer proof than this of the continued creative vitality of the Italian city state. But the character of Venetian economic life was changing. In the early 1600s, the decline of Venetian trade was generally recognised. In 1610 a proposal was put before the senate to give foreign merchants extensive trading rights in the Venetian possessions and to allow them to acquire Venetian citizenship. But vested interest, conservatism and the fear of opening the door to religious heresy defeated this proposal and with it, perhaps, the last chance of restoring the former commercial greatness of Venice.

[1] See also below, p. 366.   [2] See also below, pp. 352–4.

Compared with the old Florentine republic, or with contemporary western Europe, Venetian politics remained in a minor key. The economic changes of the period did not disturb the social equilibrium. Given this fact, together with the superior military and naval power of Spain and the Porte, the Venetian ruling classes had little room for manœuvre, either in internal or in external politics. The differences which divided the 'old' and the 'new' families, and the 'young' and 'old' patricians, were questions of attitude and tactics, of the length to which one could go in defying Spain or the pope, but not fundamental questions of government or religion. The Cyprus war discredited the ruling groups of the older patricians and the 'new' families who had monopolised the office of doge for more than a hundred years. A loosely organised group of younger men, mainly from the 'old' families, managed to reduce the power of the Council of Ten and its permanent executive committee, the Zonta, in 1582–3. The leaders of this group, Leonardo Donato and Nicolò Contarini, spiritual descendants of the earlier Venetian religious reformers, Sadoleto and Gasparo Contarini, now began to steer the republic on a more anti-Spanish, anti-papal and pro-French course. They forced the rejection in 1585 of an attractive Spanish offer to Venice to take over the Portuguese spice trade. They feared, with justice, that the republic would become as much a satellite of Spain as Genoa had become. They recognised the succession of Henry IV and did much to persuade Sixtus V to alter his policy towards France.[1] In 1605 they took up the challenge of the papal attack on the republic's control over its clergy. It was a quarrel over jurisdiction, like the many quarrels between Spain and the papacy. Unlike these latter, it led to a complete breach and a papal interdict over the republic (1606). The newly elected pope, Paul V (Borghese), thought he could, once for all, establish the maximum claims of the Holy See in the smaller Italian states. Spain did her best to goad him on, out of her traditional hostility towards Venice. The republic replied by electing Donato as its doge. The Jesuits, as the pope's most dangerous agents, were banished. Fra Paolo Sarpi, the friend of Donato and Contarini, brilliantly attacked the doctrinal justification of the papal action. It was the most serious crisis of Catholicism in Italy. But when Spain threatened war and Henry IV would give only diplomatic support, Venice accepted French mediation and a compromise on the immediate points at issue. In effect, however, Venice had won. The republic maintained the full independence of her secular government from clerical interference. In the following decade, Venice was to face one more attack by Spain, this time on the very existence of her political independence. This too the republic overcame. For the Italians of the early seventeenth century, it was the Republic of St Mark, and not the princely houses of Savoy and Medici, which stood as the champion of what remained of Italian liberty.

---

[1] See below, pp. 303–4.

263

2. *The problems of the Netherlands and France to 1585*

When in 1520 Charles V left Spain after his first visit to his new kingdom, the towns of Castile rebelled against the Flemish domination of their country.[1] In 1559 the roles were reversed. It was the Netherlands which had suffered a foreign succession and were alarmed by Spanish domination. Yet such a foreign domination did not exist, any more than it did in Spain in 1520.

Philip II's residence in the Netherlands, from his father's abdication until 1559, was not a success. He appeared as foreign to the Netherlanders as his father had at first appeared to the Spaniards. His government's demands for money for the French wars led to prolonged and exasperating wrangles with the States General, the joint sessions of the provincial estates. The nobles and patricians in the assemblies of the estates blocked every attempt by the government to introduce new and fairer types of taxes which would no longer fall most heavily on the poorer people. In 1557/8 the States General made a grant of 800,000 florins *per annum* for nine years, but only on condition that their own commissioners should control the collection and expenditure of the money. Some of the provincial estates, notably Brabant, Flanders and Holland, had done this before and had built up their own financial machinery. Now it was to be extended to all the thirteen provinces normally represented in the States General. The purpose was primarily the practical one of preventing money earmarked for the payment of troops from being used to pay the government's debts. Flanders and, later, Holland were opposed to the new system because they feared the predominance of Brabant in its administration. Nor did the new financial organisation, headed by the Antwerp banker Anthony van Straelen, work particularly efficiently or honestly. The government was bound to regard it as a serious infringement of its rights and a dangerous advance in the power of the estates.

Just before Philip's departure for Spain, the States General demanded the withdrawal of the *tercio* of three thousand Spanish troops. The king had wanted to maintain them in the Netherlands, both as an effective defence force against France and as a reliable weapon against possible opposition in the country itself. All the opposition to Habsburg imperial policy, to the wars, the heavy taxation, the extension of government power at the expense of old privileges,[2] was concentrated on this one issue. Philip had to give way, but he did so grudgingly and late. From then on, he determined that the States General could not be trusted.

The only sign of direct Spanish domination had now been removed. The government which the king provided on his departure was an almost purely Netherlands government in the Burgundian tradition. He appointed his half-sister, Margaret, wife of Ottavio Farnese, duke of Parma, as the

[1] See vol. II, pp. 304 ff., 318 ff. [2] See vol. II, p. 318.

new governor-general. Margaret, an illegitimate daughter of Charles V, was herself born in the Netherlands and her appointment seemed to continue the tradition created by the emperor with the appointment of his aunt, Margaret of Austria, and his sister, Mary of Hungary. The high nobility, members of the Order of the Golden Fleece, occupied the provincial governorships. Several of them, including the popular wartime hero the count of Egmont, the prince of Orange, and their friend, the count of Hoorn, became members of the Council of State. The high nobility had long since outgrown their purely provincial interests; they saw the best chance of advancement in the greatness of their prince. For more than half a century, the Habsburgs had relied on them to further their policy of centralising the government of the seventeen provinces. Philip thought he could count on their continued loyalty. At the same time, he did not fully trust them. In his secret instructions to Margaret of Parma, he commanded her to take all important decisions with the advice only of Granvelle, of the secretary of the Privy Council, Viglius, and of the ultra-loyal Walloon, the count of Berlaymont. Ultimate authority resided, of course, in Madrid, and the king, as everyone knew, disliked taking decisions.

From the very beginning, Margaret's government was faced with a religious and a financial crisis. Heresy was spreading rapidly. There was nothing new in this. The established church in the Netherlands had long been notorious for its worldliness and for its inadequacy in ministering to the religious needs of the population. Erasmus and his friends had sought to reform the church from the inside and to instil into it the spirit of piety, enlightenment and peace. They had great influence on the educated classes and their spirit persisted even when, from the 1520s, more radical reformers began to appear. It was against these, the Lutherans, the Anabaptists and, later, the Mennonites, that the government of Charles V directed ever more rigorous *placards*. Hundreds paid for their faith at the stake; yet persecution remained sporadic and only very partially effective. Except for the Lutherans, the new sects had not usually touched the ruling classes of patricians and nobles. Yet many of these, and especially those influenced by Erasmian ideas, felt a growing revulsion against the practice of burning their fellow citizens for their religious beliefs. The *placards* were never executed systematically and the episcopal Inquisition remained highly unpopular.

But from about 1560 the situation changed. For the first time, Calvinist preachers began to appear in considerable numbers. Soon they could assure Calvin that the sale of his writings was increasing rapidly. The peace with France brought contact with the French Protestants. Calvin himself wrote: 'I, too, am a Belgian.' From Geneva, from Germany and from England the propagation of his teaching in the Netherlands was organised almost as vigorously as in France. For the first time, too, the preachers began to make a large number of converts from among the patrician and noble classes. Socially, Calvinism was 'respectable' in a way the Baptist sects could never be. As Catholic observers rightly saw, the preachers were particularly successful where there was unemployment and economic discontent among workers and artisans; but they mistook the nature of Calvinism when they argued that religion was only a pretence to cloak economic ambitions. It was precisely its religious appeal which enabled Calvinism to become a movement including all classes and then to draw to itself ambitious nobles or hungry weavers. It was this characteristic which made the Calvinist movement much more formidable and dangerous to the established order than the earlier heresies.

The development of Calvinist organisation was much slower than in France.[1] The dangers to the preachers and to the members of Protestant conventicles were real; nevertheless, they were coming more and more into the open. The mood of the country was such that the government dared not pursue a consistent policy of rigorous suppression of heresy. It seems that the Calvinists organised a definite propaganda campaign to make people believe that the king wanted to introduce the Spanish Inquisition. Philip had no such intention. He knew it would be far too dangerous. Besides, as he wrote to Margaret in 1562, the Netherlands Inquisition was less merciful than the Spanish, for it condemned to death even those heretics who were penitent. He never understood the peculiar terror and abhorrence which the Spanish Inquisition and its procedure inspired in the whole of Europe. But even before the Calvinist danger had become acute, he had determined to strengthen ecclesiastical authority and the fight against heresy by a complete reorganisation of the Netherlands church. In 1561 the pope published the bulls for the erection of fourteen new bishoprics. The right of election was taken away from the cathedral chapters and vested in the crown. Some of the oldest and richest monasteries, especially in Brabant, were to provide the newly appointed bishops with their episcopal revenues.

There was much to be said for the plan. It made the church of the Netherlands independent of the archiepiscopal sees of Cologne and Rheims, both outside the king's jurisdiction, and it gave a better organisation to a church which was notoriously weak and badly staffed. But the plan proved to be exceedingly unpopular. The abbots of the monasteries clamoured loudly against their loss of independence and income. The nobles saw rich prizes of patronage and careers for their younger sons slipping from their grasp and handed over to the hated lawyers and theologians. They joined the Calvinists in representing the scheme to the people as a first step towards the introduction of the Spanish Inquisition. Since the latter part of the emperor's reign, the high nobility had seen the control of the empire monopolised by Spaniards and Italians. All the more fiercely they now

[1] See below, pp. 281–3; also above, pp. 100–2.

strove to assert their power in their own country. But Philip had allowed them only the shadow of power. Now the new primate of the Netherlands church, the archbishop of Malines, would have the first voice in the assembly of the estates of Brabant, and this new archbishop was Cardinal Granvelle.

For William of Nassau, sovereign prince of the small state of Orange on the lower Rhone, and the richest of the Netherlands magnates, this was not just a matter of personalities. His family had served the Habsburgs for generations and he himself had been a great favourite with the emperor. His politics had been no different from those of other great lords in the Netherlands. Together with Egmont and Hoorn, he had for years quarrelled with the estates of Holland over tax exemption of their properties in that province. As governor of Holland and Zeeland he had always supported the authority of the central government against the estates. Later, he was to claim that his opposition to Philip II began when, during the negotiations for the Peace of Cateau-Cambrésis, Henry II spoke to him of a plan of the two kings to join forces in putting down heresy in their dominions. But it seems probable that only gradually he came to see the full danger of Philip's policies for the Netherlands. The champion of narrow class interests developed into the defender of the liberties of all the king's subjects. William's religious convictions have been a matter of dispute. But there is no question that, like most of the educated nobility of the Netherlands, he detested all forms of religious persecution. More clearly, and earlier, than his noble friends he saw the implications of Philip's plan to reform the bishoprics: an enormous increase in the power of the crown. With complete control over the Netherlands church, the king would be able not only to make religious persecution much more effective, but also to dispense more and more with the co-operation of the nobility and the estates. As yet, Orange was not prepared to co-operate with the Calvinists. Their intolerance repelled him. His upbringing and his marriage to Anna of Saxony, daughter of the famous Elector Maurice,[1] made him rather seek the support of the Lutheran princes of Germany. His opposition to royal absolutism was still largely that of the great lord whom his king would allow only the shadow and not the substance of power. It was Granvelle who seemed to personify the royal absolutism. From 1561 Orange, Egmont and their friends tried to overthrow the cardinal.

For the government, this opposition was the more serious as the financial crisis left Margaret and Granvelle little room for manœuvre. The servicing of the enormous government debt, the legacy of the French wars, swallowed up ordinary revenue and the 800,000 florins a year of the nine-year grant by the States General. Troops and officials remained unpaid, and government authority in the country deteriorated dangerously. Margaret had to

[1] See vol. II, pp. 185, 332, 357.

appeal to the estates for financial help and every appeal became a constitutional crisis, giving the estates and the high nobility a chance to attack Granvelle and the government's religious policy. Philip reacted, true to his character, by trying to stir up faction strife and by intriguing with one part of the high nobility against the other, even though Granvelle himself warned against the dangers of such a course of action. Not all the seigneurs had joined Orange's league against the cardinal. The duke of Aerschot, with the whole widespread family connection of his old Walloon house of Croy, and several others of the Walloon nobility resented the political leadership of Orange and Egmont and remained loyal to the government. As in France, the parties tended to crystallise around the personal rivalries of the great noble houses.[1]

In 1564 the prince of Orange's league of the great lords, helped by a personal intrigue of Margaret of Parma against Granvelle, achieved their first political objective, the recall of the cardinal and his retirement to his estates in Franche-Comté. Granvelle never returned, though later he was still to serve his master faithfully in Italy and Spain; but for the nobles it was a hollow victory. The cardinal's party in the government accused the lords of incompetence and corruption, probably with some justice. Though Orange and his friends were now the government's spokesmen in the assemblies of the provincial estates, the deputies remained as intransigent to the lords' financial demands as they had been to the cardinal's. They insisted on a more liberal religious policy and on the summoning of the States General to deal with all the country's problems. The lords supported these demands. All sides sent complaints to Madrid and thus increased Philip's distrust of the Netherlanders. As early as 1563 the duke of Alva had recommended cutting off the heads of half a dozen great lords. But as yet there was no alternative to government by consent. Philip had no means of carrying out Alva's suggestion, even if he had so desired. In the event, he tried honestly, though with his usual exasperating hesitations, to work with the nobles and meet at least some of their demands—all of them, so Egmont thought when he visited Madrid in 1565. Orange saw the situation more clearly. Philip would not really abdicate his control over the government to the nobility; nor would he make concessions on the religious question. In two letters to Margaret in October 1565, Philip put an end to all hopes of any Netherlands equivalent to an Edict of Amboise.[2] The edicts against the heretics must be enforced, the king wrote, and the Netherlands Inquisition must continue to function. Margaret was not to summon the States General until the religious situation had improved. Finally, since the lords had wished for an increase in the membership of the Council of State, he now appointed the duke of Aerschot, Orange's most powerful opponent among the Netherlands nobility. It took Margaret a whole week to summon up enough courage

[1] See below, pp. 283–4.   [2] See below, p. 286.

to publish the king's orders. She was right in her apprehensions. Philip's letters were the signal for revolution.

The weakness of the Netherlands government, especially after the departure of Granvelle, had given the Calvinist preachers their chance to exploit the growing social tensions of Netherlands society.[1] The lower nobility began to join the reform movement in large numbers and rapidly gave the religious conventicles the military character which had already made the Huguenots such a formidable power in France.[2] Open mass meetings were held, with the women in the centre and the men, armed with every conceivable weapon and commanded by a noble member of the congregation, standing guard. The court at Brussels, undoubtedly with events in France before their eyes, began to fear open rebellion or, at least, the seizure of some important towns by the Protestants. In November 1565 the members of the lower nobility formed a league, the Compromise, with the object of inducing the government to abolish the Inquisition and to moderate the edicts against the heretics. The leaders were men of almost the same social standing as the great lords of the Golden Fleece: Brederode, wild and hard-drinking, with Calvinist sympathies, and Louis of Nassau, brother of the prince of Orange, leaning rather towards the Lutherans. The Compromise, as its name indicated, was intended to, and did, include Catholics who disliked the government's religious policy. From the beginning, there was talk of using force, if the government should not agree to their demands. The two hundred noblemen, who rode into Brussels on 3 April 1566 to present their petition with its four hundred signatures, did not, however, do much more than toast their new nickname of *gueux*, beggars, at numerous brave banquets. The majority of the lower nobility still stood aside, especially in the southern provinces.

The real revolution was started by the lower classes in the towns. Artisans' wages had caught up with rising prices; but those of unskilled workers had not. The textile and the shipping industries, depending on foreign supplies and on export markets, were subject to violent booms and depressions. The Seven Years War between Denmark and Sweden (1563–70) and the temporary closing of the Sound to shipping had brought on one of these depressions. Anglo-Netherlands quarrels over mutual restrictions on each other's trade, English piracy in the Channel, and Granvelle's sensitivity to the English merchants' support for the Antwerpers in their resistance to the new bishoprics boiled up to a Netherlands embargo on the import of English cloth and the English removal of their staple from Antwerp to Emden (1564). In Antwerp there was heavy unemployment and a sharp fall in wages. The winter of 1565–6 added famine, which the people blamed on the grain speculators and on the government. During the spring and summer of 1566 prices came down, but people remained afraid. In Antwerp and in the textile towns and villages of Walloon

[1] See vol. II, p. 318. [2] See below, p. 282.

Flanders they flocked in their thousands to the Calvinist preachers and their consoling and exciting sermons. Was it not intolerable that the Lord's elect should be excluded from the churches of their own towns and that these churches should be filled with idolatrous images and with the gold and silver which greedy prelates had wrung from the poor by a monstrous tithe? In July the radical wing of the Compromise agreed to co-operate with the Calvinist burgher communities. In August there was another, unexpected, rise in food prices. On 10 August rioting broke out. In Antwerp, and throughout Flanders and many other parts, crowds invaded the churches and monasteries and smashed pictures, statues and altars. There is some evidence that it was an organised movement, but it is not conclusive. Where the municipal authorities stood firm, as in Amsterdam, they found it easy enough to maintain order and protect the churches. Elsewhere, as in Ghent, it seems that the city fathers preferred the spoiling of the churches to the threatened sacking of their own houses. The country was seething with rumours of vast hordes of armed Protestants marching on the cities and wreaking vengeance on priests and magistrates. The hordes never materialised.

The government in Brussels hesitated for two weeks. Margaret had no troops and it was not immediately clear on whom she could rely to restore order. But the Catholics and moderates in the Compromise had been thoroughly frightened by the outbreaks and now hastened to assure the governor-general of their loyalty. Margaret was able to persuade the leaders of the Compromise to dissolve their association in return for a promise to abolish the Netherlands Inquisition and moderate the edicts against heresy. Philip sent some money, and Margaret was now able to raise troops. In the autumn of 1566 and in the following winter, Brederode's armed bands were dispersed and the Catholic nobles defeated the popular Calvinist movements in Walloon Flanders. The majority of the high nobility, including Egmont, took a new oath of loyalty to the king. Only those most compromised fled abroad. Orange thought it safer to join them. He had tried to pursue a moderate policy by supporting the demands of the opposition but upholding the government's authority by foiling Brederode's attack on Antwerp. His policy had failed, and he was bitterly denounced by Catholics and Calvinists alike.

It was a commonplace of sixteenth-century statecraft that rebellions should be crushed in their infancy. The Scottish and French governments had failed to do this, and the disasters which followed were there for every sensible Catholic statesman to see. In the summer of 1566 Philip II decided to send his best general, the duke of Alva, with a large force of Spanish and Italian troops to the Netherlands to reassert his authority. As always, it took time. Margaret, convinced that she had now broken the opposition, adjured her brother to leave well alone. There were doubts in Madrid about the wisdom of committing such a large part of the king's military resources so far from their base and from the main enemy, the Turk. The Netherlands nobility still had friends at court. But Philip had made up his mind, and the Gómez faction hoped to see Alva sink in the quicksands of Netherlands politics.

Alva arrived in Brussels on 22 August 1567 and effectively took over from Margaret of Parma. To the Iron Duke the problem he was asked to solve appeared threefold. He must punish the leaders of the opposition for *lèse-majesté*; he must make the administration of the towns and provinces completely dependent on the central government; and he must secure a stable and permanent financial basis for his government and his army. The first aim was easily achieved. In September the duke arrested Egmont and Hoorn, all privileges of the Order of the Golden Fleece notwithstanding. The king himself followed suit by arresting Hoorn's brother, Montigny, in Madrid. A newly constituted court, the Council of Troubles, soon to be known as the Council of Blood, tried and condemned altogether some 12,000 of those who had taken part in the movements of the previous year. As usually happens on such occasions, informers flourished. Mutual trust, the social cement of any society, began to break down. Alva's was a deliberate policy of terror and, in the short run, it worked. Not a single town rose to support the prince of Orange when he invaded the Netherlands from Germany in 1568. Alva took the opportunity to have Egmont, Hoorn and several other nobles executed in the market square of Brussels. After that, he was able to deal at his leisure with Orange's ill-paid and undisciplined troops. As a general, the prince was no match for the duke.

Alva's second aim met with immediate opposition. Provincial governors and town councils resented the government's interference in their administration and its disregard of their privileges. Open resistance was out of the question; but the hostility of even the most loyal Catholics was unmistakable. Alva complained more and more bitterly to the king of the 'satraps' Aerschot and Noircarmes, and even of the former yes-men Berlaymont and Viglius. Alva's policy was producing an unexpected result: the birth of a new party, the *politiques*, who were Catholic and royalist but who put the independence of their country first and religion second. Alva was under no illusion about Philip's political practice. Sooner or later the king would listen to his opponents in the Netherlands and to their friends at court who were his enemies, just as he had listened to the duke himself against Margaret of Parma.

It was Alva's financial problem, however, which presented him with his most immediate difficulties. He demanded the payment of a once-for-all tax of a hundredth penny (i.e. 1 per cent) on real property. Secondly, he intended to introduce a 10 per cent import, export and sales tax on all merchandise. This tax of the tenth penny, like the Spanish *alcabala*, was to be permanent and was to make the government independent of the estates. It is a sign of the extent to which sixteenth-century governments rested on consent and the co-operation of the governed that even Alva did not possess the power and the machinery simply to levy these taxes. He had to summon the States General in March 1569, but it was to meet for only one day, simply to approve the new measures.

The plan misfired badly. The estates agreed to the tax on property but refused the tenth penny. Alva threatened dire punishments and those estates which were constituted only of nobles and patricians gave in. The merchants could, after all, pass most of the taxes on to the consumer in the form of higher prices. But in Brabant, where the artisans were represented in the estates, the taxes were rejected. In the big towns of Flanders and the Walloon provinces, the deputies who had voted for the taxes began to fear for their lives, just as had happened in Castile in 1520.[1] Caught between Alva's anger and the people's fury, the estates and town councils entered upon a policy of passive resistance. The governor-general had, in the meantime, himself become convinced that the 10 per cent sales tax would be disastrous to the trade of the country; or he may have been worried by the evident cooling of the king's enthusiasm for this plan to beggar his subjects. Alva therefore progressively modified the tax until it began to look more like the type of taxes which towns and provinces had themselves been imposing. But to the majority of Netherlanders it remained objectionable: it was still a perpetual tax and, above all, it was still appallingly heavy. Everywhere the resistance to the tax was hardening. Aldermen denounced it in the town halls, shopkeepers cursed it in the market squares and priests fulminated against it from the pulpits. In the end, Alva's famous tenth penny, to which many historians have ascribed the economic ruin of the Netherlands, was levied even in its attenuated form only very sporadically in a few small towns, and in most provinces not at all.[2] The estates sent deputations to Madrid and offered Alva annual grants of two million florins on the basis of the traditional forms of parliamentary taxation. Alva agreed to negotiate on this basis, aware that he was losing the king's backing for his own proposals. Immediately, he was engulfed in all the exasperating parleys, bargains and delays which had made the lives of previous governor-generals such a misery. When in 1572 Holland and Zeeland fell to the Sea Beggars and Ghent and Bruges were on the point of rebellion, Alva had to give up the tenth penny altogether and with it all hope of making the Netherlands pay for his military establishment. This burden now fell on Spain and the king's own treasury and this at the very time when Spain was making her greatest efforts against the Turks.

[1] See vol. II, p. 319.
[2] J. Craeybeckx, 'De Staten van Vlaanderen en de gewestelijke Financien in de XVI eeuw', in *Handelingen der Maatschappij voor Geschiedenis en Oudheidkunde te Gent* (1950); also 'Alva's Tiende Penning, een Mythe?', in *Bijdragen en Mededelingen van het Historisch Genootschap te Utrecht*, Dl. 76 (1962).

Orange had organised the military and diplomatic offensive against Alva from his brother's principality of Nassau. He had become convinced that Philip's autocracy could be overthrown only by force. What he wanted to put in its place is far less certain at this point. Perhaps William was not entirely clear about it himself. But he was now committed to a fight *à outrance*: where many on his side were willing to compromise with the king, he was convinced that Spanish power in the Netherlands must be completely destroyed. For the next sixteen years, until his death in 1584, he pursued this aim with complete singleness of purpose. Philip saw himself entrusted by God with the preservation of his subjects in the true Catholic religion. To accomplish this divine purpose he felt in duty bound to use his royal powers, if need be, to the point of the most ruthless political tyranny. William, for his part, saw himself as the defender of his own aristocratic rights and liberties, of the rights and liberties of his order and, ultimately, of those of his country and of the individual conscience against political absolutism and religious persecution. There was no bridge between these two concepts. The court of Madrid misunderstood William's motives, attributing them to mere ambition; but it was right in seeing him as the driving force behind the revolt, without whose determination and political ability it might never have survived.

Louis of Nassau was in touch with Coligny and Walsingham, then English ambassador in Paris. There seemed to be no hope of success without French or English help. Louis, at least, did not hesitate to bribe potential allies with the promise of some of the seventeen provinces. The nobles who had fled from the Netherlands organised a naval force, the Sea Beggars (*gueux de mer*). From Emden, La Rochelle and England their ships preyed on Spanish and Netherlands commerce. Their activities, and the trade war between England and the Netherlands which followed Elizabeth's seizure of four ships with £85,000 Genoese money for Alva (December 1568), did much to increase the economic malaise of the Netherlands and the discontent of the lower classes. In April 1572 the Sea Beggars seized the small port of Brill in Holland. Then they set out systematically to capture the towns of Holland and Zeeland. In most cases the pattern of events was remarkably similar. The patrician councils of the towns had nearly all large Catholic majorities who were loyal to the government, even though they detested Alva's religious persecution and heavy taxation. The great mass of the burghers were with them in preferring peace and loyalty to war and revolution. Organised as *schutters* in the citizen guards, they proudly maintained that they were sufficient to protect their own towns and they therefore opposed the entry of Spanish garrisons. Alva, short of money and troops, had no choice but to accept this position. In May 1572 Louis of Nassau captured Mons, near the French border. With the French government dominated by Coligny, Alva had to fear a full-scale French invasion. Orange was preparing to attack him from Germany. Alva turned south to deal first with the most dangerous threat. He besieged Mons and annihilated a small Huguenot army sent to its relief. The massacre of St Bartholomew (24 August 1572) finally removed his fears from this front. Orange's offensive once more collapsed and Alva was now free to turn north.

It was already too late. The Beggars in Holland and Zeeland could rely on a small but determined minority of fanatical Calvinists in the town councils and on the sympathy of sections of the *schutters*. Calvinist preachers and organisers worked among the townspeople, making converts especially among the sailors, shipbuilders and fishermen. When the Beggar forces approached a town, the Calvinist minorities would open the gates to them and force the authorities to treat. In most towns the Beggars entered by agreement. Where the strategic situation allowed, a determined council could prevent their entry. Thus Amsterdam maintained its loyalty to the king until 1578 and Middelburg resisted a Beggar siege for eighteen months. Its burghers showed no less heroism in their loyalty to Philip II than did those of Leiden in their famous resistance to him (1574). Once the Beggars were inside a town they rapidly broke their agreements with the authorities. Public preaching of the reformed faith was followed by the conversion of churches to Protestant use, by image-breaking and by brutal attacks on monasteries and convents. Some of the *gueux* leaders used terror as a deliberate policy, just as Alva did, until Orange stopped them. Loyalist and moderate magistrates and officers of the citizen guards were replaced by Beggar officers and ardent Calvinists. The number of convinced Calvinists remained small for a long time. Only very gradually, through the work of schools, propaganda and official pressure, was the majority of the population won over to the new faith. In July 1572 the estates of Holland met at Dordrecht and recognised the prince of Orange as their governor, nominally in the name of the king.[1]

The revolution now had a firm territorial basis. Holland and Zeeland were ruled by their estates in combination with their governor. Orange recognised that, effectively, his authority derived from the estates and no longer from the king. But the towns, and through them the estates, were still controlled by the patricians. On the religious side, Orange could not fully control the Beggar movement with its popular following and establish full toleration for Catholics, as he wished. Politically and militarily, he could still use the *gueux* for his wider plans of overthrowing the Spanish government in the whole Netherlands.

Alva's counter-offensive, in the winter months of 1572–3, was formidable and ruthless. He gained notable victories and reconquered a number of towns. In the end he failed because he lacked sufficient sea-power. The

[1] My interpretation of the revolution in Holland and Zeeland follows, roughly, the views of P. Geyl, *The Revolt of the Netherlands* (London, 1932), and of H. A. Enno van Gelder's many studies of the period.

heart of Holland and Zeeland remained impregnable to land armies, protected as it was by the great rivers and by flooded marshes. In 1573 Philip acceded to Alva's repeated requests for recall. His policy had failed and his enemies in Madrid had undermined the king's confidence in him. He never regained it, even though he was to conquer Portugal for his master.

The new governor-general, Don Luis de Requesens, immediately broke with Alva's policy of terror. He issued a general pardon and finally abolished the chimerical tenth penny. But Philip refused to make concessions on the religious issue, and so the struggle against Holland and Zeeland had to continue. Again the royalist armies, composed of Italians, Germans and Walloons, as well as Spaniards, achieved striking successes in the field and again they failed against the Beggars' superior naval power. In the loyal provinces, Requesens was faced with the growing opposition of the old privileged classes who saw in the government's difficulties their opportunity to regain their lost power. More and more, he had to depend on Madrid for money to pay his troops.

Spain could not carry this increased burden. Philip had managed to double his revenues since his return, by increasing the *encabezamiento*,[1] by imposing new export taxes and by large subsidies from the clergy. Nevertheless, rising prices and the wars in the Mediterranean and Granada had pushed up government expenditure even more rapidly. In 1573 the government informed the Cortes that its debts were close on fifty million ducats (they had been about twenty million at the abdication of Charles V). Perhaps one-third of all revenues was swallowed up by payments of interest on this sum. Philip now forced the protesting delegates of the Cortes to raise the *encabezamiento* to more than double its previous amount (1574). But the resources of the Castilian *pecheros* were exhausted. Several towns resorted to the imposition of the *alcabala* in place of the *encabezamiento*, and its yields fell far short of the government's expectations. On 1 September 1575 Philip's government had to suspend payment on its debts.

Spain's second bankruptcy caused a financial crisis in Genoa and Antwerp and threw out of gear the whole complicated credit structure on which the transfer of money from Spain and Italy to the Netherlands depended. The results were disastrous. The unpaid armies in the Netherlands mutinied. When the governor-general died (5 March 1576), the regiments got completely out of hand. The king's authority in the Netherlands collapsed with the collapse of his finances. When, later, Spanish finances partially recovered, owing to the vast increase of silver shipments from the New World, the king's authority was also partially recovered.

This was not, of course, the whole story. In the Council of State, the *politiques*, with the duke of Aerschot as their leader, seized the initiative. They outlawed the mutinous regiments, and the estates of Brabant raised

---

[1] See vol. II, pp. 320 f., for the technical terms used here.

troops of their own. On 4 September 1576 these troops, in conjunction with the citizen guard of Brussels, arrested the Council of State. Its *politique* members were released and gave their authority to a further revolutionary move, the summoning of the States General by the estates of Brabant. Its immediate tasks were to protect the country from the mutinous soldiers and to end the civil war with Holland and Zeeland. In the first of these objectives the States General signally failed. On 4 November 1576 Spanish troops entered Antwerp, killed over seven thousand people and subjected the town to several days of plunder and murder. Neither Antwerp nor Spain fully recovered from the material blow and the moral outrage. A few days earlier the representatives of the States General and of the prince of Orange had arrived at a compromise. The Pacification of Ghent (published 8 November 1576) stipulated the withdrawal of all foreign troops from the Netherlands, government only with the consent of the States General, the suspension of the edicts against heresy, and the settlement of the religious question by a future States General. The continued predominance of Calvinism in Holland and Zeeland, and of Catholicism in the other provinces, was thus tacitly acknowledged. The 'Peace of the duke of Aerschot', like the 'Peace of Monsieur' in France, in the same year,[1] was the high-water mark of the influence of the *politiques*.

Faced with the bankruptcy of his policy of the last ten years, Philip was as usual loath to take decisions. He appointed his brother as Requesens's successor, hoping that Don John's tremendous prestige would make a solution possible. But, from the spring to the autumn of 1576, he did nothing to intervene in the Netherlands nor even to support Gerónimo de Roda, his Spanish representative on the Council of State. Don John arrived in November, without money or troops. It was clear that, at least on the political side, he and the king would have to make serious concessions. In February 1577 Don John signed the Eternal Edict with the States General. The Spanish troops were to be sent away, but the Catholic religion was to be restored in all provinces, without reference to the States General. Holland and Zeeland immediately protested, recalled their delegates from the States General and refused to recognise Don John as governor-general.

For the next months, Don John tried to establish his authority. The States General and the great nobles, however, were unwilling to give up the power they had just gained. Don John was intelligent enough to know himself utterly unsuited to his exasperating task. 'They fear me and regard me as choleric; I detest them and regard them as the greatest scoundrels', he wrote in February 1577. He knew now that neither the States General nor the king would sanction his plans for the liberation of Mary Queen of Scots. On 24 July 1577 he reverted to the more congenial role of soldier

[1] See below, p. 292.

and captured Namur. The war had started again. For the moment, it seemed to be no longer a civil war but a national war against Spain.

Orange's ideal of the union of all the provinces against Spain had been achieved—but only at the cost of the homogeneity of his revolutionary movement. In Holland and Zeeland, the patricians of the towns had never had to share power with the guilds. The Beggar movement had made use of the artisans; but they were neither numerous nor politically experienced enough to act on their own. The patrician town councils, having accepted the reformed religion, or replaced one group of patrician councillors by another, had remained in control of the towns, and through them, of the assembly of estates. In the large industrial towns of Flanders and Brabant, on the other hand, the artisans, through their guilds, had a constitutional voice in the government of their towns and a long tradition of upholding it by revolutionary action. Neither they nor the high nobility of the south were amenable to control by the Beggar movement, nor willing to accept Orange's policy of limited revolution and religious toleration. Here was a fundamental difference in the social and political structure of the northern and the southern provinces which foreshadowed the ultimate division of the Netherlands.[1]

The towns of Flanders and Brabant had obtained the restoration of all privileges and these included much greater powers for the guilds.[2] At the same time, the magistrates of the towns were still the old Catholic patricians, often appointed by Alva himself. From August 1577 social and religious revolutions broke out in Brussels, Antwerp, 's Hertogenbosch and Ghent. In Brussels the popular element in the city government chose a War Council of Eighteen which soon came to dominate it. Other towns followed this example and chose their own Councils of Eighteen. They were usually dominated by the Calvinists. The now familiar pattern of events repeated itself. The mobs were allowed, or incited, to sack churches and monasteries; Catholic magistrates were replaced by Calvinists; the Councils of Eighteen appointed their own creatures as captains of the citizen guards; and Catholic burghers were terrorised into silence.

Nowhere was the revolution carried so far as in Ghent. Fired by the demagogic preaching of Peter Dathenus, and organised by the able and ambitious lord of Rijhove and by the self-appointed popular tribune, Jan van Hembyze, the Ghenters carried their revolution through the length and breadth of Flanders. With the help of native sympathisers, they set up revolutionary Calvinist governments in Bruges, Ypres, Oudenaarde and other towns.

The political revolution of 1576 had become a social and religious revolution and this broke the common front against Spain. To the duke of Aerschot and his friends it seemed that the towns had set up a political

---

[1] I would like to thank Professor and Mrs E. Kossmann for drawing my attention to this important point.　　　　　　　[2] See vol. II, p. 316.

and religious tyranny even more odious than that of the Spaniards. The great lords had overthrown Spanish rule in the south, only to find themselves as powerless as before. In the autumn of 1577 they invited the emperor's brother, the Archduke Matthias, to become governor-general; but when they had installed him in Brussels, they found that he preferred to work with the prince of Orange, whom the States General had appointed as his lieutenant.

The old jealousy between the Croy and the Nassau flared up again. In January 1578 Don John inflicted a crushing defeat on the States General's troops, commanded by the nobility. In the mutual recriminations which followed the battle of Gembloux, the lords complained, with justice, that the States General failed to pay their troops. Singly, or in family groups, they began to make their peace with the king or assumed an independent position, as 'malcontents', looking to France and the duke of Anjou for support.

Orange did his utmost to prevent the breach and to moderate the revolutionary movements. In August 1579 he entered Ghent in force and, with the support of Rijhove and the moderates, disarmed the Eighteen. Hembyze and Dathenus fled. But the harm was done. In January 1579 the Walloon nobles formed the Union of Arras and in June this Union came to terms with the king.

Don John had died in October 1578 and Philip appointed his nephew, Margaret of Parma's son, Alexander Farnese, to succeed him. For the first time he had found a governor-general who had all the qualities needed for this most difficult post. Farnese, at 33, had none of Don John's self-doubts nor any of his romantic visions of captive queens rescued and kingdoms conquered for himself. He was as convinced of the justice of the king's cause as Philip himself, although in temperament and religious beliefs he was nearer to his grandfather the emperor than to his uncle the king. Superbly confident in his own abilities, he rejected Philip's proposal to make him commander-in-chief while re-appointing his mother, Margaret, as governor-general. The king had to give way and, for once, delegated sufficient powers to his new governor-general. Farnese had a free hand to make any concessions he saw fit, except in questions of the king's ultimate authority and in the maintenance of the old religion.

In the south the nobles were sufficiently powerful to carry the Walloon provinces with them into the Union of Arras, despite some resistance in the larger towns. Farnese had to agree, once again, to send all foreign troops away and to govern with the consent of the estates. The Walloon nobility seemed to have maintained all the gains of the Pacification of Ghent, which, indeed, they regarded as the basis of their Union. But the war continued and the king's foreign troops had to be recalled yet again. This inescapable necessity, and Farnese's skilful strategy, gradually weighted the balance of political power decisively in favour of the crown.

The northern provinces formed their union at the same time (January 1579) and on the basis of their own interpretation of the Pacification of Ghent. It was a Calvinist and a constitutional interpretation, even though the union was formed against the opposition of the estates of Catholic Gelderland. The Union of Utrecht (Holland, Zeeland, Utrecht, Friesland, Gelderland, Drenthe, Overijssel and the province, but not the city, of Groningen) gave political power to the estates and to the house of Orange. The balance of power between them, however, remained the subject of conflict for more than a century.

Orange himself had originally favoured a closer union of the northern provinces. The actual union was concluded against his wishes, for its uncompromising Calvinism made it virtually impossible to achieve his ideal of uniting all provinces on the basis of a religious peace. Farnese's military successes, moreover, induced the prince to look once more to France for help. To obtain this, he was prepared to offer the sovereignty of the Netherlands to Henry III's brother, the duke of Anjou, for the king himself declined it. Such plans were regarded as high treason in Madrid. Philip declared Orange an outlaw and put a price on his head. Orange answered with his 'Apology', the first consistent, and highly imaginative, statement of the 'black legend' against Philip II and Spain. The pamphlet war now reached new heights, both in the level of argument and in shrillness of tone. The Calvinists and anti-royalists had the better of this propaganda warfare throughout the conflict. The royalist side was inhibited by its unwillingness to debase the king's authority by arguing about his policy with his subjects. In 1581 the States General renounced their allegiance to Philip II. 'God did not create the people slaves to their prince,' thus ran the Act of Abjuration, 'to obey his commands whether right or wrong, but rather the prince for the sake of his subjects, to love and support them as a father his children or a shepherd his flock.' Perhaps the wording was deliberately modelled on that of the instructions which Philip used to give to his viceroys, for it is strikingly similar.

The duke of Anjou, the new sovereign to whom the provinces now swore a reluctant allegiance, had been the leader of the *politiques* in France; but his ambitions were personal. All parties could therefore use him for their own ends. Henry III, fearing Anjou's influence in France, was glad to divert his energies abroad and, at the same time, make trouble for Spain without committing himself. Elizabeth had similar reasons in her enjoyable marriage negotiations with the duke; and if these also created trouble in France by raising Anjou's prestige, so much the better. Orange and the States General needed Anjou's name and troops, but would grant him no power in the government of the Union. More and more, the Netherlands became the focal point for all the political and religious struggles of western Europe—the only place where, as yet, France and England dared to challenge the hegemony of Spain. Flanders, Brabant and the north-eastern provinces became the battle-ground of international armies: Germans, Scots, English and French on the side of the States General; Spaniards, Italians and Germans on the royalist side. Only for the Netherlanders was it still a civil war.

Systematically Farnese set about his task of reconquest. There were no more massacres to terrorise the population. If a town returned to obedience to the king and the old religion, the governor-general promised the citizens their lives, property and many of their local privileges. Town after town surrendered on these terms. Anjou's troops were both unsuccessful and unpopular. The duke himself found his relations with the States General as frustrating as Don John had done. In France he was taunted with the concessions he had made to heretics and commoners. He reacted like Don John. In January 1583 he attempted to seize Antwerp. The *coup* failed miserably and Anjou lost what little prestige he still commanded.

As military reverse followed on military reverse, the extremists in Flanders once more gained the upper hand. Four years after their flight, Hembyze and Dathenus returned to Ghent (August 1583). The dictator-ship was re-established. But, just as it was to happen in later revolutionary movements, the struggle for power inside the movement became more important than the struggle against the common enemy. Hembyze and Dathenus opened negotiations with Farnese and started replacing Calvinist officials with Catholics. This was too much for their own supporters. In March 1584 they arrested Hembyze, and on 4 August the old dictator was executed. But the revolution was lost; six weeks later Ghent surren-dered to the Spaniards. In March 1585 Brussels fell and in August Antwerp capitulated after a siege of thirteen months.

From then on, the issue between the rebels and the Spaniards became almost entirely a military one. The period of revolutions was over. In the south, Calvinists and Catholics no longer intermingled in the former explosive mixture. Farnese expelled the Calvinist preachers and many thousands of laymen followed them to the northern provinces, or to England and Germany, for a variety of religious, political and economic reasons. A reorganised and purified church was able to win back to Catholicism the great majority of the population, and this without the use of the Inquisition. The contemporary penchant for burning the hetero-dox could be safely indulged against Baptists and witches, without causing political repercussions. It was a practice in which, at least in the case of witches, the Protestant countries did not lag behind. At the same time, the idea of religious peace, of the co-existence of Catholics and Protestants in one political community and with equal rights, had died. Orange, its greatest protagonist, fell to the bullets of a fanatic (10 July 1584). He had failed to preserve the unity of the Netherlands; but he had succeeded both in keeping alive the resistance to Philip II's political and religious absolutism and in co-operating, as head of a government, with an assembly of estates. It was a remarkable achievement for a conservative aristocat turned revolutionary. No other revolutionary leader of the sixteeth century could rival him in his understanding of the political forces, both of his own country and of Europe, nor in the diplomatic skill with which he made them serve his own ends. He could not always control these forces; but, in the course of the struggle, he imposed his personality on his own side until, in the end, all the old distrusts were stilled and all parties accepted his leadership, however much they might quarrel with his tactics. Much of William's motivation and many of his aims remained obscure to his contemporaries, as they have also remained obscure to historians. In this sense, his posthumous sobriquet, the Silent, is apt. But it was always clear what he fought against: despotic government and religious persecution. His reputed dying words, 'Oh God, have pity on my soul and on this poor country', were broadcast throughout the provinces. All parties could now claim him for their own. His actual achievement, and the power of the myth attaching to his name after his death, created a political pattern which made the Union of Utrecht a viable political structure despite the medieval particularism of its constituent towns and provinces.

In France the crisis following the end of the Habsburg–Valois wars had developed even more rapidly than in the Netherlands. Its causes were essentially similar. After the bankruptcy of 1557, Henry II squeezed another seven million livres in extraordinary taxes out of his unfortunate subjects. Nevertheless, the limit had been reached. There were peasant revolts in Normandy and Languedoc. The nobles, though exempt from taxation, had spent their incomes and mortgaged or sold their estates in the king's service or the heavy ransoms demanded of noble prisoners after the disaster of St Quentin (1557). Peace left many without income or employment. Unlike the English gentry, they or their younger sons could not make their fortunes in trade. Both tradition and a specific law of 1560 forbade such a course. The luckier ones could enter the church; for the French church had become a part of the enormous patronage system of the crown and the high nobility, so that, as people said, 'bishoprics were sold like cinnamon and pepper'. But the unlucky ones swelled the growing number of those who were clamouring for church reforms.

In the towns, the small artisans and shopkeepers had been hit by heavy taxation and by the periodic collapse of rural purchasing power which followed bad harvests such as that of 1557. The journeymen saw food prices rising faster than wages and found that the growing influence and rigidity of the guilds blocked the advance of the majority to mastership.

Such conditions provided a fertile field for the Calvinist preachers. Their sermons, their Bible readings, and their services with communal snging of psalms, attracted ever greater numbers. Too often, the local curés could not emulate the preachers' eloquence nor satisfy the spiritual longings of a people whose lives had become insecure. Yet, just as in the Netherlands, the appeal of the reformed religion cut across class divisions. Many of the richer bourgeois and professional men, and more especially their womenfolk, were drawn towards the new doctrines.

From 1555 Geneva sent an increasing number of preachers into France. They were all Frenchmen and a considerable proportion were noblemen; for it was Calvin's deliberate policy to convert the nobility. Wherever a Protestant community was established, it elected its elders and deacons to assure the discipline of the faithful, administer its funds and, in general, look after the physical and spiritual welfare of its members. The pastors of the larger communities, or groups of smaller ones, were appointed by Theodore Beza or by Calvin himself. Thus, spiritual control was centred in Geneva and the whole movement had the characteristics of an international as well as of a national, party. After 1559 the nobility joined the movement in large numbers, especially in the south. By the beginning of 1562 the majority of the Calvinist communities had placed themselves under the protection of a local seigneur. His influence would bring new converts, especially from the country population which had been comparatively untouched by the new religion. More important still was the military element introduced by the nobility. The religious conventicles became military cadres. Mass meetings of armed men, protected by the local nobility and their retainers, began to invade the churches and to celebrate their services in open defiance of public authority and of the feelings of the majority of the Catholic population. Nor did this happen only in the south. In May 1560 their assemblies in Rouen were said to be 20,000 strong. The figure may be exaggerated, but the royal commander, with 5,000 troops, could not prevent the scaffolds and gibbets he had set up from being torn down.

The Huguenot cadres were now organised on a provincial and national basis on the pattern of the religious communities with their provincial and national synods. The synod of Clairac, in November 1560, divided the province of Guienne into seven colloques, each with its colonel. In 1561 the synod of Sainte-Foy decided on the election of two 'protectors' for the regions of Toulouse and Bordeaux. Under these, there was a whole hierarchy of communal leaders, each strictly responsible to his immediate superior. By 1562 this organisation was more or less fully developed in Guienne, Languedoc, Provence and Dauphiné, and it existed at least in outline in the rest of France. Inevitably, the control of the movement tended to shift from the preachers to the nobles, despite Calvin's misgivings and his efforts to prevent it.

This organisation could not have been built up had it not been for the weakness of the government. Henry II had been determined to destroy the Protestants. Their growing success had been one of the reasons why he had negotiated the peace with Spain. The government in Paris, however found it as difficult as the government in Brussels to persuade its local Catholic officials to execute the edicts against their Protestant neighbours and fellow-countrymen. Many sympathised or frankly joined the movement; still more disliked persecution. Throughout the years 1560 and 1561 the Vicomte de Joyeuse, acting governor of Languedoc, wrote to the government with increasing gloom about his waning authority, the unreliability of his officials, and the increasing power and influence of the Huguenots, who were insulting loyal Catholics by claiming to act in the king's name.

The situation might still have been restored if the government had vigorously backed its provincial governors in their struggle against the Huguenots. But this was precisely what the government could no longer do. Henry II died, on 26 July 1559, from an injury received in a tourna-ment. Francis II was only 15: legally of age, but clearly too young to rule himself. A political crisis was now added to the social, financial and reli-gious problems of France. Francis I and Henry II had governed with the aid of the high nobility. With the help of royal favour, the house of Guise had amassed huge estates in the east and the house of Montmorency in the north and in the Île de France. The Bourbons had managed to hang on to most of their property in the south and in Picardy, despite the mis-fortune of the treason committed by the Constable Bourbon in the reign of Francis I. As ministers and provincial governors, these great lords had built up a vast network of clientage among the local nobility. Municipal and provincial officials looked to them for advancement in their careers. As long as Henry II lived, the inevitable rivalries of the great lords were fought out within the constitutional limits of court intrigue. Now Francis II threw himself unreservedly into the arms of the Guises, the uncles of his wife, Mary Queen of Scots. Duke Francis of Guise, the defender of Metz and conqueror of Calais,[1] and his younger brother Charles, the cardinal of Lorraine, were a formidable team; but their ascendancy was bound to be challenged. As descendants of the house of Lorraine, they prided them-selves on their foreign origin in order to emphasise their loyalty to the French crown and their equality of status with all French princes. Their rivals made it an effective propaganda point against them. The old constable, Anne de Montmorency, resented his exclusion from power. The Bourbons openly demanded power for themselves. They were the nearest relatives of the Valois, princes of the blood who could claim the constitutional right to govern during a royal minority. Anthony, the head of the family and, through his wife, king of Navarre, lacked the personality and will power to become an effective party leader and was both too vain and too vacillating to become the reliable tool of any one else. His younger

[1] See vol. II, pp. 357, 249.

brother, Louis, prince of Condé, attempted to make up for his deficiencies. As early as 1555 he had visited Geneva and shown his interest in religious reform. Yet his motives and sincerity have remained controversial, not least because Calvin himself came deeply to distrust them. There is no doubt about his ambition for himself and his house nor about his appreciation of the political possibilities of the Huguenot movement. When he took the title of protector-general of the churches of France, a great part of the enormous influence of the Bourbon connection was added to the Huguenot party. It was further strengthened when the constable's nephew, the Admiral Gaspard de Coligny, brought to the Huguenots at least a part of the Montmorency clientage. Condé was thus the leader of a party formed by the union of aristocratic influence with the military organisation of the Calvinist communities and financed by the backing of wealthy bankers and the voluntary contributions of the faithful. The members of this organisation were fired by a religious faith kept alight by skilful propaganda, and organised in a strict communal discipline that held together in a common purpose nobles and artisans, soldiers and peaceful burghers. This was a political instrument such as no 'over-mighty subject' had ever commanded before. In Coligny, moreover, the Huguenots had a leader whose motives were never suspect. Like his uncle the constable, Coligny had spent his life in the service of his king, a brave soldier, an excellent organiser and a strict disciplinarian. His conversion had been slow and marked by strong internal conflicts. He had little of Orange's abhorrence of absolutist government. When he finally decided to take up arms, it was not to fight a political system, still less to fight his own king, but rather to obtain liberty of conscience and worship for his co-religionists and, if possible, to free the king from his evil advisers who were persecuting true religion. Coligny's singleness of purpose gave to the Huguenot movement in France a unity such as the Calvinist movement in the Netherlands never achieved.

Throughout the short reign of Francis II political and religious passions rose alarmingly. There was much local violence and the outrages committed by both parties led to bitter recriminations and further violence. The government was faced with a debt of over 40 million livres; but the States General of 1560, summoned to give financial help, proved as difficult to handle as its counterpart in the Netherlands. Condé had many friends in the assembly. The third estate refused to vote taxes, but demanded that it should determine the country's religious policy and the composition of the government itself. From March 1560 the government gave up its official policy of imposing religious unity by force and issued a series of edicts, granting liberty of conscience, but prohibiting armed assemblies. Neither side was satisfied. No one, not even the chancellor, L'Hôpital, who opposed force in matters of religion, thought that a state could live with two religions. There had not yet been time for a party of *politiques* to develop. Those who held no strong religious views or dis liked persecuting men for their opinions still hoped for a solution from a general or a national council of the church.

In March 1560 the first big *coup* attempted by the Huguenots, the conspiracy of Amboise, misfired completely. Condé was arrested on the somewhat doubtful grounds of implication. But the government's weakness had become very obvious. 'I never saw state more amased than this,' the English ambassador reported from the court at Amboise; 'they know not whome to mistruste, nor to truste.' The Guises only maintained their position by giving much more power than before to the queen mother, Catherine de Medici.

Francis II died on 5 December 1560. Condé was immediately released and the Bourbon claim to the regency for the ten-year-old Charles IX was now much harder to resist than in the case of Francis II, who had been nominally of age. The queen mother, however, was determined to control the regency herself. Catherine de Medici, half Florentine and half French, had long since identified her personal interests with those of the French monarchy. She was convinced that she must follow the example of Blanche of Castile, the mother of St Louis, and preserve the authority of the French crown intact for her children. Only the monarchy could give France stability and preserve her independence from Spain. Every faction, however good its intentions, would necessarily work to the detriment of the monarchy. Hence, neither Guise nor Bourbon must dominate the government. Above all, she must win time for tempers to cool and for her sons to grow up. This was the aim which Catherine pursued consistently, though in a bewildering succession of tactical twists, during her sons' minorities, and even afterwards. To achieve it, she was prepared to use every means to keep her own power. It is impossible to know how far this power became for her an end in itself. Catherine's field of manœuvre, however, was dangerously narrow. She could no more rule without the high nobility than could Margaret of Parma. Like Margaret and Philip II before 1567, she could only play court politics, for her government had no money to raise an effective army of its own. For eighteen months Catherine tried to reconcile the princes or, when this did not work, to balance them against each other. All the time she had to look over her shoulder at Philip II, who threatened to intervene against the Huguenots.

On 29 November 1560, after much pressure from the cardinal of Lorraine, Pius IV finally published the bull reconvening the Council of Trent. But events in France moved too rapidly for Catherine to await its outcome. In the summer of 1561 she induced Protestant and Catholic theologians to meet at Poissy and attempt to arrive at an agreed position. The 'colloquy' failed, not so much because Catherine regarded religion as a branch of politics and thought that theologians could be induced to manœuvre and compromise like politicians, as because both sides wanted to secure the support of the monarchy but were quite unwilling to accept it as an arbiter between them. It was essentially the same difficulty that Charles V had faced, and Catherine understood it as little as the emperor had done.[1]

In the autumn of 1561 the Guises and the Montmorencys, now in alliance, withdrew from the court. Catherine had mismanaged her relations with the irascible constable. When the old man was faced with the choice between the detested but orthodox Guises and his beloved but heretical nephew, he chose the Guises. Together, they won over Anthony of Bourbon with the promise of help for the recovery of the Spanish part of his kingdom of Navarre. Both Catholics and Huguenots were arming and clashes were becoming more frequent. Catherine's manœuvres had left her powerless between two armed camps. She redoubled her efforts for peace. The Edict of January (1562) formalised her compromise agreement with the Huguenots: Protestant assemblies were allowed outside town walls and Protestant services in private houses. It was the greatest concession yet to the Huguenots, and it caused corresponding resentment in the Catholic camp. One more incident touched off civil war. On 1 March 1562 the duke of Guise's retainers surprised a Protestant service at Vassy and killed some thirty persons. At that point Catherine lost control over events. Condé's forces assembled at Orléans. He was able to count on the support of over two thousand Protestant churches. The Huguenots surprised Lyons, Tours, Blois, Rouen and other towns. But Guise and Montmorency entered Paris at the head of their own armies. In May there was open fighting.

There had not been a civil war in France for a hundred years, and many found it deeply shocking. The nobility on both sides were determined, so wrote de La Noue, one of the Huguenot leaders, in his memoirs, to fight the war with the courtesies due to gentlemen. Negotiations never ceased, thanks mainly to the queen mother. When the war was over, all parties combined to expel the English from Le Havre, which Condé had handed to them in return for military and financial help.[2] Yet both armies had committed atrocities and acts of deliberate terror, and the disillusionment was great. The Pacification of Amboise (19 March 1563) granted the Protestants liberty of conscience, but the celebration of services only to nobles and their households, and to the bourgeois only in one town in each *baillage* and *sénéchaussée*. Calvin and Coligny bitterly reproached Condé for accepting conditions which favoured his own class at the expense of the mass of the Protestant communities. The peace left more suspicion and fear than ever.

Only the queen mother had come out of the war with enhanced power and reputation. She had also been lucky. Navarre was killed at the siege of Rouen; both the constable and Condé had been taken prisoner by

[1] See vol. II, p. 307.   [2] See above, pp. 220–1.

286

their opponents. The duke of Guise was assassinated by a Huguenot fanatic (18 February 1563). Under torture, the assassin implicated Coligny. Coligny denied having instigated the murder, but rejoiced that the Lord had struck down this great enemy of his evangel. Nine years later, there were to be many who rejoiced at the murder of Coligny and his friends, though they, too, would not have commanded it.

With some of the great personalities out of the way, Catherine could now effectively assert her own authority in the name of the king. For four years she worked hard to maintain peace; but she could not allay the fears of both sides, nor prevent sporadic outbursts of local violence. The resolutions of the Council of Trent convinced many on both sides that a theological solution of the religious problem was no longer possible. A conference at Bayonne (1565), between Catherine on the one side and her daughter Elizabeth, wife of Philip II, and the duke of Alva on the other was widely (and wrongly) regarded as the establishment of a Paris–Madrid axis for the express purpose of destroying the Protestants in France and in the Netherlands.

All the Huguenot fears seemed to be justified when in the summer of 1567 Alva marched his army from Milan to the Netherlands, along the eastern border of France. Personal rivalries at court played their part in increasing mutual suspicion. There is no evidence that the French Catholics planned an attack; but Condé and Coligny thought so and decided to strike first by capturing the king (September 1567). Once again, the Huguenot organisation worked smoothly and the Protestants took over a number of towns. But the main *coup* against the court failed and open war broke out. More even than the first civil war, it became part of the European struggle between Protestants and Catholics. The government obtained help from Alva and introduced Swiss troops. The Elector Palatine sent his son, John Casimir, with German *reîtres* (*Reiter* = horseman) to help the Huguenots. They were to become a regular feature of the civil wars and greatly added to their ferocity. The war ended with the Treaty of Longjumeau (23 March 1568) and the re-establishment of the Edict of Amboise. The king agreed to pay off the *reîtres*.

It was no more than an armistice of a few months. At court, L'Hôpital and the moderates were discredited. The constable had fallen. The Guises were back in power and found a powerful ally for their aggressive policy in the king's younger brother, the duke of Anjou (later Henry III). Neither side was willing to abide by the terms of the treaty. The Huguenots were still on the offensive. When they could not dominate a region completely, they infiltrated into public offices, until there was a Huguenot hierarchy of officials intermingled with the royal administration, owing allegiance, not to the king, but to Condé and Coligny. 'Thus they could, in one day, at one definite hour, and with all secrecy start a rising in every part of the kingdom', wrote the Venetian ambassador, with only slight exaggeration.

It turned into the longest and most ferocious war yet fought. Anjou defeated the Huguenots at Jarnac and Montcontour (1569); but their organisation held firm, and Condé's death at Jarnac gave them the added advantage of a unified command under Coligny. A brilliant strategist, though only a moderate tactician—he lost most of the pitched battles he fought—Coligny kept his army in being by a war of rapid movement which prevented the superior forces of the royalists from dealing the Huguenots a fatal blow. He had, moreover, the great advantages that he could recruit German *reîtres* even without money, for the Treaty of Longjumeau had shown that the king would eventually have to pay them off. By contrast, Catherine's generals bickered with each other and were all too often unwilling to pursue the war to a final victory, for fear of losing their profitable commands. The government's financial weakness made it impossible to keep large armies together for long enough to exploit tactical successes. The royalist nobility, moreover, had friends and relatives in the Huguenot army. Neither side wished for the total ruin of the other.

The Edict of Pacification of St Germain (8 August 1570) once more restored the *status quo*; but, for the first time, the Huguenots were given the right to garrison four towns as security: La Rochelle, Montauban, la Charité and Cognac. Catherine changed course once again. Philip II had snubbed her marriage proposals for her daughter Margaret and for Charles IX. The French ambassador in Spain reported how the Morisco revolt had shown up the military weakness of the Catholic king. He could be safely snubbed in turn. Catherine therefore arranged for the marriage of her daughter Margaret with the young Henry of Navarre, hoping, with characteristic optimism, that a Valois–Bourbon marriage alliance would settle the internal troubles of the kingdom. At the same time, she started negotiations for a marriage between Elizabeth I and Anjou. Nothing came of this; but the Anglo-French rapprochement led to the Treaty of Blois (19 April 1572), a fully fledged defensive alliance. It included provision for the transfer of the English cloth staple from Antwerp to Rouen. Nothing came of this plan; but it was clear enough that the treaty was directed against Spain and the Netherlands, and Alva's government in Brussels was highly alarmed.

In the summer of 1571 Coligny appeared at court and rejoined the king's council. More consistently than Catherine, he had seen the solution of the kingdom's troubles in a vigorous anti-Spanish policy. If only all Frenchmen could combine against the old enemy of the kingdom, their more recent hatred might be forgotten. Since 1568 Coligny had been in close touch with Louis of Nassau. The Sea Beggars had used La Rochelle as a base and combined their exploits with those of the Huguenot privateers. Coligny promised Nassau to support his attack on Alva. The Beggars' successes in Zeeland and Holland in the spring of 1572, and Nassau's capture of Mons and Valenciennes, seemed to present a golden chance.

Best of all, Charles IX himself supported this policy enthusiastically. The melancholy and romantic young man had been captivated by Coligny's powerful personality. Jealous of his younger brother's military successes, he now dreamt of even greater exploits for himself.

But Coligny had misjudged both the internal and the international situation. The hatreds born of three civil wars could not be stilled by a simple display of jingoism. The Guises had never forgiven him for his alleged complicity in the murder of Duke Francis. Catherine and Anjou were increasingly jealous of his personal influence over the king. The Spanish ambassador and the papal nuncio worked feverishly against him. Catherine was becoming seriously alarmed at the prospect of open war with Spain. The battle of Lepanto had more than restored Spanish military prestige. Alva commanded a formidable army in the Netherlands and made short shrift of the small force which the Huguenots had sent for the relief of beleaguered Mons. Little help was to be expected from England or the German princes. Elizabeth had balanced the Treaty of Blois by a gesture of goodwill to Alva. Early in March she had expelled the Sea Beggars from England—with the paradoxical, but to Elizabeth highly pleasing, result that they captured Brill and started the effective revolt of Zeeland and Holland. The council and its military experts agreed with Catherine; but Coligny, secure in the king's favour, persisted. The Huguenots began to talk of changing the king's council. They had fought three civil wars with the limited objective of security for themselves and their religious practices. Now, in peace time, they seemed about to capture the government of France.

Catherine planned her stroke with all the economy of the experienced politician she was. The Guises were readily induced to have Coligny murdered. Once this dangerous man was dead and his fateful influence over the king had gone, the balance of political power would be restored, with the queen mother again having the decisive voice, and France could withdraw from disastrous adventures against Spain. On 22 August 1572 the assassins wounded Coligny, but failed to kill him. Immediately Paris was in an uproar. Thousands of Huguenot gentlemen had come to the capital for the wedding of Henry and Margaret—the marriage which was to have ended the civil strife. They now demanded revenge for the outrage committed on their leader. The king himself visited the wounded Coligny and promised punishment for the culprits. The plot had turned against Catherine. It was all too clear that she and the Guises would be implicated. Her reaction was the unpremeditated act of desperation.

On Saturday 23 August, she convinced the king that all Huguenot leaders must now be killed. All the Catholics in the council agreed. It seems likely that, even now, Catherine only thought of doing away with a comparatively small number of Huguenots. But at this point she once more lost control over the course of events. Anjou, the young duke Henry of Guise, and the provost of the Merchants of Paris organised the massacre for the same night. It was easy. The murderous proclivities of the Paris populace were well known; the Huguenots were unsuspecting. Who, indeed, could have suspected such a monstrous deed? Yet some such action had been discussed, though never planned, in Catholic circles for years. Neither Catholics nor Huguenots had clean hands in the matter of smaller massacres. On the night of 23–24 August, St Bartholomew's Eve, and in the following days, several thousand Huguenots were murdered. This time, Guise made sure of Coligny's death, waiting outside the admiral's house until the assassins had thrown his mangled body through the window. Of the leaders, only Navarre and the young prince of Condé were spared, both on abjuring their Protestant faith. The massacres spread to the provinces and several thousand more perished. The exact figures have always remained a matter of dispute.[1]

Even the duke of Alva was shocked, but certainly not displeased. Masses of thanksgiving were said in Madrid and Rome, and even the Venetian senate voted, by 162 to 2, to celebrate the joyful event by a procession. The Venetians had second thoughts fairly soon, and so had Catherine. The murder of Coligny had fitted into her plans; the massacres had not, for they destroyed the political balance in France and delivered her again into the hands of the Guise faction. She boasted of the deed to Philip II and the pope, rightly judging that it would be held to her credit. She excused it to Elizabeth I and to the German princes as self-defence and as a plot of the Guises. Almost immediately, she started negotiating once more with the Huguenots; not surprisingly, without success. The resumption of the civil war was therefore inevitable. The cardinal of Lorraine promoted the publication by the Italian Capalupi of *Lo stratagemma di Carlo IX* (Rome, 1572), a fanciful account of French royal policy, purporting to prove that the massacres were premeditated. Lorraine calculated, quite correctly, that the book would become a kind of devil's bible for the Protestants which would make their future co-operation with the monarchy much more difficult. As so often happens, the extremists on both sides were playing into each other's hands.

The fourth war of religion, mostly an unsuccessful siege of La Rochelle by the royalists, ended once more in a compromise when Anjou needed peace in order to take up the crown of Poland to which he had been elected (1573). It was only now that the Huguenot organisation reached its full development, in a broad arc stretching from Dauphiné through Provence and Languedoc to Béarn and Guienne. As in the Netherlands, the successful revolution tended to become localised, both by an alliance with provincial feeling against an interfering central government and by the logic of the military situation. Again as in Holland and Zeeland,

[1] The best modern account is P. Erlanger, *Le Massacre de la Saint-Barthélemy* (Paris, 1960); English translation by A. O'Brian, *St Bartholomew's Night* (London, 1962).

political authority came to reside in representative assemblies. They acted in conjunction with the princes, Condé and Navarre, after they had fled from court and returned to Protestantism (1574 and 1575 respectively). Huguenot propaganda now laid far greater stress than it had done formerly on constitutional theories against the absolutism of the French monarchy. But the Protestant movement had passed its peak. Outside the southern provinces it was declining.

It was able to survive owing to its alliance with the *politiques*. What Alva's Council of Troubles had done over a number of years, the massacres in France did in a few days: they persuaded many Catholics to seek a way out of the horrors of religious and civil strife by sacrificing the religious rather than the political unity of the state.[1] The *politiques*, or Malcontents, like the other parties in France, were a mixed group and not nearly as well organised as the Huguenots or, later, the League. Among them were the Montmorency family with its clients, the moderates and Erasmians among lawyers and government officials, the bankers and merchants whose business had suffered from civil war, and all those among the Catholic nobility who hated the Guises. Their leaders were influential, but personally unattractive. The duke of Alençon, youngest of Catherine's sons and later, as duke of Anjou, notorious for his intervention in the Netherlands, saw in the *politiques* a convenient instrument to further his political ambitions. The constable's son, Montmorency-Damville, was governor of Languedoc and interested more in his own authority in the south than in that of the crown. A Catholic without religious interests, he permitted effective toleration under his authority. Politically, he allied himself with the king against the Huguenots, or with the Huguenots against the king, as occasion arose. The only consistent part of his policy was his jealousy of the house of Guise.

The civil wars continued intermittently and with shifting alliances. As the Venetian ambassadors saw it, war had now come to be built into the social and political structure and habits of French society. The great princely houses, the Guises, the Bourbons, the Montmorencys, knew that war increased their hold over the central government or, at least, over the provinces which they governed. The lower nobility were impoverished by inflation and by the devastation of their estates. They could hope to recoup their fortunes only in war and in the service of one of the great lords. Now that every town and province had become a frontier in the civil war, the formerly pacific French population had been trained to warfare. As the marauding armies interrupted trade and made life insecure, an increasing number of young men came to prefer the life of the plunderer to that of the plundered.

[1] H. A. Enno van Gelder, 'De Nederlandse opstand en de Franse godsdienstoorlogen', in *Verslag van de Algemene Vergadering van het Historisch Genootschap te Utrecht* (1930), p. 29.

In 1574 Charles IX died at the age of 24, haunted, so it was said, by the spectres of the massacres. Anjou returned post-haste from Poland to wear the crown as Henry III. Intelligent, but without his mother's persistence and capacity for hard work, he was not the man to impose himself on the faction leaders. His extravagance made him unpopular with the taxpayers. His sexual proclivities and the favours which he bestowed on his *mignons*, brave and capable though some of them were, together with his growing distaste for warfare, made him despised by the aristocratic and military society of France. While the great lords went to war with their retainers and clients, the crown had to pay for most of the professional troops and was ruining itself. In 1576 Henry III and Catherine came to the conclusion that the Huguenots could not be crushed. Alençon negotiated a very favourable treaty for them: the exercise of their religion everywhere outside Paris and the residence of the court, eight places of security and mixed commissions in the *parlements* (*chambres mi-parties*) to deal with cases involving Protestants.

The 'Peace of Monsieur' (i.e. Alençon) was the French counterpart to the Pacification of Ghent. In the Netherlands, Catholic extremism was represented by the monarchy. Its religious intransigence, together with the acceleration of the religious and social revolution in Flanders and Brabant, led to the breakdown of the compromise peace. In France, the monarchy had now become suspect to many Catholics. In consequence an independent Catholic movement appeared which, in its turn, became revolutionary and anti-royalist. Local Catholic unions, or leagues, had been formed by local authorities, nobles and prelates as early as 1560 and 1562. After the Peace of Monsieur these local associations were organised into a nation-wide League or Holy Union. Where the Huguenot party had been built on the alliance of the militarised Calvinist communities with the Bourbon family connection, the League was built on the alliance of the military Catholic nobility in their local unions with the Guise family connection. Where the Huguenots looked to Geneva for spiritual guidance and to England and the Protestant princes of Germany for material help, the Leaguers looked to Rome and to the Catholic rulers of Spain and Savoy. Thus, all revolutionary movements of the period were linked to powers and interests outside their national boundaries. This added to their strength, but it also set up tensions within the movements that greatly increased the difficulties of unified leadership.

The League of 1576 was founded as a Catholic party of the nobility, with essentially conservative aims. Henry III and his successors were to be preserved in their authority, according to their coronation oaths; the provinces and estates were to have their ancient rights restored to them. This was not very different from similar feudal programmes in the middle ages. The League's articles dealing with its organisation, however, had a most unmedieval ring. All members were to be closely linked in mutual protection and obedience to their chief, without respect for any other authority. They were to contribute arms and men and hound down any defaulter, while the League would protect them from all reprisals. Every member had to take an oath to observe these articles, on pain of anathema and eternal damnation. In many parts of France the League was broadened to include the clergy and the third estate and, just as in the Huguenot movement, the lower orders were enrolled to provide mass support.

The power of this new party became immediately apparent in the States General of Blois in 1576. It manipulated the elections and intimidated the voters. Leaguer *baillis* and *sénéchaux* tried to prevent the Huguenots from attending electoral meetings. Within the assembly, they organised an adroit attack on the king's powers in the name of the old privileges of the estates and provinces. Their inability to win direct control over the government had turned the extremist Catholics, like the Huguenots, into an anti-absolutist party.

Henry III was very conscious of the League's threats to his independence and he knew of its close links with Madrid. To draw its teeth and, if possible, to make it serve his own ends, he declared himself its chief in place of the duke of Guise (January 1577). But the Catholic nobility had no intention of exchanging their vague obligations to serve the king for the very precise and far-reaching obligations they would have to him as chief of the League. The organisation which had been created to coerce the king disintegrated in his hands when he tried to use it for his own purposes. Henry got little help from the League and no financial support from the States General in his renewed war with the Protestants. If this was disappointing, it was still better than leaving such a weapon in the hands of Henry of Guise. Moreover, the inevitable divergence of aim between the Huguenots and the *politiques* allowed the royal armies considerable successes. In the Peace of Bergerac, the 'King's Peace', the Huguenots lost many of their lately won concessions. The king declared all leagues dissolved.

A *modus vivendi* now seemed possible. Catherine worked ceaselessly for it, travelling through the southern provinces and negotiating with *politique* governors and Huguenot chiefs. Local fighting never ceased completely; but the old queen mother managed to prevent all but one short open war (1579–80). Since both Henry III and his brother, now duke of Anjou, were childless, Henry of Navarre was willing to bide his time in the hope of succeeding to the throne. Anjou found in the Netherlands a promising field for his ambitions, with the prospect of an English marriage and a crown on the further horizon. The French military nobility of all parties willingly followed his call to seek plunder abroad or, since they had long since ceased to be very particular in such matters, on their way through their own country. Guise, too, was looking abroad, dreaming romantically, like Don John of Austria, of liberating his cousin Mary Stuart. Philip II gave him good words, as he did the Scottish and English

Catholics, but did nothing practical to help him. It could never be an object of Spanish policy to help the French establish themselves in the British Isles. Until he was strong enough to attack Elizabeth I without French help, Philip would plot against her life, but go to great lengths to prevent an open breach, for fear of an Anglo-French alliance against him. Henry III and Catherine, for their part, were mortally afraid of the power of Spain. They supported the prior of Crato in the Azores and Anjou in the Netherlands, though they officially disavowed him and constantly quarrelled with him over his complaints of insufficient support. It is not really surprising that, in his irritation with French policy, Philip opened negotiations with Henry of Navarre to restart the civil wars in France. Navarre was too intelligent to fall into this trap.

The situation, however, remained tense. Nothing had really been settled. There was open warfare only in the Netherlands; but the great powers were manœuvring for position and building up their 'fifth columns' inside their opponents' territories. In France none of the parties was satisfied nor had given up hope of bettering its position. With relative peace and a stable currency, after monetary reforms in 1577, economic life was beginning to recover, especially in the western seaports which handled most of the Spanish-Netherlands trade. But the tax burden increased, rather than diminished. Between 1576 and 1588 the *taille* was doubled and the *gabelle*, the hated tax on salt, was trebled. Peasants, artisans and shopkeepers were ruined, while the great merchants and bankers (many of them Italians and Spaniards), the tax-farmers, and the king's favourites grew rich. The great political and social crisis of 1559 was only now reaching its climax.

3. *The French succession and the war with England*

The truce with the Porte and the conquest of Portugal marked a turning-point in Spanish policy. The greatest danger to Spain was no longer in the Mediterranean but in the Atlantic. France and England were supporting her enemies in the Netherlands and in Portugal. Drake and the English pirates were wickedly and illegally disrupting Spanish trade with her colonies and robbing the king and his subjects. The pope, Cardinal Granvelle and Philip's Spanish advisers were pressing for a more aggressive policy. Gradually, the king himself became convinced that the defence, both of his own interests and of the church, demanded more active Spanish intervention in western Europe.

The immediate occasion for the change in Spanish policy was the death of the duke of Anjou and of the prince of Orange (1584). Even before Anjou's death, the United Provinces (i.e. the members of the Union of Utrecht) had once more approached both Henry III and Elizabeth I with offers of the sovereignty over the Netherlands. Henry III again refused.

William's death and the fall of Antwerp made help urgent if the Union was to be saved. On 20 August 1585 Elizabeth therefore, while likewise refusing the sovereignty, agreed to send five thousand troops, under the command of the earl of Leicester, to the Netherlands. Leicester and two other Englishmen were to have seats in the Council of State. Brill and Flushing, commanding the estuaries of the Meuse and the Scheldt, were handed over to the English as bases and as security for the repayment of the English government's expenses. Elizabeth had driven a hard bargain and had still not yet broken completely with Spain. But, for the first time, she was committed to fight Philip II openly and, as it turned out, committed more heavily than she had bargained for.

In France, Anjou's death upset the precarious equilibrium of the previous years. Henry of Navarre was now the immediate heir to the throne. Faced with the spectre of a heretic king, the Catholics resurrected the League. It started as a secret society of a small number of fanatical Catholics among the Parisian bourgeoisie, mostly priests and professional men. Its discipline, dedication to the cause, and puritanical insistence on the personal virtue of its members were as severe as in any Calvinist community. When this society had built up a strong party among the artisans, guilds and public officials of Paris it entered into relations with Guise and the Catholic princes. Immediately, the old League of 1576 reappeared all over France. The signal was a declaration of the old cardinal of Bourbon, the cat's-paw of Guise, claiming the succession against the heretic Henry of Bourbon. In town after town, the Leaguers removed royalist commanders and governors and replaced them by their own men, on the pretext of insuring a firm anti-Huguenot policy. Not for the last time, a moderate government fighting a revolutionary movement found itself outbid by an extremist party on its own side.

On 31 December 1584 Philip II concluded the Treaty of Joinville with Guise and the League. They agreed to recognise the succession of the cardinal of Bourbon and jointly to destroy heresy. Philip was to advance the League 50,000 ducats a month and give military help, if necessary. In return, the League promised to help Philip recover French Navarre, Cambrai and other towns to which he laid claim, and to continue the alliance after victory. Philip II had thus achieved what his father had always vainly striven for: alliance with a Catholic France under the leadership of Spain; but he had got it only from one party in France. The treaty itself remained secret; but the League's contacts with the Spanish ambassador, Bernardino de Mendoza, were evident. Henry III and Catherine were thoroughly frightened and once more veered towards the League. On 7 July 1585 Catherine and Guise concluded the Treaty of Nemours in which the king promised to abolish all previous edicts of pacification with the Huguenots. Navarre had now no choice but to start the civil war again.

Not only was Guise now financially dependent on Spain for his French policy; he also had to give up all his Scottish and English plans so as to be able to concentrate on the French succession question. This left Philip II free to pursue his own plans. Now that there was no longer any fear of French intervention, it seemed most logical to move against England. The English queen was under sentence of excommunication; she was oppressing her Catholic subjects; and she was keeping prisoner a queen whose title to the English throne was regarded by most Catholics as better than her own. It seemed, moreover, that only English help enabled Philip's rebellious subjects in the Netherlands to defy him. Religious, moral and strategic reasons thus combined to lead Philip into the 'enterprise of England', the invasion whose success must lead to the decisive defeat of Protestantism, to the restoration of the king's authority in the Netherlands, and to the strengthening of the Spanish leadership of Catholic Europe.

Philip's decision transformed the civil wars in France and the Netherlands into open European war. Since the French monarchy had surrendered its initiative to the League and since the League was dependent on Spain, the political opposition to Spain was now left entirely to the Protestants. For the first and last time, the lines of political and religious division coincided completely. To the whole of Europe it seemed that the decisive phase of the great struggle was now beginning.

The invasion of England was not a new idea. Philip's admiral, the marquis of Santa Cruz, had urged it already in 1583. From the spring of 1585 Philip began to plan it seriously. His financial position had improved since the bankruptcy of 1575. Shipments of silver from the New World had increased beyond all previous hopes.[1] The Spanish government received the quint (a 20 per cent tax) and other dues directly. The rest was shipped to Spain on private account and most of the money flowed into the hands of a comparatively small number of rich merchant and banking houses. They accumulated capital out of all proportion to their commercial needs. The Venetians and the Dutch merchants, in their heyday, carried on international trade with far less capital than the Ruiz, the Spinola or the Fugger had accumulated. The siege of Antwerp and the Dutch blockade of the Scheldt, together with the Protestant privateers in the Channel and in the Atlantic, made trade routes precarious and reduced investment opportunities. Even mining did not usually call for the investment of hundreds of thousands of ducats. Thus, the great financial houses could employ their capital only in government loans— a very profitable, but very precarious, form of investment. The Spanish government, in particular, could therefore obtain relatively cheap loans of enormous sums in the international money markets. These formed the basis of the vastly increased military and naval activities of the period. In 1576 the Fleming Oudegherste had proposed to Philip II the establish-

[1] See above, p. 25, for figures.

ment of banks in every part of his empire and the co-ordination of their activities by a council in Madrid. As in the case of most other proposals for the economic integration of the Spanish empire, nothing came of it. Philip II remained at the mercy of the bankers and their highly speculative bill-of-exchange transactions.[1]

When Leicester landed at Flushing (December 1585), the situation in the Netherlands was critical. Farnese—from 1586 he was duke of Parma— was advancing methodically against the Holland and Zeeland defences in the south. In the north-east the royalists had held Groningen from 1580, when its governor, the count of Rennenberg, joined the malcontents and made his peace with the king. In the other eastern provinces the Catholics were still strong and the authority of the States General precarious. The Union itself was dangerously disunited. The revolt against the king had been, among other things, a revolt of the provinces against a centralising government. Now the provinces were not minded to give up their newly won autonomy to another effective central government. Utrecht, Gelderland, Overijssel and Friesland were jealous of Holland and Zeeland and their dominating role in the Council of State and the States General. Holland was paying for about two-thirds of the whole war effort and was, in its turn, impatient of the susceptibilities of the poorer provinces. The victory of the reformed religion had left unsettled the relations between church and state. The regent class in Holland, the oligarchs who controlled the towns, had accepted Protestantism, but were, by upbringing and tradition, Erasmian and tolerant, just as they had been before the revolution. By contrast, the Calvinist preachers were intolerant and exclusive, claiming the right to supervise the religion and morals of people and magistrates alike. They were supported by the religious refugees from Flanders and Brabant and by precisely those classes, the petty bourgeoisie, the artisans and the workers, whom the regents had successfully excluded from power after making use of them in the revolution of 1572. The clash between the state and the Calvinist church therefore overlapped with a political and social struggle between oligarchic and popular groups.

Orange had lived and grown with these struggles. Through his personal prestige and the exercise of an astonishing political virtuosity, he had managed to remain above the party conflicts and prevent them from disrupting the Union. Leicester did not understand them and allowed himself to become the leader of one of the factions. At first there was much goodwill from nearly all parties. The States General made him governor-general and gave him wider powers than they had allowed to Anjou or Don John (January 1586). But immediately it became apparent how equivocal his position was. His acceptance of the office went beyond his instructions. Elizabeth refused to accept it for a long time, and the earl's authority suffered in consequence. But there was worse to come.

[1] H. Lapeyre, *Simon Ruiz et les 'asientos' de Philippe II* (1953), pp. 14 ff., 103 ff.

Elizabeth was still clinging to her policy of negotiating with Spain. She had sent Leicester to the Netherlands to bring pressure on Philip II, so as to obtain a reasonable settlement for herself and for the United Provinces. The Netherlanders, on the other hand, had lost all illusions about the possibility of such a settlement. They wanted to involve England in their war with the king. Between these divergent aims, Leicester's mission came to grief.

He quarrelled with Holland and Zeeland when he attempted to prohibit their trade with Spain and with the southern provinces—the famous *handel op den vijand*, the trade with the enemy which, so the merchants argued, allowed them to finance the war. The preachers regarded it as treason, and Leicester agreed with them. In April 1586 he established himself in Utrecht, the centre of the anti-Holland party. He helped to overthrow the oligarchy in the city itself and allied himself with the preachers and the popular party. With their help, and with the army, he hoped to bring the regents of Holland to heel. But he quarrelled with the Netherlands army commanders; his actions against Parma were almost uniformly unsuccessful; his troops were unpaid and mutinous. Desperately, he begged Elizabeth to send him more money. But the queen had paid as much as, or more than, she had promised. Her financial resources were limited and she was more anxious for peace than for war. In December 1586 Leicester returned to England to obtain more money and to restore his shaken position at court.

By January 1587 Wilkes, the English representative at the Hague, reported that 'we begin to grow as hatefull to the people as the Spaigniard himself who governeth his townes of conquest with a milder hand than we doe our frendes and allyes'. When English commanders betrayed Deventer and the fortifications of Zutphen to Parma, the States General took action. Jan van Oldenbarnevelt, newly appointed pensionary of Holland, engineered a purge of Leicester's partisans in the Council of State and had Orange's young son, Maurice of Nassau, appointed commander-in-chief. But English help remained more necessary than ever, and Elizabeth was persuaded to send the reluctant Leicester once more on his 'most perylous and most crooked voyage', as he called it (July 1587).

He continued to rely on the Calvinists, and his relations with the States General and the generals deteriorated still further. They accused him of negotiating with Parma. He denied it, but it was true. Elizabeth was willing to make concessions to Spain which the Netherlands could not accept. Leicester blamed Holland and Zeeland and threw English troops into a number of Dutch towns. For the third time, a governor-general was attempting a *coup* against the States General and again it failed. Elizabeth's policy of negotiation had lost him the support of his own party, the Calvinists and the popular movement, even in Utrecht. At the end of 1587 he left the Netherlands, broken as much by the incompatibility of aim of the two countries he had tried to serve as by his personal insufficiency for the role he had been asked to fill.

Leicester's departure sealed the victory of the alliance of the urban oligarchies with the Netherlands military commanders. The popular movement was everywhere defeated. The States General was now convinced that the policy of offering the sovereignty to a foreign prince did not work. In the controversies of the Leicester period, the Dutch pamphleteers had developed the theory of the sovereignty of the States General. This body now decided to exercise it and to obtain foreign help only by way of alliances. In 1589 Oldenbarnevelt persuaded the estates of Utrecht, Gelderland and Overijssel to elect Maurice of Nassau as their governor. Since 1585 he had been governor of Holland and Zeeland. His cousin, William Louis, exercised the governorship in Friesland. The particularist tendencies of the provinces in the States General were therefore balanced by the unifying role of the house of Orange and of Maurice in particular. But the precise nature of their relation, as of that between church and state, was not settled and was to lead to renewed conflict once the immediate danger from Spain was past. For the moment, however, this danger still outweighed all other considerations, even the bitter feelings between the Dutch and the English, and kept alive the uneasy alliance.

It is generally held that Philip II should have concentrated all his resources on the reconquest of the northern provinces at this moment, and that he might well have succeeded. Philip, however, had decided to strike at England first. Mary Queen of Scots had written to Mendoza (20 May 1586), making over her rights of succession to the English throne to Philip and asking him to take her under his protection. This gave the king the final moral justification which he craved for his plans. Parma agreed with him at first. From the early months of 1586, when both Parma and Santa Cruz presented detailed plans, preparations for the great expedition went ahead. The difficulties were enormous and Philip and his advisers were under no illusions about them, least of all about the superiority of English naval gunnery and the tactics the English were likely to pursue. Santa Cruz demanded 150 warships and 360 cargo and auxiliary ships, over 90,000 men and 2,200 pieces of artillery, all at an estimated cost of little less than four million ducats. These estimates could not possibly have been fulfilled and were drastically scaled down when it was decided that Parma's army in the Netherlands was to make the actual invasion. Yet it remained the greatest combined operation ever planned up to that time.

Inevitably, there were delays. The costs outran the estimates. Drake's raid on Cadiz (April 1587), pestilence and bad weather held up the preparations and every day's delay cost 30,000 ducats for just the pay and maintenance of the troops. In the first five months of 1587 alone, Philip sent two and a half million ducats to Parma, and yet the duke owed his troops several months' back pay. The Spaniards resented having an Italian as commander-in-chief, and there was the usual ill-feeling among Philip's ministers and generals. By the autumn of 1587 Parma had become convinced that the 'enterprise of England' had no chance of success. Philip himself veered between hysterical commands for action and his more usual inability to take decisions. In February 1588 Santa Cruz died. Philip had many experienced captains, but none of them of a rank to command the obedience of the others. The experience of the Granada and Lepanto campaigns had shown that only a prince or a very great lord would be obeyed. He could be given technical advisers if, as Don John had been, he was inexperienced himself. This, rather than his alleged preference for nonentities, was Philip's reason for appointing the duke of Medina Sidonia as commander-in-chief of the Armada.[1] The duke lacked Don John's spirit, but no Don John was available, and in courage and resolution he proved himself worthy of the finest Spanish traditions.

It was essential for the success of the expedition that France should be kept neutral. The renewed civil war therefore played into Philip's hands. From his point of view, it went excellently. Navarre defeated the royalists at Coutras (20 October 1587), while Guise annihilated Navarre's German allies a month later. Only Henry III had lost further prestige. In January 1588 the Guises imposed even harder terms on him than before as the price for the continued alliance. Henry had promised aid to Elizabeth if she were attacked. He might not give it; but Philip had to make sure that he was not even in a position to do so. Nor did the League trust him. They later claimed that they had planned a *coup* in Paris as early as the spring of 1587 or even earlier. Its timing, however, was controlled from Madrid, through Mendoza's contacts with Guise and the League committees in Paris, to coincide with the sailing of the Armada. Guise was to gain control of the king and Philip promised that he would then recognise the duke and the League as the provisional government of France, until the cardinal of Bourbon was crowned. He would help with money and troops, if necessary.

The Armada was expected to sail at the beginning of May 1588, though it did not, in fact, leave Lisbon until 30 May. On 9 May Guise rode into Paris, in defiance of Henry III's orders. Henry had a chance to arrest him, but hesitated. In the capital tension was at fever heat. The Leaguers had been rapidly gaining in strength and confidence. Their growing tyranny over the city has been brilliantly chronicled by Pierre de L'Estoile, their bitter enemy. The Paris mob, which had already proved its talent for murderous pogroms, was being systematically roused by the League preachers—for once the oratorical equals of the Calvinists—until every misfortune and every crime was attributed to the Calvinists and the *politiques*. There were rumours that Épernon, the king's favourite, was

[1] E. Herrera Oria, *Felipe II y el Marqués de Santa Cruz en la Empresa de Inglaterra* (1946), p. 87.

plotting with the Huguenots to set fire to the city. On 11 May Henry moved French and Swiss troops into Paris, but with orders not to take any action against the population. The next day, the Parisians threw up barricades and blockaded the isolated contingents of royal troops. The action had been carefully planned by the League committees and was directed by Guise. The king had to appeal to him to prevent a massacre of his troops. On the following day, Henry fled from Paris and Guise remained in control of the capital. The main object had been achieved. Henry was no longer in a position to intervene in the Armada campaign. The *coup* drew Épernon and his forces away from Picardy, towards the king and Paris, and gave the League their chance to occupy the province and cover Parma's flank against a possible attack by the king.

This success did not save the Armada from disaster (August–September 1588). For Spain it was not only a terrible moral and material blow: it also broke all hopes of an agreement with Elizabeth and ranged England irrevocably in the ranks of the Catholic King's enemies. He made plans for a renewed attack on England; but, more and more, his attention came to be focused on France. Here, it seemed, all Spain's failures might yet be triumphantly retrieved. Once more, Philip doubled the stakes. But Parma was convinced that he was only compounding his previous mistake.

During the summer and autumn of 1588 the League's power in France was constantly growing. Henry III had no choice but to maintain his alliance with Guise, and on the duke's terms. But the news of the defeat of the Armada restored his nerve. In September he dismissed eight of his closest advisers. They had been Catherine's creatures and this palace revolution marked the end of the queen mother's influence. The States General met at Blois in October 1588, for the first time since 1576. The League had again a well-organised majority in all three estates. They attacked Henry's administration on a wide front; they wanted decisions taken jointly by the three estates to have the force of law; they pressed the king to pursue the war against the Huguenots with more vigour and, at the same time, demanded sweeping reductions in taxation. Henry held Guise responsible for all his humiliations. The last straw was the duke of Savoy's attack on French-occupied Saluzzo. The king thought the attack was inspired by the League. He was wrong; for Charles Emmanuel was, as usual, only indulging his passion for power politics and nearly wrecked the Catholic alliance by causing a patriotic revulsion of feeling in favour of Henry III.

Guise had been warned not to trust Henry; but he was riding on the crest of popular favour and political success and despised the weak king. In his usual nonchalant way, he walked unarmed into Henry's trap, in the château of Blois, and was assassinated before the king's eyes (23 December 1588). His brother, the cardinal of Guise, was arrested and murdered the next day. Catherine lay ill when Henry brought her the triumphant news.

She remained sceptical about its effects. She died on 5 January 1589. The event 'made no more stir than the death of a goat', said L'Estoile.

There was an immediate revulsion against the king. The Sorbonne declared him guilty of murder and tyranny and absolved all Frenchmen from their allegiance to him. The League became an openly revolutionary party. They recognised Guise's brother, Charles, duke of Mayenne, as lieutenant-general of the realm for the cardinal of Bourbon, who was Henry III's prisoner. In Provence, the *parlement* declared for the League and the towns renounced their allegiance to 'the assassin Henry III'. Elsewhere it needed the appearance of Leaguer troops to overawe the loyalist provincial *parlements*. The League had a strong party in the council of almost every town. With the help of Mayenne's troops, or with the force provided by the retainers of the local Leaguer nobility, revolutionary governments were set up in almost all the major towns of the kingdom. Secret or open League committees, composed of members of the three estates, supervised the councils and imprisoned nobles and officials suspected of royalist sympathies. In Toulouse, always fanatically Catholic, the *capitouls* (mayor and corporation) declared for the League and, when the *parlement* wanted to maintain the king's authority, the mob invaded the court and murdered the president and the advocate general.

In Toulouse, as in other towns, there had grown up a fierce rivalry between the *parlement* and the corporation. The civil wars and the general insecurity had induced many of the wealthier burghers to withdraw capital from trade. They sent their sons to study law and bought offices for them. But the members of the high courts had progressively closed their ranks to outsiders. Their offices had tended to become hereditary, and the growing number of lawyers found their careers blocked. They had to fall back either on royal offices in the provinces or on municipal offices. Where, before the civil wars, town councils had been controlled by wealthy merchants, they were now run by a class of professional lawyers with political ambitions to which the merchants had never aspired. Half the deputies of the third estate in the States General of 1588 were *avocats* who, with their friends, controlled the municipal governments of France. They became enthusiastic supporters of the League ideas of popular (i.e. non-aristocratic) government and of municipal and provincial autonomy.

It was in Paris that the revolution was carried to its furthest extremes. The League organisation in each of the sixteen quarters of the city set up a committee charged with police functions and the supervision of the municipal officials. These committees, in turn, formed a central committee, called the Sixteen after the number of quarters in the capital, but with an actual membership of up to fifty. The Sixteen introduced the first revolutionary reign of terror that Paris was to experience. To co-ordinate the movement over the whole country, the Sixteen sent their agents to the provinces and received those of the provincial towns. The general council of the League thus controlled the whole network of autonomous Leaguer towns in France.

Henry III completely failed to follow up such advantage as he had gained from the murder of the duke of Guise. Within three months, his writ ran only in the towns of the Loire valley. In April 1589 he accepted the logic of the situation and allied himself with Henry of Navarre. With combined forces they moved on Paris and started the first siege of the capital. Paris seemed lost to the League, when a fanatical friar, Jacques Clément, struck down the king (1 August 1589). As he was dying, Henry III recognised Navarre as his successor if he agreed to become a Catholic. The three persons mainly responsible for the massacre of St Bartholomew had died within the space of eight months, two of them by assassination.

France now had two kings, the Huguenot king of Navarre, Henry IV of France, and his prisoner, the cardinal of Bourbon, whom the League and the Catholic powers recognised as Charles X. Henry had been a very different Huguenot leader from Coligny. His mother had brought him up as a Protestant, but he had none of Coligny's intense and compelling religious conviction. He made up for it by a grasp of political realities and a sense of opportunity which rivalled that of William of Orange. Where Coligny had imposed himself on his followers by his singleness of purpose and his severe integrity, Henry won men by a personal magnetism compounded of courage, military competence and, not least, personal charm. His manner masked an authoritarian temperament as strong as that of Philip II. He kept it well under control until he could afford to indulge it. He sought even less than Coligny had done to overturn the political institutions of France or to weaken the crown to which he himself hoped to succeed. He had made his position clear, in March 1589, when he declared that he agreed to be instructed in the Catholic faith but refused to give up his beliefs simply to gain a crown, or thirty crowns. He would never impose his religion on Catholic France, he said, but his Huguenot co-religionists would equally not be converted by the sword. This declaration was insufficient for a large number of royalists who deserted him for the League or for an uneasy neutrality. Henry had to raise the siege of Paris.

There was now a good chance of preventing Henry's succession if all the Catholic parties could co-operate. But their interests were too divergent. Philip instructed Mendoza to put forward his own claims to the throne of France, or those of his daughter, Isabella Clara Eugenia, together with his claim to be recognised as protector of the Catholic religion in the kingdom of France. The pope, however, thought that this protectorate belonged to himself. The tense relations between Philip II and Sixtus V now deteriorated alarmingly. They had never been good, for Sixtus had tried throughout his pontificate (1585–90) to keep some degree of independence for the papacy against the overwhelming power of Spain. He had confirmed Navarre's excommunication in 1585, when he thought that Henry III and the League were really co-operating against the Protestants. But Philip's open intervention in France, after the death of Henry III, made the pope afraid that the only Catholic power which could possibly counterbalance Spain would lose its independence. This was the argument put to him by the Venetians, who were the first Catholic power to recognise Henry IV, and he was impressed by it. Philip II, for his part, argued that he was offering all his resources for the defence of the church. How feeble were the pope's own forces by contrast. As the weaker part, he should follow the stronger; it was the least the king could expect. Early in 1590 Spain and the papacy were nearer a complete breach than they had been since the time of Paul IV.

Sixtus V died on 27 August 1590 and the election of a more tractable pope now became a matter of vital importance for the success of Philip's plans. Up to this point, he had not directly interfered in papal elections. His representatives in Rome had simply been ordered to further the election of a pious pope and to exclude any candidate who was pro-French. This time, his ambassador, the count of Olivares, presented the conclave with a list of names from which alone they might choose. The majority of the cardinals received pensions or revenues from Spain or the Spanish dominions in Italy. Their families depended on Spanish patronage for their advancement. To a greater or a lesser degree, they were sensitive to Spanish pressure. Olivares applied this pressure skilfully and ruthlessly, both in the election of Urban VII (Castagna), who died after twelve days, and in the long and bitter contest over the election of Gregory XIV (Sfondrato). Olivares went far beyond his instructions; but Philip did not disown him—a foretaste of the position under Philip III, when Spanish policy was made by ambitious and self-willed viceroys and ambassadors in Italy and Germany. Gregory XIV was an ardent supporter of the League. He sent money and troops to France, as well as backing the League with the moral authority of his office. His death, in October 1591, was a serious loss to Spain; but, once more, Olivares had his own candidate elected.

In the end, Spanish tactics were self-defeating. When Innocent IX died in December 1591, there had grown up a determined opposition in the college of cardinals against allowing the pope to become 'the king of Spain's chaplain'. In the most closely fought and dramatic of all recorded elections, Philip's preferred candidate was defeated (January 1592) and the conclave elected the young Cardinal Aldobrandini as a compromise candidate. Clement VIII was not anti-Spanish, but he was no longer dependent on Spain like his predecessors. His political views were formed under Sixtus V, who had bestowed the cardinal's hat on him. He could not immediately withdraw his help from the League, but he was not unwilling to listen to Henry IV's emissaries. The king would have to prove the sincerity of his return to the church before the pope would absolve him. But the door to reconciliation was no longer closed.

Philip might temporarily control the papacy: he could not equally control his other allies. The death of the cardinal of Bourbon (May 1590) brought a host of claimants to the French crown into the field. Charles Emmanuel of Savoy and the duke of Lorraine soon withdrew from the race by modestly limiting their claims to kingdoms in Provence and Champagne, and they sent their troops into these provinces. Mayenne had his own designs on the French crown, but did not see eye to eye on this matter even with his own family. He distrusted the Spaniards, yet could not do without their help. In March 1590 Henry defeated him at Ivry and then began the siege of Paris for the second time. Supplies ran out and thirteen thousand were reckoned to have died of hunger. But the League preachers and the régime of terror of the Sixteen prevented a surrender. In September the duke of Parma with his Spanish veterans relieved the city. Spanish armies now operated in Brittany and Languedoc. It looked as if France would break up like the Netherlands. In 1592 Parma once more intervened to save Rouen from Henry.

Mayenne could not even control his own party, the League. More honest and less romantic than his brother had been, this fat and ambitious aristocrat lacked Duke Henry's personal magnetism and his ability of gaining both the confidence of his fellow noblemen and the enthusiastic admiration of the popular sections of the League. The aristocratic members of the general council of the League were becoming increasingly uneasy about the revolutionary and democratic policy of the Sixteen. L'Estoile was not alone in resenting the appointment of 'small tradesmen and a bunch of Leaguer scoundrels' to the captaincies of the citizen guards and to high municipal offices. Already in February 1589 Mayenne had tried to counterbalance the popular wing in the general council by appointing to it fourteen members of the Parisian *haute bourgeoisie* and the *parlement*. The Sixteen answered by setting up a Committee of Public Safety, with ten members, selected by themselves. In November 1591 they struck against their most hated enemy in Paris, the *parlement*. Brisson, its president, and two councillors were arrested and executed for alleged treason. The act was justified, in a very modern fashion, both by the highly doubtful claim that the other members of the court had agreed with it and by the argument that treason against the public must be punished even by illegal means if legal ones were not sufficient.

This act made the breach between the nobles and the Sixteen irreconcilable. Mayenne arrested several of the Sixteen in December 1591; but he refused to act against the preachers or to destroy the Sixteen completely. Yet his attempt to hold together and balance the aristocratic and the revolutionary wings of the League was doomed to failure, just as was the similar attempt by the prince of Orange in the parallel situation in Flanders and Brabant ten years earlier.

The break-up of the Catholic front became most apparent in the States General of 1593. Mayenne had summoned it, with much reluctance, under pressure from Philip II. The Spanish ambassadors put forward the claims of the Infanta, arguing that the need to prevent the succession of a heretic justified setting aside the Salic Law, which reserved the succession to males. But Mayenne was offended and the delegates were hostile. They preferred to negotiate with Henry. With superb timing, the king now announced his decision to return to the Catholic church. The ceremony took place at St Denis on 25 July 1593. The only effective bond between the different sections of the League, fear of a heretic king, had now disappeared. France threw herself into the arms of the king, as the Leaguer Jean de Tavannes said. Henry was liberal in his bribes of money, estates and offices to the commanders and towns who accepted his authority. It was much cheaper than having to conquer them, he told the scandalised Sully. The lower nobility, lacking the bargaining counters of the princes and generals, had for some time begun to play for safety by placing a son in each of the opposing camps.

Paris was isolated. The interurban organisation of the League was broken by Mayenne's intrigues and by Henry's renewed advance in 1594. Mayenne had undermined the position of the revolutionary leaders by his 'Thermidor' of 1591. They were left with only one ally, the Catholic autocrat, Philip II of Spain. It was the *reductio ad absurdum* of revolution and it was its end. Parma had died in December 1592 and the Spanish armies in the Netherlands were no longer in a position to come to the rescue when Henry marched on Paris for the third time. He entered his capital, almost unopposed, on 22 March 1594. As on every other occasion, he took no revenge on those who had opposed him so bitterly. Only a small number of the preachers and leaders of the League were banished for a short time.

It was the paradox of the revolutionary movements of the sixteenth century that they were led by men who were not revolutionaries. Condé and Navarre, Orange, Guise and Mayenne did not create the organisations of their parties. Their aim, as that of many aristocratic rebels before them, was to capture the existing machinery of state, without overturning the social order or radically changing the political, or even religious, structure of their country. Yet they found themselves carried far along the path of political and social revolution by the parties of which they were the leaders. The lower nobility, who formed the most active elements in all the movements, together with the rich burghers and impoverished artisans of the citizen guards, were the real revolutionary forces. They were effectively revolutionary by virtue of their economic ambitions and their religious beliefs. Religion was the binding force that held together the divergent interests of the different classes and provided them with an organisation and a propaganda machine capable of forming the first genuinely national and international parties in modern European history; for these parties never embraced more than a minority of each of their constituent classes. It was through religion that they could appeal to the lowest classes and the mob to vent the anger of their poverty and the despair of their unemployment in fanatical looting and in barbarous massacres. Social and economic discontent were fertile ground for recruitment by either side, and popular tyranny appeared both in Calvinist Ghent and in Catholic Paris.

In the long run, not even religion could reconcile the nobles with popular dictatorship and one side or the other was driven into alliance with the former common enemy. The result was, in every case, the break-up of the revolutionary party and the defeat of the popular movement. Where the nobles and the patricians in the towns managed to maintain control over the revolutionary movement, they also managed to achieve a great part of their political and religious aims. But, once firmly in the saddle, they could afford to abandon the greater part of their revolutionary organisation. Only in the field of religion did they carry their revolutions to the full conclusion. Yet neither with the Dutch Calvinists nor with the French Huguenots did the radical wing succeed in setting up a rigorous theocracy on the Geneva model. When the parties lost their revolutionary impetus and their preaching its social content, they rapidly lost the support of the lower classes. The devastations caused by the wars of the League and the increasing misery of the French peasants produced a growing number of peasant movements directed against the seigneurs and their rents, against the clergy and their tithes, and against the tax collectors and their *taille*; but they took no account of religion or the political parties. These *jacqueries* culminated in the movement of the Croquants in central and southern France in 1594–5. They fought a pitched battle against a league of seigneurs, formed for the sole purpose of defeating them. This and many similar outbursts in the seventeenth century throw a sombre light on the rural society and the tax system of France; but they remained without political effect until the revolution of 1789.

In January 1595 Henry IV declared war on Spain. He succeeded where Coligny had failed, in unifying France against her external enemy. In September Clement VIII was finally induced to absolve Henry, after overcoming his anger at the Gallican church which had claimed the power to do this without the pope. The papal absolution brought most of the remaining Leaguers onto the king's side. Mayenne made his peace in October, and only the duke of Mercœur in Brittany held out until 1598. In international relations, as in the internal affairs of France, the war with Spain was a victory for the *politique* idea of the primacy of the demands of the state over those of religion. The European state system was beginning to crystallise. Only ten years before, the Dutch had still been searching for a foreign sovereign. Now, the United Provinces of the Netherlands were accepted as equal partners in an alliance by the king of France and, with some reluctance, by the queen of England. Effectively, Spain was no longer engaged in putting down a rebellion and in intervening in a civil war, but in open warfare against the major powers of western Europe.

The strain of this war proved too much for Spain's financial resources. The Cortes of Castile, powerless but outspoken, had as early as 1588 demanded to know whether France, Flanders and England would really be better if Spain were poorer. Five years later their irony was even sharper when they petitioned the king to withdraw his armies from the Netherlands and France, for in this way the rebels who refused to accept the holy Catholic faith would be most effectively punished, 'for if they wanted to be damned, let them be'.[1] In 1596 Philip's government went bankrupt for the third time and once again the crisis spread through all the financial centres of Europe. Yet the effects were temporary. Silver imports from America were still rising and on this basis Philip could continue to borrow. Whenever the Spanish armies could be paid, they still proved their tactical superiority. They captured Calais, over the possession of which Henry IV and Elizabeth had bitterly quarrelled (April 1596). A year later, they took Amiens. It took Henry six months of the most strenuous efforts to re-capture the city. Honour was now satisfied on both sides, and the papal nuncio was able to negotiate the treaty of Vervins (2 May 1598). Spain gave up Calais and, in most other respects, the conditions of Cateau-Cambrésis were restored. In 1559 the French had regarded that treaty as a major defeat; in 1598 they spoke of Vervins as 'the most advantageous treaty that France had concluded for five hundred years'. It was a sign of the dread which Spanish power had inspired in Europe during the reign of Philip II.

Elizabeth complained of Henry's breach of faith in concluding the treaty with Spain, just as the Dutch had complained about her negotiations with Philip in 1586–8. With some justice, both England and France distrusted each other; but the nuncio's hope of a Franco-Spanish alliance against England was much too optimistic. Henry maintained a benevolent neutrality towards England and continued underhand support to his Dutch allies.

Since the defeat of the Armada, the war between England and Spain had gone on without decisive advantage to either side. English attacks on the Iberian mainland in 1589 and 1596 (Essex's famous expedition against Cadiz) were spectacular but strategically ineffective. In between these dates, English commitments to Henry IV in Normandy and the attempt to hold Brittany against the Spaniards prevented attacks on Spain. Philip sent new and powerful armadas to invade England in 1596

[1] C. Sánchez-Albornoz, *España un enigma histórico*, II (Buenos Aires, 1956), 346.

and 1597; but they were wrecked by storms. English captains could maraud profitably in the Caribbean and off the Azores, or fight gallant actions against great odds like Grenville in the *Revenge*. But the Spaniards reorganised their navy and adapted their ships to English tactics. Their control of the ocean routes to the West Indies held. The English could capture isolated ships; but all the great treasure convoys got through safely.

In 1601 the Spaniards made one more attempt to attack England where they could expect local help. The idea of a Spanish landing in Ireland was not new: it had been seriously considered during the preparations for the Armada campaign. Tyrone's and O'Donnell's rebellion presented a splendid opportunity. The two Irish leaders were in contact with Spain. Already in 1596 they had asked the Archduke Albert to become their sovereign. The Irish rebellions had become an increasingly serious problem for the English government. Money and troops which could have been used in the naval war against Spain were diverted, as they had earlier been diverted to help Henry IV. But, as usual, the Spaniards acted too late and with insufficient forces. The rebellions in Munster and Connaught had already been defeated. The Spaniards could not break out of the small port of Kinsale where they had landed in September 1601. Tyrone and O'Donnell marched south from Ulster to join them, but were crushingly defeated by the lord deputy, Mountjoy. On 2 January 1602, the Spaniards surrendered on honourable terms.

The Spaniards had not found co-operation with the Irish easy. Both sides now blamed each other for the defeat. For both it was the end of their hopes. O'Donnell fled to Spain and Tyrone submitted to the lord deputy. For the time being, at least, Ireland was pacified. When James I, shortly after his accession in 1603, offered to negotiate with Spain, Philip III grasped the opportunity to end a war he could no longer hope to win. The Treaty of London (19 August 1604) marked the end of Spain's attempt to overthrow Protestantism in England. But she had successfully defended Portugal against all English efforts to upset Philip II's succession and she had retained intact her monopoly of the West Indian colonies and their trade. As in the case of the Treaty of Vervins, honours were even.

Philip II had calculated that success in either his English or his French plans would mean certain success against the rebellious provinces of the Netherlands. Parma, in Brussels and nearer the scene of action, saw the same interconnection of the political problems but drew the opposite conclusion: Philip's English and French plans would fail, and with their failure would be lost all chance of conquering Holland and Zeeland. Only with the greatest reluctance he led his army to the relief of Paris and Rouen, knowing that he was disastrously weakening his northern front against the Dutch. He returned from Rouen a dying man. Parma had been Philip's best general and, to the end, he remained undefeated. By his firmness and moderation he had lifted the king's cause out of the moral bankruptcy into which Philip's intolerance, Alva's terror and Don John's ambitions had plunged it. But Philip ignored his nephew's advice and in the end betrayed him, as he had betrayed so many of his best servants. Parma's enemies at court exploited his opposition to the king's policy. They blamed him for the defeat of the Armada. The Spanish captains in the Netherlands resented their Italian commander. He died just in time (2/3 December 1592). Unknown to him, the count of Fuentes was already on his way to relieve him of his post and send him back to Spain. Philip would not even trust him to retire to Italy as the duke had pleaded, for some time, to be allowed to do.

Fuentes, the brother-in-law of the duke of Alva, dismissed Parma's Italian and Flemish councillors and appointed Spaniards, in direct contravention of the Treaty of Arras. Once more, the old duke of Aerschot and the Belgian nobility protested, but to no avail; nor did the short-lived governor-generalship of the Archduke Ernest, the brother of Matthias, alter the situation. But the Spaniards could no longer wage a successful war on two fronts. The young Maurice of Nassau had reorganised the armies of the United Provinces. Methodically, he drove the Spaniards from Groningen, Overijssel, Gelderland and their bridgeheads north of the Rhine and the Meuse. Between 1590 and 1595, while the king's armies were fighting in France, he destroyed the favourable offensive position against Holland and Zeeland which Parma had built up with so much effort and skill.

From then on, the strategic position remained stable. In 1600 Maurice invaded Flanders; but the Flemings did not rise to support him. In 1604 the Spaniards, once more led by an Italian, the Genoese Marquis Ambrogio Spinola, captured Ostend. After that they also could make no further progress. Both north and south had now achieved reasonably defensible fronts.

None of the protagonists in the long struggle in the Netherlands had foreseen that it would lead to the permanent division of the country. For all their jealous defence of their local rights, the provinces had felt themselves bound in a common destiny under their common ruler. Yet, by the end of Philip II's reign, thirty years of war had hardened differences in religion, in the social and economic structure of society, and in political customs until north and south were separated not only by the lines of soldiers and fortresses but by an unbridgeable gulf of incomprehension and indifference. Just before his death, Philip made over the Netherlands to his nephew, the Archduke Albert, brother of the Emperor Rudolf II and of the Archdukes Matthias and Ernest, and betrothed him to his favourite daughter, the Infanta Isabella Clara Eugenia. The sovereignty of the archdukes, as the couple came to be called, was severely limited by secret agreements: the king retained the ultimate authority. Yet, in practice, they enjoyed a great deal of independence, and the weak government of Philip III followed their lead more often than it led, just as it did in the case of its viceroys and ambassadors in Italy and Germany.[1] The archdukes brought the Walloon nobility once more back into the government. Twice, in 1598 and 1600, they enlisted the help of the States General of the southern provinces to induce the northern provinces to return to their old allegiance, offering them complete autonomy and the exercise of their own religion. The attempts broke down over Madrid's unwillingness to let the southern exiles return and over the northern provinces' distrust of Spanish intentions. As Oldenbarnevelt saw it, it was ultimately a question of power. This became very clear when the archdukes overrode their States General's protests about increased taxes and ignored its demands to control government finances. The States General in the south was not summoned again until 1630. The provincial estates continued to meet. The nobility, the towns and the corporations retained many of their old privileges—sufficient to make them content with the régime of the archdukes and unwilling to risk another rising for the sake of union with the north. Belgium, with its own traditions and loyalties, was beginning to emerge.

In the north, all was self-confidence and optimism now. Military successes were matched by economic expansion. Amsterdam began to take over Antwerp's role of an international trading and financial centre. The refugees from the south brought new industrial skills and commercial contacts. The economically most important trade of the United Provinces was in Europe. The most spectacular development, however, was the appearance of Dutch ships in the Indian Ocean. Despite the war, Spain had not been able to do without Dutch goods and shipping, even for the supplies of her armies in the Netherlands. This trade was fiercely attacked in both camps, but it was highly profitable. In 1595 Philip II placed an embargo on Dutch ships in Spanish and Portuguese ports and confiscated a number of them in Lisbon. But even before this blow fell, the Dutch had decided to bypass the Iberian ports and to fetch their spices directly from the Indies. A number of companies competing for the East India trade were formed in the last years of the sixteenth century. Mainly for political reasons, Oldenbarnevelt induced them to combine. In 1602 the fabulous United East India Company was launched—for nearly two hundred years one of the world's most successful trading ventures. The Dutch now began to build their own empire at the expense of Portugal and Spain. Once again, they were taking by force what Spain was not allowing to its own loyal subjects; for the Belgians remained strictly excluded from the trade of the Spanish empire. The advantages of political independence could not have been more strikingly demonstrated. The United Provinces were entering their 'golden century'.

[1] For the internal history of the Spanish empire under Philip III, cf. vol. IV, ch. XIV.

But the war had to be brought to an end. The Anglo-Spanish treaty had left the United Provinces without an active ally. The Spanish government suffered yet another bankruptcy (1607). There was no means of raising the 30,000 ducats per month which Spinola demanded if the war was to go on. The archdukes started to negotiate. After forty years of warfare, the difficulties were immense. In the northern Netherlands, Maurice and the merchants of Amsterdam who had grown rich in the war feared for their influence and profits. Philip III was reluctant to let down the Catholics in the United Provinces and to acknowledge the sovereignty of rebels. The inevitable court opposition to Spinola and the archdukes opposed the peace. Dutch demands for the closing of the Scheldt and for free access to the Indies threatened the economic existence of the Spanish empire itself. Henry IV acted as mediator, but had his own designs on the sovereignty of the United Provinces. Thus it took two years of hard bargaining to reach a compromise. The Dutch gained most of their points; but only for the duration of a twelve-year truce (1609–21). Before its expiration Europe had plunged into another generation of war.

The three treaties, of 1598, 1604 and 1609, marked the failure of Philip II's grandiose plans of defeating Protestantism by establishing the political hegemony of Spain over western Europe. He had not started out with any such ambition. It was rather a policy which had crystallised in the last twenty years of his reign out of his reactions to a number of more limited problems and opportunities. To its achievement he had sacrificed the treasures of the Indies and the blood and property of his Spanish subjects. When he died on 13 September 1598, Spanish government debts were estimated at 100 million ducats. Interest payment on this sum amounted to about two-thirds of all revenues. The finances of the Spanish government never fully recovered and, in the seventeenth century, staggered from inflation to deflation of the coinage and thence to renewed bankruptcies. The fundamental weakness of the Spanish economy could not be remedied.[1] The crushing tax burden on the *pecheros* inhibited investment and economic growth. The social prestige of soldiers, ecclesiastics and civil servants drew the most enterprising elements of the population away from agricultural and industrial production. The success of a handful of merchants and financiers could not counterbalance this tendency. 'These kingdoms seem to have wanted to become a republic of enchanted men living outside the natural order of things', wrote the economist and moralist Cellorigo in 1600. Since the Spaniards could not themselves supply their colonies with the textiles, arms and other manufactured goods which they wanted and were willing to pay for in good silver, they had to import these things from their allies, rivals and even enemies. The Spaniards' zealously guarded monopoly of trade with their colonial empire did not prevent the rest of Europe from sharing in its profits.

[1] Cf. vol. II, pp. 320 ff.

Philip II had no eyes for these problems. He lived from crisis to crisis and gambled on the increasing yields from the silver mines of Potoís, always hoping for the great political success which would allow his treasury and his subjects a long respite for recovery. Yet the sacrifices had not been wholly in vain. He had defeated and contained the great Ottoman offensive in the Mediterranean. He had preserved Italy from attack and had given her a long period of peace. In the Iberian peninsula, he had continued the work of unification, begun by the Catholic kings, by adding the crown of Portugal to those he had inherited and by curbing the excessive liberties of Aragon. Most important of all in his own eyes, he had won great victories for the Catholic church. England and Scotland, indeed, were lost and so were the seven northern provinces of the Netherlands although, he hoped, not yet irretrievably. But he had saved Brabant and Flanders when they too had seemed lost. He had prevented the spread of heresy in Spain and Italy. Perhaps, he had also saved France; for had not his interventions forced Henry IV to buy Paris with a Mass? Everywhere in Europe, he had stiffened the resistance of the church against Protestant attack and helped it to win back lost ground. The Spain of the 'golden century', with its wonderful achievements in painting, in literature, and in religious and moral thought, was a self-confident society, a society which saw itself as the moral leader of Catholic Christianity, proud in the knowledge that its kings were the arbiters of Europe, that its soldiers defended Christendom from Turks and heretics, and that its sailors and missionaries were conquering continents for Spain and Christ.

Unlike the Netherlands, France had maintained her political unity; but only just. The Huguenots were disappointed and alarmed by their leader's conversion. They tightened their political and military organisation. There was talk of renewing the civil war: the 3,500 Huguenot gentlemen could still put 25,000 fighting men into the field. Henry IV may not have been sorry to see their threatening attitude. It made it easier for him to convince the Catholics of the need for a settlement. He had made incompatible promises to both sides; but he had publicly and often admitted his obligations to his old party and his determination not to impose either religion by force. The Edict of Nantes (April/May 1598), formulated after much bargaining, was in the tradition of the previous edicts granting limited toleration. The Protestants were granted freedom of conscience and the right to worship where they had worshipped before, except in and around Paris. They were also given the right to hold all public offices and in the *parlement* of Paris a special chamber was constituted in which ten Catholic and six Protestant councillors judged all cases involving Protestants. To guarantee the observance of the edict, they were allowed to garrison some hundred places of security at the expense of the royal treasury. In return for these concessions, Catholic worship was to be allowed where the Protestants had prevented it before.

It was a compromise which did not satisfy either side. The *parlements* refused to ratify the edict. The king had to make some concessions, to persuade, to cajole and to threaten, before they finally agreed. He showed himself at his most brilliant in this crisis. Clement VIII thundered his disapproval. The 'leap across the ditch' which he had taken with Henry's absolution could also be made in reverse, he threatened. But he needed French backing in the acquisition of Ferrara for the Papal States and, like the French Catholics, he finally gave in with bad grace.

The Huguenots had failed to convert France. Their 2,000 congregations of 1562 had sunk to less than 800. The northern and eastern provinces were almost wholly lost to them—one of the League's definite achievements. In the south, however, from Guienne through Languedoc to Dauphiné, they remained strong, a state within the state, and this in an age when few men believed in toleration as anything but a regrettable necessity and when nearly everyone was convinced that a healthy state must have no rivals within its boundaries. *Sub specie aeternitatis*, the Edict of Nantes may be regarded as a milestone in the history of toleration. To most contemporaries, it was a temporary shelving of the problem of co-existence of two religious faiths in one body politic.

The most urgent task facing Henry IV in 1598 was the economic and political reconstruction of France.[1] Most contemporary observers agreed that France recovered remarkably quickly from the terrible devastations of the last stages of the civil wars. The country's greatest wealth, her fertile soil, had not been destroyed. Hard work restored the abandoned fields and rebuilt the burnt houses. By 1609 France exported so much grain that it 'robbeth all Spain of their silver and gold that is brought thither out of their Indies', as the English ambassador reported. Sully, the king's old Huguenot comrade-in-arms, reorganised the administration of the royal finances. It became more efficient and a little more honest, but taxation was only a little less heavy than it had been during the civil wars. Sully made no fundamental changes in the French system of taxation. The *taille*, a personal tax, became more and more a peasants' tax. The nobles did not pay it and an increasing number of bourgeois obtained exemption by office-holding, by buying letters of nobility, or simply by usurpation. Sully managed to have a surplus of as much as one million livres a year, in budgets of perhaps 30 million, and Henry boasted of his accumulated treasure. But the hoard deprived the country of much-needed capital, and the heavy rates of taxation, as the estates of Normandy complained, weighed in peace-time on the country as if it were still at war. The sums which the government spent with much boasting on the rebuilding of roads and bridges and on the navy were a fraction of the king's household expenses. For the majority of the French peasants, there were few of the 'chickens in the pot' which Henry wished for them.

[1] Cf. J. H. Mariéjol in E. Lavisse, *Histoire de France*, VI, ii (1905).

Henry's heavy household expenses were not, indeed, all frivolous. He had to spend large sums in pensions to the nobility, to attract them to his court and to assure himself of their loyalty. The civil wars had been only a temporary solution of the economic and social crisis of the French nobility. Many had spent their fortunes in the service of one or other of the parties. Prices were still rising and it was difficult to adjust rents to keep up with them. Younger sons could rarely be provided for. There were still careers in the church. But the church, too, had lost much property during the civil wars and Catholic opinion was now beginning to demand a higher standard from its clergy than many semi-literate country gentlemen could attain to. Their honourable habits of violence and plunder were now frustrated by the king's peace. They found some compensation in duels fought in contravention of royal edicts and often organised as pitched street battles, in which they could kill each other by the hundred every year.

The high nobility, the towns, and great corporations like the *parlements* presented even greater problems. Henry had no difficulty in dispensing with the States General. At its last meeting, in 1593, it had fought not so much for a permanent political order as for the victory of an ecclesiastical policy in conjunction with a foreign state. Henry's victory therefore left it without power or support in the country to oppose his absolutism. The revived power of the crown appeared less as a suppression of ancient rights than as a victory over a foreign state. Contemporary political thought, especially as expressed by the lawyers, was now almost unanimous in its support of royal absolutism. In the Netherlands the anti-Catholic party had necessarily been anti-royalist. Its victory therefore led to the establishment of constitutional government in the United Provinces. In France both extremist parties had been, to some extent, anti-royalist and therefore constitutionalist. The royalist-*politique* party was, in consequence, anti-constitutionalist, and this was true especially during the League's attack on the monarchy. The victory of the *politiques* was therefore a victory for absolutism and the divine right of kings. 'The finest privilege which a people may have is to be in the good graces of its king', Henry said to the provincial estates of Burgundy.

But, in practice, it was not so simple. The last Valois kings had lost many crown rights, through grants or simple usurpation. Henry IV himself had been prodigal with them when he bought the support of the Leaguer nobles and towns. There were towns, and not only Huguenot ones, where his troops might not enter and where his writ ran only by favour of the local magistrates. The governors of provinces had usurped the appointment of crown officials. Henry's old allies, Montmorency-Damville in Languedoc and Lesdiguières in Dauphiné, ruled their provinces like princes. There was no short cut to the restoration of royal authority. Henry won it back piecemeal, by constant pressure and by skilful exploitation of favourable circumstances in individual cases. The great seigneurs were rigorously excluded from his council. Sully, though created a peer, came from a minor noble family and was a Huguenot and therefore without following among the Catholics. In any case, he was very unpopular. Henry's other councillors came from the nobility of the robe, the 'penne and inkhorne gentlemen', as the English ambassador said. They had been formerly servants of Henry III or of the League and were now devoted to the new king's service. The high nobility were dissatisfied with their exclusion from power, and especially the royalists and *politiques*, who felt, with some justice, that the king was more generous to his former enemies than to the friends who had stood by him in his adversity. The two most dangerous conspiracies of the reign were headed by Henry's old allies, Marshal Biron and the duke of Bouillon.

The crown did not even have full control over its own officials. No other country had as many as France, from the councillors of the *parlements* at the top to the officers of the *sénéchaussées* and the *bailliages* and down to the humble guild and market officials. The crown sold these offices for their revenues and for the status they gave their holders, and constantly created new ones. It was estimated that there were more than 50,000. During the civil wars, sales of and appointments to offices had become part of the aristocratic patronage system and the princes of the League had used it skilfully to win supporters in the towns. When the succession of Henry IV became certain, office-holders appointed by the League began to fear for the legality of their position and deserted the League for the king. This movement explains much of the political landslide of 1593–5. In 1604 Sully introduced the *paulette*, an annual tax of 4*d*. in the £ on the value of offices, payment of which made the offices hereditary. The original purpose of the tax was probably financial; but it had the effect of making officials less dependent on the patronage of the high nobility and, for this reason, it was later defended by Richelieu. It also associated a large section of the propertied classes with the monarchy and the government of the country. As the English ambassador wrote in 1609, the king was 'sharing the booty gotten from the common people...with the clergy, nobility, gentry and officers of justice...At least in time of peace they go jollily with it; but yet not without danger, if the times should change.'[1]

War-weariness and Henry's intelligence and determination, coupled with his great personal charm, allowed the monarchy to regain many lost positions. But the political situation remained unstable. The king's death and a renewed minority, as many observers had foreseen, threw the fate of the French monarchy once more into the balance.

Henry IV had concluded the peace with Spain because he needed it for his work of reconstruction and because he had achieved his immediate

[1] Sir G. Carew, 'A Relation of the State of France', in T. Birch, *An Historical View of the Negotiations between the Courts of England, France and Brussels* (1749), p. 462.

object, the restoration of the frontiers of France. The old hostility, how-
ever, remained, for the ultimate problem of power in western Europe had
not yet been settled. Since neither side could afford open war, both now
directed their policies towards the small states on the borders of France:
Savoy, the Swiss cantons, Lorraine and the German principalities on the
Rhine. Here was the strategic route, the famous Spanish Road by which
Spain kept open her communications between Italy and the Netherlands.
When the Dutch and the English blocked the Channel there was no other
route, except much further east, through the Valtelline; but this route was
considered neither politically safe nor topographically convenient. Both
sides therefore used every diplomatic trick to retain or gain control over
the Spanish Road and, from time to time, also over the Valtelline. Only
once did they slide into open warfare. When Charles Emmanuel failed to
return Saluzzo, which he had occupied in 1588, Henry invaded Savoy.
The threatening attitude of Spain induced him to conclude a rapid but
not unfavourable peace. He gave up Saluzzo in return for Bresse, Bugey
and Gex, French-speaking Savoyard territories west of the Rhône (Treaty
of Lyons, 17 January 1601). It meant at least a temporary French withdrawal from Italy and left Charles Emmanuel free for his last, unsuccessful, attempt on Geneva (1602). But the Spanish Road had now, at one
important point, been reduced to a narrow tongue of Savoyard territory,
the Pont de Grésin in the Val de Chézery, which preserved the link between
Savoy and Spanish Franche-Comté. The French could, and on occasion
did, quite easily cut this link.[1]

The Spanish peace with England and the truce with the United Provinces did nothing to diminish Franco-Spanish tension. When a dispute
arose over the succession of the duchies of Juliers, Berg and Cleves, and
involved the emperor with the Protestant Union, Henry IV decided to
intervene, to prevent an extension of Habsburg power on the lower Rhine.
The diplomatic situation was not favourable. England and the United
Provinces would not break with Spain. The Protestant princes of Germany
did not look with enthusiasm on French intervention in Germany. Charles
Emmanuel, with his eyes on Milan, urged Henry on; but his previous
career did not inspire confidence either in his strength or in his reliability.
Yet Henry seemed determined on a show-down. New and highly unpopular
taxes were imposed; the army was put on a war footing. His attitude
towards Brussels and Madrid became increasingly threatening. With the
archdukes he had a personal quarrel. He had pursued the beautiful wife
of the young prince of Condé. Condé had fled to Brussels taking his rather
unwilling lady with him. The archdukes saw their honour engaged and
refused to send them back to France. Another of Henry's light-hearted
love affairs had suddenly taken a grave political turn. Condé, whose name

[1] I wish to thank Mr Geoffrey Parker for much of the information contained in this
paragraph and for drawing my attention to the detailed literature on the Spanish Road.

evoked great Huguenot memories, was nearest in succession to the throne after Henry's children by Marie de Medici, and grounds might always be found for impugning their legitimacy. Even then, war was not yet certain. It would not have been the first time that Henry had used his love affairs to cover more subtle political designs. His real intentions have remained a mystery. He was about to leave Paris to join his army, when he was struck down by the dagger of Ravaillac (14 May 1610). Like the assassin of Henry III, Ravaillac was convinced that he was performing a pious deed. Henry's eldest son, Louis XIII, was not yet nine. The regency government of his mother, Marie de Medici, immediately came to terms with Madrid.

Henry IV's death postponed but did not prevent the outbreak of renewed European war. Many issues had been settled in the fifty years since the Treaty of Cateau-Cambrésis. France had remained Catholic. England had maintained her independence and her own brand of Protestantism. The northern Netherlanders had won theirs, at least provisionally. But the great political crisis of the mid-sixteenth century had not yet been resolved, neither in the internal structures of the states of western Europe nor in their relations with each other. It was not to be fully resolved for another fifty years.

CHAPTER X

THE AUSTRIAN HABSBURGS
AND THE EMPIRE

THE Peace of Augsburg in 1555 marked a pause for breath in German affairs, with the failure of the Emperor Charles V either to establish an effective monarchy in the empire or to suppress the Lutheran heresy. Rather than be a party to the registration of the double defeat, Charles relinquished the authority to promulgate the legislation implementing the peace to his brother Ferdinand, the first of a line of rulers whose authority was to endure on the eastern marches of Germany for some three and a half centuries. The basis of Ferdinand's power lay in the lands that had been ceded to him and his descendants by his brother: the Austrian archduchy proper with its double set of institutions 'above and below the Enns', the various Alpine provinces extending from Tyrol and Vorarlberg to Styria, Carinthia and Carniola, and the scattered remnants of the ancient Habsburg patrimony in Swabia and along the upper Rhine. In addition, Ferdinand by his marriage to the heiress of the Jagiellons had acquired a claim to the crowns of Bohemia and Hungary with their dependencies, a claim subsequently fortified by a show of election by the parliaments of the two kingdoms, though there was some opposition in Bohemia and a great deal in Hungary. The possessions over which he directly asserted his sway thus extended impressively over much of central Europe, from Alsace to the Carpathians, from Silesia and Lusatia in the north German plain southwards to the Adriatic. In 1558 he was formally elected emperor in succession to his brother, and thereby won in addition a venerable authority over not only the rest of Germany but also northern Italy, parts of what are now eastern France and the Netherlands. Unhappily the real power that Ferdinand might expect to wield was much less than the sum total of his dignities might suggest. How tattered was the constitutional structure of the empire, we shall see. As to his lesser titles, most of Hungary lay in the hands of either the prince of Transylvania or the Turks, who since 1541 had occupied the capital city Buda and the central portion of the kingdom. Bohemia and its associated provinces were the playground of a powerful and unruly aristocracy. Even in the hereditary lands proper, the estates were far from docile. Most serious of all, the decay of the church and the infiltration of heretical

(*Editorial Note:* The author wrote, and would have preferred to have had printed, the words 'Reich' and 'Kaiser' in this chapter; but for the sake of uniformity has agreed to their replacement by 'empire' and 'emperor'.)

doctrines had everywhere complicated existing problems. Such was the general situation that faced Ferdinand, his son Maximilian II (1564–76), and his grandson Rudolf II (1576–1612).

On these three princes the verdict of historians has been critical, though, for sovereigns whose authority rested on the caprice of heredity, Ferdinand and Maximilian at least acquitted themselves better than most. None proved an outstanding political leader, though Ferdinand was an active and in some ways attractive man, more balanced than his elder brother, while Maximilian was lively, gifted and of an independent turn of mind; further, he knew how to compromise and how to make friends, and he avoided the extreme of religious partisanship. The family sensitivity to the arts was especially marked with Maximilian and Rudolf, but the latter proved disastrously unequal to the daunting demands made upon him. After receiving at Vienna the homage of his estates, he retired to the Hradschin at Prague and in the course of his long reign he became increasingly reluctant to leave the seclusion of this hilltop palace. He found pleasure in the company of scholars and pundits of various types, from Kepler, Tycho Brahe and John Dee to the most arrant of charlatans, and in the collection of curios and works of art. His wholehearted siding with the Catholics lost him much of the respect that his temporising father had received from the Protestants. But in his actions he grew increasingly dilatory: his intervention in the Cologne war, the fiercest German crisis of his reign, was so long delayed that it produced no effect. After 1594 he ceased to appear before the Reichstag. From the end of 1598 his mental stability became doubtful. From 1600 he was dependent upon menial servants for his contacts with the outside world; he was afflicted by long bouts of melancholy during which he ceased to discharge public business, while his ministers could gain no access to him and even foreign envoys found it difficult to procure an audience. As his malady grew upon him, he became less and less aware of the urgency and even the reality of his responsibilities, more and more overcome by suspicions and superstitions and incapable of more than petulant forays into politics. Government came to a halt, and ultimately the other members of the arch-house were goaded into the concerted action that led to his supersession. The personal concern of the emperors with German affairs, marked as it was with Ferdinand I and Maximilian II, thus dried up under Rudolf II. With him as emperor, the empire came gradually to possess little more than the shadow of an executive.

In each generation, Habsburg political weakness was enhanced by the division and subdivision of the family lands. What Charles V committed to his brother was no more than the provinces that had come to their grandfather Maximilian I from his ancestors. The whole Burgundian inheritance, though lying chiefly within the empire, passed to his son Philip of Spain, as did the duchy of Milan, likewise an imperial fief.

Charles indeed seems actually to have considered making arrangements for the imperial title to pass to Philip on the death of Ferdinand and thereafter to rotate between the two branches of the family, though fortunately this plan was not pursued. The Netherlands had been the financial mainstay of Charles V and the loss of their revenues was a source of weakness keenly felt by the Austrian Habsburgs. Ferdinand had continued the rudimentary efforts of his grandfather Maximilian towards centralising the government in the hereditary lands, and there had even been a project for erecting them into a single kingdom. Yet he in turn jettisoned even this precarious approach to constitutional unity and by his will he divided his possessions among his three sons. To his second son, the Archduke Ferdinand, there thus passed in 1564 the lands in south-west Germany and the Alpine provinces of Tyrol and Vorarlberg, the former with its strategic position athwart the route to Italy and its valuable copper and silver mines; the Archduke Charles, the third son, secured the other Alpine provinces of Styria, Carinthia and Carniola. The succession of the eldest son, Maximilian II, to the thrones of Bohemia and Hungary as well as the empire had already been arranged by Ferdinand before his death, but apart from these he inherited no more than the Austrian archduchy on the Danube. He thus had very meagre resources to sustain his dignity as emperor and also to defend the eastern flank of Christendom against the Turk. He in turn had six sons, but at this point the imprudent splitting of the Habsburg lands stopped. His eldest son, Rudolf II, succeeded to all his dominions and in 1578 was able to buy off the claims of his five brothers.

To offset this partitioning of the Habsburg possessions there was undoubtedly in every generation a strong feeling of family solidarity. It linked Maximilian II and his brothers, the Archdukes Ferdinand and Charles, just as much as it had knit together Charles V and his brother Ferdinand I. There were private family agreements and frequent intermarriages to re-unite every generation of cousins and testify to the strength of the dynastic tie. Maximilian II, for example, married a daughter of his uncle Charles V, and subsequently he became the father-in-law of his cousin Philip II of Spain and thus grandfather of Philip III, who in turn married another Austrian Habsburg. The Spanish branch was at a disadvantage owing to the intermittent threat of a failure of male heirs. For ten years, between the death in 1568 of Don Carlos and the birth of the future Philip III in 1578, Maximilian was heir presumptive to the Spanish and Burgundian inheritance. This expectation furnished him with good cause for hesitating to show more than very limited sympathy to heresy in his own dominions and even during the lifetime of Don Carlos it lay behind the despatch of two of his sons, including his heir Rudolf, to complete their education in Spain. It is not necessary to follow further the close pattern of inbreeding and consultation followed by the Habsburgs: the point is that the constant renewal of alliances helped in every generation to re-create the family solidarity that persistently guided the actions of individual princes from the time of Charles V onwards.

But more than family solidarity was needed to stave off the perpetual menace of the Turks, now firmly installed in central Hungary. The Austrian Habsburgs in this period were at a heavy disadvantage owing to their position as guardians of the eastern flank of Christendom against the infidel. Formal war was brought to an end by Ferdinand I in 1562, but with a treaty that left the enemy his conquests and bound the emperor to the humiliating payment of an annual tribute. Peace did not long endure, for in 1566 the intrigues of the prince of Transylvania led to the appearance of Sulaimān I in person at the head of a large army in Hungary, and the invasion of Austria seemed imminent. This was averted by the death of the aged sultan and in 1568 another agreement renewed the terms that had been reached six years earlier. There was outright war again during the thirteen years from 1593 to 1606, when an important treaty was made between sultan and emperor at the Hungarian town of Sitvatorok.[1] The latter paid an indemnity (disguised as a 'gift') and the frontier rectifications favoured the Turk; but the annual tribute came to an end and further formal conflict was averted for over half a century. On the land frontier between Islam and Christendom the distinction between formal war and peace was always very blurred. The authority of the sultan never sufficed to restrain his local commanders from forays and exactions, and it was seldom safe to assume that a large-scale invasion was not in fact brewing. There existed during the later sixteenth century in western Hungary and Croatia a broad strip of wasted countryside across which there was waged an unending conflict, commemorated on the Christian side by a collection of folk-tales and epics in which the exploits of local heroes and warriors were recounted. Behind the front, the tale was a weary one—of conscripts levied from the peasantry of the Habsburg hereditary lands, of taxes exacted from an exhausted population, of brutal mercenaries who cared little whether the countryfolk among whom they lived were friend or foe. At a higher level, there was the impecunious emperor compelled perpetually to seek money from the Austrian estates or from the Hungarian or Bohemian parliaments, or to procure aid from his brothers or uncles who ruled in the Alpine provinces. Beyond them, he risked the sharpening of political tension in Germany by convoking the Reichstag to ask for subsidies to finance his defences. In the further background, there stretched a diplomatic network from Poland to Persia and the golden chains that bound him to his incomparably richer Spanish cousin.

It is difficult to exaggerate the significance of the perpetual Turkish menace for Ferdinand I and his two successors. It is the most important external factor to be borne in mind when evaluating their policy inside

[1] See below, pp. 360–5.

Germany. A second weighty disability lay in the divided and intractable nature of the lands they claimed to rule in virtue of their family connections. The division of the inheritance has already been explained, but something must now be added with regard to the temporising policy they often had to follow in matters of religion. Indeed, a faithful yardstick by which their weakness might be measured is provided by the history of their dealings with their Protestant subjects in these territories. Hungary was perhaps a special case. It was an independent kingdom, unquestionably outside the empire; only its western fringes lay within Habsburg power and even here little could be done to prevent the propagation of first Lutheran and later Calvinist and even anti-trinitarian doctrines. In 1606 Rudolf II ultimately had to acquiesce, though with great reluctance, in the grant of full toleration for Lutheranism and Calvinism in his third of the country.[1] But Bohemia, too, was difficult to bridle. It likewise was an independent kingdom, and whether or not it lay within the empire was disputed by lawyers until the eighteenth century. It had been the classic land of heresy in the fifteenth century, and the doctrines of the next period soon took root there also. In the second half of the sixteenth century, Lutheranism predominated in Bohemia, but there were also Utraquists of various shades, Bohemian Brethren and Calvinists, while the orthodox Catholics were reduced to a disorganised minority and the propaganda of the Jesuits made no more than slow headway. The proud Czech landowners who had chosen Ferdinand I as their ruler were not afraid of admitting a foreigner with absolutist notions to the throne—they were sufficiently sure of their own power—and the dependence of the Habsburg kings on their purses, which were opened only when the parliament met at Prague, made certain a continuance of their liberties. Indeed, the need to keep on the right side of the oligarchs at Prague influenced at times the general policy of not only Ferdinand I but also Maximilian II.

In Austria and the Alpine provinces, the Habsburgs had a freer field for action. No original contributions to Protestant doctrine were ever made in this region, though from the 1520s onwards it was accessible to Lutheran views. The church was in poor condition to resist. Its property was heavily taxed by the government to pay for defence against the Turks, and often the prey of noble despoilers. Parish priests were frequently underpaid and ignorant, religious houses in decay, and the bishops, who bore at least some responsibility for the plight of their clergy, were apt to be distant prelates knowing little of their far-flung dioceses. It was a definite drawback for the church in the Danubian archduchy that it lay chiefly within the jurisdiction of the bishop of Passau and the archbishop of Salzburg, both of them imperial potentates ruling their own principalities beyond the frontier. Even in the later part of the century, they were not always very zealous, and as a result of their status as foreigners

[1] See vol. IV.

there was always liable to be friction, with a political tinge, between the spiritual and secular authorities in Austria. The Reformation in the Habsburg hereditary lands was introduced chiefly by the nobles, save in Tyrol where the peasants were most affected. The process was marked by the raising of demands by the estates, summoned regularly to vote money for the Turkish war, that the Word of God should be freely preached; by the introduction of Lutheran ministers to hold services in the castles of the landowners and to educate their children; and ultimately by the presentation to country livings of doctrinally doubtful or downright heretical priests. By the third quarter of the century, much of the country-side had fallen away from the traditional religion in all the Habsburg hereditary lands, especially Austria above the Enns. The bearers of the historic Austrian family names—Stahremberg, Windischgrätz, Traut-mannsdorff, for example—were now often Protestants. Only in the towns, whose citizens pulled much less political weight than the landowners, was the government able to hinder—though not to bar—the progress of Lutheran views. It was also possible to uproot the first seeds of Anabaptism and extremer heresies, since the Austrian nobles, unlike those of Bohemia and Moravia, gave them no support.

In the face of this onset of heresy, Ferdinand I acted with circumspection. His own faith did not waver, thanks no doubt in part to his Spanish upbringing. But such military resources as he possessed could not be spared from the task of guarding the eastern frontier, even for the suppression of heresy among his nobles. He took measures to arrest the further decay of church life, and for the rest he could but hope that the Lutheran heresy would in due course wither and perish as its forerunners had done: for a man of his generation, this was reasonable enough. Timely concessions might, he felt, hasten the process and accordingly his envoys at the Council of Trent pressed for a reform of the church, as well as for the grant to priests of the right to marry and to the laity of the communion in both kinds. For Maximilian II, the outlook was less simple, nor was his mind so closed to new ideas. Lutherans filled influential positions in his entourage, though how far he himself absorbed their views he discreetly concealed. He did not wish to alienate his nobles as he observed his cousin Philip II to be alienating the Netherlanders. He accepted the fact of the religious cleavage, and though he had no mercy for extremist sects he impartially encouraged both the revival of church life among the Catholics and the building of an official Austrian Lutheran church. He went so far as to procure a couple of Lutheran theologians from north Germany to organise the latter and to frame a liturgy for it. In 1568 the Austrian nobles, within certain limits, were permitted in principle to follow the Confession of Augsburg and in 1571 the use of the new liturgy was authorised for them on their properties as well as in their castles—it was a limited freedom, but the concession was great enough to anger the Catholics. It was only with the accession of Rudolf II that the policy of granting relaxations to the Lutherans came to an end and was bit by bit altered to one of increasing restrictions upon the exercise of their religion. Meanwhile, the Archduke Charles in 1578 had to give way to his Lutheran nobles and townsfolk, and not until his son Ferdinand came of age in 1596 could the extirpation of heresy in Styria, Carinthia and Carniola effectively begin. The Archduke Ferdinand in Tyrol had the easiest task, since he was faced by markedly weaker opposition. By the end of the century, heresy was thus in process of elimination from the Alpine lands, by the conversion of most and the expulsion of the stiff-necked few, and only in a handful of remote valleys could the peasants quietly cling to their Protestant faith.

Although the Habsburg princes, with the possible exception of Maximilian II, were all faithful sons of the church, the ultimate triumph of Catholicism in their family dominions owed only a moderate debt to their favour. Neither Ferdinand I nor Maximilian II sought directly to do more than limit the progress of Lutheranism, and Rudolf II from his distant palace at Prague could do no more than dismiss Protestant office-holders at court and in the administration, enforce the laws restraining the exercise of Lutheran worship and extend his patronage to the leaders of the Catholic revival. The march of the Counter-Reformation in the Habsburg hereditary lands, as in other parts of Germany, was a remarkable social movement, the spearhead of which was provided by the missionary and educational work of the Jesuits and other religious orders. The ultimate direction came from Rome, where the *Collegium Germanicum* for the training of priests had been founded in 1552. The reformed papacy was willing to spare more attention to German affairs and from the pontificate of Gregory XIII onwards it maintained in Germany four nuncios, each in a different region. The business of these emissaries included, besides the representation of the pope at the courts of Catholic princes, the supervision of the local church organisation, the watching of episcopal and other elections and the general encouragement of the faithful. The *Congregatio Germanica* was founded in 1573 to provide a headquarters at Rome for all this activity. In Germany itself, the most fertile centre of the Catholic revival was the university of Ingolstadt in Bavaria, now under Jesuit influence; although Ferdinand I had invited the Jesuits as early as 1541 to Vienna, their settlement there was not so influential as the college at Ingolstadt. A new generation of faithful and instructed Catholics was gradually built up and from them it was possible in due course to recruit zealous priests and bishops and so in turn to proceed to revive parochial life in the spirit of the Tridentine Fathers. By the last quarter of the century, the Catholic resurgence had acquired sufficient momentum to set about the final reduction of heresy. To analyse the inner springs of the movement is an elusive task for the historian, who can only point to such assiduous lives as that of the Jesuit saint, Peter Canisius, or chronicle the opening of schools and universities and the revival of pious practices.

The leader of the Catholic revival in Austria was Melchior Khlesl, the son of a Protestant Viennese baker, who was in youth converted by a Jesuit and subsequently rose to be chancellor of the university, bishop and finally cardinal. His most effective office was that of commissary for the bishop of Passau in the Habsburg lands from 1580 onwards, until in 1602 he became bishop of Vienna. In later life he was drawn into high politics and he played a not entirely happy part in the government and family affairs of the Habsburgs in the early seventeenth century. But it was under his guidance that Vienna and the smaller Austrian towns were in the later sixteenth century recovered definitively for Catholicism. In the rural districts, however, Catholic pressure and propaganda made at first no headway. Together with the fiscal and other oppressions that followed the re-opening of the Turkish war in 1593, they helped to provoke the peasants' revolt the next year. This bloody upheaval (1594–7) threw the landlords, Lutherans included, into the arms of the government. Gotthard von Stahremberg, under whose command the rebellion was put down, was himself a Protestant. His victory paradoxically opened the way for the Catholic recovery of the countryside, so that by the early seventeenth century the nobleman with his Lutheran chapel in his castle was the only significant survivor of the heretical onset that had once almost engulfed Austria; and his position was a precarious one, with his peasants alienated and the government increasingly intolerant in its policy. In Hungary and Bohemia, decisive military victories were necessary before the heretical nobles could eventually be brought to heel. But by 1600 Lutheranism was in a fair way towards extinction in the Alpine lands; and even in Austria it was now being closely hemmed in by the Catholic revival. With this religious transformation there disappeared one dangerous link that had in the past united the estates of the various provinces against the arch-house. The Habsburgs thus profited appreciably by the progress of the Counter-Reformation in their dominions, though they lacked—so far—the power and the personalities to exploit fully the favourable situation thus being created, or indeed even to pursue a firm or consistent policy at all.

The imperial title embodied a very ancient ideal and in the later sixteenth century it still carried with it an immense appeal and some authority. But the princes of the empire, in name the vassals of the emperor, were at one in a determination never to allow the evolution of a unitary state in Germany, on the French or English model, that would rob them of their long-developed autonomy. Yet there existed the framework of an authentic imperial constitution whose component parts were alive, and various attempts were made in the sixteenth century, from the time of Maximilian I to that of Maximilian II, to discover a basis of agreement that would make them more efficient. Although these efforts met with little success, the curious imperial institutions in their limited way functioned to some purpose during the first quarter of a century or so after the conclusion of the religious peace in 1555. There was a quiet discarding of much of the cosmopolitan panoply of earlier times and the structure of the empire was enabled to dovetail more neatly into the needs of the German governing class. In official documents the empire was now commonly described as 'the Roman Empire of the German nation', and it was symptomatic of this new national status that Ferdinand I and his successors were crowned neither at Rome nor by the pope but at Frankfurt by the archbishop of Mainz, and simply as 'German king': they then assumed the further and legally admissible title of 'Roman Emperor elect'. The realm over which their authority was recognised coincided more than formerly with the confines of German speech. The ancient suzerainty over northern Italy was hardly more than a diplomatic argument, the dukes of Lorraine from 1542 had turned to France rather than eastwards, and since the position of Bohemia was for all practical purposes that of a foreign country, there were few Slavs living within the empire. On the other hand, Maximilian II could still interest himself, admittedly to no practical effect, in the problem of the return of outlying non-German districts to his jurisdiction—whether the three bishoprics of Metz, Toul and Verdun, since 1552 in French occupation, or Livonia, the prey of contending neighbours from 1558 onwards.

The office of emperor was elective, although in fact during the sixteenth and seventeenth centuries it passed in agreed fashion from one generation to the next of the Austrian Habsburg family: to smooth the succession, it was customary for each emperor to secure during his lifetime the election and coronation of his eldest son as 'king of the Romans'. Although the lawyers ascribed the universal powers of a Roman emperor to him, his office was in fact greatly circumscribed by various restraints. All the emperors from Charles V onwards had to subscribe before their formal election to a charter of liberties (*Wahlkapitulation*); these documents on each occasion grew more elaborate and virtually turned the emperor into a constitutional monarch, entitled to wield his authority only with the consent of the Reichstag, or at least of the electors. The latter comprised three ecclesiastics: the archbishops of Mainz, Trier and Cologne; and four laymen: the count palatine of the Rhine, the margrave of Brandenburg, the duke of Saxony and the king of Bohemia. Their peculiar privileges tended to set them apart from the other princes of the empire, though the latter were jealous of their essential equality. The princely estate numbered some eighty members, fifty being ecclesiastics and thirty laymen. Next came the middle nobility of the empire; there were about 150 of these, some of whom, such as the counts of Oldenburg or East Friesland, were potentates as great as the majority of the princes. Below these again was the confused medley of knights of the empire, perhaps two thousand or more, each holding his territory of the emperor directly, even though it might be no more than a hilltop castle with a few cottages at its foot. Many of these were thus less powerful and rich than the great nobles owning allegiance to one or another of the empire princes. Finally there were the sixty-six free cities of the empire, little urban republics varying in size from major economic centres such as Lübeck or Nuremberg to mere fortified villages in the Black Forest. Not all German cities by any means were free of the empire; many had lost their independence in the later middle ages and some of the most famous lay inside the dominions of one or another of the princes.

The constitutional significance of the estates was expressed chiefly through the imperial parliament, the Reichstag. Its importance in German history had seldom or never been so great as now, for, owing chiefly to the Turkish threat, the emperors frequently found themselves obliged to summon it in the hope of raising money. It thus became a forum for the ventilation of the grievances of the estates, especially in matters of religion, and for the discussion of matters of general German interest. It met in one of the free cities, mostly at Regensburg, and sat in three houses. The first of these comprised merely the six electors (the king of Bohemia joined them only for the choosing of a new emperor), sitting in lordly isolation. In the second house there sat the other princes of the empire, each with one vote: there was a tendency in this period to refuse to create extra votes when the territories of a princely family were partitioned, though it was not logically pursued. Three representatives of the middle nobility were also allowed a seat in this house; the knights of the empire had no voice whatsoever in the Reichstag. The third house contained delegates from fifty-one free cities, though the validity of its right to concur or dissent in legislative matters was in dispute. Statutes binding on the empire were enacted when the archbishop of Mainz had brought the first two houses to agree on their wording: when imperial consent was given, they were then promulgated in the form of an agreement between emperor and estates. An older form of enactment, however, also survived and by this method the statute was simply published as an imperial edict—a good example of this being the regulation for ecclesiastical reservation that formed part of the religious peace.[1] The Reichstag also possessed the right to grant revenue to the emperor. The tax it voted was known by the peculiar name of 'Roman months', since it had originally been applied to defray the expenses of the emperor on his journey to Rome for the coronation. Now, it helped to maintain the imperial troops keeping the Turks at bay.

For a generation or so after 1555, the Reichstag remained capable of fruitful legislation. It was able to give some expression to an embryonic economic policy and at its best it was the clearing-house of German politics. The custom of sending proxies, though growing, had not yet become so widespread as to prevent its sessions from providing opportu-

[1] See below, pp. 337–8.

nities for personal contacts and informal discussions. It was able to delegate complex or contentious problems to a small working committee (*Deputationstag*) that met during recesses and could deliberate in a more businesslike way than the full assembly. Unhappily, meetings of the Reichstag were to prove increasingly ineffective in bridging the gap between the contending religious faiths. The Protestants held the initiative into the reign of Maximilian II, but the Reichstag of 1576 provided the occasion for the emergence of a determinedly Catholic party. Once the clear split on confessional lines had hardened, it was evident that in the second house the Catholics could count on the larger number of votes, while in the first the attitude of the elector of Saxony, often followed by his Brandenburg colleague, was generally moderate and favourable to whatever policy the emperor supported. Hence the more militant Protestants were tempted in the end to challenge the majority principle and so to disrupt the working of the assembly. The official business for which the Reichstag met was chiefly the granting of money to the emperor to finance his defences against the Turk, but once in session the princes were soon at odds over the fulfilment of the arrangements connected with the religious peace. In the last years of the century, each session surpassed its predecessor in bitterness and constructive legislation became virtually impossible. At the Reichstag of 1594 the Catholics carried their points by vote and the emperor got his subsidy; three years later, another Reichstag was followed by the refusal of the Elector Palatine and his allies—the 'corresponding princes'—to accept responsibility for the payment of a subsidy voted by the majority. Whatever the justification for this—and the political arguments were not without weight—it was tantamount to a denial of the authority of the Reichstag in one of its most important functions and historians usually reckon it as a milestone on the road to war. But it did not by itself rob further sessions of the Reichstag of all utility.

The empire possessed law courts as well as an executive and a legislature. The acknowledged court of the empire was the *Reichskammergericht* (chamber tribunal), a product of the reforming movement of the late fifteenth century whose final form was fixed in 1555. It was a court of appeal for Germany in only a limited sense, since its use was reserved for nobles and cities free of the empire; their subjects could be heard only in the rare instances when they were alleged to have been refused justice at home. Nevertheless, it did have some influence upon the course of German law, both in the maintenance of uniformity and in the entrenchment of the principles of Roman law. It was a creature of the estates of the empire rather than of the emperor, who merely nominated its president and four out of the two dozen other judges. It sat at Speier on the middle Rhine, at a respectful distance from the Austrian Habsburg lands. Down to 1588 its proceedings were annually reviewed by a *Visitationskommission* (appellate commission) appointed by the Reichstag. The defects of the *Reichskammergericht* were always marked and they tended to increase. The stipends of the judges were furnished by taxes levied in theory on the estates, which in fact were never fully paid. Consequently the judges were normally below establishment in number and the more experienced and effective among them were always liable to be lured to positions elsewhere, where salaries might be larger and more secure. The business brought before the court was considerable, and cases tended to drag on and on. The famous suit of the abbot of Fulda against the bishop of Würzburg, for example, was pending for twenty-five years before a verdict was given in 1602.[1] It is thus not surprising that the emperor should have attempted to supplant this snail-like body by a law court that should be both more efficient and more under his own thumb. This was done by Ferdinand I in 1559, when he turned his own court council into an imperial law court, the *Reichshofrat*; this body was undeniably more efficient but distrusted because of its complete dependence upon the emperor. It exercised a jurisdiction concurrent with that of the *Reichskammergericht*, and its activities markedly widened from the 1580s onwards.

Since the empire thus possessed in some sort not only an emperor but also a legislature and law courts, it may be asked on what administrative or military bodies it could rely for the enforcement of statutes or legal verdicts. The answer must be—on none. The constitutional reforms of the reign of Maximilian I had indeed given legal sanction to the institution of a number of local security organisations, known as Circles, with arrangements on the model of the empire for self-help in the maintenance of the peace; but the Circles operated effectively only in Swabia, Franconia and the Rhineland, where the small feudatories could co-operate without fearing that a powerful neighbour might exploit the Circle arrangements as a means of dominating them. One purpose of the elaborate *Executionsordnung* (security statute) of 1555 had been to enable the institutions of Circle and empire to be invoked against disturbers of the peace, but the application of this measure was a very slow and difficult business. The whole administrative and coercive apparatus of the modern state, with which the justices of the peace in England or the *gens de robe* in France were already long associated, was hitched in Germany not at all to the archaic and defective constitution of the empire but to the territories nominally subject to it, and in particular to those ruled by the more powerful or enterprising families. Nevertheless, the constitutional structure of the empire remained very important. There was, of course, the possibility that at some future date a capable emperor might discover the means to abolish the liberties of the estates and so create a unitary monarchy in Germany. But meanwhile, the existing laws and usages provided a framework within which the princes, knights and cities jostled each other and

[1] See below, pp. 339–40.

pursued their rivalries. There was a certain balance of power—between emperor and estates, between princes great and small, between Protestant and Catholic, even between law and disorder; and after the strife that marked the later years of the reign of Charles V, few were ready to risk toppling it over once more. The rules of the game—as allowed by the imperial constitution—might sometimes be circumvented or in an extremity openly defied, but nearly everyone paid lip-service to them and their existence provided for all a better security than the law of the jungle.

Within the frontiers of the empire there lay in the later sixteenth century several principalities of European importance, often ruled by men who as a result perhaps of the religious revival—Protestant and Catholic—were more conscientious or industrious than their grandparents and less prone to seek power by force of arms than by the development of an apparatus of government that should endow them with full control over the lives of their subjects. The historian anxious to study the origins of modern administrative technique in Germany must accordingly turn to the internal development of the Austrian archduchy, or the duchy of Bavaria, or the Saxon and Brandenburg electorates, for example, and not to the constitution of the empire. The greater princes were in fact marching towards full autonomy. They had their own legal systems, and with the *privilegium de non appellando* they were protected against any citation by their own subjects before imperial tribunals. They ran their own military forces—standing armies were yet to come. They were now elaborating their own internal administrative systems. The religious peace of 1555 had in addition legalised their power to make their subjects conform to either Lutheranism or Catholicism as they might be directed.

While it is difficult to generalise about the administrative progress of these leading states, some features common to all deserve mention. The essential weapon for the authority of the prince was everywhere his council, and in the most advanced principalities this was already being staffed by jurists and professional men rather than noblemen before the end of the fifteenth century. Princely councils in the sixteenth century thus tended to be boards of administrators well versed in the recently received principles of the civil law, using them to decide legal cases, and ready to turn them in defence of the rights of the prince against landowners, towns and church. In many principalities, an inner circle of two or three confidential advisers gradually took shape, to deal with the highest matters. Such 'privy councillors' were emerging officially in electoral Saxony by 1574, in Bavaria by 1582, and in Brandenburg by 1604. The council also kept a tight grip on the church. In Lutheran states there was no doubt of the supreme power of the prince; but also in the Catholic lands, from Bavaria downwards, the prince straitly controlled the organisation and personnel of his church, and no pope would dare gainsay him. Financial administration was also evolving as a specialised branch of princely government, with regular audits and with various departments supervising the collection of revenue from excise, forests, mines, and so forth. Parallel to the princely chamber that administered the patrimonial revenue, there was in the later sixteenth century frequently to be found a chamber of the local estates, for the supervision of the land or other taxes that they had voted for extraordinary needs. The power of the estates was in most principalities on the wane. In Bavaria and elsewhere, the chamber of the estates tended to be milked regularly for the benefit of that of the prince, until the distinction became blurred and faded away; but this evolution was not yet universal. In the creation of a professional class of administrators and in the organisation of the constitutional framework of the state, the Habsburgs in their hereditary lands frequently led the way and Austrian methods of government were imitated in various parts of Germany.

Which and where were the territories that were thus graduating as modern states, with administrations comparable to those now in process of development in western Europe? No exclusive list is possible, though it may be stated that with one or two exceptions they all lay inland and in the eastern part of Germany, where free cities and petty principalities cumbered the ground less thickly than to the west. The great bulk of the small rulers had no resources for supporting the new techniques of government and they continued to stagnate with a simple household type of rule until they were extinguished by Bonaparte in the early nineteenth century. There were perhaps a dozen or so secular principalities with resources available to support a more elaborate and effective administration and sufficient to sustain an individual political character. Among these, there stood out more particularly in the politics of the later sixteenth century, besides the hereditary lands of the Austrian Habsburgs of which something has already been said, the Saxon and Palatine electorates and the duchy of Bavaria. It may help to make clear the course of imperial politics if some attention is now given to these territories, each of which had a very important part to play.

The elector of Saxony ruled rather more than half the medieval duchy of that name: he belonged to the younger or Albertine branch of the family, while his cousins of the Ernestine and elder line controlled the remaining western portion. The electoral dignity had recently been transferred by Charles V from the elder to the younger branch and there remained much bitterness to separate the cousins. The elder line—usually referred to as 'ducal Saxony' in contrast to 'electoral Saxony'—provides a classic instance of the decay of family power through the division of the inheritance in each generation. Owing to the progressive fragmentation of its territory it subsided into a group of small principalities, while electoral Saxony retained its unity, which was guaranteed by the enforcement of a primogeniture rule. The output of the mines of the Erzgebirge had long given the electors of Saxony a useful, though now diminishing, financial prop, just as the Austrian Habsburgs had benefited from the production of metals in Bohemia, Hungary, Tyrol and Carniola. From 1553 to 1586 electoral Saxony was ruled by Augustus I, a staunch Lutheran, a methodical administrator of the new type, and in external affairs a politician of caution and of coldly calculated moderation. He used his position to complete the appropriation of various pieces of church territory adjacent to his dominions. But he also remained on good terms with successive emperors, and was especially intimate with Maximilian II. No doubt the consciousness that he owed his electorate to imperial favour had something to do with this, but he could in any case only profit by maintaining friendly relations with his neighbour the tolerant king of Bohemia. Electoral Saxon influence was thrown in moments of crisis fully into the scales in favour of compromise and peace —for instance, in 1569 when events in France and the Netherlands seemed to presage a new outbreak of religious strife in Germany.

In old age, Augustus grew hostile to the Protestant extremists under Calvinist leadership and he made an attempt to rally the Lutherans by sponsoring in 1580 the publication of a precise confession of faith drafted by approved theologians—the *concordiae formularis*.[1] Unfortunately, not all the Lutheran princes and cities agreed to it, so that in the ensuing years German Protestantism was split into three groups—Lutheran supporters and opponents of the formulary of concord, and Calvinists. Augustus's son and successor, Christian I, turned away from the formulary and under the influence of his minister, Dr Nicholaus Krell, took into favour the doctrines formerly developed by Philip Melanchthon. He also reversed the cautious foreign policy of his father and incidentally demonstrated during his short reign (1586–91) the pivotal position of his electorate by helping to bring about in 1591 the 'Torgau alliance', a confederation of the Protestant princes of the empire. This alignment was provoked by the continued presence of Spanish troops in the Rhineland. Its main purpose was to despatch forces to help Henry IV of France, but there seemed every prospect that such an army would be used also in Germany. It was thanks to the disappearance of the conciliatory Saxon voice that this cleavage of the German princes into two clear-cut religious factions was momentarily achieved, and the premature death of Christian was an important factor in now averting a general war. As his son and successor Christian II was minor, electoral Saxony fell under the government of regents, who fortunately returned to the traditional conservative and temporising policy. Krell was disgraced and later put to death.

The Palatine electorate was no less prominent than the Saxon in the politics of the period, though in a very different fashion. Its territories were smaller and less compact. They comprised two distinct portions—

[1] See above, pp. 82–4.

the Lower Palatinate on the middle Rhine, in the centre of the most disturbed region of Germany, and the Upper Palatinate, just to the west of the Bohemian frontier north of Bavaria. The Reformation had been only recently introduced when Frederick III (1559–76) succeeded to the electorate, and he found a medley of religious tendencies at large in his dominions. During the years 1562–4 he began to impose a new uniformity by remoulding his church in Calvinist style. This was a startling innovation and by imperial law illegal, since the religious peace entitled the princes to make their choice between Lutheranism and Catholicism only. The installation of Calvinism in the Rhenish Palatinate was full of implications. It not only gave this novel and fiery persuasion a firm foothold within the empire but also brought the elector into close touch with the Calvinist rebels in France and the Netherlands. The emperor, backed by the pope, did his utmost to set the machinery of the security statute of 1555 in motion, but without success, since nobody was prepared to use force against the elector. He accordingly went his way, which was a bold and independent one matching his sober but fanatical faith. Inside his principality, he impartially expelled monks, nuns and Jews. Externally, he pursued lively quarrels with his ecclesiastical neighbours the bishops of Speier and Worms, and to the west he embarked on a forward policy. With the aid of English subsidies, troops were sent under the command of members of his family on various occasions to succour the Huguenots in France—an additional underhand objective, never realised, being the seizure of the French-occupied bishoprics of Metz, Toul and Verdun. The adventurous projects of Frederick were in flagrant contradiction with imperial law, and they created much tension in the Rhine valley, but there was no means of bringing them to an end. The brief reign of his son Ludwig (1576–83) swung back the Palatinate to Lutheranism, but under his youthful successor Frederick IV Calvinism was restored. Meanwhile, Calvinism was making headway elsewhere: it was adopted by the count of Nassau-Dillingen in 1578 and by the free city of Bremen in the early 'eighties.

Like the Rhenish Palatinate, the duchy of Bavaria was ruled by a branch of the Wittelsbach dynasty, though the cousins by no means shared the same ideas in either politics or religion. Bavaria comprised in the sixteenth century a compact and sheltered block of territory on the upper Danube and its indivisibility was guaranteed by the acceptance of the rule of primogeniture by the ducal house from 1578 onwards. It population of less than a million was roughly comparable with that of contemporary Scotland. The dukes with whom we are now concerned were Albrecht V (1550–79) and Wilhelm V (1579–97), both of them cultured princes who patronised artists and musicians, notably the composer Orlando di Lasso, and whose Maecenas-like prodigality was a persistent cause of financial troubles. Both proved stout protagonists of the Counter-Reformation and

334

the personal piety of Duke Wilhelm grew so intense that in the end he abdicated and retired to a monastery. As in other parts of Germany, so in Bavaria the religious question in the mid-sixteenth century bore a markedly political tinge. Duke Albrecht was faced by the problem of a church far gone in laxity and disarray, while in his estates he had to deal with some forty or fifty landowning nobles among whom Lutheran ideas had made considerable headway—conditions comparable to those confronting his neighbour the Emperor Ferdinand in Austria. In concert with Ferdinand, he tried to procure concessions from pope and council, and he was on friendly terms with some of the Protestant princes of the empire; he preferred the pursuit of art and scholarship to the despatch of business and for some years he attempted to compromise with his nobles. But with the appointment in 1558 as his chancellor of Simon Thaddäus Eck, a good friend of the Jesuits, his policy hardened. In 1563 he boldly withstood his estates and followed this up by the seizure of the small imperial enclave of Ortenburg, whose count was also a landowner within the duchy and prominent among the Protestants there. Here the duke found evidence that allegedly incriminated many other of his nobles, who were forthwith arrested and tried. The constitutional opposition of the estates was broken and the way now lay open to the enforcement of religious uniformity. Avowed Protestants were before long forced to choose between exile and conversion, and attendance at Mass by the end of the century had become virtually a state duty. The reform of the church likewise proceeded, with Jesuit guidance, but under strict ducal supervision.

The political crisis of 1563–4 proved a turning-point in Bavarian history. It was not only that it enabled the duke finally to uproot heresy: there were also fateful political consequences. Ducal prerogative was henceforward not seriously threatened by any encroachments on the part of the estates, which were summoned less and less frequently and finally ceased to meet early in the next century, while administrative reform provided a backbone to the religious and political unity of the duchy. This internal renovation helped the dukes to step forward and play a major part in the politics of the empire, so that the later sixteenth and early seventeenth centuries marked the apogee of Bavarian influence in German affairs. Locally, the dukes presided over the Landsberg League, an association of principalities to maintain the peace in southern Germany. Further afield, the religious cleavage offered new opportunities: since three temporal electors were Protestants, and the emperors were embarrassed by their commitments and in any case unprepared by their characters to offer real leadership, Bavaria was able to take its place as the unquestioned champion of the Catholic cause within the empire. At Rome, Bavarian influence was strong. Even with the Austrian Habsburgs relations were close and friendly. The bittersweet rivalry that sharpened the relationship of the courts of Munich and Vienna down the centuries was briefly interrupted.

The neighbouring houses were connected by family ties, Duke Albrecht having married a daughter of Ferdinand I, while his daughter married the Archduke Charles of Styria; to his father-in-law and subsequently to his brother-in-law Maximilian II, he was an intimate and trusted councillor. The future Emperor Ferdinand II was educated along with his Bavarian cousins at Ingolstadt.

The most fruitful field for the extension of Bavarian power was provided by the ecclesiastical territories of the empire, most of which, as we shall see, were rescued for Catholicism. Imperial church lands had for centuries provided endowments and careers for the cadets of the foremost German families, not all of them in holy orders when elected. But since the Protestants were now ineligible for most of these plums, there remained all the more for the Bavarian and other Catholic houses. Duke Albrecht fully exploited the extended opportunities, tirelessly collecting for his younger son Ernest a series of benefices held in plurality. This young man had no vocation for the priesthood, being not outstandingly pious and far from chaste; but he was warned that, the duchy being now indivisible, only in the church could he hope for endowment. For clear political reasons, no pope could afford to refuse the requests for the necessary dispensations and confirmations now sought by the court of Munich. Prince Ernest began his remarkable career with a canonry at Salzburg when he was aged eleven, and he later accumulated the bishoprics of Freising, Hildesheim, Liège and Münster, as well as the archbishopric and electorate of Cologne. He thus willy-nilly became a great potentate in north-west Germany, with Spanish and papal backing as well as support from his father and brother. There were in subsequent generations frequent parallels to this episcopal pluralism; a major preoccupation of Wilhelm V was the provision of benefices for his younger sons, and family influence proved pertinacious enough to ensure the uninterrupted tenure of the electorate of Cologne by cadets of the Bavarian house from 1583 to 1761.

The political tension ubiquitous in sixteenth-century Germany cannot be ascribed to any single cause. Religious antagonisms had much to do with it, and so had the precarious balance of power within the imperial constitution. There were also the ceaseless local rivalries between princes, counts, knights and cities, springing from the most diverse roots, whether religious, fiscal, dynastic or merely personal. No complete survey of all these feuds or of the incidents to which they gave rise can be attempted in these pages, but it is possible to make some general observations and to map some of the contours in the decline of the empire as an effective body politic. The affirmation (though not in so many words) by the religious peace of 1555 of the famous *cujus regio ejus religio* principle as far as the temporal rulers were concerned enabled them to establish the faith of their choice—Lutheran or papist—in their dominions, without legal question. This undoubtedly lent some stability to conditions in eastern and northern Germany, where the principalities were large and preponderantly secular. There was no great obstacle to prevent such magnates as the electors of Brandenburg and Saxony or the dukes of Bavaria and Mecklenburg from enforcing their will upon their subjects. It was otherwise in the valleys of the Main and of the Rhine, where petty princedoms, church lands and free cities were crowded together and where at the time of the promulgation of the religious peace the frontier between Catholic and Protestant was neither clear-cut nor stable. An additional reason for unrest in western Germany was the propinquity of the Netherlands, where from 1568 onwards Calvinist rebels were fighting to maintain themselves, and also of France, where the civil wars were largely though not wholly connected with religion. Frontiers in sixteenth-century Europe were often indefinite things, and of the western marches of the empire this was especially true. The possibility of these various wars merging into a general conflagration was never remote. The Protestant cause, in both France and the Netherlands, drew soldiers from Germany, and Calvinism filtered eastwards from both countries. In the hour of French weakness, the Palatine princes sought territorial aggrandisement at French expense, just as Henry IV was later preparing to invade Germany to strike at the Habsburgs. Spanish troops from the Netherlands were used to support the Catholic cause in the Rhine valley—which was in any case part of a vital line of communication connecting Genoa with the Netherlands.

At the time of the religious peace in 1555, the forces of the Counter-Reformation had as yet barely begun to mobilise in Germany. Heresy was everywhere still encroaching. Among the greater lay princes, only the Habsburgs and the dukes of Bavaria and of Jülich-Cleve remained faithful to Catholicism. Almost all the free cities had defected. Especially precarious was the position of the ecclesiastical principalities, to which we must now turn. The bishops and abbots who held land directly of the emperor owed their office first to election by chapters of canons or monks, mostly of noble birth. Then came subsequent confirmation by emperor and pope. Once in the saddle, they were masters sometimes of widespread territories. They were open to pressure, especially in the north, by their more powerful lay neighbours, but in the west and south their independence was fortified by some spirit of local patriotism among their estates. Lutheran princes used familiar tactics to tighten their grip on nearby sees: they put forward their own relatives or clients according to the accustomed procedure, save that the elected candidate as a Protestant could not expect papal confirmation and ruled the territory as permanently unconsecrated 'administrator'. When the time was ripe, outright annexation by the secular neighbour would follow. Ferdinand I and the Reichstag had at the making of the religious peace attempted to crystallise the existing situation by the crucial clause that laid down the principle of 'ecclesiastical reservation'. By this, a Catholic prelate resolving to embrace Lutheranism was legally bound to vacate his office. The Lutheran princes had protested at this enactment and they never recognised the validity of the principle, which would have put an end to their acquisition of church lands. On the other hand, Ferdinand had sought to reassure them by a separate declaration, to which the Reichstag was not a party and whose legal weight was therefore slight, that where Lutheranism had already gained a footing in ecclesiastical territory it was not his wish to disturb it. This compromise, wholly satisfactory to nobody, offered a doubtful barrier to the further transfer of imperial ecclesiastical principalities from one persuasion to the other.

The future of the imperial church lands was thus in 1555 very uncertain. In the following years, the Catholics watched with helpless dismay the introduction of equivocal or openly heretical nominees into various northern imperial sees and abbeys. For instance, Lutheranism was imposed upon the archbishopric of Magdeburg in 1561–2 and upon the bishopric of Halberstadt in 1564, and the way was thus being prepared for the ultimate absorption of these principalities into the electorate of Brandenburg. Further south, in the border zone between Protestant and Catholic, there lay in Franconia and the Rhineland the richest and most important ecclesiastical territories. These were still ruled by Catholic prelates, though neither their cathedral chapters nor their estates were immune to Lutheran influence and the outlook was dark. Among these clerical princes were numbered the archbishops of Mainz, Trier and Cologne, who as electors filled the highest positions in the empire after the emperor. Further, since three of their four temporal colleagues were now Protestant, it was they who maintained the Catholic majority in the electoral college. The defection of any one of these would have meant not only the installation of heresy along the strategic and commercial highroad of the middle Rhine but also the possibility of the election of a Protestant emperor, with all that this implied for European politics. The efforts to enforce the principle of ecclesiastical reservation in western Germany reached their climax in the 'eighties with the fierce struggle for the electorate of Cologne. But before tracing the course of this crucial conflict it is necessary to glance briefly at two other threats to the peace of the empire that arose further east.

The first startling breach of the peace within the empire, following the settlement of 1555, occurred in Franconia. Here the imperial bishoprics of Würzburg and Bamberg and other ecclesiastical principalities had recently proved incapable of protecting themselves against marauding neighbours, in particular the Margrave Albert Alcibiades of Brandenburg-Kulmbach. This wild princelet had tried to carve out for himself, at their expense, a principality in the Main valley—an enterprise cut short only by his death in 1557. Among his followers had been the knight Wilhelm von Grumbach, who now transferred himself to the service of the senior prince of ducal Saxony. This new patron intended with the aid of French subsidies to make use of Grumbach to eject his cousin the elector of Saxony from his dominions. This project became impracticable with the end of the European war in 1559. But Grumbach had already begun his lawless career by invading the territories of the see of Würzburg and procuring the murder of its occupant, and now he was able with scant hindrance to prolong his depredations within and around its frontiers. It was impossible to follow up the outlawry proclaimed by the emperor, and the machinery prescribed by the security statute could not be set in motion. The princes of the Franconian Circle shivered in their exposed position, unable to help themselves, and the new bishop of Würzburg was in severe straits. In the end, it was the elector of Saxony, acting from motives of self-protection, who with the authority of the emperor made an end in 1567 to the mischief: Grumbach was captured and put to death and his patron imprisoned for life. But it had taken eight years to suppress the disorders, which had caused an immense stir throughout Germany, and both the helplessness of the ecclesiastical princes and the feebleness of the imperial arrangements for the maintenance of the peace had received full illustration.

The next episode also concerned the bishopric of Würzburg, though taking its origin in its neighbour the imperial abbey of Fulda. The abbot was ruler of a considerable principality to the west of the bishopric, in which Lutheranism had for a generation more than maintained a foothold. The few remaining monks had deserted the cloister and established themselves in separate households in the town, the clergy gave the communion in both kinds and taught the Lutheran catechism, while the landowners of the principality were avowed Protestants. In 1570 the monks elected to the vacant abbacy Balthasar von Dernbach, a young man still in his twenties, believed to be Lutheran in sympathy. He at once found himself confronted by the clear alternatives of either giving the Lutherans free rein, with the ultimate secularisation of the abbey in prospect, or putting an end to their worship. He chose the latter course, modified his religious views—he appears to have had little or no theological training—and embraced Catholicism with all the enthusiasm of the convert. He invoked the aid of the Jesuits and in 1573 founded and endowed a college for them at Fulda; meanwhile, he forbade the delivery of the cup to the laity in the town and soon made evident his intention to put an end to Lutheran practices in the principality. Thus there was at once raised the validity of the imperial promise that the Lutherans already established in church lands should not be disturbed. The monks and nobles of Fulda appealed for support to the neighbouring Protestant princes, who thereupon urged the abbot to drop his policy and dismiss his Jesuits; instead, he in his turn leant on powerful allies that included the duke of Bavaria. For a while in 1574 it looked as if serious strife might develop in central Germany. The emperor himself was invoked and ordered the princes not to interfere with the abbey of Fulda. In the end, war was averted by the decision of the ever amenable elector of Saxony not to pursue the matter. The pope ordered the monks to their obedience, the abbot kept on his way and the crisis passed.

The radical measures of Abbot Balthasar did not cease to provoke the Protestants in Fulda, but he would doubtless have continued to get the better of his adversaries had it not been for the unexpected intervention of a third party—his neighbour Julius Echter von Mespelbrunn, bishop of Würzburg from 1573. Bishop Julius likewise was a youthful prelate, born in 1545, a product of the Jesuit college at Cologne and a zealous Catholic. But he was also a cunning lawyer—and a careerist who had delayed for two years after his election before accepting ordination and consecration. He approached the abbot with a proposal for a pact of inheritance—a characteristic German device by which the survivor of the pair should succeed to the office of the other. This was intended to lead to the permanent union of bishopric and abbey and thus to the formation of a single and larger and therefore better protected Catholic principality. On the rejection of this scheme by Abbot Balthasar, the bishop entered into alliance with the discontented nobles and monks of Fulda, invaded the principality and in June 1576 forced the abbot to resign. It was a good illustration of the way in which territorial greed afflicted even ecclesiastical princes. It implied also a setback for the Catholic cause, since for the moment at least Bishop Julius had to loosen the reins at Fulda to reward his allies. The storm broke over his head sooner and more violently than he possibly expected: Abbot Balthasar appealed to pope and emperor and cited the bishop before the *Reichskammergericht*. A prolonged lawsuit followed and after a quarter of a century the verdict was given in favour of the abbot, who resumed his sway in 1602. Meanwhile, Bishop Julius had to hand Fulda over from March 1577 to an imperial administrator, under whose rule the progress of the Counter-Reformation was again forwarded. The subsequent exemplary career of Bishop Julius points the moral of the story: he ruled at Würzburg with a strong hand, expelling heretical preachers, quelling the pretensions of his canons to a share in the government and, Medici-like, laying the foundations of princely absolutism. His long reign—he survived until 1617—was marked by a pronounced Catholic revival and also by much prosperity, commonly ascribed to his beneficent rule. He is best remembered as a discerning patron of the arts, the founder of a university and an assiduous builder of churches and other buildings fashioned in the well-known 'Julius-style' baroque of Franconia.

The struggle for control of the ecclesiastical principalities raged at its most violent in the contest for the electorate of Cologne, the bastion both of the Rhineland and of the imperial constitution. The principality of the archbishop elector was a large one, embracing lands both along the Rhine and in Westphalia, the former abutting on the Spanish Netherlands.

There had been some infiltration of heresy, though Catholicism remained preponderant, and Cologne itself—it was not subject to the archbishop but was a free city of the empire—housed a Jesuit headquarters. The estates of the principality were knit together by a sense of local solidarity which helped to fortify a spirit of independence in the territory. The twenty-four canons of the cathedral, in whose hands the power to elect the archbishop lay, were in many cases connected by family ties with the landed families of the region, and they also collectively constituted the first house of the estates. In 1562 the chapter elected as archbishop Count Friedrich von Wied, a churchman of the old school who believed that it might still be possible by judicious concessions to entice the heretics back to the traditional faith and who was therefore out of sympathy with the doctrinal definitions and condemnations of the Council of Trent. This attitude brought him into trouble with the papal nuncio, Commendone, and the other Catholic princes, and in 1567 he escaped from his predicament by resigning. The canons chose as his successor an energetic and hard-drinking young nobleman, Count Salentin von Isenburg, who was an undoubted and even brutal partisan of the Catholic side, even to the point of serving with Alva in the field as a paid mercenary captain. But he was not prepared to alter his way of living, or even to accept ordination, and so he ruled at Cologne, somewhat brusquely, as 'archbishop elect' only. Throughout his tenure of the electorate there was a general expectation that he would not stay long, though some of his Protestant neighbours tried to persuade him to marry and yet cling to his principality. These he disappointed. In 1577 his long-expected abdication occurred and he retired to rule his paternal inheritance and take a wife. Once more, the canons had to make their choice of an archbishop.

This time, the troubles in the Netherlands and the gathering power of the Catholic reaction gave the election an unwonted political significance. The duke of Bavaria had had his eye on the electorate of Cologne since the abdication of Archbishop Friedrich, and with the support of Philip II of Spain and of the pope he put forward as his candidate his second son, Prince Ernest, already bishop of Freising and of Hildesheim. To press his claims, there came to Cologne not only the papal nuncio and an imperial commissioner but also envoys from Madrid and Brussels and from the sister sees of Mainz and Trier. There was a large Catholic faction among the canons. But this was not the point. Chapter and archbishop were traditionally at loggerheads at Cologne as elsewhere, and the high-handed methods of Archbishop Salentin had exacerbated this enmity. The canons were therefore not minded to instal as his successor anyone with the strong backing enjoyed by a Bavarian prince. They were moved not at all by the needs of high politics and only to a secondary degree by the claims of religion; their primary interests centred on their stipends and perquisites and the administration of cathedral property. There were in fact only three out-and-out Protestants among them, men in touch with neighbouring imperial princes who hoped to pull the electorate over to heresy. But there was a much larger number who disliked the prospect of being reduced to Tridentine standards of discipline by the representative of a great princely house, and their vote was decisive. The successful candidate, by a narrow margin, was not Prince Ernest but another young man, Gebhard Truchsess von Waldburg, nephew to Cardinal Otto Truchsess, formerly bishop of Augsburg and an early patron of the Jesuits. He was indisputably Catholic, but not too strict in his principles. On election, he submitted to ordination and consecration though, like Prince Ernest, he never personally discharged any priestly functions. After some hesitation, pope as well as emperor confirmed him in office.

At first Archbishop Gebhard conducted himself with discretion. But a dangerous situation arose when early in 1580 he began to cherish the idea of marrying a nun with whom he had fallen in love. His first notion was to resign his archbishopric in order to do so, but the same voices that had vainly tempted his predecessor to marry and yet keep his preferment were again raised, this time with more success. The local factors were favourable enough: the Dutch were maintaining themselves to the west, the count of Nassau and other Protestant tempters were on his eastern flank, and there was some heresy in the electorate, especially the Westphalian portion. It was the significance of the archbishopric in both imperial and international politics that made the project so reckless. When in the summer of 1582 Gebhard set about securing allies, the elector of Saxony and other moderate Protestants hung back. On the other hand, the Catholic side had been fortified by the election of Prince Ernest to the neighbouring see of Liège in 1581, and in January 1583 the cathedral chapter of Cologne, moved less by religious zeal than by a chronic suspicion of all archiepiscopal actions, took the initiative in resistance by summoning the estates of the electorate. Gebhard meanwhile formally granted toleration to Protestants, celebrated his wedding by the Lutheran rite, and then withdrew to the Westphalian part of his territories, where he prepared to defend himself. In March the pope deposed him from his archbishopric and ordered the chapter to proceed to a new election. This time, solicited by pope, emperor and the Catholic princes of the empire, the canons bowed to the claims of Prince Ernest, though only after a widespread distribution of pensions and bribes. The papal nuncio later confessed that he had never met a more mercenary lot. The successful candidate himself was worthy of them; he would have preferred to pursue his pleasures elsewhere and only a papal command sufficed to make him break off his latest amour and proceed to Cologne. His ceremonial entry into the city closed the first phase of the grotesque but fateful episode. There followed a long and ill-led war, in which Spanish troops from the Netherlands played the decisive part. Neither side could pay its soldiers punctually and they lived on the country: towns were sacked, vanquished combatants slain, heretics expelled and the region wrapped in misery. Not until 1589 did the last of Gebhard's garrisons surrender. But long before then Prince Ernest had won general recognition as elector of Cologne.

The success of the Catholic party at Cologne, together with the revival of Spanish power under Parma in the Netherlands, marked a turning-point in the history of the imperial bishoprics that covered so much of north-west Germany. There was no hope of saving from the Lutherans the archbishopric of Bremen, for it was full of heresy and surrounded by Protestant territory. But it was possible in part to rescue the bishoprics of Paderborn and Osnabrück, which with Bremen fell vacant in 1585; their chapters indeed turned down Prince Ernest, but chose at Paderborn a good Catholic, at Osnabrück a less certain one. Prince Ernest was enabled to gather his fifth see the following year, when he was elected bishop of Münster. The effect of these changes was not only to create Prince Ernest's great pluralist principality, but also to secure the encouragement and enforcement of Catholicism over some thousands of square miles of country between the Rhine and the Weser, from Bonn to within a few miles of the North Sea. It was a heartening development for the Catholic cause all over Germany. In the opposite direction, further up the Rhine, there was another decisive sequel to the Cologne struggle. Both Archbishop Gebhard and his three Protestant allies among the canons of Cologne were also members of the cathedral chapter of the imperial see of Strassburg. When the Catholic canons tried to expel the latter, they resisted; and since the townsfolk, unlike those of Cologne, were Lutherans, they were able to maintain themselves within the capitular buildings (*Brüderhof*). The chapter was henceforth cleft in twain, and when in 1592 the bishop died there was a double election, the Lutherans choosing a cadet of the Brandenburg Hohenzollerns, the Catholics the cardinal of Lorraine, who was already bishop of Metz, Toul and Verdun and to some extent represented the vanguard of a renewed French political advance. Here the emperor was able to intervene as mediator, thanks to the proximity of the Habsburg hereditary lands in western Germany. In 1598, the cardinal of Lorraine finally concluded a bargain with the emperor by which he was recognised as bishop while the Archduke Leopold was named as his successor. Since the Catholics had thus been brought to agreement, it was now possible to edge out the Hohenzollern claimant, who was finally bought off by a money payment. Thus the see of Strassburg was also preserved from heresy, though at the cost of admitting French influence.

There remained one ultimate crisis before the hardly won Catholicism of north-west Germany and the Rhineland could be guaranteed—the succession to the duchy of Jülich-Cleve, the only large secular principality in the region. Its territories were inextricably intertwined with those of the electorate of Cologne and other church lands, and it was hardly conceivable that it could be lost to Catholicism without damage to its neighbours. The conflicting claims of various parties to the Jülich-Cleve inheritance were complicated in the extreme and no full examination of their rights can be attempted here. Suffice it to explain that the problem of the succession first became pressing after the Cologne war. The old Duke William had ruled since 1539 and he was now weary and ill. When younger, he had wobbled in matters of religion and three of his four daughters had married Protestant princes; both Lutheranism and Calvinism had taken some root in his principality, though heresy was far from predominant. He was now firmly within the Catholic fold, as was his only surviving son, John William. But from 1589 onwards it was apparent that the latter was losing his reason and unfit to govern. With an aged prince and a mad heir, the scene was now set for a series of startling events that shook the political fabric not merely of the empire but of Europe. When the old duke died in 1592, claims to the regency were asserted in various quarters, but in agreement with the estates of the principality it was awarded, under imperial supervision, to the madman's wife, a Bavarian princess of impeccable Catholicism though not beyond scandal in her private life. She was murdered by conspirators in 1597, but it proved possible to provide John William with a second Catholic wife, this time a Lorraine princess, who in turn took up the reins. When in 1609 the mad duke died, the Protestant representatives of two of his sisters, belonging to the houses of Brandenburg and Neuburg, prevailed—in the face of emperor, empire and the threatened thunderbolt of a French intervention that was averted at the last moment by the murder of Henry IV. Meanwhile, the inhabitants had been brought back to Catholic uniformity, sometimes with the brutal and illegal help of Spanish soldiers from the Netherlands. In the end, the Jülich-Cleve problem was resolved when a cooler generation accepted the novel argument that princes and their subjects need not necessarily profess the same religion. Long before then the triumph of the Counter-Reformation in the Rhineland had been assured.

One final point remains to be made. The survey of the field of German politics in this chapter has taken us through the struggle for the Rhineland and Franconia. But there were other though subsidiary routes, from some of which the political landscape would have been visible from a different angle.[1] The free cities of the empire shared the uncertainties of the ecclesiastical principalities and their history also throws much light on the nature of political events. The English traveller of the period might gape in admiration at the palaces and stone mansions of such famous places as Augsburg or Nuremberg, and reflect on the wealth of the Germans. But

[1] Some account of economic and social aspects will be found in the succeeding volume of this *History*.

he also noted the stout walls with look-out turrets manned throughout the day, the arrangements for the instant sounding of the alarm, the well-stocked civic arsenals and the practice of storing a supply of provisions for a year—all symptoms of acute political insecurity. By the middle of the sixteenth century, the government of all the free cities was Lutheran save at Cologne and Aachen, and even here there were numbers of heretics; to balance this, in many others there were sizeable Catholic minorities. Confessional friction was to be met everywhere. At a number of Swabian cities, as at Ulm in 1569, the Catholics were extruded from the remaining churches in their possession. Heresy was driven underground at Cologne by the expulsion of nonconformists. At Aachen, the immigration of heretical refugees from the Netherlands led to a series of interventions and compromises that until 1598 enabled adherents of the opposing faiths to live side by side. Tension proved too great in the end and Aachen, like most of north-west Germany, reverted wholly to Catholicism. Religion in the early seventeenth century was to prove the undoing of the free city of Donauwörth, where the missionary work of the Jesuits enabled the Catholics by 1600 to muster an enlarged and determined minority. The subsequent bickerings between the Protestant town council and the Catholic militants led in 1607 to the intervention of a formidable neighbour—the duke of Bavaria—as the official agent of the emperor. The duke subsequently reimbursed himself for the expenses of his interference by the annexation of the city: as neat a piece of power politics veiled by religious principles as could be found in Europe. The episode caused a great flutter in imperial politics, and in addition to its bearing on the confessional rivalry it illustrated the persistent weakness of the free cities in an epoch when the power of the princes was continuing to grow.

Thus in the later sixteenth century the house of Austria with its insecure and divided inheritance and its preoccupation with the Turkish menace lacked the power to assert itself in the empire. Its sovereigns presided over the political structure of a great country that was in the main still prosperous, though the reality of power lay chiefly with a disunited oligarchy of princes. The imperial constitution functioned to some modest effect under Ferdinand I and Maximilian II, but the partisanship, the lack of political realism and finally the sheer madness of Rudolf II helped to clog and discredit its working. The Cologne war provided a precipice in the descent from the forms of law to unmitigated violence. But the basic cause of the deterioration in German politics lay with the polarisation of religious enmities around, on the one hand, the new faith of Calvinism and, on the other, the Catholic revival, with the Jesuits to the forefront. Calvinism had not taken root in Germany at the time of the religious settlement in 1555, nor was the significance of Jesuit activities fully apparent at that time. The Catholic revival demonstrated its power by its rescue of north-west Germany: although there remained nests of heresy in Catholic lands, the line of demarcation between the creeds was by the early seventeenth century crystallising along a frontier that might in 1555 have seemed to the Catholics highly optimistic. The mounting enthusiasm of either party was registered chiefly in parishes, schools and universities all over Germany, but the history of the confessional conflict has in this chapter been related in terms of politics and personalities, since it was events in the world of imperial princely animosities and of international diplomacy that permitted it to unfold. These were the elements that provided the ultimate and inescapable mould into which the religious rivalries were gradually gathering.

CHAPTER XI

THE OTTOMAN EMPIRE 1566–1617

THE Ottoman empire had attained under Sulaimān the Magnificent (1520–66) the summit of its power and splendour. Now, during the period that followed his death, strains and stresses originating both within and without the empire gave rise to notable changes in the structure of the Ottoman state. The general trend of events after 1566 cannot be understood, therefore, without reference to some at least of the essential characteristics of the Ottoman régime as it was in the reign of Sultan Sulaimān.

The household of the sultan was far more than a domestic organisation designed to meet the private and personal needs of the monarch. It included also much more than the apparatus and adornments of an imperial court. The household embraced within itself the personnel of the central administration and of the great executive offices of state; of the higher ranks in the provincial administration; and also of the armed forces of the central régime—the Janissaries, the mounted regiments of the household (sometimes known as the Sipāhīs of the Porte) and the various specialist corps such as artillerists and engineers. The numerous personnel of this household had in general the status of *ghulām* (pl. *ghilmān*), a term better interpreted as 'man of the sultan' than as 'slave', since it in no wise implied, as the English word 'slave' might suggest, a position of inferiority, but was on the contrary a mark of privilege and prestige within the state. A basic principle observed in recruitment to the household was the exclusion of Muslim Turkish subjects[1] of the sultan from the ranks of the *ghilmān*. To be born non-Muslim and non-Turkish was an essential qualification for entrance into this dominant élite. There were several sources of recruitment available to the sultan: captives of war taken in the course of land or sea campaigns against the Christians; captives acquired by gift or by purchase; and, in addition, the children of the *devshirme*, the child-tribute levied at intervals from the subject Christian—and, in respect of ethnic origin, above all from the Slav and Albanian—populations of the empire. The recruits drawn from these sources, being as a rule no more than children or youths in point of age, became converts to Islam, not simply as the result of direct compulsion, but also by the pressure of their new environment, by force of example, and by the prospect of advancement in the service of the sultan. The actual road that a recruit might follow would depend, in large degree, on his possession or lack of high

---

[1] To the Muslim-born subjects of the sultan was reserved, however, exclusive control of the Muslim religious, legal and educational institutions of the empire.

intellectual and physical qualities. Of the recruits the best endowed went into the palace schools, there to be instructed in the Muslim faith and in the arts of war, statecraft and administration. After long years of training, and in the prime of their young manhood, the most gifted amongst them would be sent out as governors (*sanjak-begi*) of provinces. Some of them might rise in the course of time to the rank of governor-general (*beglerbegi*) over a number of sanjaks and then, if fortune favoured them, to the status of vizier, with a seat in the Diwān, that is, the Council of State which controlled the great affairs of the empire. The most exalted office—the grand vizierate—would now be within their reach. Few, however, amongst the recruits chosen for education in the palace schools attained to high eminence. Service in the subordinate offices of the court and of the central administration or in the mounted regiments of the household was the lot which awaited most of these more favoured recruits.

The captives of war and the *devshirme* children not selected for the palace schools underwent some years of hard physical labour on lands belonging to the state, above all in Asia Minor. These recruits—known as the '*ajemioghlanlar* ('foreign youths')—would be recalled in due course to Istanbul, a large proportion of them being now destined to enrolment in the corps of Janissaries after a rigorous training in the profession of arms. The household of the sultan also included the Sipāhīs of the Porte,[1] the mounted regiments, six in all, two of them numbering in their ranks men born Muslim, but hailing from lands outside the confines of the Ottoman empire, the other four regiments being composed of recruits drawn in general from the palace schools. Amongst the personnel of the specialist corps, the armourers, artillerists and engineers, could be found captives of war, children from the *devshirme*, and also renegades of Christian origin.

Two notable characteristics of the system must be stressed here. First, that the status of *ghulām* was not heritable, children of men who belonged to the imperial household being in general excluded from the system and absorbed into the Muslim population of the empire; and second, that the *ghilmān*, with some exceptions, received as their means of subsistence not landed estates, but fixed salaries paid to them in cash at regular intervals out of the revenues of the central régime.

The sultan had at his command, however, a warrior class far more numerous than the armed forces of the imperial household and distinct from them in status—the 'feudal' horsemen known as sipāhīs and located in most, but not all, of the provinces of the empire. These horsemen came to war at the call of the sultan and, in reward for their fulfilment of this obligation, held fiefs adequate to maintain them as efficient soldiers. A fief

[1] The term 'Sipāhīs of the Porte' is an expression of convenience used to designate the mounted regiments of the imperial household—the *spahi di paga* (paid sipāhīs) of the Italian sources, who are not to be confused with the 'feudal' horsemen, also known in general as 'sipāhīs' (on whom, see below, pp. 373–4).

consisted of a nucleus called *kilij* (sword) and of further allocations of land described as *terakki* (increase). The *kilij* gave the minimum of revenue considered to be sufficient for the maintenance of the sipāhī himself, grants of *terakki* being added one at a time to the *kilij* in order to augment the total revenues of the fief as a reward for long and meritorious service. Each sipāhī had to provide his own equipment of war—arms, tents, beasts of burden and the like. Moreover, as his fief grew in value, he was obliged to bring with him on campaign, in proportion to his revenues, one or more mounted soldiers (*jebeli*) maintained and furnished with arms at his own expense.

There were, in relation to the 'feudal' horsemen known as sipāhīs, two main grades of fief: (i) the *tīmār*, yielding from between 2,000 and 3,000 to 19,999 akçes[1] per annum; and (ii) the *zi'āmet*, ranging in value from 20,000 to 99,999 akçes per annum. The right to grant tīmārs and zi'āmets had rested, in former times, with the beglerbegs. The central régime, in the course of time, reserved to itself, however, the assignment of all such fiefs save the lowest grades of *tīmār*, appointment to which was allowed to remain within the competence of the beglerbegs. Each sipāhī might hope, through good service, to rise from the lower to the higher grade of fief.

The sipāhī had no absolute right of possession in respect of the lands which constituted his fief—such lands belonged in law to the state. He enjoyed only the usufruct of the land, the right to receive certain defined dues, in cash and in kind, from the peasants who lived and worked on the soil. The status of sipāhī was, within limits, hereditable. A fief would be granted in normal circumstances to one of his sons—sometimes, indeed, more than one son might be given a small fief. If a sipāhī died childless or left sons not competent to perform the duties of a soldier, the *kilij* of his fief might go to the most deserving of the *jebeli* men-at-arms who had fought in the retinue of the dead sipāhī. Enrolment within the 'feudal' class was not restricted, however, to members of old-established sipāhī families and to the *jebeli* warriors associated with them: for example, the sons of some amongst the high dignitaries who belonged to the household of the sultan and held the status of *ghulām* had the right to receive a *tīmār* or a *zi'āmet*, the size of the grant depending on the rank of the father; a Muslim volunteer, too, might be given a fief in reward for exceptional valour on the field of battle; and, not infrequently, personnel from the palace schools also passed into the 'feudal' system.

The sipāhīs in each province of the empire where the 'feudal' system was in being had their own officers chosen from amongst themselves. Of these officers the most important was the *alay begi*,[2] who, amongst other duties, mustered the sipāhīs of the province at the beginning of a

---

[1] The akçe, or asper, was a small Ottoman coin of silver. According to the rate of exchange operative in the time of Sulaimān the Magnificent 60 akçes equalled one Venetian gold ducat.

[2] *Alay* (Turkish) = an array of troops.

campaign. The rank of *alay begi* was the highest that a sipāhī could attain. Appointment to the great offices in the provincial administration—of *sanjak begi* and *beglerbegi*—was reserved to members of the privileged élite who had the status of *ghulām*. The sanjak begs and beglerbegs, in addition to the performance of the executive and administrative duties inherent in their office, also commanded the sipāhīs of their province in time of war. These high officials enjoyed the revenues of large fiefs known as *khāss* (special), which gave 100,000 akçes and more per annum. It was laid down that sanjak begs should receive not less than 200,000 and beglerbegs not less than 1,000,000 akçes a year—moreover, the longer their service the higher were the revenues assigned to them, additional lands being allocated as *terakki* to their fiefs. The minimum *khāss* granted to a *sanjak begi*, or to a *beglerbegi*, on the occasion of his first appointment to such a rank, corresponded therefore to the *kilij* of a sipāhī holding a *tīmār* or a *zi'āmet*. Each *sanjak begi* and *beglerbegi* had to furnish and bring to war *jebeli* warriors in proportion to the value of his fief—some of these great officials indeed maintained retinues much larger than was in fact demanded of them. There was, however, in relation to the fiefs called *khāss*, no right of inheritance, even to a limited degree, as in the case of the *tīmār* and the *zi'āmet*. The *khāss* fiefs pertained not to the individual, but to the office of *sanjak begi* or *beglerbegi* and thus changed hands as one incumbent succeeded another.

It will be evident that in such fields of action as war, politics and administration a preponderant measure of power and privilege in the Ottoman state rested with the *ghilmān*, the 'men of the sultan'. The 'feudal' sipāhīs, although constituting in effect a privileged aristocratic element in the life of the provinces, found themselves excluded from the highest levels of power and prestige within the state—an exclusion which, again in relation to war, politics and administration, embraced indeed the great mass of the Muslim-born subjects of the sultan.[1] A line of division so paradoxical in character might obtain a more or less general acceptance as long as all went well with the empire and the system as a whole worked to the obvious advantage of its members, whether of Muslim or of non-Muslim birth. It was to become blurred, however, and to an increasing degree obliterated, when the tide of Ottoman affairs began to take an adverse course. The years 1566–1617 saw the Ottomans confronted with new and unfavourable circumstances which brought about a profound transformation in some of the institutions of their empire. This transformation marked, in fact, the first phase in a long and slow process of decline.

There were amongst the Ottomans themselves men who sought to discover the reasons for the decline. One of the *'ulemā* (the Muslim theologians and jurists learned in the *sharī'a*, or sacred law of Islam), a

[1] See, however, p. 347 n. above.

Bosnian named Hasan al-Kāfī, lamented in his small treatise on the art of government, written in 1596–7, that justice was becoming ill administered in the empire, that incapable men untested in long years of service rose to the highest offices of state and that the Ottoman armies had lost much of the obedience and discipline, the courage and skill, which distinguished them in former times; the sultans had fallen into a life of ease and self-indulgence, viziers intrigued one against the other, the influence of women had become marked in the conduct of affairs; there was no regular mustering of the armed forces and their equipment, the soldiers often committed grave excesses against the subject populations of the empire, and failure to adopt the latest techniques of warfare had led to defeat in battle with the enemies of Islam; negligence, corruption, favouritism and greed now bade fair to ruin the Ottoman system of government. A similar diagnosis of the ills that beset the empire can be found in the famous *Risāle* or memorandum which Koçu Beg submitted to Sultan Murād IV (1623–40)— a memorandum wider in scope, however, and more elaborate than the little treatise of Hasan al-Kāfī. Some of the arguments that Koçu Beg advanced can be summarised thus: the sultans have ceased to lead their armies in war and to attend the Diwān or Council of State; favourites attain to high office over the heads of able and experienced men; intrigue and corruption, now rife amongst the viziers and great dignitaries of the central régime, have filtered down through all levels of the administration; the harem exercises, all too often, a pernicious influence on the course of affairs; ostentation and luxurious living have done much to undermine the moral fibre of the dominant class in the empire.

The criticisms of such men as Hasan al-Kāfī and Koçu Beg contain a solid element of truth. It cannot be denied that, save on rare occasions, the sultans who followed Sulaimān the Magnificent neither led their armies in time of war nor overburdened themselves with a constant attention to the great affairs of state. Their negligence facilitated beyond doubt the growth of manifold abuses. The women of the harem, for example the *Wālide Sultan* (the mother of the sultan on the throne) and the *Khāsseki Sultans* (the consorts who had borne the sultan a male child), made and unmade the fortunes of the high officials who secured or lost their favour. Princesses of the Ottoman house, married to viziers or other dignitaries of exalted rank, strove to advance the careers of their husbands and the interests of their children. The spirit of faction and intrigue, grown strong amongst the great personalities of the central régime, determined all too often the policies of the government even in matters of serious concern. Abuses like the over-frequent appointment, dismissal or transfer of high officials meant that the Ottoman administration became less efficient than it had once been. To a modern historian, however, these factors, which have so large a place in the treatises of Hasan al-Kāfī and of Koçu Beg, will stand out rather as symptoms than as fundamental causes of the Ottoman decline. Koçu Beg, it is true, examines in some detail problems of a deeper significance—the increase in the number of the Janissaries, the introduction into their ranks of Muslim-born subjects of the sultan, the growing confusion evident in the 'feudal' system and in the financial affairs of the empire—and yet these factors, too, are in some measure the overt symptoms and not the basic causes of a decline the real origins of which must be sought elsewhere.

Of all the forces that now contributed to deform and break down the 'classical' institutions of the Ottoman state, thrusting them into new and unfavourable lines of evolution, none was perhaps more important than the strain arising out of prolonged and arduous warfare. The tide of Ottoman conquest, which had been so strong for almost three centuries, came to a virtual halt in Asia and above all in Europe during the years 1566–1617. It was an event formidable in its consequences. The Ottoman state had been founded on the frontier between Islam and Byzantine Christendom; its *raison d'être* was the *jihād*, or war against the Infidel, on behalf of the Sunnī or orthodox Muslim faith. To the Ottomans, whether men of the sword or men of religion, the advancing frontier had given, over and above the material rewards of conquest, a distinctive ethos and purpose which exercised a profound influence on the evolution of their political, religious and social life. The Ottoman war machine, the administration, the systems of land tenure and taxation had been geared to the needs of an expanding state. Now, as the onward tide of warfare slowed down—a process first visible in the later years of Sulaimān the Magnificent —these institutions failed to harmonise with the new and unfamiliar stresses of a frontier that was becoming static.

The main event in the reign of Selīm II (1566–74) was the conquest of Cyprus, an island which had been under Venetian rule since 1489. It was not difficult to discover arguments in favour of a new war against Venice— for example, the friction that existed along the borders of the Venetian enclaves on the eastern shore of the Adriatic, the failure of the Signoria to deal with the so-called Uskoks (a band of corsairs operating from Segna (Senj) in Dalmatia), or the harbouring in Cyprus of Christian corsairs who infested the waters of the Levant, assailing Muslim commerce and the sea-borne traffic of Muslim pilgrims bound for Mecca. The Grand Vizier Mehemmed Sokolli strove to avert the outbreak of war, but a number of influential personalities—amongst them Piāle Pasha, Mustafā Pasha and Uluj 'Alī Pasha—convinced the sultan that Cyprus might be won without undue trouble and expense. Selīm II had renewed in 1567 the formal state of peace existing between the Porte and the Signoria at the time of his accession to the throne. The Mufti Abū'l-Su'ūd now issued a *fetwā* (a legal judgement based on the principles of the *sharī'a*, or sacred law of Islam), declaring that it was permissible to break treaties of peace when the purpose in view was to recover control of lands which, like

Cyprus, had once been under Muslim rule. Some members of the Venetian Senate urged that Cyprus be ceded in exchange for compensation in Dalmatia and Albania and new commercial privileges in the Ottoman empire; others proposed that an attempt be made to placate the sultan and the great dignitaries at the Porte with lavish gifts; but at Venice, as at Istanbul, the war faction gained the ascendant. The Signoria trusted indeed that, in the event of an armed conflict, assistance would be forthcoming from the other Christian states and was thus emboldened in the spring of 1570 to meet a formal Ottoman demand for the cession of Cyprus with a refusal so uncompromising that it closed the door to the prospect of further negotiation.

A powerful Ottoman force, under the command of Mustafā Pasha, landed in Cyprus during the month of July 1570. Meanwhile Pope Pius V had been labouring hard to bring about an alliance between Spain and Venice. A deplorable spirit of distrust, procrastination and intrigue marked, however, the course of the negotiations. It was soon made clear that, as in the years 1537–40,[1] so now the interests of Spain, preoccupied with her ambitions in North Africa and with the defence of the western Mediterranean against the corsairs from Algiers, and of Venice, intent on preserving the remnants of her old imperium in the Levant, did not coincide. Philip II of Spain, in answer to the pleas of Pope Pius V, agreed at last to send a squadron to the aid of the Signoria, but it was not until the end of August 1570, at Suda in Crete, that the Spanish and papal contingents joined the Venetian fleet. A vigorous prosecution of the campaign was not to be achieved, however, in the face of the dissension so rife in the high command of the Christian armada. On the arrival of the news that Nicosia in Cyprus had fallen to the Ottomans on 9 September, the entire force, then not far from Castellorizo on the southern shore of Asia Minor, sailed back to Crete and thence to Italian waters, having done nothing of importance.

There now followed, during and beyond the winter of 1570–1, a series of further negotiations between Spain, the papacy and Venice. A formal league signed on 15 May 1571 envisaged an extension of the war to include operations in North Africa as well as in the eastern Mediterranean. A new Christian armada assembled at Messina in September 1571—but it was too late to save Cyprus. Famagusta, the last major Venetian stronghold in the island, surrendered to the Ottomans on 1 August 1571 after a siege of almost eleven months. The Christian armada, under the command of Don John of Austria, did achieve, however, one notable success—the virtual destruction of the Ottoman fleet at the famous battle of Lepanto fought on 7 October 1571. Although it broke the initiative that the Ottomans had held at sea since the battle of Prevesa in 1538, Lepanto must be considered as a triumph symbolic in character rather than positive in its actual consequences. The season for naval warfare in the Mediterranean

[1] See vol. II, pp. 519–20.

353

was now too far advanced for the Christians to undertake an immediate exploitation of their success, all the more since at Lepanto their own vessels and crews had suffered no small damage and loss. During the winter and spring of 1571-2 the Ottomans, making a supreme and sustained effort, built and equipped a large new fleet which, in 1572 off Cerigo, Navarino and Modon and under the able guidance of Uluj 'Ali Pasha, frustrated the attempt of the Christians to win a second and this time decisive battle against their Muslim foes. The Christian armada was in fact able to achieve nothing of importance in the campaign of 1572.

Venice, dissatisfied with the outcome of a war at once expensive and unsuccessful and burdened with the loss of her trade to the Levant and of the essential supplies of grain that she was accustomed to draw from the Ottoman empire, now sought peace from the sultan and in March 1573 obtained it in return for the cession of Cyprus and the payment of a large sum in war indemnities. Spain, left to fight alone against the Ottomans, turned her attention towards North Africa. The Emperor Charles V had established a protectorate over Tunis in 1535, the harbour fortress of La Goletta becoming the main instrument of Spanish control. Uluj 'Ali Pasha had marched overland from Algiers to Tunis in the winter of 1569-70, the Muslim prince whom Spain supported there had fled for refuge to La Goletta, and the Pasha had seized and garrisoned the town. Don John of Austria, sailing from Sicily, brought Tunis once more under Spanish domination in October 1573—a brilliant success, but one destined to be of no long duration. Uluj 'Ali Pasha appeared before Tunis with a large fleet in July 1574 and after a short siege took both the town itself and the fortress of La Goletta. The Ottoman conquest of Tunis in 1574 was an event of some significance. It marked in fact the virtual end of a long conflict waged between Spaniard and Ottoman to decide whether North Africa was to come under Christian or remain under Muslim rule. Algiers, Tunis and Tripoli, dependent on the sultan and now poised on the verge of their golden age as corsair states, stood as a visible sign that the issue had been resolved in favour of the Muslims and that the Spanish *conquista* along the African shore, begun in the time of Isabella of Castile and Ferdinand of Aragon, had terminated in failure.

The war of Cyprus exacted from the Ottomans a large expenditure and no inconsiderable loss of men and munitions at Nicosia, Famagusta and Tunis. It cost them, too, the almost total destruction of their effective naval forces at Lepanto and an enormous effort thereafter to build in haste a new fleet strong enough to meet the Christian armada on equal terms. An ample reward, none the less, had fallen to the Ottomans in the acquisition of Cyprus and Tunis. The long war against Persia, extending over the years 1578-90, demanded of them, however, a far more lavish expenditure of resources—and for a success ambiguous in character and brief in duration, as the future course of events was to reveal.

The campaigns of Sulaimān the Magnificent against Persia had brought within the Ottoman empire Iraq and also, in Asia Minor, the regions around Erzerum and Lake Van.[1] A peace concluded at Amasia in 1555 made over these conquests to the Ottomans. There was now little reason for the Porte to fear a revival in Persia of the drive towards religious and political expansion in Asia Minor which had distinguished the reign of Shah Ismā'īl (d. 1524), the founder of the Safawid state. And yet the old causes of tension and distrust retained much of their earlier force—the odium dividing the Ottomans, as Sunnī or orthodox Muslims, from the Persians, who adhered to the Shī'ī form of Islam; the presence in Ottoman-controlled Asia Minor of numerous elements pro-Shī'ī in belief and therefore suspect to the government of the sultan; and the endless irritation arising out of local quarrels in the ill-defined frontier zones which separated the Ottoman and the Persian territories. Moreover, with the passing of the years, the antagonism between the two states had begun to assume a more complex character. The sultan and the shah vied with each other for the allegiance of the small principalities, Christian as well as Muslim, situated in the Caucasus, the western areas of this wide region falling under Ottoman and the eastern areas under Persian influence. Ottoman statesmen sought to establish and consolidate an effective *entente* with the Uzbeg Turks of Transoxania—Muslims of the orthodox belief and avowed enemies of the Safawid régime, which had wrested from them control over the great province of Khurāsān in north-east Persia. At the same time the conviction that in the armies of the shah an apt instrument might be found to hinder the Ottoman advance against Christendom became en-grained in the political consciousness of Europe. There was from time to time an exchange of ambassadors and of diplomatic correspondence between Persia and such states as Austria, Venice and Spain, but diffi-culties of communication made it almost impossible to organise a united front against the Ottomans.

A new factor which made itself felt within the broad context of the Ottoman/Safawid antagonism was the advance of the Muscovites towards the Black Sea, the Caucasus and the Caspian Sea. Ivan IV subdued Kazan in 1552 and Astrakhan at the mouth of the Volga four years later. Musco-vite forces thrust southward as far as the river Terek, which flows a little to the north of the High Caucasus. The tsar had thus created a situation that the Porte could not ignore. Muslim merchants and Muslim pilgrims to Mecca and Medina from the lands of the north often found it difficult to pass through Safawid Persia into the Ottoman empire. Now it seemed that the routes leading to the shores of the Black Sea might also become less accessible to them. The sultan, as *Khādim al-Haramain*, or protector of the two sacred cities, Mecca and Medina—a status which gave him a vast prestige in the world of Islam—was under the obligation to defend

---

[1] See vol. II, pp. 516–17, 524–6.

23-2

the religious interests of the Muslims. He had, moreover, to take into account the obvious disadvantages, political and economic, that a continuation of the Muscovite advance would bring to the Ottoman empire. Ottoman forces tried to conquer Astrakhan in 1569, but without success. Among the unrealised objectives of the campaign was the construction of a canal between the Don and the Volga. Such a canal would have given to the Ottomans a continuous water route extending from the Black Sea along the Don and thence down the Volga to the Caspian Sea. There can be little doubt that the statesmen at Istanbul had much more in mind than the reduction to Ottoman control of the lands around the lower Volga. Access to the Caspian Sea would mean direct contact with the Uzbeg khans of Transoxania and freedom to transport men, guns and munitions into the heart of the Caucasus and into northern Persia. The failure of the Astrakhan campaign, it is true, denied to the Ottomans the use of the Don and the Volga in the event of a new war against the Safawids. It did not diminish, however, their preoccupations with the strategic possibilities of other routes to the north of the Caucasus. Ottoman forces would in fact march from the Crimea across the Kuban steppe to the shore of the Caspian Sea during the course of the great conflict with Persia which began in 1578.

The campaigns of Sulaimān the Magnificent had underlined the formidable nature of the difficulties confronting the Ottomans in their wars against Persia—the long distances to be traversed, the harshness of the climate and of the terrain, the brief duration of the campaign season, the serious problems of logistics to be overcome and the high rate of loss in men, animals and supplies.[1] To the Ottoman soldier such warfare, over and above the normal risk of death, wounds and sickness, brought exposure to extremes of heat and cold (a German travelling in the empire during the years 1553–5 saw at Istanbul men who had lost their feet as a result of frost-bite contracted on the eastern front); it also meant hunger in regions laid waste by the Safawids and at times, with most of the camels, mules and horses dead, the abandonment of arms, tents and munitions. Moreover, the prospect of a rich reward in the form of plunder was small, since the forces of the shah, pursuing their usual tactics of retreat, harassment and evasion, took care to denude the towns and the land itself of all that might assist or benefit the foe. It is evident from the historical sources of this time that the eastern campaigns had little appeal for the rank and file of the Ottoman armies, and this despite the efforts of the central régime to stimulate their morale, even to the extent of procuring from the Sunnī, or orthodox, *'ulemā* legal pronouncements, i.e. fetwās, which equated the Shī'ī with the Christians as enemies of the true faith, and declared it lawful therefore to sell as slaves, Shī'ī Muslims captured in war—a measure so extreme that it was fated to evoke no effective response.

---

[1] See vol. ii, p. 526.

The forces of the shah made use of 'burnt earth' tactics, avoided in general all risk of a major engagement, harassed the Ottoman columns and withdrew deep inside their own territories. It was thus almost impossible to win a rapid and decisive success against them. To seize Tabriz and then abandon it, as the Ottomans had done on several occasions, was of little avail. The statesmen at Istanbul found themselves confronted in fact with a difficult choice: to rest content with the eastern frontier as it now was or to enlarge the range and character of their objectives in the event of a new war. There was but one real alternative to the frustrating sequence of hard-fought advance and laborious retreat experienced in earlier campaigns—a grand offensive mounted and sustained at whatever cost in Ottoman resources, human and material, to achieve the outright conquest and permanent occupation of the wide lands beyond Erzerum and Lake Van.

One factor which counted for much in the ultimate decision of the Ottomans to renew the conflict was the growth of a serious crisis inside Persia during the last years of Shah Tahmāsp (1524–76). The Turcomans from Asia Minor and northern Syria who rallied to the cause of Ismā'īl, the founder of the Safawid state, had obtained in Persia the position of a privileged military aristocracy.[1] As the religious fervour which gave a dynamic force and cohesion to the Safawid movement in the time of Ismā'īl began to decline, inter-tribal feuds made their appearance amongst the Turcomans. Moreover, during the reign of Tahmāsp, the son of Ismā'īl, various Caucasian elements, from Georgia and Circassia and from Shirvān and Dāghistān, became more and more important in the affairs of the court and in the armed forces of the state, thus constituting a new and dangerous threat to the predominance of the Turcomans. After the death of Tahmāsp the tensions existing within the Turcoman tribes and between them and the Caucasian elements in the régime erupted into open and embittered violence.

It was to be a conflict fought out under the guise of dynastic quarrels, each of the two main factions, Turcoman and Caucasian, using princes of the blood as pawns in the struggle for power. An attempt of the Caucasians in alliance with one of the Turcoman tribes, the Ustājlū, to raise their own candidate to the throne ended in failure when their protégé Haidar Mīrzā, a son of Tahmāsp, was slain in May 1576. Ismā'īl, also a son of Tahmāsp, now ascended the throne as the choice of the Turcoman faction. His brief reign of less than two years witnessed the execution of almost all the male members of the Safawid house and of some of the most powerful amongst the great amirs and dignitaries of the state. Such unbridled violence, productive of increased fear and distrust, together with the suspicion, abhorrent to his Shī'ī subjects, that he was inclined to favour the Sunnī form of Islam, brought about his downfall and death in November 1577.

---

[1] See vol. I, pp. 404–6, for a brief account of the formation of the Safawid state.

The spirit of intrigue and dissension remained alive throughout the reign of Muhammad Khudābanda (1577–87), a prince, who, suffering from an ailment which had left him half-blind, was little more than a tool in the hands of the Turcoman chieftains. It affected also the small principalities of the Caucasus, Christian as well as Muslim, some of which, after long years of subjection to Safawid influence, had become identified with one or the other of the factions at the court of the shah, and this to such a degree that their resistance to the Ottoman offensive begun in 1578 tended—apart from the actual fortunes of the war—to fluctuate with the course of the feuds which still beset the Safawid régime. To some of the high dignitaries at Istanbul, prominent amongst them being Mustafā Pasha and Sinān Pasha, it seemed that a most opportune moment had come to settle once and for all the long contention with Persia. Sultan Murād III (1574–95) listened to their arguments and, despite the counter-advice of the grand vizier, Mehemmed Sokolli, who feared the consequences of so ambitious an enterprise, resolved to attempt the permanent conquest of the broad region between the Black Sea and the Caspian Sea.

Erzerum, to which men and munitions could be brought either along the land routes through Asia Minor or else by sea as far as Trebizond, was to be the main Ottoman base during the years of the Persian war. Here in the summer of 1578 the Ottoman commander-in-chief Mustafā Pasha concentrated a large number of Janissaries and of Sipāhīs of the Porte, and also the 'feudal' sipāhīs of Erzerum, Diyārbekir and Sivas, of Dhū'l-Kadr, Karamān and Aleppo. The Ottomans had chosen as their first major objective the subjugation of Georgia and the territories adjacent to it—a wide area divided at this time into the principalities of Kartli (including Tiflis), Kakheti, Imereti, Samtzkhé or Meskhia (including Akhaltzikhé, the Altun Kal'e of the Ottoman sources), Guria and Mingrelia. Mustafā Pasha, having defeated the Persians near Lake Çildir in August 1578, occupied and garrisoned Tiflis later in the same month. Moving now in the direction of the lands that border the Caspian Sea, Mustafā Pasha won a further battle against the Persians which enabled him to force a passage across the river Kanak (or Alazan) and then took Arash, a point of great strategic value, since it controlled the line of march from Tiflis towards Shamakhi in Shirvān and Derbend in Dāghistān and also the routes leading to the Safawid fortresses of Ganja, Erivan and Tabriz. At Arash Mustafā Pasha, before withdrawing to winter quarters at Erzerum, made arrangements for the administration of the territories thus far overrun and for the future conduct of the war: Kartli, with Tiflis, was to become an Ottoman province; Kakheti to remain under the rule of a Georgian prince dependent on the sultan; at Sukhum an Ottoman Pasha would have control of affairs in the lands along the eastern shore of the Black Sea; the reduction of Shirvān and Dāghistān, as yet unsubdued, was entrusted to a separate force under the command of Osmān Pasha. During the course of the Ottoman withdrawal towards Erzerum the princes of Imereti, Guria and Samtzkhé offered their submission to Mustafā Pasha. The Ottomans had achieved much in this first major campaign of the war, but their success was far from complete. The years 1579–84 saw them engaged in laborious and expensive operations designed to consolidate their hold on Georgia—operations which involved the construction of a great fortress at Kars in 1579, the capture and refortification of Erivan in 1583 and the establishment in 1584 of less elaborate defences on the routes leading into Tiflis, for example, at Gori, Tomanis and Lori. Moreover, the Ottomans had to undertake each year large and often hard-fought 'convoy' campaigns bearing reinforcements of men and material to the garrisons at Tiflis and elsewhere, which found themselves time and again blockaded and harassed by the Safawids and their Georgian allies.

Meanwhile, Osmān Pasha had fought a series of brilliant campaigns in the region bordering the western shore of the Caspian Sea. Although he was able to defeat the Persians on the river Kura in 1578, the forces at his command proved to be inadequate for the conquest of Shirvān. Withdrawing into Derbend, which controls the narrow coastal route, about six miles wide, between the mountains of Dāghistān and the inland sea, Osmān Pasha maintained himself there, almost isolated and against great odds, throughout the years 1579–83. At last he received, late in 1582, reinforcements sufficient for him to assume the offensive, the flower of the troops of Rumeli moving now from Kaffa in the Crimea across the Kuban and Terek rivers to Derbend—a formidable march that took almost twelve weeks under the repeated harassment and raids of the Kalmyk and Çerkes (Circassian) tribes to the north of the Caucasus. Osmān Pasha, on the river Samur in 1583, won a great battle which drove the Persians from Dāghistān and also out of Shirvān, where Shamakhi and Baku soon surrendered to the victorious general. Ordered now to reassert Ottoman control over the Crimea—the Tatar khan had evaded his obligations as a vassal of the sultan, refusing to send his horsemen to the war in the Caucasus—Osmān Pasha crossed the Kuban steppe, held Kaffa until a naval force under Uluj 'Alī Pasha came to his assistance, and then installed a new khan on the throne. Murād III welcomed the famous soldier at Istanbul with the highest tokens of esteem and favour and in July 1584 raised him to the grand vizierate in reward for his incomparable services.

The Ottoman campaigns of 1585–8 had as their main purpose the conquest of Azerbaijān. Osmān Pasha, in the face of a stiff resistance, broke through to Tabriz in 1585, seized and fortified the town and then died in the course of an arduous retreat under sustained pressure from the Safawid forces. Tabriz, Tiflis and Erivan had now to meet the weight of a Persian counter-offensive, but their garrisons, although reduced to sore straits, held out until the new Ottoman commander-in-chief on the eastern front, Ferhād Pasha, was able to relieve them in 1586. The last great campaign of the war, carried out in 1588, witnessed the fall of Ganja and of the fertile region of Kara-Bagh to the Ottomans. Meanwhile, in 1587, subordinate operations conducted from Iraq under the guidance of Çighāla-zāde Sinān Pasha, the beglerbeg of Baghdad, resulted in the occupation of two provinces—Luristān and Hamadhān—on the western borders of Persia.

The feuds that divided the Safawid régime flared out into renewed violence during the last years of the war. Hamza Mīrzā, a son of Shah Muhammad Khudābanda prominent in the resistance to the Ottomans, was slain and Muhammad Khudābanda himself forced in June 1587 to relinquish the throne in favour of another of his sons, 'Abbās (1587–1629). Moreover, in 1588 and 1589 the Uzbeg Turks of Transoxania invaded Khurāsān, capturing Herāt, Mashhad and Nīshāpūr. The urgent need to overcome the factions within the state and to drive out the Uzbegs convinced Shah 'Abbās that the war against the Ottomans must be brought to an end, whatever the cost might be. Under the terms of a peace concluded in 1590 the shah ceded to the sultan Tabriz and the territories dependent thereon in Azerbaijān, Ganja and the Kara-Bagh region, Shirvān, Georgia, Luristān, and Shahrazūr in Kurdistān.

As the war against Persia drew towards its close, a new conflict began to take form along the Ottoman frontier in Europe. A state of peace had existed between Austria and the Ottoman empire since 1568, but the endless raids and counter-incursions of Muslim *ghāzi* against Christian marcher lord continued unabated in the ill-defined zones along the border, giving rise to tensions ever liable to break out into more serious warfare.[1] The *Kleinkrieg* of the frontier was now assuming, e.g. in 1587 near Koppan, Buda and Kanizsa and in 1588 at Szikso, dimensions which threatened to undermine the suspect and unquiet peace. Hasan Pasha, the *beglerbeg* of Bosnia, raided into Croatia and besieged Sisak (Sissek) on the river Kulpa in 1591 and again in 1592. Meanwhile, some of the great dignitaries at Istanbul, most prominent amongst them being the influential Sinān Pasha, urged the sultan to make war on Austria. Murād III yielded at last to their insistence when the fateful news arrived that the ghāzis of Bosnia had been routed with great loss at Sisak in June 1593, Hasan of Bosnia being numbered amongst the slain.

A major offensive on the Danube was a severe test of Ottoman skill and resource in war. As in their Persian, so too in their Hungarian campaigns, the Ottomans had to meet and overcome formidable difficulties of time and distance, of climate, terrain and logistics.[2] Moreover, the actual warfare itself was now far less fluid in character than it had been in the earlier years of the reign of Sultan Sulaimān. The Habsburgs of Austria sought to erect a strong defensive barrier against the Ottomans. As archduke of

---

[1] See vol. II, pp. 521–2.   [2] See vol. II, pp. 514–15.

Austria and later as emperor (1558–64), Ferdinand I encouraged Germans and also Slav and Hungarian refugees from the lands under Ottoman rule to settle in the Christian border zones, granting to them religious and financial privileges in return for their services as guardians of the frontier. Out of these first tentative measures there emerged the Croat and Windisch marches, extending from the Adriatic along the Unna and Kulpa rivers and thence to the higher reaches of the Sava and the Drava—a defence system furnished in the course of time with a fully organised military apparatus of its own and financed after 1578 largely by revenues levied in Carniola, Carinthia and Styria. The more effective resistance thus made possible to the Christians, the progressive strengthening of their border defences, and the continuing recruitment of refugee Slavs and Hungarians as *limitanei* did much to evoke from the ghāzis of Bosnia the violent reaction that led to the war of 1593. The government at Vienna strove also to improve and strengthen the main fortresses still left in Christian hands— for example, Kanizsa, Raab, Komorn and Erlau. At the same time a network of small forts—palankas—came into existence, protecting the more important routes, the river crossings and the approaches to the large fortified towns. As the prospect of rapid conquest diminished with the passing of the years, the Ottomans perforce created for themselves a similar defensive armature based on a number of great fortresses like Belgrade, Temesvár, Stuhlweissenburg, Buda and Gran, each of them controlling minor strongholds situated at points of strategic value. Muslim and Christian now stood ranged one against the other behind the defences which marked out their respective zones of domination. The frontier in fact was hardening along more or less stable lines.

Not the least of the difficulties that the Ottomans had to face was the character of the troops opposed to them. The emperor, exploiting the international ramifications of Habsburg influence, was able to draw into his service some of the best soldiers of the time, the German, Walloon and Italian mercenaries, turbulent, it is true, and hard to control when ill paid, but none the less professionals expert in the most advanced techniques of warfare. Hasan al-Kāfī indeed noted with regret that the Christians, through their use of new types of hand-gun and cannon, as yet neglected by the Ottomans, had won a definite advantage over the armies of the sultan.

Moreover, despite the vast changes which the Reformation wrought in Europe, the modes of sentiment and belief deriving from the old ideal of a *Corpus Christianum* designed to unite in one common allegiance, regardless of race and language, all nations that held the true faith, retained even now some of their ancient force. At the call to arms against the Muslim foe numerous volunteers, Protestant as well as Catholic, still came to serve on the Hungarian front. One Christian was to describe the war of 1593 as a conflict fought *pro aris et focis, pro patria et religione*. The

Emperor Rudolf II, in declaring his armies to be the shield of all Christendom, but echoed the conviction of his contemporaries. The immense interest aroused amongst the Christians is reflected in the popular demand for works, old and new, analysing the strength and weakness of the Ottoman empire and in the appearance of innumerable *Zeitungen* and *Relationes* written in German, Latin and Italian and then translated into other languages and all of them narrating, often with much detail and on the basis of first-hand information, the events and fortunes of the war. A Venetian author of this time, Lazaro Soranzo, expressed indeed far more than a personal judgement when he stated that the conflict begun in 1593 was the greatest affair then happening in the world: *la presente guerra e il maggior negotio, c'hora corra nel Mondo.*[1]

The great Hungarian war which followed the rout of the Bosnian ghāzis at Sisak lasted for thirteen long and arduous years (1593–1606). Throughout most of this time the Ottomans had to face a grave situation on the lower Danube, where in 1594 Moldavia, Wallachia and Transylvania, hitherto dependent on the sultan, rose in revolt and made common cause with Austria. The defection of the three principalities constituted a serious menace to the lines of communication running from Istanbul to Belgrade, Buda and Gran, for the Danube was of high importance as a water-route much used in the transport of guns and munitions to the Hungarian front. It also denied to the Ottomans the rich supplies of grain and meat, of horses and other beasts of burden which came to them from Moldavia and Wallachia. A not inconsiderable portion of the Ottoman war effort was therefore directed perforce towards the defence of the river line, and this to the obvious advantage of the imperialist armies operating on the middle Danube. The entente now established between the three Danubian states and Austria rested, however, on a most insecure foundation. Sigismund Bathory, the prince of Transylvania, had acquired from the Jesuit influences surrounding his youth the ambition and zeal to lead a new resistance to the Ottomans. He also wished to reassert old Hungarian claims to control over Wallachia and Moldavia—a desire that ran counter to the aims of Michael, the energetic voivode of Wallachia. The Habsburgs, too, had their own objectives and, as heirs to the ancient Hungarian realm which came to an end at the battle of Mohács in 1526,[2] would miss no favourable occasion to bring Transylvania under their direct rule. A further complication was the interest and, at times in the course of the war, the armed intervention of Poland in the affairs of Moldavia. Sigismund Bathory, unstable of purpose, abdicated the throne of Transylvania in favour of the Emperor Rudolf II and then reassumed it, thus increasing the confusion which reigned north of the Danube. Michael of Wallachia, professing to act on behalf of the emperor, overran Transyl-

---

[1] L. Soranzo, *L'Ottomanno* (Ferrara, 1599), Proemio, VI.
[2] See vol. II, pp. 512–13.

vania in 1599 and Moldavia in 1600. His success called forth a Polish intervention in Moldavia and also in Wallachia itself and, in addition, a combined resistance in Transylvania of the Hungarian elements there and of imperialist forces now sent to their aid. On the murder in 1601 of the Voivode Michael there followed in Transylvania some four years of imperialist control involving measures against the Protestant religion and the local estates, confiscations designed to break the influence of the great nobles and, in addition, the appointment of German and Italian officials as the instruments of a centralised Habsburg régime. The end result was that Transylvania, led by Stephen Bocskai, the ablest of the lieutenants of Sigismund Bathory, abandoned the alliance with the emperor and sought a new entente with the sultan. This change of alignment had a marked effect on the course of the long Hungarian war, since it so eased the situation of the Ottomans that their armies now recovered, during the last phase of the conflict, the territories lost earlier to the imperialist forces. It brought about also the emergence of a Transylvania soon to enter into a brief golden age as a state endowed with a large measure of independence in relation alike to the emperor and to the Ottoman sultan.

The first years of the Hungarian war went ill for the Ottomans. It is true that the great fortress of Raab fell to them in 1594, but this gain was more than counterbalanced when in 1595 Gran—the northernmost bulwark of Ottoman rule on the middle Danube—surrendered to the imperialists and at the same time a full-scale campaign directed against Wallachia, now ranged on the side of the emperor, came to a disastrous end with the rout —at Giurgiu on the lower Danube—of the Ottoman forces under the command of Sinān Pasha. So grave was the outlook that Mehemmed III (1595–1603) was induced to take the field himself in the next year. As their main objective for the campaign of 1596 the Ottomans chose the Hungarian fortress of Erlau situated close to the narrow corridor of land through which ran the imperialist lines of communication with Transylvania. Erlau surrendered to the sultan on 12 October 1596, before the imperialists, who had brought together a powerful concentration of forces, could arrive to relieve it. There now followed the greatest field battle of the war. At Mezö-Keresztes on 26 October 1596 the Ottomans, at first driven back almost to the verge of disaster, routed the Christians in a final desperate assault. This battle, although it led to no immediate consequences of note (the campaign season was in fact far advanced), denied to the imperialists all hope of a rapid conquest which would evict the Ottomans from the Hungarian lands under their control.

The war became now a laborious conflict of sieges demanding of Muslim and Christian alike an exorbitant expenditure in men and material. The imperialists reconquered Raab in 1598, but failed in a determined attempt to seize Buda. This same year saw the Ottomans engaged in a vain effort to capture Varaždin. A notable success came to the Ottomans, however, in 1600 with their conquest of Kanizsa, a fortress almost impregnable in its encircling marshes. The Christians in 1601, though repulsed with severe loss in their endeavour to regain Kanizsa, besieged and took Stuhl-weissenburg, only to lose it to the Ottomans in the following year. The main operations of 1602–4 centred around Buda, which the imperialists strove in vain to reduce, and Pest, which the Ottomans sought to re-capture—it had fallen to the Christians in 1602. Not until 1605, when Transylvania aligned itself once more on the side of the sultan, did the conflict enter into a more decisive phase. The Ottomans, in the course of this year, fought the last major campaign of the war, recovering Gran, together with several lesser strongholds, amongst them Visegrád, Vesz-prém and Palota.

At Vienna, as at Istanbul, the desire for peace was now dominant. The revolt of Transylvania against Habsburg control had turned the tide of war in favour of the Ottomans. It was clear that Austria would gain little and might indeed lose much from a continuation of hostilities. An agree-ment negotiated in June 1606 resolved the differences existing between Stephen Bocskai and the Emperor Rudolf II. Bocskai—to whom the sultan in 1605 had promised Transylvania and also the Hungarian throne —was to retain Transylvania for himself and his heirs, the pretension to the title of king being allowed to lapse in silence. The sultan also was eager to end the long conflict on the Danube. Asia Minor had been aflame with rebellion since 1596. Moreover, in 1603 Shah ʿAbbās of Persia had begun a new war against the Ottomans with the aim of reconquering the large territories ceded to the sultan in 1590. Until there was peace with Austria, the Porte would be free neither to stamp out the fire of insurrection nor to halt the Safawid advance.

Peace was made between the emperor and the sultan in November 1606. The long war brought into the foreground one basic fact—that the Ottomans, despite a most lavish expenditure of their resources, had failed to break the resistance of the Habsburgs. Their formidable war machine, extended beyond its effective range, was ground almost into exhaustion on the far-off plains bordering the middle Danube. The actual location of the peace conference, and still more the terms of the peace itself, revealed how much the relative balance as between Austria and the Ottoman empire had altered, since the golden years of Sulaimān the Magnificent, to the advantage of the emperor and to the detriment of the sultan. Hitherto Austria had been forced to send ambassadors to Istanbul when seeking agreement with the Porte. Now the conclusion of peace was not to have the appearance of an act of grace and favour from the sultan to a sup-pliant foe. The final conference took place on the Hungarian frontier between the Christian fortress of Komorn and the Muslim fortress of Gran, on neutral ground at Zsitva-Torok, where the river Zsitva flows into the Danube. Here the Ottomans assented to terms which reflected not so much their concern over the dangers confronting them in Asia Minor as their recognition that the war begun in 1593 was ending for them in virtual failure. The emperor, after a single and final 'gift' amounting to 200,000 gulden, was to yield no more tribute to the sultan, as he and his predecessors had done since the time of Sulaimān the Magnificent. Henceforth the sultan would accord to the emperor, in all future diplomatic intercourse, his full rank and titles, that is, was to accept him as an equal. Each side retained the territories then under its control. The Ottomans continued, therefore, to hold the Hungarian lands subject to their rule in 1593 and now added to them two fortresses, Erlau and Kanizsa—a meagre reward for thirteen years of arduous conflict.

The long wars against Persia and Austria had—over and above their immediate outcome—a disadvantageous effect on some of the basic institutions of the Ottoman state. One factor of great importance was the character of the warfare itself. The conquest, with a view to permanent occupation, of large territories in the region of the Caucasus demanded of the Ottomans the construction of numerous fortresses and the establishment of garrisons adept in the use of firearms and the arts of siegecraft. On the Hungarian front the Ottoman war machine was committed to a laborious offensive against fortresses often manned with expert professional soldiers skilled in the latest techniques of warfare. Under these conditions the role of the Ottoman sipāhīs, the 'feudal' warriors of the sultan, tended to become less significant than it had been heretofore. Now on the eastern and still more on the western front, the dominant need was for foot soldiers trained to use firearms and for specialist troops such as engineers and artillerists. The 'feudal' sipāhī, fashioned and moulded in accordance with the old traditions of the Ottoman state, was ill at ease in the new warfare. The changed circumstances of war made inevitable a large increase in the paid forces of the central Ottoman régime, in the Janissaries and the other specialised corps of the imperial household.

The forces of the central régime bore time and again the brunt of the severest hostilities. Under the difficulties of warfare on the eastern front the rate of loss, for example amongst the Janissaries, through death, wounds and sickness became high indeed. The conditions prevailing on the western front must have been still more harsh—one Christian was to describe the Hungarian war as 'a slaughter-house of men'[1]—and here too the élite troops of the imperial household had to endure grave losses.

The combined effect of the need to increase the paid forces of the central régime and the need to make good the high casualties suffered in the long wars of this time was disastrous. It soon became clear that the traditional sources of recruitment—captives acquired through war, gift or purchase

[1] A. Tarducci, *Delle Machine, Ordinanze et Quartieri Antichi et Moderni* (Venice, 1601), p. 38.

and, in addition, the *devshirme* or child-tribute levied from the subject Christian populations of the empire—would in no wise suffice to meet this twofold demand. Nor did the adoption of expedients—for example, the throwing into battle of the *'ajemioghlanlar* or 'foreign youths' (the young recruits to the corps of Janissaries), before their training was complete—offer more than a transient relief from the dire pressures of war. The Porte was therefore driven to countenance a solution which blurred and broke down the barrier hitherto existing between the *ghilmān* and the Muslim-born elements in the state: now began the inclusion, on a large scale, of Muslim-born subjects amongst the Janissaries and the other paid troops of the central régime and the creation of new bodies such as the *culcardasi*, or 'brothers of the *kul*' (that is, of the *ghulām*), recruited from the same Muslim sources and assimilated in privilege and status to the 'men of the sultan'. This departure from the 'classical' system of Ottoman rule brought in its train a serious impairment of that *esprit de corps*, that efficient skill and discipline amongst the *ghilmān*, which had contributed so much towards the greatness of the Ottoman state.

The years 1566–1617 saw the emergence, in relation to the Ottomans, of new factors and new influences—some of them markedly adverse in character—within the realm of commercial, economic and social affairs. To the south, in the distant waters of the Red Sea, the Indian Ocean and the Persian Gulf, the protracted if spasmodic warfare between the Ottomans and the Portuguese was drawing to its close. Ottoman vessels, under the command of 'Alī Beg, sailed from the Yemen in 1580 to raid the Portuguese-dominated Maskat in the 'Umān. 'Alī Beg in 1584 moved down the coast of East Africa as far as Malindi. He repeated the venture in 1589, this time reaching Mombasa, where his squadron succumbed, however, to the assault of a superior Portuguese fleet from Goa in western India. Thus ended the last Ottoman endeavour to challenge the domination of Portugal over the waters of the Indian Ocean. It had long since become clear that the Portuguese had not the resources to win for themselves a complete control of the ancient trade routes running from India through the lands of Islam towards Europe. Their penetration into the Indian Ocean in the wake of Vasco da Gama disrupted for some considerable time the rich transit trade through the Red Sea and the Persian Gulf to the harbours of the Levant. None the less, as the tide of events revealed more and more the limitations of Portuguese power and influence, this traffic began to revive: the spices and the other exotic products of the East now flowed both around the Cape of Good Hope and also, once more and on a large scale, through Suez and Basra towards the shore of the Mediterranean Sea. Aleppo, indeed, became after 1550 a flourishing emporium dealing in spices and in the much coveted silk of Persia, while Alexandria in Egypt, too, prospered to the extent that it recovered no small measure of its former wealth and importance. This revival, however, of the old transit trade had no long duration. The advance into the Indian Ocean of maritime nations much stronger than the Portuguese—the English and the Dutch—was to ensure in the not distant future the undeniable predominance of the sea route around Africa.

The English and, after them, the Dutch now began to penetrate into the Mediterranean Sea. English merchant vessels had sometimes previously ventured into the waters of the Levant, sailing under the aegis of those Christian states, such as Venice and France, which possessed commercial privileges within the Ottoman empire. As yet the circumstances did not exist, however, which would favour the growth of close and profitable trade relations between London and Istanbul. The merchants of England had no grant of privileges from the sultan. Their voyages to the Mediterranean long continued to be precarious enterprises. There was no powerful organisation at home to foster their interests. Not until the middle years of the reign of Queen Elizabeth did a more auspicious state of affairs become evident. The merchants had now to hand an adequate financial mechanism in the form of chartered joint-stock companies, increased resources of capital and, arising from the obvious revival of the old transit traffic through the Middle East, a strong interest in the possibilities of trade with the Levant. William Harborne went to Istanbul in 1578 as the representative of the London merchants Edward Osborne and Richard Staper. He obtained from the grace and favour of Sultan Murād III in 1580 a grant of 'capitulations', of commercial privileges similar to the ones that France and Venice enjoyed in the Ottoman empire. Osborne, Staper and their associates received from Queen Elizabeth in 1581 a charter incorporating them as a company of merchants trading to the Levant. The privileges secured from the sultan in 1580 had, and would retain, a provisional character until England appointed and maintained a permanent diplomatic representative at the Porte. Harborne became the first accredited agent of the Levant merchants at Istanbul in 1583 and also, at the same time, the first 'orator', or ambassador, of England to the Ottoman empire—an office that he held until 1588.

Neither France nor Venice desired to see established in the Levant a new rival to their own interests. Moreover, if the sultan allowed England to conduct an independent trade within his dominions, the two Christian states would lose the valuable dues of consulage that Englishmen had hitherto paid for permission to traffic under the French or under the Venetian flag. The ambassador of France and the *bailo* (representative) of Venice at Istanbul strove with all the means at their command to ruin the negotiations of Harborne, but in vain, since Murād III confirmed in 1583 the grant of trade privileges that he had made to England three years before. The Ottomans realised no doubt the advantages, both economic and political, to be drawn from close contact with a Christian state powerful at sea and hostile, like themselves, towards the house of Habsburg. None the less, it is surprising that Harborne, within the brief space of two years (1578–80), should have surmounted all the difficulties which confronted him at Istanbul. One factor did much to facilitate his success.

The long years of conflict with Persia and later with Austria demanded of the Ottomans an enormous expenditure in munitions of war—so enormous indeed as to create a genuine shortage of such materials. English merchants had the means and also the will to make good deficiencies of this kind. The Spanish ambassador at London, Bernardino de Mendoza, noted in 1579 that the Ottomans received from England quantities of tin, a metal indispensable in the manufacture of bronze cannon. Other cargoes sent out from England to the Ottoman empire included broken bells and images (plunder from English churches despoiled in the course of the Reformation), iron and steel, lead, copper, arquebuses, muskets, sword-blades, brimstone, saltpetre and gunpowder. One Englishman—a captive of the Ottomans from 1603 to 1605—wrote that the Janissaries had 'not one corne of good powder but that whyche they gett from overthrone Christians, or els is broughte them out of Englande' and that the English 'keepe 3 open shoppes of armes and munition in Constantinople...Gunpowder is solde for 23 and 24 *chikinoes* the hundred; in Englande it costeth but 3 pounde. Tinne in Constantinople beareth the same price. Muskettes are solde for 5 or 6 *chikinos* the peyce; in Englande they buy ordinary ones for 2 markes, the best for 18 shillings.'[1]

Trade was no doubt the initial motive force that brought the English to the Levant, but political considerations also exerted a strong influence during the embassies of William Harborne, the first ambassador (1583–8) of England at the Porte, and of Edward Barton, his successor in that office (1588–98). Harborne and Barton, time and again, entreated the Ottomans to begin a naval offensive against Spain in the interests of England and the other Protestant states. Barton, moreover, seems to have welcomed the drift toward war between the Ottoman empire and Austria in the years before 1593. He revealed, perhaps, his true attitude when he wrote: 'In my small judgment I think it nothing offensive to God to set one of his enemies against the other, the Infidel against the Idolaters, to the end that whilst they were by the ears, God's people[2] might respite and take strength.'[3]

The trade in munitions of war brought the good name of England into much disrepute at this time. This traffic contravened the old canon law of the Christian Church Universal, which forbade the sale of war material to the Infidel. It is true that the ancient doctrine had lost almost all its

[1] *Calendar of State Papers, Spanish (1568–79)*, no. 609, and *(1580–86)*, no. 265; Sir T. Sherley, *Discours of the Turkes* (ed. E. D. Ross) Camden Misc., XVI (1936), 7, 9–10.
[2] I.e. the Protestants.
[3] I. I. Podea, 'A Contribution to the Study of Queen Elizabeth's Eastern Policy (1590–1593)', in *Mélanges d'Histoire Générale*, II (Cluj, 1938), 9.

compulsive force, but the modes of thought and sentiment deriving from it, although now in decline, still remained alive in Protestant as in Catholic Europe. Men of firm religious belief felt this commerce to be therefore 'a contraband hateful and pernicious to the whole of Christendom'. No less damaging to the reputation of England was the character of the political objectives that Harborne and Barton sought to achieve at the Porte. The propagandists who wrote on behalf of the Roman church, notable amongst them being such Catholic exiles from England as William Allen, Joseph Cresswell, Thomas Stapleton, William Reynolds, Richard Rowlands and William Giffard, had ample and, indeed, given their own particular point of view, valid reason to belabour the two ambassadors and their mistress, Queen Elizabeth, as traitors to the Christian faith. Thomas Stapleton declared, indeed, that the greatest of the impieties— *summum impietatis culmen*—attributable to the queen and her servants was their incitement of the Ottomans to attack Christendom. Propaganda of this kind achieved a cumulative effect so embarrassing to Queen Elizabeth that she was obliged to take active measures against the uneasiness and distrust that it aroused both at home in England itself and abroad in Europe. One of the most harmful of the accusations made against the queen laid at her door the blame for the outbreak of war between the Ottomans and the imperialists in 1593. The German Protestants might well remain silent while the English ambassadors at Istanbul urged the sultan to attack Spain, the most formidable of the Catholic powers. Their compliance was not, however, to be assumed in the case of manœuvres designed to bring about a great Ottoman assault on Austria—an assault that would perforce imperil their own interests, if it were successful. Queen Elizabeth, therefore, in order to counteract the discredit now gathering about her name, sent Christopher Parkins to Prague in 1593 with instructions to exculpate her before the Emperor Rudolf II. The mission of Parkins was in fact a success, since the emperor declared himself to be satisfied that the queen was not to blame for the imminent war in Hungary. None the less, the Catholic propaganda continued unabated during the years of the Hungarian conflict (1593–1606) and had repercussions even in distant Russia. The ambassador of England at the Porte, Edward Barton, accompanied Sultan Mehemmed III on the campaign of 1596 which brought disaster to the Christians at Erlau and at Mező-Keresztes. His presence in the field with the sultan was of great advantage to the Catholic agents at Moscow. The Muscovites, under the influence of papal and imperialist propaganda (the astute intelligences at the Roman curia of this time saw in Russia a potential foe—and indeed the ultimate ruin—of the Ottoman empire), communicated to Queen Elizabeth their astonishment and alarm at the conduct of Barton and also at the traffic in munitions of war. Once more the queen was obliged to defend her good name, first, in 1597 through one of her merchants trading in Russia and again in 1600 through Sir Richard Lee, whom she sent to Moscow with specious assurances that the sultan had forced Barton to go on the campaign of 1596 and that Englishmen had sold to the Ottomans no arms nor other material of war. Not until the course of events made clear the impotence of Spain to conquer England and of the Ottoman empire to subdue Austria did the war of propaganda begin to die down and the more debatable aspects of English traffic in the Levant cease to be of some significance in the field of international relations.

The years of warfare against Persia and Austria saw the Ottoman government confronted with serious financial difficulties. Revenue and expenditure were calculated in terms of the silver akçe or asper, the basic unit of coinage in the empire. The Ottomans, like the peoples of Europe, had suffered hitherto from a recurring shortage of the precious metals, gold and silver—a shortage so acute that it threatened at times to disrupt their silver-based system of coinage. To overcome such moments of stress and strain the sultans controlled the silver mines, favoured the import and discouraged the export of coin and bullion, enlarged those sectors of the state business which involved transactions in kind rather than in cash, and also resorted at need to a measure of debasement in the coinage. This situation underwent a marked change, however, when the empire, from about 1580 onward, began to feel the effects of a severe inflation.

American silver has been regarded as a major cause of the 'price revolution' which was affecting Europe at this time. The great increase in the amount of silver available brought about, so it is argued, a prolonged inflation. Silver, flowing from the Americas into Spain and thence to Genoa and Ragusa, penetrated thereafter into the Ottoman empire. As it moved eastwards through the channels of international commerce, the flood of silver left in its wake similar consequences in each of the countries that it overran, that is, a rapid rise in prices, depreciation of the coinage and debasement, counterfeiting, speculation and the like. This quantitative view of the 'price revolution', this emphasis on the sudden large expansion of the circulating medium has been subject of late to much criticism. Recent analyses have suggested that the rise in prices was not due—or at least not alone due—to the influx of precious metals from the New World, but to other factors of equal or even greater effect. Attention has been drawn, for example, to the importance of an increase in population more rapid than the parallel expansion of the means of subsistence and thus productive of grave social imbalance—and there is indeed evidence to show that the population of the Ottoman empire, above all in Asia Minor, was increasing to a considerable degree at this time. The 'price revolution' should be attributed, no doubt, to the interaction of a number of different causes rather than to the action of one single cause. It is difficult to believe, however, that the eastward movement of silver had nothing to do with the inflation which now beset the Ottoman state. It constituted, at the lowest estimate, a factor of disturbance in the complex and adverse situation now facing the Ottomans. The inflation occurred, moreover, at a time when the Porte was obliged to find and disburse enormous sums in connection with the long wars, first against Persia and then against Austria, and when it had, also, to countenance a notable expansion in the paid forces and personnel of the central régime—an expansion which meant, for the state, a further and large increase of expenditure.

The Porte, in order to alleviate the fiscal troubles of the moment, decreed in 1584 a reduction in the silver content of the akçe or asper from one-fifth to one-eighth of a dirham. This debasement of the coinage brought great, though ephemeral, profits to a government hard pressed to meet the high cost of the Persian war. It was also fraught with serious consequences. The ratio of the akçe to the ducat declined from 60 to over 200. Foreign coins, of gold as well as of silver, began to drive the debased Ottoman issues even from the internal markets of the empire. The Porte, faced with vast expenses and with a depreciating coinage, became more and more exorbitant in its fiscal measures and demands and thus aggravated the distress felt amongst the mass of the population as a result of the rise in prices.

The inflation struck hard at all classes dependent on a fixed income. Among the civil, administrative and religious personnel of the state, numerous officials, often underpaid and with their salaries in arrear, found it difficult to maintain themselves and sought relief for their troubles in malpractice and corruption. There was unrest, too, and a dangerous spirit of turbulence amongst the paid troops of the imperial household. The inclusion within the Janissaries of elements hitherto debarred from their ranks no doubt did much to undermine the old standards of obedience and trustworthiness prevailing in this famous corps. None the less, a further and cogent reason for the marked growth of indiscipline among the Janissaries—and also among the other categories of paid troops—was the fact that their wages, allotted to them in cash and at a fixed rate, had become insufficient, in view of the rise in prices, to meet their normal needs: hence their demands for large donatives and for increased rates of pay—demands too menacing to be ignored, since behind them was the ultimate sanction of revolt against the sultan and his viziers. The Janissaries in 1589 rose in rebellion when the government wanted to give them their wages not in old and good, but in new and debased, coin. Three years later, in 1592, the Sipāhīs of the Porte mutinied, because their pay was not issued to them in full. More serious still was the revolt which broke out, again amongst the Sipāhīs of the Porte, in 1603. The Grand Vizier Hasan Pasha induced the Janissaries to crush this insurrection. Their readiness to intervene—a source of much embitterment for the future between themselves and the mounted regiments of the imperial household—reflected how fast and how far the *esprit de corps* heretofore uniting the 'men of the sultan' was crumbling under the impact of adverse circumstance.

The price revolution affected, too, the 'feudal' sipāhīs, dependent for their maintenance on a fixed income accruing to them from their fiefs. Even before this time, the 'feudal' horsemen had begun to feel the strain of distant campaigns expensive to themselves in respect of supplies and equipment and at the same time less and less rewarding in terms of plunder and captives of war. It is understandable, therefore, that the inflation hit the 'feudal' class hard, and above all those sipāhīs who had tīmārs of low or moderate yield—such fiefs being far more numerous, it would seem, in Asia Minor than in the Balkans. Moreover, with the growth of intrigue and corruption amongst the personnel of the central régime, palace favourites and large-scale speculators obtained tīmārs and zi'āmets. The government at Istanbul, in its search for additional sources of revenue, seized and—through its deliberate failure to regrant them—held for its own use numerous fiefs which fell vacant in the normal course of affairs. It is from this time forward that a progressive diminution began in the number of tīmārs and a parallel increase in extent of the *khāss-i shāhī*, the domain of the sultan.

A further and potent factor in the growing disruption of the 'feudal' system was the flight of the peasants from the land—a phenomenon which meant that fiefs often became less productive through lack of labour. Even in the reign of Sultan Sulaimān, at a time when the empire was at the apogee of its power and splendour, Lutfī Pasha, in the small treatise entitled *Āsāfnāme* which he wrote after his dismissal from the office of grand vizier in 1541, felt obliged to warn against the danger of rural depopulation and to recommend that the peasants be subjected to no more than a moderate taxation and also be safeguarded from possible oppression at the hands of the provincial authorities.

The growth in the population of the empire tended to exceed the increase in the amount of land under cultivation. This factor, in conjunction with the prevailing inflation, the debasement of the coinage and the fiscal pressures now emanating from the central régime and from the provincial authorities, led to the gradual emergence, especially in Asia Minor, of a rootless class of men (known as *ghurbet tā'ifesi* or *levendāt*)—men torn from the soil, some of them finding relief for their distress in brigandage, others fleeing in their trouble to the local towns, there to form a restive proletarian element ripe for mischief, should a suitable occasion offer itself. Around Mustafā, a son of Sultan Sulaimān, had been focused in 1553 the malaise and dissatisfaction felt amongst the *levendāt* and also amongst the 'feudal' sipāhīs. After the execution, in that year, of Mustafā, the two remaining sons of Sulaimān, Selīm and Bāyazīd, came into conflict (1558–9) over the succession to the Ottoman throne. The princes, eager to build armies of their own, sought and obtained support from the 'feudal' sipāhīs and their *jebeli* warriors and also from the Muslim elements driven from the soil. A grave price was demanded, however, for this assistance. Selīm and Bāyazīd had to confer on a large number of the troops thus recruited a status which would assimilate the recipient, in rank and prestige, to the paid forces of the central régime, to the 'men of the sultan'.[1] The need to grant such a concession indicated that, under the pressure of hostile circumstance, the Muslim-born subjects of the empire had become more reluctant than ever before to acquiesce in their own exclusion from those areas of high power and privilege in the state hitherto reserved for the personnel of the imperial household. It will be evident that the onset of inflation, the harsh fiscal policies of the central government, and the increasing disruption of the 'feudal' system augmented and accelerated the flight of the peasants from the land, heightening even to the point of crisis the unrest so widespread in the provinces of the empire. There was now a real danger that, in Asia Minor, 'feudal' grievance might coalesce with agrarian discontent in the form of rebellion against the central régime and its privileged personnel—rebellion, moreover, of a most formidable kind, since it would be fought with the aid of the *levendāt*, large numbers of whom had acquired experience of warfare as irregulars serving in the campaigns against Persia and Austria. It would also be waged with assistance from the 'feudal' sipāhīs and their *jebeli* retinues expert in the art of war.

Such indeed was to be the issue of events. The 'feudal' horsemen summoned from Asia Minor for service in the Hungarian campaign of 1596 did not distinguish themselves at the battle of Mezö-Keresztes. Moreover, of the sipāhīs called to the war, no small number had failed to take the field. Çighāla-zāde Sinān Pasha, raised to the grand vizierate after the battle, introduced severe measures to deal with this situation. It is to the bitter resentment thus aroused amongst the 'feudal' sipāhīs and to the increasing turbulence of the *levendāt* that the Ottoman chronicles relating to this time ascribe the great wave of rebellion which swept across Asia Minor between 1596 and 1610. To the Ottomans the movement was known as the *Khurūj-i Jalāliyān*, the insurrection of the *Jalālī* rebels. The main architects of revolt were a certain 'Abd al-Halīm, called Kara Yaziji (the 'Black Scribe'), and his brother Deli Hasan. Their depredations extended from Ruhā (Urfa) to Sivas and Kaysari and from the region of Albistān in the south to the region of Jānīk in the north of Asia Minor. The government at Istanbul sought to separate one from the other two elements involved in the tide of insurrection—on the one hand the 'feudal' sipāhīs (most of them warriors endowed with fiefs which did not yield large revenues) and, with them, the personalities most prominent amongst the *levendāt* and on the other hand the mass of the rootless men

---

[1] See vol. II, pp. 527-30.

whom economic and fiscal pressures had driven from the land. It was indeed obvious enough that the discontent so rife in Asia Minor would become much less dangerous to the central régime once the *levendāt* rank and file of rebellion lost the co-operation of the sipāhīs. The means chosen at the Porte to attain such an outcome indicated how resolute the Muslim-born subjects of the sultan had become to force an entrance into the exalted world of power and privilege belonging, until this time, to the men of non-Muslim and non-Turkish origin, who rejoiced in the status of *ghulām*. Kara Yaziji received from the sultan an appointment as *sanjak-begi*, that is, governor of a province; later, Deli Hasan, his brother, was raised to the rank of *beglerbegi* (governor-general over a group of provinces). On these occasions, too, some at least of the more important and more intimate adherents of Kara Yaziji and Deli Hasan obtained for themselves inclusion amongst the 'men of the sultan'. Measures of this kind won, however, but a transient and partial success. New rebel chieftains made their appearance in Asia Minor, for example, in Aidin and Sarukhan, in the region of Brusa, in Karaman and in Cilicia. The need— becoming more urgent with each passing year—to take decisive action against the rebels goes far to explain the readiness of the sultan and his viziers to seek peace with the imperialists, as soon as operations on the Hungarian front had assumed a trend favourable to the Ottoman cause. Murād Pasha, able and vigorous, prominent at Zsitva-Torok and, in reward for his valuable services there, appointed to be grand vizier, crushed the revolts through a combination of fraud, treachery and force in a series of relentless campaigns (1607–10). His merciless severity stamped out most of the resistance and imposed some degree of order on a land which had endured a decade and more of spoliation. The basic causes of economic and social discontent remained, however, untouched and would continue to be active in the future.

Meanwhile, in 1603 a new conflict had broken out between the Ottomans and the Safawids. Shah 'Abbās of Persia (1587–1629), during the first fifteen years of his reign, overcame and brought under his own ruthless control the Turcoman chieftains and their tribesmen, who had dominated so long the internal life of the Safawid state. He increased in number the paid troops recruited from the Caucasus, and above all from Georgia, and introduced amongst them a more extensive use of firearms. These forces, non-tribal in character and dependent on himself alone, formed the hard core of the armies that 'Abbās mustered in order to face (1587–97) the repeated and dangerous invasions of the Uzbeg Turks from Transoxania into Khurāsān and thereafter to drive the Uzbegs back (1598–1602) into their own territories. The shah, once he had made himself the real master of Persia and also had overcome the challenge of the Uzbegs, turned his attention to the reconquest of the lands yielded to the Ottoman sultan in 1590. His endeavour, through such emissaries as the Englishmen Anthony and Robert Sherley, to establish an offensive alliance with one or more of the states of Europe against the Ottoman empire ended in failure. The moment was ripe, however, for the revival, even without Christian aid, of Safawid domination in the countries situated between the Black Sea and the Caspian Sea. Ottoman rule in the Caucasus was in effect an armed occupation limited over wide regions to control of the main lines of communication and of the more important strategic centres—a rule, save perhaps in some of the western areas long exposed to the influence of the Porte, too new as yet to have grown deep roots and still alien therefore to the mass of the people, a large proportion of whom retained their earlier and close ties with the Safawid régime. The fact, too, that the Ottoman empire was involved in war against Austria and beset, moreover, with rebellion in Asia Minor gave to Shah 'Abbās a pronounced advantage. How great this advantage was became clear when, in the brief space of five years (1603–7), the precarious edifice of Ottoman rule in the Caucasus crumbled into almost total ruin, Tabriz, Erivan and Ganja, Derbend, Baku and Shamakhi, Tiflis and even Kars falling to the armies of the shah. Not until the war with Austria had been brought to a close and the fire of revolt subdued in Asia Minor was the Porte free in fact to prepare a real counter-offensive. Ottoman resistance during these years, therefore, was spasmodic in character and of small effect. Çighāla-zāde Sinān Pasha advanced towards Tabriz in 1605, but suffered defeat in battle and then retired with considerable loss to Van and Diyārbekir. Murād Pasha, having beaten down the rebels of Asia Minor, marched to Tabriz in 1610 and ravaged the town, which Shah 'Abbās had chosen not to defend. This event proved, however, to be the sole occurrence of note during the campaign, since the Pasha soon withdrew to winter quarters at Erzerum. The truth was that, bearing in mind the vast strain of protracted warfare abroad and of hydra-headed revolt at home, neither the sultan, Ahmed I (1603–17), nor his ministers felt much desire to wage against Persia yet another major conflict, which might well be no less arduous and long and no less impermanent in result than the war begun in 1578 had been. A peace was negotiated, therefore, between the two states in 1612, the Ottomans surrendering the large territories ceded to them in 1590. Disputes over the terms of this settlement led to a renewal of hostilities in 1615. The Ottomans, in 1616, besieged Erivan and also rebuilt the fortress of Kars. Two events—the death of Ahmed I in 1617 and the rout of an Ottoman force near Tabriz in 1618—hastened the end of the war. The peace of September 1618, ratified in September 1619, reiterated in effect the articles of agreement laid down in 1612: once more the Ottomans renounced the lands yielded to them in 1590 and thus accepted a reversion to the state of affairs which had existed in the last years of Sulaimān the Magnificent.

The Ottoman empire, under the impact of forces that it was almost powerless to control, fell during the years 1566–1617 from the summit of its strength and splendour into a condition of indubitable, though as yet incipient, decline. It was perhaps an Englishman who, in relation to the Ottomans, summarised best the essential lesson of these years. Sir Thomas Roe, ambassador of England at the Porte from 1621 to 1628, made a shrewd judgement when he wrote that the Ottoman empire might 'stand, but never rise again'.[1]

[1] *The Negotiations of Sir Thomas Roe in his Embassy to the Ottoman Porte from the Year 1621 to 1628 Inclusive* (London, 1740), p. 809.

CHAPTER XII

POLAND AND LITHUANIA

O N 25 June 1572 Sigismund Augustus, the last male descendant of the house of Jagiellon which had ruled in central and eastern Europe for nearly two hundred years, died at his favourite country residence at Knyszyn. This monarch of great dignity and exceptional humanity, gifted in languages, a good stylist and orator, a connoisseur of art and a passionate collector of tapestries, left his vast kingdom, largely his life-work, without an heir. This kingdom was a sort of union of various states which had previously been independent or semi-independent but which had been united under the Jagiellon dynasty. It included the kingdom of Poland, the grand duchy of Lithuania with its Ruthenian territories, the duchy of Mazovia, royal Prussia (Danzig Pomerania), ducal Prussia, the duchy of Curland, and Livonia. This vast federation, as well as being called a kingdom, was known as the *Rzeczpospolita*, a commonwealth of various nations or states, as Sigismund Augustus used sometimes to describe it. This emphasised the fact that the union consisted of several nations differing in creed, race and language, but together making a political unity, under one king, with a central parliament and a common foreign policy. It was obvious that the immediate future would show whether the idea of union which Sigismund Augustus had fostered during his reign, and had bequeathed to his dominions in his will, would survive his death and become a source of political strength in this part of Europe.

The population of the *Rzeczpospolita* during the second half of the sixteenth century was about eight millions, and by the first half of the seventeenth century reached over ten millions. This included 200,000 in Livonia, 300,000 in ducal Prussia and 120,000 in the duchy of Curland. Without northern (Swedish) Livonia and the duchies, the area amounted to 990,000 square kilometres and was one of the largest political units in Europe at the time. The population was distributed unevenly, the density being higher in the west. In Great Poland the average was nineteen people to the square kilometre, in Little Poland twenty-three (Cracow palatinate) and twelve (Lublin palatinate), in Mazovia twenty-four, in the Lwów area ten, in Volhynia and Podolia seven, and in the Ukraine three. There was a tendency for the people to move eastwards from the more thickly populated districts; people from Mazovia colonised Podlachia and part of Lithuania, and people from other parts of Poland reached Podolia and the Kiev Ukraine. After 1582 Livonia received an increase of population in a similar way. As a result of these movements the population in some districts became mixed so far as origin, language and religion were concerned.

There was considerable social differentiation. The nobles formed the highest estate and they possessed full civic rights. They considered themselves all equal; but whatever the theory, there was inequality in practice. Economically their position varied considerably. A few dozen families owned vast domains, consisting sometimes of several hundred villages or small towns, and they exercised a predominant influence in public affairs. A large group of nobles possessed three or more villages each, but many owned only one or two. Finally, more than half the nobles owned nothing but a strip of land like a peasant; they cultivated the land themselves and only differed from the peasants by their noble status and by being independent of a landlord. There were also nobles who, for various reasons, had lost their land and become *impossessionati*. They often rented land from the *possessionati* or were used by them in the administration of their estates; some of them penetrated into the towns and mixed with the burgher population. The differences in economic position between the magnate nobles and the peasant nobles were very wide, but they all enjoyed civic rights, taking part in the palatinate assemblies and, through their representatives, in the parliaments. And so at the electoral parliament there could be seen poor peasant nobles who had come many miles on foot, and splendid processions of magnate nobles with their courts and entourage.

Geographically the nobles were scattered over the whole kingdom, but their proportion to the total population varied from district to district. The large estates of the magnates were mainly in the eastern part of the kingdom, especially in Lithuania, Volhynia and the Ukraine; there were only a few large estates in Poland proper. The highest percentage of nobles in the population was in Mazovia and Podlachia, where it was more than 20 per cent. In various districts of Lithuania the percentage was about 20 per cent. Throughout the whole commonwealth the nobles probably averaged less than 10 per cent of the population. More than half the nobles, however, were peasant nobles, owning nothing but a strip of land.

Besides the economic differences there were also differences among the nobles in education and in culture generally. Some had been educated at universities in Poland or abroad—in Italy, Germany, France. For example, among the political leaders, John Zamoyski, the crown chancellor, had once been rector of the university of Padua, and Stanisław Górka, the palatine of Poznań, had been rector of the university of Wittenberg. Some of the magnates maintained artists, architects and writers in their households, as did the king. In contrast, however, many of the nobles were uneducated, rough in manner and narrow in outlook, especially those who had to work their own land.

Another distinction among the nobles was between families who held seats in the senate and those who did not. Membership of the senate, though not hereditary, was in practice confined to a limited number of the more influential families; however, the king did occasionally introduce into the senate some noble who might be expected to be more loyal to his policy.

The nobility, so aware of the principle of equality among their own ranks, were not at all anxious to extend it to the other estates by granting them full civic rights. They held the Aristotelian theory that the lower orders should naturally play a less prominent part in affairs of state. This did not apply to the clergy, who still enjoyed their medieval ecclesiastical privileges, though these were being whittled away; for example, the ecclesiastical courts had been deprived in 1565 of the *brachium seculare*, the assistance of the state in the execution of their indictments, which considerably weakened their power. At the same time the archbishoprics, bishoprics and most of the cathedral chapter offices always went to members of the nobility. In 1607 the same applied to the prelates of collegiate churches. Nevertheless there was always tension between the ecclesiastical estate and the nobility as a whole.

The peasants formed the most numerous group in the community, some being landholders and some not. There would be about a dozen or so landholders in a village, and the conditions of tenure would be regulated either by customary law or by contract. Those who had no land of their own to cultivate would work on the lord's demesne or on the holding of some other peasant, being paid in kind or sometimes in cash. They might hold a house and small plot of land for their own use or they might be dependent on their employer for their accommodation.

The peasant holdings were much smaller than they had been in the four-teenth and fifteenth centuries, usually about half a *łan* (about 20¾ acres) or sometimes only a quarter, corresponding to fifteen or seven *morgs* of land respectively. The peasants were tied to the soil but a fair amount of illegal migration went on in search of better conditions, legal action some-times being taken to bring runaways back, and sometimes not. Apart from the obligation of providing gifts in kind, for example, eggs or poultry, rent was in cash and labour service involving the use of their own animals. The fall in the value of money during the sixteenth century was to the peasants' advantage, but the landlords, having enlarged their demesnes, had in-creased their demands for labour services and by the end of the sixteenth century these labour dues had come to vary considerably in different parts of the country and were sometimes very different even in neighbouring villages. The labour services of a peasant holding half a *łan* varied between two and three days a week, although occasionally even more was exacted. Those peasants who had a small plot of land provided manual labour only.

This increase in labour service was regarded as a breach of contract on the part of the landlord, but it took place gradually and did not provoke any mass protest. There is evidence of local protests. In 1574, for example, the peasants of Łukowa, Obsza, Różaniec and Zamch made a protest against the increase of labour services and similar abuses, and in 1604 those of Wieprzec and some other villages did the same. As the empty areas of the eastern provinces became colonised, many new villages and small towns were settled in Podolia, Volhynia and part of the Ukraine. Their inhabitants enjoyed better economic conditions than those in Poland proper. They were usually given a long period free of money rent at the beginning, and labour services were practically non-existent.

The peasants on the royal domains could appeal to the king from their local bailiff courts; and the king often agreed to their demands for injustices to be removed. The peasants on private estates could not appeal to the king. They were completely dependent on their own lords, ecclesiastical or lay, who organised courts of justice for them, sometimes issuing ordinances to be followed and sometimes allowing the village communities a measure of self-government.

The towns increased their population considerably during the sixteenth century, although they remained smaller than those in western Europe. Cracow by the end of the century had more than 28,000 inhabitants, Poznań had about 20,000, Danzig over 70,000, Warsaw about 20,000, and Lublin and Lwów each had more than 10,000, as did Elbląg, Toruń and Bydgoszcz. In Lithuania the largest town was Wilno, with about 25,000 inhabitants. Polotsk had about 7,500, Brest 6,000, Kiev 4,000, Vlodimir 4,000 and Grodno 3,500. All over the country there were small towns with only about 1,000 to 3,000 inhabitants, engaged in agriculture as much as in trade. While at the beginning of the seventeenth century some smaller towns were showing signs of decline, the larger ones made steady progress until the middle of the century. The larger towns were royal boroughs and the smaller ones were usually privately owned. About a hundred towns were founded by private owners during this period, including Zamość (1580), notable for its Renaissance architecture.

The town hall was the most important building in the town and was the centre of municipal life. Many were built or rebuilt in the Late Renaissance style, but in the smaller towns they would be built of wood. Many new churches were founded by burghers or nobles. Justice was administered by special municipal courts. The town council was responsible for the government and the finances of the town. It usually provided piped water and also public baths. These town councils were mainly in the hands of the patricians (the wealthy merchants and master craftsmen), though representatives of some lower groups had by this time been admitted in some cases. The lords in the private towns and the crown representatives in the royal boroughs were suspicious of middlemen and themselves regulated prices, imposing their regulations on the town councils. This growing intervention had a damaging effect on the economic development of the towns.

During the sixteenth century most of the towns lost their medieval privileges, but Danzig succeeded in preserving hers. The citizens of Danzig were able to influence prices generally by their control of exports, to the great detriment of producers; in Danzig itself they had a monopoly of trade with overseas merchants and prevented the inland towns and the nobility from any direct contact with them. The privileged position of Danzig contributed greatly to the financial difficulties experienced by the merchants of the inland towns, who were already harassed by the fact that the nobles had succeeded in freeing themselves from the obligation to pay toll and customs duties when disposing of their own products or buying for their own needs.

Besides the economic and social differences, the community was deeply divided by religion. The frontier between the Catholic and Orthodox churches in Europe passed through the country and more recently the Protestant sects had revived interest in religious problems and won converts from both Catholics and Orthodox; there was also a great increase in controversial literature. Non-Christian religions were represented by the Jews and Karaites, and by the Muslims who had settled in Lithuania.

As well as the religious differences, there were differences in language. More than half of the population were Polish-speaking and they lived mainly in the central and western palatinates, adjacent to the Polish-speaking people beyond the western frontier. The sparsely populated south-east was inhabited by Ruthenians (Ukrainians) together with settlers from other provinces. In the eastern part of Lithuania there were White Russians and in the north the Lithuanians proper. In Livonia Latvians, and in the north Estonians. The German-speaking people were settled mainly in ducal Prussia, in the towns of Livonia and royal Prussia, and in some towns of Great Poland, where they had become partly polonised. All over the kingdom, the population of the towns was mixed and included Jews, Italians and Scots, and in the south-east Armenians also.

It had been customary to elect the king in the time of the Jagiellons, but the way in which the election was to be carried out had never really been settled and when the convocation parliament met in January 1573 it decided against any system of representation and preferred the *viritim* method of direct individual voting. Great emphasis was laid on freedom of election and on the necessity of everybody being quite free to express his opinion: 'Not force, not gold, not acclamation, but fair argument, the common good, and persuasion, should hold sway.' This electoral parliament consisted of the senate, whose members came from all over the kingdom, and the palatinate assemblies, where the actual voting took place. The palatinate assemblies each consisted of all the nobles from that particular palatinate who were present at the parliament, including senators, and also representatives from certain towns. The documents bearing the votes and the seals of the voters were taken from the palatinate assemblies to the senate, which was used as a clearing-house. After the votes had been taken it became clear that an overwhelming majority was in favour of Henry of Valois, brother of King Charles IX of France, and the minority finally gave way so as not to allow 'our country to be ruined and ourselves be the cause of bloodshed', in the words of John Firlej, the leader of the opposition. He thereupon, in his capacity as crown marshal, proclaimed Henry king elect.

The election of 1573 was on the whole characterised by discipline and good sense. There were some 40,000 voters present, and about seventy pamphlets of one kind or another were printed and circulated, including more than 1,200 copies of the French ambassador's speech. Apart from one short period of confusion, the marshals had been able to keep good order and the food supply for 100,000 people was well organised.

The next two elections, however, in 1575 and 1587, were by comparison chaotic and disorderly, although the numbers were much smaller—in 1575 there were only about 15,000 voters present. This was partly due to a change in procedure, as the nobles decided to meet in one single assembly, without the senators, in order to avoid the influence the senators had previously exercised in the palatinate assemblies. This resulted in two quite separate bodies, between which co-ordinated action was very difficult to establish. Moreover, the large assembly of nobles proved unworkable in practice and the orderly discussion which had characterised the first election was replaced by shouting and acclamation. The general tension was heightened by foreign intrigues, bribery, and the presence of the magnates' armed retainers. The minority refused to give way, so that on each of the two occasions two candidates were declared king elect—in 1575 Stephen Bathory, prince of Transylvania, and the Habsburg Maximilian II, the Holy Roman Emperor; in 1587 Sigismund Vasa and the Habsburg Archduke Maximilian.

All three elections were greatly influenced by the international situation which had developed during the last years of the reign of Sigismund Augustus. He had built up a political system based on an understanding with Sweden (1568) and with Turkey. John III of Sweden had married Sigismund's sister Catherine, and Sigismund wanted his help against Russia, not only on the Livonian frontier but also in blockading the Baltic to stop the supply of arms and ammunition. In 1568 he renewed a previous treaty with Turkey, who was threatened by Russia on her north-eastern frontier and by the Habsburgs in south-east Europe. He also sought the friendship of France, who had had a treaty with Sweden since 1541 and who renewed her treaty with Turkey in 1572. There are some indications that he envisaged a member of the house of Valois succeeding him on the throne. His interests clashed with those of the Habsburgs over Hungary and on the Baltic over Prussia and Livonia, and since 1566 he had been openly following an anti-Habsburg policy. He consequently refused to support the anti-Turkish league in 1571–2. In these circumstances the policy of the majority of the voters during the first three elections was based on two main points: anti-Habsburg feeling and the wish for peaceful relations with Turkey, which they thought would be impossible to maintain with a Habsburg or Muscovite candidate. The French, Swedish and Transylvanian candidates, on the other hand, fitted easily into the international situation. It was also thought that the Baltic question, to which great importance was attached, would be settled more satisfactorily by the French or Swedish candidate. Deeply rooted sentiments of loyalty towards the house of Jagiellon favoured Sigismund Vasa, who was the son of Catherine, the sister of Sigismund Augustus, and who was firmly supported by Sigismund's other sister, Bathory's widow, Queen Anne.

The reigns of the elected kings covering the period 1573–1632 varied considerably in length and also in character. Henry of Valois reigned for less than two years and was in Poland for less than five months (1573–5); Stephen Bathory reigned for ten years (1576–86); and Sigismund III Vasa, who was only twenty-one when he was crowned, reigned for forty-five years (1587–1632). Whatever differences in approach there may have been, these three kings had one thing in common. The crown of Poland and Lithuania could not banish from their minds the thought of their native countries, and this had a far-reaching effect on both domestic and foreign policy. Henry neglected the kingdom of Poland in order to make sure of his succession to the French throne. Bathory was always making plans against the Turks who were threatening his native Transylvania. Sigismund, during the whole of his long reign, subordinated the interests of Poland and Lithuania to his own overwhelming desire to be king of Sweden. This attitude was bound to give rise to political opposition and to disturb the domestic affairs of the country, especially the relationship between king and parliament, and there was a steadily growing feeling that a national dynasty was necessary.

After three elections it became obvious that these periods of interregnum led to a disquieting instability both in the domestic life of the country and in international relations. The foreign princes who competed for the throne during an interregnum continued their intrigues and their interest in the country when the election was over. The newly elected king not only had to pacify the country and bring internal affairs under control but was also faced with the difficult task of dealing with foreign plots, wasting time and energy which could have been put to a more constructive purpose.

Henry was elected unanimously and so had no competitors to fight, and internationally he seems to have established his position quite satisfactorily. Internally, however, he ran into difficulties owing to his efforts to take back the over-large concessions to the nobility that had been made to secure his election.[1] During the negotiations which took place while he was still in Paris he repudiated a considerable amount of the financial

[1] See also vol. ii, p. 474.

responsibility accepted on his behalf by his ambassadors during the election and he was prepared to continue the struggle when he reached Poland. He planned to go by sea to Danzig and obtained permission from Elizabeth I of England for his passage and that of his fleet and 4,000 Gascon infantry destined for military operations in Livonia. The king of Denmark, however, acting on inspiration from Moscow, put obstacles in his way and, as soon as the renewal of the truce with Moscow disposed of the immediate need for an army, he travelled by land through the Holy Roman Empire, taking with him as his advisers some of the leading French politicians, the duke of Nevers, the marshal de Retz, and de Pibrac. He was crowned at Cracow in January 1574. He aroused strong opposition by his flat refusal to confirm the *Articuli Henriciani* in his coronation oath, because they contained certain limitations to his power, and some palatinates refused to administer justice in his name. He had no time to solve this problem, as he found it necessary to return to Paris on the death of Charles IX in June 1574 in order not to lose his succession to the French crown. The French had envisaged the two kingdoms being united under Henry, but the Poles became impatient at his absence and proclaimed an interregnum. Henry's election also had its effects on France as he was thereby obliged to raise the siege of La Rochelle. Moreover, the Protestants who had elected Henry, as Thuanus relates, drew up the *Postulata Polonica*, intended to improve the position of the Protestants in France. Charles IX, however, was not anxious to accept these proposals, seeing them as an attempt to intervene in the internal affairs of France.

Stephen Bathory was elected on 15 December 1575, and crowned on 1 May 1576. He immediately took steps against Danzig, which was refusing to recognise him as king. The issue was an economic one. An act of the parliament of 1570 had suppressed the monopolistic privileges which Danzig had enjoyed, and had incorporated the town into the economic life of the kingdom as a whole. The townsmen of Danzig had taken the opportunity of the interregnum to regain their lost position and made their acceptance of Stephen conditional on their privileges being restored. Otherwise they would continue to support the Habsburg candidate, and in this they were backed up by Denmark. Armed intervention was necessary before they could be made to accept Bathory, and Danzig was made to pay an indemnity. The king, however, promised to put the question of their lost privileges on the agenda for the next parliament. With the early death of his competitor, the Emperor Maximilian, on 12 October 1576, the political situation was completely under Stephen's control and the last of Maximilian's supporters accepted his authority.

The situation after the election of Sigismund III was not so easy. He landed at Oliwa near Danzig in October 1587, was welcomed by the town council of Danzig, and slowly moved south towards Cracow. Here the political situation was greatly confused. The Habsburg Archduke Maximilian, younger son of the late Emperor Maximilian II, crossed the Silesian frontier with the intention of using force to secure the throne for himself. However, the crown chancellor, John Zamoyski, was able by a swift movement to save Cracow, and the Habsburg army was finally annihilated at the battle of Byczyna (24 January 1588). The archduke was taken prisoner and remained in captivity for almost two years. As Bishop Goślicki was not slow to point out, this Habsburg disaster took place in the same year that the Spanish Armada was destroyed.

The Habsburgs, however, did not easily forget the Polish throne. After prolonged negotiations a peace treaty was concluded on 19 March 1589, according to which the Habsburgs, especially Maximilian, were to renounce all designs upon the Polish crown and also to stop intriguing within the kingdom. They were also to promise never to help Moscow against Poland or Sweden. The treaty was ratified by Sigismund III, then by the Emperor Rudolf II and most of the members of the house of Habsburg. It had been hoped that the parliament of 1589, by approving it, would bring about a final pacification both at home and abroad, but Maximilian's unexpected behaviour prolonged the unsettled period until 1598. In spite of the difficulties created by foreign intrigues and internally by the system of election, which could easily have led to the disintegration of the whole state, the various nations remained loyal to the idea of common *Rzeczpospolita* built up by Sigismund Augustus and the territorial links between them appeared to become even stronger.

An analysis of the concept of kingship accepted in Poland-Lithuania at this time brings to light various elements. Authority was conferred on the king-elect by the community of the electors, as is made clear by the *Denuntiato electi regis* of 1573: 'We conferred on him the title of king of Poland...and handed over to him the government of this kingdom.' On the other hand, the coronation service bestowed on the king-elect the character of the holder of a divine office when, as a true king and lord, he was crowned with 'the sacred crown' and anointed with sanctifying oil: 'Christ anoint this king unto his authority.' At the same time he was reminded that his kingdom and his power had their origin in God. There was also a medieval contractual element, as is shown by the coronation oath, the *Pacta Conventa*, and the *Articuli Henriciani*, all of which he had to accept as a condition of his election. In the coronation oath the king promised to hold and keep the laws and customs of the kingdom. The *Pacta Conventa* set out the king's personal obligations, for example, to provide an army, build up the navy, educate a certain number of youths, and pay certain treasury debts. The *Pacta Conventa* of 1573 was signed by Charles IX of France as well as by Henry and had rather the character of an international treaty. Later it lost this international character, although it kept the same name and its original form, and its contents were drawn up in agreement with the candidate concerned. The *Articuli Henriciani* called for constitutional reforms which consisted, in fact, of limitations of the royal authority. Among other things the king had to summon parliament for an ordinary session once every two years, and he was not to carry on a war or levy taxes without its consent.

Notwithstanding these limitations, the authority left to the king was fairly extensive, as the duke of Nevers pointed out in the report he prepared for Henry, and the personality of the king remained of the utmost importance. Henry succeeded in diminishing the threat to the king's authority which was created by the *articulus de non praestanda oboedientia* of the *Articuli Henriciani*, by insisting that it be understood in such a way as to remove its immediate danger, but although the constitutional effect of the article was softened, the psychological effect on the nobles remained. Later on, the king was to be warned three times before any action could be taken against him and the clause was stated in these terms in 1607 and 1609. In practice this deprived the *articulus* almost entirely of its significance. During his short reign Henry managed, against opposition, to introduce financial reforms in the royal domains which would increase his income, and he had various other reforms in mind. Bathory stood firm during the parliamentary debates and on several occasions succeeded in exacting a much higher tax than had previously been granted. When he was reminded of the contractual relationship he retorted that the estates had first to remember their duties and obligations arising from the contract, and once he had been elected king by them he had no intention of being ruled by anybody. Ostroróg, the castellan of Poznań, made the same point to the nobles during the reign of Sigismund III, who was fully conscious of his royal dignity and prestige, to such an extent that it sometimes irritated the nobles. Sigismund's position, however, suffered considerably in the long run on account of his foreign policy, which led the majority of the nobles to distrust him.

The king had various powers and prerogatives. He was commander-in-chief of the armed forces and had the supreme military authority in his hands. Since he was responsible for peace and order in the kingdom, any assembly summoned without his permission was illegal and the organisers liable to punishment. In any case of disagreement between his ministers, the king was the arbiter. The privilege of operating printing presses could be given to whom he chose. Above all, the distribution of all the higher offices, secular and ecclesiastical, belonged to the king and this was a potent source of influence. Bathory co-operated with Zamoyski and his followers and most of his nominees were chosen from this party, to the dissatisfaction of the family of Zborowski and others. When Sigismund III found co-operation with Zamoyski unsatisfactory, he started appointing his own followers to senatorial seats. One result of this was that the Protestants were more or less passed over, as they were for the most part behind Zamoyski, and later on they supported Zebrzydowski and his rebellions. Bathory organised supreme courts of appeal; in 1578 for Poland, in 1581 for Lithuania. Royal Prussia came under the jurisdiction of the former in 1585 and the Ukraine in 1589, retaining the Ruthenian language. The towns did not come under the jurisdiction of these appeal courts as they had their own courts. In this way the king delegated judicial work which he was unable to cope with, keeping the more important issues for himself in the court of parliament. The king had a predominant influence in practice on foreign policy.

The greatest restriction on the king's authority was the need to work through parliament (*sejm*) in some matters. The question of peace or war could not be decided, in practice, without the consent of parliament, nor could taxes be levied. Both Stephen Bathory and Sigismund III found this their greatest difficulty. When they needed taxes for the continuation of their wars, they were dependent on the decision of parliament and if this went against them their plans had to be abandoned or postponed. Both kings tried to co-operate with parliament; they summoned it every second year according to law and sometimes even for an extraordinary session. Like his predecessor Sigismund Augustus, Bathory was able to influence the lower house by his speeches and often won them over to his plans, especially when Zamoyski and his party were on his side. Sigismund III was not so successful; gradually a spirit of suspicion grew up between him and parliament, making the majority of the nobles uncooperative and often leading to open rifts. In the upper house, the senate, the king played a more decisive role and was often able to direct national policy. He had the right to wind up the discussion when the senators had expressed their opinions. In any case the king had the right to oppose and to veto the resolutions of both houses if he objected to them.

In 1606 Sigismund hoped with the support of his king's party to introduce some sound and badly needed reforms, including an increase in the standing army, regular annual taxes which would not require parliamentary approval each time, and certain reforms of parliament itself and of its procedure. He proposed to enforce the majority principle in voting. This had not been observed during the last few parliaments and proceedings had been disrupted by the unwillingness of the minority. He also wanted to place some limit on the length of the speeches and so shorten the debates. The king's proposals had the support of most of the senators. Bishop Szyszkowski, referring to the parliament of 1605 which had been completely disrupted by the intransigence of a small minority, asked ironically, 'Is this freedom? Rather is it oppression by a minority.' He wanted to reform the *modum tractandi et concludendi* of the debates. The crown marshal Myszkowski, the Lithuanian chancellor Lew Sapieha, the crown chancellor Pstrokoński and others all spoke in favour of reform. They were also interested in social reform, maintaining that the peasants were in a state of destitution. They thought that the nobles should pay taxes as well, as it was not right that the whole of the financial burden should rest on the shoulders of the peasants, 'our poor and tormented subjects'.

However, feeling against the Habsburgs, and mistrust of the king for plotting with them, led to strong opposition from the majority of the nobles, who were suspicious that he might be plotting against them in internal affairs also by trying to introduce an *absolutum dominium* to their disadvantage. They therefore rejected all the reforms he proposed. The tragic confusion of these two factors had a disastrous effect on the future of the kingdom. Zebrzydowski, the palatine of Cracow, a Catholic whose ambition was to play Zamoyski's role in politics, and Prince Janusz Radziwiłł, the leader of the Calvinists, took advantage of the anti-Habsburg feeling to start a rebellion against the king in 1607. They defended the privileges and liberties of the nobles, which they wished to enjoy at whatever cost to the state. Stanisław Stadnicki, for example, had as his main concern to retain the principle that 'each landlord should be *absolutus dominus* on his own estate'. The king, supported by the hetmans, Stanisław Żółkiewski and Charles Chodkiewicz, crushed the rebellion at the battle of Guzów, but did not follow up his military victory by pressing his point on the political side, and the reforms were again postponed.

Both Bathory and Sigismund may be regarded as constitutional monarchs co-operating with parliament, with the rare virtue of being able to listen patiently to the incredibly long orations which even parliament itself was unable to curtail and which often made the debates quite fruitless. Sigismund III had no intention of abolishing parliament but only wished to bring in certain reforms to make it more workable. Meanwhile, however, the constitution was gradually being transformed, not by means of reforms but by the course of events. The opportunity of establishing a strong government was lost. The king was gradually losing his authority and the nobles took to holding illegal meetings over which he had no control.

Alongside these constitutional problems there were the religious divisions which had been multiplied by the Reformation and which took up an increasing amount of parliamentary time. The Catholic church was by now beginning to set its house in order and move over to the offensive. Its sixteen dioceses (increased to seventeen in 1613), under the two metropolitan sees of Gniezno and Lwów, varied widely in size and in endowment. Some, like Cracow, which covered 56,000 square kilometres, were too large for pastoral work to be carried out efficiently. Some, again like Cracow and its chapter, which owned 3,850 square kilometres of land and more than 300 villages, were well endowed; others, like Kiev and Kamieniec, very poorly. The leaders of the Catholic hierarchy, however, enjoyed considerable political influence. The primate, the archbishop of Gniezno, was not only supreme in ecclesiastical affairs but also, as *interrex* during an interregnum, summoned the convocation parliament, and on certain other occasions had the right to summon the senate. The bishops had seats in the senate and were often appointed, by king or by senate, to serve on important commissions. The rest of the Catholic clergy took no part in parliament but held provincial and diocesan synods. These were especially frequent after the Council of Trent, whose decrees were accepted by the hierarchy in 1577, the king having accepted them as early as 1564. The synods helped to bring about a moral reform and a religious revival among the clergy throughout the country.

With the coming of the Jesuits a new system of education was introduced. Between 1564 and 1610 they established some twenty or thirty colleges and at the beginning of the seventeenth century almost 10,000 boys were being taught in them. The university of Wilno was under their control, with Peter Skarga as its rector. Their attempts to establish an academy at Poznań in 1611 and later at Cracow were opposed by the university of Cracow, which had itself established several colleges elsewhere in the country. The Jesuits were entrusted by the pope with two papal missionary colleges, at Braniewo (Braunsberg, 1578) and Wilno (1587), to train priests for Scandinavia and Livonia. Most of the priests so trained were Swedish; a few were British. Zamoyski founded a university in Zamość in 1580.

The Orthodox church was in a less healthy condition. Its seven bishop-rics, under the metropolitan of Kiev, and its monasteries were fairly well endowed, though again the endowments varied widely in size. The bishops, however, were not members of the senate. Their nomination was in the hands of the king, who usually endorsed the suggestions of the various protectors. Indeed, in 1592 Prince Constantin Ostrogski, the palatine of Kiev and an influential Orthodox magnate, received a special privilege from Sigismund III by which the king promised to appoint as bishops only candidates put forward by the prince. The palatine was regarded as the lay protector of the church and in 1597 even received the formal title of exarch from the patriarch of Constantinople. Ostrogski's letters show that the church at this time was going through a serious crisis, with a lack of adequately trained clergy and leaders. In 1576 he established a college of a Greco-Slavonic type at Ostróg. Other schools at Lwów and Wilno were founded by the lay fraternities. Lukaris, who eventually became patriarch of Constantinople, was one of the teachers at Ostróg. Bishops Pociej and Terlecki and some of the leading laymen sought the solution, however, in union with Rome and were encouraged by the apostolic nuncio, Bolognetti; the Jesuits were also working for union. Peter Skarga, in his book *The Unity of the Church* (1577), envisaged the retention of the oriental Slavonic rite, which was eventually approved by the pope. Ostrogski seems not to have been unsympathetic but his approach was different, as seen in his letters of 1583 and 1593. He envisaged a union on a much wider scale, which would include the patriarchates of Constantinople and

Moscow and the Orthodox church in Moldavia. Meanwhile, however, negotiations were being carried on along other lines and without his being consulted by the bishops, and the agreed conditions for union which were sent to Rome were on the narrower lines. Ostrogski thereupon opposed the whole idea of union and renewed his contacts of 1584 with the Protestants. He wrote to Prince Christopher Radziwiłł in 1595 asking for Protestant co-operation against the proposed union and in 1599 a 'confederation' was formed between Protestants and Orthodox to co-ordinate their activities. In 1596 the conditions for union with Rome were officially accepted at the Orthodox synod of Brest, but two of the Orthodox bishops, supported by some laymen, including Ostrogski, refused to sign. Those Orthodox who did not want the union experienced hardship, and it was not until 1607 that the king once more confirmed the rights of his Orthodox subjects. Even then their position was not entirely satisfactory. It is significant that the Orthodox were behind the king during the rebellion of 1606–7.

Protestantism was fairly widespread. In 1591 there were about 800 Protestant churches in use, apart from those in royal and ducal Prussia and in Livonia, where there was a Lutheran majority. In Great Poland, where the Lutherans were fewer, influential families such as the Ostroróg, Górka and Tomicki acted as their protectors. They claimed some adherents among the nobility, but were established mainly in the towns. Conditions were similar in Lithuania. The colleges at Danzig and Toruń, actually intended for German-speaking Lutherans, attracted Lutherans from all over the country. There were smaller colleges at Bojanów and Wilno.

The Calvinists were by this time well settled in. They were strong in Little Poland among the nobles and townsmen; less strong in Great Poland; and again stronger in Lithuania, where Prince Radziwiłł the Black became their protector and sponsored the well-known Bible of Brest. By the end of the sixteenth century the Calvinists had about 250 churches in Little Poland and 140 in Lithuania and had well-established colleges at Pinczów, Secymin, Kiejdany and several other places.

By 1570 the Bohemian Brethren, who in 1548 had taken refuge in Poland and settled in the district of Poznań, had sixty-four churches in the area and were developing their activities under the protection of Leszczyński and others. Leszno became their main intellectual centre, especially after Jan Amos Komenský (Comenius) became the rector of their school.

During the reign of Sigismund III there had been an increase in the number of Arians, also known as Anti-trinitarians or Polish Brethren. They were divided into a number of opposing lines of thought, of which the Socinians were the most numerous. Raków, with its college and printing press, became the centre of Polish Arianism, and its influence extended to various provinces, especially Volhynia where there were several schools.

Their supporters were usually from the lesser nobility and included some townspeople. Four hundred representatives took part in the synod of Rakocin in 1612, and in 1618 there were about 460. The discussions were led by eminent Arians, many of whom played an important role in the international anti-trinitarian movement. The Arians had as their influential protector John Kiszka, castellan of Wilno. They accepted a free and rationalistic interpretation of the Bible. Some of them rejected the divinity of Christ and denied the right of Christians to bear arms or to take part in civil government. In the social field, influenced by the Moravian Anabaptists, they condemned luxurious living, oppression of the peasants and the privileges of the rich. The catechism of Raków, published in 1605, was later translated into various languages.

In 1570 at Sandomierz an agreement was reached between the three principal Protestant churches. The Calvinists and Bohemian Brethren had had an understanding since 1555 and they were now joined by the Lutherans, and thus a common Protestant front was created. The Arians were excluded. A *consensus mutuus* was agreed on but each denomination retained its own organisation and its order of services. It was agreed to hold general synods in common and also to prepare a common catechism, but this last project was never realised. Opposition, however, arose among the German-speaking Lutherans, who were inclined to copy the uncompromising attitude towards the Calvinists adopted by the Lutherans in Germany. On account of this the agreement of Sandomierz was short-lived and at the last general synod in 1595 at Toruń the Lutherans withdrew from the agreement. In the same year, however, a rapprochement was made with the Orthodox which to a certain degree strengthened the position of the Protestants.

Relations between Catholics, Protestants and Orthodox were regulated by the principle adopted by the 'Confederation' of Warsaw in 1573 during the interregnum, at which it was agreed that there should be peace between the various faiths (*pax inter dissidentes de religione*) and that bloodshed should be avoided. The massacre of St Bartholomew was remembered with horror. This 'peace of Warsaw' was signed by Protestant, Orthodox and Catholic laymen; the only bishop who signed was Francis Krasiński *ob bonum pacis*. It was confirmed by Henry after his election and by his successors, and became the keynote of religious policy.

It seems as if the principle *cuius regio eius religio* may have also been implied in the settlement of 1573 but only so far as landed estates were concerned; it did not affect the national policy of religious freedom as a whole. There were cases where the lord adopted the new faith, expelled the Catholic clergy and closed the church, or used it for reformed services, although new churches were often built for this purpose. Only rarely were the people forced to accept their lord's new religion, although it seems that they were occasionally punished for avoiding the reformed church and going further afield to find one of the old faith. Jacob Sieniński complained that Radziwiłł forced the Arians on his estate to attend the Calvinist church, and similar complaints were occasionally made against Catholic landlords. It sometimes happened that a particular church changed its religious character two or three times in fifty years or so, on account of changes of landlord or changes in the landlord's religious allegiance; in the later part of the period these changes were often in favour of the Catholic church. Some landlords, however, preferred to respect the convictions of their peasants or burghers. Zamoyski, a Catholic, gave permission for the establishment of Armenian and Greek churches, as well as a synagogue, in his own domains of Zamość and Szarogród; and Ostrogski, an Orthodox, helped to establish Catholic and Protestant churches as well as a mosque, in Ostróg.

The kings followed the same line of policy. Bathory supported the Catholic church and the Jesuits, but also employed Protestants and used them as advisers. His great competitor and enemy during the election of 1571 in Transylvania, Gaspar Békés of Kornyát (1520–79), was an Arian; after some years he came to an understanding with Bathory, settled in Poland, and became the king's most loyal adviser. Sigismund III and his aunt Anne, widow of the late king, maintained the most close and friendly relations with his sister, Anne Vasa, who was a Protestant and Sigismund's closest adviser during the early years of his reign. She had a Protestant chapel in the Wawel Castle and later, when Sigismund married, he bestowed on her the royal domains of Brodnica and Golub, where she established a centre of Protestantism, and she often acted as protector to the Protestants. This spirit of moderation within the royal family was probably not without influence on the life of the country as a whole.

At the time Sigismund Augustus died Protestant influence in public life, especially Calvinist influence, was fairly strong. Protestants were in the majority in the lower house, and of the lay members of the senate seventy were Catholic, sixty Protestant and three Orthodox. There were twenty-four Protestant printing presses as against twenty-one Catholic, and a number of Protestant schools had been established, but the majority of rural population was almost untouched by the Reformation. At the same time the Catholics were at last beginning to consolidate themselves. This may be attributed to various causes, including the unspectacular but steady work of the Dominicans, the reforms introduced by the synodical statutes, the bishops' pastoral visitations, and later the activity of the Jesuits. The number of converts to Catholicism increased.

The principle underlying the 'Confederation' of 1573 worked satisfactorily for many years, although from time to time violent incidents took place, due to the action of extremists of one party or the other. The Calvinist church at Cracow was destroyed in 1574 and again in 1587. The king condemned such actions and ordered the guilty to be punished.

Bathory especially took a firm stand; he was not prepared to see any faith being propagated 'by force, fire or sword instead of by teaching and good example', he said. But as time went on similar incidents happened at Wilno and at Cracow in 1591, and at Lublin and at Wilno in 1611. On the other hand Lutheran attacks took place at Danzig, Toruń, Elbląg and Riga against the Catholics, and also sometimes against the Calvinists. These events gradually led to an atmosphere of mutual recrimination. The Protestants blamed the administration for being too slow with judicial proceedings and claimed that the *processus confederationis* promised in 1573, which provided for the establishment of special courts and procedure for that type of crime, had not yet been enacted by parliament. The Catholics, on the other hand, showed no signs of becoming reconciled to the losses they had experienced over the last sixty years—churches with land attached, *ius patronatus*, tithes, ecclesiastical jurisdiction, etc. The hierarchy, anxious to regain at least some of the lost privileges, tried to come to some agreement with the nobles and prepared a document, the *compositio inter status*. The nobles as a whole, however, were not willing.

The religious question was discussed by several parliaments but the Catholics were divided, some following a more rigorous line while the majority, under the leadership of Zamoyski, joined with the Protestants in supporting the principle of the Warsaw 'Confederation', agreeing with Zamoyski that peace and order were of primary importance and that all differences, including religious differences, should be subordinated to them. As a result neither *processus* nor *compositio* was passed by the parliament, as no common agreement could be reached, but temporary arrangements for short periods were agreed in 1593 and 1596. Finally, however, a sort of *processus* was passed by the parliament in 1631 and thus religious wars were avoided during this whole period.

The foreign policy of Poland-Lithuania centred largely upon the Livonian question, which is dealt with in another chapter. Here it must suffice to say that for most of this period Poland's relations with her Baltic neighbours hinged upon that question. So far as relations with Russia were concerned, however, in Sigismund's reign the emphasis shifted from Livonia to the Lithuanian claim to the districts of Smolensk and Siewier, which Lithuania had lost to Russia early in the sixteenth century. In 1582, after some months of hard bargaining, a ten-year truce was signed at Yam Zapolski; Livonia and Polotsk were left to Bathory and Velikie Luki went to Russia. Russia would not make a proper peace on these conditions, but was prepared to prolong the *status quo* by renewing the armistice; this she did in 1591 for twelve years and in 1601 for twenty. The Polish and Lithuanian statesmen, however, faced as they were with a steady deterioration in their relations with Sweden, made a far-reaching offer to Russia, which seems to have been meant quite seriously. This offer was first made in 1584 after the death of Ivan the Terrible and was repeated in 1601, this time by Lew Sapieha, the chancellor of Lithuania, who went to Moscow for this purpose.

The proposal was for a union between Poland-Lithuania and Moscow, with a treaty of friendship, a common foreign policy, freedom to settle and marry anywhere in the two countries, toleration for the Catholic and Orthodox minorities, and similar clauses. It was envisaged that at first there would be two sovereigns but that the survivor should become sole and common monarch. The Russians, in their counter-proposal, rejected all the more liberal articles and the whole issue became confused by the course of events. The time of troubles in Russia, and the unofficial support given to the two Demetriuses in their claim to the throne by some of the Ukrainian and Polish magnates, both Orthodox and Catholic, and later Sigismund's own claim to the throne of the tsars, as the descendant of Juliana of Tver, eventually led, in the second decade of the seventeenth century, to the long wars between Russia and Poland-Lithuania, resulting in the gain of Smolensk.

Relations with the Habsburgs were not very satisfactory, especially during the first decades of the reign of Sigismund III. The treaty of Będzin and Bytom of 1589 lost its significance when Maximilian escaped and after crossing the frontier refused to take the oath. He and other members of his family started intriguing once more to gain the Polish throne for the house of Habsburg, in spite of the fact that Sigismund III had by this time been crowned for two years. They revived the 'Austrian' party to work inside Poland for the Habsburgs; they tried to get Sigismund's father, John III of Sweden, to persuade his son to relinquish the Polish throne and turn the whole of his attention to Sweden; and they also initiated direct negotiations with Sigismund for the same purpose. The situation, however, became greatly confused by the disagreements among the Habsburgs themselves—there were at least two Habsburg competitors for the Polish throne, Maximilian and Ernest. The Emperor Rudolf II, at the beginning at least, remained faithful to the treaty of 1589 and would not support Maximilian's claims. The strongest support Maximilian had came from Philip II of Spain, who had not ratified the treaty and wished to see Habsburg influence established in this part of Europe at any price. Meanwhile Ernest managed to get into contact with Sigismund and, as the Habsburg candidate to the Polish-Lithuanian throne, secretly promised him that if he would relinquish the throne and return to Sweden he would sign a treaty of friendship with Sweden, abandon all claim to Estonia and pay Sigismund a sum of 400,000 gulden. Sigismund was particularly anxious not to endanger his Swedish succession and went so far as to consider returning to Sweden directly after his meeting with his father at Reval, but decided otherwise. Soon after this Maximilian discovered these secret negotiations and in 1592 he made them public. Great concern was felt among the Habsburg supporters in Poland, who were divided between Ernest and Maximilian, and there was serious disquiet throughout the whole country, especially among Zamoyski's followers. It was felt that 'foreigners negotiate over us between themselves'. Feeling against the Habsburgs hardened and opinion also turned against the king for his part in the affair. At Zamoyski's instigation parliament was summoned in 1592 to enquire into the whole question; violent attacks were made on all who had been involved in the Habsburg plot, and the king's authority and dignity suffered considerably, and there remained ill-feeling between him and the majority of his subjects. These two factors, feeling against the Habsburgs and the fear that the king might have a secret understanding with them, were among those that led to Zebrzydowski's revolt a few years later.[1] At this parliament of 1592 Zamoyski spoke very strongly against the Habsburgs' claim to the throne. He had already tried in 1589 to get them barred by act of parliament from ever being accepted as candidates. The king made a declaration to the effect that he had no intention of leaving the kingdom; but, though Ernest was very soon made governor of the Netherlands by Philip II, Maximilian did not renounce his claim until 1598.

The Hohenzollerns had managed to draw some advantage from the Polish-Lithuanian fighting in Livonia and Sweden. Albert Frederick, the son of Albert, the first duke of Prussia, took an oath of allegiance to Bathory in 1576, and the latter in 1578 extended the succession to the Prussian fief to the electoral line of the Hohenzollerns in the event of the extinction of the Ansbach line. According to the agreement of 1525 the succession to the fief had been limited to the Hohenzollerns of Ansbach and this extension was arranged to meet the wishes of the margrave of Brandenburg, as Bathory wished to be on friendly terms with the Hohenzollerns in view of his approaching campaign in Livonia against Moscow. Albert Frederick was suffering from mental incapacity and Bathory appointed as his guardian and as administrator of the duchy the Elector George Frederick. In 1589 Sigismund III confirmed Bathory's arrangements, both with regard to the guardianship and with regard to the extension of the succession to the fief. The death of George Frederick in 1603 provided an opportunity of appointing somebody more favourably inclined towards Polish interests, but Sigismund was too much afraid of the attitude of the Hohenzollerns towards his wars with Charles of Sweden to take this opportunity and in 1605 he appointed the new Elector, Joachim Frederick. Sigismund's decision was made without consulting parliament and it was felt generally among the nobles that the king had lost a good opportunity of linking the duchy of Prussia more closely to the crown, especially as the Prussian estates were dissatisfied with Brandenburg rule and had appealed to the king several times since 1566. The issue was brought up during the parliamentary debates and protests were made,

[1] See above, p. 388.

but Sigismund was either unable or unwilling to change his decision. Moreover, in 1611 John Sigismund, son of Joachim Frederick, was invested with the fief of Prussia and so the electoral line of the Hohenzollerns gained control of the duchy. Sigismund III did, however, strengthen his position of suzerain in Prussia (*ad corpus regni pertinens*) by enactments made in 1605 and 1611, laying down that appeals could be made in certain matters from the ducal to the royal court; that the king had the right to intervene in certain internal affairs; that the duchy was to con- tribute 30,000 złoty annually to the royal treasury and the same sum whenever taxes were levied in the kingdom; that navigation on the Warta through Brandenburg territories was to be free for Polish merchants; and finally, that the duchy was to be incorporated into the Polish crown in case of the extinction of the electoral line of Hohenzollern.

There was a general desire to maintain peaceful relations with Turkey and Bathory renewed the peace treaty with her in 1577. Peace was, how- ever, threatened several times, mainly by Cossacks raiding Tartar and Turkish territories. They were sometimes encouraged by the emperor (e.g. in 1594), who intended in this way to create difficulties between Turkey and Poland. The Tartars usually took their revenge and in 1590 Turkey even contemplated going to war. This was only averted through the good offices of Barton, the English ambassador (not to deprive Holland of Polish corn), and in 1591 the peace treaty was renewed again. The conflict between the interests of Turkey, Poland and the empire with regard to Moldavia, Wallachia and Transylvania sometimes went so far as to lead to armed intervention.[1] These three powers were competing for control over the Black Sea area, and trying to establish their influence there. They opposed and paralysed the efforts of Michal of Wallachia to unite the Roumanian lands. Zamoyski was able to occupy Moldavia in 1595 and to introduce, as his candidate for the hospodar's throne, Jeremy Mohyla, against the will of the Turks and the emperor; in 1600 his brother Simon Mohyla, acceded in Wallachia, so that Polish influence extended to the Danube. Zamoyski wanted to expand his influence also in Transyl- vania, again contrary to the wishes of the emperor and the Turks. After 1615 the Turks were able to introduce their own candidate in Moldavia, in this way extending their influence further to the north. After the Polish victory at Chocim in 1621, an agreement was reached whereby the Turks promised to keep the Tartars from attacking Poland and the Poles to do the same with the Cossacks. Meanwhile the imperial army interfered in Transylvania.

By the first decade of the seventeenth century the international situation inherited from the last two Jagiellons had been completely transformed. The Russo-Swedish treaty of 1609 worsened Polish-Lithuanian relations with Sweden, which had already been deteriorating. The treaty made by

[1] See also chapter XI above.

Poland-Lithuania in 1612 with Austria showed that the anti-Habsburg policy had been abandoned. Poland-Lithuania became involved in the wars with Turkey and the wars which were continually going on with Sweden and Russia.

The military responsibility which Sigismund Augustus had undertaken in the Ukraine in the south-east and in Livonia in the north involved the organisation of defence in those two areas to protect the population from the constant danger of attack. The heavy burden which this represented can be gauged from the fact that during the years 1572–1610 more than thirty major Tartar invasions took place in the south, as well as a number of less important ones.

In 1564 a sort of standing army (*wojsko kwarciane*) about 4,000 strong was authorised by king and parliament, but this was not really adequate. The feudal levy of nobles no longer worked satisfactorily and so the army had to rely mainly on mercenaries, not only for infantry but also for cavalry. These mercenaries were recruited from all parts of the kingdom and also from abroad. Bathory modernised the army and in 1578 introduced new infantry formations of peasants from the royal domains. He also reorganised the artillery and technical services and considerably developed military cartography. He used a number of Cossacks, organised in special detachments, and also used the Tartars who lived in Lithuania. The large entailed estates, such as those founded by Zamoyski and Ostrogski, included defence clauses in their charters. Part of the income was to be used to maintain several hundred soldiers, to repair the castles and strongholds and to provide them with the necessary arms and ammunition. Around the castles tracts of land were distributed to knights who had to be prepared for military service if needed.

The use of mercenaries raised certain difficulties for the king and lengthened the time needed to get an army together. The king needed the approval of parliament, and summoning parliament was itself a lengthy business. If approval was given, the taxes then had to be collected, which took several months. Altogether it was hardly possible to raise an army in less than a year and sometimes it took even longer. The seventeenth-century state machinery was too cumbersome and made it practically impossible for the king to carry out any sort of imperialistic policy.

The economy of the kingdom depended mainly on agriculture, based on labour services which by the end of the sixteenth century had almost everywhere replaced the previous rent system. The output, especially of cereals, was increased year by year to meet the growing export demand. This, however, depressed the economic position of the peasants, as more and more labour service was imposed on them. Conversion of land to arable, mainly in the east, increased the labour shortage. Many villages were settled in Podolia, Volhynia and parts of the Ukraine, as well as in other parts of the kingdom, and the economic position of the settlers in the east was better than that of the rest of the country. Zamoyski alone founded more than sixty villages.

As the manorial system became established, the character of the knight nobles completely changed; they became more farmers than knights and as time went on they became more and more interested in agriculture. At first they adopted the traditional methods of husbandry from the peasants, but later a number of handbooks were published advocating better methods, of which that by Anzelm Gostomski, published in 1588, was the best. For the most part they used the three-field system. The chief crop was rye, although oats, barley and wheat were grown. Hemp and flax were also grown, partly for export and partly for the manufacture of linen. Cattle-farming was more developed in the eastern part of the kingdom, as corn was more difficult to transport, since the outlet to the Black Sea had been lost and the river route to Riga had not yet been properly established. But it also flourished in the south at the foot of the Carpathian mountains and in some other districts. Apiaries and fish-ponds were often important additions to farming. The most important fish-breeding centre was in the duchy of Oświęcim.

The manorial system gave certain monopolies to the lord as feudal rights. He owned the flour-mill which the peasants of the district had to use, he had a monopoly of distilling and controlled the sale of spirits, and these privileges strengthened the economic position of the lord of the area and made the peasants more dependent on his economy. There was also a close association between the landowners and the iron industry. Iron ore was exploited in various parts of the country, mainly in the district of Częstochowa, Radom and Zamość. Usually the rights to mine ore, to extract iron from it, and to produce ironware were rented from the landlord by small producers. The capital necessary for mining, and for building the forges and foundries, was provided by either party or by both. Rent was paid in cash, or sometimes in goods. The ironworks, however, were usually quite small and seldom employed as many as thirty workers, skilled and unskilled. They produced iron bars, ironware or tools especially needed in farming. Cracow, Danzig, Lwów and other towns established foundries in which cannon, cannonballs and guns were manufactured for their own use and for supply to the army. Bells were also cast to meet the need of the churches.

The paper industry developed rapidly during this period to meet the growing demand of the printing presses; glass, cloth and linen goods were manufactured, mainly for local markets. Various types of goods were made in the towns by craftsmen and small producers, who were organised in the craft guilds, which remained in existence—new ones were even founded. The goods produced by them covered the needs of the lower classes, and those of the middle class nobles and burghers. The richer nobles and burghers, however, bought more expensive imported articles, involving a constant drain of money out of the country. To stop this and make the country economically self-sufficient Zamoyski encouraged the production of luxury goods and at the parliament of 1605 he pointed out that it would be better to use the raw material inside the country rather than export it as they were doing. Morocco, cordovan and other expensive kinds of leather were in fact manufactured at Zamość at a much lower cost than imported leathers. Tapestries and fine quality carpets were made in Mazovia, Zamość and, later, Brody, in the last two places under oriental influence. Various kinds of tents were also made for the use of the army. Clocks and other articles involving intricate workmanship were made, and expensive Turkish-style saddles were produced at Lwów. In some fields the craftsmen reached quite a high standard.

Sometimes the town council, as at Lwów, would prohibit the import of certain goods which were produced in sufficient quantity locally. Bathory granted patents of monopoly to various people for the manufacture of particular things which had not until then been produced. Altogether it seems clear that there was at the time a trend towards the mercantilist principle of self-sufficiency, which was practised locally although it had not been generally adopted by the government. There was, however, insufficient investment of capital in industry, which was probably due, at least in part, to the fact that local demand was diminishing with the deterioration of the condition of the lower classes.

Lead and silver were mined at Olkusz and Chęciny and foundries were built there. Production grew steadily until the middle of the seventeenth century. At the beginning of the sixteenth century the yearly output of lead was only 3,000 *centners* (1 *centner* = approximately 50 kilogrammes), but by the end of the same century it had reached 20,000 and by half-way through the seventeenth century 50,000. The corresponding figures for silver were 250, 1,500 and 6,000 *grzywnas* (1 *grzywna* = 200 grammes). Small producers gradually disappeared in favour of enterprises run on capitalistic lines.

Salt mines were developed near Wieliczka and Bochnia. They were organised on a capitalistic basis, with a yearly output of more than 200,000 *centners*. More than 1,000 workers and supervisors were employed, with a weekly wage according to their qualifications. There were also a number of salterns in the south-east at the foot of the Carpathians, mainly in the hands of the king but sometimes worked by small private producers. These were all organised as a single enterprise employing about 1,000 people and managed on capitalistic lines, with the admixture of some feudal elements.

The large estates which emerged during the sixteenth century, especially in the eastern provinces, played an important part in the economy of the country. The largest belonged to the Radziwiłł, Ostrogski, Zasławski, Wiśniowiecki and a few other families. Some of them were formed as entails. Probably the best organised were the estates of John Zamoyski. In addition to his private estates he held part of the royal domains in tenure, making a total of 17,479 square kilometres and including twenty-three small towns and 816 villages. Most of this land was in the Zamość and Bełz districts but some of it was scattered through other provinces. These estates were efficiently organised with a large number of administrative staff and labourers, divided into smaller economic units, but the whole enterprise remained under his personal supervision and guidance. Equal attention was paid to corn and cattle and to the development of industry. About 3,700 lasts of corn were available each year for export after the needs of the estate administration had been met. Most of it was transported down the Vistula in barges made on the estates; that from Livonia was transported partly to Riga and partly to Pskov; and that from Great Poland went by the river Warta to Stettin. Horses were bred for the local market, and especially to meet the needs of the army; cattle, especially oxen, were bred to supply the peasants with draught animals. Some were exported and some left for the local market. Sheep were bred for their wool, which in ten establishments was manufactured into cloth for the peasants on the estates. There were more than 110 fish-ponds in which fish were produced for local markets; honey and wax were also produced. Seventeen foundries manufactured ironware, especially tools for agricultural purposes. Five glass-houses supplied glass products, and about 130 flour-mills driven by water-power were used by the peasants. A score of saw-mills were in use and there were also establishments for bleaching linen. The whole enterprise was organised on the basis of self-sufficiency, with an annual budget, and with an emphasis on economic working and reasonable expenditure.

Maritime and overland trade, especially the former, were both expanding considerably during the second half of the sixteenth century and the beginning of the seventeenth. The overland trade routes from the east passed through Lwów in the south and Wilno in the north, and met, further west, either at Poznań or at Cracow. From there they went on towards Wrocław or Frankfurt, and finally reached Leipzig and Nuremberg. Another system of routes developed from south to north, from Hungary through Nowy Sącz, Cracow, Warsaw and Toruń to Danzig, from Moldavia through Lwów, Sandomierz, Toruń and Danzig, and from Silesia to Poznań and Danzig.

Transport by land was expensive and waterways were on the whole more important, especially for long distances, the rivers being used even for transporting the army. The river most used was the Vistula with its tributaries and this was the reason for Danzig developing into the most important Baltic port at this time. The river Warta was used for transport to Stettin, and in the north-east the river Dvina was used as a route to Riga. Once the kings realised that they were unlikely to be able to obtain an outlet to the Black Sea they made every effort to get the whole of the Dvina inside their frontiers so that it could be used as a transport route for Lithuania and, in conjunction with the Dnieper, for the Ukraine. The Niemen was also used to a certain extent for transport to Königsberg. Poland-Lithuania at this time absorbed by far the major part of the Baltic trade, and the greater part of it was concentrated in Danzig. According to the toll register at the Sound, shipping at that port accounted for 59 per cent of all the vessels engaged in the Baltic trade from 1562 to 1574. A small amount must be credited to the other Polish and Livonian ports, and the remainder was destined for other Baltic countries.

The chief export from Danzig and other ports was corn, especially rye. From 1555 it was exported at a rate of about 14,000 lasts a year, and at the beginning of the seventeenth century it amounted sometimes to more than 100,000 lasts a year (in 1618 it was 129,000). Wheat, oats and barley were also exported, but in smaller quantities. The most important type of export after corn was timber and its by-products, together with naval stores such as tar, pitch, cordage and potash. During the second half of the sixteenth century less potash was exported by way of Danzig but more by way of the Dvina and Riga. Exports also included wax, flax, hemp, linen, hides, leather and all kinds of fur, as well as copper, lead, iron and steel.

The principal imports through the Baltic ports were better quality cloth, herrings, salt, wines and southern fruits. The turnover of trade in Danzig alone during this period reached an average of about 10 million złoty a year.

The Baltic trade with Poland-Lithuania was mainly in the hands of Dutch and Frisian merchants, with England holding second place. In 1585, of the ships plying from Danzig through the Sound, 52 per cent were Dutch, 24 per cent from East Friesland, 12 per cent from England and Scotland. The English merchants, competing with the Hansa towns, opened negotiations with Elbląg (Elbing) in order to obtain a new market. The Eastland Company was established in 1579 and a staple for English goods was set up in Elbląg. The merchants were to be allowed to trade freely without the limitations imposed in Danzig. This move was supported by Elizabeth I and it was also encouraged by Bathory, as it aimed at breaking Danzig's trading monopoly. In 1583 a treaty was signed between Elbląg and the Eastland Company and it was expected that the king and parliament would officially confirm it. Danzig, however, seeing its privileged position threatened, made every effort to prevent the king agreeing to it and applied to Zamoyski for his influence. As a result the king did not confirm officially the agreement reached between Elbląg and the Eastland Company. He did no more than confirm the rights which the English merchants had prior to the arrangement with Elbląg. Danzig had won and its trading monopoly was kept secure, and for this it agreed (1585) to pay

401

half its annual toll income to the king. The king was occupied at the time with plans against Turkey and wished to have peace in the north.

The overland trade with the German principalities and Bohemia and Moravia consisted mainly of oxen (at the beginning of the seventeenth century to the number of 60,000 a year), pigs and horses. There were also linen, various kinds of leather·in great quantities, honey and wax. Iron-ware and some textiles were imported. Exports to Turkey included lead, arms, knives, furs and certain kinds of cloth. Silks, carpets and other costly oriental goods were imported. From Russia furs and oriental goods, including China tea, were imported and iron goods, cloth and paper were exported.

By the beginning of the seventeenth century the demand for the more expensive products, both imported and home-produced, was growing, but the demand from the lower classes was steadily diminishing. Nevertheless it seems that the balance between exports and imports was kept, although a great deal of money went out of the country in return for luxury goods instead of being invested in industry or other enterprises. On the other hand, the monetary crisis which slowly developed also worsened the position of the peasants, as well as of the lower classes of the nobility.

The responsibility for relieving poverty was not accepted by the state, as Modrzewski (*De republica emendanda*, 1558) had vigorously suggested it should be, but was left to ecclesiastical and private charity. There were hospitals in town and country, founded and maintained by monasteries, landlords or burghers, but they were not very well equipped. In times of special hardship caused by war or famine, or if peasants suffered loss from fire, etc., they were usually freed for a time from their duties in money or kind. They were sometimes granted loans or given help in kind.

The court had an important part to play in the life of the country. Bathory said it ought to be 'a model and a mirror of noble deeds and virtuous living', and Luke Górnicki, by paraphrasing and adapting to Polish conditions Castiglione's *Il Cortegiano* in 1566, put the ideal of a good courtier into currency. Although the monarchy was elective, the court was maintained with royal dignity and splendour. The atmosphere varied with the personality of the king—that of Henry's court, imbued with the French spirit, is in sharp contrast with the more austere customs under Stephen Bathory and the rigid etiquette and pompous ceremonies, modelled on the Spanish court, which characterised the court during the reign of Sigismund III. The household was not so large as under the last Jagiellons but the tradition of making the court the centre of art and culture was maintained, and the kings encouraged artists and writers.

Bathory rebuilt Łobzów, just outside Cracow, and Sigismund III laid out a park there in the Italian style. Sigismund also built, among other buildings, a palace at Warsaw to Abrahamowicz's designs. He both collected and commissioned works of art, again principally Italian, and his example was followed by some of the magnates and rich burghers. The leading native artists, such as Wojciech Borzymowski, Christopher Boguszewski, Martin Kober, and the Italian-born Thomas della Bella, were very much influenced by foreign schools. The musical tradition established by Wacław Szamotulski at the court of Sigismund Augustus was also continued by his successors, who maintained a court orchestra as well as the Wawel cathedral choir and, later, the royal opera. Of the leading composers, Nicolas Gomółka and Martin Leopolita still adhered to the polyphonic style, but Nicolas Zieliński used the new antiphonal 'Venetian method'.

These years also saw a large output of historical writing, both in Polish and in Latin, dealing with both the recent and the more remote past. Stryjkowski, writing about Poland, Lithuania, and Russia (1582), gave the first account of Lithuania's history and in 1584 Bartosz Paprocki published a work on Polish heraldry. The two first interregna were described by two Protestant writers, Świętosław Orzelski (1572–6) and Reinhold Heidenstein (1572–1603), and the reign of Sigismund III by Paul Piasecki and Stanisław Łubieński. The history of the Reformed church was written later by Andrew Węgierski (Regenvolscius), and Stanisław Lubieniecki dealt with the Arians. Among political writers and politicians, some tried to justify the social inequalities by appealing to Aristotle, but it was Cicero, with his theory of civic rights and the inequality of professions, who was most frequently cited. Many writers deplored the oppressed condition of the peasants, as, for example, Sebastian Petrycy, in the Commentaries to his Polish translation of Aristotle, and Peter Skarga, who said: 'Woe to you who pass unjust laws and legalise unlawfulness in order to oppress the poor...' But almost all writers supported the electoral system, even though all thought that reform was necessary and Luke Górnicki, in *A Dialogue between a Pole and an Italian*, suggested replacing *viritim* voting by a representative system. Yet even the strongest advocate of stable monarchy and strong government, Christopher Warszewicki, in his *De optimo statu libertatis* (1598), wanted to keep parliament. He wanted, however, to make it workable and he emphasised the duties of the subject: 'For some there is perhaps the pleasure of making the law, but for all it is far more necessary and more useful to obey the law and to carry it out.'

CHAPTER XIII

SWEDEN AND THE BALTIC

A COMPARISON between the countries round the Baltic and those round the Mediterranean in the middle of the sixteenth century sheds light on conditions in the north at a time when the political situation was vastly different from the present one. Though in varying degrees, the European countries on the Mediterranean all had an ancient cultural heritage, and during the last few centuries they had evolved a new culture—the Renaissance—in conscious relation to classical antiquity. The former political disunity was partly overcome in France, was on the way to being overcome in the Iberian peninsula, but was still acute in Italy. At the eastern end of the Mediterranean, on the other side of an 'iron curtain', lay the cultural world of the Orient. For centuries it had given many impulses to southern Europe. Now the links were broken, and most of Europe's trade with the Far East followed new routes.

Similarly, in the middle of the sixteenth century the eastern and western sides of the Baltic belonged to different cultural spheres in religion, education, language and custom; the main line of demarcation was between Russia on the one side, and her neighbours Sweden-Finland and Poland on the other. But the dissimilarities to southern Europe were enormous. The northern countries were economically and culturally primitive compared with those in the south. The refinement of the Renaissance had as yet left only small traces in northern Europe, primarily in art. The Reformation's programme, however, had quickly and effectively reached northern Germany, Poland and Scandinavia, spreading not so much among the masses as in certain social groups—particularly the middle-class townspeople—and within government circles. The Counter-Reformation won back Poland but not the other countries. The victory of the Reformation meant that old cultural bonds were severed and that the most important international influence over northern Europe came to an end—with nothing ready as yet to be put in its place.

Economically the contrast was just as great. Except for the Hanseatic towns of northern Germany and the Baltic, the countries in the north were undeveloped nations of peasants. The Sala silver mine in Sweden was a very modest counterpart of the stream of precious metals in the south, and its yield diminished rapidly. The chief Scandinavian exports handled by the Hansa derived at first from furs and stock-raising. Norway also supplied dried fish, and Sweden iron and copper. These two Swedish exports, however, expanded greatly in the latter part of the sixteenth century and the beginning of the seventeenth.

While in southern Europe the frontier between east and west was closed more and more tightly and new prospects opened up in other directions, this was not the case in the north. The economic and political relations between the countries west and east of the Baltic became increasingly important. The trade with Russia attracted attention far and wide, even in western Europe. Contacts of various kinds were tried out, experiment followed experiment, and one plan came on top of the next, particularly where Sweden was concerned. At an early stage (1557) Russia attacked the Teutonic Order in Livonia and in 1558 captured the town of Narva on the river Narova, which flows into the Gulf of Finland.[1] Russia had thereby penetrated to the immediate vicinity of the Baltic. A new political situation had arisen.

The Teutonic Order in Livonia had no chance of survival. Russia had struck the first blow and as a result Russian trade routes to the Baltic were opened up. Fear within the Order grew and the Teutonic Knights began to look round for help from outside. As a result, all the neighbouring powers were soon drawn in. Livonia's fate was of great concern to Poland. Denmark, too, showed an interest, managing to acquire the island of Ösel off the Estonian coast for Prince Magnus, the younger brother of the Danish king, Frederick II. The chief mercantile town of Estonia, Reval, which belonged to the Hanseatic League, appealed to the Swedish king for help. Gustavus Vasa was reluctant to intervene in affairs of the Order, but his son Eric XIV, who succeeded him in 1560, immediately lent a sympathetic ear to Reval. Herein lay the seed of a widespread conflict between the interests of the Baltic states.

During the sixteenth century the main line of communication between the North Sea and the Baltic passed through Öresund, the Sound. The export routes for the Russian market led to the Gulf of Finland and the Gulf of Riga, and for the Polish and Lithuanian market to the ports in the south-east of the Baltic, Riga and the Prussian towns. The more southerly routes from eastern Europe were by land through Cracow and Leipzig; they are of great importance in another context. A new northern highway to the White Sea was found by English merchant adventurers during the 1550s.

Ever since the middle ages Russia's overseas trade had been in the hands of foreign merchants. In the very early days trade had been through Novgorod; later Reval in Estonia, Riga in Livonia, and the Prussian towns, chiefly Königsberg and Danzig, came into the picture. Russian goods were in great demand in western Europe: hemp and flax, hides and costly furs, wax and tallow. A Swedish historian, Artur Attman, has analysed the Russian market of that time, its production areas and outlets. Reval had corn as its chief article of export and, to a lesser degree, wares

[1] See vol. II, chapter 18.

from the Russian interior. Riga exported mainly flax and hemp from Russia, and the same applied to Königsberg, which obtained its export goods from Lithuania and Russia. Danzig was Poland's and Lithuania's big port, with timber, tar and corn from the Vistula area as chief export articles, but Russian goods also were shipped from Danzig, being taken there from Estonian and Livonian ports.

This economic-strategic state of affairs was in many ways decisive for the northern kingdoms. The key position was held by Denmark, since olden times ruler of the Sound, the two coasts of which she controlled up to 1658. When the Union of Kalmar came to an end, this dominion over a vital trade route was of even greater importance, especially as during the sixteenth century the Netherlands increased their trade in this region and England, too, began to show a mercantile interest there. Moreover, Denmark held the island of Gotland in the centre of the Baltic. Her ancient territory also comprised the provinces which have been Swedish since 1658—Skåne, Blekinge and Halland. Bohuslän was included in the Norwegian part of the realm. Sweden's encirclement became even plainer when Denmark reached across to Estonia and seized Ösel.

Sweden, whose only access to the sea in the west was across a narrow strip of land round the mouth of the Göta river, was therefore largely dependent on Denmark for her connections with western Europe. Since the eastern part of the Swedish kingdom, Finland, stretched right to the Novgorod Russian frontier, Sweden at this time had strong leanings to the east, and all through the middle ages this orientation had been conspicuous in the country's foreign policy.

At the beginning of the period dealt with here, three deaths of political significance occurred in Scandinavia. The captive Christian II of Denmark, symbol of the tendencies overcome by the nobility,[1] died in 1559; Christian III of Denmark, who had been on good terms with the nobles and reigned under their influence, died in the same year; and Gustavus Vasa of Sweden in 1560.

The oath of accession that determined the powers of the new Danish king, Frederick II, gave further power to the council and confirmed the economic privileges of the aristocracy; the reins of government were in their hands. In Sweden the accession of the new king, Eric XIV, caused no change in the constitution and administration as a whole, but the position did alter in that Eric's half-brothers, the Dukes John and Charles, enjoyed a certain independence through their private duchies. The dissension was aggravated by John's position as duke of Finland; when he married Catherine Jagellonica, sister of the Polish king, Sigismund Augustus, his involvement on the eastern side of the Baltic became even plainer.

Christian III of Denmark and Gustavus Vasa of Sweden had both built

[1] See vol. II, chapter 5.

up a new system of administration, which made possible more settled state finances and gave the king a better control of the country. Denmark based her foreign position on mercenaries and a strong fleet; the money for these came largely from the toll collected from ships passing through the Sound. Gustavus Vasa had started to create an army of Swedish soldiers, tested in the war against Russia in 1555–7, and he also laid the foundation of a navy. Eric XIV pressed on with these plans. At this period the nobility, headed by the council, had greater influence in Denmark than in Sweden. The Swedish council played a smaller part than the Danish, and the *Riksdag* still had importance in Sweden. Antagonism between royal power and nobility was to be a recurrent theme in Swedish history between 1560 and 1612 and the *Riksdag* thereby had certain opportunities of asserting itself.

In broad outline this is the background to the course of events to be described here: the establishment of Sweden's dominion on the Baltic, which during the next period was to lead to the country's position as a great power.

Gustavus Vasa had always held that it was vital to acquire diplomatic and mercantile contacts on the other side of the powers that excluded Sweden from direct communication with central and western Europe, that is, Denmark, which controlled the Sound, and Lübeck, which still had the final say in Sweden's foreign trade. But he also tried to maintain good relations with Denmark, confirmed by an alliance in 1541.

His son Eric, however, even when he was heir to the throne and had his seat in the town and castle of Kalmar in the south-east of Sweden, had observed what he took to be an encirclement on the part of Denmark. He had taken particular notice of Denmark's hold on the river mouths in Blekinge and Skåne. Before his accession he had also seen the diplomatic possibilities of his unmarried state and had entered into marriage negotiations with Elizabeth of England before she became queen. Furthermore, both his father's Russian war and his brother John's Finnish duchy had drawn his attention to the east. A conjunction between east and west was in his mind and was mentioned openly when the advantages of a marriage with him were urged upon Elizabeth by his envoys in England. Russia's conquest of Narva and Reval's appeal to Sweden spurred him on to intervene in the events in the Baltic. A strong foothold on its east coast would enhance his prospects of gaining support in the west, the south, and on the other side of Denmark-Norway, and would give him a key position in relation to the trade with Russia.

Internal conditions in Sweden made Eric still more eager. Duke John (later King John III) was carrying on an active foreign policy of his own from his seat in Åbo. As security for a loan to his brother-in-law Sigismund Augustus of Poland, he received a number of fortified castles in Livonia, as it were in the rear of the position that Sweden now occupied in northern Estonia. This led to open civil war. Eric sent troops against John, took him prisoner and put him in custody in Gripsholm Castle in the spring of 1563. By then Sweden's seizure of Reval and most of Estonia (1561) had given rise to serious complications of foreign policy. Denmark and Poland were both Sweden's rivals for the spoils of the disintegrating Teutonic Order, and relations between these countries and Sweden grew rapidly worse. There was a further complication. Eric tried to guard Reval's position as a vital port for the shipment of Russian goods—and also that of the Finnish town of Viborg—by demanding that all trade in the Gulf of Finland should be under Swedish control. He tried to back up this demand by blockading Narva, where the Hanseatic merchants could now trade direct with Russia. This situation caused a clash between him and certain Hansa towns, especially Lübeck. Sweden's occupation of Estonia thus had consequences which Eric, with his sanguine disposition, hardly expected.

During the years of increasing tension between Sweden and her neighbours, Eric's hopes of forming political ties in Denmark's rear were also frustrated. In keeping with the political traditions of the age, he had given them the form of marriage negotiations, not only in England but also in Scotland and Hesse. But though his wooing of Elizabeth was favoured by his having begun it before her accession and though it was viewed with interest in certain English circles, it was doomed to failure. Posterity takes this for granted, but it was less obvious at the beginning of the 1560s when Elizabeth's gift for using her person as a lure in diplomatic negotiations was not yet fully revealed. The bait that Eric and his envoys held out was the possibility of directing most Russian exports by way of Sweden. Since English merchants were turning their eyes to the White Sea route, it was natural to tempt them with such prospects. It was unfortunate that Denmark controlled the Sound, especially as the Danish king, too, was courting Elizabeth; but Eric XIV pointed out through his ambassadors that a canal could be built right across Sweden (as indeed it was nearly three hundred years later).

The advantages of a Swedish marriage, however, were not sufficiently plain, either to Elizabeth or to her advisers. An improvised attempt to bring about a marriage with Mary Queen of Scots does not seem to have been meant very seriously on Eric's part. A third attempt (1562–3) to win an important ally in Denmark's rear also came to nothing. This was a proposal to Christina, daughter of Landgrave Philip of Hesse, one of the most prominent Lutheran princes. When hostilities flared up in the Baltic area Sweden was still alone. Equally vain were later efforts to gain support by means of a courtship in Lorraine; the dowager duchess was the daughter of Christian II of Denmark and maintained a claim to her father's kingdom.

It came to open warfare between Sweden and Denmark in the autumn of 1563. The traditional view of this struggle is that the young, ambitious kings in the two northern kingdoms which had long been rivals gave vent to their feelings in an armed conflict. This was an age that thought in symbols, so it was quite in keeping that a dispute about the two countries' coats of arms should help to fan the flames. Denmark had not renounced the claims on Sweden made by her kings ever since the Union of Kalmar, and in 1546 Christian III had incorporated the Swedish arms—three crowns, a common medieval heraldic device associated with the Magi— in the Danish. As a protest against this, Eric XIV included the arms of Denmark and Norway in two quarters of the Swedish coat of arms, with the justification that for a short period in the middle ages Norway had had the same king as Sweden, and that Denmark's arms—three lions—did not symbolise Denmark but the newly won Reval.

This dispute about the national emblems was regarded in former times as one of the main causes of the war that broke out in 1563. It is plain from what has been said above that the war had its origins elsewhere. Both Denmark's mastery of the Sound and Sweden's striving for a hold on Russian trade through the ports on the east coast of the Baltic were economic realities well known to both governments. When Denmark also showed an interest in the crumbling Teutonic Order, with a view to tightening her stranglehold, and Sweden was trying to form an alliance with foreign powers in the south and west, a clash was unavoidable. In September 1563 Frederick II of Denmark launched an attack against Sweden's most vulnerable spot—her only port to the west, Elfsborg on the Skagerack, situated not far from the present big port of Gothenburg, which did not then exist. The civil war between Eric and his half-brother John was a weapon in the hands of the Danes, who had the additional advantage of trained mercenaries and experienced military leaders. At this same time the conflict between Sweden and Lübeck flared up. Lübeck would not tolerate Sweden's pretensions to control the Russian trade and regarded the Swedish encroachment in Estonia, especially the alliance with Reval, as a threat to her own trade in the east, which had been vital to her for so many years. Finally, the ruler of Poland had to react to the fate that had overtaken his brother-in-law, Duke John, and to Sweden's intervention in Estonia; on this front, too, hostilities were unavoidable. So began the Seven Years War of the North (1563–70), as it is usually called. The expansionist aims of the northern countries had inevitably collided.

It is unnecessary here to follow the Swedish–Danish war in detail. It was a terrible tragedy, with savage depredations in all quarters which resulted in bitter feelings on both sides of the frontier and fed the widespread hatred hatched out by propaganda as well as a hundred years of fighting under the Kalmar Union. There was barbaric logic in the depredations, both sides aiming to lay waste those parts of enemy territory useful as military bases; the Swedes, moreover, had to break through the Danish encirclement. Both high commands carried out this programme with macabre tenacity of purpose. The young Swedish army stood up well to Frederick II's mercenaries, and in Eric XIV Sweden had a competent military organiser and 'chief of staff', though he was of no use as a leader of troops since he was apt to lose his nerve in the presence of the enemy. And on the Swedish side there was no one to match the Danes' commander, Daniel Rantzau, a gifted strategist of Holstein descent.

The biggest tactical successes were won by Denmark, while the Swedes compensated for their reverses on land by victories at sea. Eric had worked hard to build up a modern fleet and, after initial setbacks, it was possible for the capable admiral, Klas Kristersson Horn, to keep open the routes to northern Germany and ensure vital supplies. For a long time, therefore, the struggle was even and both antagonists showed signs of exhaustion.

Eric XIV was a man of great talent but he lacked a sense of reality in weighing his political ideas. Like no one else in Sweden at that time, he had European culture at his fingertips: he was a musician and composer, he had read the classics widely and was well versed in astrology, the fashionable science of the age. But his theoretical mind made it hard for him to understand that politics is the art of the possible. In him, too, the acute suspiciousness that was a family failing of the Vasas often took the form of persecution mania; violent changes of mood flung him constantly from reckless self-assertion to deep depression.

His advisers, chiefly his secretary Jöran Persson, the son of a priest, guarded—often by extremely harsh means—the interests of the central government against the administrators and the nobles. A bitter conflict arose between the king and certain groups of the aristocracy: members of the Sture family, which had produced the regents at the end of the middle ages, and other supporters of Duke John. In 1567 the king had several of the most prominent men put to death; it was then found that his mind was unbalanced. After his recovery he legalised his long-standing liaison with Karin Månsdotter, a girl of peasant stock. Duke John had been let out of prison during his half-brother's insanity and now (1568), together with his younger brother Duke Charles, placed himself at the head of a rebellion of the nobles, in the middle of the Danish war. Eric was seized in Stockholm, deposed and put in prison, where he spent the rest of his life. He died in 1577.

After Eric's dethronement the nobles were the undisputed masters. Duke John was elected king and the *Riksdag* sanctioned the transfer of the crown to him as John III. Having confirmed the nobility's privileges, the new king's first task was to seek peace with Denmark. In the winter of 1567–8 the Danish troops under Rantzau had thrust far into the eastern part of Sweden, whose conduct of the war was hampered by the internal fighting. The terms were harsh, but were mitigated by the fact that Denmark was just as exhausted as Sweden. At the peace of Stettin (1570) a stiff ransom had to be paid for Elfsborg, which the Danes still held. And the plans for Swedish domination over a part of the Russian trade had to be shelved. True, Sweden retained Estonia, and relations with Poland were good from now on, as was only natural when the new Swedish king was the Polish king's brother-in-law. Denmark's efforts to get a foothold in Estonia had also failed. But Eric XIV's two main ideas—to gain an opening to the North Sea and to control the trade routes to Russia—had come to nothing as yet; the trade to Narva was again free for Lübeck and others, and Denmark's grip on the entrance to the Baltic was unbroken. Moreover, during the war the Sound toll had been changed (1567), being assessed now on a ship's burden and cargo, where before it had been a ship toll. This meant greater economic gain to Denmark, and Elsinore (Helsingør), where the toll was collected, became a key point for the control of the Baltic trade.

Eric XIV had tried to maintain tolerable relations with Russia, in a crisis even intimating that he was prepared to hand over John's wife, Catherine Jagellonica, to the tsar, Ivan IV, who at one time had been an unsuccessful suitor for her hand. It is therefore not surprising that John III and Ivan IV were now at daggers drawn, and they exchanged notoriously abusive letters. But John was of no mind to abandon his brother's plans to gain control of the Russian trade. He merely sought new ways. Under his direction Swedish expansion to the east was aimed straight at Russia, while he could count on Poland as a friendly power. Trade with the countries east of the Baltic was growing in importance, stimulated also by the price revolution that had repercussions even in the north of Europe in the latter part of the sixteenth century. More and more west European merchants made their way to the Baltic states. The traditional products of the Russian market, together with the timber and corn exported from the south-east corner of the Baltic, were increasingly in demand. Also merchants not only from England but by degrees from the Netherlands as well took the fairly new route along the Norwegian coast to the new port, Archangel, founded in 1586.

Under these conditions it was natural that Sweden continued to expand eastwards. John III soon blockaded Narva again and resumed the old demands for control of the routes in the east, for the time being in concert with Poland and without being disturbed now by Denmark, who, though clinging to her aspirations here, was unable to pursue them. However, the initiative in the east was seized by Russia, who attacked Swedish Estonia. Only with a mighty effort and great sacrifice did Sweden hold her ground, Scottish and German mercenaries being thrown into the fight. Towards the end of the 1570s the new king of Poland, Stephen Bathory (1575–86), he too a brother-in-law of John III (he had married Catherine Jagellonica's sister Anna), vigorously countered the Russian attack and won Livonia once and for all. Poland thereby gained control over the vital trade route that led to Riga. The Polish war eased Sweden's position and, after the French-born Pontus de la Gardie had taken command of the Swedish troops, a series of decisive victories were won against the Russians. With the capture of Narva in 1581 all the strategic positions on the Gulf of Finland were in Swedish hands and the Narva blockade could be made effective. But the result was disappointing; most of the Russian trade went through the Polish ports and some of it through Archangel. A truce was agreed on between Russia and Sweden in 1581, and the following year Poland and Russia signed a peace treaty which confirmed Poland's possession of Livonia. Sweden and Poland had not directly supported one another, but each had benefited by the other's policy.

It was only with great difficulty that Sweden had been able to wage war in the east. True, production of certain coveted Swedish exports had increased. A more up-to-date method of refining iron had resulted in bar iron instead of the primitive *osmund* iron, and the export of this refined product doubled during the latter part of the sixteenth century. The production of copper also rose, especially during and after the 1580s, when the big mine in Dalarna (Stora Kopparberg) gave bigger yields, first because of new veins and then because of improved techniques. But in a country which still depended mainly on a barter economy, it was not easy to raise money for a policy of foreign expansion of the kind Sweden had now embarked on and the government was constantly grappling with severe financial problems. The internal conflicts that had marred Eric XIV's reign had ceased for a time, but the nobles were not content with their gains from the new privileges, nor did they have the desired influence over the government which the Danish nobles of that time possessed. Another seed of internal strife was that Gustav Vasa's youngest son, Duke Charles, asserted his independence as the holder of a duchy in central Sweden containing several vital iron-producing areas.

John III, however, was not minded to give up his political plans abroad. He pursued them along two lines, the first being a dynastic combination that was to unite Sweden and Poland and enable them to dominate the eastern part of the Baltic; the second being to see that Sweden commanded the Russian trade route through Archangel.

John's marriage to the Polish princess Catherine gave him the idea of the dynastic union. When Stephen Bathory died in 1586, John put forward Sigismund, his son by Catherine, as candidate for the Polish throne. At first the Reformation had gained ground in Poland, but the Counter-Reformation had hit back and the Roman Catholics had won the day. Sigismund had been brought up as a Catholic. John himself, who had only superficial Lutheran sympathies, had drawn up a Catholicising liturgy which he wished to introduce into Sweden. In addition, he had begun a series of negotiations with Catholic powers during the 1570s, his aim being partly to gain some of the legacy from his queen's mother, Bona Sforza of

Milan. His aesthetic ambitions, expressed mainly in his building of stately castles in a Renaissance style, concurred with his theological interests. To him there was nothing impossible or unpalatable about a dynastic union between Protestant Sweden and re-Catholicised Poland. He succeeded in getting Sigismund, who bore the old Polish royal name, elected (1587). At the election Poland had put forward the claim that Estonia should be united with Livonia. This would have given Poland control of the Russian trade routes through the Gulf of Finland and also a favourable military position. However, John would not accept this claim—naturally enough, with his foreign policy—and the matter was deferred until such time as Sigismund became king of both countries.

The personal union planned between Sweden and Poland-Lithuania can be called the third phase in Sweden's Baltic policy during the sixteenth century, if the acquisition of Estonia in 1561 and the conquest of Narva in 1581 are regarded as the first two. Sigismund's election as Polish king accentuated Sweden's leanings to the east, and a united kingdom of the kind envisaged might have had a very strong political and commercial position. But the union also involved new problems. These were already apparent soon after Sigismund's accession, and only a few years later they became so aggravated that they gradually changed the entire course of Swedish foreign policy.

John III's second scheme in connection with Russian trade was prompted by the increasing importance of the relatively new route through Archangel. The account books of the toll collected by Denmark in the Sound at this time show that about 2,000 Netherlandish and 130 English (and a smaller number of Scottish) ships sailed annually through the Sound in both directions. In England an Eastland Company had been organised in 1579 to carry on trade with Prussia, Poland and the Baltic states. For the White Sea trade, the figures available are naturally not so exact, but it has been estimated that two or three score of ships, mainly English, sailed to the far north every year, and the number gradually increased. The route certainly had a growing importance. In addition, it was free and uncontrolled, even if Denmark did assert that she had a right to exact compensation for loss in toll money from the ships that, instead of going through the Sound, sailed to the White Sea across 'the Danish king's main'—the waters along the west and north coast of Norway. The tsar had given the English merchants, who were organised in the Muscovy Company, a monopoly of the north Russian trade, which, however, was lost later, in 1586. The frontiers in the far north were ill defined, and John III considered he had certain territorial rights even there. Ambitious plans were made, but they fell through. Yet the project of a Swedish expansion towards the White Sea was to recur, showing how well prepared and comprehensive these plans were. They were aimed deliberately at controlling the whole of Russian trade with western Europe.

The internal conflicts in Sweden during the 1580s, already referred to, became more acute during John III's last years. The precarious state of the country's finances took the form of a continued depreciation of the currency which caused wide concern. John's efforts to get his new liturgy accepted in 1576 led to violent discord between its supporters and opponents. Several of the latter were forced to leave their clerical offices and a bitter polemic was waged. The leader of the opposition was Duke Charles, who held steadfast to 'the pure doctrine' and denied the liturgy a footing in his duchy; he was not without Calvinistic leanings. There were thus three conflicting factions in Sweden: the king, the duke, and the nobility, with the council in the centre. A new generation of nobles had grown up; the most cultured of them had studied on the continent, were interested in history—especially the part formerly played by the nobility—and were familiar with the current political doctrines of the Monarchomachs, for example, the French Calvinists' theories about rebellion and the sovereign power of the people. They were openly in sympathy with the medieval aristocratic constitutionalism that had played such an important part during the Kalmar Union.

During the 1580s the composition of the parties kept changing. First, the king and the aristocracy joined forces against Duke Charles, who had his power within his duchy curbed and was excluded from membership of the council that was to rule Sweden whenever Sigismund, future king of the union, was in his other realm. After his accession in Poland Sigismund found himself in difficulties, since Sweden obviously had no intention of giving up Estonia. He went to meet John at Reval (1589). In desperation over the awkward state of affairs, John demanded that his son should leave Poland and return with him to Sweden. But the Swedish lords of the council who were present in Reval vigorously opposed this, at the same time complaining of the way John ruled. John had to give in, and Sigismund returned to Poland.

The result was an immediate breach between John and the council; the king turned for support to Duke Charles, revoking the decrees against him, and the brothers made common cause against the nobility. Certain lords of the council were removed from office and the *Riksdag* was summoned to ratify the new policy. Although unwilling to sanction all the king's measures, it did give him and his brother some support. Their alliance continued until John's death in 1592 and there was no reconciliation with the deposed lords of the council.

The position pending the arrival of the new king in Sweden was therefore extremely complicated. The nobility, headed by the displaced lords, mustered their resources. Most of the clergy had set themselves against the liturgy and Catholicism. Duke Charles was again master of his well-administered and united duchy and had no intention of renouncing his status as a semi-independent prince in the kingdom.

A new protagonist now came on the scene: Sigismund. He was not going to have his inherited power in Sweden weakened, particularly as he had unpleasant memories of the aristocracy from the first years of his reign in Poland. He also planned to restore Catholicism to Sweden, being accompanied by a group of similarly minded advisers. The most prominent of these was the papal nuncio Malaspina, a leading figure of the Counter-Reformation. John III's idea of bringing about Swedish expansion by means of a dynastic union had led to a position which he had not foreseen.

Sigismund could count on a widespread popular opinion favourable to the king and on several loyal supporters among the nobles, especially in Finland. But opposition to his plans was also to be expected. The Lutheran clergy, at a synod in Uppsala in March 1593 when all 'heresies' had been denounced, had organised their resistance to possible Catholic action. Duke Charles and the council had patched up their quarrels, determined to safeguard their power against any plans the new ruler might have for strengthening the power of the monarchy. In September 1593 Sigismund's Polish fleet arrived in the Stockholm archipelago. At his coronation in Uppsala in 1594, attended also by Duke Charles with a large following, he was to meet his subjects.

The struggle between royal power, duke and aristocratic constitutionalism was thus centred round a religious bone of contention: would the king get his way in securing the right of public worship for non-Lutherans—chiefly his Polish followers—or would the *Riksdag* be able to exact a promise from him that he would conform to its own religious views? Politics and religion were combined in a manner typical of the age. The king was forced to yield, and had to listen to strong words from the nobles on absolute monarchy: '...Little hath been heard in Sweden hitherto that hereditary kings should reign *absolute*.' Disappointed and dejected, Sigismund soon returned to his Polish realm, while Duke Charles and the council—that is, the nobility—assumed joint rule of Sweden during his absence. No final, precise form of government had been adopted, although many proposals had been mooted. For the time being, however, the duke and the council were more or less agreed to act together in guarding the country's rights against Sigismund's real or imagined actions in favour of absolutism and the Counter-Reformation.

But this alliance was too weak to last. At the *Riksdag* in Söderköping (1595) it already began to crack. The duke, more rigorously than the council, upheld the independence of the home government against the king and he made good use of the commons' support in order to get his way. The internal conflict soon grew more bitter. Klas Fleming, the governor of Finland, John III's old duchy, refused to accept the form of government brought about by the duke. Charles demanded a settlement with Fleming, but the council wavered. With Charles's approval the peasants in Finland rose against Fleming (1596–7), but the revolt was brutally crushed. The duke now challenged the council and appealed to the *Riksdag*, which met at Arboga (1597); of all the lords of the council, only one attended. From then on, Duke Charles and the commons formed a hostile front against Sigismund and the aristocracy. Soon the tension was so great that several lords of the council fled to Sigismund in Poland. They accompanied him when he sailed to Sweden with an army in 1598. Several clashes with the duke's troops decided nothing. Sigismund suddenly gave in, handed over to his uncle the lords who had deserted and returned with his army to Poland, leaving the government of Sweden unsettled. The duke captured the towns and castles still loyal to the king in Sweden and Finland; arraignments and bloodshed followed, and at the *Riksdag* in Linköping (1600) several of the indicted lords were sentenced to death by an extraordinary court of the estates and executed. Aristocratic constitutionalism was temporarily overthrown and Sigismund, fully occupied by affairs in Poland, did not resume the struggle. The union with Poland was irreparably broken. John III's ambitious plan had led to results which were the very opposite of those intended.

In one respect, however, the original aim had been furthered. Just as the rupture between Sigismund and his Swedish subjects became apparent, Sweden derived great benefit from the personal union with Poland. As already pointed out, Sweden's war with Russia had previously—at the beginning of the 1580s—been favoured by Poland's fight with the same country. There had been a truce between Sweden and Russia since 1581, but war broke out again in 1590. The Swedish attacks were directed against the areas vital to trade round Novgorod and Pskov, and against the White Sea in order to gain control of the northern trade route. But they came to nothing and peace was signed in 1595 at Teusina, while the union between Sweden and Poland was still in force and gave the Swedes a favourable basis for negotiation. Their real goal had not been reached, but Narva was retained and it was agreed in principle that trade could be carried on freely to Viborg in Finland and to Reval, while only Swedes could trade to Narva. It seemed as if the object of the Baltic policy had been achieved, but the actual gains turned out to be smaller than expected. From now on Russian trade was conducted through the ports held by Poland and through Archangel. Sweden's position on the Gulf of Finland, however, had been firmly established.

Despite the breach with Poland, Sweden did not give up her original plans. Duke Charles (later King Charles IX) picked up the threads of his brothers' designs; he had, moreover, taken an active part in the negotiations with Russia. But the plans had become both more far-reaching and more risky because of events in Sweden during the 1590s. Eric XIV had fought Poland but had tried to maintain friendly relations with Russia, even at the cost of drastic concessions. John III had from time to time fought at Poland's side but Russia had been his arch-enemy in the east.

When Charles IX became king of Sweden, relations with Poland were definitely hostile; the question was how the situation with Russia would develop. Eric XIV had waged a hard struggle against Denmark in order to break the encirclement of Sweden. Both sides had exhausted themselves, but the conflict was not fought out. The continued Swedish expansion in the east, while not a direct provocation to Denmark, had entailed complications with that country. In particular the Swedish plans to reach the Arctic Ocean and the White Sea had caused misgivings on the other side of the Sound. How far did Charles IX intend to pursue his predecessors' schemes?

Like his elder brothers, Charles had a fascinating, rather problematical nature. Inherited from his father's side he had the orator's persuasive gift—lacking in Eric XIV and John III—of winning the support of the common people for his policy, the faculty of presenting a propaganda that was effective and convincing. Neither Eric nor John had been able entirely to exploit the *Riksdag* in the political struggle for power and to gain its support, although the former in particular had made efforts in that direction. Charles no doubt looked on himself as the one who fulfilled and completed his father's work, and his political methods, sometimes cynical, did not exclude a sense of what was right and of Swedish political tradition. For all his domineering ways he really tried to co-operate with the *Riksdag*, whose authority was indeed behind his rule. The latest research makes it clear that his conception of politics generally was not far removed from aristocratic constitutionalism; the violent personal conflicts between him and the lords of the council do not preclude this.

The Swedish *Riksdag* began once more to play a prominent part in the country's political life. As before, it consisted of four estates: nobles, clergy, burgesses and peasants. It met irregularly, when the political situation seemed to demand it, and during the first decade of the seventeenth century relatively often: in 1600, 1602, 1604 and 1607. Its role during the quarrels of the 1590s, and the king's need to submit important problems to it, stabilised its position in the Swedish constitution. The council likewise regained some of its importance: new lords were appointed in place of those who had been removed. Council and *Riksdag* also considered questions of foreign policy, the council's attitude sometimes being rather cautious.

As already mentioned, it was Charles IX's intention to pursue the expansion eastwards begun by his two elder brothers. No agreement had been reached with Poland about the contention for the throne nor was the question of Estonia settled, and Poland still laid claim to this area. Charles decided to carry the war east of the Baltic, with Swedish Estonia as base; the town of Reval and the Estonian nobility were Protestant and loyal to Sweden. However, the campaigns against Poland, carried on in Livonia, were full of setbacks. Charles was not a competent general, and the Polish

417

cavalry won victory after victory. After initial success in 1601, when the Swedish troops swept forward to the Düna, the Livonian estates acclaimed Charles in 1602; but Polish troops then marched in, drove the Swedes back, and pressed into Estonia. In 1605 Charles again attacked Livonia and began to besiege Riga, one of the ports most vital to the Russian trade, but he was routed at Kirkholm (Salaspils) and had to return to Sweden with what was left of his army. The war went on for the next few years without any decisive results. The most effective part of Charles's strategy, showing the consistency of his plans, was no doubt the blockade of Polish ports that he tried to carry out. However, the war was soon to be transferred to a new front.

In the history of Russia the beginning of the seventeenth century is marked by civil war, rebellion and party strife. The outward reason for this was that the old dynasty had died out with Theodore, Ivan the Terrible's son, in 1598. He was succeeded by his brother-in-law Boris Godunov, the main character in Pushkin's drama and Moussorgsky's opera. A younger son of Ivan IV, Demetrius, had been killed in 1591, but in 1604 a pretender to the throne appeared who made out he was Demetrius; he was supported by Poland and by Boris's opponents among the boyars and various groups of the population. Poland hereby carried her war against Russia onto Russian soil. Boris died in 1605; his son Theodore was murdered soon afterwards and the pseudo-Demetrius was killed in the following year. One of the boyars, Basil Shuisky, was now elected tsar but his power was severely limited. In the years that followed two new pseudo-Demetriuses raised rebellion one after the other and Basil was deposed in 1610. These stormy events formed the background to Charles IX's Russian foreign policy.

Boris Godunov had taken the initiative towards negotiations with Charles in 1599 and they were continued during the next few years. Boris refused to recognise the Peace of Teusina and wanted to have it revised. Charles for his part was anxious to keep his gains in the east, especially Narva, but at the same time wanted to maintain reasonably good relations with Russia. The attacks against Boris by the first pseudo-Demetrius and his Polish helpers altered the position in Sweden's favour, and the tsar grew more amenable towards Charles. Negotiations continued until Boris's death and were resumed with Demetrius, without leading anywhere. In Charles's view the situation was critical, and it was at this time that he thought of trying to win Turkey as an ally against Russia, an idea which later became a tradition in Swedish foreign policy. With Basil's accession as tsar, however, the position swung round again in Sweden's favour, Basil and his supporters being hostile to Poland.

Charles IX now had two possibilities of carrying out his Russian policy; everything hinged on relations with Poland. He hoped mainly for support from the new anti-Polish régime, but the ferment and internal dissensions in Russia brought home to him the fact that such unstable conditions were nothing to build on. He reasoned that direct intervention might lead to more lasting results.

In the development of Swedish foreign policy outlined here, two areas of Russia were of special importance: round Ladoga and the eastern part of the Gulf of Finland, and the outlet to the north on the White Sea. The internal troubles in Russia might offer a chance of gaining the desired influence over these areas. In the matter of Arctic Ocean policy Charles IX had carried out John III's ideas, and by so doing he had come into conflict with Denmark-Norway, as will be seen later on. This was the position when he decided on direct intervention in Russia, torn by civil strife. Fresh negotiations were begun in 1608 when Basil, disturbed by the successes of the second pseudo-Demetrius, showed interest in a Swedish alliance. Early in the new year of 1609 an agreement was reached and a treaty was signed in February. The Peace of Teusina was confirmed and an alliance entered into against Sigismund and Poland; an army 5,000 strong was to be sent to Russia, after which the fortress and province of Kexholm (Käkisalmi) were to be handed over to the Swedes. This province comprised the western shore of Lake Ladoga and north thereof and held a key position in relation to the Russian trade routes. With this treaty Sweden pursued both the fight against Poland and the already traditional aim of command over Russia's outlets.

This was a fateful initiative that Swedish foreign policy had taken. The provocation against Poland led to immediate action by Sigismund; it was hastened by the successes of the Swedish troops, side by side with the Russian, when under the command of Jacob de la Gardie—son of the Pontus de la Gardie who had captured Narva in 1581—they put to flight the second pseudo-Demetrius's forces and pushed on through Novgorod to Moscow. Poland now declared war on Russia; her armies besieged Smolensk and pressed towards Moscow. De la Gardie was defeated at the battle of Klushino in June 1610, the Poles took Moscow, and Tsar Basil was dethroned.

The Russian boyars were grouped in opposing factions. One of these now put forward Sigismund's son, Wladislaw, as candidate for the tsar's crown. This would bring about a united eastern front and spell ruin to Sweden's foreign policy. Among the boyars, however, was another faction which was bitterly hostile to the Poles and could not accept the choice of Wladislaw; moreover Sigismund had doubts about his son's fitness to be tsar. The anti-Polish party in Russia entered into negotiations with de la Gardie, and when the latter in return for Swedish help demanded that the new tsar should not be dependent on Sigismund, Charles IX's young son Gustavus Adolphus was put forward for tsar (1611). De la Gardie, however, expected little from this candidature; what mattered to him was to gain the territories aspired to by Sweden. Leading his troops towards

419 27-2

Novgorod, he took the city and agreed with the local authorities that they should place themselves under the protection of the Swedish king and for their own part offer the throne to one of Charles IX's sons—Gustavus Adolphus or the younger Charles Philip—pending a general Russian election. This was yet another astonishing countermove to the Polish dynastic policy, but de la Gardie had conducted these negotiations on his own account and it was now a question of how the leaders of foreign affairs at home would react to these ambitious plans. Word of them did not reach Stockholm until Charles IX was dying. A dynastic combination curiously similar to John III's Polish–Swedish plan three decades earlier seemed for a moment to make the Swedish dream of control over the Russian trade come true. But it was only a short-lived hope.

Charles IX's foreign policy resembled that of his elder brother, Eric XIV, in that it was like an avalanche: one mass dislodged and swept away the next. A conquest of Novgorod and northern Russia would have meant that part of the traditional plan had been realised, and a dynastic union would have completed it. But, as in Eric's time, there were complications. The most serious were the relations with Denmark and the decisive factor here was the Arctic Ocean policy inaugurated by John III and carried on by Charles IX. Antagonism between Denmark and Sweden had not ceased with the peace of 1570; the position was unchanged. Eric's attempts to gain support in the rear of Denmark were resumed by Charles, who sought an alliance with various Protestant powers—with the Hansa and princes in northern and western Germany, with the Dutch and England—but without success. To the western European countries, who saw in the Baltic trade an increasingly vital part of their economic policy, Denmark, still in control of the Sound, was unquestionably the chief power in the north. The fact that Shakespeare laid the scene of *Hamlet* at Elsinore shows that this toll port was of current interest in western Europe.

Since 1588 Denmark had had a new sovereign, Christian IV, who came of age in 1596. The country's foreign policy had followed old lines. A chain of fortresses had been built in order to secure the hold on Sweden's outlets in the south and west: from Kristianopel, in the east of Blekinge, to Bohus, north of Sweden's narrow passage to the North Sea. But Charles IX with Dutch assistance founded the new town of Gothenburg on Sweden's strip of land in the west and its citizens were granted privileges to trade with Lapland, to sail to Russia by way of the White Sea and to fish in the north. There was consistency and logic in this extension of the old plans: after Sweden had gained control of the Narva trade and it had proved a disappointment, the next step was in the direction of the White Sea. The founding of Gothenburg was part and parcel of the White Sea plans, which have already been touched on in connnection with the Russian policy. Charles's concern with the northern waters was combined with an interest in Lapland and in reindeer-breeding—while still duke he had even sent reindeer herds to Germany. After Olaus Magnus's great work on the ethnographical curiosities of Sweden had been published in Italy in the middle of the sixteenth century, Lapland's exoticism had fascinated many, but it was the political considerations that really mattered to Charles.

The thought that Sweden might establish a base in Swedish Lapland, thus gaining control of the Arctic Ocean coast and the northern outlet from Russia, was of course goading to Denmark, who had always claimed the right to dominate the route round the Norwegian coast to the White Sea. Sweden's expansion in the east heightened the tension, and Denmark made overtures to Poland. There were no fixed frontiers in the regions of the far north and, after the peace with Russia at Teusina, Sweden demanded possession of part of the Arctic Ocean coast. This was regarded by Denmark as a threat to her rights over 'the Danish king's main'. The fact that Denmark, Norway and Poland—apart from England—are the three countries forming the background to the *Hamlet* drama of that age reflects important facets of the foreign political situation in northern Europe, seen from the English viewpoint.

Denmark still had several questions to raise during the negotiations conducted with Sweden after Charles IX came to the throne. The Swedish claim to have the final say in the Narva trade, the Swedish blockade of the Polish ports, especially Riga, and other strategic measures concerning trade, all irritated the neighbouring power, and Charles IX's rightful position as ruler in Sweden could also be called in question. Negotiations were carried on from the beginning of the new century, but no reconciliation was reached. Christian IV wanted war, not least because of the critical position for Sweden that her policy in the east had led to about 1610 and because of the danger to the Danish–Norwegian domination in the Arctic Ocean inherent in the Sweden expansion. Early in 1611 the Danish king put before his council a plan for war against Sweden, having a good excuse in Charles's unwillingness to settle matters by negotiation. The position was similar to that at the start of the Seven Years War of the North: with no support from the west or south, but with serious and unpredictable conflicts in the east, Sweden faced an attack from Denmark. The latter still had the initial advantage geographically and strategically and was determined to retain her key position on the Sound and on the route to Russia round Norway. Christian IV attacked in the spring of 1611. Sweden was then involved in the intricacies of her eastern policy, which fully occupied her foremost military leader Jacob de la Gardie, and her king was laid low with illness. Charles IX died in October of the same year. The Danish assault was directed chiefly at the important fortress and town of Kalmar, in the south-east of Sweden, where Eric had once had his seat as duke. Its commander capitulated to the Danes. Sweden's position, not least because of the previous discord between Charles and the council, appeared very critical; this internal state of affairs, moreover, seems to have been one of the reasons why Christian IV attacked at that particular juncture. Charles's consistent and ruthless pursuit of his elder brothers' foreign policy had led Sweden to the brink of disaster. About the same time—Kalmar fell to the Danes at the beginning of August and de la Gardie made his pact with Novgorod at the end of July 1611—the situation came to a head on both fronts. The troubles of the 1560s recurred in a worse form. It was up to the young heir to the throne, Gustavus Adolphus, and the Swedish council to decide whether, in spite of everything, to keep to the course already embarked upon or to relinquish the gains of Sweden's eastern expansion and retreat. The decision influenced the next decades in the history of the Baltic area.

When Charles IX died (October 1611) he was succeeded—under the terms of the succession law passed at the *Riksdag* at Norrköping in 1604—by his eldest son Gustavus Adolphus, who as king took the title of Gustav II Adolf. At this time he was sixteen years old, and according to the order of succession he would 'half' come of age when he was eighteen and be of full age when he turned twenty-four. He was a precocious, highly gifted boy who, ever since he was ten, had listened to deliberations on vital questions of state. When the *Riksdag* met at Nyköping at the end of 1611 he was, despite his youth, acclaimed as fully empowered king. His powers were determined by his royal oath. In this were stated the matters that he was not to decide without the consent of the council and the *Riksdag*. This consent was needed in order to enact laws, to start or end a war, and to form alliances. No extra taxes were to be levied, and no soldiers were to be conscripted, without asking the council and without the agreement of those affected by these measures. Gustavus Adolphus undertook to abide by the ancient law from the fourteenth century. All the privileges of the estates were to be retained. For the nobility, these were set out in detail in 1612. The noblemen's sole right to higher office was laid down and their economic privileges were extended; the peasants on their estates were in general freed from any but the regulation taxes and from recruitment as soldiers, while those of their peasants who belonged to or lived near their principal lands were freed from all services to the crown; these devolved instead upon the noblemen. The nobility, especially the higher aristocracy, had thereby attained the political and economic position it had striven for during the latter part of the sixteenth century. At the same time the king's secretaries, who had played an important part ever since Jöran Persson in Eric XIV's time and, most recently, under Charles IX, lost their influence. The new generation of nobles who thus took up their dominant position in Swedish politics were led by Axel Oxenstierna, the chancellor, one of the five high officers of state with traditions going back to the middle ages: *drots* (lord high steward), administration of justice; *marsk* (marshal), the army; *amiral* (admiral), the navy; *kansler* (chancellor), the king's council;

and *skattmästare* (treasurer), public revenue. All these vacant posts were filled in 1611.

This reshaping of the Swedish administration and the formation of this partially new constitution were carried out in the midst of war. The Danes' successes were still considerable. Elfsborg was captured in the spring of 1612 and Sweden was thereby cut off from the North Sea, as she had been during the Seven Years War of the North. An attempt by the Danish fleet in the same year to take Stockholm failed, however. As time went on, and Sweden was not conquered as quickly as expected, the heavy cost of the German mercenaries in Danish service became a severe drain on Denmark's finances. Peace talks were therefore begun through the mediation of England, who was not happy about the disturbances in the Baltic and the prospect that Denmark might further increase her power there. Peace was signed at Knäred in 1613 and the terms for Sweden were harsh. She must give up all claim to territory on the Arctic Ocean coast and allow Danish ships to trade freely to the ports of Livonia and Courland, especially Riga. Further, Denmark would retain Elfsborg with a large slice of territory until Sweden had paid the sum of one million *riksdaler*—equivalent to the value of the country's harvest for four years—during a period of payment that extended to 1619. For nearly a decade, therefore, Sweden was quite cut off from the Skagerack and North Sea.

Problems equally desperate remained unsolved in the east. A large embassy from Novgorod had come to Stockholm shortly before Charles IX's death, but the Swedish government was uncertain what attitude to adopt to the dynastic policy that de la Gardie had taken it upon himself to initiate. At first Gustavus Adolphus accepted the candidature for Russian tsar, but during 1612 decided to hand it on to his younger brother, Charles Philip, who had been mentioned in Russia as an alternative. Axel Oxenstierna was extremely sceptical about this means of expansion in the east and subsequent events were to prove him right. Charles Philip did embark upon the journey to Novgorod in the summer of 1613, but stopped in Viborg in eastern Finland to await developments. In the meantime the Poles were driven out of Russia, following the failure of a new campaign by Sigismund, and in February 1613, during confused party quarrels, Michael Romanov was elected tsar; by May he was master of Moscow. At the beginning of 1614 Charles Philip returned to Sweden, after it seemed certain that the new régime in Russia would last. Sweden was back where she started from. De la Gardie still held Novgorod with a Swedish force a couple of thousand strong, but to carry through the action was difficult for a country which at the same time had to find the ransom for Elfsborg.

Peace talks with Russia were entered upon, with England as go-between; the mediator was John Mericke, agent of the Muscovy Company in London and familiar with Russian conditions; the Dutch also took part for a time in the talks. The result of the Peace of Stolbova (1617) was that Russia confirmed Tsar Basil's surrender of the province of Kexholm and, further, ceded Ingermanland; Sweden thus gained not only control over the entire coast round the inmost part of the Gulf of Finland but also a favourable frontier for Finland and one of the primary goals in her eastern policy. Gustavus Adolphus emphasised to the *Riksdag* the economic importance of these acquisitions. But the position now was different from what it had been sixty years earlier. Since then Russia's trade by way of the Neva and the Gulf of Finland had declined heavily and the most important outlets now were through the White Sea and Riga, which belonged to Poland. The efforts to dominate the White Sea had come to nought, partly owing to the Danish war and partly because the English mediator was working to keep this route free. So far, the Swedish policy of conquest in the east had not kept pace with the trade policy in the realisation of its aims.

From 1614 to 1616 there had been a truce between Poland and Sweden although indirectly both countries had been opponents in Russia. Negotiations were started but they fell through, and Sweden intended to attack on the Polish front once a favourable peace with Russia had been attained. The war was resumed in 1617 and on the Swedish side soon appeared to be conducted along lines that followed previous thrusts. This continuation of the Swedish struggle for supremacy over the eastern European outlets belongs, however, to the next chapter of history.

It remains to be seen how Sweden could carry out payment of the heavy ransom due to Denmark for Elfsborg. It was made possible principally by two circumstances: the steadily increasing production, at the Stora Kopparberg mine, of copper, which was more and more in demand on the international market; and closer contacts with this market, brought about mainly by the Dutch. Sweden was favoured by the fact that the Dutch were worried by Danish domination—which if anything had increased—in the Baltic area and by the burden imposed by the Sound toll. It was cramping to their efforts to enlarge the ever more profitable trade with the cities on the east of the Baltic that *dominium maris Baltici* should be in the hands of a single power which controlled the only way out. By a kind of monopoly the Swedish state now bought up the copper produced in the country and exported it (in 1615 about 1,600 tons) in return for payment in the currency in which the Elfsborg ransom was to be paid. The Netherlands acted as intermediary and also supplied Sweden with the loans necessary to meet the payments in the prescribed order. In addition, heavy taxes were levied: the king and the princes of the blood paid nearly a third of their annual income, a peasant two *riksdaler*, a farmhand one and a servant-girl a half; in a crisis the king, his kinsmen and several of the nobles gave their private silver to be made into coins. The records in connection with Elfsborg's ransom give a valuable picture of conditions in Sweden at the time. The payments were all made by the stipulated date and at the beginning of 1619 Denmark restored the fortress of Elfsborg with adjacent territory to Sweden. This was the last time that the country's direct link with the Skagerack was threatened.

The contacts with the Dutch also took on a political colour. As early as 1614 a Swedish–Dutch defence pact was signed at The Hague. It had special significance in that it was connected with a somewhat earlier defensive alliance between the Dutch and Lübeck, which also felt disturbed by Denmark's supremacy. The aim of the Swedish–Dutch pact was to preserve freedom of trade and uphold the allies' liberties and rights in the Baltic and North Sea. It was valid for fifteen years. Sweden had at last obtained the long-sought aid outside the Baltic area that had been one of the purposes of Eric XIV's negotiations in England, Scotland, Hesse and Lorraine. At this time it was the Dutch who had the biggest trade interests to guard in the Baltic, interests which seemed to be threatened by Denmark. This was the circumstance that brought Sweden the support she desired; a contributory factor had been her increased influence over the east coast of the Baltic as a direct result of expansion. Such influence might well grow stronger.

The Swedish kingdom as it existed at the beginning of the seventeenth century was still largely an agricultural country of medieval structure. The cultivated districts had grown, however, and Finnish settlers had colonised forest areas in central Sweden. The peasant's life was intimately connected with the changing seasons, with sowing and harvest. The farm produced almost all he needed, salt for the preservation of food being the only commodity that had to be procured from outside. Barley and rye were the main crops, and coarse black bread, salt meat and fish the staple diet, washed down with water, milk or ale; fresh meat relieved the monotony in the summer and at slaughter-time. Only about 5 per cent of the population lived in towns. Attempts have been made to estimate Sweden's population, based partly on the records of the two Elfsborg ransoms. They vary between nearly 430,000 and 830,000 (excluding Finland) for the period round 1570; for the year 1632 the figure 850,000—with 350,000 for Finland—has been arrived at. These figures are not exact, and are probably on the high side.

The kingdom had a source of strength in the administration that had been created since Gustavus Vasa's time. Local government was in the hands of reeves or bailiffs, who as a rule were not nobles, and they kept accounts which were carefully checked; the role of the nobles in local government grew smaller and they were remunerated for their central services to the state by donations of crown land and by incomes from taxes. Their economic privileges also played a part. Herein lay the seed of the development that marked the next period, when the need of compensating the nobles for their increased services could be met only by rapidly increased donations of land and tax incomes—the only means available in a state with barter economy of bringing about a workable remuneration system for the country's foremost servants in central administration, diplomacy and the army. The Swedish noblemen were acquiring a new position in the community. Most of them gave up their occupation as country squires, and Axel Oxenstierna's generation—even the previous one to some extent—trained themselves to be public officials, civil servants and officers. Every nobleman, it is stated in Gustavus Adolphus's privileges of the nobility, should 'have his children brought up in learning, virtue and experience'. Through the nobility's right of precedence to important posts and through the new remuneration system, Sweden's foreign policy of expansion had significant social consequences.

About 1615 Sweden was faced with a vital choice. Was her foreign policy to be kept within the old framework and the country to become once more of no account in the Baltic—she had had to grant Denmark the right to the Swedish coat of arms' Three Crowns at the Peace of Knäred, a momentous renouncement in an age that thought in symbols— or was the expansion to continue, the conquest of the Russian outlets to be completed and a final settlement with Denmark to be reached? There was very little hesitation. Aspirations to political power, hopes of a mercantile key position and bright prospects of a career for the government officials were all linked with a revived national romanticism in the spirit of what Swedish scholars called 'the old Goths' and, in the young king, with a firm belief in the country's and his own potentialities. The war with Poland was resumed, the immediate aim being to gain control over one of the most important east European trade routes, that by the Düna to Riga. The encouraging experience of the copper export, and the diplomatic contact in western Europe achieved at long last, augured well for the future. Sweden's struggle for *dominium maris Baltici* entered its decisive phase.

CHAPTER XIV

EDUCATION AND LEARNING

THE educational achievements of the post-Reformation period must be set against a background of widespread ignorance. It is probable that half the men and more than half the women were illiterate even in the more advanced European states. East of Vienna, north of the Baltic, conditions were a good deal worse. Illiteracy was found more in the country than in the towns, more among women than men, more among the poor than the well-to-do, but it existed everywhere and at nearly all social levels. To have received any degree of systematic teaching was a prerogative of the fortunate or the unusually persistent.

All the same, it is possible to maintain that the opportunities for instruction open to the young were more extensive than they had ever been before, and that they were eagerly utilised. We shall find it convenient to consider them under three heads: popular education, apprenticeship, and the training offered by universities and schools. We know only a little about the first and a good deal about the last; but they were of equal importance for the future of Europe.

Popular education may be defined for our purposes as education acquired independently of Latin. Its range varied greatly. While the majority of those who were ignorant of Latin remained ignorant in most other respects, some could claim to be well informed and an exceptional individual could attain to the many-sided learning of a Palissy. But in nearly all cases non-Latinists who made some progress in their studies did so through private reading. They were autodidacts. Teaching on the basis of the vernacular was limited to certain elementary subjects: reading, writing, simple arithmetic and the catechism. It was unambitious. And of all the sectors that made up the educational life of the time, it was without question the worst organised. Some continental cities ran special schools for children who were not going to learn Latin; and now and again we hear of individual masters hired on the cheap by town councils to teach reading and accounts. Boys were expected to be able to read their own language before embarking on Latin, and many grammar schools provided special classes for this purpose. But except in Scotland such classes were generally confined to those who intended to go on to the grammar course. This was a field where official effort accomplished little. People helped each other.

Classes to teach young children their letters were a common feature of life. Sometimes the teachers were well-intentioned persons who gave their services free. More often they were poor men or women out to make an honest penny. A few were properly educated but many were themselves barely literate. We hear also of more professional pedagogues who hung out their sign and took older pupils—girls or apprentices whose education had been neglected. Some of this teaching may have been efficient. Much was certainly amateurish and careless. That a relatively large number of people knew how to read, write and count was due to the casual and ill-organised efforts of thousands of humble individuals. Such were the uncertain foundations not only of the popularity of vernacular literature but also of technical advance and the diffusion of general knowledge.

Some measure of elementary education was sought after by all who wished to raise themselves a little in the world. By contrast the benefits of apprenticeship, like the benefits of Latin, were enjoyed by a much smaller group. In assessing the educational importance of apprenticeship, it is necessary to remember that the institution had a dual purpose. The exemptions enjoyed by the sons of existing masters, the property qualification imposed on outsiders, and the restrictions which excluded the children of husbandmen and labourers show that its purpose was as much to control entry to the skilled crafts as to train the entrants. Moreover, the training given varied in value. In some of the cruder crafts it did not go beyond the mastery of certain mechanically imitated skills and the moulding of the apprentice's character to a conventionally accepted pattern. All the same, apprenticeship must be considered as an important element in education since in certain fields the training went far beyond these simple limits. Such technical works as Biringuccio's *Pirotechnia* (1540), Digges's *Pantometria* (1571), Zimmermann's *Probierbuch* (1573) were appearing in all the major languages. They influenced workshop methods, and ambitious beginners must have turned to them for help. Buying and selling and the keeping of accounts—a commonplace in many trades—demanded even in their simplest forms literacy and an acquaintance with simple arithmetic; and commerce on a large scale could not be conducted without substantial background knowledge. Already in the fifteenth century such general works on mathematics as the *Summa* of Luca Pacioli had discussed accounting, and in the Italian trading communities treatises on letter-writing with a legal and commercial slant had long enjoyed considerable vogue. A hundred years later we come across works like John Browne's *Marchants Avizo* (1589). Providing not only a formulary, but extensive notes on business practice, it ran into several editions. The merchant class was also to the forefront when it came to learning foreign languages. This is shown by the prefaces of several contemporary grammars and conversation manuals, and we know that pupils of Saravia's Southampton French school went from 'arts to marts'. It is not surprising, therefore, that merchants and other craftsmen sent their sons to grammar schools to give them some intellectual training as a preliminary to apprenticeship. The scope of vocational instruction was expanding rapidly, and it is the apprentices who were among the most zealous readers of those easy handbooks of general information which men like Thomas Hill were producing on subjects that ranged from astronomy to apiculture.

Turning from vernacular instruction and apprenticeship to the education based upon Latin, we enter a different world. Here we have to consider, not the unorganised efforts of individuals, but a multiplicity of well-established institutions; and these institutions were in 1550 at the middle point of a long process of development which began in the fourteenth and was not to end until the nineteenth century. Consequently, to understand the significance of the changes taking place in the schools and universities between 1550 and 1600 we have to look at both the past and the future.

Although the educational institutions of the middle ages were of many sorts and kinds and little attempt was made to co-ordinate them—we should be wrong to talk of anything like a uniform system—it is nevertheless possible to trace, after the thirteenth century, a pattern which, if it never became universal, was common enough to be described as dominant. The universities were multiplying in number, and the education which the society of the day valued was the education they offered. This consisted at its highest level in the three great disciplines of theology, law and medicine, and at a lower level there was the faculty of arts—logic accompanied by a greater or less amount of rhetoric or mathematics. Arts studies were a preparation for the higher faculties, but they also served as a general education for a multitude of the lower clergy. Once established, a university usually brought under its control not only higher instruction in its immediate neighbourhood but also the teaching of grammar beyond the elementary stage. Imparting the rudiments of Latin was the only task left to the schools in university towns. At the same time, the grammar course was in a great number of cases reduced to the learning of an unclassical and colourless Latin for daily use. Rarely pursued beyond the age of fourteen or fifteen, when students switched to logic, it lost its earlier formative connection with literature. Logic was the subject and the university was the institution which shaped men's minds.

What we see after 1550 is an advanced stage of the revolt against this pattern. That revolt had developed gradually. Already in the fourteenth century, the Italian humanists had claimed that a general education was more valuable than a professional one and had argued that such an education ought to be based on literature rather than logic. Their programme had been to gain control of the teaching of rhetoric in the universities and by improving its quality, to elevate its status. Their ideas came to dominate the intellectual life of the time, but for over a hundred years they made little impression on organised education. Humanists who taught rhetoric extended the range of their lectures to include classical authors, and Greek made its appearance as a subject studied outside the normal curriculum; but logic continued to dominate the arts course, and the pre-eminence of the professional faculties remained unshaken in all the important universities. It was not until the end of the fifteenth century, when the Renaissance moved north of the Alps, that more radical changes were introduced.

At this juncture, we must note another and distinct line of development. The medieval universities had initially been centres of instruction and nothing more. They did not seek to guide the moral growth of their pupils. Then, in the fourteenth century, men came to feel that education ought to include an element of character training. This feeling found institutional expression in the regulated lives of the newly founded colleges which brought an increasing number of university students under their care; and at the end of the fifteenth century character training became an integral part of the humanist programme.

If the humanists had continued to centre their attention on the universities, their adoption of this idea, though still important, would not have had revolutionary results. But the north had fewer universities than Italy relatively to its population. In some areas, such as the Netherlands, the schools played a major role in educational life. Inevitably, therefore, as soon as humanism spread north of the Alps, school reform began to interest its champions, and the new classical learning with its literary culture, the new collegiate concern for moral improvement, made their influence felt at an earlier age level. The importance of schools like Deventer, St Paul's and the Collège de Guyenne lay in their offer of a training which intellectually and morally had some claim to be regarded as a preparation for life and so could stand as a rival to the logic-centred university discipline.

The next advance occurred as a result of the Reformation. The revolt against Rome gave a fresh impetus to the changes introduced by the humanists, in both the universities and the schools. In Italy university conservatism had been able to resist the assaults of the new learning because the power of the state had not effectively intervened anywhere in favour of reform. But once the battle had begun between the rival faiths, and governments were interested in the maintenance of particular religious beliefs, the stage was set for state intervention. In Protestant Germany and Catholic Spain the theological faculties came to dominate university life. Law and medicine surrendered their old predominance, while Greek and Hebrew, the instruments of biblical exegesis, were now firmly established in the faculty of arts. The Protestants, moreover, suspicious of Aristotle and inclined, because of their interest in preaching, to set a high value on eloquence, went far in subordinating logic to rhetoric as the principal arts study; and since many of their leaders were humanists, the rhetoric they introduced was based on an imitation of the classics. To some extent then, if we make allowance for the fact that in the reformed universities linguistic and literary learning was made to serve the purposes of religious controversy, the Reformation may be seen as having furthered the work of the Renaissance. In many places, however, where rival beliefs were equally matched, the effect of their struggles was not reform but a deadlock which strengthened academic conservatism and merely rendered the universities less capable of carrying out their tasks.

The achievements of Melanchthon and Ximenes must not be allowed to obscure the fact that in general Catholics and Protestants alike found the universities difficult to control. The grammar schools with their smaller and less eminent staffs, drawing their pupils from a limited area and securely under the thumb of the local administration, proved much more convenient instruments where it was intended to ensure that the young would follow the faith of their fathers. The Protestants realised this before the Catholics. Several Calvinist teachers—notably Buchanan and Cordier —had been associated with that most ambitious of humanist experiments, the Collège de Guyenne, which aimed to combine a school course with a complete arts curriculum; and the reorganisation of Guyenne (1534) was followed shortly by Sturm's exclusively Protestant and much more influential foundation at Strassburg (1538). Sturm drew on the practice of the Paris university colleges such as Montaigu and on his own experiences in the humanist school run by the Brethren of the Common Life in Liège. He reproduced all the conventional features of the new pedagogy, the use of classical Latin, the addition of Greek, the careful division into classes (originally eight, later nine), the insistence on promotion by merit, and attention to the boys' moral welfare. He also tried, as at Guyenne, to follow the grammar course by five years of higher studies for which the logic and rhetoric learnt in the two top grammar classes served as an introduction. But his fame does not rest merely on having adapted humanist ideas to Protestant purposes. In two respects at least he advanced decisively beyond the point reached by his predecessors. At Strassburg the moral training advocated by the humanists assumed a specifically sectarian form. The school was not satisfied with turning out good men. Its aim was to turn out good Protestants. And at the same time, the classical curriculum was pruned of its more pagan elements. It was reduced to the study of the ancient languages and ancient eloquence. Sturm transformed the humanist tradition in this field; and he deserves to be remembered because the efficiency of this transformation made the grammar school into an educational instrument perfectly suited to the needs of the religious struggle of the time. The constitutions of the Strassburg school were rapidly imitated—at Lausanne (1547), at Pinczow in Poland (1556), at Geneva (1559), in Germany and later in England. But the most important beneficiaries of Sturm's example were not his co-religionists. Historians of the Society of Jesus have maintained that Loyola was not indebted to the organisation at Strassburg and that the resemblances between his programme and Sturm's are due to their having followed the same humanist models. But the fact that the two used their models in the same way suggests a closer affiliation. The Jesuits took children at ten instead of six. They had five classes instead of nine. They began Greek earlier. But in respect of the two essential characteristics of the new education, the blending of intellectual and religious training and the subordination of historical and literary knowledge to rhetoric, their colleges—the first was opened at Messina in 1548—were the Catholic counterparts of Strassburg.

Thus the year 1550 found Europe in the throes of an educational revolution whose formative phase was largely over. The foundations of a new order had been laid, and the development which was to characterise the next half century was, in the main, the dissemination of existing reforms. Its landmarks were the new constitutions of the University of Salamanca (1561–2), the imperial privilege granted to the Strassburg Academy (1566), the founding of the University of Leyden (1575), the establishment of substantial grammar schools in Protestant Germany and England, and above all the amazing increase in the number of Jesuit colleges. There were nearly 250 of them by 1600. But if the period was remarkable primarily for the multiplication of institutions whose main features had been fixed earlier, there were also certain changes in the character of these institutions which, slight as they were, deserve notice. Before 1550, the form the new schools were to take was still uncertain. The curriculum at St Paul's (1512) and at Wolsey's foundation at Ipswich (1528) had been limited to Latin speaking, reading and composition. Maurice of Saxony's ambitiously conceived Pforta, Meissen and Grimma (1543) had added Greek and logic. Sturm (1538) had planned a fourteen-year course with everything required for an arts degree and Loyola's *Constitutiones* (1552) had envisaged the possibility of a similar range of instruction. It was left for the next half century to bring order out of this chaos. When Sturm and the Jesuits came to put their more extensive plans into practice, they found it difficult to attract students to their advanced classes since they had no degrees to offer, and they were forced to seek university status for their institutes of higher study, setting these in a class apart. Simultaneously, most of the purely Latin schools came round to adding Greek. Consequently, by 1600 the normal form of secondary training was either a simple 'grammar' course—Latin, Greek and rhetoric—or a 'grammar' course with the addition of logic, arithmetic and cosmography, all at a very elementary level. The curriculum had moulded itself to the requirements of the six-to-sixteen age range. Meanwhile the universities ceased to concern themselves with grammar teaching and the average age of their students began to rise, so that the schools were left in free possession of their chosen field.

If the thirteenth century was the age of the universities, the sixteenth deserves to be known as the age of the grammar schools. They embodied the educational aspirations of the men that had slid from humanism into religious strife. We can define their aim in the words of Erasmus as eloquence conjoined with piety. More exactly, they had three principal aims: the teaching of classical Latin, the teaching of rhetorical skill, and the promotion of religious fervour; and these three aims, though pursued independently, were woven into a single discipline.

The education of the grammar schoolboy began necessarily with his learning to read. Some did so at home or in a little private school; but there were always a few who had not received such preliminary instruction, and for these the grammar master often arranged a special class. They used hornbooks, which contained an alphabet, a syllabarium and the Lord's Prayer, or primers which added to the above a wider selection of reading matter including the Creed and the Commandments. These works were published for the most part in the vernacular. But they appeared also in Latin, for some grammar-school masters insisted on that language even for beginners. The point which deserves attention is that, whatever the language used, the texts were of a religious character. We have here a crude example of a method much favoured by sixteenth-century educators. Wherever possible, they liked to kill two birds with one stone, and in particular they liked to choose their material so as to impart linguistic skills and pious habits simultaneously.

When a child had mastered his letters, he entered the lower school, which comprised in most cases rather less than half the total number of classes—four out of Sturm's nine, three out of Eton's seven, two out of the Jesuit five. Here he learnt Latin grammar and enough vocabulary to write easy compositions and read the easier Latin authors. By the middle of the century the medieval favourites had virtually disappeared from the classrooms of western Europe: only nine of the 295 printed editions of the *Doctrinale* of Alexandre de Villedieu date from after 1525. The first stage of the grammar reform accomplished by the humanists was now over. Correct usage was established as the norm. But the majority of school-masters still clung to those early humanist grammars which, aiming primarily at the elimination of incorrect Latin, had faced their readers with ill-defined rules and monstrous lists of anomalies. The second stage of the reform, which involved the presentation of morphology and syntax in a form the learner could easily master, was only just beginning when the royal proclamation of 1540 made the use of the revised version of Lily's grammar compulsory in English schools. Compiled originally for St Paul's by Colet, Erasmus and others, this work contained a substantial section in English, concentrated on essentials and employed such memory aids as tables. Its authorisation represented a triumph for the new pedagogy. For a long time this triumph stood alone. Pellisson's 1535 revision of Despauterius, which enjoyed a certain vogue in France and Italy, was not much better than the 1510–15 original; and when the Jesuits, who spent years looking for a grammar, found one answering to their requirements—

it was the shortened version of the *de Institutione* of Alvarez (1583)—they discovered that many of their teachers were unwilling to abandon old favourites like Despauterius or Lebrija. There was progress in grammar teaching, but it was surprisingly slow.

Composition in the lower school took the form of simple sentences which were translations from the vernacular or variations on an original suggested by the master. At this elementary stage the most important activity after the learning of the grammar was naturally reading. Like the *Donat* and the *Doctrinale*, the *auctores octo* of the medieval tradition lingered awhile—'Cato' in particular was often re-edited—but by the latter half of the sixteenth century they were passing out of use. The utilitarian morality of the fables, the stoicism of 'Cato', did not measure up to the ethical standards set by the Reformation. And this was not their only defect. If the men of the time were sensitive to the needs of Christian morality, they were also more interested than their predecessors had been in the mechanism of learning and they had discovered that one must proceed from the simple to the complex, especially when attempting to teach the young. It was their aim to replace the medieval school texts by reading which was at once more pious and better graded to suit the development of the pupil's mind. The catechism presented itself as an obvious work for school study. But the catechisms which each faith produced to guide its theologians were too complicated for classroom use. So simplifications were produced. The history of Nowell's catechism is typical. Compiled in 1570, it had a long, a middle and a short form in Latin. All except the first were translated into Greek, all except the last into English. If we add the prayer-book catechism which took the place of an English translation of Nowell's short version—the two were in any case similar—we have seven variants. No English school seems to have read fewer than four and some attempted the entire set.

But catechisms, however simplified, could not be made into ideal instruments for language teaching. If schoolboys were to speak Latin, they had to be provided with a vocabulary suited to their interests, as well as with habits of mind necessary for their salvation; and the realisation of this fact produced those typical textbooks of the period—the school colloquies. The simplest of these, the only one of a wholly elementary character, was the *Confabulationes Pueriles* of Evaldus Gallus. It appeared, accompanied by vernacular translations, in a great many languages—there exists for example a Hungarian edition (1531)—and in a revised form it was still being used by Charles Hoole in 1660. But it is not a good specimen of the genre since the first steps in word-learning did not give educationists much chance to display their skill and they preferred to devote their energies to a level above the elementary. Here the pioneer works had been the *Paedologia* of Schade (Mosellanus, 1518) and the *Colloquia* of Erasmus (1519–30). Schade had stressed the element of actuality. His dialogues give an excellent picture of German student life. Erasmus had introduced ideological criticism of current abuses. But both proved too difficult for younger boys and neither provided the sort of moral training that was thought suitable. So experiments continued. Vives (1538) introduced the principle of using dialogues graduated in difficulty and Châteillon (1543), rewriting biblical stories in dialogue form, offered religious reading matter which, unlike the catechism, was planned to serve the purposes of language teaching. Then in 1564 appeared the work which united all the virtues of its predecessors, being at once a model of good Latin, graduated in difficulty, interesting to the young, and rich in moral lessons. Written by the Protestant schoolmaster Mathurin Cordier, this collection of *Colloquia*, provided variously with French, German, English and Dutch translations, was to see twenty editions in the sixteenth, sixty-four in the seventeenth, fifty-six in the eighteenth, and twenty-seven in the nineteenth century. It can fairly claim to have been the most popular school-book outside the middle ages.

The only texts of classical origin to enjoy as great a vogue as the colloquies were the various selections from Cicero's letters. Jesuit schools used these selections in preference to contemporary texts, though one of their best teachers, Spanmueller (Pontanus), had composed some excellent dialogues, as useful for Catholic as Cordier's were for Protestant youth; and the Protestant schools used Sturm's selection from Cicero alongside Cordier or Châteillon. Other authors, Terence, 'Cato', 'Aesop' (in humanist translations), appear occasionally in lower school curricula; but they did not have the same vogue as the other works we have mentioned. The grammar-book, the colloquy and the Cicero selections were the mainstay of elementary instruction.

The business of writing involved, for the humanist, analysis, memorisation and synthesis; and the schools had something to contribute in each of these departments.

The boys in the higher forms made the acquaintance of a large number of Latin authors. Cicero—his *Epistolae, de Amicitia, de Senectute, de Officiis*—and Caesar and Sallust were the favourites; but many curricula recommended also Justin, Curtius, the speeches from Livy, Quintilian and Cicero's *Partitiones* and *Paradoxa*. Jesuit schools paid special attention to Cicero's speeches and to the *de Oratore*. Terence, Virgil, Horace, the *Metamorphoses* and *Tristia* of Ovid were read as often as the most popular prose writers. They appear in many more curricula than the other classical poets or those humanists—Alciat, Thomas More, Mantuanus and Palingenius—who are sometimes regarded as the typical reading-books of the Renaissance.

The data provided by the curricula in school statutes must admittedly be accepted with reservations. The mention of an author is not evidence that his work was effectively studied. Schools varied in their efficiency.

At Winchester, under the famous headmaster Christopher Johnson, the fourth form did in fact read the *Georgics* in the course of a year; and the great Jesuit colleges, which had a master for each form, probably covered a substantial portion of their official programme. But in a school like Eton in 1560, where two men shared the responsibility for seven forms, the time at a teacher's disposal would not have allowed him to cover in class much more than thirty pages each of the books set for any particular year. The remaining part of each text must have been read privately by the boys if it was read at all. What we do know for certain, however, is that reading was always a preparation for writing. Schoolboys worked note-book in hand, and they were trained to notice the detail rather than the total purport of the texts before them.

A schoolboy could not be expected to follow Erasmus's note-taker through the entire range of ancient literature. The little he could glean from his own reading had to be supplemented somehow. So we find schools making extensive use of handbooks in which linguistic and rhetorical material from the classical writers was to be found ordered in a readily accessible form.

The most important of these handbooks were the dictionaries. Humanist effort had done much to transform lexicography, weeding out incorrect usages, providing references to authorities, omitting such material as belonged more properly to an encyclopedia. But the feature which most clearly distinguishes the dictionaries of the later sixteenth century from those of the fifteenth is the addition of vernacular interpretations. The immensely popular polyglot compilation of the Italian Calepino (1502) was repeatedly extended until by 1590 it covered eleven languages. Alongside it existed a host of works for use in particular countries—the Latin–Spanish dictionary of Antonio de Lebrija (1492), the Latin–French of Robert Estienne (1538), the Latin–German of Rauchfuss (Dasypodius, 1531), the Latin–English of Eliot (1538) revised by Cooper (1552), while Robert Estienne in France (1544) and Withals in England (*c.* 1554) produced short versions specially for the use of schoolboys.

Supplementing the dictionaries as aids in finding the right word or the telling idiomatic phrase were the treatises on style. Extensive use was still made of the great humanist textbooks, the *Elegantiae* (first printed 1471) of Lorenza Valla and the *de Copia Verborum* (1511) of Erasmus, as well as of more recent works like the *Elegantiarum Flores* (1558) of Aldo Manuzio the younger. At the same time, the growing tendency to restrict imitation to Ciceronian models received a powerful stimulus from the *Observationes* (1535) of Nizzoli, re-edited in 1568 as the monumental *Thesaurus Ciceronianus*.

Other handbooks helped with the selection and accumulation of subject-matter. If you wanted to elaborate some simple idea, you could find gnomic material from Greek and Latin in the *Adages* of Erasmus or its numerous imitations, poetic imagery in Mirandula's *Flores* (1538), myths in Natalis Comes (1568) and Cartari (1556). Another mine of information was Charles Estienne's historical, geographical and poetical dictionary (1561). Recent research had shown that many of the classical references, not only in schoolboy themes, but in the best literature of the time, came from these miscellanies. By the close of the Renaissance, it was not unusual for the heritage of antiquity to reach its devotees second-hand, fragmented and alphabetically classified.

Composition—the arrangement of one's material for various purposes—was still taught largely through imitation; and here the popular textbooks were, first, the formularies—Erasmus, Hegendorff, Diether—which provided models for letters, and then the exercises, in a Latin translation annotated and augmented by Lorich (1542), of the fourth-century Greek rhetorician, Aphthonius, which gave examples of the different prose genres.

This love of imitation, which went with a neglect of the formal study of rhetoric, did not, however, remain unchallenged. It dominated the Jesuit schools. But outside the Jesuit order, La Ramée's *Dialectica* (1543), discussing in general terms how to invent and order arguments, became increasingly popular, first in France, then after 1580 in Germany and England. The abandonment of imitation, useful principally to the Latinist, in favour of a theoretical approach whose conclusions could be applied to vernacular writing, was inevitable at a time when the new literatures were growing in importance; and by the next century the triumph of Ramist methods was assured.

Greek was taught along the same lines as Latin. It remained throughout the century an upper school subject, though the Jesuits after 1591 made some attempt to introduce it simultaneously with Latin. Improvements in method came slowly. The *Lexicon* of Scapula, the first to be written for school use, did not appear until 1579 and the pioneer grammar of Clenardus remained universally popular until Gretser (1593) and Camden (1597) wrote the works which replaced it. Beginners read the Greek catechism and Cebes, passed after a year to Isocrates, Demosthenes, Plutarch, Lucian and finally to Homer, Thucydides and Plato. Nor were the Church Fathers forgotten. Basil, Chrysostom, Gregory Nazianzen appear in the curricula of both Jesuit and Protestant schools. But it is evident that Greek was not learnt as thoroughly as Latin. The time devoted to its study was relatively short and reading was often done with the help of Latin translations. Effectively, Greek, not introduced in many schools until about 1575, was an ancillary to Latin, an additional source of illustrative material for Latin composition. And the same is true of the other subjects which we see occasionally mentioned. If bright pupils here and there learnt a little Hebrew, if the top forms in the larger Jesuit or German Protestant colleges tried their hand at logic, cosmography and mathematics, such studies never went beyond the elementary stage. They never seriously affected the rhetorical character of the sixteenth-century course.

That course did not provide an introduction to the historical, social and scientific disciplines which govern our thinking today, just as it did not—in spite of its humanist orientation—provide more than a very limited insight into the realities of Graeco-Roman life. What it did foster was a moral outlook in harmony with Christian belief. It promoted facility in speaking and writing. It gave educated men all over Europe a common language, a common stock of ideas, a shared vicarious experience related to the normal run of human interests. In the context of the period, these merits were sufficient to assure its success.

Turning from secondary to higher education, we find that the religious and nationalist interests which encouraged the rise of the grammar schools harmed rather than helped the universities. At the secondary level, the need had been for new schools, and the discipline created to meet contemporary requirements had been educationally satisfactory. The situation was very different where the universities were concerned. They existed in substantial numbers. There was no great call for new foundations. To adapt the system to what the times demanded meant changing established institutions; and the changes were in a large degree for the worse.

The division of Europe into increasingly centralised political and religious units deprived the universities of their traditionally international character. They became local centres, serving the state in whose territory they were placed. An extreme instance of this development shows the Brandenburgers forbidden in 1564 to attend any university but Frankfort-on-Oder. The number of students to each foundation declined in consequence. In Germany, twenty teachers and four hundred students were considered a reasonable establishment; and even at Oxford the total of determining bachelors rarely rose above a hundred a year during the reign of Elizabeth.

State control meant also that special attention was paid to the interest which governments everywhere had most at heart—the maintenance of whatever form of the Christian religion happened to be locally dominant. Theology acquired a predominant position in every university. A specialist study in the middle ages, it was now regarded as part of a churchman's normal training and so attracted large numbers of students. Its professors were held in high regard and they often exercised a dangerous supervision over the opinions of their colleagues in other faculties.

The importance accorded to theology—though it led to a complementary decline of legal and medical studies—would not have mattered if the theologians had been capable of benefiting by their opportunity. But the requirements of controversy imposed a rigid traditionalism on Catholic

438

apologetics and led to bitter disputes among the Protestants.[1] The Cambridge quarrel between Whitgift and Cartwright was a pale shadow of the struggles between Lutherans, Calvinists, Zwinglians and Anti-trinitarians which rent the continental universities. In Paris, the partisans of the League intrigued to displace their reformist colleagues. These were not the conditions in which true learning could flourish and no one had any attention to spare for useful reforms. Such innovations as were introduced often fell victim to the hostilities aroused by religious conflict. The interest in mathematical studies which La Ramée fostered at the Collège de France was crushed by the men who hated him for his Protestant opinions. The Edwardian reorganisation of the Oxford curriculum was set aside by the moderates who came to power under Elizabeth. Apart from the new position of theology, the official pattern of studies remained as a result almost universally medieval.

We cannot, however, conclude that higher education had entered upon a period of decadence: for signs of progress were not wholly absent. In addition to their academies at Strassburg, Geneva and Edinburgh which eventually acquired university status, the Protestants founded Jena (1558), Helmstadt and Leyden (1574), Dublin (1591), while Marischal College (1593) revived the fortunes of Aberdeen. The Catholic record—thanks to the Jesuits—was even longer: Mexico (1551), Lima (1551), Dillingen (1554), Douai (1562), Pont-à-Mousson (1572), Wilno (1578), Würzburg and the Gregorian in Rome (1582), Graz (1585). Several were concerned primarily with theology. But Wilno, supported by the Academy at Zamość, and the two Latin American universities faced the novel problem of carrying the culture of Christian Europe into untried territories.

Moreover, the medieval curriculum, though outdated, was singularly elastic. Humanist teaching, for example, had been introduced as a natural part of the rhetoric and philosophy course, and after 1550 it gained acceptance nearly everywhere. Even Oxford and Cambridge, whose examinations retained a medieval form, allowed it to flourish in individual colleges so that it came gradually to dominate the education of the average undergraduate. Science similarly made some progress, under the aegis of the *quadrivium* and the traditional medical course. The Jesuits, inspired by their missionary experiences, made a point of encouraging geographical studies. Salamanca had a chair of astronomy and used Copernicus's treatise as a set book. Italy produced eminent mathematical professors. England could boast of Caius, Recorde and a scientific enthusiasm which produced Humphrey Gilbert's plan for an Academy and Gresham's College (1596). Anatomy flourished at Padua, Bologna, Basel, Montpellier and Salamanca. Dissection was now a common practice; and an interest in plants, stimulated by Dioscorides, led to the opening of several botanic gardens.

[1] See also chapters III and IV above.

Legal studies had lost ground heavily when the canonists were driven from the Protestant universities and the civilians in their turn incurred the suspicions of the Inquisition. But here again the general decline was relieved by a revival of canon law in Spain and by some distinguished teaching of civil law at Bourges, Geneva and—after the appointment of Gentili—at Oxford also. Badly organised, constantly misdirected by powerful interests, the university system was still sufficiently vital to reflect, if only in a marginal way, the preoccupations of the wider world of learning.

The gap between education and learning, between the attempts to transmit and the attempts to extend man's intellectual heritage, was particularly wide in the sixteenth century. The curriculum of the school and universities did not cover even the traditional field of human knowledge, much less the new subjects which were being explored on every side. And while many learned men depended on educational institutions for a livelihood, many others had no such contacts, but were supported by professional earnings, patronage or private means. It was a situation where great advances could be made in learning without much reference to what was taught in the classroom.

Our survey of sixteenth-century learning will be most conveniently made subject by subject. But as with education, mention must be made first of certain general influences. Of these, the most important were once again the religious controversies. The rival denominations looked to the learned to provide them with arguments in support of their doctrines and claims; and the pressure they exercised resulted in considerable attention being paid to theology and to certain branches of history and political thought. At the same time, the fact that religious opinion was divided meant that subjects which were marginal to religious issues could develop more freely than before. Their students no longer found it necessary to devote time and effort to reconciling new discoveries with an official cosmology. Ecclesiastical authorities still tried to control legal, philosophical and scientific thinking, but such attempts at control were spasmodic and, though they could be disastrous in individual cases, they had not in general the compulsive force which the Christian tradition had exercised during the middle ages.

The other influences we need to consider were less widespread in their effects. But nationalist zeal, the admiration for antiquity created by the humanists, the growing respect for factual knowledge and technical achievement, all helped to determine what problems were studied and what methods were used. They affected the interests of the reading public; and with the growth of the book trade, those interests were now for the first time important in shaping the pattern of scholarship.

Theology was pre-eminent both in the number of its students and in the volume of their writings. Apart from the debates on church government, which belong rather to political thought, the weightiest controversies centred round the relations of the divine and the human will, the Catholics struggling with the problem of efficacious grace, the Protestants with predestination. The most important new contribution was made on the first of these topics by the Jesuit Luis de Molina, on the second by the Dutchman Arminius. Both were concerned to safeguard the freedom of the human will against a rigidly logical determinism. The eucharist was another focus of controversy. The Council of Trent affirmed its sacrificial nature which many Protestants denied. It also affirmed the doctrine of transubstantiation against views which ranged from consubstantiation to the Socinian remembrance theory. Finally, certain heterodox thinkers attempted to evolve a rationalised Christianity. Advocating reason and tolerance and retaining only such dogmas as were necessary to ensure the personal benefits of religion, Fausto Sozzini emerged as an opponent of dogmatism and sectarian strife. His doctrines received notable support in eastern Europe, where their unorthodoxy was emphasised by Simon Budny, a brilliant Polish theologian whose writings show him to have been far in advance of his age.

The study of the Bible had been prosecuted with great vigour since the beginning of the century and Robert Estienne's famous edition in 1540 saw the work that the scholarship of the day could do on the text effectively completed. But the textual corrections in that volume and oppositions of doctrine made fresh translations desirable. In England, the Geneva (1560), the Bishops' (1568), and the Rheims versions presented respectively the Calvinist, Anglican and Roman Catholic points of view. Lefèvre's French translation was amended by the theologians of Louvain (1582) and Budny's Polish version (1570) had an anti-trinitarian slant. The study of the Fathers, that necessary complement to Bible reading and theology, made relatively slow progress after the excellent start given to it by Erasmus. The Greek editions produced by the younger Froben and the Morels and the younger Frédéric Morel's translations filled an obvious gap. In the Ukraine the scholars collected by Ostrogskhi began to translate the Greek Fathers into Slavonic. But the great age of patristic learning lay still in the future.

In philosophy, we see the many-sided development of a complex heritage. One influential achievement was the revitalising of scholastic metaphysics by the Jesuit Francisco Suárez. His eclectic *Disputationes Metaphysicae*—they owe as much to Scotus and Ockham as to Aquinas—did more than any other work to preserve scholasticism as a living force in European thought. Moving within the limits imposed by his faith and his method, but moving there freely, he displayed a fertility and subtlety beyond the reach of his less orthodox fellows, men like Cesalpino and Zabarella, leaders of the Averroist and Alexandrist schools in Italy, who, hampered by their dread of ecclesiastical censure, confined themselves to indicating difficulties without offering solutions. Another important development was that reform of logic teaching in Paris whose complexities research is only just beginning to disentangle. The logic of the medieval arts faculties had been based on the twelfth-century *Summulae* of Petrus Hispanus. That had affinities with the 'mathematical' logic of the present day, but, lacking an adequate system of symbols, its exponents had lost themselves in a tangle of cumbersome definitions; and a humanist revolt against them had gathered force in the fifteenth century. The Rhinelander Roelof Huysmann (Rudolphus Agricola, 1444–85) treated the subject as a branch of rhetoric, revived interest in probability and in topical logic, which was essentially a mnemonic device for facilitating the discovery of arguments. His lead was followed in Paris by Sturm and Pierre La Ramée (1515–72). The latter was concerned, however, not so much with logic as with the systematic ordering of knowledge. His much-advertised Method, beginning everywhere with broad definitions and working down through successive divisions to particular instances—an arrangement capable of spatial representation as a pyramid—reduced what men had to learn to pedagogically convenient forms, but at the cost of rigid distinctions between disciplines. Another feature of his complex system was its presentation of thought as a private activity, visile in character, therefore diagrammatic, quantitative and independent of words. It separated the content of ideas from their verbal expression. La Ramée was not competent to explore the philosophical implications of his doctrines. As a philosopher he was negligible. But his Method and his preference for non-verbal thinking were to have a startling influence. New England Puritanism, the *Great Didactic*, the Royal Society, were all to carry the Ramist stamp.

Scholasticism and Ramism originated in the universities. Another substantial current of thought had less respectable antecedents. It derived from those neoplatonist speculations, tinged with animism and often linked with occult practices, which had delighted fifteenth-century scholars, and its exponents suffered heavily from ecclesiastical disapproval. The importance of animism for the progress of natural science will require discussion elsewhere, but the scientific thinkers whom it attracted laid themselves open, like Paracelsus, to extensive persecution. Similarly Muret, who approached the subject through literature, found his lectures on Plato banned in Rome (*c.* 1565), while the best-known systematic exponent of animism, Giordano Bruno, was imprisoned and burnt (1600). The animist doctrine that everything is unique and a direct manifestation of the Godhead invited attack because, leaving no room for general laws or for the possibility of mediation between God and man, it undermined the claims of Christianity and the visible church.

If we leave the revival of scholasticism out of account, the philosophy of the late-sixteenth century claims our interest principally for its services to empiricism. Telesio's somewhat fanciful *de Natura Rerum* (1565), neo-platonic in its affiliations, stated that all true knowledge comes from sense data. Nizzoli's attacks on Aristotelian logic aimed to rehabilitate rhetoric; but his insistence that general concepts were no guide to the nature of things had the incidental effect of establishing individual facts as the main source of truth. Ramism was concerned with the ordering of these facts and with their liberation from the trammels of language. The animist theory of individual uniqueness supported Nizzoli and so did scepticism, which developed independently of the universities. Its main exponents, Montaigne and the Toulouse doctor, Francisco Sanchez, coupled their denial of the possibility of real knowledge with a respect for the approximate knowledge gained through observation. Starting from different premises, these theories all contributed to a climate favourable to the growth of scientific modes of thought.

Some interest also attaches to another system of a different sort—the neo-stoicism which became popular in the countries most affected by the religious wars. But stoics like Lipsius and du Vair cannot be classed with the speculative philosophers. They were primarily moralists, seekers after a rule of life in difficult circumstances.

The forces which hampered philosophy encouraged the development of political thought. Earlier, both Luther and Calvin had supported the absolutist claims of the Renaissance state, having found that the reformed religion could not be established without the help of a strong secular power. Now, their successors were discovering that religious minorities could not survive if the secular power could not be challenged. The task of the 1550 generation was a reassessment of the relations between the rulers and ruled. The concepts they employed were borrowed from medieval writers, but shifts of emphasis provide an element of novelty.[1]

The writing of history was subject to the same influences as political thought. But here our interest is in the development of method. Some of the humanist historians had admittedly overvalued style, neglected accuracy or been too fond of battle-pieces and imaginary orations. But Biondo had explored the possibilities of archaeology, Aeneas Sylvius those of ethnography. Guicciardini had learnt from his classical models to analyse political intrigue. Polydore Vergil had made a brave attempt to accumulate and sift his sources. The humanists had been experimenters, and a student of their works was likely to find them full of fertile suggestions. But they did not evolve a coherent methodological tradition, and so we cannot, when we come to the post-Reformation period, talk of the rise of a 'new school' of historiography. The successors of the humanists were men of diverse attainments who followed with an ever-increasing skill the different lines indicated by their predecessors. There was a slow transformation rather than a sudden change.

[1] See below, chapter XVI.

Chronicles, a form of history associated with the middle ages, were still popular after 1550, not only in Russia and Turkey, but in Voisin's France and Holinshed's England. Similarly, we find the Pole Kromer (1555) and the Scotsman Buchanan (1582) composing national histories which make their mark as masterpieces of humanist Latin. Barros (1553-65), writing about the Portuguese in India, imitated Livy. Hurtado de Mendoza in his *Guerra de Grenada* (1572) took Sallust and Tacitus as his models. A general view of the period shows, however, that these chronicles and classical imitations were no more than survivals, for all their popularity. Other trends were in the ascendant. The Dutch lawyer, Sleidan, commissioned by his fellow Protestants to prepare a documentary account of the Reformation, completed his task by 1555. Bullinger described the beginnings of the movement, Knox (1566) its Scottish triumphs. Crespin in France (1554) and Foxe in England (1559-63) provided their co-religionists with a martyrology. These men were naturally eager to set the Protestant cause in the best possible light, and so they were attracted to the arts of the advocate: to vivid narrative, a parade of evidence, and arguments which were superficially persuasive rather than rigorously logical. They were not impartial, and they were often careless about checking the truth of their facts.

These characteristics were also present in certain partisan writers who took a more remote past for their subject. The authors of the *Magdeburg Centuries* (1559-74) set out to demonstrate the bygone shortcomings of the Roman Church; and the method they chose was to pile example upon example, seeking to convince by the weight of their evidence. But they accepted statements favourable to their thesis without any sort of check and they were not above suppressing inconvenient facts. Their charges were answered by Baronius, the Vatican librarian. Having a treasure-house of unpublished archives at his disposal, he produced an even more impressive collection than his opponents. The twelve folios of the *Annales Ecclesiastici* (1588-1607) were a landmark in the documentary study of church history. But the contagion of partisanship had spread: and the learned Baronius, though more laborious, more scholarly and more honest than the Magdeburg collaborators, was also at times guilty of distorting the truth.

These incursions into religious controversy, though they encouraged partisanship, can be seen to have acted as a forcing-house promoting habits of documentation, analysis and clear statement. We must not, however, attribute too great an importance to them or ignore the substantial contribution which other fields made at the same time to the development of historical method. The sixteenth century was the springtime of antiquarianism. Fauchet, Leland, Bale, Stow, impelled by patriotic feeling, but also by a spontaneous enthusiasm, explored the almost virgin field of local remains. They sought after facts for their own sake; and the wealth of their discoveries found lasting memorials in Pasquier's *Recherches de la France* (1560–1621) and Camden's *Britannia* (1586). Simultaneously, men's general understanding of the past deepened as historians widened the field in which they looked for connections between phenomena. Here the most important advance was a clearer realisation of the role of geographical influences. Bodin discussed these influences in his *Methodus ad facilem historiarum cognitionem* (1566), but it was the Spaniards and the Portuguese writing about their overseas territories who first demonstrated in detail how climate and natural resources can give shape to a culture; and in this respect the literature of travel, as in Hakluyt's collection, also had much to contribute.

Progress in other ancillary studies made a smaller impact, but the numerous humanist monographs on the Roman family, the *Comitia* and the law courts, and the researches of Bodin, Hotman and Thomas Smith on medieval and contemporary institutions undoubtedly helped to provide historical interpretation with a firmer basis. Vasari's *Lives of the Painters* (1550) were mainly useful because of the light they shed on a neglected department of human activity. But a biography like Ribadaneira's *Loyola* (1572), the autobiographies of Loyola, Cardan, Cellini and St Teresa, and Montaigne's *Essais* reflect an interest in the individual which led to the abandonment of the static psychology of the Romans and laid the foundation for a subtler analysis of human motives.

Mention must also be made of one specific achievement of importance. The Roman *Fasti* were discovered in the Forum in 1546–7. Their first editors, Robortello and Sigonio, used them to correct the chronology of Livy; and before long the chronological framework of ancient history was more nearly established on an orderly basis in J. J. Scaliger's *De Emendatione Temporum* (1583).

Historians were also learning to write better. In part this was due to the general improvement of vernacular style. But it was also an indirect result of the spread of literacy. By the end of the sixteenth century the man of action, not possessed of any special literary training, who took up his pen to describe his personal experiences was no longer an uncommon phenomenon. These untutored attempts were often very realistic and vivid and, being the raw material of the contemporary historian, they came gradually to have a growing influence on formal writing. The manner as well as the matter of history was insensibly transformed.

The period also saw substantial innovations in legal studies. The enactments of the Council of Trent and the work of the Congregation appointed to interpret them (1564) laid the foundations of the *ius novissimum*, the canon law of the Roman church in the modern period of unquestioned papal supremacy. The Protestants, faced by the problem of reconciling ecclesiastical law with the responsibilities of an established church, struggled on their side with projects of reform, which remained, however, largely abortive. Civil law was also affected by the collapse of the medieval order. Many legal conceptions had become outdated with the gradual passing of feudalism. A return to the Justinian Code stripped of its medieval accretions—the course recommended by the humanists—proved impossible, since the existing social order differed substantially from the ancient. It is against this background that we must set the work of the continental jurists as they tried first to interpret the laws of antiquity within their proper setting and then to extract from these laws, when correctly interpreted, a body of basic principles. The Spaniard Agostino and the French professor Turnebus continued the humanist analysis of Roman legal institutions. Cujas edited the Theodosian Code, Godefroy the *Corpus Iuris Civilis*; and in his *Paratitla* Cujas tried to condense into axioms the elementary principles of law. Coke in England tried to solve the same problem of simplification. Like Cujas he relied on his historical sense but took common, not Roman, law as his starting-point. None of these attempts were wholly successful, but they did much to adapt the confused legal heritage of Europe to the requirements of modern society.

There was one important problem, however, which could not be solved by the conservative methods of a Coke or a Cujas. The breakdown of the universal church had left the dominant national states facing each other without an arbitrator, and some system had to be found to regulate their relations. The problem had attracted the notice earlier of Francis of Vitoria but the man who in this period contributed most to its solution was Gentili, the Italian who became professor at Oxford. He found a basis for international law in the *ius naturae* and worked out some of its detailed applications, preparing the way for the work of Grotius.

In classical studies we have the beginnings of what is called the great age of scholarship. The principal activity of the heirs of Erasmus was the editing of texts and the interpretation or correction of difficult readings. Except for Phaedrus (1596), the better-known Latin and most of the better-known Greek authors had already appeared in print. Two dozen volumes, including 'Anacreon' and 'Longinus' (1554), Marcus Aurelius (1558), Bion and Moschus (1565), now filled the more obvious gaps. But many *editiones principes* had been carelessly produced and, even with the good ones, the discovery of new manuscripts and improvements in critical method opened up rich possibilities for the corrector. Robortello (1557) composed the first treatise on textual criticism, and publishing miscellaneous readings became the highroad to a reputation. It brought fame equally to the mature Vettori and to the twenty-two-year-old Lipsius and Canter. New editions poured from the printing presses. Lambin's *Lucretius*, Vettori's *Aeschylus* and *Aristotle*, Lipsius's *Tacitus*, Joseph Scaliger's *Manilius*, Casaubon's *Athenaeus* were held to rank among the chief glories of the age.

Other branches of humanist study made small progress by comparison.

446

Some of the work already mentioned in the historical and legal field was of lasting value, but, except for Scaliger's treatise on chronology, none of it was of the first importance. Ciceronianism was still a live issue and the points debated by Erasmus and Bembo were taken up again by Muret, La Ramée, Lipsius and Gabriel Harvey. The task of the imitator who wanted to use nothing but Ciceronian phrases was made easy by the publication of Nizzoli's *Thesaurus* (re-edited 1591), and, supported by the authority of both Sturm and the Jesuits, Ciceronianism had triumphed in the grammar schools. But outside the schools, among serious writers, it lost ground rapidly, as we can see from Lipsius's abandonment of the Ciceronian period in favour of Seneca's hopping style. The long-continued interest in this odd controversy becomes explicable once we realise that Ciceronianism involved assumptions of cardinal importance for the development of the vernaculars. The theory that there was a 'classical' period in the history of every language, when it approached nearest to perfection, coupled as it was with beliefs about the natural superiority of Latin, threatened to undermine the hope of producing great modern literatures. For why should a writer struggle with a language that was still immature, when a perfect instrument lay ready to his hand? The acceptance of the Ciceronian period as an ideal threatened, furthermore, to condemn uninflected languages like French and English to using a form which did not suit their natural structure. And finally there was the point that, in the teaching of composition, imitation was for the sixteenth century still largely an alternative to the study of formal rhetoric, and it was rhetoric, as expounded by La Ramée, that the vernacular writer found genuinely useful. Consciously or unconsciously, the anti-Ciceronians were fighting the battle of the new literatures.

Similar interests were involved in the discussion on Aristotle's *Poetics*. This neglected treatise leapt into prominence during the middle years of the sixteenth century and owed its popularity to literary rather than academic circles. Though it was edited several times, the editions and the commentaries were far outnumbered by the works on poetic theory which it inspired. The Aristotelian concept of art as generalised experience provided a rational defence against the denigrators of the fictional element in imaginative literature, and Aristotle's detailed comments on epic and tragedy were a help to writers who wished to introduce these literary forms in the vernaculars. That most of the critics followed Castelvetro in seeking to derive rigid rules from Aristotle's generalisations is a mark of the normative, almost authoritarian, spirit which characterised the decadence of humanism. The versatile genius of Patrizzi—*Della Poetica* (1586)—was alone in advancing a more organic view of literary and cultural achievement.

The last two departments of humanist study which call for some mention were archaeology and linguistics. In the former some attention was paid to inscriptions, but the principal objects of interest were the monuments and statues of Rome. This was the age of the first illustrated accounts of these antiquities by Lafreri, de Cavaleriis and Vacca. Since Rome represented their country's past, it is possible that these men were inspired less by humanist zeal than by the spirit which had guided Pasquier and Camden. In linguistics, few of the numerous scholars who worked on grammar and syntax looked beyond the needs of the classroom. But the age had one major achievement to its credit: the Greek *Thesaurus* of Henri Estienne (1572); and one theoretical treatise deserves to be remembered: the *Mithridates* (1555), in which Gesner introduced the comparative method of language study.

Looking at classical learning as a whole in this period, we are bound to notice the gap which separates Joseph Scaliger and Casaubon from Erasmus and Bembo. The leading humanists of 1500 had been intellectual pioneers, many of whom held positions of public importance. Their successors a century later were academics, out of touch with the most fruitful speculations of their day. This crippling contraction of interests seems to have been due to the interaction of several causes. Many branches of knowledge were now progressing beyond the level they had reached in classical times. Their devotees were not led, as they had been a century earlier, to interest themselves automatically in Greek or Latin; and now that knowing the text of Galen, Justinian or Archimedes no longer served to put a man in the front rank in medicine, law or science, the humanists on their side tended to neglect these aspects of their speciality. The conditions which had made the classics a key to all learning were ceasing to operate; and as they vanished, other forces actively promoted a further narrowing of interests. The cult of textual criticism was greatest in those countries where the largest number of university posts were open to classical scholars. Competition for professional status led the humanists to concentrate on that branch of their work—the correction of texts— in which the skill and industry of the contestants could be most effectively measured. And religious intolerance also helped to make this choice desirable. Paleario was arraigned as a heretic in Rome. Lipsius had his difficulties in Protestant Leyden. Speculation was dangerous. The emendator was less likely to offend.

The study of Hebrew and other oriental languages lagged far behind classical learning. Their importance for Christianity assured them a place in universities and in the more ambitious grammar schools. But their students were content with a modest level of achievement, and the extensive literature on these subjects consists for the most part of simple grammars. Scholars well known in other fields, like Bellarmine and Flacius, Catholics like the Benedictine Génébrard, professor at the Collège de France, Protestants like Chevallier at Lausanne, Italian exiles like Stancari and Tremellio, Jews like John Isaac at Cologne, all tried their hand at expounding the elements of Hebrew. A few—Palma Cayet, one of La Ramée's pupils, and the Italian Caninio—extended their labours to cover other Eastern languages. But the serious study of Eastern traditions was left for the most part to the Jews themselves. Some important Talmudic scholars, Joseph Qaro and Azariah dei Rossi, the historian Joseph ben Joshua, and the mystic Isaac Luria, belong to this period.

Neglected by the official academic world, the study of the living languages made only slow progress. A man who wanted to learn a foreign tongue or to master the correct use of his own could find books to help him. Even such a distant and unfortunate nation as the Hungarian had its grammar and its dictionary. Intending writers were encouraged to use the vernaculars. Henri Estienne's treatises on the virtues of French, Thomas Wilson's attempt to explain the mysteries of rhetoric to his compatriots, had the backing of many similar works. But between these products of a utilitarian and a literary approach remained a gap which in the absence of help from the universities private effort went only a little way to fill. The Italians, whose interest in their mother tongue dated back to Dante, had made some progress with its systematic study already by the fifteenth century; and in the sixteenth, the French followed their example. Meigret initiated a debate on orthography (1542). Henri Estienne attacked the practice of borrowing from the Italian (1578). Bourgoing made a beginning with the comparative study of the romance languages (1583). But even in France, and certainly elsewhere, much still remained to be done.

Science is the subject of a separate chapter, and no more need be said here of its achievements than will enable us to assess correctly the importance of the non-scientific works which we have been discussing. The latter half of the sixteenth century was the age of Mercator, Galileo, Stevin and Viète, when the foundations were laid for the discovery of the circulation of the blood and the manufacture of the first telescope. The scientific progress of these fifty years made a remarkable contribution to the shape the future was to take. Measure against that contribution the lasting influence of Suárez on the Catholic, of Hooker on the Anglican, mind, Grotius's debt to Gentili, Bentley's to Scaliger, Montesquieu's to Frycz and Bodin. It still stands as undoubtedly impressive. But what is even more enlightening is to set, one against the other, the contemporaneous achievements of science and theology. The scientific studies of the age, meanly endowed, were pursued only by a devoted few. They produced results which are still recognised as indispensable. Theological learning, rendered attractive by preferment and power, commanded the wit and energies of an ambitious multitude: but with everything in its favour, it failed to leave more than a tiny mark on our intellectual heritage. For once the gods were not on the side of the big battalions.

It has been convenient in discussing education and learning to speak of

Europe as a unified whole, but something must now be said about the differences which existed between its several areas. Elementary education based on the vernacular was best organised in Scotland, where Knox's excellent scheme, though hamstrung by lack of support, left its memorials in parish schools that provided a genuine preparation for grammar studies; in Protestant Germany, where Melanchthon's influence was felt; in Bohemia, which was self-consciously nationalist; and in the traditionally literate Swiss Cantons and Netherlands. England lagged some way behind, and so did the Latin and the Scandinavian countries. In Poland and the independent parts of Hungary, vernacular teaching was confined mostly to the German settlements. In the territories under Turkish control, and in Russia, as Ivan IV's complaints show, it was virtually non-existent.

The Latin schools had been revivified by the Protestant reformers and the Jesuits. Since religious conflict acted as a spur to educational zeal, the areas furthest from the points where Catholic and Protestant powers came in close contact—Scotland, Scandinavia, the Iberian peninsula and south Italy—were by 1600 those with the fewest foundations. But even in France the royal edict which recommended that a school be established in every town was generally disregarded, while Ireland, a backward country at grips with a foreign invader, and Hungary, where a flourishing educational system had wholly collapsed under the twin impact of Turkish invasion and Protestant hostility, constituted special cases of a remarkable neglect. In eastern Poland, which then extended well into present-day Russia, the religious rivalries of the west were complicated by the presence of a Greek Orthodox population. At Ostróg in Volhynia an attempt was made in 1570 to set up a trilingual lyceum—Slavonic, Latin and Greek—and in 1586 the Orthodox Brotherhood of the Assumption founded a Latin school at Lwów, meeting Roman Catholic pressure with its own weapons. Further east, in Russia proper, secondary, like primary, education was unknown except in a few seminaries. Ivan IV persuaded an ecclesiastical congress (1551) to pass a measure calling for greater efficiency in the training of priests, but this had never been carried into practice.

Generally speaking, the religious struggle had an adverse effect on the universities from which they gradually recovered as one or other party was safely established in power. This, at any rate, happened in Great Britain, Germany and Switzerland, though in all cases the recovery was slowed up by dissensions between the Protestants themselves. In France where the religious wars were the most bitter, the period of decline lasted to the final years of the century, having begun rather later than in Germany. Law teaching, however, flourished reasonably in the provinces. The Italian universities and the Spanish were both efficient above the average; the former because they managed to retain a certain measure of independence, the latter because the impeccably orthodox could always, like Suárez, allow themselves a fair measure of freedom. Neither group, however, reached the same high degree of competence as Louvain or the newly founded Leyden. The trading interests of the Netherlands, their cosmopolitan character and their tradition of relative tolerance formed a more favourable environment for academic achievement than existed elsewhere.

The diversities of the educational system must be considered alongside the distribution of learned activity. Theologians, political thinkers (particularly those dealing with the relations of church and state) and historians were to be found in every country. Scientists, philosophers, lawyers (other than canonists) and the best of the classical scholars came, with a few exceptions like Brahe and Suárez, from a central area comprising north Italy, Switzerland, France, the Netherlands and southern England. The connections between this general pattern and the work of the universities are not hard to trace. History and political thought were not represented in the university curriculum. They progressed under the impulsion of nationalist and sectarian interest independently of the efficacy of academic training. The other branches of knowledge in which the learned men of the day made their mark came within the range of university studies; and in their case, there is a correspondence, country by country, between the general progress made in a subject and the attention that subject received in the local available centres of higher education. If eminent theologians were to be found all over Europe west of the Beresina, it was because theology had an honoured place in every university. If the majority of philosophers, lawyers and scientists came from what we have called the central area, it was because the universities of that area pursued philosophy (other than scholastic thought), civil law and science more earnestly than their neighbours. If Germany, which had been distinguished in science and the humanities during the previous half century, now fell behind in these subjects, it was because of the decline of her universities before Melanchthon's reforms took effect and because of the importance given to theology after these reforms. If Spanish scholars shone in scholastic philosophy and canon law, it was because Spain had retained these medieval emphases in her university course.

The interconnections of organised education and learned achievement certainly deserve notice. But the moment we take a wider view, consider the intellectual life of the period at all its levels, if only within the relatively narrow geographical limits of Europe, and consider also the role of the period in the general development of the European mind, then this academic learning, whether in the universities or outside of them, loses much of its apparent importance. We cannot fail to recognise that a greater interest attaches to the remarkable growth of the vernacular literatures and to the spread of literacy outside the limits of a clerkly class. This was an age when the diffusion of culture counted for more than its improvement. The preachers who educated as well as stirred their audiences, the compilers of religious manuals—in certain parts of eastern Europe these were the only products of the local printing presses—the dramatists, translators and chroniclers of romantic tales, the Hills and the Mizaulds, busy purveyors of miscellaneous information, were the powerful architects of the future.

Admittedly, a great deal was lost in the process of popularisation. The subtleties of the theologians reappeared as catchwords. The speculations of the neoplatonists served to lend a false profundity to astrological claptrap. The translators did a valuable job in making by the end of the century the best of the classical writings, with the exception of certain lyrical and dramatic works, available at least in French and Italian and often in other languages as well. But translations did not represent the final stage in the popularising of the classical heritage. The *Metamorphoses*, the tales of Troy and the Fleece were retold in a thousand forms until at the lowest level they appeared scrimped and vulgarised in trumpery storybooks; and for large numbers of people, including whole nations like the Hungarian, these poor stories were the main source through which they knew antiquity. As for the disseminators of scientific knowledge, the very sources they used—Galen, Pliny, Ptolemy—were themselves out of date.

But these deficiencies were unimportant. The education of the European middle class was not to be accomplished in one, two or even three generations and its preliminary stages could not in any case have extended much beyond making books more familiar and education less of a specialist mystery. The vernacular writing of the time achieved this. It achieved what mattered; and after another two centuries, the classical heritage which the humanists preserved, the discoveries of scientists, the scholasticism which Suárez refurbished, were all integrated into the emergent middle-class culture, just as the creation of the grammar schools and the reshuffling of the medieval universities, undertaken to provide defenders for religion, were steps towards those later reforms that built the educational systems of the industrial revolution. To contemporary observers the period of the Counter-Reformation seemed full of plans and parties dragging mankind in directions which were diametrically opposed. The future, they thought, would belong to those that pulled the hardest. But we can see that the pull was all the same way. Or as near as may be. The waters ran down twisting and widely deflected channels, but in the end they all found a common issue.

CHAPTER XV

SCIENCE

THE earlier half of the sixteenth century saw the publication of important and even revolutionary new works in various fields—notably the
De Revolutionibus Orbium Coelestium of Copernicus and the *De
Humani Corporis Fabrica* of Vesalius, both published coincidentally in
1543—and the introduction of new ideas and methods in other fields
besides astronomy and anatomy. The work of Paracelsus and Fernel in
medicine, of Belon and Rondelet in zoology, of Carden and Tartaglia in
mathematics, of Nuñez, Oronce Finé and Gemma Frisius in navigation
and cartography, was all complete by mid-century. The major work of
Kepler, Galileo and Harvey was not begun until 1610 or later. The men
of the later sixteenth century were consolidators and continuers rather
than innovators. With the exception of Tycho Brahe and William Gilbert
there are few great names or startling ideas; yet it was in this period that
the men who were to make the scientific revolution of the seventeenth
century grew to manhood and it was by the scientists and scientific literature of this age that they were trained and prepared for innovation.
Fabricius of Aquapendente, a respectably second-class scientist himself,
has more often been remembered as the teacher of Harvey than for his
own accomplishments. Yet, though the scientists of the later sixteenth
century were in general of no very original turn of mind, they had an
important role to play: they provided a necessary and salutary link between the respect for authority which prompted the innovations of the
earlier sixteenth century and the consciousness of novelty that prompted
the innovations of the seventeenth century. The interest in antiquity continued strong: it was only after 1550, indeed, that the works of the
Hellenistic mathematicians were made completely available for assimilation, and the influence of Archimedes was particularly important. Much
Greek science still had the power to provide a starting-point for research;
but, however slowly, respect for antiquity was tempered by a consciousness
of novelty, perhaps helped by the opening up through exploration of a
world the ancients never knew; and dependence upon authority became
mixed with a delighted and virulent iconoclasm, often presented with the
full flow of Renaissance exuberance and vituperation.

In a sense, all science in this period was mathematics, medicine or magic.
Mathematics, in the universities and in the newly founded humanist colleges
and lectureships, meant applied and practical mathematics even more
often than pure theoretical mathematics: that is, theoretical astronomy,
navigation, cartography, mechanics, ballistics, fortification, surveying

and even astrology, which gave the *mathematicus* his frequently dubious reputation. Medicine was a university subject which included within its surveillance botany and, later, chemistry, as well as anatomy and physiology; outside the university was surgery, a well-regulated craft, and Paracelsan iatrochemistry, concerned with the manufacture and use of chemical remedies, associated with the iconoclasm and heterodoxy of its initiator. Magic held the most singular place in this age; for magic was now classed as black, white and natural, and though black and white magic were no novelty, natural magic—the esoteric investigation of natural forces—ravished many more souls than that of Faust. Natural magic was more respectable than black or white magic, but still touched with some of the illicit glamour of magic in general, and the sixteenth century was perfectly conscious of the difference between magic and natural science even while professing that both were of equal importance. Natural magic was half mysticism, half experimental science; wholly serious, widely practised, producing the popular picture of the scientist as half mage and half sage which has never wholly disappeared. Few experimental scientists of the age were immune from its fascination: at one extreme lies John Dee, astrologer to Queen Elizabeth, original and competent mathematician, who later left England to wander wildly on the continent, a confirmed spiritualist at the mercy of his medium; at the other, Tycho Brahe, outwardly the most modern and rational of strictly observational astronomers, who yet believed that alchemy and astrology had as much to offer as pure astronomy to the knowledge of the true inwardness of nature. At the end of the century Kepler maintained this tradition, wandering easily between number mysticism and mathematical astronomy, to show that in itself natural magic was no necessary hindrance to the advance of science, though the 'new' scientists of the age were already turning to that acute rationalism that characterises the scientific revolution. Natural magic extended thus from mysticism to experimental science, and continued until it joined with engineering, in which the excellent tradition begun earlier in the century and so brilliantly exemplified by Leonardo da Vinci was continued in the work of the clockmakers, astronomical instrument makers and mechanicians.

One marked characteristic of this period is an enhanced interest in the popularisation of science, partly through works in the vernacular, partly through picture-books to catch the fancy, partly through appeal to the faculty of wonder, and partly through the demonstration of the useful aspects of the learned sciences. Whereas earlier scholars translated from Greek to Latin in an effort to make the classics of Greek science available to an academic but non-specialist audience, now these same scholars translated the classics into the vernacular with the avowed purpose of reaching both the 'practical man'—artisan, navigator, engineer—and the gentleman, who as courtier, diplomat and promoter influenced the course of events in the world of learning and the world of practice. Thus a French Euclid (translated by Peletier, humanist, poet and mathematician) was published in 1559, an English Euclid in 1570, and an Italian Euclid (by Commandino, able mathematician and scholar) in 1575. Not only scholars made vernacular translations: there were also professedly non-learned men, making use of the humanist translations into Latin. Thus Hero of Alexandria's *Pneumatics* (influential because of the prefatory discussion of the physical nature of air, as well as because of its careful description of ingenious hydraulic and pneumatic machines and toys) was first made widely available by its translation into Latin by Commandino in 1575; this translation was then turned into vernacular Italian by a number of practical men, the first of whom, Aleotti, used it as a vehicle for publicising his own mechanical contrivances. The intention of both sorts of translator was clear: to introduce a new audience to the old wisdom. Humanism may have begun as an aristocratic and exclusive movement, the preserve of the few; but by the mid-sixteenth century scientific humanists, at least, had turned the passionate proselytising spirit, so characteristic of all humanism, in the direction of the wider dissemination of learning and were almost pathetically eager to educate those who could not educate themselves. Almost all the works on applied mathematics and engineering in this period, whether written in vernacular or in Latin, combine denunciation of 'pure' learning, useless in itself, with complaints of the obtuseness of the ordinary man—seaman, artisan, mechanic, gunner—who persisted in using old, rule-of-thumb methods instead of adopting the new methods discovered by scholars all too eager to impart their learning. Robert Norman, the compass-maker, the first artisan to write on magnetism, might complain that all too few learned works made use of the knowledge of the practical man; the learned mathematician, when he wrote on applied mathematics, usually felt that the practical man refused to listen to his undoubtedly greater theoretical knowledge. It was, in fact, precisely in this period that a rapprochement between scholar and craftsman was first, however tentatively, effected, and effected through the intense efforts of scholar and layman alike.

In this popularisation of knowledge two subjects enjoyed the especial advantage of appealing to the gentleman as well as to the artisan: engineering and cartography. Engineering lent itself to the production of beautiful picture-books illustrating real or imaginary devices; who would not, in a newly mechanical age, enjoy looking at the many lovely examples of Renaissance book-making? There was Jacques Besson's *Theatre des Instrumens Mathematiques & Mechaniques* (Lyon, 1579) with its ingenious and complex power machines; Agostino Ramelli's *Le Diverse et Artificiose Machine* (Paris, 1588) issued in a bilingual French and Italian form, with dozens of pumps, mills, cranes, bridges, fountains and war machines worked by water, man or wind power; Fontana's description of how he set up the Vatican obelisk (*Del Modo Tenuto per Transportare l'Obelisco*, Rome, 1589), with its handsome pictures and interesting text; and a host of lesser works, all based partly on Greek and medieval tradition, partly on the Late Renaissance love of complex mechanical contrivances. Such were the *Machinae Novae* of Faust Veranzio, some copies of which exist with the descriptions of the machines in Italian, Spanish, French and German, as well as Latin; the *Novo Theatro di Machini et Edificii* (Padua, 1607) of the architect Zonca; *Le Machine* (Rome, 1629) of Branca, also an architect; and, in a slightly different tradition, the *Architettura Militare* (Brescia, 1599) of Francesco Marchi. The list could be much extended; while the Italians maintained their lead in the invention and description of machines, in the early seventeenth century the French and Germans began to produce works dealing with pneumatic and hydraulic devices. The Dutch and Spanish excelled in useful works on navigation in the earlier sixteenth century; in the latter half of the century the English began to replace them in this field, as their ships were dominating the high seas. Indeed, the number and popularity, at home and abroad, of English works on navigation and cartography is remarkable; and, though Holland remained the centre of the map trade, the best map-makers kept in close touch with the English market. Maps, especially in England, were as popular as works on machinery in Italy; as John Dee wrote in the Preface to Henry Billingsley's English Euclid:

While some, to beautifie their Halls, Parlers, Chambers, Galeries, Studies, or Libraries with; other some, for things past, as batels fought, earthquakes, heavenly fyringes, & such occurrences, in histories mentioned: therby lively as it were to vewe the place, the region adjoyning, the distance from us, and such other circumstances. Some other, presently to vewe the large dominion of the Turke: the wide Empire of the Moschovite: and the litle morsell of ground, where Christendome (by profession) is certainly known. Litle, I say, in respecte of the rest, &c. Some either for their owne journeys directing into farre lands: or to understand of other men's travailes. To conclude, some, for one purpose; and some, for an other, liketh, loveth, getteth, and useth, Mappes, Chartes, and Geographicall Globes.

Indeed, the original motive for the production of books of maps was to provide information and entertainment for gentlemen at home; the seaman was content with a single chart, often traced from a printed map. Slowly, in fact, engineer and theoretical cartographer and navigator were displacing the astrologer from his medieval position of court scientist—though John Dee successfully combined both roles—and mathematics extended its scope in the popular mind.

The natural sciences had less scope for popular appeal, except for natural history and herbals, both of which continued in an older tradition. Travel literature, though extensive—this is the period of Hakluyt's great collection, *The Principall Navigations, Voyages and Discoveries of the English Nation* (1589, with second part 1598–1600)—was more often concerned with superficial description and account of the dangers braved than it was with the flora and fauna of the landfall. Nicolas Monardes's account of the Spanish new world, published early in the century, was translated into English by John Frampton, appearing in 1575 under the beguiling title, *Joyeful Newes out of the New Founde World*. This did describe new plants and animals, as did José d'Acosta's *Natural and Moral History of the Indies* (i.e. Peru and Mexico) published in Spanish in 1591, with an English edition in 1601 and a French edition in 1606. Raleigh's first colonial expedition to Virginia included not only Thomas Harriot the mathematician, who ably described the country in *A Brief and True Report of the New-founde Land of Virginia* (1588), but also John White, whose drawings and sketches of the Indians, the flora and the marine life of the area are charmingly and delightfully done.

Though many scholars were so vividly aware of the need to popularise their learning, yet the bulk of their activity was naturally devoted to the serious development of the theoretical aspects of their science. In all fields there was a flood of books, learnedly presented, primarily in Latin, dealing with what contemporary mathematicians, astronomers, natural philosophers, physicians and natural historians saw as the major problems of their respective fields. Some of these have interest only as showing how the past lingered on; more were concerned, however tentatively, with what proved to be the necessary steps in the development of more advanced understanding of particular problems.

The most interesting aspects of mathematics in the later sixteenth century are undoubtedly in its applications—to astronomy, to navigation, to cosmography, to physics—but the advances in pure mathematics, though unspectacular, are by no means negligible. Mathematical activity in this period may be said to have had three main aspects: first, assimilation and extension of advanced Greek mathematics; second, the improvement and extension of symbolism; and third, the solution of more and more types of algebraic equation.

Hellenistic mathematics still had much to offer the sixteenth century and new and accurate Latin translations to replace or supplement medieval versions were of value. These were made by competent mathematicians. For example, Federigo Commandino (1509–75), mathematician to the duke of Urbino, did useful if not important work on the centres of gravity of solids, using Archimedean methods of analysis, but was more influential through his series of excellent translations: of Archimedes (Venice, 1558; Bologna, 1565); Apollonius with the commentaries of Pappus and Eutochius (Bologna, 1566); Pappus (Pisa, 1588); and, as well, a number of non-mathematical treatises. These translations, for example, stimulated his disciple, Guido Ubaldo del Monte (1545–1607), to sound work on Archimedean problems. Similarly, Francisco Maurolyco (1494–1575), one of the best geometers of the period, undertook an extensive and elegant study of conic sections, treating them as actual plane sections of the cone, a study stimulated by, though in reaction to, the work of Apollonius; and he applied his mathematical discoveries to his exploration of optics. A new impetus was given to algebraic studies by the publication of the first Latin translation of Diophantus in 1575, printed at Basle, in the translation of Xylander.

Algebra was undoubtedly the most rewarding branch of mathematics for the sixteenth century. Although modern symbolism was not developed until the next century, much progress was made towards its formulation in this period. Indeed, each mathematician experimented with a new symbolism; while this tendency rendered each new work difficult to read, it was yet the means by which a general system was ultimately worked out, incorporating the best formulation for each particular case. The German algebraists (*cossists*) of the first half of the century, like Michael Stifel (d. 1567), took the lead in trying to standardise notation and began, for example, the modern sign for a square root; this symbolism was first used in Italy by Christopher Clavius (1537–1612), a sound but unoriginal worker. Throughout the century the struggle was continued to find an adequate symbolism for roots and powers, a struggle which reflects the increasing understanding of the relations between the two operations. Similarly, the famous work of Simon Stevin (1548–1620) on decimal fractions (*De Thiende*, 1585) is important less for its novelty (for decimal fractions had been long known) or for its symbolism (Stevin's was extremely clumsy) than for its convincing demonstration of the superiority of decimal over common fractions for simplicity and clarity of manipulation. A logical development of this search was the invention of logarithms by Napier (1614), and Briggs (1617), which enormously simplified calculation.

The earlier half of the century dealt amid public and rancorous dispute with the solution of cubic equations of certain types. The later sixteenth century was more concerned with methods of rendering the known methods of solving equations of all types more general. Raffaelo Bombelli was one of the few to accept (in his *Algebra* of 1572) the existence of imaginary roots, which permitted him to deal with hitherto irreducible equations, but he had little influence until the next century. Real generalisation was not achieved until the work of François Viète (1540–1603), whose *Introduction to the Art of Analysis* of 1591 is the earliest work of true symbolic algebra. Here, for the first time, symbols were used for both known and unknown quantities, thereby permitting truly general results to be formulated. Viète also did important work in the analysis of equations and the introduction of general methods of solution. The algebraic contributions of Thomas Harriot (1560–1621) were similar; he was perhaps influenced by Viète's work, which he carried further in some directions, as for example in decomposing equations into their simple factors. As he did not recognise negative or imaginary roots, his work lacked real generality; and his *Art of Analytical Practice* was only published in 1631, ten years after his death.

An odd characteristic of mathematics in this period, which makes it particularly difficult to assess the relative importance of individual mathematicians, is an extraordinary nationalism, most uncharacteristic of science as a whole. One reason for the isolation into national schools was the growth of symbolism, which failed, in this period, to become international. A second is the result of the fact that much work of this period only became fertile in the hands of some later mathematician: thus Viète's work was the source of inspiration for Descartes, while Harriot's work was the origin of the work of the English school, especially Wallis, who naturally therefore made exaggerated claims for Harriot's originality, claims much disputed by French historians of mathematics. This was the more possible as much work circulated in manuscript and was only published posthumously. What is important to realise is that, though minor, the contributions of mathematicians in the later sixteenth century did provide the basis for the exuberant growth of mathematics in the succeeding century.

Astronomy in the later sixteenth century presents a somewhat different aspect from mathematics, for the inspiration of Hellenistic science had here been exhausted by Copernicus, and astronomers were forced to wrestle with a quite extraordinarily difficult problem. Firm in three hundred years' education in the heliostatic hypothesis, moderns often fail to grasp the essential improbability of the Copernican theory. For Copernicus was not only turning the science of astronomy upside down, as Luther had protested: he was turning upside down man's whole normal view of the world. Ptolemaic astronomy was Everyman's astronomy mathematised; Copernican astronomy bore not the faintest resemblance to everyday, common-sense astronomy, which deals with such a manifestly geocentric universe that elementary astronomy still begins with what is, after all, the only universe we can know from direct observation. It is therefore no wonder that many of the best astronomers of the sixteenth century rejected the Copernican theory on grounds of common sense as much as on grounds of religion and physics, nor that many Copernicans of the period were more remarkable for their mysticism than for their rationalism. Even Copernicans recognised that the new doctrine was unsuited to elementary presentation, and Copernicans who lectured on astronomy, like Michael Maestlin (1550–1631) or Galileo (1564–1642), agreed with Robert Recorde's decision in the *Castle of Knowledge* (1556) that a scholar ungrounded in Ptolemaic astronomy did not have the astronomical equipment to appreciate the new hypothesis. When one looks at the problem in this light, it is hardly surprising that most astronomers failed to become Copernicans; the wonder is rather that so complex and mathematical a theory received such wide dissemination and that

Copernicus was referred to so frequently and in general with such respect. It is true that many references to Copernicus are really references to the Copernican or Prutenic Tables compiled in 1551 by Erasmus Reinhold which were based on the Copernican theory—though Reinhold was not himself a Copernican—and which were markedly superior to the older Alphonsine tables. But on the whole scientists were by no means slighting or derogatory in their references, which must be in part a measure of the acuteness of the need for a new astronomy, widely felt even before 1500.

Not all praise of Copernicus indicates acceptance of his theory, for all serious astronomers recognised his ability and were more appreciative of his observational skill than the modern historian is inclined to be. And, until the end of the century, there was little reason to reject his hypothesis on theological grounds, except among extreme fundamentalists. The number of references are, however, some measure of the interest with which Copernicus's theory was discussed, though many astronomers discussed the hypothesis eagerly and even favourably without feeling it necessary to commit themselves publicly to what was, after all, still a hypothesis, unsupported by observation. Indeed, a convinced Copernican had obstinately to believe in spite of observational evidence. Michael Maestlin, Kepler's teacher, remained a Copernican even though he could himself detect no stellar parallax; and he was an able observational astronomer, the first to give a correct explanation of earthshine. Among other scientists who adhered to the Copernican theory may be mentioned Christopher Rothmann, astronomer to Landgrave William IV of Hesse-Cassel, who wrote no Copernican treatise; and J. B. Benedetti who spoke well of the theory from second-hand knowledge—he was, after all, not an astronomer and his major contributions were in mathematical physics. In France there were few discussions of Copernicus, except for those of Pontus de Tyard (c. 1521–1605), a member of the Pléiade, who was assigned the scientific section of the encyclopedic discussions conducted in the informal academy that flourished in and about Henry III's court in the dark days of the religious wars. Pontus was sympathetically inclined towards Copernicanism partly because, like Giordano Bruno later, he found it consistent with the Lucretian doctrine of the plurality of worlds. There was of course Kepler (1571–1630), whose *Cosmographical Mystery* of 1596, with its appendix of the *Narratio Prima* of Rheticus, the first disciple of Copernicus, proclaimed its author an uncompromising Copernican. The *Cosmographical Mystery* also proclaimed its author to be an able mathematician and a convinced number mystic—for its central thesis was that there is a geometrical relation between the distances of the various planets from the sun, a relation that could be expressed in terms of the spheres inscribed and circumscribed about the five regular Platonic solids. Certainly, it displayed both conviction and great mathematical skill, and it served to introduce the young Kepler to Tycho and to Galileo, though it is but a slight work compared to Kepler's later efforts. Kepler is one of the few, in this period, to argue for Copernicanism on primarily mathematical grounds.

Perhaps surprisingly, England, previously undistinguished in astronomy, saw a very great interest in Copernicus, rather more interest than was to be found on the continent. Robert Recorde, while finding Copernicanism too difficult for the young scholar, praised Copernicus as 'a man of greate learninge, of muche experience, and of wonderful diligence in observation'.[1] John Dee (1527–1608), in his prefatory remarks to John Feild's *Ephemeris anni 1557*, particularly praised Copernicus's skill in observation. Edward Wright (*c.* 1558–1615) was reputed a Copernican by his contemporaries, though he wrote only on navigation. The first real exposition of Copernican theories in English (the first in any vernacular) was contained in a curious little work by Thomas Digges (d. 1595) called *A Perfit Description of the Coelestial Orbes*; this was one of the appendices he added to the 1576 edition of his father's *A Prognostication Everlasting*, which provided tables for the perpetual prediction of weather and disaster by astrological considerations. This association of Copernicanism and mysticism was not uncommon in the period. The *Perfit Description*, which was reprinted seven times by 1605 as part of the *Prognostication*, is virtually an English translation of most of the first book of Copernicus. To this Digges added some brief comments, and a diagram of the universe interesting for its declaration that the sphere of fixed stars extends infinitely up, without boundary, to 'the pallace of foelicitye', that is, to the firmament, the theological heaven. The Christian mysticism associated with this first statement of the infinity of the Copernican universe (not a part of Copernicus's own theory) makes one wonder if Giordano Bruno might not have been influenced by Digges. Such an abolition of the celestial sphere, as Digges knew, implied that the stars, being at varying distances, must be of varying sizes, but he found no difficulty in imagining that many were very large. Digges was clearly an out-and-out Copernican. The nature of William Gilbert's Copernicanism is more difficult to assess. His contemporaries classed him as a Copernican, but there is no written evidence to show whether he thought in terms of a heliostatic universe. His studies on magnetism had convinced him that Aristotle erred in assigning souls only to the heavenly bodies, to the exclusion of the earth, for his own discovery of terrestrial magnetism showed that the earth, too, was animate. The sixth book of the *De Magnete* (1600) is, in fact, devoted to a passionate defence of the diurnal rotation of the earth; for since the earth is endowed with magnetism, it must be capable of motion. And, he says, it is far easier to believe that the earth turns on its axis every 24 hours than it is to believe that the whole of the heavens with the sun, the planets and the fixed stars rotates every 24 hours. This argument he repeated in

---

[1] *The Castle of Knowledge* (London, 1556), p. 165.

the posthumously published *New Philosophy of our Sublunary World* (1651) in which, as Francis Bacon remarked, he made a philosophy out of the loadstone. For here (writing presumably about the same time as in the *De Magnete*, for he died in 1603) he suggested that magnetism might extend to the moon and thereby account for the tides, and perhaps it might be magnetism which kept the planets in their orbits. This is interesting and novel, and Gilbert's theory of a magnetic soul seems to have had some influence upon Kepler; but it is not necessarily Copernican.

Until the end of this period there was little religious objection to Copernicus. Luther, to be sure, had denounced the hypothesis on biblical grounds, since it was the sun and not the earth which Joshua had commanded to stand still, and Luther's friend and disciple Melanchthon in *Elements of Physical Doctrines* (1549) had declared it contrary to the Bible and to natural philosophy. This emphasis on scriptural authority had some influence upon other Lutherans besides Tycho, but it was not binding. Calvinists and Anglicans were free to make up their own minds on the question and until 1612 the Catholic church made no official pronouncement. Indeed, until 1600 Catholic theologians had no interest in doing so, in spite of the increased emphasis on biblical authority that emerged from the decisions of the Council of Trent. Thus in 1584 the Spanish theologian Diego de Zuñiga (Didacus à Stunica) published a *Commentary on Job* in which he was able without difficulty to argue that the Pythagorean theory, as it was still commonly called, was not contrary to scripture. It was the case of Giordano Bruno which, more than anything else, focused attention on the heretical possibilities of the Copernican hypothesis. Bruno was not a scientist, nor learned in science, but an original and highly heterodox philosopher whose soaring pantheism was in advance of his age, though it was to be enormously influential upon later philosophers. Bruno was enamoured of unity, divine and natural, and it was because Copernicanism offered cosmological unity that he favoured it. He also accepted Lucretian ideas of the infinity of the universe (Bruno was the first Copernican to believe in an infinite physical, as distinct from Digges's infinite theological, universe) and of the plurality of worlds. It was not for his Copernicanism but for his pantheism and his heresy that the Roman Inquisition imprisoned him and, after wrestling with his indomitable spirit for eight years, burned him at the stake in 1600. Yet, to the Inquisition, Copernicanism and heresy were thereafter closely associated, if not inseparable.

The one original astronomer of this period—for the mature work of Kepler lies just outside its limits—was Tycho Brahe (1546–1601), who was not a Copernican, though he referred to Copernicus with great respect. Tycho, indeed, was far more remarkable as an observational than as a theoretical astronomer, though this is not an appraisal he would have cared for, and in fact his observations had far-reaching theoretical implications. As he recalled in his *Astronomiae Instauratae Mechanica*[1] of 1598, he began reading elementary astronomy for pleasure while studying classical literature at Leipzig, to help him make more accurate observations. He was bothered by the fact that while the available tables were reasonably accurate for the fixed stars—though he was later to make his own, far more accurate, star catalogue—they were grossly inaccurate for the position of the planets, a situation strikingly confirmed by his observation in 1563 of the conjunction of Saturn and Jupiter. Fired by the desire to improve this situation, he had better instruments made and gradually immersed himself in scientific pursuits. Alchemy he found for a time more absorbing than astronomy, until the sudden appearance of a new star in Cassiopeia in 1572 settled the matter once for all. His account of his observations (*De Nova Stella*, 1573) won him the patronage of the king of Denmark, who with extraordinary generosity made him feudal lord of the island of Hveen, where he built the great astronomical observatory of Uraniborg. Here he worked from 1576 to 1597, surrounded by able assistants, with a complete range of the best astronomical instruments of the age.

The nova of 1572 naturally excited enormous interest, since it was in such a well-known constellation and was, at first, as bright as Venus. Tycho, Digges and Maestlin all studied it carefully with a view to detecting any parallax, and all, failing to find any, concluded that it lay in the sphere of fixed stars. Not all astronomers agreed; some insisted that it did move visibly, and others (including Dee) that it must be moving in a straight line away from the earth, a more rational explanation of the change in brightness than the idea that it was a totally new star. Tycho's study was the most thorough: he carefully noted the colour changes (characteristic of novae) as it faded, and most firmly insisted that it was situated in the theoretically unchanging heavens. Tycho was thus led to an anti-Aristotelian position through observation, and this attitude was fortified by his studies of comets. The later sixteenth century was a wonderful time for astronomers; seldom can there have been such a concatenation of heavenly events all visible to the naked eye. Tycho was able to observe six comets between 1577 and 1596 with the accurate new instruments he built at Uraniborg, and with the accurate new techniques he developed. With so much heavenly agitation, it was no wonder that there was a tremendous public interest and a flood of books on popular astronomy predicting disasters worthy of the unsettled state of the times. Tycho, though a devout believer in astrology, felt that there were not yet enough reliable observations to permit accurate predictions; this was one reason for the study of astronomy. Nevertheless, rough predictions were possible and, as he declared in his public lectures to the University of Copenhagen in 1574,

[1] Transl. and ed. by Hans Raeder, Elis Stromgren and Brent Stromgren as *Description of his Instruments and Scientific Work* (Copenhagen, 1946).

these were of use to mankind, since when one understood the influence of the stars, one could resist and avert the threatening evils. As late as 1598 he summed the position up as follows:

After I at length obtained more accurate knowledge of the orbits of the celestial bodies, I took Astrology up again from time to time, and I arrived at the conclusion that this science, although it is considered idle and meaningless not only by laymen but also by most scholars, among which are even several astronomers, is really more reliable than one would think; and this is true not only with regard to meteorological influences and predictions of the weather, but also concerning the predictions by nativities provided that the times were determined correctly, and that the courses of the stars and their entrances into definite sections of the sky are utilized in accordance with the actual sky, and that their directions of motion and revolutions are correctly worked up.[1]

From this it is clear that Tycho, in spite of what is sometimes said, was as much a believer in astrology as the ordinary man of his day; but equally that his belief in astrology only strengthened his interest in observational astronomy and its rational interpretation. His observations on comets were described in careful detail, as carefully as the measurements which convinced him that, since the comets showed no parallax, they were therefore not in the sublunary sphere (as Aristotle had thought and his followers insisted) but in the outer spheres. They were, in fact, normal celestial bodies, moving in a manner comparable to the motion of the planets. Besides contradicting Aristotelian physics, this introduced a new problem, for the motion of comets around the sun necessarily meant that they cut across the orbits of the planets, impossible if the planets were located on crystalline spheres. Tycho was willing to relinquish crystalline spheres without, apparently, worrying about the question which then arose, of what kept the planets in their orbits; his assistant Kepler was later to conclude that it was an *anima motrix* drawing the planets toward the sun.

In the treatise *On the Recent Phaenomena of the Aethereal World*, dealing primarily with comets, Tycho described for the first time his own system of the world, which he claimed to have devised five years earlier. (Questions of priority arose because in 1588 Nicolas Reymers, a fairly obscure astronomer, published his *Fundamentum Astronomicum*, in which he presented the Tychonic system with the addition of the diurnal rotation of the earth; a virulent and inconclusive controversy resulted, in which Tycho and Reymers accused each other of plagiarism.) Tycho could not accept the idea that the earth might have motion: there was no observational evidence in favour of it; common-sense physics was against it (for he believed that a stone dropped from the top of a tower could never hit the ground immediately below its point of fall if the earth were moving, a point to be argued at length by the next generation); and scripture un-

[1] *Astronomiae Instauratae Mechanica*, p. 117.

doubtedly opposed it (Tycho was a Lutheran). The Tychonic system was a rational and natural replacement of the weak points of the Ptolemaic system with observational likelihoods, while retaining the geostatic universe so much preferable in Tycho's view to the uncomfortable terrestrial restlessness of the Copernican theory. According to Tycho, all the planets revolve in orbits around the sun; the whole solar system then revolves about the earth–moon system. This was mathematically equivalent to the Copernican system, but easier to accept, provided that one was willing to dispense with crystalline spheres. For the drawback of the Tychonic system was that the orbit of the solar system about the earth crossed the orbits of Mars and the inner planets, a state of affairs only possible if there were indeed no crystalline spheres, as Tycho's cometary researches had indicated. This system is remarkable for its simplicity and its reasonableness and, with the diurnal rotation of the earth replacing the rotation of the fixed stars (a notion unacceptable to Tycho himself), was widely accepted in the early seventeenth century by those who found the Ptolemaic system out of date and the Copernican system too novel for acceptance.

An important use for astronomy was, as it had been for many centuries, its assistance in calculating the date of Easter. Ever since the thirteenth century there had been an uneasy awareness that the Julian calendar was inaccurate, which meant that the date of Easter and of other movable holy days no longer conformed to the specifications decreed by the Council of Nicaea. Easter was reckoned from the first full moon after the vernal equinox; at the time of the Council of Nicaea (A.D. 325) the vernal equinox had already moved from the original 25th of March to the 21st of March; by the sixteenth century the difference between the official calendar and the solar calendar was ten days more, a situation bound to worsen as time went on. Various church councils had discussed the matter, but it was generally agreed among scientists that astronomical knowledge was insufficient to rectify the problem. Under Pope Gregory XIII a new system was at last developed and accepted. This had been devised by Luigi Lilio, a Neapolitan physician and astronomer; he died before the new calendar could be officially accepted, and its adoption was ultimately supervised by Clavius, who published a detailed account of the calculations in *An Explanation of the Restoration of the Roman Calendar by Gregory XIII* in 1603. Essentially the reform consisted in eliminating three leap years in every four hundred years, by making centurial years leap years only when they were divisible by four hundred—thus 1600 was a leap year, but 1700, 1800 and 1900 were not. The method of calculation of Easter was reorganised: Lilio based his calculation on 'epacts', that is, on the phase of the moon obtaining on the first of January of each year, an arbitrary method which gratified Renaissance love of number mysticism and did also satisfy the conditions laid down by the Council of

Nicaea. Catholic countries adopted the new calendar quickly, though most showed reluctance; Protestant countries in general held out until the eighteenth century. The new calendar was an achievement of technical astronomy, but even more of the efficiency of church administration.

The most important, as well as the most difficult, branch of applied mathematics and astronomy was navigation, with its associated field of cartography. Navigational methods improved perforce under the necessities of Atlantic voyages, but the chief improvement was in the skill of individual seamen rather than in the theory and practice of navigation as a whole. It was an obvious and fertile field for the application of science; yet the suggestions for improvement made in the first half of the sixteenth century by such men as Oronce Finé in France, Gemma Frisius (1508–55) in the Low Countries and Pedro Nuñez (1492–1577) in Portugal were mainly of importance for the influence on the mathematical practitioners of the later sixteenth century, who, unlike their teachers, were able to make practical suggestions which bore fruit. The spectacular success of English navigation led English mathematicians and instrument makers to an enormous interest in ways to aid the seaman in his gallant passage through as yet uncharted seas, and England challenged the Low Countries as a centre of interest for this sort of endeavour.

The writers of the earlier half of the century had tended to suggest methods which, though basically sound, were too refined under the conditions prevailing at sea. Thus Gemma Frisius had suggested the use of clocks to determine longitude and there had been other suggestions based upon observation of eclipses, conjunctions, or the motion of the moon in relation to the fixed stars. These the seaman found far too difficult to apply on the ships of the day, nor did anyone ever try to install the complex chair, mounted on gimbals to permit steady observation, which Jacques Besson designed.[1] A sweeping criticism of this sort of invention was made by Robert Hues (1553–1632), an Oxford graduate who made two voyages across the Atlantic; as he commented in 1594, the determination of longitude by the known motion of the moon

is an uncertaine and ticklish way, and subject to many difficulties. Others have gone other wayes to worke; as, namely, by observing the space of the Aequinoctiall houres betwixt the Meridians of two places, which they conceive may be taken by the helpe of sunne dials, or clocks, or houre glasses, either with water or sand, or the like. But these conceits long since devised, having been more strictly and accurately examined, have beene disallowed and rejected by all learned men (at least those of riper judgments) as being altogether unable to performe that which is required of them. But yet for all this there are a kind of trifling Imposters that made public sale of those toys or worse, and that with great ostentation and boasting; to the great abuse and expense of some men of good note and quality, who are perhaps better stored with

[1] In *Le Cosmolabe, ou Instrument Universel, concernant Toutes Observations qui se peuvent faire Par les Sciences Mathematiques, Tant au Ciel, en la Terre, comme en la Mer* (Paris, 1567); there is a picture of the device on p. 29.

money than either learning or judgment. But I shall not stand here to discover the erroures and uncertainties of these instruments. Only I admonish these men by the way that they beware of these fellowes, least when their noses are wiped (as we say) of their money, they too late repent them of their ill-bought bargaines. Away with all such trifling, cheating rascals.[1]

Sailors did not altogether reject astronomical methods; indeed, by the mid-sixteenth century determination of latitude by observation of the meridian altitude of the sun or by means of the circumpolar stars was so common that the method of parallel sailing could be widely adopted. This consisted in making the required latitude as soon as convenient, and then sailing along this latitude east or west until the ship bumped into its objective; though this might increase the length of the voyage, it was safer than trying academic methods of longitude determination. Academic men might protest that great circle sailing was shorter, but actually this saved too little distance, generally, to be worth the trouble caused, and it ignored the direction of the prevailing winds which seamen had learned by experience. Determination of latitude was facilitated by the invention of the backstaff, described by John Davis in *Seamen's Secrets* in 1594, especially when in the next century this was improved into Davis's quadrant.

In the later sixteenth century three new methods were introduced to improve the seaman's knowledge of his longitude: the invention of the log, the investigation of magnetic variation, and the improvement of the sea chart. The first and last helped the seaman by making it easier for him to navigate by dead reckoning and in this period dead reckoning was far more accurate than any method that could be devised for longitude determination at sea. The log was an English invention and for long remained an English monopoly. It was first described by William Bourne (who did not invent it) in *A Regiment for the Sea* in 1573; as there were six editions of this book by 1600, the log received plenty of publicity even though it was not discussed by others until the early seventeenth century. The log, with its line knotted at measured intervals, was a vast improvement as a method for determining the speed of the ship over the older methods, such as watching a bit of flotsam going by the ship in a period fixed by pacing out the deck. In actual practice, the length of the line between the knots, the calibration of the sand-glass used for timing, and the estimated length of a degree of terrestrial arc (necessary for accurate dead reckoning) were all inaccurate. Seamen commonly were content to have it so, provided they erred to keep the ship actually behind the estimated position; as they said, it was better to be a day's sail from their destination than even the length of a cannon shot ahead of it. Among the first to point out the need for accurate measurement of a minute of arc of

[1] *Tractatus de Globis et eorum usu*, from the English edition of 1638 (published for the Hakluyt Society, London, 1889).

a great circle of the earth was Edward Wright, a Cambridge-trained mathematician who had accompanied the earl of Cumberland on his expedition to the Azores in 1589. Wright made an astronomically based estimation; actual measurement of the earth's surface was not undertaken until the next century.

Atlantic sailing had drawn attention to the variation in the compass; for while in most of Europe the compass pointed east of true north, the western Atlantic then had westerly variation. William Gilbert in the *De Magnete* argued that the westerly variation found by the Dutch in Nova Zembla indicated that there was a north-east passage through the arctic sea. For Gilbert believed that variation was the result of the attraction of the compass needle by large land masses (a natural consequence of his establishment of the fact that the magnetic pole was terrestrial, not celestial) and a westerly variation would have been impossible in high latitudes had there been a large continental land mass to the east. As the fact of variation became known early in the sixteenth century, compass-makers habitually set the needles askew on their compass cards so that the cards pointed to true north at the place of manufacture; writers on magnetism and navigation bitterly denounced this practice, which made it more difficult than necessary for the seaman to know where, in fact, he was. There were many suggestions made that the variation of the compass might be used to determine longitude; in fact Simon Stevin's *The Haven-finding Art* (1599, in Dutch with an English translation in the same year by Wright) is entirely devoted to the proposition that the position of any place at sea can be found provided that the latitude and the compass variation are known. Although Gilbert agreed with Stevin that this was a possibility, since he thought the variation was constant for any one place, he did not think this a good method of navigation, for he thought seamen incapable of making sufficiently accurate observations. Gilbert preferred inclination (dip) as a navigational aid. This phenomenon had been discovered by Robert Norman, a London compass-maker: he always mounted his needles before 'touching' (magnetising) them, and found that magnetisation caused the point of the needle to incline toward the earth, inconveniently so when the needle was long. He described his observation carefully in *The Newe Attractive* (1581), together with a declinometer. Gilbert wrote of Norman's work in detail and believed that measurement of the dip was an easy way of determining latitude when the sky was overcast; as he wrote:

We may see how far from unproductive magnetick philosophy is, how agreeable, how helpful, how divine! Sailors when tossed about on the waves with continuous cloudy weather, and unable by means of the coelestial luminaries to learn anything about the place or region in which they are, with a very slight effort and with a small instrument are comforted, and learn the latitude of the place.[1]

[1] *On the Magnet* (New York, 1958, facsimile of the Chiswick Press edition of 1900).

But the use of the dip, like the use of the variation, was destined to prove worthless because of secular variation, a fact discovered only some thirty years after Gilbert wrote.

Gilbert's remarks amply illustrate the fact that the learned scientist was extremely eager to help the practical man, however and wherever he could. To this end he frequently wrote in the vernacular or translated suitable texts into the vernacular, especially into English. The French first provided the English seaman with his 'Rutter' (routier), a handbook of useful information on courses, landfalls, shoals, tides, etc. This was replaced after 1588 by a 'Waggoner', an English translation of the Dutch *Mariner's Mirror* published in 1583 by Lucas Janszoon Waghenaer, a collection of sea charts for the European coasts together with full sailing directions and tables of the new moons and the declination of the sun, a catalogue of fixed stars (about 100) with positions, directions for making a cross-staff and for copying a chart, and rules for finding the meridian altitude of the sun. This was an invaluable navigational aid, deeply appreciated, as the many editions testify.

The charts in a Waggoner were all 'plane charts', that is, they used no projection but mapped the earth as if it were flat rather than spherical. A sphere, as Ptolemy knew, cannot be represented as a plane surface without distortion, and obviously the distortion grows worse around the poles, since the meridians converge towards the poles, whereas on a plane chart they are all the same distance apart, whatever the latitude. Many writers, like Pedro Nuñcz, had commented on this and Nuñez had suggested the advantages of a loxodromic chart, that is, one in which a line of constant compass heading (a rhumb line) is straight. Sailing by rhumbs was clearly desirable, but a loxodromic course could not be readily plotted on a plane chart—though it could on a globe, so that globes were often advocated and occasionally used as navigational aids. But to obtain a true loxodromic chart a mathematical projection of a sphere was required. Nuñez could not calculate the method of doing this, nor, indeed, could Mercator, though the first loxodromic chart was drawn by him. Mercator was a mathematician, educated at Louvain under Gemma Frisius, who turned his mathematical knowledge to the production of maps, charts and globes. (In this he differed from his contemporary Ortelius (1527–98), who merely collected and published maps without having any knowledge of how to draw or engrave maps and charts.) Mercator's skill was considerable; he was, for example, one of the first globe-makers to work out theoretically the proper relation between the length and width of the gores which were pasted on the globe: he divided the world into twelve gores, each of which he cut off 20 degrees from the poles, making two extra circular sections to cover the poles, which ensured more accurate conformity of the map to the spherical globe than was normally the case. He perceived that to make a plane surface conform to a sphere the parallels ought to be spread out as one got further away from the equator, and in his chart of 1569 'for the use of mariners' he did so. But what reasoning he used to deduce the correct spacing he did not say. The chart was useful, but before others could be drawn a method needed to be devised. Even Mercator did not use the form again; the maps in his *Atlas* (the first use of the word for a collection of maps), published in three parts in 1585, 1590 and 1595, were either plane charts or drawn to quite different projections. It was left to Edward Wright to understand the method of cylindrical projection and to explain its mode of construction and use. This he did in *Certaine Errors in Navigation* (1599), the errors being, as the subtitle indicates, those 'arising either of the ordinarie erroneous making or using of the Sea Chart, Compasse, Crosse Staff, and Tables of declination of the Sunne and fixed Starres', which he therefore 'detected and corrected'. Chief among these errors was the use of the plane chart; he therefore explained the Mercator projection; supplied the tables of rhumbs; showed how, with the use of table and chart, to find the distance from one place to another, latitude and longitude being known; and showed seamen how to plot a course on the new chart to the best advantage. Wright gave a really excellent explanation of what the Mercator projection was:

Suppose a sphericall superficies with meridians, parallels, rumbes, and the whole hydrographicall description drawne thereupon to bee inscribed into a concave cylinder, their axes agreeing in one. Let this sphericall superficies swel like a bladder, (whiles it is in blowing) equally alwayes in everie part thereof (that is as much in longitude as in latitude) till it apply, and joyne it selfe (round about, and all alongst towardes either pole) unto the concave superficies of the cylinder: each parallel upon this sphericall superficies increasing successively from the equinoctiall towards eyther pole, until it come to bee of equall diameter with the cylinder, and consequently the meridians stil widening them selves, til they come to be so far distant every where ech from other as they are at the Equinoctiall. Thus it may most easily be understoode, how a sphericall superficies may (by extension) be made a cylindrical, and consequently, a plaine parallelogram superficies.[1]

Wright also drew a map to illustrate the use of this projection, published later by his friend Hakluyt, but his table of rhumbs and methods of construction had already been used by the Dutch map-maker Jodocus Hondius (1563–1611), who had access to Wright's manuscript while in England. Hondius had promised not to publish anything on the problem without Wright's permission but, as he confessed to the mathematician Henry Briggs, 'the profit thereof moved me', and it was partly because of the use made of his work by Hondius that Wright finally published the *Certaine Errors*.[2] (Others besides Hondius knew of Wright's work and mentioned or made use of it, as did Blundeville and Harriot.) The Mercator projection, as elucidated by Wright, now became a method of construction which could be utilised by the more mathematical map-makers, like

[1] Part I, chapter 2 (unpaged).　　　　[2] *Certaine Errors*, Preface.

Willem Blaeu. Blaeu (1571–1638) had studied with Tycho Brahe; and, when he was commissioned by the Dutch States General to write a complete seamen's guide, he first drew charts on the new projection and then, in 1612, published *The Light of Navigation*. Only sea charts, at first, were drawn on the Mercator projection; the cheap, often pocket-sized, collections of maps which appeared in such numbers after 1600 were mainly copies of much older maps and charts. Indeed, if the Mercator projection appears to have come into wide use only slowly, this is mainly because the number of so-called map-makers competent to draw their own maps—as did Mercator, Hondius, Blaeu and Christopher Saxton (who made his own survey of England between 1574 and 1591)—remained small and most map-makers were in fact copyists and publishers who only slowly came to copy the more complicated Mercator maps. By the middle of the seventeenth century, however, this contribution of the later sixteenth century was firmly established.

Mathematical physics in the later sixteenth century pursued paths already partly travelled, developing the immediate past in dynamics and the remote past in statics. In dynamics the medieval theory of impetus had been improved by, for example, the work of Tartaglia on ballistics; now J. B. Benedetti (1530–90) further developed a mathematical and overtly anti-Aristotelian theory. Thus, for example, he argued that the relative speed of two falling bodies was dependent not upon the difference in their absolute weights, but the difference between their specific gravities; and that the rate of fall of a body was dependent not upon its absolute weight, but its relative weight. The relative weight was the true weight less the resistance of the medium, whereas for Aristotle it was the true weight divided by the resistance of the medium. For Aristotle motion in a non-resisting medium, a vacuum, had thus been meaningless; Benedetti realised that in a vacuum all bodies should fall at the same speed and that a vacuum was thus a dynamically possible concept. Benedetti's dynamics was not yet Galilean dynamics, but his impetus physics deeply influenced the young Galileo. The outstanding figure in the revival of ancient statics was the Archimedean Simon Stevin. Stevin was a most versatile figure in the world of pure and applied mathematics, and his work on centres of gravity and hydrostatics goes far beyond the work of Archimedes. In his rejection of perpetual motion, in his elucidation of the equilibrium of bodies on an inclined plane, in his discovery of the hydrostatical paradox (that the pressure of a fluid upon a solid body varies with the area of the body and the height of the column of fluid, and not with the volume of fluid), Stevin prepared the way for the further development of these problems a generation later in the hands of such men as Descartes and Pascal.

In a very real sense, the natural sciences were, in this period, a by-product of medicine. Botany was primarily valued for the knowledge it gave of herbs useful as remedies, zoology for the anatomical insight it could give into the construction of the human body. There are exceptions to this rule: thus Carlo Ruini, a senator of Bologna, published in 1598 the first comprehensive treatise on the anatomy of an animal, *On the Anatomy and Diseases of the Horse*, which attempted for the horse what Vesalius had attempted for the human body, and equally successfully. One has only to compare Ruini's beautiful illustrations with the pathetically poor plates of the horse published earlier to see how well he achieved his aim. But this was unusual. In general even zoological anatomists like Ulisse Aldrovandi (1522–1605) or his pupil Volcher Coiter (1534–c. 1576), whose best work is on bird anatomy and embryology, were never unmindful that the real interest of such work was for ultimately medical ends; Aldrovandi was a lecturer on pharmacology at Bologna, while Coiter's portrait shows, by its inclusion of muscle dissections, that he valued his work in human anatomy most highly. Similarly, herbals and botanical works, often filled with lovely examples of Renaissance appreciation of nature, still tended to emphasise utility, as Theophrastus had done. The great interest of this, as of the preceding ages, was human anatomy and physiology on the one hand and medical and surgical practice on the other.

Most university appointments, of course, were in the medical faculties, and Padua particularly kept the tradition founded by Vesalius. Thus even Fabricius of Aquapendente (1537–1619) was more noted for his contributions to human anatomy than for his extensive work on embryology. And perhaps rightly so, for embryological work, in this period, however good, was a continuation of an old tradition. One could but copy Aristotle and open eggs on successive days, tracing the development of the chick as carefully as possible. Coiter and Fabricius both followed this method, noting much that Aristotle missed, but in default of microscopes not discovering anything that made a revision of basic theory essential. Fabricius also studied the developing embryo in human and animal subjects, relating his work to the prevailing interest in the blood vessels, heart and lungs. The doctrine of the pulmonary circulation had been taught by his predecessor, Realdo Columbo (d. 1559), but how much still remained to discover is indicated in Fabricius's own work on respiration and in his best known (and shortest) treatise, *On the Valves in the Veins* (1603). Fabricius was not the first to notice the valves, but he was the first to recognise them for what they are and to discuss them thoroughly in print. It is highly revealing of the wealth of machinery commonly available and the extent to which mechanical contrivances had made mechanical conceptions part of the scientific consciousness that Fabricius did recognise these structures as valves and see that they existed to regulate the flow of the blood stream. Secure in his conviction that the blood flows in both directions in the veins, he never adequately tested the actual functioning

472

of the valves, but assumed that they act only intermittently, to prevent all the blood from rushing into the extremities under the influence of gravity. It was left to Harvey to extend the mechanical analogy and to realise that these valves ensure unidirectional flow of the blood in the veins, and that toward the heart.

Somewhat enigmatically outside the main tradition, perhaps merely because he belonged to Pisa and Rome rather than to Padua, was Andrea Cesalpino (1519–1603), who dealt with the physiology of the blood and lungs in a rather different way. Cesalpino had studied under Realdo Columbo (who taught at Pisa as well as at Padua) and must have learned of the pulmonary circulation from him. His own views were presented in his *Peripatetic Investigations* of 1588, an ardent defence of Aristotelian doctrines, in which he was anxious to exalt the heart over the brain (in the matter of sensation) or the liver (in the matter of blood supply). In this work he discussed the pulmonary circulation at length; was the first to use the word 'circulation'; and correctly demonstrated that when a limb is ligatured the veins swell above the ligature. He concluded that in sleep (when the passions are quiescent) the veins send all their blood to the heart; when the subject is awake and the passions active, only some of the blood in the veins goes to the heart. Indeed, in the posthumously published *Practice of the Art of Medicine* (1606), he specifically said that the blood goes forth from both sides of the heart. Had Cesalpino been more interested in human physiology and less in Aristotelian defence, he might have investigated further and thought more clearly. What influence he had upon Harvey—who never mentioned his work—is not determinable. Cesalpino's botanical work (*On Plants*, 1603) is also a mixture of what is original and what is intensely Aristotelian; he is particularly good in his analysis of the structure of plants and the kinds of fruit they bear.

Both medical and surgical practice changed considerably in this period, though it is generally difficult to assess the value of the change in terms of cures wrought. Paracelsus had, earlier in the century, tried to found a new school of medicine, based upon mysticism, rejection of orthodox methods, and the introduction of chemical remedies. The mysticism is extreme and often, even for the sixteenth century, obscured the doctrine in the eyes of more rationally minded men; as the English surgeon William Clowes remarked pertinently, 'I had here likewise thought good to have spoken somewhat of Paracelsus, but I must confess his doctrine has a more pregnant sense than my wit or reach is able to construe; only this I can say by experience, that I have practiced certain of his surgical inventions, the which I have found to be singular good and worthy of great commendation.'[1] But the problems of assimilating Paracelsan medicine lay in

[1] *Selected Writings of William Clowes (1544–1604)* (ed. F. N. L. Poynter, London, 1948), pp. 46–7.

more than its mysticism, for chemical remedies, particularly in the first years of their introduction, were rightly suspect for their danger and violence. Even mercury, really useful in treating syphilis, was poisonous in excessive amounts, and a useful dose was difficult to administer successfully. Antimony, the favourite emetic of the Paracelsan school, was extremely violent and its chemistry was not understood until the very end of this period. Very few writers were thoroughly Paracelsan; more were like Alexander von Suchten, who praised antimonial medicines extravagantly in his *Book of the Secrets of Antimony* (1575), but was anxious to show that his knowledge was based more on experience than Paracelsus, though he admired him; or Joseph Du Chesne (Quercetanus), physician to Henry IV, who sometimes annexed good recipes to his pro-Paracelsan polemic. Antimony was much more thoroughly understood, both chemically and medically, after the publication of the *Triumphal Chariot of Antimony* of 'Basil Valentine' in 1604. The way was paved for the medico-chemical textbook by the *Royal Chemistry* of Oswald Croll (1580–1609), first published in 1608 and much reprinted throughout the first half of the seventeenth century, and, pattern of all later chemical textbooks, Jean Beguin's *Tyrocinium Chymicum* of 1610.

While the improvements effected by the introduction of chemicals into the pharmacopoeia were at best dubious, there is no doubt that the sixteenth century saw a marked improvement in the practice of surgery. Surgeons were more important, better educated and more in demand; this was partly the result of the new disease syphilis, which came within the surgeon's practice because the early symptoms were external, and partly the result of the increasing demand by captains and generals that they be accompanied to battle by a private surgeon, who thereby gained much experience. The barber-surgeons, who are the most notable in the sixteenth century, were all trained as army surgeons; their increase led to new regulations for the practice of surgery and the rise of a class of men well educated, if not academic. England and France especially saw improved surgical education and regulation about the mid-sixteenth century; and in England the London apprentice was required to attend lectures given at the Barber-Surgeons Hall by men like John Caius and William Clowes. New methods developed quickly under the influence of new experience; it was, for example, only in 1514 that Giovanni da Vigo publicised the method of treating gun-shot wounds with cautery, under the assumption that they were poisoned; thirty years later the French surgeon Ambroise Paré (1510–90) was writing strenuously and effectively against such methods. The English surgeon Thomas Gale (1507–87) was perhaps influenced by Paré, perhaps by experience, when he counselled mild dressings without cautery in *Certain Works of Chirurgerie* in 1563. Paré's rediscovery of the value of ligaturing arteries to stop haemorrhage in amputations was publicised by Jacques Guillemau in 1594; the first

English discussion of this method was published only two years later by the leading English surgeon of the day, William Clowes (1544–1604), who read of it in Guillemau's book and described it in his own casebook, *A Profitable and Necessary Book of Observations*. The possibility of applying common sense and skilled technique to an endless variety of cases made surgery in the sixteenth century a more exciting field of endeavour than it was to be again until the nineteenth century. Hence the casebooks of the more enterprising surgeons of the period, fascinating reading because of the skill displayed as well as because of the pungent criticism of conventional medicine and of the physicians, who jealously guarded their rights and refused to allow the surgeons to meddle with internal medicine. These men were by no means the illiterate barbers of an earlier age and their choice of the vernacular for their writings was as much in protest against the university Latin of the physicians as it was in a desire to reach the widest possible audience.

Much of what the seventeenth and later centuries have classified as experimental science lay, in the sixteenth century, within the province of natural magic. Natural magic, in spite of Francis Bacon's favourable view, was by no means identical with experimental philosophy, though it perhaps pointed out the road; it was rather mysticism and experiment combined in a characteristic blend. Many natural philosophers turned impatiently from traditional and slow methods of pursuing knowledge and looked to magic as a quicker route to the understanding of nature. With Marlowe's Faust (with whom they were contemporary) they could cry, 'Philosophy is odious and obscure, Both law and physik are for petty wits, Divinity's the basest of the three, 'Tis Magic, Magic, that hath ravished me.' The university curriculum seemed sterile even to sober men, so it is hardly surprising if the wilder spirits turned to a more promising, if dubiously permissible, form of learning. The sixteenth century regarded natural magic as distinctly mystic and heterodox, but useful and worthy of study, and the same man might combine magic and rational science without finding it at all difficult to reconcile the two. John Dee was an able mathematician and made important contributions to navigation; yet he was an astrologer and spiritualist. For him the link was natural magic, which he called Archemastrie, and which he praised extravagantly:

This Arte, teacheth to bryng to actuall experience sensible, all worthy conclusions by all the Artes Mathematicall purposed, & by true Naturall Philosophie concluded: & both addeth to them a farder scope, in the termes of the same Artes, & also by hys propre Method, and in peculiar termes, proceedeth, with the helpe of the foresayd Artes, to the performance of complet Experiences, which of no particular Art, are hable (Formally) to be challenged...*Science* I may call it, rather, than an Arte: for the excellency and Mastershyp it hath, over so many, and so mighty Artes and Sciences. And bycause it procedeth by *Experiences*, and searcheth forth the causes

475

of Conclusions, by *Experiences*: and also putteth the Conclusions them selves, in *Experience*, it is named *Scientia Experimentalis*.[1]

When words and mathematical arguments failed, then, Dee believed, 'the *Archemaster* steppeth in, and leadeth forth on, the *Experiences*, by order of his doctrine *Experimentall*, to the chief and finall power of Naturall and Mathematicall Artes'. For Dee—and for other natural magicians—the key to the understanding of the more difficult natural forces was experience or experiment. Though Kepler hoped to penetrate the secrets of the motion of the celestial bodies by means of Pythagorean number mysticism, most men agreed that experience, whether sense experience or mystic experience, was the true key. Natural magic was confined to precisely those areas where logic and mathematics failed to provide a clue, that is, to the unexplained properties of matter and the mysterious forces of nature. Alchemy, optics, astrology, pneumatics, hydraulics, geology, magnetism, electricity—these, where mysterious things occurred, with no mathematical law to explain why, were the areas of philosophy that natural magic professed to comprehend in terms of experience. And scholastic philosophy, confessedly ignorant, did not dispute its competence.

It should be remarked, however, that natural magic was still magic, and still mystic, even though it was half way to experimental science. Experience might be subjective as well as objective; alchemy was both the mystic search for the philosopher's stone and the rational search for useful medical remedies (though even the latter had its mystic aspects). Natural magic was esoteric learning. J. B. della Porta (*c.* 1535–1615) carefully separated the two in his definition, saying,

There are two sorts of Magick: the one is infamous, and unhappie, because it hath to do with foul spirits, and consists of Inchantments and wicked Curiosity; and this is called Sorcery...The other Magic is natural; which all excellent wise men do admit and embrace, and worship with great applause; neither is there any more highly esteemed, or better thought of, by men of learning.[2]

Yet his Academy of the Secrets of Nature was suspected of dealing with illicit mystic arts, and probably correctly. The mystic aspect explains why, for example, Dee published reluctantly, because he felt that scientific knowledge should be imparted only to the initiate. How far this feeling penetrated is attested by Tycho Brahe's comment on his alchemical work:

I have also made with much care alchemical investigations, or chemical experiments. This subject, too, I shall occasionally mention here, as the substances treated are somewhat analogous to the celestial bodies and their influences, for which reason I usually call this science terrestrial Astronomy...I shall be willing to discuss these questions frankly with princes and noblemen, and other distinguished and learned people, who are interested in this subject and know something about it, and I shall

[1] Preface to Henry Billingsley's English translation of Euclid (London, 1570).
[2] *Natural Magick. In XX Books* (London, 1669), pp. 1–2.

occasionally give them information, as long as I feel sure of their good intentions and that they will keep it secret. For it serves no useful purpose, and is unreasonable to make such things generally known. For although many people pretend to understand them, it is not given to everybody to treat these mysteries properly according to the demands of nature, and in an honest and beneficial way.[1]

Yet, at the same time, men were beginning to turn away from the secrecy, which they must have recognised made them suspect of worse practices than they aspired to. Porta's *Natural Magick*, published in 1558 (in four books) and then, after many editions, in an expanded version in 1589, was frankly a popularisation of its subject; it ranged from the generation of animals to the beautifying of women, from the counterfeiting of gold to cookery, from the art of tempering steel to optics, hydraulics, pneumatics, and the wonders of the loadstone. Porta rather curiously combined trickery, the delusion of the senses, with a critical spirit of experimental investigation. He was interested not in the way things are, but in the way they appear to be: so his study of optics was concerned with making near things seem far, or far near, and this is why he described lenses and the camera obscura. His interest in the loadstone was primarily in the design of toys; yet he tested experimentally the superstition that garlic affected the action of the loadstone and found it, as he suspected, nonsense. Combined with Renaissance enjoyment of knowledge for its own sake, knowledge for fun, is an equally Renaissance parade of learning, and Porta could quote Archimedes as enthusiastically as any mathematician of his day. This popularised natural magic is, admittedly, at a low level; but on all levels alchemy and optics and pneumatic machines were described and discussed with an openness that foreshadows the propaganda for the experimental learning of the next century.

At the scientific extreme of natural magic, where it nearly merged with experimental science, lies the great work of William Gilbert on magnetism. The *Treatise on the Loadstone and Magnetic Bodies* was learned, not popular, science, yet Gilbert in his review of the literature of magnetism did not exclude Porta or indeed any natural magician. His almost lyrical disquisition upon the magnetic soul of the earth, as well as his conviction that magnetism was an animating and universally pervasive force, bring his underlying philosophy very close to natural magic. At the same time, this is the first original treatise on magnetism since the thirteenth century, and the first thorough examination of electricity, which Gilbert was the first to distinguish clearly from magnetism. He demonstrated the magnetism of the earth; showed that the compass pointed to the terrestrial, not the celestial, pole; declared that perpetual motion by a loadstone was impossible; demonstrated the artificial production of magnetism (by hammering an iron bar laid in a north–south line); identified the loadstone with iron ore magnetised by the earth's magnetism; and discussed the

---

[1] *Astronomiae Instauratae Mechanica*, p. 118.

utility of magnetism to navigation and astronomy. His electroscope was at the same time a useful scientific instrument and the kind of engaging toy common to natural magic. While learned men accepted this as a great and important treatise in natural philosophy, the layman saw in it a superb piece of natural magic, and the smiths of London promptly made a great loadstone which could lift an anchor of 24 pounds weight, a spectacular method of making manifest one of the occult forces of nature. Seventeenth-century physicists like Robert Boyle (1626–91) were to seek to explain such occult forces in purely material terms; Gilbert was content to demonstrate the existence of occult and esoteric forces and the ways in which they worked. This was still natural magic, not the natural philosophy which seeks to understand as well as to describe.

Evidently, in experimental physics as in mathematical physics, a completely new point of view was required before natural philosophy could claim to have created a scientific revolution. The sixteenth-century scientists eagerly enquired into many fields and rejoiced in the idea that they were taking all learning to be their province. They saw where the ancients pointed, and followed; where the ancients failed, and they tried to succeed. But though they improved on the work of antiquity, they seldom broke free from it with a new method of approach. Thus they were much more mechanically minded, far more familiar with machines, than were the ancients; but though engineering flourished, the mechanical analogy and concept so characteristic of much of the best seventeenth-century science was only sparingly applied—the case of Fabricius shows how tentatively this notion was pursued. Perhaps only in natural magic was the sixteenth century truly original, and natural magic could not be scientific without ceasing to exist in all but name. John Wilkins published his *Mathematical Magick* in 1648, but it is not much more like Porta's work than are the *Letters on Natural Magic* of David Brewster, published in 1834. Natural magic in the hands of someone like Gilbert very nearly became experimental natural philosophy, but it did not quite do so. Gilbert was too firmly rooted in the sixteenth century to transcend its thought and limitations; for that one must look to Galileo. But Galileo, though educated in the sixteenth century, was a generation younger than Gilbert and his *Sidereus Nuncius* was only to appear in 1610, seven years after Gilbert's death. The fact that Galileo did transcend the framework of contemporary thought is a measure of his genius. For the essence of the scientific revolution did not lie only in achievement: it lay much more in a totally new frame of mind which made the achievement possible.

The difference between the later sixteenth century and the mid-seventeenth is well revealed by the different modes of association between scientists exercised in the two periods. In general, sixteenth-century groupings, which only appear after the mid-century, were informal. They tended to be of three sorts: either the old Renaissance master–disciple, almost master–apprentice, relation; or the patron–protégé relationship, where the rich man maintained or subsidised a scholar for his own edification, entertainment or prestige; or the relationship of initiates in a secret society, suspect and suspicious. The first is well exemplified by Tycho's Uraniborg, to which young scholars flocked from all over Europe for a year or two's training and research; the second by Harriot in his relations with Raleigh, for Harriot was the leader of a group of philosophers, natural, magical and theological; the third by the vague group supposed to have been organised by Gilbert, or the more formal Academy of the Secrets of Nature founded by della Porta and suppressed by the pope on suspicion of practising the black arts. These groups were at best devoted to instruction, at worst to mysticism; something of the idea of the initiation of a layman into the secrets of a master of knowledge lay behind all of them. There is nothing like the grouping together of free and equal spirits dedicated to the independent or collective pursuit of scientific knowledge, profoundly rational, bitterly opposed to magical, academic or secret learning, which is so characteristic of the first half of the seventeenth century.

In sum, one may say that the sixteenth century sought knowledge of things, and found what they sought, but no more. This knowledge was of many kinds, the results of a restless desire to know, to know especially Nature. So, in general, the science of the sixteenth century was descriptive and practical. It was not analytical; it was not even particularly synthetic. The astronomers, anatomists and natural magicians all saw where the problems lay, but they could not formulate these problems in terms that would admit solution. They could not yet find the method whereby the workings of nature could be understood in rational, simple terms, nor frame a system of the world (for Tycho's was not based upon fundamental principles, but was merely saving the appearances as well as might be). That was left to the next generation, which took such a brilliant step forward that it is properly regarded as the creation of a revolution. But even revolutions have to have origins, and the men who made the revolution were dependent upon the advances of their immediate predecessors. Many of the first generation of revolutionary scientists looked to a man of the preceding generation as his teacher and master who had, he thought, directed and encouraged him along the new roads to knowledge. Though the scientists of the later sixteenth century had not, in fact, found the clue to the successful study of nature, they had begun to break with the old ways, and they had indicated a number of possible and impossible paths. Above all, perhaps, they had shown how much it was possible to know, and at the same time how much there was still to learn. They gave to their pupils an overwhelming faith that the workings of nature could be understood, and, strong in this faith, their pupils found the method and the understanding.

CHAPTER XVI

POLITICAL THOUGHT AND
THE THEORY AND PRACTICE OF
TOLERATION

OUTSIDE Italy political thinking in the sixteenth century was focused on problems raised by the Reformation. In the first place the ordinary individual was forced into an altogether novel situation, and one fraught with the most serious consequences to his peace and security. For the first time humble individuals had to make a decision *for themselves* as to which of the various claimants was indeed the true church. There had, of course, been heretical movements in the middle ages. But even the most serious of these, such as the Lollard movement in England or the Hussite in Bohemia, had been localised. They precipitated no general crisis of conscience. To the great mass of the faithful, Rome was the citadel of the Catholic faith and those beliefs condemned by her were rejected without hesitation as indubitably heretical. Where there were no doubts, there were no decisions to be made. But in the sixteenth century Rome's authority itself was challenged, and great congregations, Lutheran, Calvinist, Anglican and Unitarian were organised, besides lesser sects such as the Anabaptists. Distinctive theologies were developed, noticeably by Calvinists and Unitarians, and rival theologians thundered mutual denunciations of their adversaries as heretics and children of Antichrist. Moreover, most of these churches took the traditional view that it is the duty of the secular arm to destroy the heretic, a duty which most princes in the earlier part of the century, for various mixed motives of their own, were ready enough to discharge. Any individual, therefore, however obscure, in making a decision as to what he believed, and to which church he adhered, risked exposing himself to the extreme penalties of loss of life, liberty or estate. Many so chose, and secular rulers found themselves involved in an attempt to stamp out heresy which, because unsuccessful, increasingly plunged their principalities into disorder. For them also, therefore, there was a practical problem of the utmost consequence. Should they, could they, destroy the heretic within their borders? It was the immediacy and intimacy of these problems that gave to the debates of the sixteenth century such vitality and such tension.

These new and unfamiliar predicaments, then, determined the lines upon which political thinking in the second half of the sixteenth century developed. The controversies of theologians, and the spectacle of so many churches claiming a monopoly of the truth, undermined the dogmatic certainty as to the absolute distinction between truth and error on which the conviction of the rightfulness of persecution was based. Before it ever became a political necessity, toleration was debated in principle and the compulsion of the individual condemned in the name of sanctity of conscience. In the second place, just because, both in theory and in practice, princes accepted the obligation to destroy heresy, what was originally a private and personal problem of discerning what was true became a public and political one of determining one's allegiance. It took the form of a debate on the right of resistance. On the subjects' side, those who had experienced, or feared they might have to experience, the rigours of the heresy laws and were not minded to submit meekly, justified rebellion by restating the doctrine that authority derives from the community. Their concern was with the rights of individuals. Princes on their side, threatened by the dissolution of their principalities should they persist in the attempt to coerce the heretic, developed the doctrine of sovereignty, or the doctrine of the independent and self-subsisting character of the state. Their concern was with the need for order. It was on these two debates, the debate on toleration and the debate on the right of resistance, that political thinking in the second half of the sixteenth century was focused.

On 21 July 1542 Paul III published the bull *Licet ab initio*, reconstituting the Holy Office of the Inquisition in Rome as a central authority for the whole of western Christendom. It was empowered to deal with the lapsed and the suspect and all those thought to be adherents, patrons or advocates of heretics. It could inflict imprisonment, confiscation or death, and call upon the ecclesiastical and temporal authorities to execute sentence. The bull did not, of course, initiate a policy; it only organised more efficiently the traditional one being pursued with varying degrees of intensity in different parts of the west. In France, for instance, men and women had been burned ever since the condemnation of Luther's writings in 1521, and since the affair of the *placards* in 1537 persecutions had been severe.

It was not so much the consequences of the bull that were of first importance as the affirmation of principle contained in the preamble. It restated briefly the case for persecution as presented by Aquinas.[1] He likened heretics to false coiners and heresy to treason, and argued by analogy that if the secular crimes, which merely threatened the safety of body and goods, are punishable by death, how much more should be the sin which endangers souls. The argument rested on a series of assumptions: that there is an absolute distinction between truth and error, whereby the single dogmatic system of the church expresses uniquely that which is true; that all other systems are not only error, but dangerous error, because acceptance of the true doctrine is the sole means to salvation; that acceptance of this truth is an irreversible act since once it is received it cannot be unlearned, but only perversely denied; that, the church being a corporate

---

[1] *Summa Theologica*, Secunda Secundae, quaest. XI, art. iii.

whole, the defection of any one member of it injures the whole body. These assumptions were so universally made in 1542 that there was no need to recite them in the bull. All that was required was to draw the conclusions, that the destruction of the heretic was necessary in order to preserve the Christian faith from damnable error and that obstinate and perverse corruptors must be treated in such a way as would not merely remove them but deter others from like offences. The whole argument was dictated by concern for the church, not for the predicament of the heretic.

But neither the bull nor the executions for heresy consequent upon the ideas on which it was based caused any controversy among Catholic writers. Paul III's action was the logical application of generally accepted principles and followed the established practice of the medieval church.

An altogether new situation was created ten years later when Calvin was instrumental in getting Michael Servetus burned in Geneva for heretical opinions on the Trinity. In his *Defensio* of 1554, writen to justify his action, Calvin took exactly the same stand as Paul III. The manifest and obstinate heretic must be destroyed as the rebel against truth who would betray others to their damnation. For Calvin's values were traditional. His intention was to replace one dogmatic system by another as absolute and exclusive in its claims as that which it was intended to supersede. He was, if anything, even more emphatic on the duty of the secular magistrate to act as the sword of the church and root out the ungodly at its direction.

But Calvin's action, unlike Paul III's, caused an immediate outcry among Reformers. Servetus's death came as a severe shock to Protestant opinion. He was the first person to be burned at the instance of a reformed church. Hitherto the Reformers had thought of themselves, not without some admixture of spiritual pride, as enjoying the monopoly of being persecuted for the truth's sake. It could not but be appreciated that Servetus's execution raised the question of persecution in its purest form. His doctrines were unmixed with any sort of social subversiveness—as were those of the Anabaptists, for instance—which might justify an attack on him as the enemy of order. The offence for which he died was that he held peculiar views on the Trinity. But he had made no attempt to propagate these views; he had expounded them obscurely in Latin, in a book addressed to learned persons; and, as Castellion pointed out, what he had to say passed unnoticed even by them till Calvin saw fit to draw attention to it for the purposes of refutation. Indignation over the incident precipitated a controversy among Reformers in which all the principles involved were brought to light. However traditional their values and conservative their intentions might be, Calvin and the other early Reformers struck at the root of medieval conceptions of authority when they submitted the dogmatic system of the medieval church to their private judgement and rejected its sacramental system in favour of a doctrine of the sufficiency of a personal experience—of justification or of election—for salvation.

The first persons to see that Calvin's action revealed a problem of heresy were a handful of remarkable men who all, by accident or attraction, made some sort of sojourn at Basel in the middle years of the century. The most influential was Sebastian Castellion, a former disciple of Calvin's, who opened the controversy by condemning persecution for opinions; Giacomo Acconcio, an Italian military engineer who found his way to England in that capacity and who wrote a book on the evils of dogmatic controversy, which he analysed with remarkable psychological insight; and Faustino Sozzini or Socinus, the theologian of the Unitarian churches. To Aquinas's question 'whether heretics are to be persecuted' they returned an emphatic negative. In marked agreement with one another they broke new ground by formulating a defence of toleration. They were led into doing so because they reversed the traditional viewpoint. Their concern was not for the safety of the church as a whole, but for the predicament of the individual 'heretic'.

The fundamental problem, therefore, was seen to be the problem of truth—what do we know, and how do we know it? In the *De Arte Dubitandi* Castellion laid the foundations of the argument against persecution by drawing a distinction between knowledge and belief. We can only have knowledge of what is true, and that depends on either sense experience or 'demonstration', that is, the logical consequences deducible from accepted premisses. But we can believe what is not true. Belief is based not on evidence or demonstration but on faith, and faith is the acceptance on trust of the word of an authority recognised as such by the believer concerned. It begins where knowledge ends, for what is or can be ascertained belongs to the realm of knowledge. Christian faith is therefore a virtue because it depends on an act of the will to believe, rather than upon an inescapable conclusion of the reason. Bodin, writing at the end of half a century of indeterminable controversy, put a more sceptical version of this view into the mouth of his natural philosopher Toralba. Theologians have tried many times to bring religion into the province of science and to show that its principles can be demonstrated from certain premisses to necessary conclusions. They have always failed; and, had they succeeded, faith would have been destroyed in the very act. For faith, according to these same theologians, is an act of simple acquiescence which requires no proof here on earth of the things of which the blessed have knowledge.

But if religious truth is based on faith and not knowledge, how were those things which must be believed to be determined? To what authority must this act of simple acquiescence be made? To say that God spoke not through an infallible church but in the inspired word of the Scriptures did not solve this problem of authority; it only altered its form and made it a question of the interpretation of the Scriptures. In the face of the evidence there were many who could not agree with Calvin's contention in the *Defensio* that the Scriptures need no interpretation. He argued that to suggest that they did was to imply blasphemously that the Lord God Almighty had failed of his intention to make any revelation at all. Those who could accept neither the Catholic belief in an infallible church nor the Calvinist view of the Scriptures necessarily adopted a position distinct from either. They claimed the right of each of the faithful to interpret for himself in accordance with the light that was in him and as his conscience should dictate. They were individualists of the sixteenth-century type, not in spite of themselves, as was Calvin, but consciously and deliberately. They were the apostles of self-sufficiency.

Castellion opened the attack on Calvin for the burning of Servetus by publishing in 1554 the *De Haereticis an sint persequendi*, under the assumed name of Martin Bellius. The book was a collection of passages from various writers from St Augustine to contemporary reformers such as Sebastian Franck. The dedication was to William of Hesse, and in a long introduction Castellion expounded his own views. He and all those who subsequently came to share his views started by denying Calvin's doctrine that there is an absolute division in the human race between the pre-destinate damned and the predestinate redeemed, and based their arguments on the assumption that it is the divine intention that all men should be saved. They held that it followed that the matter of the faith must be within the comprehension of all, and therefore simple, because they held that each must find it for himself in the Scriptures. They argued that the gospel of Christ was in the first instance preached to the poor and the lowly, and received by the poor gladly, whereas the learned in the persons of the scribes and pharisees rejected it. From this it was argued that what is comprehensible to the uninstructed and universally agreed among Christians is the moral content of the gospels, the way of life revealed in Christ. It is by their 'fruits' and not by their beliefs that we are told true believers may be known.

It was a short step from this insistence on right conduct rather than right opinions to an attack on dogmatic systems as such. This attack was made with great force and great eloquence by Socinus, especially in his *De fide et operibus*. Though both he and the congregations deriving from his teaching in east Europe and the Low Countries were distinguished in the eyes of contemporaries by their anti-trinitarian doctrine, they themselves regarded all dogma as of secondary importance. For Socinus the essence of the faith was not that men should have right notions of the nature of God—such as exact views of the mode of the inherence of the two natures in Christ—but a right disposition of the heart to embrace the way of life revealed in Christ. This is the message of the gospels, and the mark of the believer, to live after that model. The whole superstructure of dogma therefore elicited by either Catholic or Calvinist theologians was rejected, not so much on the grounds that it was false as that it was not necessary to salvation to be believed, and therefore irrelevant. The assumption that the theological and ethical elements in Christianity can be disjoined was the distinctive mark of 'Socinians'. To most believers they were mutually implied.

Dogma was also attacked on the ground that insistence on it generated schisms because men are not and never have been agreed about the precise doctrinal implications of the gospels. Castellion deduced that it is a matter of opinion simply. Acconcio launched a most effective attack on controversy as breeding schism. In 1561 he wrote the *Strategematum Satanae* in order to show that the persuasion that in one's own speculations one has found the truth to the exclusion of all others is a device of the devil to make men commit the sin of pride. From this follow anger, envy and the lust for power, as all doctrinal controversies show. Once a disputation starts, men seek not the truth but the triumph of their own views.

Such principles cut away the grounds upon which any man may be justly punished for his beliefs, for the basic assumption of an absolute and objective truth which only perversity could reject was denied. Truth is subjective; it is for each individual that which he can believe. What we are bidden to do, said Acconcio, is to seek the truth with humility. Each man believes that he has it. But it cannot be demonstrated that he has it, nor, if he has, that what he believes is necessary to salvation.

The distinction drawn between knowledge and belief therefore involved not only a distinction between what is demonstrated to be true and what is accepted as true, but also a distinction between what can be objectively proved and what is subjectively embraced by conviction. 'Socinians' therefore emphatically and logically denounced the forcing of men's consciences as a sin against the light. To persecute those who do not agree with you because you are persuaded that you alone have the truth is to commit the very error of the pharisees in crucifying Christ.

It is clear that the actual situation was responsible for this revolution of thinking. Castellion could say in 1554, what would have been unthinkable a century earlier, that there is no criterion whereby 'heresy' may be defined. The true believer in one place becomes the heretic in another; if one travels about, and wishes to escape the charge, one must change one's faith as one does one's money.

Carried to its logical conclusion, the argument implied the unqualified toleration of all beliefs whatsoever. Only very rare individuals wished to go as far as that. Most controversialists assumed that there is an ultimate objective truth that all men are capable of receiving, and the test is the test of agreement. Thinking within the framework of Christendom, and writing for a Christian society, they were able to assume that whereas men differed about doctrines, because they agreed that Christ was the Son of God and his life and teaching the pattern of all excellence, this is the matter of the revelation which is self-evidently true. When they argued that it is the moral teaching of the gospels and not their doctrinal implications that must be believed, the ground for their conviction was not only that it is this aspect of the gospels which is comprehensible to the simplest, but that it is the only aspect which commands universal agreement.

But Bodin, who was distinguished in everything that he wrote by the extensiveness of the field he surveyed and the originality of his conclusions, was aware that this was not so. He argued with passion both in the *Six livres de la République* and the *Heptaplomeres* that men must have religious beliefs; atheism is the supreme human catastrophe. But he demonstrated in the latter work that if the test of truth is universal agreement then Christianity is in no better case than any other religion. By including in his colloquy not only a Catholic, a Lutheran and a Calvinist but also a Mohammedan, a Jew, a philosopher and a sceptic, he widened the discussion to include the whole then-known field of beliefs. When, therefore, it is asserted as self-evident that Christianity is true, the Mohammedan, significantly a renegade Christian, objects that it is not accepted by the majority of men. Moreover, later in the discussion there is a long attack on the pattern of holiness exemplified in the life of Christ, that is, on precisely that aspect of the gospels which it was generally supposed commanded universal approval, as being unacceptable to many men and repugnant to their ideal of heroism. At the conclusion of the debate it is discovered that the only matter on which all are agreed is that the Decalogue is a succinct statement of those fundamental truths which are not simply matters of opinion but are recognised intuitively and are therefore universally true. The Jew, the Mohammedan and the Christians agree because they accept the Old Testament as the inspired word of God; the philosopher and the sceptic, because they hold that there is a natural religion known to all men as rational beings, the 'law written in the heart of the gentiles' of St Paul (whom the philosopher quotes), which is reducible to the moral precepts of the Ten Commandments. All of them concede in the end that once one proceeds beyond this point there is no agreement, and one is in the realm not of truth but of opinion. Opinions may be firmly held, but they are in the last resort incommunicable save to those already disposed to hold them. The sceptic observes that provided the First Commandment is obeyed and God is worshipped, he for his part is prepared to do so under any of the forms men practise.

But the *Heptaplomeres* is unique. Nowhere else in the sixteenth century can one find that union between a passionate conviction that men must believe in God and at the same time that extreme detachment as to the form in which that belief is expressed. So little did it represent any phase of sixteenth-century thinking that Bodin dared not publish it, and for long after his death it was known only in manuscript copies.[1] Its great interest lies in the fact that it is the comment of a man of original and capacious mind who saw more clearly than most where the argument was tending. If the church is to be based on agreement among individuals as to what they think to be true, then there must inevitably be an indefinite number of churches; for there is nothing self-evident in the mathematical sense about the truths of religion such as compels the concurrence of all reasonable men. Once this is admitted, one cannot claim privilege for any particular form of religion. What Bodin's personal convictions were must always be a matter of speculation. He excluded Christianity from the sphere of natural religion and based it on faith or the submission to authority. But what that authority is which can instruct men in those things of which the blessed have knowledge, he never indicated.

This was the fundamental way in which the case against persecution was approached, by an attack on the whole conception of heresy. But a good deal of the argument was focused upon the more immediate question of the appropriateness of a policy of persecution as a way of dealing with heretics, supposing they can be discerned. Calvin, defending the execution of Servetus, based his case on the express commands of God to the Israelites to slay the blasphemer and the idolator and on such examples from sacred history as the destruction of the prophets of Baal by Elijah. But Castellion dismissed the Old Testament as irrelevant to Christians living under the new dispensation, and appealed from it to the New Testament. Because Christ's teaching was directed to forming men's conduct rather than their opinions, there is no command in the New Testament to kill men for their beliefs. Instead, we are bidden to forgive one another until seventy times seven. The parable of the tares directly commands us not to attempt to root out the ungodly for fear of destroying the faithful at the same time. Persecution is dangerous; given the fallibility of all human judgements, what is destroyed may so easily be truth and not error.

Even more serious, as was frequently pointed out in view of the contemporary abundant evidence that fear could secure conformity, it forced men into the sin of hypocrisy. Persecution, being contrary to the express word of God, produces the fruits of unrighteousness. This is inevitably so because the means bear no relation to the end. In his preface to his translation of the Bible, dedicated to Edward VI, Castellion referred briefly to the absurdity of using the earthly weapon of the sword of compulsion for spiritual warfare which can only be waged by the word of persuasion. A few years later, in the *De Haereticis*, he included as an argument to this effect Luther's sermon, *Von weltlicher Obrigkeit*. Luther started from the doctrine of the separation of powers. There is the kingdom of God under

---

[1] The Latin version was first published in 1857 by L. Noack in an inferior text. R. Chauviré published an early French version, with a critical introduction (Paris, 1914).

Christ, and the kingdom of the world under the magistrate, and it is the latter alone which has the power of compulsion. 'Heresy is a spiritual thing which no iron can cut, no fire burn, and no water drown.' Violence is irrelevant because the spirit is not accessible to force. Each man is responsible for believing what he can and what he must, and another can no more determine what that should be than he can enter heaven or hell for him. And if what a man believes is error, 'God's word is the sole recourse against heresy, and if this does not avail, worldly constraint is vain, though the world be inundated with blood'. Force can only constrain the hand and the tongue and so set men on the road to perdition by compelling the weak to give the lie to conscience. It is to be noticed that in this version of the medieval doctrine of the separation of powers, Luther and Castellion were thinking not so much in terms of institutions and their jurisdictions, but of two distinct disciplines and their appropriate use.

These views recommended themselves in the first instance to the temperamentally unfanatical and enquiring Italians of the late Renaissance, the men whom Calvin contemptuously called 'Nicodemists' because they escaped persecution by outward conformity in the matter of Catholic worship on the ground of the indifference of dogma. Their dispersal after the publication of the bull *Licet ab initio* led to the foundation of churches whose confessions of faith were based on their teaching and included religious toleration as one of their principal tenets. Most of the Italians followed Lelio Sozzini (Laelius Socinus) to Poland and were responsible for the organisation of the Unitarian congregations in Poland and Transylvania. In Holland, on the other hand, there was a spontaneous local revolt against the rigidity of Calvinist theology, especially against the dogma of predestination. The Remonstrants, through their spokesman Coornhert, opposed compulsory confessions of faith on the ground that no doctrinal system could be, or should be, enforced, and criticised Calvinists for ignoring the spiritual and personal character of Christianity which requires the soul's free acceptance of the living word of God through faith.

In all this discussion the argument turned on the ethics of persecution in relation to the defence of true religion. But the actual situation not only suggested a rejection of the assumptions upon which persecution was based, but for the first time created conditions in which it was impracticable. Castellion already in 1554 sounded a note of warning to kings and princes. Persecution breeds those very disorders which, as a matter of duty and in their own interests, they must seek to remedy. In 1562, with the spectacle before his eyes of a France sunk in an anarchy of conflict from which there seemed no issue, he composed the *Conseil à la France désolée* in order to point out, with terrible urgency, that persecution is not only wicked, but futile. It was not possible for either side to give effect to an intention to 'root out the ungodly' and destroy its opponents; the two sides were too evenly matched. The only possible solution to the intolerable misery of France would be the acceptance of the principle of mutual toleration. Bodin put doctrinal controversies among the causes of the disruption of states; the passions generated can only issue in armed conflict, and controversy about matters not susceptible of demonstration, because of its inconclusiveness, breeds doubt to the point of atheism, and atheism strikes at the very root of all authority. When Bodin himself wanted to compose an elaborate religious disputation and came to write the *Heptaplomeres*, he excused it on the ground that it was to be confined to a private discussion among learned persons only.

Secular rulers, whether German princes, French statesmen, or the kings and queens of England, did not need to be reminded that religious disputes have political repercussions. But their concern was not for truth but for order, and as the century progressed it became increasingly clear that any attempt to respond to the demands of Catholic or Calvinist leaders and root out the ungodly merely plunged a divided society into anarchy. Sooner or later responsible rulers were bound to repudiate any such obligation. This was first done in a remarkable speech by the French chancellor, Michel de l'Hôpital, made on the very eve of the Wars of Religion at the opening of the estates of Orléans in 1561. It was remarkable for its implications rather than for what it actually said. He silently rejected, on the one hand, the Catholic and Calvinist doctrine that the king is under an obligation to establish or defend true religion and, on the other, Luther's doctrine that, things of the spirit being beyond the competence of the secular ruler, he is precluded from taking any action in the matter whatsoever. De l'Hôpital took his stand upon the state and its interests. It is the business of the statesman to maintain peace and order. He is the only competent judge of what conduces thereto and has power to act accordingly. The French government was therefore under no compulsion to attempt to establish any religion by force, because such attempts were patently leading to disorder. But neither was it precluded from taking any action it thought fit in relation to religious disputes, if it could thereby promote peace. His point of view found precise expression in the Edict of Nantes in 1598. On his authority as king, and in order to restore peace, Henry IV permitted the practice of two religions in his realm and determined the areas in which this might be done.

Whether he realised it or not, what de l'Hôpital said (and also what the French government implied by its action in 1598) had far-reaching implications. He was asserting that the state exists in its own right as the guarantor of peace and security and as such determines its own actions without reference to any prior spiritual authority of which it is the instrument. Fourteen years later Jean Bodin, a servant of the crown, and an adherent of the party of the *politiques*, who subscribed to these views, made explicit in his *Six livres de la République* the implied dogma of the sovereignty of the state. The distinguishing mark of the state is sovereign power, a power which is in its essence unlimited, undivided and unconditioned, for, if any have power to impose limits and conditions, that very fact makes him or them the true sovereign. Those in whom this power is vested therefore make law and frame policy at will, institute to all office, are the source of justice and its final resort on appeal, are entitled to exact oaths of allegiance and command the obedience of the subject without qualification. It is true that Bodin requires his sovereign to be subject to the dictates of divine and natural law. But he does not identify this law with the doctrine of any organised church. This law is for him those moral principles epitomised in the Decalogue, whose sole claim to absolute validity he was concerned to demonstrate later in the *Heptaplomeres*.

It can be argued, of course, that, in preserving the priority of the moral order, he had not got so far as Machiavelli and his Italian contemporaries in seeing the state not only as existing in its own right but also as a law unto itself and the standard of action for all its citizens, whereby patriotism becomes the supreme virtue. Bodin most profoundly believed in the priority and universality of the moral order. It is the end of the state to establish the right regimen which enables its citizens to find justice and truth as well as peace and security. But the authority of a ruler who does not attempt to do this is irregular rather than invalid. He includes tyranny among the various possible forms of the state and will not allow the subjects of the tyrant any right of forcible resistance. He makes no reference to the church or the prince's relation to it. But he was clearly of opinion that to the prince belonged the determination of the policy to be pursued in matters of religion, since the very existence of the state depends on its rulers being able to prevent disruption through dissension. He advises the prince to forbid disputations altogether, as destructive of both religion and order. Bodin's doctrine of sovereignty, then, involves a doctrine of the autonomy of politics. He sees the state as the only organisation with power to direct men to their ends. In so far as men mutually recognise principles of justice and an impulse to worship God, it is the state's business to secure conditions under which men may do so. This is what he means by saying that its laws must conform to divine and natural law.

It is evident that it was the problem of anarchy, into which France was being plunged as a result of the attempt to establish true religion by force, that drove Frenchmen to develop a doctrine of the sovereign state. Machiavelli had no more to do than to systematise established and familiar Italian practice when he treated the ruler as a law unto himself. For Frenchmen, a revolution in thought and practice was required. Francis I and Henry II had accepted the role of executor of the church in the destruction of heresy and so admitted the priority of spiritual ends. Henry IV put the peace and order of the realm first and treated heresy accordingly.

In Germany, of course, the princes' right to establish by law that form of religion which they deemed desirable had been officially recognised at Augsburg in 1555 by the adoption of the principle of *cuius regio eius religio*. But the issues there were less clear than in the great monarchies to the west. The fragmentation of political authority made it possible for each prince to disregard the dissident minority among his own subjects. He could establish 'true religion' without risking temporal disaster, for the recalcitrant could be relied on to withdraw to some neighbour state of their own persuasion. In Germany, therefore, there was no body of literature produced in which the claims of the state as such were the subject of discussion. The conflict there had not been so much one between the princes and their subjects—save for such sporadic outbreaks as the Peasants' Revolt or the Anabaptist rising in Münster—as one between the princes and the emperor, and so was solved in terms of the particular rights of a group of rulers.

But the English government, like the French, had to try to solve— it could not evade—the problem of religious differences. Elizabeth and her advisers were as secular in outlook, and as exclusively concerned with order, as were the *politiques*. But their problem presented itself in a rather different form. A unique situation was created in England by the claim to the royal supremacy 'over all persons and in all causes as well spiritual as temporal' under which a distinctive form of public worship was established by law. The action of the English government appeared much more revolutionary in its implications than anything done in France, for it would seem to reject the traditional view, still generally held, that there was a necessary separation between church and commonwealth and to have required a doctrine of state sovereignty much more absolute than anything demanded by the French situation. French kings went no further than to determine the legal position of the churches whose origins were unquestionably independent.

In fact Elizabethan statesmen tried to avoid revolutionary theories by insisting on the exclusively secular character of the state and relegating religion as such outside politics. But they were nevertheless driven to compromise themselves because they were persuaded that unity of public worship was a condition of public order. 'Is it meet that every man should have his own fancy to live as him list?' exclaimed Whitgift, and went on to enlarge upon the 'intolerable contention and extreme confusion' which would follow if this were allowed, and the danger to which the commonwealth, beset by external perils, would be exposed. In the interests of public order, therefore, a revised rite was imposed by law and attendance at public worship required on pain of a fine. Fines were increased for hearing Mass, and persistent frequenting of 'conventicles' incurred the sentence of banishment by the act of 1581. But heresy ceased to be an indictable offence, and no one could be required to make any statement as to what he believed save only beneficed clergy, and then only as a condition of entering into the benefice. It was consistently maintained throughout the reign that it was the queen's intention to promote a decent and seemly order in externals. It was as consistently maintained that it was not her intention to dictate what a man should believe or to enquire into tender consciences.

The bull of deposition of 1570 made it much more difficult to frame a policy which should observe this distinction between belief and practice and leave the former untouched. Thereafter to be a Roman Catholic was *ipso facto* to be required to repudiate the queen's claim to obedience as the legitimate sovereign of the realm. By the Act for Retaining the Queen's Subjects in Obedience of 1581 those who took the initiative in reconciling subjects to the see of Rome became liable to the penalties of high treason, because such action was regarded as withdrawing subjects from their allegiance. In a pamphlet published in 1583 under the title *The Execution of Justice in England*, defending these measures, it was insisted that the Jesuit missionaries were prosecuted not for their religion but for endangering the queen's throne. It was added that no action had been taken, nor was contemplated, against any persons for accepting the pope's spiritual supremacy provided they did not make it grounds for repudiating the queen's authority. The very severe treatment of Jesuits, especially during the last decade of the reign, always took the form of treason trials. Whatever the justice of any particular conviction, the principle on which the government acted was that laid down by Locke a century later in his first *Letter on Toleration*: the state is only concerned with religious beliefs when they issue in action detrimental to its interests, but in that case it can take such action as it thinks necessary to defend them.

In fact it proved impossible to satisfy numbers of the queen's subjects that what men believed, and the forms under which they worshipped, could be so distinguished. Those who agreed that the concerns of the state are purely secular—a small minority—objected in principle to the establishment of forms of worship by law. This group were the Separatists, and their first systematic apologist was Robert Browne. In his *Treatise of Reformation* (1582) he emphatically asserted the indifference of the state to religion and denounced any attempt on its part to make provision as destructive of the true character of the church. He held a version of the doctrine of election. Faith is the establishment of a relationship between God and the individual soul whereby the regenerate are separated out from the sinful world. A church is a voluntary society of such individuals. In *The Book which Sheweth* and *The True and Short Declaration* he elaborated the idea of the 'Gathered Church'. He attracted a following which acted upon its principles and proceeded to associate into little independent communities for the purpose of worship. In 1592 Francis Johnson, pastor of the London church, and fifty-three of his congregation incurred the sentence of banishment for frequenting conventicles.

Such doctrines precluded any attempt by the state to establish a church, as Browne pointed out. Any attempt to set up a church by compulsion must be the work of the magistrate and not of the Spirit, and therefore not a church at all. He freely denounced the established church for being a political device, and the bishops for their lack of spirituality. His views entailed a belief in toleration in principle. If regeneration is a consequence of the free operation of the Spirit and the church a community of the regenerate, it follows that there must not only be no attempt to compel or punish men in the matter of their religion, but that they must be as free to associate and to determine forms of association as they are to believe. It is to be noticed that this is not quite the same defence of toleration as was made on the continent. The emphasis is different. Browne was not so much concerned to preserve the integrity of the individual in his search for truth as to remove all lets and hindrances to the free operation of the Spirit. He faced more squarely than did his continental brethren the consequent dissolution of the one authoritative church into an indeterminate number of voluntary associations.

The vast majority of the queen's subjects held no such views. They agreed with her that the ruler is vitally concerned with the matter of church order. But both the extreme Catholic and the extreme Protestant refused to accept the authority of the actual church established by law. They held that it had no validity because a thing of her own devising, to serve her own purposes; whereas her duty was to establish *true* religion, and what that was, was not for her to determine. The authority of the established church was rejected, on the one side, because the spiritual supremacy of the pope in Christendom was denied and, on the other, because its episcopal organisation did not conform to that presbyterian form of church government claimed to be prescribed in the Scriptures. Moreover, though both Roman Catholics and Puritans alike were reluctant to admit it, their political allegiance was involved. The bull of deposition clearly implied that the secular state could claim the allegiance of Christian subjects only if it framed its policy in accordance with the requirements of the church. And the puritan Cartwright could only have meant the same thing when he said in his *Second Admonition to Parliament* that 'the Commonwealth must agree with the Church, and the government thereof with her government'.

Resistance, therefore, to Elizabeth's government was focused on her religious policy, on the ground that in establishing the church in the form she chose, or in establishing the church at all, she exceeded the authority proper to the secular ruler. The problem of sovereignty in England was therefore the problem of the royal supremacy. If resistance was to be condemned, both the fact of a church by law established, and the form that it had taken, had to be defended. That defence was first taken up by Anglican bishops. They at once found themselves involved in the whole question of the authority of the secular ruler. It was the need to show that

493

this extended to the prescribing of forms of public worship that gave its distinctive—and 'inexportable'—form to the English version of state sovereignty.

The discussion started on the level of particular controversies. Bishop Bilson in his dialogue *The True Difference between Christian Subjection and Unchristian Rebellion* (1583) replied to Cardinal Allen's *Defence of English Catholics*; and Whitgift engaged Cartwright in his *Answer*, and *Defence of the Answer* of 1572. The position taken up by each of them in rebutting the political Augustinianism of the extreme Catholic and Calvinist position was not to deny the dogma of the separation of the spiritual and temporal spheres or the priority of the spiritual order in respect of final ends, but to redefine the terms and, in so doing, profoundly modify the concept of authority in either context.

The true Catholic church, said Bilson, that church which cannot err, is the whole congregation of the faithful, and its mind is expressed in the 'ancient and godly rules of Christ's Church generally received by all good Christians'; or, as Whitgift thought, in enduring tradition, 'that which hath been believed at all times and in all places by all persons'. Final authority is in the *consensus fidelium* directly expressed. On these grounds post-patristic developments in the medieval church were rejected as corruptions of this original deposit of faith and not commanding universal agreement. This is what Whitgift in his *Defence of the Answer* called the substance and matter of church government, the universal and unchanging dogmas of the faith, to be accepted absolutely by all Christians, princes as well as the rest. Over matters of faith and the administration of the sacraments both he and Bilson were emphatic that princes who bear the temporal sword can have no jurisdiction whatever. Rather their function is to be the church's 'aids and defences' against enemies.

But to the church in this sense of the body of the faithful, neither Bilson nor Whitgift would allow any distinctive organ of government. Neither the pope, said Bilson, nor even a general council can bind it. The authority of the spiritual sword whereby it is governed is vested in no person, or body of persons, but in the Word simply. Whitgift therefore distinguished the 'substance and matter of church government about which it is occupied, and the form to attain the same'. Whereas the former is universal and unchanging, the latter should be 'disposed according to the state of times, places and persons'. And the disposer, they both agreed, is the Christian prince. Bilson held extreme divine-right views. Princes are instituted to their office directly by God, in virtue of which they receive the temporal sword which is the power, not merely of compulsion, but of all effective action. Therefore, it is a power which necessarily extends over matters ecclesiastical as well as material. The prince's office, he held, was as much an office *in* the church as that of the bishop. He must protect it by punishing all heresies and schisms and order it by determining forms of worship upon the advice of bishops and pastors. Whitgift in his *Answer* therefore boldly enunciated the revolutionary doctrine of the identity of the Christian commonwealth and a Christian church considered as organisations. 'I perceive no such distinction of the Commonwealth and the Church that they should be counted as it were two several bodies governed with divers laws and divers magistrates, except the church be linked with an heathenish and idolatrous commonwealth.'

The exception is important. Just because it is the universal church of Christ which is the 'right end of all earthly states', it is only the Christian prince in a Christian community who can effect a particularisation of it in time and place. As a Christian magistrate, it is his obligation to do so, and what he does must be conformable with Christian faith and practice as it has been handed down from the foundation of the church. The diversity of rites to be expected if every Christian prince has power to order public worship was accepted as in no way destroying the unity of the Holy Catholic and Apostolic Church, 'for the Communion of Saints standeth not of external rites'.

Anglican bishops in general were not reformers in the continental sense. They repudiated any desire to form the church *anew* after any model, scriptural or otherwise. For them the Church of England was a continuing member of the historic Catholic and Apostolic Church as it had always subsisted. They did not therefore make the distinction between truths necessary for salvation and those matters which the individual could decide for himself. As has been seen, Whitgift did not think it seemly that every man should have his own fancy to live as him list. What they did distinguish was the authority of the church in matters of faith which all claiming the name of Christian must accept; and the authority of the Christian prince in matters of church order, to which the subject must submit, provided always that what is ordered 'makes no breach in faith'. The priority of divine law to positive law meant, therefore, something much more definite for them, despite the identification of church and commonwealth, than it did for Bodin. They identified it with the creeds and the sacraments of the historic Christian church.

In this way it was argued that there are no grounds for resisting either the fact of the royal supremacy or the way in which it had been exercised under Elizabeth. But the argument was stated dogmatically and as such did not satisfy the greatest of all the English controversialists, Richard Hooker. His controversial purpose was the usual one of exposing the error of the puritans in appealing from the tradition of the church to private conscience. But Hooker was not content to make assertions: he wished to show cause. In *The Laws of Ecclesiastical Polity*, therefore, he set out to examine the immediate and contemporary situation in its universal context, the principles of right order as they are known to men as rational beings.

The radical disagreement between him and the puritans can be traced back to opposing views as to what the human predicament is, expressed in terms of the fall of man. For Calvin and all those Protestant sects which derived from his theology, man's free will and his rational insight were alike totally corrupted by the fall. Both will and reason are enslaved to the passions, so that men have no means of knowing truth save by revelation nor capacity for virtue save by the arbitrary operation of divine grace. To the creature so fallen, God is only perceivable as inscrutable will, pre-determining the fate of all his creatures 'selon son bon plaisir'. Grace, therefore, where it is bestowed, abrogates corrupted nature. It is only the small company of the elect and the justified who have the truth; the great majority of mankind are in outer darkness, sunk in their natural condition of ignorance and sin.

Hooker took a much less extreme view. More especially, he believed that men have in their rational faculty a sure guide, within its own field of operation, to both truth and goodness; for in virtue of this faculty all men participate in the divine nature. Therefore all men, fallen as they are, naturally seek truth and are inclined to virtue. Castellion had made the same point in his *De Arte Dubitandi* when he asserted dogmatically that it was only the will that was corrupted by the fall; sense and intellect were uncorrupted, though impeded in their perfect operation by the mis-direction of the will. Hooker builds his whole argument on the assumption of the validity of reason and its priority to will.

The Laws of Ecclesiastical Polity opens, therefore, with a discussion of the perceived rational order of the universe. It is an order because its regular operation is governed by the eternal law which God has set down for Himself and all His creatures to follow. The particular modes of operation of each kind of creature derive therefore from the eternal law. These are the laws of nature, obeyed of necessity and involuntarily by their several agents. Men, made uniquely in the image of God, are governed by the law of reason, as voluntary agents. Hooker's concept of reason was Thomist. He thought of it not simply as the calculation of means to ends which are essentially irrational, but as intuitive knowledge of values. Therefore, because it is the faculty whereby men know what is true and what is good, reason indicates the ends to which will is directed. Men exhibit their fallen nature not so much in the total enslavement of the will to the passions as in that disorder that makes them seek the lesser good of immediate satisfactions rather than the higher good which is that mode of conformity with God intended for each of his creatures. Sin is not desiring evil for evil's sake—no rational agent, Hooker held, could do so. All things in heaven and earth are of God, and good after their kind. Sin is introducing disorder into the divine harmony by disturbing the hierarchy of values, and preferring the lesser to the greater good.

From these premisses Hooker deduced the authority of the collective over individual judgement. The puritan contention that it is the elect only who have the truth seemed to him intolerable pride and presumption. Reason is of God, and given to all men as men. A general persuasion of the truth of any matter is sufficient evidence that it is the truth: 'That which all men at all times have learned, nature herself must needs have taught... for the voice of all men is as the sentence of God Himself.' Hooker, like Bodin, made universal agreement the test of truth and for the same reason, that it must be based on rational insight. But he used the idea for a very different purpose. Bodin used it to demonstrate the uncertainty, because of the lack of unanimity about most of the things men believe. Hooker used it to establish the authority of collective over individual opinion.

By bringing the state within the natural order, Hooker could conclude that it was at once a manifestation of divine providence and a contrivance of human reason. Men are 'naturally inclined to seek communion with others', partly from an imparted sociability and partly in order to supply wants by mutual assistance. Therefore, they live in politic societies, and such societies imply government; that is to say, the instinctive impulse to associate issues in a deliberate and conscious effort at organisation. It follows, therefore, that the forms of law and government are devised by men and established by agreement. Any particular politic society is 'an order expressly or secretly agreed upon touching the manner of their union or living together'. And, men being what they are, fallen creatures, they need not only a recognised government, but positive laws which give 'regiment', or compulsive force, to the law of reason. Positive law, unlike natural law, however, is conditioned by time and place, for it is shaped by 'sundry particular ends'. But its foundations, like those of the forms of political society, are consent. 'Laws they are not which public approbation hath not made so.' Hooker therefore rejected the doctrine of many of his Anglican contemporaries and successors that government is directly *de jure divino*. Forms of government and forms of law are determined by human wisdom, for reason is the God-given means by which men can order their lives in society.

But though Hooker founded the state and all its works on consent, his doctrine was not individualist. It did not spring from any theories about natural rights, nor involve the counting of heads or majority rule. His mental world was much nearer to that of Aquinas than to that of Locke. No one man, as an individual, can of right command any other man. But the totality of individuals that make up a politic society can corporately command the several members of the community. Only the whole is greater than the part and the part is ordained to the whole. So little has *individual* consent to do with the authority of the commonwealth over its members that, however old laws and institutions may be, they are assumed to be based on the consent of those to whom they apply until there is a general agreement to alter them, because until that happens they have the authority of the collective wisdom over particular predilections. Hooker therefore rejected any right in the individual, or group of individuals, to resist either the established order which was generally approved or ancient traditions that had stood the test of time.

But Hooker, of course, was a rationalist after the thirteenth- and not the eighteenth-century model. Reason is a sure guide, but not a sufficient guide if men are to attain to their final end, which is union with God. Like Aquinas, he held that this supernatural end required a supernatural law to direct men to its attainment. There is a divine law based not on the operation of reason but of grace. But for him, as for Aquinas, grace does not abrogate nature, but perfects it; the limitations of the reason are transcended by revelation and the disordered will perfected by grace.

These premisses brought Hooker to the point where he could consider the puritan claim to disobey the laws of England relating to public worship. It was here that he parted company with St Thomas and contemporary Thomists like Suárez and Cardinal Bellarmine. Like Whitgift and Bilson, he distinguished the church universal, consisting of all those united in the Christian faith, from the church considered as an organised society of such persons. The church in the first sense is of God and belongs altogether to the sphere of divine law. In the latter sense he brought it within the sphere of natural law. It is a supernatural society in that it exists for a supernatural end, and the doctrine and discipline whereby that end is to be attained are therefore the concern of divine law. But as an organised society its foundations are the same as those of a political society, that is to say, a natural inclination to associate and general consent to the bond of association. Upon these grounds Hooker concluded with Whitgift that the church and the commonwealth are one. They cannot be disjoined by reference to ends, for natural and supernatural are ordered hierarchically. Nor can they be distinguished by reference to the persons constituting them—where 'the whole commonwealth doth believe', that very fact makes it a church.[1]

Till all Christians unite into a single state, 'the Church of Jesus Christ is every such politic society of men as doth in religion hold that which is proper to Christianity'. In the interests of order a unitary society requires a single government. In England that government is the crown in parliament and the care of religion is as much its concern, being a Christian commonwealth, as the maintenance of order.

His doctrine, of course, was not Erastian and did not in any sense imply a theory of the autonomy of politics. He emphasised that both the church and the commonwealth are societies organised by man to give effect to a higher law whose realisation is their end. The laws and institutions of the commonwealth are only valid in so far as they are based on the law of

[1] For a discussion of the authenticity of the later books of *The Laws of Ecclesiastical Polity* see C. J. Sisson, *The Judicious Marriage of Mr Hooker*, ch. IV (Cambridge, 1940).

reason; the laws and institutions of the church are only valid in so far as they are based on divine law. The just order of Elizabeth's government in temporal affairs was not in dispute and Hooker did not give it his attention. But her religious establishment was questioned, and the central books of the *Laws of Ecclesiastical Polity* are devoted to the detailed demonstration of the truth of Whitgift's assertion that 'in the Church of England we have all points of religion necessary to salvation...as purely and perfectly taught as ever they were in any Church sithence the Apostles' time'. It carried no weight at all with any of the puritans, for they could not accept his assumption of the validity of the reason and all that followed from it. Their concept of law was voluntarist, not rationalist; they looked for truth not in the collective judgement of reasonable men but in the illuminated elect; they admitted no distinction between matters of faith and matters of church order, for they held that all these things indifferently were laid down in the Scriptures.

In defending the royal supremacy Anglican clergy concurred in the official view that the sovereign authority of the crown included authority to determine by law the form of public worship, and they also agreed that unauthorised forms could not be tolerated. But the grounds of their conclusions were different. So far were they from regarding the state as a purely secular affair concerned only with order and indifferent to religious beliefs that they argued that a Christian commonwealth was *ipso facto* a church within the universal church and that the Christian magistrate united in his person power over temporal and ecclesiastical affairs. The exalted notion of sovereignty that was implied was reinforced by the very general belief in divine right. Rebellion against the ruler appointed by God was not only a crime but a sin. Hooker was peculiar in his generation, not only among Englishmen but in the west generally, in basing the duty of obedience on consent. The doctrine that authority to command is founded on the consent of those commanded was everywhere connected with the vindication of the right of resistance.

The insistence on the claims of authority and the duty of obedience in both England and France was the direct reaction to religious strife of those who valued peace and order. Such insistence would not have been necessary had there not been powerful groups who lived by other values. To the ideal of order was opposed that of liberty. As a political concept it was developed not by 'Socinians' and those who believed on principle in liberty of conscience but, paradoxically, by Calvinists who utterly rejected the whole concept of toleration.

Calvin himself, when he came to discuss temporal authority in the last book of the *Instituts de la Religion Chrétienne*, condemned resistance utterly on the ground that it involves rebellion against that order which, because it is there, must be so by divine dispensation. The magistrate is 'vicaire de dieu' and to resist him is to resist the ordinance of God. At the same time he laid upon the magistrate the obligation of establishing true religion as his first duty and punishing the wicked as his second. But as soon as a situation arose in which a strong Calvinist minority had every prospect of protecting itself against persecution by resisting it—that is to say in France, in Scotland, and in the Low Countries—the duty of establishing true religion was stressed at the expense of the duty of submission to the heretic or wicked ruler.[1] It was done by extending the obligation to the community in general.

This is clearly illustrated in the anonymous *Vindiciae contra tyrannos* of 1579.[2] The author has travelled a very long way from Calvin. The 'powers that be' are no longer thought of as representing directly and in all circumstances the inscrutable will of the Almighty. The secular state is described as the outcome of a mutual covenant entered into by prince and people with God to establish true religion. Each is the guarantor of the other. The prince's part is to establish true religion and punish the heretic and blasphemer; the people's, of compelling him to do so by resisting any action of his detrimental to that end. It is, of course, assumed that these engagements present no practical difficulties because true religion is manifestly that taught by the Calvinist church.

It was an easy step from the doctrine of resistance on grounds of religion to resistance on political grounds, and that step was taken by most leading Calvinists in the last quarter of the century. Calvin's simple Pauline teaching was refined upon in two ways. In the first place the prince's function was no longer thought of as simply the punishment of wicked men, but in positive terms as the maintenance of the order of justice, the counterpart in the secular sphere of his obligation to establish true religion in the spiritual sphere. In the second place, and even more subversive of Calvin's doctrine of the relation of the subject to the ruler, though the powers that be are ordained of God, the people act as the agents of the divine action. With writers such as Theodore Beza and the author of the *Vindiciae contra tyrannos*, the transition is made from a theocratic to a secular theory of the state, conceived of in terms of popular right.

This development can first be seen in Beza's *Du droit des magistrats* of 1576. All power is of God; the obligation to obey, therefore, is an obligation to God. But Beza distinguishes the office and the person holding it. The authority attached to an office is by divine right; but the provision of persons to fill that office belongs to the people. The particular ruler is therefore instituted by the people, and as such answerable to them for the right use of his authority. Three years later the author of the *Vindiciae contra tyrannos* carried the argument a step further by inquiring into the foundations of this popular right. He goes back to the very old hypothesis of an original and natural condition of innocence. But there are certain

[1] See above, pp. 94–100.
[2] Translated as *The Defence of Liberty against Tyrants* by H. L. Laski (London, 1924).

novel and significant features about his treatment of the theme which look forward to the later concept of the state of nature rather than back to the old concept of a Golden Age or the Garden of Eden. Men by nature, he says, love liberty and hate servitude. They therefore do not submit to any curtailment of that liberty save for some advantage, such as defence or the maintenance of the order of justice. Such a step became necessary when the words 'mine' and 'thine' were first used and disputes arose about property. Kings were therefore instituted to defend the community as a whole from outside attack and the weaker members within it from the depredations of their stronger neighbours. A covenant was therefore entered into between the people and the king by which he engaged absolutely to rule justly and the people were engaged conditionally to obey so long as he did so. The old distinction between the king and the tyrant, that the tyrant rules according to his own arbitrary will and the king according to the law, is preserved. But the meaning of the distinction has changed. The priority of law follows not so much from the assumption that it is to be identified with the order of justice, but from the fact that it is the act of the people, making provision for the common advantage. The people are the source of law as well as of government, because the common good is better provided for by the collective wisdom of the many than by the particular wisdom of any individual. The king therefore receives the law, as well as his office, from the people. He is its guardian and its organ; the law is the soul of a good king and gives him motion, sense and life. His coronation oath solemnly engages him to keep his covenant with his people and do justice according to the law they devise.

It is quite clear that this is a contract of government and not a social contract. It is assumed that the natural condition of men is a social one and that it is the people collectively who institute a king and covenant with him. This is evident from what the author says on the subject of resistance. The heretic or tyrant king must be resisted and deposed. But this duty belongs not to any private individual, but to the magistrates as holding public office, for they alone can act on behalf of the community as a whole and are responsible with the king for the public welfare. 'Private and particular persons may not unsheath the sword against tyrants, because kings are not established by particular persons but by the whole body of the people.' Should the magistrates fail to act, then the individual has no remedy but in prayer, submission or flight. Beza agreed. Both authors were fully alive to the danger of anarchy should it once be conceded that the individual may determine for himself when the covenant has been broken and that his duty requires him to resist the prince.

The way out of the difficulty was to postulate that all holders of office, as public persons, share in the obligations of sovereignty. If the king, as supreme magistrate, fails of his duty, then it devolves upon the lesser magistrates, his subordinates. It was a view very generally held. In the

Vindiciae contra tyrannos a distinction is drawn between officers of the king who have charge of his person and officers of the kingdom who have charge of the commonwealth. The latter derive their authority from the people, are responsible for the preservation of rights under the covenant, and for raising the standard of resistance in the name of the people should the king fail of his duty to religion or to justice. Bodin made the same point when he argued that public office belongs to the commonwealth and not to the prince—who has the power only of the provision of persons—and that holders of office are therefore individually responsible for seeing that justice is done and cannot excuse themselves by pleading royal commands.

What is forward-looking in this account is the concept of liberty. Calvin's doctrine that man's primitive liberty was lost with the fall, and the present condition of mankind is one of enslavement to sin and to government, has been altogether abandoned. Life and liberty have become indefeasible rights and the mark of man: 'The law of nature teaches and commands us to maintain and defend our lives and liberties, without which life is scant worth the enjoying, against all injury and violence.' Government is no longer thought of as the divine punishment and remedy for sin, but as the means by which rights are secured. Obedience due is no longer an unlimited obligation to submit to a discipline divinely ordained, but a limited obligation to obey the ruler appointed by the community only so long as he serves the purposes for which he was instituted. Liberty, that is to say, is conceived of in political terms, as secured by government. But it is clear that when Beza and the author of *Vindiciae contra tyrannos* substituted popular right for divine right as the immediate source of authority in order to justify resistance, neither of them founded popular right in any doctrine of individual natural rights. Both condemned individual resistance. Liberty is the collective right of the whole community to choose its own rulers and make its own laws for the common good. The Frenchmen were thinking in terms of corporate Calvinist communes which offered corporate resistance to the French monarchy.

A Scotsman, however, George Buchanan, in the *De jure regni apud Scotos*, anticipated in all essentials the later doctrine of natural rights. He starts his argument from the natural sociability of man. Men are by nature sociable; the voice of nature is the voice of God; and the highest form of association, 'assemblages of men called states, united upon the principles of justice', is that form of association most pleasing to God. A society presupposes government, and he proceeds to argue that that government must be of popular origin. In doing so, he emphasises not so much men's natural liberty—as has been shown, this can be thought of in collective terms—but their natural equality, which is essentially a relationship between individuals. 'By the law of nature an equal has neither the power nor the right of assuming authority over his equals, for I think it but justice that among persons in other respects equal, the returns of command

and obedience should also be equal.' If all men are by nature equal, none
has a natural right to command another. But what cannot be assumed can
be given. On this basis he argues that the people are the source of all law
and institute to all public office, and the end for which they submit to a
ruler and bind themselves by laws is for the securing of advantages in
common and reciprocation of benefits. The order of justice is, in other
words, a relationship of equality between individuals, and it would seem
to be implied, though it is not explicitly stated, that the parties to the
covenant under which a king is instituted must be individuals also. The
implication becomes even clearer when he takes the unusual step of
justifying tyrannicide. The king who violates his covenant becomes a
tyrant and a public enemy. Destruction of such a one is the justest of all
wars and may be undertaken not only by the whole people in a public act,
but by any individual among them. The dangers of preaching tyrannicide
are obvious. But if George Buchanan's egalitarianism meant that he
thought of each member of his free society severally agreeing to institute
a king upon conditions, breach of the covenant involves a breach of faith
with each one of them, and it could therefore be logically deduced that
each one of them was entitled to act in the matter.

Buchanan's otherwise not very profound work has this special interest
that in it the disentangling of a purely secular theory of the state from its
religious origins is complete. There is no section, as there is in the *Vindiciae
contra tyrannos*, on the obligation of a king to establish true religion or the
duty of resistance on the part of the subject to the heretic ruler. This aspect
of the sixteenth-century state is passed over in silence. The state is founded
in men's natural sociability, and popular government in their natural
equality. It exists to secure benefits, and resistance is conceived of purely
in terms of resistance to injustice.

In the next century the heirs of this generation of Calvinists proceeded
to draw conclusions from these premises about the necessary form of the
state, and to contend for the unique validity of representative institutions.
Such a claim was made already in the sixteenth century, though not in the
context of the right of resistance. The conflicts in the second half of the
sixteenth century between kings and the organs of government through
which they ruled generated for the first time since classical times an
interest in forms of constitution, more especially the relationships of the
monarch to the estates, diet or parliament of his realm. The discussion
therefore tended to be focused on particular situations and their historic
background rather than on general philosophical concepts. Bodin took
the initiative in reconsidering, in the light of his concept of the state,
Aristotle's division of constitutions into six basic types. Because sovereignty
was the mark of the state, he would allow only three simple types of
commonwealth: monarchy where the sovereign is a single person; aristocracy where a minority group rule; and democracy where the majority do

so. But he went on to make a distinction of his own between the form of the commonwealth and the mode of its operation or, as he said, between the state and the government. Any one type of commonwealth can function through machinery normally characteristic of one of the other two. This analysis allowed him to give a much more exact and penetrating account of the varieties of actual constitutions than Aristotle's simple sixfold division. More especially, he could by this means reconcile his strong preference for monarchy as the only reliably effective form of commonwealth, because of its unity and despatch, and his conviction that some system of estates increases stability because it is the means by which subjects can express their aspirations and ventilate their grievances. France and England, therefore, he describes as monarchies functioning democratically and he holds that this is the form of constitution to be preferred above all others because the most stable.

Bodin's preference for what we should call constitutional monarchy was dictated purely by considerations of expediency. For him all the possible forms of constitution were equally legitimate and all actual systems of law and institutions the inevitable products of environment. So far was he from attaching any particular validity to popular institutions that he insisted that the obligation to obey had nothing to do with consent. All power is of God, and neither the community as a whole nor the individuals that make it up play any part in the institution of rulers, who derive their authority from God, or in the formulation of law, which derives its authority from the ruler. The function of estates, therefore, in a constitutional monarchy is purely advisory.

But in this, as in other discussions, few writers in the last quarter of the century could examine the situation with Bodin's philosophical detachment. Most of them, like De Seyssel or Du Haillan for instance, were frankly concerned with a particular case, that of the French monarchy, and in expounding a view of it which conformed to some preconceived theory of right order. Of all such writers François Hotman is the most interesting because he identified a system of estates with liberty and regarded liberty in this sense as the essential mark of the valid state. The theme of his *Franco-Gallia* is the contrast between tyranny, as exemplified in the forcible subjection of the Franks to Caesar and the general character of subsequent Roman rule; and liberty, that condition obtaining among the Franks, the Greek city states, the Germans, the English, and the Aragonese, where the people were ruled through popular assemblies. It is significant of future developments that the contrast between tyranny and legitimate government is not here a contrast between arbitrary government and the rule of law, but between a government of repression based on force, which exists to satisfy the ambitions of the ruler and is contrary, therefore (it is assumed), to the will of the people, and a government directed to the common good because based on the will of the people and therefore sustained by their loyalty. Such a government, Hotman goes on to argue, is only secure where sovereign power to make and unmake kings, declare war and peace, make law, and confer all honours and offices belongs to a common council or estates. 'It is an essential part of liberty that the same persons at whose cost and peril everything is done should have it done likewise by their authority and advice, for what concerns all should be approved by all.' He believes this to have been the ancient order among the Franks from the time of the election of Pépin in 751, but to have been gradually eaten away by the growing autocracy of the king. This has been manifested in the developments of the practice of making office heritable and the transference of the power of approving and registering laws from the common council to the *parlements*, that is to say, to the body of lawyers who are the king's creatures. Such a government, he assumes throughout, is tyrannous because autocratic. Freedom is the necessary mark of the rightly ordered government, and that is only secured when government is in the hands of representative estates, or their predecessor, the 'common council', which he identifies with the Frankish folkmoot and which he thought was perpetuated in the great council of the Capetian kings. Though François Hotman was only concerned to discuss the French constitution, it is clear that in his mind freedom is conceived of in political terms and is identified with representative institutions.

The debate on the constitution in England was deferred till the next century, for it was only then that the conditions of civil commotion and strife that engendered it in France were reproduced in this country. When it came, it was essentially the same debate, between divine-right absolutists on the one hand and popular-right libertarians on the other, with Hobbes —so different in other respects—exhibiting the same peculiarity as Hooker in combining absolutism with a doctrine of the necessarily representative character of authority. It is not surprising that Bodin's *Six livres de la République*, the *Vindiciae contra tyrannos*, and Hotman's *Franco-Gallia* were all translated into English and the experience and the literature of the French Wars of Religion freely used in the English debate.

In the second half of the sixteenth century specifically medieval attitudes to political obligation were giving way to specifically modern. In the middle of the century, whether the writers were Catholic, Lutheran or Calvinist, the emphasis was on obligation, both of the ruler and of the subject, because the state and all other institutions were judged from the point of view of their place in the scheme of salvation. They existed *de jure divino* for the purpose of discipline. At the end of the century the emphasis was shifting to rights. The state was increasingly regarded as belonging to the order of nature, brought into existence by men for the securing of certain advantages. Already Hotman and Buchanan were attaching an absolute value to liberty, and Bodin to liberty and possessions without relating them to any scheme of salvation. The doctrine that it is the function of the state to secure to the individual the enjoyment of his natural rights did not emerge into full consciousness till the seventeenth century. But Hotman, Bodin and Buchanan all assume that respect for the liberty and possessions of the subject is the mark of the rightly ordered state.

The change was an aspect of the new individualism of the sixteenth century. Hooker was harking back when he treated the part as ordained to the whole, and the political society that sustains their physical and moral well-being as prior to its several members. Most of his contemporaries regarded the individual as a radically self-subsisting unit. This attitude manifested itself first in the field of religion, in the exaltation of the individual conscience above the authority of the corporate body of the church, and in the affirmation of the principle of toleration. Before the end of the century it was manifesting itself in the field of politics as well. The dogma of the natural equality between men, with the inference that the authority of the ruler is based on the consent of his subjects and that the powers he enjoys are limited to what they have bestowed upon him, is the counterpart in the state of the dogma of the sufficiency of the individual conscience in matters of religion. Both mark a decline in the older sense of corporateness. The conception of the church as the congregation organised as a corporate whole under a divinely constituted authority which is the directive of all its members was being challenged by the conception of aggregations of individuals united by an agreement as to the beliefs which they share in common. The unified nation state, which superseded the pluralism of the corporate life of medieval political society, was an aggregation of individuals united by agreement over the laws and institutions under which they were willing to live. In the sixteenth century the constitutive principle of the reformed churches was the confession of faith in which were defined those beliefs that were agreed to be necessary to salvation; all doctrine and practices not included were each member's private concern. In the seventeenth century the constitutive principle of the state was very widely held to be a contract by which the ends for which a political society was instituted, and therefore the limits of the obligations of the contracting parties, were determined. Preoccupation with the need for discipline, and therefore for the recognition of authority, was giving way to preoccupation with liberty and the securing of rights. Proof of an argument was less and less sought for in the Scriptures as revealing the will of God, and more and more in history as evidence of human experience.

CHAPTER XVII

COLONIAL DEVELOPMENT
AND INTERNATIONAL RIVALRIES
OUTSIDE EUROPE

I. AMERICA

THE age of the *conquistadores* was already over when Philip II ascended the throne of Spain and the Indies. The leaders of the great *entradas* were nearly all dead. Some died prematurely of their wounds and their exertions, some by the knives of jealous rivals. A few—Cortés was one of them—spent their middle age in bored and litigious retirement. Not one was long allowed to administer for the crown the provinces he had conquered. Already by 1558 an administrative service, civil and ecclesiastical, had been created and was rapidly growing in numbers, efficiency and cost. The *conquistadores* had no successors in their own violent mould. Miguel López de Legazpi, who in 1561 undertook the conquest of the Philippines, had been an official in Mexico; his highly successful *entrada* was notable for diplomacy and organising ability rather than for skill in war and was, indeed, almost bloodless. Francisco de Ibarra, conqueror of Durango, and Francisco de Urdiñola, who founded Saltillo and settled Coahuila, were typical of the later generation of *conquistadores*, no strangers to violence on occasion, but *entrepreneurs* in silver-mining and cattle-ranching, organisers of settlements, rather than conquerors of semi-barbarous empires. There were, in fact, no empires left to conquer. In North America, Coronado's expedition of 1540 had revealed nothing but arid hills and apparently boundless prairies, occupied by great herds of 'wild cattle' and a scattering of equally wild Indians; no place for men who lived by their swords or by their wits. The prosperous though comparatively modest towns of the Pueblo Indians in New Mexico and Arizona possessed silver mines and offered a possible prize to a *conquistador*; but they were not known until Espejo explored the upper Rio Grande in 1582. An expedition under Juan de Oñate 'took possession' of New Mexico in 1598; but the possession was little more than a formality, and in fact the Pueblos were little disturbed by Spaniards, except for Franciscan missionaries, for another hundred years.

In South America, the dripping pine woods of southern Chile and the vast rain forests east of the Cordillera placed severe obstacles in the way of explorers and offered little obvious attraction. García Hurtado de Mendoza led a successful expedition against the Araucanians of Chile in 1557, but its results—and its intentions—were primarily punitive and military, measures of frontier defence. A number of new settlements were made in the eastern Andes in the 1560s and 1570s (notably Caracas in 1567); but Maldonado's attempts to explore and settle in the upper Amazon basin were—as might be expected—total failures. Nor did Orellana's famous journey down the river lead to settlement near its mouth. The swampy coast-land of Guiana was supposedly the threshold of the country of 'El Dorado'; but in the later sixteenth century that elusive dream appeared only to a few visionaries among Spaniards, such as Hernando de Berrio, governor of Trinidad, who later, as Sir Walter Raleigh's prisoner, communicated his own gold-fevered enthusiasm to his captor. Berrio founded a few small forts; but there was no serious attempt at Spanish settlement, either in Guiana or in Trinidad.

On the long coastline of eastern South America the Portuguese were thinly settled on their sugar plantations and in their little rustic towns. Their principal rivals were not Spanish but French, who, after some years of visits to the coast to cut brazil-wood, in 1555 established a settlement, with Coligny's backing, on Rio de Janeiro bay. The settlers survived Portuguese attacks until 1567, when Mem de Sá, the ablest of the sixteenth-century governors of Brazil, finally drove them out and founded the city of São Sebastião on the shores of the bay. The Portuguese were better placed than other Europeans for obtaining slaves from west Africa, and by the end of Mem de Sá's government the pattern of 'great house', slave quarters and cane fields was established and was spreading. By 1580 there were some sixty sugar mills in operation. The population included about 20,000 Portuguese, 18,000 settled Indians and 14,000 negro slaves. The union of the Spanish and Portuguese crowns made little difference. In a *carta patente* issued at Lisbon in 1582, Philip II undertook to leave both the commerce and the administration of the Portuguese colonies in Portuguese hands, and in general he kept his promise. The Portuguese in Brazil were left to themselves in the sixteenth century; not until the seventeenth did the growing returns from sugar attract Spanish attempts at bureaucratic control, and Dutch aggression.

The Spaniards had never shown much interest in their own section of the coast, and showed even less after 1580, when they no longer had cause to fear Portuguese encroachment. The site of Buenos Aires was occupied intermittently from 1537 and the settlement received its permanent corporate foundation in 1580; but Buenos Aires was interesting more to smugglers than to settlers. It was a back door to Peru, a possible channel for clandestine trade with Brazil. This, of course, was no recommendation in Spanish official eyes. Buenos Aires got no encouragement from Lima or Madrid, and for many years remained a mere village. The other late sixteenth-century settlements in what is now Argentina—Santiago del Estero, Mendoza, Córdoba, Salta—were settled, not from the coast, but by people who came over the mountains from Peru. All were modest agricultural settlements, whose chief function was to supply mules, grain and meat to the mountain mines of Upper Peru. Even Asunción in Paraguay, which had been settled originally by people coming up the river, had little regular contact with the Atlantic coast, and that little was clandestine. In the late sixteenth century it lost what little trade it had to Buenos Aires. All these small settlements survived with difficulty. They had no mines and little trade, for the shipping of metropolitan Spain at that time made no use of the Rio de la Plata, and was indeed forbidden to go there. They never became important centres of expansion or conquest, and down to the eighteenth century unsubdued Indian tribes continued to be a serious nuisance, sometimes a serious danger, in their near neighbourhood.

The slowing down of Spanish exploration and expansion in the Americas in Philip II's time was not, however, simply the result of a growing conviction that there was nothing left worth exploring; for of that no one could yet be sure. Nor had the race of *conquistadores* become extinct. It is true that in any developing colonial empire the free-lance captain must sooner or later give way to the official, the soldier of fortune to the capitalist or the settler (or both), the pioneer missionary to the parish priest; and that in the Spanish empire these replacements were begun in the later years of Charles V and largely completed under Philip II. Nevertheless, there were still plenty of adventurers in Spain and the Indies who were able, and in other circumstances would have been willing, to explore, conquer and settle beyond the known frontiers of empire. The precious metals were not an indispensable attraction. Spaniards were perfectly capable of establishing agricultural colonies, and had done so successfully in Chile, in Antioquia, and in the Puebla valley in central Mexico. That expansion almost ceased, that California, New Mexico and Florida were not settled until much later, that Argentina was ignored, that Virginia was left to the English, was due in large measure to governmental caution, to a deliberately restrictive policy.

All the *conquistadores* had been in some sense agents of the crown. Without royal recognition of their authority and subsequent royal confirmation of their actions, they could not reward their followers or maintain discipline in their motley armies. There were always jealous rivals and disloyal lieutenants, ready to seize upon any apparent flaws in a leader's title to command. Hence their care to maintain an appearance of strict constitutional legality. Cortés never forgot this lesson and died in his bed a rich man. Gonzalo Pizarro—an able and popular captain— forgot it at a crucial point in his career and lost his head in consequence. No *conquistador*—especially under the stricter rule of Philip II—could hope to make a successful *entrada* without the approval either of the king or of the king's representative, the viceroy. Under Philip II such approval was rarely and grudgingly granted. General legislation, moreover, laid down rules and conditions which made *entradas* of the old ruthless kind almost impossible. The *Ordenanzas sobre Descubrimiento* of 1573—the celebrated and humane code promulgated by Philip II for the guidance of *conquistadores*—laid down that 'discoverers by land or by sea shall not engage in war or conquest, nor support one Indian faction against another, nor become involved in quarrels with natives, nor do them any harm, nor take any of their property, unless it be given willingly, or by way of barter'.[1] No man could emulate Cortés, still less Pizarro or Nuño de Guzmán, according to such rules.

This deliberate discouragement of armed expansion reflected in some measure the reaction of the royal conscience against the brutalities of the original conquests; brutalities which had been brought to public notice by missionary friars in a steady stream of humanitarian propaganda. A resounding controversy over the status of the Indians, between the Dominican missionary Las Casas and the worldly humanist Sepúlveda, had concluded at Valladolid as late as 1551. The bench of theologians and jurists appointed to judge between them had reached no firm conclusion, but on the whole the honours had rested with Las Casas. In some measure, also, the new policy reflected Philip's own temperament and convictions. That great and cautious king inclined naturally to consolidate before expanding, to look before leaping. Insistent, as his predecessor had never been, on collecting the fullest and most detailed information about every part of his empire, he was aware of the hollow frontiers of the Indies, of great areas of unexploited and unexplored land within the boundaries of settled provinces, of wild, unsubdued tribes within striking distance of key places—the isthmus of Panama and the mountain roads by which the silver trains came down from Zacatecas to Mexico and Vera Cruz, from Potosí to Arequipa, from Cuzco to Lima. A widespread and dangerous revolt occurred among the Zacateco and Guachichile Indians in northern New Spain as late as 1561. Nor were Indian revolts the only source of internal danger. In Peru a series of civil wars between Spanish chieftains had ended with the execution of Gonzalo Pizarro in 1548; but the establishment of order throughout the viceroyalty was a slow and difficult process. Not until 1560 could the viceroy report that the southern realms were at peace and armed colonial feudalism put down; not until fifteen or twenty years later, in the days of the great Francisco de Toledo, was an organised and workable administration finally established.

It was natural that Philip should wish, in the interests of security, to hold up further conquest until existing provinces could be peopled with industrious Spaniards and settled Indians, and administered by methodical and obedient civil servants. Above all, the discouragement of expansion arose from recognition of the growing importance of the Indies as a source of royal revenue. The crown had drawn some income from the Indies from

[1] *Colección de Documentos inéditos...de Indias* (Madrid, 1864–81), XVI, 142.

the beginning; customs duties, Indian tributes, and the like, however, were trifling. Even the royal 'fifth', levied on the small quantities of precious metals mined or looted from the Indians, was comparatively unimportant until the last years of Charles V's reign. In the middle years of the sixteenth century, however, immensely productive silver mines were discovered at Zacatecas and Guanajuato in northern New Spain and at Potosí in what is now Bolivia. Various forms of crude mass production quickly took the place of primitive washing, and extensive plant—extensive for those days—was set up for extracting the silver from the ore, increasingly by the *patio* or mercury amalgamation method. A veritable torrent of silver began to flow towards Spain and the royal silver tax, the *quinto*, became in a few years a major source of revenue. The numbers of Spanish immigrants, attracted by the silver rush, increased, and other heads of taxation also became vastly more productive. At the time of Philip II's accession his income from the Indies was nearly 10 per cent of his total revenue and was increasing. In the light of Philip's vast debts and enormous commitments in Europe, it inevitably became a major aim of royal policy to increase the Indies revenue more and more rapidly; to concentrate Spanish capital and ingenuity and Indian labour upon silver-mining and other revenue-producing activities; and to insist upon the development of existing and profitable provinces, rather than allow the dissipation of energy in distant and speculative new *entradas*.

A general system of government—administrative, judicial, financial—for the Indies had been firmly established in Charles V's time.[1] Philip II made relatively few innovations in civil administration. He established three new *audiencias*—Charcas (1559), Quito (1563) and Manila (1583). The numbers of colonial officials increased greatly during his reign; an increase necessitated partly by the general development of the Indies, partly by the meticulous and detailed reporting, record-keeping and consultation on which the king insisted. In particular, Philip greatly elaborated the treasury organisation and the system for auditing the royal accounts, both in the Indies and at the centre. He instituted a tighter central—indeed personal—control over appointments, and systematised, in the interests of the crown, the existing practice of the sale of fee-earning offices. These sales became an important source of revenue; in the seventeenth century the practice was to spread to more senior and responsible offices and to become a serious abuse, but in Philip II's time it was always limited and carefully controlled. In many other ways, the king sought—often against the advice of the Council of the Indies—to increase his income from the new world. The *alcabala*—the unpopular but lucrative Spanish sales tax—was extended to the Indies in 1575 and came to rival the *quinto* as a source of revenue. The net receipts from the Indies mounted steadily, despite the mounting increase in the cost of administration. In 1585—admittedly a

[1] See vol. II, p. 572.

peak year—they amounted to nearly a quarter of the total revenue of the Crown.

This constant and strenuous endeavour to increase the revenue from the Indies ultimately depended for its success upon the labour of the native Indians. The abundance of well-organised labour had been one of the chief original attractions of the mainland kingdoms, and in the early years Spanish settlers had grown accustomed to an extremely lavish use of labour. Throughout the sixteenth century, however, the Indian population declined; a slow, continuous decline, punctuated three or four times during the century by catastrophic plunges due to major epidemics which left the population permanently enfeebled and depleted. Tentative figures have been worked out only for central Mexico,[1] but there is little doubt that the story was much the same in all provinces where Indians were in regular contact with Europeans. At the same time, the numbers of Spaniards, and of *mestizos* who passed for Spaniards, slowly but steadily grew through natural increase and immigration. In New Spain alone, numbers increased from about 50,000 in the middle of the century to over 100,000 at the end, and their demands upon Indian labour, with the development of silver-mining, cattle ranching and European-type agriculture, grew more than proportionately. The frequent and detailed legislative enactments which regulated Indian affairs were inspired, therefore, not only by a paternal concern for Indian welfare (though this was genuine enough) but also by the necessity of using a dwindling labour supply in the most economical and efficient way. The great smallpox epidemic of 1545–6, which afflicted both New Spain and Peru, was followed in 1549 and 1550 by legislation taking the power to exact forced labour out of private hands and entrusting it to public authorities. Viceroys and *audiencias* might authorise the levy of gangs of labourers from Indian villages, to be employed (and paid) either by government or by private employers for short periods and for specific purposes—mining, food production, building and miscellaneous public works. In addition, 'idle' Indians were to be compelled to offer themselves for regular wage employment. The viceroyalty of Peru at this time was still in a disturbed state; but in New Spain these somewhat loose arrangements worked tolerably well for the next twenty-five years. This was the period of the first great expansion of silver production. The Indian population remained relatively stable; there were no epidemics and decline was relatively gradual. Indian labour was supplemented by a considerable import of negro slaves and general conditions were relatively prosperous. In the years 1576–9, however, another disastrous epidemic swept New Spain and demonstrated, contrary to general belief, that negroes had no greater immunity to disease than Indians. A frantic search for labour ensued. The wages of 'free' labour naturally increased very greatly. The casual and occasional levy of *repartimiento* labour in New

[1] See vol. II, p. 583, n. I.

Spain was turned by Enríquez, the viceroy of the time, into a fixed and regular levy, and the numbers demanded steadily increased. In Peru the reorganisation was more drastic still. The worst epidemic there occurred at a time when the rich surface veins at Potosí were becoming exhausted, when deeper shafts were required to get the ore and better techniques to reduce it. The great mercury mine at Huancavélica was being vigorously developed as a complement to Potosí. More and more labour was needed, both to work the mines and to bring to the barren mountains of Potosí the food and fuel which the miners required. The *mita* organised for these purposes by the viceroy Francisco de Toledo demanded the labour, at any one time, of about one-seventh of the surviving adult male Indians of the province. About 14,000 labourers, and their wives and children, annually made the journey to Potosí. These *mitayos* were in addition to free miners, who worked either for wages or on their own account, and slaves; but the slaves had also been decimated by disease. Toledo insisted on a hospital being provided for the *mitayos* with a resident doctor; but according to Capoche, the contemporary historian of Potosí, they feared the hospital more than the mine.

From 1576 the uses to which *repartimiento* labour might be put were necessarily restricted mainly to mining and food production. The ambitious church-building which had been characteristic of New Spain for three quarters of a century ceased almost entirely. For the first time since the Conquest food shortages appeared. The city markets depended on Indian producers for maize, fruit, vegetables, poultry, fodder, firewood and many other essentials; but Indian villages, half depopulated and deprived of much of their surviving labour supply by the *repartimiento*, could hardly feed themselves and had little surplus, either for sale or as tribute for their *encomenderos*. Wheat was grown for Spanish consumption by Spaniards employing Indian labour, and through lack of labour its production also declined, so that government was obliged from 1578 onwards to operate public granaries with powers of compulsory purchase and price-fixing. Meat, which had been cheap and plentiful, became scarcer and dearer, though for different reasons. Livestock, especially sheep and goats, grazing uncontrolled on open range, tend to multiply to the limit of subsistence and then to destroy the means of their subsistence. Vast areas in central Mexico and in the upland valleys of Peru, including much land which before the Conquest had been under crops, were turned first into open pasture and then into bare and eroded wilderness. The practice of trans-humance increased in consequence, with further damage to Indian cultivation and a widening of the ruined areas. Numbers of sheep, and a prosperous woollen industry, declined sharply towards the end of the sixteenth century throughout the Indies (and, incidentally, in Spain). Cattle, less destructive than sheep, maintained their numbers; but the ranchers moved on to fresh ranges, further from the cities, so that supplies of meat became less and less readily available, and the profits of ranching more and more dependent merely on hides and tallow. After 1576, therefore, the easy opulence of the middle years of the century disappeared. In 1596 yet another disastrous epidemic brought another downward plunge in the economy of New Spain. From the reports of the viceroys it is clear that in the last years of the sixteenth century the surviving Indian population was permanently near starvation, and in years of bad harvest some of the Spanish cities also experienced near-famine conditions. These conditions were to occur at intervals throughout most of the seventeenth century.

The steady shrinkage in the Indian population forced the Spaniards to produce their own food instead of relying upon Indian sources. *Encomiendas* which had been princely fiefs became exiguous pensions, hardly worth the cost of petitions to the crown. The large, self-contained, Spanish-owned and Spanish-managed *hacienda* was the logical answer to food shortage, particularly in the mining areas where Spaniards were concentrated. *Repartimiento* labour was too temporary and too uncertain for the work on *latifundia* of this type, and towards the end of the sixteenth century wage labour became increasingly common both on the land and in the mines. By leaving their villages and seeking employment among Spaniards, Indians could evade the burden of *repartimiento* and tribute, which automatically became heavier as the village population declined. Labour was also increasingly bound to estates and mines by debt peonage, since in hard times Indian labourers would readily accept advances of food, clothing or money, to be repaid in labour. These advances were very rarely repaid in full; they created a new status, a permanent hereditary obligation. For all these reasons, the old self-contained Indian communities broke up rapidly wherever the *haciendas* grew. The government—though it legislated occasionally against advances to Indians—in the long run had no choice but to acquiesce. These changes in social and economic circumstances were reflected in the ecclesiastical policy of the crown. Under Charles V the tasks of evangelisation and of church government in the Indies had been entrusted to missionaries of the mendicant orders. The friars had identified themselves in large measure with Indian interests. They had lived among Indians and preached in Indian languages. Their policy, and that of the crown, had been to preserve the Indian communities and their lands intact and to protect them—subject to the payment of tribute and the rendering of limited services—from contact with lay Spaniards. In this way they had found a *modus vivendi* with a colonial society dominated by *encomenderos*. In time, however, their exclusive paternalism became as obstructive of economic and administrative development, and as irritating to the king, as the *encomienda* itself. Under Philip II royal policy changed abruptly. The Indians—as Sepúlveda and his followers had always advocated—were to be hispanicised as well as christianised. They were to learn Spanish and to be integrated, as artisans and labourers, in Spanish society. To this end, for ecclesiastical purposes they were to be brought under ordinary parochial care. The Mexican church councils of 1565 and 1585, dominated by the bishops and supported by the crown, gradually but firmly enforced the decree of the Council of Trent that no cleric might have jurisdiction over secular persons with cure of souls unless he was subject to episcopal authority. Step by step the power and privileges of the orders were reduced and those of the secular clergy increased. The number of the secular clergy also increased, partly as a result of increased immigration, partly through the appearance of a class of Creole clerics, who now had the advantage of universities (both Mexico and San Marcos de Lima were founded in 1551) and the discipline of the Holy Office, established in the Indies in 1572. A secular, bureaucratic, partly Creole ecclesiastical hierarchy had little fervour for missionary work in remote provinces and no interest in preserving the more accessible Indian communities from lay Spanish contacts. The ideal of a specifically Indian Christianity, founded upon primitive innocence, faded from view. With it went the hope of a native priesthood. The imaginative experiments of the Franciscans in Indian higher education were largely abandoned. The famous Indian college of Santiago Tlatelolco, founded in 1536 and backed by the first two viceroys and by some of the more liberal *encomenderos*, survived many vicissitudes down to 1576; but the epidemic of that year carried off most of its students, its staff lost heart, and it never recovered. By the end of the century its buildings were ruinous beyond repair, save for two rooms which housed a primary school for *mestizo* children. Its fate was symbolic. Mendieta, the chronicler of the Franciscans in New Spain, looked back to the reign of Charles V as a golden age and to Cortés as the Spanish Moses; a description which would have surprised that astute soldier of fortune greatly, could he have read it. By the end of the sixteenth century the friars—staunchest of friends to the simple Indian, so long as he remained simple—were left with but two alternatives: to retire peacefully to their convents or to transfer their missionary enthusiasm to the colonial frontiers among the less civilised natives, as many of them eventually did.

The Indies in the last quarter of the sixteenth century thus passed through a series of very damaging demographic, social and economic crises. During the same period Spain itself entered upon an economic and demographic decline which was not arrested until the beginning of the eighteenth century. The inability of Spain to absorb colonial exports of hides, dyes, sugar and other products may well have contributed to the falling off in production of these commodities in the Indies. Similarly, the growing inability of Spanish industries to provide manufactures for the Spanish cities of America in sufficient quantities and at competitive prices added to the difficulties arising from deficits in colonial production. Fewer economic opportunities and a worsening of living conditions in Spain also encouraged more Spaniards, both laymen and clerics, to migrate to the Indies where, bad though economic conditions may have been, food was still more plentiful throughout the late sixteenth century and most of the seventeenth than in Spain. Because of the nature of colonial society, these immigrants meant little, if any, addition to the labour force in the Indies, but rather an increase in the number of people to be fed. Finally, the fiscal straits of the Spanish crown forced it to press continually for more funds, which the American communities provided with increasing difficulty and almost entirely in silver, with baneful effects upon the monetary situation in Spain. Through their coincidence in time, the economic and demographic crises in Spain and the Indies thus interacted to the disadvantage of both.

Throughout this period of mounting internal difficulty, with its unavoidable shifts of policy, the one continuous thread, the one fixed aim of government, was the safe and regular shipment of silver to Spain. Conversely, the silver shipments were the principal attraction for hostile privateers in war and pirates in peace. Until the last decades of the sixteenth century, the rivals of Spain were not much concerned to capture Spanish territory in America; the empire seemed too powerful and too distant for overt attack, and the costs too high. The other maritime peoples of Europe sought more simply to deny silver, the sinews of war, to the Spaniards and to acquire it for themselves; to steal it by force of arms at sea or to earn it by illicit trade. As a result, international rivalry in the New World was for long concentrated in the Caribbean sea-lanes, through which passed eastbound the silver and the tropical products of the Indies, and westbound the European wine, oil and manufactured goods upon which the comfort of the New World Spaniards largely depended. Throughout Charles V's long contest with France, the shipping of the Indies had been an object of French attack. The sack of Havana by Jacques Sores in 1555 had come as a severe shock. One of the first preoccupations of government thereafter was to protect the harbours and passages of the West Indies by fortification, and the shipments of silver by the provision of armed convoy. It is true that at the outset of Philip's reign, the Treaty of Cateau-Cambrésis settled, mostly in favour of Spain, the questions over which the two powers had officially been fighting; but the Spaniards could not be sure that peace would endure for long or that the French government would be able, or even willing, to control such of its privateer captains as chose to take to piracy on their own account. Nor was piracy the only problem. According to the economic theories of the time, illicit trade presented an almost equally dangerous threat.

The colonists—avid for slaves and manufactured goods of all kinds, with a good deal of specie at their disposal, yet confined in law to dealing with a rapacious and inefficient monopoly—offered a perfect interlopers' market, worth considerable risk to enter. In the 1560s smuggling by foreign traders became for the first time a serious problem for Spanish government in the Caribbean. The interlopers were not French for the most part, but English, led initially by the versatile and ingenious John Hawkins. Hawkins organised four trading voyages to the Caribbean between 1562 and 1568, and commanded three of them himself. He carried cloth and general merchandise from England, and slaves whom he purchased directly from dealers on the West African Coast. He proposed to sell his goods and slaves to Spanish settlers in the Indies and to secure cargoes of sugar, hides and silver for the return voyage to England. Hawkins's plan thus anticipated the triangular voyage of later times and defied the monopolistic regulations of both Portugal and Spain. He did not, however, intend mere tip-and-run smuggling; still less, open piracy. He seems to have entertained serious hopes of securing licences from Spain which would legitimise his activities. England and Spain were at peace and traditionally friendly. Hawkins was known in Seville and had friends and business correspondents there. He was prepared to pay all lawful dues; and in return for a licence to trade he offered his services to the Spanish crown as a privateer, to assist in clearing pirates and foreign smugglers from the West Indian waters. In particular, he appreciated the strategic importance of the Florida Channel and knew that the French were trying to establish a settlement on the coast of Florida, under René de Laudonnière, which could become very dangerous to Spanish shipping. Hawkins hoped to demonstrate the value of his services by destroying this colony at the beginning of its career.

Hawkins's plan failed completely in its larger aspect, though as business ventures his first two voyages were highly successful. He was right in assuming that Spanish planters and minor government officials would be glad to do business with him. On the last homeward trip, however, he was driven by continued bad weather into the Gulf of Mexico and obliged to seek shelter at San Juan de Ulúa, the port of Vera Cruz. Here he was caught by a convoy arriving from Spain. Most of his fleet was destroyed in the ensuing battle, and he himself reached England in January 1569, after great hardships, with only fifteen surviving companions. This battle, and the subsequent ill-treatment of English castaways, did much to arouse anti-Spanish feeling in England. The whole episode made clear that the Spanish government would tolerate no interlopers of any kind in American waters; any foreigner was a pirate and would be treated as such if caught. Foreign traders in the West Indies, therefore, must go secretly or go well armed. Meanwhile—and this may have been one of the reasons for Hawkins's failure—fresh dispositions in the area showed that the Spaniards could do for themselves what they refused to allow Hawkins to do for them.

The co-ordination of land and sea defences in the Caribbean, whether against privateers, pirates or smugglers, called for a unified command; and this was entrusted in the 1560s to Pedro Menéndez de Avilés, one of the ablest sea commanders of the time. Menéndez's first important appointment was the command of the escort of the homeward-bound fleet of 1555-6. In 1561 he was appointed captain-general of the *Armada de la Carrera de Indias*, and in that capacity he took out and back in 1562 the largest fleet which until then had crossed the Atlantic—forty-nine sail, of which six were men-of-war. During the next two years he was engaged in advising the crown upon the regulations for the Indies trade which were promulgated between 1564 and 1566. His proposals fell under three main heads: compulsory convoy for transatlantic sailings; the provision of fortifications and naval dockyards at the principal ports of the Indies; and the organisation of cruiser squadrons—*armadillas*—based in the Indies, to patrol the main trade routes.

A system of convoyed fleets had been in use in war-time since 1542. At that time the total volume of Spanish shipping crossing the Atlantic annually each way amounted to about 10,000 modern capacity tons. Between 1542 and the outbreak of war with England the volume roughly doubled. Most of the ships were comparatively small. The largest rarely exceeded 600 tons, though the tendency through the century was for the average size to increase. The number of ships leaving San Lúcar varied greatly from year to year; the annual average in Menéndez's time was between sixty and seventy. These were big fleets by sixteenth-century standards, calling for considerable powers of organisation. Menéndez made convoy compulsory at all times except for urgent sailings of fast and well-armed ships which might be made licensed exceptions; and gave to the system the fixed and characteristic routine which it was to follow for more than a hundred years. A fleet for New Spain was ordered to leave San Lúcar every May, and usually entered Caribbean waters by the Mona passage. Once inside the Caribbean, ships for Honduras and the Greater Antilles parted company. The main body passed south of Hispaniola and Cuba, through the Yucatán channel and across the Gulf to Vera Cruz. It was one of these *flotas* which caught Hawkins at San Juan de Ulúa. The Isthmus fleet left San Lúcar in August and set a slightly more southerly course, passing through the Windward Islands. Some ships put into small ports on the Main, but the main body anchored off Nombre de Dios (later off Puerto Bello), where it unloaded goods for Peru and loaded silver. It then retired to the sheltered harbour of Cartagena. Both fleets normally wintered in the Indies. The Isthmus fleet began its return passage in January, steering north-west—usually a comfortable reach with the wind on the starboard beam—until it could round Cape San Antonio and put into Havana. Meanwhile the Mexican *flota* in February made its tedious three- or four-week beat against the trade wind from Vera Cruz, for *rendezvous* at Havana in March. Havana guarded the only convenient exit from the Gulf of Mexico for sailing ships. The fleets refitted and victualled there, and endeavoured to sail in company for Spain in the early summer in order to get clear of tropical waters before the hurricane season. The fleets beat out through the Florida channel— a tedious and dangerous stretch—and stood to the north until they could pick up a westerly wind for the transatlantic crossing. Each convoy was escorted by warships, from two to eight in number according to the international situation and the shipping available, and relied on these escorts for protection against marauders lying in wait in the Bahamas or the Azores.

Havana was the pivot of the convoy system, at least for the homeward passage, which chiefly interested Spain's enemies. Menéndez made it an almost impregnable fortress, safe against enemy attack for over two hundred years, with a dockyard capable of building light warships of local timber and of refitting any class of ship. He destroyed the French settlement in Florida which had attracted Hawkins's attention, and built in its place the Spanish fort of San Agustín; and he strengthened the local defences of Santo Domingo and Santiago in Cuba. Both in the work of fortification and in the organisation of naval patrols, his plans were constantly delayed by lack of money. No attempt was made to station a squadron permanently in the Caribbean until 1582, when two galleys were sailed and rowed across the Atlantic from Lisbon to Santo Domingo. One was wrecked shortly after arrival, and the crew of the other mutinied. Galleys, whether based on Santo Domingo or, later, on Cartagena, proved only moderately effective. Oarsmen were hard to recruit and maintenance costs were high. From the turn of the century the crown was repeatedly urged by its naval advisers to maintain a fleet of true sailing warships in the West Indies, but no effective action was taken to this end until the 1630s, when repeated naval disasters had made the need both painfully and belatedly obvious. Vital though the Indies were to Spain, the exigencies of war in Europe tended constantly to rob them of ships, and only the energy and persistence of a Menéndez could ensure them even a measure of defence.

The years which Menéndez spent in the West Indies were years of intense activity and, on the whole, conspicuous success. He died in 1574; but his work in fortifying bases and drilling and organising the trans-atlantic convoys was carried on by a series of able and energetic successors (including a son and a nephew) and enabled the Spanish colonies to survive intact, their communications with Spain unbroken, through a long and wasting naval war.

Throughout the period of Menéndez's greatest activity in the West Indies the task of protecting and policing Spanish Atlantic shipping routes grew steadily more troublesome and expensive. Although internecine religious war had removed France temporarily from the international arena, French corsairs were still active on their own account, and English raiders were growing bolder, their rapacity intensified and reinforced by religious hatred. Soon the revolt of the Netherlands and open war with England were to bring the warships and privateers of the two strongest North Atlantic maritime powers to the Caribbean in formidable strength and were to loose another naval genius, Francis Drake, upon the Indies and in independent command of voyages of reprisal.

Drake became the central figure in the attack on the Spanish Indies, as Menéndez was the central figure of their defence. He personified in his own day and afterwards the maritime genius and the Protestant religion of his countrymen. He created the legend of the bold corsair and the rich, defenceless Spaniard, which was to affect English policy in the Caribbean for many generations. He was the hero and the model of a host of poor gentlemen in England, small landlords who had been driven by inflation and social change to take to privateering, to 'get a ship and judiciously manage her'. For Spaniards, 'El Draque' was a name to frighten children. In sober fact, Drake evolved a coherent strategic West Indian plan in place of a series of small and uncoordinated raids; he carried his plan into effect with great, though not complete, success; he did great damage, acquired great booty, and seriously weakened the fighting power of Spain without, however, breaking the Spanish monopoly of territorial possession in the Caribbean.

Drake began his acquaintance with the West Indies as an illicit trader and was with Hawkins at San Juan de Ulúa. Thereafter he became a more or less authorised privateer and his next two voyages, in 1570 and 1571, combined slave-running with systematic reconnaissance. In 1572, the year after the expulsion of the Spanish ambassador from England, Drake sailed on his first serious raid, the famous voyage on which, with two small ships and seventy-odd men, he took Nombre de Dios by surprise and captured three mule-trains crossing the Isthmus loaded with silver from Peru. The booty was enough to make every man in Drake's company rich for life.

In 1574—the year of Menéndez's death—the English and Spanish governments patched up a grudging reconciliation. English captains continued to visit the Caribbean, trading with smaller settlements and with the Maroons, cruising with letters of reprisal, or making minor raids. None of them achieved success comparable with Drake's. Their government left them to fend for themselves as pirates, and a number of them—including Drake's friend John Oxenham, who made a bold attempt on the Isthmus in 1576—were caught and executed by the Spaniards. Menéndez had succeeded, if not in making the Caribbean a Spanish lake, at least in making it a dangerous cruising-ground for mere raiders. Drake, who never regarded himself as a pirate, left the West Indies alone in those years. From 1577 to 1580 he was away on his great voyage of circumnavigation,

In which he accomplished in one voyage what Dias, da Gama and Magellan had done separately over years. It was a prodigious achievement; but apart from the capture of the *Cacafuego*, its effects upon the American situation were moral rather than material, future rather than immediate. It added greatly to English maritime prestige; it revealed a route to the Pacific round Cape Horn, a passage less hazardous, though for the ships of the time not much less, than Magellan's Strait; it broke the Spanish monopoly, hitherto a real monopoly and not merely a legal one, of navigation off the Pacific coast of the Americas; it added enormously to the colonial anxieties of the Spanish government, by showing that the Isthmus, and the riches to which it gave access, could be attacked from both sides.

Drake did not appear again in the Caribbean until 1585, when war between England and Spain was already certain. The 'Indies voyage' of that year was no mere raid, but a full-scale naval operation carried out by a fleet of more than twenty sail. The plan was similar to that which the French had projected thirty years before, but never put into effect. It included, first, an attack on Santo Domingo and on the port towns of Tierra Firme, in particular Cartagena; then a land attack on Nombre de Dios and Panama in conjunction with the Maroons, in order to control both ends of the land route across the Isthmus; and finally the capture of Havana. Drake hoped to hold both Havana and Cartagena with permanent English garrisons. Success would break up the whole communication and supply system of the Spanish Indies. It would deny to Spain for many years, perhaps permanently, the means of making war in Europe and would throw the Indies open to English exploitation. The conception of such a plan is evidence, already by the end of the sixteenth century, of the importance of the West Indies in the international rivalries of Europe. Over and over again, for more than two hundred years, English, Dutch and French admirals and statesmen mounted plans similar, in whole or in part, to that of Drake. Some achieved partial and temporary success, as Drake did; but the Caribbean proved too big, the islands too scattered and too wild to be mastered in a single campaign. The commander of large-scale amphibious operations, moreover, faced more serious health difficulties than the tip-and-run raiders of earlier times, for his men had to live and fight ashore in large numbers for a considerable length of time. Armies and navies coming fresh from Europe wasted away in the fearful mortality of tropical campaigning. The Spaniards, the mosquitos, and the climate worked together to defeat every attempt.

Santo Domingo, the administrative capital for the West Indies and Tierra Firme, was one of the largest cities in the Spanish empire, impressively laid out with stone buildings and spacious streets and plazas. It was fortified and had a small garrison of trained soldiers. Its capture was by far the most ambitious feat yet undertaken by an English commander in the West Indies. Drake took the place by tactics similar to those used earlier by Sores at Havana, but with a force more than ten times the size of that of Sores. The damage to the prosperity of the city was heavy and permanent. All the principal buildings were gutted, the guns and stores of the fort taken away, and the ships of the island guard squadron burned in the harbour.

Drake's next major objective, Cartagena, was a much smaller town than Santo Domingo, but strategically much more important and likely to be a richer prize, for it was a collecting depot for goods and treasure to be loaded for Spain. It was well defended, and Drake's attack, in the teeth of brave and well-organised resistance, was perhaps the most brilliant of all his amphibious operations, involving intricate and dangerous pilotage and synchronised landings through heavy surf. In the course of the fighting, however, the English forces were reduced by casualties and sickness from their original number of 2,300 to about 800 fit men. There could be no question of holding Cartagena with an English garrison. Drake decided to abandon his attempt on the Isthmus, and to make for the Cayman Islands and thence for Cape San Antonio, where, with his ships refitted and men refreshed, he hoped to intercept the *flota* from New Spain. The weather in May was bad, however, and the *flota* slipped through unmolested. Judging Havana too strong to be attacked, Drake sailed for home in June 1586, only pausing to destroy the fortifications which were being built at San Agustín, on the site of the ill-fated French settlement in Florida.

The 'Indies voyage', though it failed in its larger aims, did great material damage to Spanish possessions and even greater damage to Spanish prestige. The Spanish authorities did not fail to note the lessons of their defeats. In the 1590s the defence forces of the Indies were all strengthened both by land and by sea, despite the urgent need for ships and troops in Europe. A beginning was made by Antonelli, the best military engineer of his day, on the immense fortifications of Puerto Rico, the windward bastion of Caribbean defence, not so much because of the direct importance of the place to the Spaniards as because of the vital necessity of denying its use to Spain's enemies. At the same time, communications between the Caribbean bases were improved by the provision of fast despatch boats. When in 1595 another great fleet left England, under the joint command of Drake and Hawkins, on what was to be for both their last Indies voyage, they found the Spaniards ready and able to resist. The English were defeated at San Juan del Puerto Rico (though curiously enough, a less able leader, Cumberland, succeeded in taking the place— but not in holding it—three years later). They abandoned their project for a second attack on Cartagena. On the Isthmus—where the Spaniards had abandoned Nombre de Dios for the more defensible harbour of Puerto Bello—a picked party of 750 men set out overland for Panama, but were driven back to their boats by a combination of heavy rains and Spanish ambushes. After Drake's death off the coast of Veragua, Sir Thomas Baskerville, his successor in the command, was intercepted in the Florida Channel by a powerful fleet under Pedro Menéndez Marqués and had to fight his way out in a running battle, the first naval action between regular fleets to be fought in the West Indies. The action was inconclusive; but it cleared the Caribbean of invaders at a time when Spain was suffering heavy defeats in Europe and could not have spared ships or men to reinforce the West Indies.

The attempts made by the French and the English in the sixteenth century to break the Spanish monopoly of trade and territorial power in the West Indies were thus, on the whole, failures; or, at least, their successes were only temporary. Sporadic raiding continued and an extensive but still risky smuggling trade had developed. The Dutch, in particular—newcomers to the Caribbean—being denied access, by their war with Spain, to Portuguese sea salt, began in the very last years of the century a lucrative trade to the coast of Venezuela, bringing manufactured goods, and returning to Europe with tobacco and hides in addition to the salt which they dug from the natural pans at Araya. The Spaniards could still retaliate, however. In 1605 Luis Fajardo captured twelve Dutch ships at Araya and for a time closed the trade. In any case Venezuela and the islands were marginal provinces; the main sources of Caribbean trade remained virtually untouched.

In 1596, at the Treaty of the Hague, France under Henry IV, England and the United Provinces formed an alliance against Spain which seemed strong enough to dismember the Spanish empire; and a joint English and Dutch fleet promptly destroyed a whole American convoy lying in Cádiz harbour, thus stopping communication between Spain and the Indies for nearly two years. This alliance, also, failed to fulfil its promise; the French backed out and made their peace separately in the Treaty of Vervins in 1598. According to later accounts, Henry IV tried to secure a share of the American trade in this treaty. There is no contemporary evidence of these attempts; if made at all, they were unsuccessful. Spain, exhausted as she was, lacking the men, the ships and the money to back her vast responsibilities, still would not consider the open admission of foreign traders to her Caribbean preserves. The West Indies continued to attract adventurers, and in increasing numbers; but their enterprise was still confined to smuggling and raiding, activities which lapsed easily and naturally into piracy.

The profits and the dangers of West Indian voyages together help to explain the long reluctance of English and French adventurers to emulate the Spaniards and establish settlements of their own in areas unoccupied by Spain. The hope of booty in the West Indies was high enough to cause a lack of both private capital and public support for more constructive ventures elsewhere; and would-be settlers and merchants were handicapped by the danger of being held liable for the raids of the privateers. This was not the only explanation, of course. Another was the idea that since the Spaniards had occupied, and could defend, all the richest and most populous parts of America, nothing remained that was worth the danger and expense of annexation. It is true that this was not certainly known. Raleigh, for one, did not believe it and saw himself as a potential *conquistador*; but Raleigh was exceptional, and Guiana, the no-man's-land of great rivers between Spanish Venezuela and Portuguese Brazil, bred illusions. The motives which chiefly impelled men to explore the North American coast in the 1570s and 1580s did not immediately suggest the establishment of colonies. The fisheries were, it is true, a valuable attraction; but fishermen did not concern themselves with settlement. The north-west passage to 'Cathay' promised trade, not colonisation. Gold and silver certainly attracted Englishmen as much as Spaniards; but even the mercurial Elizabethans—and most certainly the queen herself—were aware of the hopelessness of prospecting at random over a vast continent. The fiasco of Frobisher's three voyages of 1576–7–8, with their cargoes of spurious gold, put inventors off gold-hunting for many years.

A new interest in American colonisation for its own sake first appeared among Englishmen who had gained relevant experience in Ireland. Ireland was on the way to America. Many of the west-countrymen who attempted American settlements—Gilbert, Grenville, Raleigh—had been prominent in the settlement of Ireland and thought naturally of applying their experience in more promising surroundings, among less intractable people. Land was the greatest single outlet for speculation and investment in sixteenth-century England, but speculative dealings in land had made it dear and many estates were unprofitable because of cumbersome tenurial arrangements and the heavy burdens placed on land held by feudal tenures from the crown. Some of the 'Ireland' group saw in America the prospect of acquiring vast estates, lightly encumbered, which they could rule with the power of feudal nobles. The Indians might (and did) prove too few and too primitive to supply a labour force; but homestead emigrants— people displaced from the land in England—might conceivably be persuaded that life among heathen Indians was preferable to life among Irish papists.

In the patent issued to Humphrey Gilbert in 1578—the first charter for the founding of a British colony—mention was made both of discovery and of conquest, but the destination of Gilbert's expeditions was left undefined. His intentions can only be deduced, partly from subsequent events, partly from his writings. The famous *Discourse of a discoverie for a new passage to Cataia* reads like an advertisement for Frobisher's Cathay Company and shows no interest in colonisation; but, though not published until 1576, most of the *Discourse* was written ten years earlier, before Gilbert went to Ireland. His letters and petitions of 1577, on the other hand, reflected not only his Irish experience, but also the influence of academic geographers, notably the celebrated John Dee, and contained far more imaginative and comprehensive proposals. Gilbert seems to have intended two settlements, one on the northern, the other on the southern part of the east coast of North America. The southern settlement was to be a base for heavy raids upon the Spanish Indies, the northern a staging-point on the way to 'Cathay'. In addition, the northern project was linked with the possibility of commanding the Banks fisheries. There was know-ledge as well as imagination behind this idea; throughout sixty years of fishing on the Banks, Englishmen suffered in competition with Portuguese, Spaniards, French and Dutch because they had no access to cheap and plentiful supplies of salt. They relied, therefore, on drying their catch ashore, instead of salting it down wet in cask at sea. While, therefore, English fishermen were in a minority on the Banks at sea, they were numerous and strong on the Newfoundland beaches, where they estab-lished their summer camps and drying-stages. On this predominance, a territorial lordship could perhaps be based. The whole scheme had a majestic coherence. It was an Atlantic counterpart to what Drake, in the same year, set out to accomplish in the Pacific. Nothing much came of it in practice. On his last voyage, in 1583, Gilbert 'took possession' of Newfoundland, and since nobody seriously disputed the claim, Newfound-land remained British; but at the time, the 'possession' was a mere formality and can have meant little to the fishermen. On the return passage Gilbert was drowned. It might have gone hard with the Indians had he succeeded in founding a colony. In Ireland he always behaved with ferocious severity towards a conquered people.

Raleigh at once undertook to carry forward his half-brother's originating ideas, concentrating his attention upon the southern sector of the North American coast. He secured in 1584 a charter with even fuller powers and sent out an exploratory expedition in the same year. In 1585 a second expedition, commanded by Grenville, established a settlement on Roanoke Island, among the shoals and inlets of the Carolina Banks. It was an unsuitable place, lacking a deep-water anchorage. As usual in these early enterprises, the promoters underestimated the needs of the settlers for supplies and support from home. The settlers soon became discouraged; and when Drake, on his way home from the Indies voyage, appeared off Roanoke, they took passage to England in his ships. Grenville's relief expedition arrived a few weeks later to find them gone. In 1587 Raleigh sent out a new colony of over a hundred men and women with instructions to go to Chesapeake Bay, where the anchorage was better. They settled once more upon Roanoke, however, and were left to their own devices. A small relief expedition early in 1588 failed to get across the Atlantic, because of pirates; the Armada crisis intervened to prevent Grenville sailing with a stronger force; and it was not until 1590 that an expedition reached Roanoke, to find that the colonists had disappeared. To this day no one knows what happened to them. That was the end of sixteenth-century English attempts to settle in North America. They had all been purely private attempts. The queen contributed nothing to them except the name Virginia; though it is fair to add that without her favour Raleigh would not have had the means to embark on projects of settlement at all. Raleigh himself transferred his attention to Guiana. His expeditions to Guiana, and his attempts to justify them, gave to the world a masterpiece of English prose, *The Discovery of the large, rich and beautiful Empire of Guiana*, in which, incidentally, he paid handsome tribute to the courage, skill and pertinacity of the Spaniards. Raleigh, however, after years at court, was no *conquistador* and no match for his rival Berrio in surmounting the hardships of tropical exploration. He founded no colony in Guiana. His contemporaries, Leigh, Harcourt, Roe, fared no better, though their hopes were more modest, and centred upon tobacco-planting rather than upon El Dorado. In the end, years later, it was the Dutch who succeeded.

In all colonisation, two sets of factors are necessary for success: the private, spontaneous, largely economic urges; and the directing, protecting, sometimes limiting policy of government. The two are equally essential; without the one, the other can accomplish little. Neither was present in sufficient strength, either in France or in England, in the sixteenth century. Patrons, prospectors, merchants, for the most part, failed to see their interest in colonial ventures overseas. It is true that in England a land–labour problem existed and was growing more acute; but homestead emigrants long continued to find an outlet in Ireland rather than in the Americas. At the same time, a long-term constructive policy of settlement appeared unattractive to English governments when compared with the quicker returns and greater dividends to be gained by raiding. Governmental support and organisation in England never advanced in the sixteenth century beyond the primitive urge to oppose Spain wherever she claimed to rule. One of Gilbert's most persuasive petitions in 1577 had been entitled *A discourse on how her Majesty may annoy the King of Spain* —by an unprovoked attack on the Spanish and Portuguese fishing fleets. The Roanoke ventures, similarly, as far as government was concerned, were merely flanking movements in the attack on Spain, of secondary interest. In France after Cateau-Cambrésis, the people most interested in raiding the Spanish Indies or in founding American settlements were Huguenots from the Atlantic ports; and in a country torn by religious strife, Catholic governments neither could nor would support the colonising activities of dissident groups. So, at the end of the sixteenth century as at the beginning, the only settled colonies in America were those of Spain and Portugal, loosely united after 1580 under the Spanish crown. No other nation had achieved anything in the way of permanent settlement and only a few visionaries had contemplated anything worth achieving.

The early years of the seventeenth century saw the beginning of a far-reaching change, both in France and in England. In those years European settlement on the Atlantic coasts of North America first took root. For the first time, private capital and governmental support joined to make permanent colonisation possible in areas where no semi-civilised docile native labour force existed. One reason for this change of attitude was the growing suspicion that Spain had been overrated; that Spanish power was largely an illusion, maintained by prestige and American bullion. The Spaniards were short of ships, and many of the ships they had were obsolescent. Shortage of materials, shortage of trained artificers, conservatism in design and manufacture, had caused them to fall behind both English and Dutch in the development of ships and of ordnance. Deeply committed as they were in Europe, they were short also of fighting men, sailors and soldiers. The silver fleets, and the sea-lanes through which they passed, were well defended; but the very concentration of warships and garrisons in the West Indies made it impossible for Spain to defend its pretensions to monopoly elsewhere in the Americas. Moreover, the Spaniards had lost interest. In 1590 they had searched diligently for the Virginia settlement in order to destroy it, not knowing that it had already disappeared. There were plans for settling and fortifying on Chesapeake Bay, to forestall further English attempts there. The plans came to nothing and the opportunity was lost. By 1602, believing the danger to be past, the government was again discouraging expansion, and responsible officials were even thinking of abandoning, as worthless, their own colony of Florida. English promoters were right when they argued that in eastern North America the Spaniards need not be attacked; they could be ignored.

Another reason for the change of attitude in England was a new assessment of the economic and social advantages to be gained by western planting. The old, unsophisticated desire for land and hope of gold remained strong; but, in addition, colonies in America might produce other goods of which England stood in need: cheap food, especially fish; luxuries such as wine and dried fruit, normally imported from France or the Mediterranean; tobacco, an American product rapidly gaining popularity in Europe; above all, strategic supplies such as timber, hemp and pitch, which normally came from Baltic sources and might be cut off by a hostile naval power. Conversely, colonies would be an exclusive market for English manufacturers; even the Indians might be brought to 'civility' and taught to wear broadcloth. Colonies would cure unemployment—prevalent as the result of changes in agrarian organisation—by drawing off the (supposedly) surplus population and turning paupers into useful labourers or smallholders. Conscientious nonconformists, with no desire to plot against the crown, might find places where they could worship in peace. Leading Catholics had supported Gilbert, and Dissenters were later to settle in New England. There was something in it for everyone—government, investors, emigrants. Finally, a great volume of shipping would be needed, an employment for seamen in peace and a source of naval strength in war.

Propaganda played a great part in creating this new optimism. The concentration of English interest upon America was largely due to the life's work of the younger Hakluyt. He was the prime organiser of geographical publishing. We owe to him nearly everything we know of the early American voyages. He was the one continuing figure linking the two waves of Virginia enterprise—the abortive attempts of the 1580s and those which gained a permanent footing after the turn of the century. His interest had first been kindled by Gilbert's projects. His early tract, the *Discourse of Western Planting*, was a bold plea for making North American colonisation a matter for the enterprise and resources of the state as well as of private persons. The plea had little immediate effect, because Hakluyt's opinion was not shared by the queen or her immediate advisers; but for nearly forty years Hakluyt continued to write, to record, to publish, and to advise. He knew most of the leading adventurers personally. The *Principall Navigations* is a monument of historical enquiry, of careful preservation and scholarly editing of original accounts. No other seafaring nation possesses anything like it. To Hakluyt's contemporaries, it was not only a record of past achievements but an incitement to fresh endeavours. His work was complementary to that of scientific navigators such as John Davis and of the geographers and mathematicians, among whom John Dee—who also had direct access to the queen—was pre-eminent. He was followed by a host of other pamphleteers, many of them able and persuasive. The later Elizabethan poets and playwrights in turn took up the song. Gradually influential men in England, statesmen, courtiers, financiers, came round to Hakluyt's way of thinking. No colonies ever had a better 'press' than Virginia and Newfoundland.

The death of the old queen accelerated the swing from raiding towards settlement. James I made peace with Spain in 1604 and insisted on his subjects' keeping the peace, as Raleigh discovered to his cost. Many respectable shipowners, apt enough for privateering in war, drew the line at piracy in peace. On the other hand, the government raised no objection to peaceful settlement in places not already occupied; on the contrary. In the negotiations for the Treaty of London in 1604, James declared himself willing to recognise Spanish monopolistic claims to all territory effectively occupied by Spain, but admitted no Spanish rights in unoccupied parts of America. The principle of effective occupation was embodied in a formal clause in the truce of Antwerp in 1609, which ended for a time the war between the Netherlands and Spain. It became a principle of international law, accepted explicitly by jurists and implicitly by most maritime states. The tacit consent of 1604, as James must have intended, covered the settling activities of the English in Virginia from 1606 onwards.

All the English colonies in America were planted in places where the native population was sparse and primitive, numerous enough to be dangerous but too wild to be employed as a labour force. Sixteenth-century failures had taught promoters their lesson: that they would have to transplant whole communities with a complete labour force of Europeans. These men had somehow to be induced to emigrate. The cost of their emigration had to be paid and their tools, seed and equipment provided from England by promoters. The risk, responsibility and expense were more than a private individual or a small group of partners could undertake. Colonisation, to be successful, must be a joint-stock enterprise in which many people might invest their money without necessarily adventuring their persons. In order to float such a company, with a legal title to the soil, with authority to govern the settlers and with a claim to naval defence, a royal charter was necessary. The charters granted to the Virginia Company in 1606, 1609, and 1612 owed their form largely to the persistence and ingenuity of Sir Thomas Smythe, the great London merchant who became the company's first treasurer. They were adaptations of the type of charter normally granted to trading companies; they established a highly original and significant pattern of co-operation between the crown, the city merchants who financed the project, and the settlers. The general government of the company was entrusted to the whole body of shareholders. A man could become a shareholder in two ways: the first by investing money, by buying shares; a share was valued at £12. 10s., the estimated cost of planting one settler. Alternatively, he could become a shareholder by investing his person, by emigrating to Virginia at his own expense with his family and servants. One body equalled one share. After an initial period of common labour, land was to be distributed among the shareholders, whether emigrant or not, in proportion to their investment. The emigrant shareholders were to become planters or free farmers, paying only a small quit-rent to the company. They at first composed, and later elected, the colonial Assembly. Below them in the social scale were the indented servants—men who emigrated at the expense of the company or of individual employers, binding themselves in return to work for a fixed term of years, hoping on the expiry of their indentures to set up for themselves as tenants or freeholders.

The directors, and investors generally, hoped to draw their dividend from quit-rents, from trading on their own account, and from duties levied on the trading of other merchants. They sent out voluminous instructions concerning the planting of profitable crops, the working of mines and the provision of naval stores. These instructions were never carried out. For the first few years the colonists were hard put to it to feed, house and defend themselves, even with help from England. More than half of them died within a few months of their arrival. Probably all would have died had it not been for the inspiring leadership and the Indian connections of John Smith at the beginning, and the character of the early governors, a series of old-soldier martinets, who by savage discipline kept their people to clearing and ploughing instead of wandering about the woods hunting and searching for gold-mines. The colonists escaped from a subsistence economy near to famine by cultivation of a single cash crop, tobacco. The art of growing and curing tobacco had been acquired from the Spaniards in the course of voyages to Guiana. Tobacco grew readily in Virginia and could be sold as readily to Dutch traders, who marketed it in Europe. By its means the little town of Jamestown, planted in May 1607 on the shore of the Tidewater, lived and grew, the beginning of a great Atlantic empire.

At the same time the foundations of another and very different empire were being laid far to the north. Since the Treaty of Cateau-Cambrésis French interest in the American continent had been limited and ineffectual; but French deep-sea fishermen had been prominent in the development of the Banks fisheries, and in the second half of the century men from the Biscayan ports began a profitable fishing and whaling industry within the Gulf of St Lawrence and in the estuary of the river itself. French seamen, going ashore to take in wood and water, to dry fish or to render blubber, first discovered that profits might be made by trading with the Indians, bartering tools and small articles of hardware for the fur robes which were the Indians' principal clothing and only marketable possessions. Furs, the livery of rank and wealth, and especially beaver furs, the raw material for an extremely durable felt, were valuable commodities in northern Europe. The great river which Cartier had first explored in 1534 in the hope of reaching the Pacific had never lost its fascination for adventurous Frenchmen. Now it began to acquire a new economic significance. Tadoussac, at the confluence of the Saguenay with the St Lawrence, became the scene of a seasonal fur market, so promising that in 1588 the crown was persuaded to grant a monopoly of the trade to two of Cartier's nephews in return for an engagement to found a colony. Nothing came of this scheme, nor of several subsequent projects. In 1598 La Roche planted a short-lived colony on Sable Island; and in 1599 Chauvin made an unsuccessful attempt to found a permanent settlement at Tadoussac. With its bitter winter, its granite rock, its cold lakes and its dark fir forests, Canada was an inhospitable country for pioneers. The fishermen only knew it in the summer.

The combination of fish and fur, however, was an increasingly powerful attraction; and if the fisheries and the fur trade of the area were to be monopolised effectively by Frenchmen, there must be permanent French settlement. After the accession of Henry IV the prospect of consistent support from the crown improved. In 1605 a new patentee, de Monts, succeeded in planting on the bay shore of Acadia, now Nova Scotia. Like Virginia, Acadia had a resident historian in its early years, the lively Marc Lescarbot, who recorded the painful stages by which the colony became established. It grew into a modest community of tough, self-sufficient fishermen and peasant farmers. In 1610 it received—significant arrival—the first two Jesuit missionaries to reach New France. By 1613 it was sufficiently established to attract the jealous hostility of the Virginia Company. It was to be a bone of contention for well over a hundred years.

The St Lawrence basin was a much bigger problem. The systematic investigation of this great waterway, leading not, as they hoped, to the Pacific, but into the heart of the American continent, was the work of Samuel de Champlain and of the followers whom he inspired. Champlain came appropriately from Brouage, source of much of the salt which kept the fisheries going. Sailor, cartographer and scientist, he had no golden illusions about a northern Peru. He was one of the greatest and most practical of seventeenth-century explorers and enjoyed throughout his career the generous confidence both of his government and of his commercial backers. Through the help of an uncle who was a pilot in the Spanish navy, he made a two-year visit to the Spanish Indies in 1599–1600, and his published account of his experiences first brought him into royal favour. From 1603 until his death in 1635 he devoted himself to North American discovery. Three years of this period, from 1604 to 1607, were spent in meticulous exploration of the Bay of Fundy and the Maine coast. Otherwise, his attention was concentrated on the St Lawrence basin. He was the first European to make extensive use of Indian canoes for inland travel, a significant pointer for the future; the first discoverer of the Great Lakes; and the first to grasp the commercial possibilities of the lesser waterways—the Saguenay, the Ottawa, the Richelieu—converging on the St Lawrence. In 1608, passing by the Basque monopolists at Tadoussac, Champlain founded Quebec on the cliff commanding the narrow bend of the river a hundred miles further upstream, and proceeded to use his unrivalled acquaintance with the Indians to concentrate the fur trade in the new settlement. Quebec was a trading station rather than a colony; its inhabitants got not only their trade goods but most of their food from France. All their communications, with France and with the Indian interior, were by water. It is curious that Champlain never appreciated the strategic weakness of this water empire: the Hudson valley pointed like a spear at the heart of New France. He certainly knew, by Indian report, of an Atlantic outlet from Lake Champlain. Hudson discovered the mouth of the river which bears his name in 1609, only a year after the founding of Quebec, and Dutch traders soon began to exploit the river trade upstream from the coast. The threat to New France, however, was far in the future, and for long Quebec was the key to Canada.

The chronology of the development of French America corresponds closely to the English story. The moves of the two nations suggest either conscious mutual imitation or the tactical counter-moves of the chessboard. The great variety of the pieces and the immense size of the board were not fully revealed until long after 1610; but by that date the general pattern of the game could be discerned. The Spaniards were left in general —though by no means undisputed—possession of the Caribbean and the 'waist' of America. Tiny settlements, French on the St Lawrence, English on the Atlantic coast, were taking root and becoming jealously aware of one another's distant presence. The Dutch, freed by the truce of Antwerp, were lying off-shore to pick up whatever might be going in the way of plunder or freight. The board was set for two hundred years of armed imperial rivalry.

2. ASIA AND AFRICA

Until late in the sixteenth century, over most of Asia, except the Spanish Philippines, the only Europeans wielding military and political power and engaged in corporate commercial activity were the Portuguese. Their officials, troops, settlers and traders, and the clergy working under the patronage of the Portuguese crown, were Europe's only representatives in wide areas from east Africa to China. Their eastern empire, the *Estado da India*, an established and familiar part of the Asian scene, thus represented the first solution to the problems of organising European enterprise in a very distant East. The problems were manifold: problems of management, the creation at home and overseas of instruments of control effective over unprecedented distances, technical problems of navigation, supply and defence, the political problem of relationships with powerful, aggressive, though often mutually hostile, Asian powers, the commercial problems of attempting to secure a monopoly in the spice trade and of securing the purchasing power to sustain trade when Europe had few products suited to eastern markets, and the moral problem of combining politics and trade with Christian duty. The pioneering solutions offered were not all equally effective, though some were taken over by other European powers in Asia, but all are interesting.

The original impulse to expand overseas had come from the Crown, and the *Estado da India* remained a royal enterprise throughout the sixteenth century.[1] The main purpose was commercial, to tap Asian trade directly and secure the middleman's profits for the crown. The primacy of the commercial motive might be obscured by chroniclers who wrote in terms of a crusade against the Muslim and of personal glory,[2] or by missionaries who wrote for the edification and encouragement of the faithful, but the *Estado da India* remained throughout a trading enterprise rather than an instrument of conquest and settlement.

To handle overseas affairs various new institutions had been created in Lisbon: the India House, responsible for shipping, outward cargoes and the sale of incoming spices; the Arsenal, which recruited crews, furnished

[1] See vol. II, ch. XX, pp. 601–4.
[2] The exception is Gaspar Correa, whose *Lendas da India* emphasise commercial motives and discuss the mechanics of trade and administration.

masters and pilots, charts and instruments and arms for the voyage; the High Court of Appeal, the *Desembargo do Paço*, dealing with judicial appointments and regulations overseas; the Board of Conscience and Military Orders, which handled religious affairs. The busiest of these was the India House, where all products from overseas were separately registered and either charged duty if they were private or stored for sale if they were crown purchases. The operations of the royal factory in Flanders, in the first half of the century, and the sales by contract to merchant syndicates thereafter, were alike supervised by the India House. The House also prepared cargoes for outward-bound fleets, negotiated ship construction and supervised provisioning, and maintained the register of all persons going to the East, and copies of all correspondence therewith.

The overseas departments were supervised and co-ordinated by the five-man private council of the king, but, despite its many duties, no separate India secretaryship was created until 1569, and the post was in abeyance from 1578 to 1584. Clogging of the machinery necessarily followed. After 1580 the union of the crowns of Spain and Portugal caused further complications. The promise of Philip II of Spain to respect the separate identity and interests of Portugal and her empire meant that the detailed operations of the overseas departments were thenceforth subject to review by a new Portuguese treasury council, by the viceroy for Portugal at Lisbon, and by the secretary for Indian affairs in the Council of Portugal at Valladolid before they reached the overburdened king. If the *Estado da India* gained by being a direct concern of the crown, it also suffered from the multiplication of interlocking, often conflicting, authorities, always undermanned, always swamped with detail. Indecision and delay were built into the system.

The burden on the India House was also increased by a breakdown in the marketing system for its pepper, spices, and other oriental wares. These had been shipped twice a year to the royal factory at Antwerp and there sold to merchant syndicates, mainly south German, for distribution in Europe. The system had worked well: the Portuguese could offer a semi-monopoly of pepper and spices, while the Hochstetters, Welsers, Manlichs and Fuggers could supply the German silver and Hungarian copper which the Indian and African trade required. The growth of Antwerp as an international commodity and money market had further facilitated operations. But by the mid-sixteenth century the Portuguese grip upon the pepper trade in Asia had been seriously weakened, while in Europe French attacks upon Portuguese shipping making for Antwerp forced the crown to make increasing use of foreign, notably Amsterdam, shipping. At the same time the south Germans were hit, as purveyors of silver, by the flow of American silver, their command of the Baltic trade was challenged by the growth of Dutch seaborne trade through the Sound, and their home markets were disrupted by the Schmalkaldic War. In 1548 the Portuguese factory at Antwerp was closed, the profitable carrying trade was abandoned, and buyers for northern markets were left to make their purchases at Lisbon direct from the India House. The growth of Netherlands resistance to imperial financial demands, the Spanish state bankruptcy of 1557 and associated chain of south German failures, followed by a Portuguese suspension of payments in 1569, and then the revolt of the Netherlands, closure of the Scheldt and sack of Antwerp, all ensured that the old pattern based on Antwerp could not be restored.

The retreat from northern Europe involved a loss of profits to the crown, but more serious was a revival of Levantine trade in pepper and spices, evident in the 1540s and threatening by the 1550s. The advance of Turkish power to Aden in 1538 and to Basra in 1546 opened the way to the Indian Ocean; the Ottoman alliance with France in 1539 and peace with Venice in 1540 re-opened the routes to southern Europe. Thenceforth the old Levant trade with Asia rapidly revived. The Fuggers switched their copper exports to Venice and by 1558 they were closing down at Lisbon and experimenting successfully with spice purchases at Alexandria. At the same period the Venetian consul at Aleppo described the caravan traffic in spices from Basra to Aleppo as 'one of the primary foundations of the trade of our colony'. By the late 1560s Dutch and English observers estimated that nearly half of Europe's pepper was arriving by the Levant routes. Rising European consumption and general inflation prevented any dramatic fall in spice prices, but the cut-back in Portuguese profits was nevertheless damaging. Speculation by the great merchant syndicates further affected the Lisbon market and in 1569 the crown suspended payments in Antwerp. In 1570 King Sebastian was driven to a drastic change, the abandonment of the crown monopoly of trade in pepper and other spices. All his subjects were now permitted to trade in these articles, and Malabar ports were thrown open to purchasers. The only obligation imposed upon them was that all spices must be despatched to Lisbon, there to pay duty in the India House.

The measure was an admission that the Portuguese crown, burdened with the defence of North Africa against Muslim, and of West Africa against European, enemies and busy with the opening up of Brazil, lacked the resources to manage the whole trade between Lisbon and Goa. The revival of the Levant trade was likewise an indication that Portuguese power was overstrained in Asia. Occupied with the defence of Malacca and the Moluccas against heavy local attacks, extended by the opening of trade with China and Japan, the naval forces of the *Estado* could no longer regularly sweep the Red Sea and Persian Gulf of Turkish galleys or block new spice routes opened by traders in south-east Asia. Moreover, the eleven years of regency after King John III's death in 1557 weakened the crown's control of its servants in the East, opening the way to connivance at the smuggling of pepper and spices. As a Venetian consul explained, the spices reaching Cairo were 'allowed to pass by the Portuguese soldiers who govern India in the Red Sea for their profit against the commands of their King, for they can make a living in that region only by selling cinnamon, cloves, nutmeg, mace, ginger, pepper and other drugs'. Administrative reorganisation of the *Estado da India* by King Sebastian in 1569, and a further tightening up by Philip II after 1580, partially restored the situation in India, while anti-Ottoman revolts in Arabia and the Yemen, a renewal of warfare between Venice and Turkey in 1570, and disorders in Turkey after Selim II's death more seriously disrupted the Levant routes. Even so, spices continued to pass to the Levant in considerable quantities throughout the rest of the century.

The throwing open of the spice trade in 1570 did not lead to the growth of private Portuguese enterprise. The native merchant class, weakened by the expulsion of the Jews, could not take over from the crown, especially as the crown retained a monopoly of silver and copper exports. From 1575, therefore, the crown was driven to farming out both the purchase and shipment of spices and their distribution in Europe in India and Europe contracts. Thus the first India contract provided for the purchase of 30,000 quintals of pepper a year, the contractor putting up the capital and being paid at the India House for what he landed. The first Europe contract, angled for by Philip II, who wished to establish a staple in his Italian possessions, by the Grand Duke of Tuscany, and by the old south German groups, Sebastian entrusted to the politically innocuous hands of the German Konrad Roth, who agreed to buy 20,000 quintals a year at Lisbon, and to make a large immediate loan for Sebastian's North African adventure, to be repaid in pepper.

Few contracts turned out well. Roth, for example, was led by a shortage in Levant supplies in 1578 to make a bid for a corner in pepper by adding the India to his Europe contract. He intended with Elector Augustus of Saxony to make Leipzig the northern pepper staple, but the effort, made when both English and Dutch were preying on the sea-routes to northern Europe, proved too great and by 1580 Roth was bankrupt. Philip II, now king of Portugal, again sought to switch the pepper market from the hostile north to Italy. He offered Venice the Portuguese pepper at favourable rates and, being refused, tried Milan, Genoa and Florence—in vain. From 1591, therefore, the India contract went to Italians and the Spanish Fuggers, and the Europe contract to a consortium shared by Rovelasca, the Welsers, Fuggers and Spanish and Portuguese associates. Both contracts proved disastrous for the participants. Indian shipments, hit by Achinese attacks on Malacca and by the English capture of the rich *Madre de Dios* in 1592, were only half the stipulated 30,000 quintals a year. In Europe the ban on trade with England and Holland in 1585 was followed by the Armada disaster, the attack on Cádiz in 1596, and a blockade of the Tagus in 1598. With the Levant trade rapidly reviving from about 1590, the

Portuguese trade with Asia was already in great difficulties even before first the Dutch and then the English pushed round the Cape to the East.

The Portuguese crown had failed to retain in its own hands the management of the trade between Goa and Lisbon and between Lisbon and the markets in Europe. It had been driven out of the carrying trade to northern Europe. It had failed in its attempts to escape from the grip of the Fuggers, Welsers and their confederates. It had failed even to keep foreigners out of India: the viceroy and his officials were charged with the unpopular duty of giving priority to the purchasing operations of the India contractors, whose agents, Sasseti, Kron and their like, were firmly established in Goa and the pepper ports. It found great difficulty in safeguarding the Atlantic routes for its Indiamen against English, French and Dutch privateering attack. In Asia the attempt to hold up the profits of the pepper trade by the application of force also showed diminishing returns. The force which the crown could deploy there—guard fleets, fortress garrisons, military expeditions—had never been large. With the small Portuguese population hard pressed by the demands of North and West Africa, Brazil and the Spanish war machine, and major threats developing in Asia, decline in the East might have seemed likely to follow decline in the West.

Had the *Estado da India* depended for its survival on the trade with Europe and on the military resources which could be furnished from home, decline must have been inevitable. The physical link between Lisbon and Goa was weak in the extreme. All the men, money and goods supplied to the *Estado da India* had to be crammed into an annual fleet of four, five or six ships: some five thousand tons a year in the 1550s rising to at most ten thousand tons at the close of the century. Some three thousand men might embark with a new viceroy—his relatives, retainers and slaves, fidalgos going to take up official postings, clergy, merchants and troops— less in other years. But of these numbers on average only two-thirds reached India in safety—perhaps fewer towards the end of the century. Ships were lost in increasing numbers as the search for maximum cargo space and profits led to ever larger and more unwieldy vessels and to skimped refits. The crown's failure to provide funds beforehand also meant that many fleets sailed out of season. Even if the ships reached Goa safely, losses of men could be appalling, for many troops came straight from the slums of Lisbon, riddled with disease, to crowded ships in which sanitary discipline and medical care were quite inadequate. Since every three years there was also an exodus for home of fidalgos who had served their turn as captains, factors and the like, accompanied by their families and slaves,[1] the numbers added yearly to the total of home-born Portuguese in the *Estado* was limited indeed.

[1] Diogo de Couto notes that in 1559 two homeward-bound Indiamen had 1,137 persons aboard them: *Da Asia*, decade VII, book VIII, ch. XIII, pp. 262 ff.

It has been estimated that at any one time there were never more than six or seven thousand native-born Portuguese liable to military service within the confines of the *Estado da India*. The garrisons of major strong points—Mozambique, Ormuz, Diu or Malacca—were only a few hundred strong, and the conquest of Ceylon was attempted, and almost achieved, with less than a thousand Portuguese troops. But to these exiguous numbers from Portugal must be added local mercenaries fighting under their own leaders; *topazes*, native and half-caste Christians; large bodies of household slaves, African, Malay and Japanese; the forces of Asian allies such as Cochin or Tidore; and the *casados* or married Portuguese settlers who could always be called upon for local defence. These *casados* were allotted crown villages on condition of service at call with cavalry horses or musketeers maintained at their expense. It was with such mixed local forces, stiffened with troops from Portugal, that the *Estado da India* was able to hold and at places enlarge its possessions in this period.

The defence of the *Estado da India*, a coastal and island empire, depended ultimately upon Portuguese sea-power. This, too, was limited and never fully adequate to its manifold tasks, so that while it was dealing with Ottoman threats in the West, Malacca was left dangerously open to Achinese attack, and when attention was then turned East, the Ottomans could slip in to sack Muscat. But throughout the sixteenth century the Portuguese avoided any permanent reverse in Asian waters, other than the loss of the Moluccas, and they kept the sea-lanes open for their carracks and coasting fleets. This was not achieved with fleets from Portugal, for only an occasional galleon came out for service in eastern waters, but with ships built or purchased in Asia. A number of carracks and galleons were built in the royal dockyards at Goa, using Canara teak, masts and spars from Bassein, coir from the Maldives, sail-cloth from Gujarat. When fire destroyed the Goa squadron of twelve sail in 1555, Governor Barreto was able to replace them all with India-built ships within his three years of office. However, for all but the long-distance crown voyages, such as those to Mozambique, the Moluccas and China, carracks were not used, but caravels, galliots and foists. These, like the galleys used for coastal defence and convoy, were again India-built. Locally built, they were also locally manned, for Arabs, Malays, Javanese and Japanese, and fishermen from the west coast of India formed the major part of the crews of both navy and merchant marine. Linschoten comments, indeed, on the number of merchantmen he found with no more than captain and pilot Portuguese. Portuguese command of the main sea-routes in Asia and Portuguese occupation of key points ashore thus depended in large measure upon Asian instruments, skills and spirit harnessed and directed by Europeans. Just as the British conquered an Indian empire with Indian sepoys, so the Portuguese held the *Estado da India* with Arab lascars, African slaves and Christian *topazes*.

As a military and political structure the *Estado da India* became to a considerable degree autonomous during the course of the sixteenth century. The maritime links with Portugal were tenuous, and the degree of control which could be exercised over officials in such quarters as the Moluccas, eighteen months distant from Goa and thirty from Lisbon, was obviously minimal. In financial terms, too, the *Estado* must be considered a largely independent unit. The pepper and spice trade between Goa and Lisbon was obviously important, supplying as it did half or more of Europe's consumption, but the profit derived by the crown with difficulty provided for the European costs of Asian enterprise. The pay of officials, troops and clergy, the maintenance of guard-fleets and fortifications, the support of missionary effort in Asia—all these were met from revenues and profits generated on the spot. Some of the revenues were territorial, such as the quit-rents paid by the *casados* upon their fiefs or the land revenue drawn from temple lands and made over to the clergy. But far more important than these were the customs receipts, which by the end of the century provided almost two-thirds of the regular revenues of the *Estado*. Since trade ran in narrow channels,[1] a handful of strategic strong points could exercise a considerable control over the inter-port trade of Asia. Moreover the natural flow of trade to such traditional entrepôts as Ormuz, Goa or Malacca was reinforced by the imposition of a system of *cartazes* or safe-conducts upon Asian shipping. Since the *cartaz* had to be taken out at a Portuguese factory and specified the ports to be visited, it served to drive trade into the hands of the Portuguese customs officer. With task forces patrolling the east African coast, the approaches to the Persian Gulf, western India and the Malacca Straits, much of the sea-borne trade of western Asia was compelled to pay toll to the *Estado* in customs dues, or to Portuguese officials in the form of bribes.

To these regular revenues must also be added the profits of trade conducted by officials on behalf of the crown and applied to the service of the *Estado da India*. Thus a share in the east African ivory trade was reserved to the captain of Mozambique, that in Arab horses provided a principal part of the rewards of the Ormuz captaincy, while in 1587 the trade in Gujarat indigo was granted to the contractors who built the Indiamen. Again, the proceeds of certain voyages, the annual clove galleon to the Moluccas, the nutmeg galleon to Banda, or the very lucrative China galleon, might either be allotted to specific public purposes such as the fitting out of a fleet or the fortification of a city, or be awarded to a favoured official, or even be put up for sale.

There was also a very lively port-to-port trade in private hands, managed by Portuguese officials and settlers, alone or in partnership with Asian merchants. Much of the wealth that sustained the *Estado da India* was generated in the course of this commerce, diversified with piracy and

[1] See vol. II, p. 593.

the misuse of official authority. Knots of Portuguese merchant adventurers were to be found everywhere from east Africa to China, sometimes operating from within Portuguese territories, but often established well beyond the limits of regular settlement, away up the Zambesi, in Abyssinia, on the eastern seaboard of India at Negapatam, San Thomé and Hugli, at Syriam or in Ayuthia, scattered through the ports of Indonesia and off the China coast. The organised efforts of the official trade were everywhere matched by the smaller-scale enterprise of individuals who as merchants, pilots and masters linked a series of trading areas from the Arabian to the China Sea.

The first of these areas was that which linked east Africa with the Red Sea, the Persian Gulf and western India. Portuguese influence had early been established over the string of Arab and Arab-African island settlements from Sofala to Malindi; and, thanks to their inter-city rivalries, Portuguese naval control of East African waters was scarcely challenged for most of the century. Mozambique was the most important Portuguese settlement, a refreshment point for the galleons passing through the Mozambique channel for India, a hospital or grave for many of their scurvy-ridden crews and passengers, and a refuge for homeward-bound fleets which failed to round the Cape. It was also the base for an active trade in amber, ebony, slaves, ivory and gold. The most glamorous item was gold. The Portuguese had found Arabs at Sofala trading in alluvial gold from the Manica area, and they proceeded to drive out these middlemen and establish their own outposts at Sena and Pate, two hundred miles up the Zambesi, whence caravans of porters annually went up to the gold fairs of the Monomotapa empire or tribal confederacy of Mashonaland to barter trade beads and cottons for gold. Linschoten in 1583 estimated the annual collection of gold at nine tons. Also of great importance was the ivory trade, mainly to Gujarat, in which from 1559 the captain of Mozambique was allowed to share to the tune of one hundred tusks a year.[1] Finally, at both Mozambique and the less profitable northern staple of Mombasa, there was a regular traffic in slaves, children being purchased for a few shillings in good years or a few measures of rice in bad. They were shipped to India for sale to the settlers and fidalgos, and numbers were also despatched to Malacca and to Macau, in China, where they formed a useful addition to the fighting power of the settlement. Both the official and private trade between Goa and Mozambique, from Goa in the spring with cottons, silks, some spices, wheat and rice, and back in autumn with gold, ivory, slaves, ebony, wax and ambergris, grew steadily in importance in the last years of the sixteenth century.

Trade with the Red Sea, in Turkish hands, was officially barred to the Portuguese, and a fleet cruised against Asian ships running pepper and

---

[1] Garcia da Orta in 1562 picturesquely declared that elephants were as numerous in Mozambique as cows in Europe.

spices to that quarter. Smuggling, however, made a mockery of official control, and Portuguese individuals took their share in the trade either by despatching goods through Indian partners, or by levying bribes for winking at contraventions of the regulations. By the Red Sea came fine woollens and silks, gold and silver coin and the much sought-after Abyssinian slaves, and to it went Indian cottons, indigo, spices and drugs, and large numbers of pilgrims bound for Mecca.

South Arabia, from allied Kishin to the Portuguese factory at Muscat, provided horses, camel-hair cloth, sugar and seed-pearls, and from Ormuz, key to the Persian Gulf, came a similar list of commodities, together with dyestuffs, Persian silks and carpets. Of all Portuguese possessions, Ormuz was the most lucrative. In the 1580s, Linschoten described it as 'the staple for all India, Persia, Arabia and Turkey...and commonly it is full of Persians, Armenians, Turks, and all nations, as also Venetians, who lie here to buy spices and precious stones that in great abundance are brought thither out of India'.

In India proper some new settlements, such as Damão in the north and Mangalore in Malabar, were effected, but the overall pattern of trade was not greatly modified. The conquest of Gujarat by the great Mughal emperor Akbar in 1572 introduced a new military threat to Portuguese possessions, but the unity and order he imposed and the impetus to trade provided by the linking of Gujarat and Malwa to the Mughal centres on the Jumna and Ganges were valuable compensations. Further south, Portuguese commerce certainly suffered a temporary dislocation when the Hindu empire of Vijayanagar was overthrown by the Muslim sultans of the Deccan in 1565, for Vijayanagar had taken as many as fifteen hundred Arabian cavalry horses a year, imported through Goa. It had also absorbed quantities of copper, quicksilver, and vermilion, coral and other European luxuries, and spices, sandalwood and Chinese silk, furnishing in return fine printed cottons for the Ormuz trade, and for Europe. By the end of the sixteenth century Muslim Bijapur and Golconda had in part replaced Vijayanagar as customers, but probably not completely.[1] In the pepper and ginger lands of Malabar the Portuguese may also have lost ground, for the violence of their captains led to a dragging series of wars involving most of the coastal rulers on one side or the other and unleashed a wave of attacks upon Portuguese coastal shipping at least until 1599. The failure of the India contractors from 1575 onwards to secure much more than half the usual 30,000 quintals of pepper a year from Malabar must in part at least be attributed to these political disturbances. On balance, however, it seems doubtful whether the trade of western India had declined, and contemporary observers depict Goa at the end of the sixteenth century as still flourishing and golden.

[1] Diogo de Couto, *Da Asia*, decade VIII, chapter XV, argues strongly that the fall of Vijayanagar was a blow to Portuguese commerce.

Round the Bay of Bengal there were a number of Portuguese settlements, some regularly organised, others pirate hide-outs, but all outside the direct control of the *Estado da India*. The most southerly, Negapatam, declined greatly after the fall of Vijayanagar, but San Thomé, near modern Madras, was an active entrepôt in the trade between India, Indonesia, Burma and Tenasserim, and was notable for its fine printed cottons. Other settlements existed in Orissa, a great rice-producing area which helped feed the Coromandel coast; and at Hugli, the main Ganges port of Mughal Bengal, the Portuguese from 1580 came to occupy a large quarter of their own. Here again there was great trade in foodstuffs— rice, sugar, butter and oil—and in the very fine muslins of the Dacca region and silks from the lower Ganges. Eastwards at Chittagong and in Arakan, trade was in slaves secured in raids upon eastern Bengal. Here, and in lower Burma, the Portuguese were truly described by Linschoten as having neither government nor police and living 'in a manner like wild men. . .'.

After this string of freebooter outposts, the state reasserted its power in Malacca, a great fortress and mart at one of the main crossroads of Asia. Its purpose was to guard and control the sea-borne trade between the Indian Ocean and China Sea, for it had no commercial hinterland, depended upon sea-borne food supplies, and lived upon custom-dues. Though Malacca was always exposed to the enmity of the Malay rulers of Johore and that of the sultan of Achin in northern Sumatra, and to the economic rivalry of both, its natural advantages ensured its commercial survival. To it flowed luxury goods from Europe and the Levant, opium from western India, the plain and coloured calicoes of Gujarat, the prints of Coromandel and foodstuffs from Bengal, tin from Malaya, pepper from eastern Sumatra and from Bantam in western Java, rice from central and eastern Java, sandalwood from Timor and Solor, nutmegs and mace from the Banda group, cloves from Amboina and Ternate, gold and camphor from Borneo, and Chinese goods collected from all the Indonesian ports at which they traded, all serving to maintain a most complex structure of inter-port trade. The Portuguese in Malacca were subject to frequent and violent attack, ten or a dozen assaults and sieges in the half century by Achin, Johore and Japara in northern Java. Persistent efforts were also made to undermine its trade. When Johore's links with India were broken, its Malay ruler sought forcibly to capture the trade with the pepper ports of eastern Sumatra, with Banda and with Borneo. Similarly the Achinese, a Muslim power outside the Straits of Malacca, opened pepper plantations in western Sumatra and developed routes down that coast and by way of the Sunda Straits to the spice islands, so circumventing Portuguese control. At the same time Achin developed links with Japara, whose queen twice attacked Malacca and who exercised much influence in Muslim Banda and Amboina. Venetian reports of up to fifty Achinese ships a year sailing direct to the Red Sea with pepper and spices in the mid-1560s show how serious a threat the Achinese presented to the Portuguese monopoly.

However, the contest between Malacca, Achin and Johore was a truly triangular one, and in the last resort rivalry between the Achinese and the Malays in Johore and eastern Sumatra was even more important to those powers than their enmity towards the Portuguese. In the last decades of the century, first the Malay rulers and then the sultan of Achin sought a military alliance with the Portuguese. Commercial rivalries similarly prevented any destruction of Malacca as an entrepôt. If Johore lowered prices to undercut Malacca, Portuguese officials flocked there to buy cheap. Likewise if Japara as a trader in spices resisted Portuguese attacks on Banda and Amboina, Japara as the outlet for central Javan rice was keenly interested in the great market for foodstuffs which Malacca provided. Official Portuguese trade might be politically directed to Hindu eastern Java, but private Portuguese trade with Muslim central Java was active. Bantam as a leading Muslim state might support Muslim resistance in the spice islands, but from 1560 to 1573 it contracted to supply 10,000 quintals of pepper a year for the ships despatched by the viceroy at Goa. The rivalries of their Asian enemies and the commercial interdependence of the trading centres of south-east Asia thus enabled a handful of Portuguese at Malacca to hold their own. Despite war and the extortion and misuse of power practised by the officials at Malacca, the trade of the port, as recorded in customs receipts, seems to have grown during the second half of the century.

That growth masked, however, a radical change in Portuguese fortunes. Malacca had originally been the base from which the Portuguese pushed out to the sources of the finer spices, the Bandas, Amboina and the Moluccan islands. There, by exploiting local rivalries, they had been able to establish their political power with fortified bases on Amboina and Ternate. They had thus acquired a dominant position in the trade of cottons and rice against cloves and nutmeg, though they could never achieve monopoly, for spice production spread widely as European purchases increased, and native trade in that world of islands was indestructible.

Ternate and Amboina were, however, the end of the world for the Portuguese, a monsoon away from Malacca and yet another from Goa, so that viceregal control of Portuguese captains, factors and fidalgos was always tenuous in the extreme. The two crown voyages for cloves and nutmeg came as a result to yield less and less to the crown, more and more to its servants. From 1535, therefore, private individuals were only allowed to purchase cloves on condition that they sold one-third at a fixed price to government. Individuals promptly offered more than the crown's factor to the growers, and secured the best of the crop and left the rubbish for the crown. The crown replied by securing cloves by compulsion, as tribute from the islanders and ordered that all cloves must be cleaned before delivery. The difficulties of the crown did not end there, however, for, when the spice galleons reached Malacca and the cloves were trans-shipped, much of the crown's third was embezzled by the local officials, so that from 1562 transhipment from Malacca had to be prohibited. Even so, the returns to the crown were limited, while the fidalgo in charge of the voyage and the private merchants shipping in or sailing with the galleon raked in the real profit.

The *Estado da India* thus failed either to secure a monopoly of the trade in spices or to secure a due return to the crown for the costs incurred in administering the spice islands and fitting out the annual spice voyages. But its lack of control was to have even more disastrous results when the ill discipline and tyranny of its local officials and the intolerance of missionaries working in the area led from 1556 onwards to a wave of rebellion against the Portuguese by the mainly Muslim islanders. The Portuguese forts in Ternate, Amboina and the Bandas were successively lost, and it was only because of the rivalry of Tidore with Ternate, and the aid received from the Spaniards in Manila, that a Portuguese foothold could be retained in the spice islands, at very great expense in men, ships and treasure. Trade did not cease, for the goods which the Portuguese could provide were much in demand and there were numerous inter-mediaries through whom purchases could be made. Nevertheless, the disturbances to which the spice trade had been exposed did damage the commerce of Malacca, and might have weakened its military capacity had not the Portuguese in this same period opened up a new regular trade with China and Japan.

The Portuguese first reached south China in 1514 and for seven years enjoyed a regular trade at Canton. Then failure to understand the tribute system under which the Ming regulated China's international relations and strong-arm tactics by Portuguese captains at Canton led to a rigorous imperial ban on Portuguese trade with China which lasted for some thirty years. From 1521 onwards, therefore, Portuguese trade became a mixture of smuggling and piracy among China's offshore islands. It was here that the Portuguese made contact with Japanese operating as tolerated members of tribute missions to the Ming until the 1540s and as fellow pirates thereafter, and so came to make their way to Japan itself.

The trade with both China and Japan, irregular if sometimes very profitable, was at this period in the hands of individuals. Before a settled trade with either country could be developed some more suitable perma-nent base than Malacca was required. The Portuguese eventually found it at Macau. This peninsula had been chosen by the Chinese officials at Canton as a custom-post for foreigners suitably distant from their city. From the 1540s the Portuguese had begun to trade there surreptitiously, and in 1554, perhaps in return for assistance against pirates in the Pearl River approaches, they were permitted by the Chinese authorities to make a permanent settlement at Macau. The trade driven by the Portuguese there and in Fukien and Chenkiang was at first only an extension of that conducted with Chinese merchants at Malacca, in Siam, in Javanese ports and off the Chinese coast. Its ingredients were a few European goods such as woollens, gold thread and coral together with Indian cottons and opium, African ivory and ebony, Sumatran pepper and Moluccan spices, and sandalwood from Timor. In return the Portuguese took silk and silk stuffs, porcelain and lacquer ware, rhubarb, musk, copper and gold—all staples of the Asian port-to-port trade, and now items in the trade to Europe too. With the opening of a regular trade from Macau to Japan, however, the pattern was radically transformed.

From the 1540s legitimate Japanese trade with China had been broken off by the Ming because of Japanese violence. The result was an upsurge of smuggling which degenerated into piracy, with large-scale raids from 1545 on the Chinese coast, culminating in the sack of major cities such as Nanking. This disruption of regular Chinese–Japanese trade presented a splendid opportunity to the Portuguese at Macau, who could step in as intermediaries. From their base at Macau, with access to the great market at Canton, the Portuguese built up a prosperous trade with the *daimyo* (barons) of Kyushu, the westernmost island of Japan. The *daimyo*, already busy with the economic development of their fiefs, welcomed the Portuguese, who by 1569 had the splendid harbour of Nagasaki in their administration. Thenceforth a regular trade was conducted between Macau and Nagasaki.

Two main items formed the basis of this trade: Chinese raw and woven silks and Japanese silver. In China silver, in terms of gold, was worth twice as much as in Japan or Europe, and since China's thirst for silver seemed unslakable, the Portuguese were able to make splendid profits as bullion brokers. Here they were aided by the rapid development in this period of silver mining and smelting in Japan, and by the pouring into Europe of Spanish American silver after the discovery of Potosí in 1545. By the end of the sixteenth century perhaps 200,000 cruzados worth of silver was being despatched annually from Lisbon to China—as much as the entire Portuguese pepper investment for Europe—together with 100,000 cruzados worth a year from Japan and a further fluctuating but important amount of American silver coming by way of the Philippines. This silver was invested at Canton in raw or woven silk for Japan, for the port-to-port trade of other parts of Asia, and for Europe and Spanish America. China also supplied gold which could be profitably disposed of in Japan, or in India where the gold–silver ratio was even more advantageous than in Japan. These main items were supplemented by such specialities as musk, rhubarb, porcelain and lacquer, together with painted screens, arms and copper from Japan. Though from about 1560 the Ming ban on Chinese trading abroad was relaxed, and Chinese merchant shippers revived their overseas trade, and though with the unification of Japan under Nobunaga and Hideyoshi there was a deliberate effort to develop a Japanese merchant marine, the prosperity of Macau continued to increase until the end of the century. Here and in Malacca, India and Ormuz, Portuguese merchants could not monopolise trade, but their partnership with wealthy Chinese merchants, with the western *daimyo* and even with the regent Hideyoshi, with Javanese rulers, and with the Indian merchants of Coromandel and Gujarat was the basis of great prosperity. As a commercial structure the *Estado da India* was never more successful than at the end of the sixteenth century.

The growth of 'country' trade, linking the Asian markets with one another rather than with Portugal, gave to the *Estado da India* an autonomous vigour which compensated for the diminished support received from Portugal after the death of King John III. The resources which trade provided might frequently be wasted by the violence, rashness, pride and jealousy of the fidalgos, as in the wars along the Malabar coast and in the Moluccas. But in the second half of the sixteenth century the *Estado* gave notable proof of its defensive and even of continuing offensive power. Thus in this period in east Africa a major if futile campaign was mounted up the Zambezi. Then when in 1585 a Turk, Mir Ali Bey, utilised Arab discontent against the oppressions of the Portuguese captains-major to raise the sheikhs from Kilwa northwards, an expedition from Goa sacked Faza and Mombasa and quickly reduced the coast to submission. When Mir Ali reappeared in 1588 with reinforcements, a second fleet of twenty sail from Goa penned his forces in Mombasa, where they were gobbled up by the Zimba, a cannibal horde. Thereafter the sheikhs were ruthlessly brought to heel. The building of Fort Jesus on Mombasa, a magnificent example of Italianate military architecture, served to keep them there.[1]

Further east, though the Ottomans advancing down the Red Sea and to Basra at the head of the Persian Gulf were able to sack Muscat, take Bahrein and besiege Ormuz, the Portuguese countered by destroying three successive Ottoman fleets and by an offensive in the Red Sea, clearing their sea-routes again. In India itself the half century saw the consolidation of Portuguese power in Diu and an advance to Damão which completed their command of the approaches to the Gulf of Cambay and the rich trade of Gujarat. For a moment, as the Gujarat sultanate broke up, they even seemed poised for the capture of the great prize of Surat. Though there forestalled by a Mughal advance, they were able to hold Damão against all the threats of their new and powerful neighbour. More impressive still was the successful defence of Chaul and Goa sustained by the Viceroy Dom Luis de Ataide for ten months against the massive combined assault of the sultans of Bijapur and Golconda, helped by the naval forces of the Zamorin of Calicut. Since Malacca at the same time had

---

[1] C. R. Boxer and C. de Azevedo, *Fort Jesus and the Portuguese in Mombasa* (London, 1960).

beaten off an assault by the ruler of Achin, the years 1570–1 must be counted among the most splendid in Portuguese military annals in the East.

The last decades of the century also saw the Portuguese engaging in a new major conquest, that of Ceylon. Trade with Ceylon was long exceptional in being conducted from an unfortified factory at Colombo. However, a fratricidal struggle between three princes of the lowland kingdom of Kotte had led to the calling in of the Portuguese as purveyors of mercenary troops, and by mid-century the Portuguese had become the dominant partners in the alliance with Prince Maha Bandara or Dharmapala, who by conversion to Christianity in 1557 had forfeited Sinhalese sympathy and support. The Portuguese venture into politics now proved singularly unsuccessful, for the rival prince Mayadunne and his son Rajasinha rapidly conquered all the lowlands up to the walls of Colombo. In 1582 Rajasinha extended his authority over the upland kingdom of Kandy and in 1587–8, by an all-out siege, he reduced Colombo to most desperate straits. The Portuguese response was to install a rival claimant on the throne of Kandy, thus keeping their enemy's attention divided until death ended his career in 1593. The Portuguese, in Dharmapala's name, then rapidly regained the lowland kingdom which their ally had bequeathed to the Portuguese crown in 1580. In 1591 they also succeeded in installing their own nominee in Jaffna, the Tamil kingdom in northern Ceylon. Only Kandy remained to be brought under control. In 1594 the first captain-general of the Conquest of Ceylon, with fresh troops from India, led his men up into Kandy, accompanied by the daughter of the last king of the true Kandyan line. The capital was quickly taken and the princess enthroned. In seven years the viceroy at Goa had seen the three kingdoms of Ceylon, a country half as large as Portugal, brought under his control, in large part by the local forces of the *Estado da India*.

Within a few months, however, the captain-general had alienated the Sinhalese army and people, and at Danture, on 6 October 1594, his army was annihilated. The whole island thereupon broke into revolt. The battle was the opening of a fifty-year struggle between the Portuguese in the lowlands and the Kandyan rulers, in which the territories and resources of both were exhausted, to the ultimate advantage of the Dutch. Nevertheless, by the end of the century Dom Jeronimo de Azevedo had restored the situation and was again pressing Kandy hard, while the Portuguese parcelled out the villages in fief and exploited the valuable trade in cinnamon, arecanut, elephants and precious stones. If the attempt to conquer Ceylon was to prove unwise, the tenacity with which the struggle for final victory was waged remained a measure of the surprising vitality of the *Estado da India*.

Beyond Ceylon it was in private rather than state enterprise that the Portuguese spirit of adventure was displayed. The settlements on the east coast of India were the work of Portuguese traders only loosely linked to the Goa administration. In Chittagong and in Arakan the Portuguese frankly appeared as piratical freebooters, principally occupied with the sale of slaves taken in raids on the Ganges delta, but as masters of powerful fleets also threatening the independence of the Arakanese kingdom. Portuguese adventurers and mercenaries were also to be found in Burma and Siam, the most famous being Philip de Brito, who, while in the pay of the Arakanese, was made governor of Syriam, captured from the war-exhausted kingdom of Pegu. He soon threw off allegiance to the Arakanese and for fourteen years ruled independently, even marrying the daughter of the leading Mon chief. His power seemed so assured that early in the seventeenth century the Goa authorities established a custom house at Syriam.

East of Malacca the fortunes of the Portuguese in the second half of the sixteenth century fluctuated wildly. Many individuals found a living as merchants and skippers in one corner or another of the island world running away to Macassar and the Moluccas.[1] But the rapacity and ill discipline of the officials appointed to the Moluccas, repeatedly breaking out into violence among themselves and against their native allies, led in the 'sixties to a general native revolt. Baab Ullah, son of the murdered ruler of Ternate, with Muslim allies from Java and the Sulu and Mindanao islands, besieged and ultimately expelled the Portuguese garrison from Ternate. Under pressure from Japara and Grisee, a great Muslim teaching centre, the Portuguese were also driven from their Amboina fort on the island of Hitu to take refuge with Christian converts on the Leitimor peninsula. It was only because of the rivalry between Tidore and Ternate and with aid from the Spaniards in Manila that a Portuguese foothold was retained, at great cost, in the Moluccas. That anything was salvaged at so great a distance from Goa was perhaps remarkable. That the Portuguese could still go on to found Macau and Nagasaki was truly so.

The military and commercial achievements of the *Estado da India* must seem all the more remarkable when it is realised that the second half of the sixteenth century saw a great missionary effort mounted from Goa, an effort drawing upon both the manpower and resources of the *Estado*. From the fifteenth century successive popes had granted to the Portuguese crown the right of patronage in matters of evangelisation and ecclesiastical administration within the overseas empire. In 1534 the enlarged scope of Portuguese action in Asia was recognised by the elevation of Goa to an episcopal see with jurisdiction from the Cape to China. In 1558 Goa was raised to an archbishopric with suffragan sees at Cochin and Malacca. In 1576 a separate see of Macau was created for China and Japan and in 1588 Japan was made a separate diocese. Over the whole area the crown retained its powers under the *padroado* while Goa, as an archbishopric, continued as metropolitan centre.

[1] For their activities see M. A. P. Meilink-Roelofsz, *Asian Trade and European Influence* (The Hague, 1962).

Until the 1530s attention was largely confined to pastoral care of the Portuguese in Asia. It was only in 1534 that the first large mission field was opened to the Franciscans by the acceptance of Christianity by the Paravas, the pearl-fishers of southern India, in return for political protection. Thereafter, with the Portuguese advance to the north of Goa, further success was achieved, the Franciscans founding many houses, managing hospitals, orphanages and schools, and opening a seminary for native Christian children in Goa itself. It was with the arrival of the Jesuits in 1542, however, that missionary activity began to receive the full attention and support of the crown. In Portugal, the Jesuits, as confessors and advisers to the king, received charge of higher education and in Coimbra established a training school for missionaries. In India, too, the authorities lent their aid, first by granting minor official appointments and financial privileges to converts, and then by measures of compulsion such as destruction of idols in Portuguese territory, a ban on heathen festivals, the expulsion of Brahmans and Muslim religious leaders, and the sequestration of property devoted to the upkeep of temples and mosques. The harshest of these measures was that by which minors on the death of their father, even if the mother were living, were taken from their relatives to be brought up as Christians.[1] In 1560, largely at Francis Xavier's instigation, these measures were reinforced by the establishment of the Inquisition at Goa. It was not spectacular in operation. Inquisitors such as Affonsequa seem from their correspondence to have been more anxious about status and salaries than souls, but it was naggingly persistent.

The Jesuits not only provided a considerable accession of strength— by 1560 they were already one hundred and twenty-four in the Asian field— they brought trained intelligence, ardour and discipline. With Dominicans also arriving in considerable numbers by mid-century and Augustinians from 1572 onwards, missionary numbers and quality were greatly increased in this period. India was naturally the first area to feel the new impulse. Francis Xavier began with a two-year stay among the only nominally Christian Paravas and undertook the training of native catechists to continue the work, with one solitary Jesuit father, upon their desolate coast. He also sought to reform the morals of the Portuguese themselves. He set an example of teaching the children, established a college in Goa for the training of youths of various nations for mission work in their own countries, and set about the translation into local languages of catechisms, creed and prayers. (In this last he was a typical Jesuit, for, more than any other Order, they were at pains to master local languages, producing many early dictionaries and grammars, as well as to make some study of the religious beliefs of those whom they sought to convert.) From the 1560s onwards mass conversions, celebrated with great magnificence, occurred in the Old Conquests of Goa, north to Bassein and south to Cochin, and

[1] Informers sought out such cases, receiving a share in the orphan's inheritance as reward.

considerable efforts were made to consolidate these gains by the establishment of numerous schools and colleges, Jesuit and Franciscan. The large Roman Catholic communities today existing in the Bassein area, in Goa, in Malabar and Ceylon are the enduring fruits of their enterprise. It should be noted, however, that though Indians were admitted in large numbers to the secular priesthood, they were not recruited into the regular Orders. The Franciscans by their statutes were debarred from admitting converts, and proved loath to admit even Portuguese if locally born. The Jesuits likewise refused admission, the Visitor Alessandro Valignano forthrightly labelling all blacks, whether African or Indian, as 'naturally inclined to wrongdoing, animated by base instincts and held in contempt by European Christians'.

Another feature of this period was the attempt made to bring the ancient community of St Thomas or Syrian Christians of India under Portuguese control. The Franciscans had earlier sought to bring them closer to Rome, and from 1541 had run a college for Syrian Christian boys at Cranganore. In 1551 and again in 1555 Chaldean patriarchs had received their consecration at the pope's hands in Rome, and, when bishops appointed by the Uniat patriarch reached Goa, the Jesuits sought to force the pace and bring them within the *padroado* or patronage of the crown. Bishop Mar Joseph they twice seized and shipped to Europe as a heretic, undeterred either by royal approval of his position or by the order of Pope Pius IV that the administration of the Syrian church in India should remain with its bishops. They followed direct assault by mine and sap, supporting Mar Joseph in return for permission to create a seminary for Syrian priests. In 1585 the head of the seminary denounced the bishop as a heretic and on his death an Indian Christian was appointed his successor by the archbishop of Goa, on condition of acknowledging the supremacy of Rome and denouncing the Chaldean patriarch. Finally, at the Synod of Dampier in 1599, backed by the bought secular support of the Raja of Cochin, the archbishop introduced new formularies into the Syrian church and placed it formally under the Inquisition and *padroado*, allotting to the Jesuits the administration of the whole foothills area.

In the south the Jesuits had seemingly achieved a notable success, but in the north a still greater, the winning of the Mughal emperor Akbar to Christianity, eluded them. Akbar had met Portuguese at the siege of Surat and had been impressed. In 1579 he wrote to Goa asking for 'two learned priests who should bring with them the chief books of the Law and Gospel'. Three Jesuits were selected, the Italian Aquaviva, the Spaniard Monserrate and a Persian convert Henriquez, for this first mission to the Mughal. With earlier conversions of rulers of Ceylon, the Maldives and Malabar as encouraging portents, they set out hopefully for Agra. They found Akbar a professing but clearly unorthodox Muslim, already engaged in religious discussions with Hindus, Jains and Parsis, in which they now joined. They were well received. They were given full liberty to preach, the great Abul Fazl was appointed to teach them Persian and arrange for the translation of the Gospels, and Prince Murad was ordered to receive instruction at their hands. Nevertheless they found themselves at a loss to understand the emperor's mind, and, disappointed of his high hopes, Aquaviva left the court in 1583. In 1591 a second mission was asked for and translations of the Gospels, 'through whose holy doctrine I hope to be restored from death to life'. Again Jesuits went north, were well received by Akbar, and were allowed to open a school. However, Muslim hostility was intense, the emperor showed no readiness for conversion, and the mission was early abandoned. In 1594 a third call was made, and the viceroy, anxious about Mughal movements towards the Deccan, for political purposes persuaded the Jesuits to answer it. The mission was led by Father Jerome Xavier, who remained with Akbar until his death, still unconverted, in 1605. The permanent mission now established at the Mughal court enabled the Jesuits to interpret to Europe the high Indo-Persian culture of the empire, and it was not without political utility, but it never fulfilled the religious hopes once pinned to it.

To the westwards the work of Dominicans and Augustinians in the difficult Muslim field of the African sheikhdoms and the Persian Gulf was unrewarding, their main task being the conversion of slaves en route to Goa. A Jesuit incursion into the Zambezi ended in martyrdom, and their long struggle to win monophysite Abyssinia for Rome also ultimately failed. Their hope here was that the emperor's need of Portuguese armed assistance against the advancing Ottomans would lead to conversion from the top, but though their bishops received a hearing, and early in the seventeenth century secured the ruler's allegiance, the zeal of the first Jesuit patriarch in attacking heresy led to violent popular reaction and the expulsion of the missionaries.

Eastwards, considerable Christian communities were built up in the spice islands, but, as has been seen, many were destroyed in native risings against the tyranny of officials and missionary pressure. In Japan, however, Jesuit efforts to work through the ruling class for half a century achieved a most astonishing success. Francis Xavier in his sweep across the whole Asian mission field had reported with enthusiasm on the Japanese, 'the best who have as yet been discovered'. They were men who prized honour, astonishingly self-controlled, hospitable, curious and without the xenophobia of the Chinese, and though poor, frequently literate, which was a great help to conversion. The Japanese, for their part, found in the Portuguese fidalgo elements of the samurai, and in Jesuit discipline, self-sacrifice and indifference to fortune something akin to the Bushido code.

Xavier had landed in western Japan, where the warlords Shimazu and Ōtomo had already achieved dominance and given stability, and were intent on furthering both their military and economic strength. The new muskets which the Portuguese brought and the trade of the carracks were alike welcome, and Xavier before he left had already made a number of converts in Kyushu.

On his return to Goa, therefore, further Jesuit missionaries were despatched to this promising new field. Initially they were only a handful— still only a score by 1570—and their main work was among the poor peasantry of western Japan. However, after the trade from Macau had fallen into its regular pattern of an annual sailing by a great carrack, it was possible to hold out the bait of trade to the Kyushu *daimyo*, some of whom, such as Ōtomo Sorin of Bungo, accepted Christianity mainly for political reasons. It was from another Christian *daimyo*, Omura, that in 1569 the Jesuits received the gift of Nagasaki, whose entire administration and port revenues were entrusted to their care. Considerable success was also achieved in Funai, where a Portuguese merchant who had entered the Order used his wealth to found hospitals, and the profits of trade with Macau to support the mission.

The Jesuits were anxious, however, to reach the capital, Kyoto. In 1550 Xavier had found it racked by war, and it was not till 1559 that Gaspar Vilela secured a footing there, under the protection of the Shogun, who was probably influenced by converts in his entourage. There, and in the port of Sakai, numerous samurai converts were secured. When in 1564 the emperor ordered the expulsion of the Jesuits, they were able to seek refuge there, and even to secure a number of noble converts in the central provinces, including the important *daimyo* family of Settsu. It was through this family that Luis Frois, the greatest of the Jesuit observers and letter-writers in Japan, was introduced in 1569 to the rising Odo Nobunaga, then active in subjugating the whole of central Japan. The good impression made by Frois upon Nobunaga was of great importance, for he had just mastered Kyoto, and in 1573 was to depose the Shogun, and so become the most powerful figure in Japan. His long political struggle with the militant Buddhist sects, ending in the destruction of the Ikko stronghold in 1580, gave him a further ready point of contact with the Jesuits, who were in religious conflict with Buddhism. Thus favoured, the Jesuits made many converts in the Kyoto area, and among men of good families and in important positions. By 1580 a third of the population of Settsu was Christian; there were some 15,000 converts in the central provinces, with schools, seminaries and fine churches in the principal towns. Moreover, conversion was here uninfluenced by any consideration of commercial or political advantage.

The Japanese mission was given a further impetus by the arrival in 1579 of the Jesuit Visitor Alessandro Valignano. As in India, he placed great stress on the thorough preparation of converts, opening seminaries in Arima and Adzuchi, a novitiate in Usuki, and a college in Funai. He stressed, too, the need for missionary language training, a readiness to accept and adapt indigenous cultural patterns and to treat Japanese converts, seminarists and catechists on a footing of equality, as people apt to 'produce the finest Christianity in all the East, as in fact it already is'.

In 1582 Nobunaga was assassinated. He was succeeded by Toyotomi Hideyoshi, who carried to completion the process of unifying Japan. For some years, having crushed all military opposition in the central provinces, he was mainly concerned with administrative reconstruction, a great doomsday book of the land, and the creation of a central bureaucracy. At this time, while he was also stamping out the last remnants of Buddhist opposition, he continued to accept the Jesuits in friendly fashion and to allow conversion, even at his court. He likewise showed himself anxious to encourage Portuguese trade. Then in 1587 he suddenly issued an order for the expulsion of all Jesuits within twenty days. His motives have been disputed, but it seems probable that the Jesuit tradition of seeking converts among the ruling classes had betrayed them. Hideyoshi, secure in the centre, was now preparing to bring the outer provinces into subjection, and his first objective was Kyushu. Here the Jesuits in their relations with the *daimyo* had begun to act in a distinctly political fashion. For example, when a non-Christian clan, the Satsuma, had threatened to master Kyushu, the Vice-Provincial Gaspar Coelho had encouraged the Christian *daimyo* to seek military aid from Manila. And when, in 1586, Hideyoshi received Coelho and outlined his plans against Kyushu, the latter rashly promised naval assistance and offered to bring over the Christian *daimyo* to his side. Such assertion of political authority by the Jesuits might well explain the expulsion order. The order itself also complains of the Portuguese selling Japanese as slaves, of their attacks on Shinto and Buddhist shrines and their encouragement to the *daimyo* to compel their people to accept Christianity. However, though Coelho's first reaction was to resist by force, and to call on the *daimyo* and Macau for support, the Jesuits soon decided upon a more tactful submission. Hideyoshi did not press the matter, bribery of local officials smoothed the way, and the Jesuits returned to an unobtrusive pastoral care of their people. The expulsion order was not withdrawn, but in 1592 Valignano, returning from Goa, was well received, and by 1592 there were some hundred Jesuits at work in Japan, and even in the capital. By 1596 Valignano could report 300,000 converts in Japan, no less than 60,000 baptised since 1587.

The last great mission field to which the Portuguese sought entry was China. For long China remained obstinately closed to ambassadors, merchants or missionaries. Even after permission had been granted to the merchants to pay strictly limited visits to Canton, the requests of the Jesuits, such as that made in 1565 by their Superior, Perez, to teach on the mainland, were firmly rejected, and attempts at unauthorised entry, either from Manila or Macau, ended in near disaster. Both in Macau and Manila thoughts turned to forcing an entry with the sword, but Valignano chose the pen as his weapon. In 1579, on his instruction, the young Neapolitan Ruggiero took up the task of learning to read, write and speak Chinese. The task of acquiring both the spoken dialect and Mandarin, without effective teachers or aids, was formidable, but, as Ruggiero himself saw, it was essential to appear not as mere merchants but as scholars.

From 1580 onwards Ruggiero was able to visit Canton, where his attention to Chinese etiquette and his quiet, studious habits won him the approval of the local mandarinate. By 1582 he was able to offer them the Ten Commandments in Chinese. Then a new viceroy, charged with an inquiry into the position of Macau, summoned the Portuguese to his capital Chao-Ch'ing to explain their pretensions. Ruggiero was one of the envoys sent. His explanations, suitably backed by assorted presents, were well received. Further presents were despatched to Chao-Ch'ing, and in December 1582 Ruggiero again left, armed with a striking clock, for the provincial capital. A petition to be allowed to settle as Chinese subjects to study Chinese civilisation was presented—and accepted: the long-sought entry had been achieved. Until 1589 a small group of missionaries, including Matteo Ricci, resided at Chao-Ch'ing, disarming suspicion by their attainments, intriguing the local officials with scientific toys, careful to present their religion in a sympathetic light. Permission was then granted to visit other provincial cities, and Ricci travelled to Nanch'ang, capital of Kiangsi, and there opened a further mission centre. Meanwhile Ricci was composing and printing works in Chinese on European science and the Christian religion, studying the classics, from which he drew many of his religious terms, and attempting that compromise with Chinese custom and Confucian tradition which was later to be the cause of so much controversy. Finally at the very end of the century he reached Peking, where he was allowed to settle. The great Jesuit enterprise in China had begun.

The Portuguese were not, however, to be allowed to develop their trade and missionary work in the Far East uninterrupted and single-handed. The Spaniards had only reluctantly, and after three further costly failures, abandoned their claim to the spice islands established by Magellan's expedition. From 1559 new and more serious preparations were made for an expedition to that quarter, and in 1565 five ships with four hundred men under Admiral Legazpi reached the southern Philippines from New Spain. Cebu, where he landed, was limited in its resources and unduly exposed to Muslim attack from Mindanao, but the settlement weathered a three-month Portuguese siege, was encouraged by trade with visiting Chinese junks, and in 1571 was successfully extended north to Luzon, where a new capital was founded at Manila. Under Dominican influence, Philip II had ordered Legazpi to effect his settlement without violence and injustice. Remarkably, both in Cebu and at Manila, those instructions had been successfully followed.

The colonial regime that developed in the Spanish Philippines was in the early days much more a colony of settlement than Portuguese India had ever been. The original structure carried over from the Americas was one of estates, *encomiendas*, whose Spanish grantees levied tribute from the indigenous population. All adult males paid tribute, in labour services, goods or specie, and the *encomenderos* in return were supposed to protect them and prepare them for the reception of Christianity. Legazpi, for example, distributed two-thirds of the population he brought under control to private *encomenderos* and reserved one-third for the crown. The system was evidently open to abuse—over-assessment, violence and extortion by the collecting agency, even enslavement of the Filipinos. This last abuse was ended by the action of Bishop Salazar in 1581, supported by a papal brief, and from 1591 by royal legislation, but the burden of Spanish demands upon an underdeveloped agricultural economy was really lifted by the development of active trade with the Chinese. The Chinese brought silks, porcelain, some gold and luxury articles for re-export to New Spain, but they also brought the hardware, ironmongery, furniture, livestock and foodstuffs required by the colonists, and considerable numbers of artisans and labourers to settle in their own quarter, the Parian, outside Manila. They provided many services essential to the growth of the city, as market-gardeners, bakers and craftsmen, while the 3 per cent duty levied on their junk trade produced a large slice of the Philippines' revenues, as much as one-fifth by the early 1590s. Their swelling numbers raised problems of security, but the labour and the revenue they provided lightened the demands which had to be made upon the Filipinos. By the 1620s so many Spaniards had settled in Manila and were active in trade that private *encomiendas* were declining in number and importance, and the tribute demands had become, in effect, a moderate poll tax.

The Spaniards quite early made contact with Japanese visiting the Philippines, and the Portuguese, once so anxious to exclude them from the Moluccas, were forced by the rebellion of Ternate and Amboina to call them to their aid. But with neither Japan nor the spice islands did any important trade develop: the Japanese did not require silver and were distrustful of Spanish political intentions, the inhabitants of the spice islands wanted cottons and foodstuffs which the Philippines could not supply, and Spanish demand for spices was limited, since a trade by way of America to Europe proved uncompetitive. The trade of Manila thus settled down to a straight exchange of silver from New Spain against Chinese wares. As early as 1573 the two Manila galleons for Acapulco carried 712 bolts of Chinese silk and 22,300 pieces of fine china gilt and other porcelain, and by 1600 forty to fifty large sea-going junks were arriving yearly from China. The goods they brought were bought wholesale by a committee, under the same system as in Macau, and were then allotted to individuals according to the money they had invested. Even so, there were frequent complaints of the cost of these goods. From 1575, therefore, attempts were made to open a direct trade with China, and, especially after the union of the two crowns, to overcome the jealousy of the Portuguese and extend trade with Macau. Neither succeeded, and the grip of the Chinese shippers remained unbroken. Nevertheless, the Chinese trade was profitable and continued to grow, despite the royal regulations which sought to limit the silver exports from New Spain to the Philippines.

The Philippines can be seen as a mart where American silver was exchanged for Chinese wares, the second arm binding the commerce of the Atlantic to that of Asia. But it was also seen in Spain as a great missionary venture, for the maintenance of which the crown made very considerable sacrifices. For the first decade there were only a handful of Augustinians in the island, but the arrival of Franciscans in 1578, and then of Dominicans and Jesuits, carried total missionary numbers towards the hundred and three-hundred mark in the second and third decades. By the end of the century they had baptised perhaps half of the 600,000 Filipinos under Spanish rule.

The arrival of the missionaries introduced an element prepared, in the tradition of Las Casas, to speak vigorously against the abuses of the *encomienda* system and to curb the tendency to enslave the Filipinos. The clergy also worked hard to eradicate the indigenous debt serfdom to which the native chieftains owed their power. They also, however, brought their own demands upon their converts for labour services as porters or rowers, or in the construction of church buildings; and, supported as they were by a share in the tribute, could be themselves exploiters. The Mendicant Orders were accused of excessive demands for the administration of the sacraments, and for a while the Augustinians fell into disorder, many using their spiritual authority to secure free gifts of food and to secure trade goods at low prices. The task of suppressing such occasional abuses was made very difficult by the wide scatter of parishes: the communal life which normally sustained discipline was often impossible, and even among the carefully selected Jesuits the isolation of mission stations led to some personal lapses. Moreover, though Philip II was armed with a papal brief empowering him to enforce the subjection of regulars to episcopal authority, the Orders steadily opposed such control. Since, in the absence of any considerable secular priesthood, mission activity depended entirely on the regulars, they were the more able to defy the bishop and, being in many areas the only effective Spanish presence in the countryside, to defy the civil authority likewise. The authoritarian structure of the Jesuits was some safeguard, but the more democratic Mendicants, with their triennial elections, for a while were notably demoralised. All, however, suffered by the shortage of manpower, almost entirely Spanish since neither natives, creoles nor the locally born European were recruited, when the missions were so rapidly expanding. The attempt made in the 1580s and 1590s to group converts into larger, compact villages, as in Mexico, both for protection against raiders from Mindanao and to ease the task of pastoral care, also failed. In these early years the Philippines thus proved a difficult field. One measure did ease the situation: the division of the Philippines into separate language areas each allotted to a different Order. This had the fortunate effect of making the study of both language and custom easier. One result was the creation of codes of local custom, which were allowed to continue when not in conflict with basic Christian beliefs and practices. The second was that as the missionaries acquired some linguistic ability, the Filipinos were spared the labour of learning Spanish.

Almost to the end of the sixteenth century the Iberians, circling the world in opposite directions, maintained a near monopoly of direct contact with Asia. Nevertheless, other Europeans were busy probing the approaches. The least noticed advance was that of Russia. After the unification of the Great Russian lands under Ivan III and Ivan IV, an expansion both south and east began. Even in the late fifteenth century Moscow exchanged embassies with Herat and Persia, and, after the conquest of Kazan and Astrakhan in 1552–4, more permanent relations with the central Asian khanates and Safavid Persia were established by way of the Volga and Caspian Sea. In the same decade the Strogonov family received licence to push eastwards, and by 1581 with their Cossack troops they were across the Urals. Having destroyed the Tartar khanate on the Iritch, the way was then open for an advance by easy portages from river system to river system across Siberia. The search for new supplies of such valuable furs as black fox and sable drew Cossacks and fur trappers to Tomsk by 1604 and the borders of China a decade later.

In the enlarged fur trade which these advances opened up, the state came to play a dominant role. Furs, for example, were the staple item of the state caravans trading to Persia, where they were exchanged for silk, the monopoly of the shah. Furs were also sold by a selected body of state merchants at Astrakhan to visiting Indian, Persian and Turkish merchants. Still others were sold in Moscow to European merchants—among them English exploiting the White Sea route discovered by Chancellor in 1553.

This route had been opened while the English were seeking a route to the East which would avoid conflict with Spain and Portugal, and open new markets for the declining cloth trade; the Muscovy Company incorporated in 1555 had aimed at a voyage to Cathay. The trade which developed was in fish, train oil, tallow, flax and furs, but the original purpose was not quite forgotten, for in 1557 Anthony Jenkinson, armed with the tsar's pass for a journey to China, travelled down the Volga to the Caspian. At Bokhara he found the route east closed by war, but he noted the details of the caravan traffic to China. In 1561 he went out again, this time to prospect a trade with Persia. In 1562 he reached Kazvin, was ill received by Shah Tahmasp, discussed a possible spice trade with India merchants, and then returned by Sherwan with a stock of silks. Further Persian voyages followed in 1564 and 1565, mainly for raw silk but still with spices in mind. In 1566 favourable privileges were secured from the shah and hope of successful exchange of kerseys for silk and spices rose. A limited trade was driven: 400 lb. of cinnamon was secured in 1568, while in 1569 some thousand cloths were sold in Persia and silks and spices worth £30,000 purchased. Had the English caravan not been plundered by Volga Cossacks, such a return must have encouraged an even more vigorous Persian trade. Instead, after one more voyage in 1579, the Muscovy Company lost interest.

This was due in part to the revival of English trade with the Levant. Antwerp's decline and the revival of Aleppo and Alexandria, growing political difficulty in trading with Portugal and Spain, hopes of commercial if not military links with the Porte, had led in 1580 to the procurement of new capitulations from Murad III. In 1581 the Levant Company, backed by Burghley and Walsingham, secured a royal charter. In 1583 the capitulations were renewed and in the first five years some twenty-seven voyages were made, and very profitable cargoes, including raw silk, spices and indigo from Persia and India were secured. The Levant Company thus succeeded, where the Russia Company had failed, in tapping the trade of Asia and bypassing the Iberians.

Moreover the Company was not content to secure Asian goods only at second hand, for in 1583 it despatched merchants from Aleppo to the Persian Gulf and India. One of these, Ralph Fitch, advanced as far as Burma and the borders of Siam before returning to England in 1591. Elizabeth's second charter to the Levant Company extended its monopoly overland to the lands Fitch had discovered. Hopes of Asian trade which had flickered before the Russia Company's eyes shone bright before those of the Levant Company.

The vision again proved mirage. Where the voyages of James Lancaster and Benjamin Wood by sea to the Indies had failed, the first Dutch voyage, despatched in 1595, succeeded. In 1598 no less than twenty-two ships sailed east from the Netherlands and by 1599 four had returned with rich ladings of pepper and spices. For a moment the Levant Company hoped that the Dutch, already in the Levant, would find trade there preferable to the dangers of the sea-route and Iberian hostility. By late 1599, however, the English at Aleppo were reducing their spice purchases, and in London an East India Company was being planned to follow the Dutch round the Cape. Though delayed for a year by Elizabeth's political manœuvrings, at the close of 1600 the East India Company was chartered, the naval arm, as it were, of the Levant Company, from whom it had drawn both members and its governor.

The pattern of Dutch advance towards direct participation in the trade with Asia was not unlike that of the English. Where the latter had suffered from the collapse of the Portuguese market at Antwerp, the Dutch, it is true, had gained, for they took over much of the shipping and distribution of spices to northern Europe. But the Dutch felt the spur of Spanish hostility sooner and more keenly, and they therefore also joined in the search for polar passages to Asia, and followed the English first to the White Sea and then to the Levant. They joined likewise in Atlantic privateering and in attacks upon Portuguese West Africa. But after 1585, when Philip II with increasing strictness banned trade with Iberian ports, the Dutch were better prepared than the English to undertake the hazardous sea voyage round the Cape to the spice islands. In financial strength, administrative expertise and naval experience they were well ahead. They were better informed, too, about the sea-routes east and the pattern of Portuguese commerce in Asia. From Dutchmen in the service of the India contractors, from Linschoten, for years planted at the heart of the *Estado da India* in the service of the archbishop of Goa, from Houtman at Lisbon, they had assembled the maps, rutters and detailed information which enabled them in 1595 to make for the weakest spot, the Sunda Straits and the port of Bantam. Houtman's return from the first voyage, in safety though with little profit, was sufficient to release a flood of companies anxious to follow up success. Within seven years sixty-five ships fitted out by eight separate companies sailed, some by the Strait of Magellan, a majority round the Cape to Java and the spice islands. Their fortunes varied, some like that commanded by van Neck producing most splendid profits, others like the second voyage of Houtman ending in disaster. It soon became clear, however, that the system of separate rival voyages was harmful to all the companies. Warwijck in Madura suffered for the violence of Houtman, as did van Caeden in Achin; no one company could readily sustain the permanent factories required for successful trade; competition forced up prices and made supply uncertain; and while the fleet sent out in 1599 by the Old Company of Amsterdam carried orders which treated rival Dutch companies as though they were enemies, the Portuguese were at last preparing to expel the intruders by force. In 1597 the States General had sought to induce the companies of Holland and Zeeland to join forces; in 1599 the burgomaster of Amsterdam secured the fusion of the companies of Amsterdam and North Holland. By 1601, however, the dangers of disunion had become so apparent that the States General summoned representatives of all the companies to the Hague to consider the conditions for union. From their wranglings and discussions emerged in March 1602 the Vereenigde Oostindische Compagnie, the United East India Company, the commercial and military instrument with which the Dutch were to destroy the century-old Portuguese empire in Asia.

INDEX

Aachen, 8, 345
'Abbās, shah of Persia, 360, 364, 374–5
Abbots
  secular, 51
  territories of, in Empire, 337
Abbruzzi, bandits of, 255
'Abd al-Halīm (Kara Yaziji), leader of Turkish
  rebels, 373, 374
Aberdeen, university of, 439
Åbo, 407
Abrahamowicz, architect, 402
Abul Fazl, historian of Akbar, 550
Abū'l-Suʿūd, mufti, 352
Abyssinia, Jesuits in, 539, 540, 550
Academy of the Secrets of Nature, 476, 479
Acadia (Novia Scotia), 530–1
Acapulco, 17, 554
Acconcio, Giacomo, engineer, 483, 485
Accountancy, 428
Achin, 535, 537, 541, 542, 546, 558
Acosta, Jose d', natural historian, 457
Acquaviva, Claudio, general of Jesuits, 65,
  549–50
Act, declaration, of Abjuration (Netherlands),
  99, 279
Acts of Parliament, Statutes (English)
  of Appeals (1533), 51
  of Supremacy (1559), 114, 212
  of Uniformity (1559), 114, 212
  of Weavers (1555), 128
  of Apprentices (1563), 128
  for Retaining Queen's subjects in Obedi-
    ence (1580), 492
Addled Parliament, 135
Aden, Turks at, 534
Adiaphoristic controversy, 78–9
Administration, 126–48 *passim*
  of Spanish empire, 238, 254, 507, 510, 511
  of Piedmont and Savoy, 260
  of German principalities, 331
  of Ottoman empire, 347, 351
  of Sweden and Denmark, 406–7, 423, 425–6
Admiralty, Court of, 167
Adrian VI (of Utrecht), pope, 240
Adriatic Sea, 197, 319
Adzuchi, Jesuit seminary in, 551
Aeneas Sylvius Piccolomini, see Pius II
Aerschot, Philippe de Croy, duke of, 268, 271,
  275–6, 277, 310
Aeschylus, Greek dramatist, edition of, 446
'Aesop', in schools, 435
Affonsequa, inquisitor, 548
Africa, 24, 160
  East, 366, 539–40, 545, 550
  North, 191, 197, 251, 353–4
    Portuguese in, 247, 534
  West, Portuguese in, 534, 558
Agents, diplomatic, 151, 153, 162
Agostino, Antonio, jurist, 446
Agra, 549

Agricola, Georgius, *De re metallica* by, 24
Agricola, Johannes, reformer, 74, 75
Agricola, Rudolphus (Huysmann), 442
Agriculture, 36–8, 127
  prices of products of, 20
  in Poland, 397–8, 400
  in Sweden, 425
  in Spanish America, 513
Ahmed I, sultan of Turkey, 375
Aidin (Asia Minor), 374
Aigues-Mortes, 153
Ajemioghlanlar (foreign youths), in Ottoman
  empire, 348, 366
Akbar, Mughal emperor
  conquers Gujarat, 540
  Jesuit missions to, 549–50
Akçe (asper), Ottoman coin, 349 n., 370, 371
Akhaltzikhé (Caucasus), 358
Alay begi (officer of sipāhīs), 349–50
Alba, Fernando Alvarez de Toledo, duke of,
  243, 244, 290
  and Council of Blood, 6, 102, 291
  letters of, 7–8
  meets Catherine, 154, 222, 225, 287
  forces of, 181
  terror as policy of, 207, 274, 275, 310
  marches on Netherlands, 229, 270, 287
  difficulties of, 232, 268, 271–4
  conquers Portugal, 247, 248
  recalled from Netherlands, 275
Albania, Venice and, 182, 353
  in Ottoman empire, 347
Albert, archduke, 309, 310
Albert, duke of Prussia, 395
Albert Alcibiades, margrave of Brandenburg,
  77, 338
Albert Frederick, duke of Prussia, 395
Albistān (Asia Minor), 373
Albrecht V, duke of Bavaria, 334–5, 336
Alburquerque, duke of, governor of Milan,
  258–9
Alcabala (Spanish tax), 136, 137, 147, 271, 275,
  511
Alcalá, university of, 66
Alcazar-el-Kebir, Portuguese defeat at, 200,
  247, 248
Alchemy, 454, 463, 476
Alciati, Andrea (Alciat), humanist, 435
Aldobrandini, cardinal, see Clement VIII
Aldrovandi, Ulisse, anatomist, 472
Alençon, duke of, see Anjou, Francis, duke of
Aleotti, Giovanni Battista, engineer, 455
Aleppo, 358
  trade of, 262, 366, 534, 557
Alessandrino, cardinal, 258
Alessi, Galeazzo, architect, 257
Alexandria, trade of, 262, 366, 534, 557
Algebra, 458–9
Algiers
  Turkish barracks at, 175

559

INDEX

In coena domini (papal bull), 258
Index, congregation of the, 50
India
 Mughal (Mogul) emperors of, 164, 540, 545, 550
 trade routes from, 366
 Portuguese concerns in, 532–41, 545
India House (Lisbon), 532, 533, 534, 535
Indian Ocean, 311, 366, 534
Indians (American)
 rights of, 55, 510
 Pueblo, 507
 revolts of, 510
 population numbers of, 512–14
 Spanish policy towards, 514–15
Indies
 Council of the, 56, 511
 see also West Indies, Caribbean Sea
Indigo, trade in, 538, 557
Individualism, in political thought, 480, 506
Indonesia, 539, 541
Industry, 38–42
 for production of armour, 187–8; of fire-arms, 189, 190–1, 398
 in Piedmont-Savoy, 260
 in Poland, 398–9
Infantry, 184, 192–5
Inflation, monetary, 3, 18, 20, 24, 29, 235
 in England, 126; in France, 291; in Spain, 312
 in Ottoman empire, 370, 373
Ingermanland, ceded to Sweden, 424
Ingolstadt, university of, 66, 325, 336
Innocent III, pope, 54
Innocent IX, pope, 304
Innsbruck, 77, 187
Inquisition, Roman (Congregation of the Holy Office), 50, 61, 481; and Copernicanism, 462
Inquisition, Spanish, 23, 61–3, 67, 71, 157, 232, 243, 244, 245, 251, 268
 in Sicily, 254
 attempts to introduce, in Milan and Naples, 256
 and case of Carranza, 257–8
Inquisition, episcopal, in Netherlands, 265, 266, 268, 270
 at Goa, 548
Intendant, office of, 143, 146
Interims of Augsburg and Leipzig, 75, 76–7, 98, 101, 120
Ionian sea, 197
Ipswich, school at, 432
Iraq, 355, 360
Ireland
 rebellion in, 9, 309
 English subjugation of, 165
 education neglected in, 450
 settlements in, 524, 526
Iritch, river, Tartar khanate on, 556
Iron and steel
 Netherlands, 191
 English, 368
 Polish, 398, 400
 Swedish, 404, 412
Isaac, John, Hebrew scholar, 448
Isabella Clara Eugenia, daughter of Philip II, as claimant to French throne, 303, 306

betrothal of, 310
Isabella of Castile, consort of Ferdinand of Aragon, 54, 61–2, 249
Isenburg, count Salentin von, as archbishop of Cologne, 341
Islam, 57, 350
 converts to, 347
 Shī'ī form of, 355, 356, 357
 see also Muslims
Ismā'īl I, shah of Persia, 355, 357
Ismā'īl II, son of Tahmāsp, death of, 357
Isocrates, Greek rhetorician, read in schools, 437
Istanbul, 348, 362
 ambassadors at, 163, 164, 367, 368–9
 Austrian peace envoys at, 364
 see also Constantinople
Istruzione per i cavallegieri, 172 n. 1
Italian Wars, 149–51, 183, 210
Italians
 in Spanish service, 240, 253, 266
 in Poland, 381
Italy, 404
 economy of, 16; plague in, 23; currencies of, 28, 29; population of, 33; import of grain by, 37
 Protestants in, 59, 60; church reform in, 64–5
 resident embassies of, 153, 154; absence of Protestant ambassadors in, 157
 France and, 235–6; Spain and, 238, 253–63, 311; empire and, 319, 327
 art of fortification in, 196; fleets of, 202; education and learning in, 429–30, 449, 450, 451
Ius gentium, 168, 169
Ius naturae, 446
Ivan III, grand duke of Muscovy, 556
Ivan IV, the Terrible, tsar of Muscovy, 163, 355, 393, 411, 556
 and education, 450
Ivory, trade in, 538, 539, 540
Ivry, battle of, 9, 305

Jacqueries, 307
Jaffna, kingdom of, 546
Jagiellon family, 319, 377, 381
Jalālī rebels, Ottoman empire, 373
James I, king of England, *see* James VI of Scotland
James IV, king of Scotland, 209, 210
James V, king of Scotland, 112, 210
James VI of Scotland and I of England, 112, 129, 227
 and the Kirk, 6, 118–19
 and the Catholics, 60, 67, 116
 and patronage, 133
 sale of titles by, 143
 resident embassies of, 165
 makes peace with Spain, 309, 528
Jamestown, Virginia, 530
Jānīk, region of, 373
Janissaries, 347, 348, 358, 365
 in decline, 184
 Muslims admitted to, 352, 366
 arms of, 368
 mutiny of, 371